£20.00

A HISTORY OF BRITISH WORKING CLASS LITERATURE

A History of British Working Class Literature examines the rich contributions of working class writers in Great Britain from 1700 to the present. Since the early eighteenth century, the phenomenon of working class writing has been recognized, but almost invariably coopted in some ultimately distorting manner, whether as examples of "natural genius," a Victorian self-improvement ethic, or an aspect of the heroic workers of nineteenth- and twentieth-century radical culture. The present work contrastingly applies a wide variety of interpretive approaches to this literature. Essays on more familiar topics, such as the agrarian idyll of John Clare, are mixed with entirely new areas in the field, such as working class women's life narratives. This authoritative and comprehensive *History* explores a wide range of genres, such as travel writing, the verse epistle, the elegy, and novels, while covering aspects of Welsh, Scottish, Ulster/Irish, and transatlantic perspectives.

JOHN GOODRIDGE has been researching laboring class poetry, John Clare studies, and related fields for the past three decades. He is Vice-President of the John Clare Society and a Fellow of the English Association. He cofounded the Robert Bloomfield Society and the Thomas Chatterton Society, edits the Database of Labouring-Class Poets, and is the general editor of six volumes of laboring class poetry.

BRIDGET KEEGAN has worked on British laboring class poetry for nearly 30 years and has written and edited numerous publications on the topic. She is Professor of English and Dean of the College of Arts and Sciences at Creighton University.

A HISTORY OF BRITISH WORKING CLASS LITERATURE

JOHN GOODRIDGE
Nottingham Trent University

BRIDGET KEEGAN
Creighton University

CAMBRIDGE
UNIVERSITY PRESS

University Printing House, Cambridge CB2 8BS, United Kingdom

One Liberty Plaza, 20th Floor, New York, NY 10006, USA

477 Williamstown Road, Port Melbourne, VIC 3207, Australia

314-321, 3rd Floor, Plot 3, Splendor Forum, Jasola District Centre, New Delhi - 110025, India

79 Anson Road, #06-04/06, Singapore 079906

Cambridge University Press is part of the University of Cambridge.

It furthers the University's mission by disseminating knowledge in the pursuit of education, learning and research at the highest international levels of excellence.

www.cambridge.org
Information on this title: www.cambridge.org/9781107190405
DOI: 10.1017/9781108105392

© Cambridge University Press 2017

This publication is in copyright. Subject to statutory exception and to the provisions of relevant collective licensing agreements, no reproduction of any part may take place without the written permission of Cambridge University Press.

First published 2017

A catalogue record for this publication is available from the British Library

ISBN 978-1-107-19040-5 Hardback
ISBN 978-1-316-63798-2 Paperback

Cambridge University Press has no responsibility for the persistence or accuracy of URLs for external or third-party internet websites referred to in this publication, and does not guarantee that any content on such websites is, or will remain, accurate or appropriate.

Contents

List of Figures	*page* viii
List of Contributors	ix
Foreword	xvii
Donna Landry	
Acknowledgments	xxiii
Introduction	1
John Goodridge and Bridget Keegan	
1 When "Bread Depends on Her Character": The Problem of Laboring Class Subjectivity in the Foundling Hospital Archive	10
Jennie Batchelor	
2 "Stirr'd up by Emulation of the Famous Mr. Duck": Laboring Class Poetry in the 1730s	24
Jennifer Batt	
3 The Verse Epistle and Laboring Class Literary Sociability from Duck to Burns	39
William J. Christmas	
4 "But Genius Is the Special Gift of God!": The Reclamation of "Natural Genius" in the Late-Eighteenth-Century Verses of Ann Yearsley and James Woodhouse	55
Steve Van-Hagen	
5 Alexander Wilson: The Rise and Fall and Rise of a Laboring Class Writer	70
Gerard Carruthers	
6 Neither Mute nor Inglorious: Ann Yearsley and Elegy	85
Kerri Andrews	

7   "British Bards": The Concept of Laboring Class Poetry in
    Eighteenth-Century Wales   101
    Mary-Ann Constantine

8   "Behold in These Coromantees / The Fate of an Agonized
    World": Edward Rushton's Transnational Radicalism   116
    Franca Dellarosa

9   Transnational Ulster and Laboring Class Self-Fashioning   130
    Jennifer Orr

10 Working Class Poetry and the Royal Literary Fund: Two Case
    Studies in Patronage   149
    Scott McEathron

11 The Life of William Cobbett: Caricature, Hauntology, and
    the Impossibility of Radical Life Writing in the Romantic
    Period   176
    Ian Haywood

12 John Clare's Agrarian Idyll: A Confluence of Pastoral and
    Georgic   195
    Gary Harrison

13 "And aft Thy Dear Doric aside I Hae Flung, to Busk oot My
    Sang wi' the Prood Southron Tongue": The Antiphonal Muse
    in Janet Hamilton's Poetics   208
    Kaye Kossick

14 "The Guilty Game of Human Subjugation": Religion as
    Ideology in Thomas Cooper's *The Purgatory of Suicides*   226
    Mike Sanders

15 At the Margins of Print: Life Narratives of Victorian Working
    Class Women   248
    Florence S. Boos

16 The Newspaper Press and the Victorian Working Class Poet   264
    Kirstie Blair

17 Tensions, Transformations, and Local Identity: The Evolving
    Meanings of Nineteenth-Century Tyneside Dialect Songs   281
    Rod Hermeston

18	On the Road: All Manner of Tramps in English and Scottish Writing from the 1880s to the 1920s *H. Gustav Klaus*	296
19	Ethel Carnie Holdsworth: Genre, Serial Fiction, and Popular Reading Patterns *Nicola Wilson*	311
20	"The Young Men of the Nation": Alexander Baron and Urban Working Class Masculinity *Anthony Cartwright*	327
21	Kathleen Dayus: The Girl from Hockley *Sharon Ouditt*	339
22	"It Have a Kind of Communal Feeling with the Working Class and the Spades": Sam Selvon, Tony Harrison, and "Colonization in Reverse" *Jack Windle*	352
23	Clannish Confines: The Folk, the Proletariat, and the People in Modern Scottish Literature *Corey Gibson*	367
24	A Critical Minefield: The Haunting of the Welsh Working Class Novel *Lisa Sheppard and Aidan Byrne*	385
25	Transforming Working Class Writers and Writing: Digital Editions, Projects, and Analyses *Cole Crawford*	398
	Afterword *Brian Maidment*	413
Works Cited		419
Index		455

Figures

Plates 1 through 8: James Gillray, *Life of William Cobbett*, 29 September 1809. *page* 168

11.1 Front page of *Proceedings of a General Court Martial*, 1809. 179

11.2 James Gillray, *Smelling Out a Rat, or, The Atheistical Revolutionist Disturbed in His Midnight Calculations*, 3 December 1790. 183

11.3 James Gillray, *Search Night – or – State Watchmen Mistaking Honest Men for Conspirators*, 20 March 1798. 184

11.4 James Gillray, *A Peep into the Cave of Jacobinism*. Published in the *Anti-Jacobin Review*, 1 September 1798. 186

11.5 Samuel De Wilde, *The Porcupine's Den*. Published in *The Satirist*, 1 November 1808. 187

Contributors

KERRI ANDREWS is a Senior Lecturer in English Literature at Edge Hill University. She has published extensively on the writings of Ann Yearsley, including a monograph (2013) and the first scholarly edition of Yearsley's works (2014). She is currently working on two book-length projects: one examining accounts of women's walking, the other considering representations of laboring class poets as poets of place. She is also leading a project to produce the first scholarly edition of the letters of Hannah More.

JENNIE BATCHELOR is Professor of Eighteenth-Century Studies at the University of Kent. She has published widely on eighteenth-century women's writing; representations of gender, work, sexuality, and the body; material culture studies; and the eighteenth-century charity movement. Her most recent monograph, *Women's Work* (2010; paperback, 2014), examined the relationship between manual and intellectual labor in women's writing across the second half of the eighteenth century. She is currently writing a book on the place of *The Lady's Magazine* (1770–1832) in Romantic print culture.

JENNIFER BATT is Lecturer in Eighteenth-Century English Literature at the University of Bristol. She has published on laboring class poets, miscellanies, and magazines and is completing a monograph on the eighteenth-century laboring class poet Stephen Duck.

KIRSTIE BLAIR holds a Chair in English at the University of Strathclyde. She primarily works in the field of Victorian literature and culture, particularly poetry and poetics, and has an increasing interest in Scottish Victorian literature. She has published two monographs, *Victorian Poetry and the Culture of the Heart* (2006) and *Form and Faith in Victorian Poetry and Religion* (2012), and is currently completing a third, *Working Verse in Victorian Scotland: Poetry, Press, Community*, funded by a

Leverhulme Research Fellowship. She has published extensively on working class poetry and coedited *Class and the Canon: Constructing Labouring-Class Poetry and Poetics, 1780–1900*. From 2016 to 2018, Blair is also CI on a Carnegie Collaborative Grant, "The People's Voice: Scottish Political Poetry, Song and the Franchise, 1832–1918," with colleagues from the University of Glasgow.

FLORENCE S. BOOS is Professor of English at the University of Iowa. She is the editor of *Working-Class Women Poets of Victorian Britain: An Anthology* (2008) and two special issues devoted to Victorian working class writings (*Victorian Poetry* 39, no. 2 [2001] and *Philological Quarterly* 91, no. 3 [2013]). The general editor of the William Morris Archive, she is the author or editor of several books on Morris, most recently *History and Poetics in the Early Writings of William Morris: 1856–1870* (2015). Her *Victorian Working-Class Women's Autobiographies: The Hard Way Up* is forthcoming in 2017.

AIDAN BYRNE is Course Leader in English at the University of Wolverhampton. He holds a PhD in Welsh literature and has published on masculinity and extreme politics in Welsh 1930s literature, Welsh travel literature in the nineteenth century, the uses of jazz in contemporary fiction, and philosophy in popular culture. He is currently working on politicians' creative fictions, Welsh Appalachia, and comparative modernisms in Irish and Welsh literatures. He tweets on academic matters as @plashingvole.

GERARD CARRUTHERS is Francis Hutcheson Professor of Scottish Literature at the University of Glasgow. He is General Editor of the Oxford University Press edition of the Works of Robert Burns (2014–) and coeditor, with Liam McIlvanney, of *The Cambridge Companion to Scottish Literature* (Cambridge, 2012). With Catriona Macdonald and Kirstie Blair, he is an Investigator on the Carnegie Trust–funded project "The People's Voice: Scottish Political Poetry, Song and the Franchise, 1832–1918," which will run from 2016 to 2018 and produce a database, an anthology, and a series of essays based on the material disinterred.

ANTHONY CARTWRIGHT is a teacher and writer. He taught in secondary schools in London and in the Midlands for more than ten years and has lectured in the Creative Writing Masters course at Nottingham Trent University. The author of four novels, he is currently a First Story writer-in-residence in two schools and a visiting lecturer at City University,

London. His most recent book is *Iron Towns* (2016), and a novella, *The Cut*, will be published in 2017.

WILLIAM J. CHRISTMAS, Professor of English at San Francisco State University, is currently coediting, with Kevin Binfield, *Teaching Laboring-Class British Literature of the Eighteenth and Nineteenth Centuries* for the Modern Language Association's Options for Teaching series. His most recent essay, "Lyric Modes: The Soliloquy Poems of Mary Leapor and Ann Yearsley," appeared in *Tulsa Studies in Women's Literature* (Spring 2015).

MARY-ANN CONSTANTINE is Reader at the University of Wales Centre for Advanced Welsh and Celtic Studies. She works on Welsh and British literature of the long eighteenth century and has also written on travel writing, folk song, authenticity debates, and the Romantic movement in Brittany. Her book on the Welsh stonemason poet Edward Williams, *The Truth against the World: Iolo Morganwg and Romantic Forgery*, appeared in 2007. With Dafydd Johnston, she is general editor of the multivolume Wales and the French Revolution series. She is currently leading a four-year research project on the Welsh and Scottish Tour, 1760–1820.

COLE CRAWFORD is completing a master's in English at Oregon State University. He received his undergraduate honors degree from Creighton University with a double major in British literature and computer science. He has created a digital edition of Robert Tannahill's poetry, which includes additional online resources to support the study of Tannahill's life and work. He is collaborating with John Goodridge and his research team to design the online platform for the Database of British and Irish Labouring-Class Poets, 1700–1900. He intends to pursue a career in digital humanities support or software development.

FRANCA DELLAROSA is Associate Professor of English Literature at the Aldo Moro University, Bari, Italy. Her current research interests encompass Romantic drama and theater, laboring class writing, theater and poetry in the age of abolition. Her publications include *Talking Revolution: Edward Rushton's Rebellious Poetics, 1782–1814* (2014); *Slavery on Stage: Representations of Slavery in British Theatre, 1760–1830s* (2009); and the edited collections *Poetic and Dramatic Forms in British Romanticism* (2006) and *Slavery: Histories, Fictions, Memory, 1760–2007* (2012). She is presently coediting a special issue of the journal *La Questione Romantica*, dedicated to Rushton's Bicentenary (1814–2014).

COREY GIBSON is Lecturer in Modern English Literature at the University of Groningen in the Netherlands. He was awarded his PhD from the University of Edinburgh in 2012 and is the author of *The Voice of the People: Hamish Henderson and Scottish Cultural Politics* (2015), which was nominated and shortlisted for the Saltire Research Book of the Year Award, 2015. In 2012 he was awarded the Ross Roy Medal for his research in Scottish literary studies, and in 2013–14 he was a US–UK Fulbright Commission scholar at the University of California, Berkeley.

JOHN GOODRIDGE, FEA, is Emeritus Professor of English at Nottingham Trent University. He has published widely on laboring class, pastoral, and georgic poetry, and his books include *Rural Life in Eighteenth-Century Poetry* (Cambridge, 1994) and *John Clare and Community* (Cambridge, 2013). He is the general editor of the two three-volume series, *English Labouring-Class Poets*, and is general editor and principal writer for the online Database of British and Irish Labouring-Class Poets, 1700–1900.

GARY HARRISON, Professor Emeritus of English at the University of New Mexico, author of *Wordsworth's Vagrant Muse* (1994) and coeditor of the *Bedford Anthology of World Literature* (2004, 2009), has recently published several articles on John Clare's poetry and poetics, on teaching Romantic and world literature, and on the ecological implications of Romantic poetry. His most recently published essays have focused upon John Clare, William Wordsworth, and the "poetics of acknowledgment"; his chapter entitled "Writing Rural," on teaching the rural tradition in eighteenth- and nineteenth-century poetry, is forthcoming in Christmas and Binfield's *Teaching Laboring-Class British Literature of the Eighteenth and Nineteenth Centuries* (MLA).

IAN HAYWOOD is Professor of English Literature at the University of Roehampton, Director of the Centre for Research in Romanticism, and President of the British Association for Romantic Studies. His research focuses on the literature, radical politics, and visual culture of the eighteenth and nineteenth centuries. His books include *The Revolution in Popular Literature: Print, Politics and the People* (2004); *Bloody Romanticism: Spectacular Violence and the Politics of Representation 1776–1832* (2006); and *Romanticism and Caricature* (2013). He is also coorganizer of two research networks, "Romantic Illustration Network" and "Anglo-Hispanic Horizons 1780–1840."

List of Contributors xiii

ROD HERMESTON has taught English language at several UK universities, most recently at Sheffield Hallam University. He completed his PhD on linguistic identity in nineteenth-century Tyneside dialect songs at the University of Leeds. His research interests include the range of social meanings afforded by the Tyneside dialect in performance and print, with a strong focus on the varied responses of audiences and also readers. He is now extending his research beyond Tyneside song to the language of the wider British music hall. Rod is a former disability journalist and is also researching language and the representation of disabled people.

BRIDGET KEEGAN is Professor of English and Dean of the College of Arts and Sciences at Creighton University. She is editor of volume 2 of *Eighteenth-Century English Laboring-Class Poets 1740–1780* (2003). She is the author of *British Labouring-Class Nature Poetry, 1730–1837* (2008) and has published numerous essays and edited essay collections about laboring class poetry in general and about individual laboring class poets, in particular, John Clare and Robert Bloomfield. She has collaborated with John Goodridge over the last 25 years on various projects, including a forthcoming monograph entitled *The Occupations of Poetry: Laboring-Class Writers at Work, 1700–1900*.

H. GUSTAV KLAUS is Emeritus Professor of the Literature of the British Isles at the University of Rostock, Germany. He has published widely on nineteenth- and twentieth-century working class writing. His books include *The Literature of Labour* (1985); *Factory Girl* (1998); and *James Kelman* (2005) as well as the coedited collections *British Industrial Fictions* (2000); *"To Hell with Culture"* (2005); and *Ecology and the Literature of the British Left* (2012).

KAYE KOSSICK works for Action Language teaching English to refugees and asylum seekers. Formerly she was Senior Lecturer in English at Northumbria University. Her research interests focus on the task of recuperation and (re)presentation of work by writers hitherto marginalized by the literary hegemony. She has written on gender, class, and nation in poetry by English, Irish, and Scots writers from 1800 to the present moment. Her publications include works on Gerard Manley Hopkins, Scots writer Kathleen Jamie, and the first contemporary critique of the hitherto "disappeared" Irish poet Hannah Morison (fl. 1817). She also edited the extensive mid-nineteenth-century volume (1830–60) in the Pickering and Chatto English Labouring-Class Poets series.

DONNA LANDRY is Professor of English and American Literature at the University of Kent and a Fellow of the Royal Asiatic Society. She is the author, coauthor, or coeditor of six books, including *The Muses of Resistance: Laboring-Class Women's Poetry in Britain, 1739–1796* (Cambridge, 1990, 2005); *The Invention of the Countryside: Hunting, Walking, and Ecology in English Literature, 1671–1831* (2001); and *The Country and the City Revisited: England and the Politics of Culture, 1550–1850* (coedited with Gerald MacLean and Joseph P. Ward; Cambridge, 1999, 2006). Her most recent book is *Noble Brutes: How Eastern Horses Transformed English Culture* (2009). Landry is a member of the editorial board of the *John Clare Society Journal* and a founder-member of the Evliya Çelebi Way Project, a team of scholars and equestrians who rode across western Anatolia on horseback following the great Ottoman travel writer Evliya Çelebi, establishing a UNESCO Cultural Route (project website: www.kent.ac.uk/english/evliya/index.html).

BRIAN MAIDMENT is Professor of the History of Print at Liverpool John Moores University and Vice-President of the Research Society for Victorian Periodicals. He has written widely on nineteenth-century mass circulation print culture with particular interests in periodicals and illustration. He edited one of the first anthologies of writing by laboring class authors, *The Poorhouse Fugitives* (1987), and has continued to write on related topics. His most recent books are *Comedy, Caricature and the Social Order 1820–1850* (2013) and, coedited with Keith Hanley, *Persistent Ruskin* (2013).

SCOTT MCEATHRON is Associate Professor of English at Southern Illinois University. He has written extensively on the relationship between laboring class poetry and canonical Romanticism and, more recently, has published a series of essays on Romantic-era painters and paintings with links to Lamb, Hazlitt, and Keats. He is the editor of Thomas Hardy's *Tess of the d'Urbervilles: A Sourcebook* (2005); *English Labouring-Class Poetry, 1800–1830* (2006); and, with Simon Kövesi, *New Essays on John Clare: Poetry, Culture and Community* (Cambridge, 2015).

JENNIFER ORR is Lecturer in Eighteenth-Century Literature at Newcastle University, UK. She has published a monograph and several articles on Irish and Scottish Romantic-period literature, and her recent monograph *Literary Networks and Dissenting Print Culture* (2015), supported by the Irish Research Council, has brought to attention the role of Dissenting literary networks in the conception of transnational identity, particularly the role of laboring class Romantic circles in Ulster (1790–1830). Her current research aims to offer insights about historical migration across the Atlantic and its effect on national literary consciousness in the early American republic. She is a core contributing member of the *European Dimensions of Popular Print* project, which aims to create a pan-European taxonomy of popular print culture.

SHARON OUDITT is Reader in English at Nottingham Trent University. She has published widely on women writers in the early twentieth century and is the author of *Fighting Forces, Writing Women: Identity and Ideology in the First World War* (1994) and *Women Writers of the First World War: An Annotated Bibliography* (2000). More recently, she has been pursuing an interest in travel writing, as seen in *British Travel Writers in Southern Italy*, and is presently working on an edition of Evelyn Waugh's travel book *Labels*.

MIKE SANDERS is Senior Lecturer in Nineteenth-Century Writing at the University of Manchester. He finds an endless source of fascination and inspiration in the Chartist movement and its literature. His publications include *The Poetry of Chartism: Aesthetics, Politics, History* (Cambridge, 2009) as well as articles in *Victorian Studies, Victorian Poetry, Victorian Periodicals Review*, the *Journal of Victorian Culture*, and *Victorian Literature and Culture*.

LISA SHEPPARD is a Research Associate in Cardiff University's School of Welsh. She has previously worked as a Coleg Cymraeg Cenedlaethol–sponsored Lecturer in Welsh at the School and has taught English Literature at Cardiff's School of English, Communication, and Philosophy. Her doctoral thesis, completed in 2015, examined the portrayal of multiculturalism in contemporary fiction from south Wales, and her current research contributes to a project titled "The Welsh Language in Cardiff," led by Dr. Dylan Foster Evans. Her other research interests include bilingualism in literature, literary production and translation, postcolonial theory, and multiculturalism in minority language communities.

STEVE VAN-HAGEN is Principal Lecturer and Associate Head of the School of Humanities at Coventry University, UK. He has published on eighteenth-century writers, including Stephen Duck, James Woodhouse, Mary Leapor, and Jonathan Swift, and also publishes his own poetry.

NICOLA WILSON is Lecturer in Book and Publishing Studies at the University of Reading. She is the author of *Home in British Working-Class Fiction* (2015) and general editor of the Ethel Carnie Holdsworth series.

She has published essays on working class writing in the *Oxford History of the Novel in English* (volume 7) and *Key Words* 5 (2007) and has wide interests in the histories of reading and print culture. Her current book is on the literary and cultural impact of the British Book Society Ltd. (1929–69), the first mail-order book club to operate in Britain.

JACK WINDLE is an independent researcher with 12 years' experience of researching, writing about, and teaching British working class literature. His highly commended PhD thesis is about twentieth-century working class writing, with particular focus on its diversity of forms and its complex relationship to decolonization and the decline of the British Empire. He is currently working on a chapter about working class writing and literary theory, focusing on postcolonialism and the body, and projects to republish neglected working class texts by Jack Hilton and Len Doherty. Jack blogs about working class literature, history, and culture at proletics.wordpress.com.

Foreword

Donna Landry

It is a truth now universally acknowledged that there were English women writers before Jane Austen. Less well known is that there were laboring class writers before John Clare. Before the coming into being of the industrial working class, there were cottagers and agricultural workers, domestic servants and skilled artisans, who became published authors. Historical recovery work of the last three decades has uncovered dozens of such men and women throughout the British Isles, beginning circa 1700. The Cambridge *History of British Working Class Literature* testifies to this rich tradition. The place of working class writing in British literary history has always been marginal. Yet archival research has increasingly turned up numbers of English, Welsh, Scottish, and Irish authors, principally poets. To read their writing is to experience the silent majority suddenly finding a voice, the shepherd or washerwoman or haymaker stepping forward out of the "dark side of the landscape" toward us with tremendous energy.[1]

That the pastoral is always political nobody knows better than the shepherds themselves. During the eighteenth century, there developed a taste for rural writing that captured the national particularity of the country, with vernacular figures replacing classical models in the poetry of John Gay, Alexander Pope, and James Thomson. The countryside of Britain contains pastoral but also georgic topography peopled by plowmen and threshers, washerwomen and dairy maids, shoemakers and grooms. The democratization of the literary marketplace that made professional literary livelihoods possible and allowed women to publish also benefited the lower classes. Even the rural poor might occasionally find a voice through networks of patronage and publicity.

The place of early working class writing in Britain finds visual analogy in Paul Sandby's pen, ink, watercolor, and bodycolor picture *North West View of Wakefield Lodge in Whittlebury Forest, 1767* (Bonehill and Daniels, catalog entry 87, 207; and detail 64). The Duke of Grafton's estate is shown as a pleasure ground replete with deer and horses grazing on close-cropped lawns, a boating lake, a man and woman in an open carriage, and red-coated horsemen seeming to ask the way. At the center of the left-hand foreground of the picture, between the touristic gentlefolk and the livestock, a man and woman are collecting wood. The man has been halted in his movements by the appearance of the carriage party. He stands one-legged, having turned, one leg against the trunk, putting all his weight into stripping old wood or bark from a veteran ash tree. His body has the monumentality and sculpted form that will distinguish James Barry's 1790s figures (Kear and Thomas) and be experimented with so illuminatingly by William Blake. The woman is bending to tie up a bundle of neatly stacked wood, her back to the new arrivals. She is slight, pale, wearing a pale cap and short smock, her ankle visible, the foot encased in a black shoe. She looks beleaguered, weary, her shoulders hunched. Is she aware of the new arrivals yet? Would she take flight if she were, a huntress gathering her bag, about to flee the scene before anything untoward occurs? Although these wood gatherers might look out of place, laboring bodies exerting themselves in a pleasure park, they are emphatically *there*.

Why does Sandby focus our attention gently but inexorably on this working couple within an otherwise pastoral retreat? It happens that the Duke of Grafton was an agricultural improver, notoriously embroiled in disputes over Whittlebury Forest commoners' exercising of their customary rights, including gathering wood and hunting game (Bonehill and Daniels 206). Regardless of what Grafton might himself prefer, the location of Wakefield Lodge is enmeshed in forest custom and law, a field of power that exceeds the boundaries of the estate conceived as private land, constantly breeching them. It is characteristic of Paul Sandby to include such a reckoning of the infrastructural socioeconomic and human relations of the view portrayed. His pictures of Windsor, Edinburgh, and the military encampments that sprang up in and near London, attracting tourists, jostle the plebeian insistently alongside the polite. And the longer one studies this view of Wakefield Lodge, the clearer it becomes that the wood gatherers are its fulcrum, a darkly shadowed concentration of energy and interest, demonstrating boldly and publicly that there is a forest economy still, and one that entails arduous physical labor in the name of common rights.

So it is with laboring or working class writing. Despite the hierarchies of rank predicting and proscribing intellectual and creative achievement, exceptional figures since at least the early eighteenth century have made literary names for themselves in the British Isles. They have done so in diverse ways and by many different means and genres and, in doing so, have often changed the terms of debate within literary culture and brought about formal and aesthetic innovations as well as contributed new content to enrich and trouble patrician bias within British literary history. The Cambridge *History of British Working Class Literature* is a salutary reminder of how crucial and sometimes pivotal have been laborers' contributions to literature in the British Isles. The arc from the poets Stephen Duck and Mary Collier, the "Wiltshire thresher" and the "washerwoman of Petersfield," to the twenty-first-century Welsh fiction writers Jon Gower, Niall Griffiths, Owen Martell, and Angharad Pr, or the digital project Laboring-Class Poets Online, sheds refreshing new light on familiar terrain. The question is always asked of working class writers, as of women writers, "They may have existed, granted, but were they any good?"

That aesthetics and politics can never be entirely divorced from one another is one of the truths repeatedly revealed by the study of laboring class writing. The first chapter of this Cambridge *History*, serving as a keynote setting the agenda for subsequent chapters, addresses this question explicitly. Today the canonical inclusion of laboring class poets such as Stephen Duck, Mary Collier, Mary Leapor, and Ann Yearsley is once again being questioned on formal and aesthetic grounds. Such gifted writers as these can readily be defended. However, is it enough to focus solely on such undoubtedly exceptional writers, who were celebrated during their lifetimes as geniuses? Investigating women's petitions to the Foundling Hospital from 1760 onward, Jennie Batchelor reflects upon whether such traces of women's literacy, but also their formation and formulations of sexuality and subjectivity, should be included as part of a literary history. Batchelor proposes that the Foundling petitions "offer a salutary reminder that in privileging certain kinds of textual work above others, we risk privileging elite discourses of value around aesthetics or sexual politics or class."[2] The Foundling Hospital petitions "are more than mere historical curiosities"; they are "skillfully crafted documents that reveal the tellers' ability to manipulate language and narrative in order to secure the best chance of a successful hearing and to reimagine class-based and gendered understandings of seduction, maternity, and illegitimacy."

The entanglement of more elite authors and genres with working class literature as it insists upon a certain dissonance from the mainstream can be analogized, as I have shown, with representations of class differences in eighteenth-century British landscape art. Barrell, thinking of John Clare and those who preceded him, writes of how, by the end of the eighteenth century, pastoral or pastoral-georgic conventions had fallen out of favor with the polite classes "to be appropriated by radical writers, and by the humble poets of rural complaint, who demanded some of that leisure for the ploughman and thresher, which the shepherd and the gentleman-philosopher had long enjoyed" (Barrell, *The Dark Side* 81). These writers could in some sense give voice to those shadowy, enigmatic figures idling or laboring in the landscape – and more and more it was laboring, and looking cheerful while doing it, as the century wore on.

Thus, to find John Clare writing the following lines in "The Mores" early in the nineteenth century captures something of what was at stake in the increasing monitoring and extraction, including the extraction of grateful obligation, from the laboring poor:

> Unbounded freedom ruled the wandering scene
> Nor fence of ownership crept in between
> To hide the prospect of the following eye
> Its only bondage was the circling sky
> ...
> Cows went and came with evening morn and night
> To the wild pasture as their common right
> And sheep unfolded with the rising sun
> Heard the swains shout and felt their freedom won
> Tracked the red fallow field and heath and plain
> Then met the brook and drank and roamed again
> (ll. 7–10, 25–30)[3]

The pleasures of independence and of free time and movement across common land cannot be overestimated. For humans and other animals, the prospect of boundlessness is emancipatory, "a faint shadow of immensity" (l. 12). But nowhere in the country remains immune to the pressures of enclosure, privatization, and improvement:

> Inclosure came and trampled on the grave
> Of labours rights and left the poor a slave
> And memorys pride ere want to wealth did bow
> Is both the shadow and the substance now
> (ll. 19–22)

Clare's judgment regarding the actions taken in Helpston by agricultural improvers is as unequivocal as his joy had been in the unimproved prospect that "lost itself" and "seemed to eke its bounds / In the blue mist the orisons edge surrounds" (ll. 13–14).

Laboring class writing simultaneously benefits from new archival contexts through which to understand its genesis and reception and sheds fresh light on such contexts. Barrell has more recently traced an intricate web of conspiracies of British state power and paranoia in the wake of the French Revolution and war with France that evolved to become ever more micrologically entwined with debates about what the imagination, or imagining, might mean (Barrell, *Imagining*). Eventually, by 1796, even "imagining the king's death" could be considered treason. Barrell mentions in passing the case of Margaret Nicholson, a domestic servant who, in 1786, accosted George III alighting from his carriage outside St. James's, presenting him with a blank sheet of paper instead of a petition and attacking him with an ivory-handled dessert knife. She was pronounced a madwoman, thereby posing no political threat (Barrell, *Imagining* 354). There seemed no reason to connect her with serious protest, let alone regicidal republicanism. The following year, however, the laboring class poet Ann Cromarty Yearsley, the "Bristol milkwoman," whose work is explored in this volume by Kerri Andrews and Steve Van-Hagen, not only names Nicholson but implies, however archly, that her attack on the king may have carried political meaning. In "Addressed to Ignorance, Occasioned by a Gentleman's desiring the Author never to assume a Knowledge of the Ancients," a poem in her second volume, Yearsley ironizes her own supposed lack of education while exploring the theory of metempsychosis, whereby figures from classical mythology and history are reborn in contemporary England.[4] In a concluding twist, Yearsley substitutes an English historical figure for the ancients, with Margaret Nicholson reembodying the leader of the Peasants' Revolt of 1381:

> Wat Tyler, in Nicholson, dares a King's life,
> At St. James's the blow was design'd;
> But Jove lean'd from heaven, and wrested the knife,
> Then in haste lash'd the wings of the wind.
>
> (ll. 65–8)

To suggest the spirit of Wat Tyler was reincarnated in Margaret Nicholson may sound farcical, but the allusion also registers the possibility that Nicholson may have had a political point to make not unrelated to a venerable tradition of popular protest. As if to reinforce this reading of Nicholson, Yearsley ends the poem on a note that is both playful and defiantly personal, a defiance that also resonates politically:

> Here's Trojan, Athenian, Greek, Frenchman and I,
> Heav'n knows what I was long ago;
> No matter, thus shielded, this age I defy,
> And the next cannot wound me, I know.
>
> (ll. 69–72)

Fighting talk? Eight or nine years later, such an allusion to Nicholson might conceivably have been construed as a treasonable imagining of the king's death, but so far no evidence has emerged that anyone remembered it. Barrell's investigations shed retrospective light on the possible implications of Yearsley's poem. The poem itself offers new evidence of a laboring writer, however enigmatically, engaged in political comment.

Aesthetics and politics need to be understood as distinct categories of analysis and experience. Yet, that they can never be entirely severed from one another remains a lesson and a revelation delivered by working class writing.

NOTES

1. John Barrell adopted his title, *The Dark Side of the Landscape: The Rural Poor in English Painting 1730–1840*, from an unsigned review of George Crabbe's *The Village* in *The Gentleman's Magazine*. Following a study of the laboring poet John Clare, *The Idea of Landscape and the Sense of Place, 1730–1840: An Approach to the Poetry of John Clare*, Barrell in *The Dark Side* drew attention to how changing representations of the laboring class in eighteenth-century landscape painting might be understood as articulating tensions and conflicts registered also in contemporary writing about rural life, from John Gay's comic pastorals to the lament and loss of Oliver Goldsmith's *The Deserted Village* (1770) and the accounts of radical and "humble" writers (81).
2. A similarly powerful argument was mounted by Srinivas Aravamudan on behalf of the Sierra Leone settlers whose struggle has been obscured by scholarly fetishism of the literary genius of Olaudah Equiano; see *Tropicopolitans*, 253–88.
3. "The Mores" (written c. 1812–31), in Robinson and Powell, *The Oxford Authors: John Clare*, 167–9.
4. Ann Yearsley, Milkwoman of Clifton, near Bristol, "Addressed to Ignorance, Occasioned by a Gentleman's desiring the Author never to assume a Knowledge of the Ancients," in *Poems, on Various Subjects*, 93–9; also Yearsley, *Selected Poems*, 23–5. See also Landry, *Muses of Resistance*, 164–5.

Acknowledgments

In the last 25 years, we have worked separately and together, collaborating on numerous projects with the goal of advancing the study of working class literature as a significant, dynamic field of inquiry in English. While much work remains to be done, the publication of this volume represents something of a milestone for us in terms of achieving our scholarly goal. The preparation of this collection has given us the opportunity to draw together an international group of scholars, some already highly respected and others at the start of their careers. We are grateful to all the contributors for the time and care they have taken with their individual chapters and for what they have taught us about the breadth and depth of the tradition of British working class literature. We are also indebted to the editorial team at Cambridge University Press, in particular to Ray Ryan, for his immense patience – which we tried all too often – and for his encouragement and support during our rougher patches. Ray's vision for this and the two related volumes on Irish and American working class literature has been an inspiration to us. In addition, Joanna Breeze and Edgar Mendez provided outstanding support as we entered the production phase. Sarah Starkey, Anamika Singh, and Holly Monteith helped take the book through production, and Meghan Brawley stepped in during our hour of need to prepare the index. Finally, this book would not have been possible without Rachel Nozicka and Josie Whelan, our graduate research assistants. We wish to thank them for their exceptional support in helping to prepare the manuscript. Thanks to their tireless and careful efforts, the project has stayed on track.

Bridget Keegan wishes to thank several of her Creighton colleagues, including Rob Dornsife, Tracy Leavelle, Pam Yenko, and assistant editor Matt Reznicek, each of whom provided valuable moral support and advice. Bill Christmas has continued to be an important sounding board, giving much-needed coaching on "work–life" balance. Simon Kövesi has been –

as he always is – a source of inspiration, strength, and good humor in this and so many other projects.

John Goodridge would like to thank his colleagues and friends for their support, the contributors for their ideas and engagement, and most of all his coeditor for her patience, grace, and energy throughout the process of preparing this project.

And, of course, we would both like to thank our families for their love and care for us. We dedicate this book to them.

Introduction

John Goodridge and Bridget Keegan

This volume gathers new research from scholars investigating working class writing from the past three centuries, offering a sampling of 25 representative areas of study to give a conspectus of current critical thinking and research in the field. Perhaps the most straightforward definition of working class writing[1] is that it is writing produced by individuals who have not enjoyed social, economic, and educational advantages. By this reckoning the first English working class writer would also be the first English poet whose name we know, Caedmon (d. 680 CE), an uneducated stockman of Whitby Abbey whose vernacular "Hymn" to the Creator survives in Bede's *History* (248–51). Class is of course an evolving and elastic concept, a moveable feast. Raymond Williams's *Keywords* observes that the term first came into English in the sixteenth century in its Latin form, "classis," as "a general term for a division or group," and in its English form in the seventeenth century, when it "acquired a special association with education," a significant association in the present context. Williams dates its modern usage, describing specific social groups including the working class, to around 1770–1840, "the period of the Industrial Revolution and its decisive reorganisation of society" (*Keywords* 60–61). The *Oxford English Dictionary* (*OED*), defining "working class" as those who work for wages and "their families" and are "typically considered the lowest class in terms of economic and social status," gives as its first usage example a disapproving comment from 1735 about the stage being "a very improper Diversion to be planted among the Working Class of people" (*OED*, "working class"). Definition and example both imply a patrician view, and this sense of a category being imposed from above remains a central one. But as almost every chapter in this book witnesses, such class labels may be self-defining as well as restricting, and can provide an individual or a group of writers with a potentially empowering sense of identity. Throughout the history of working class writing we can find individuals and groups "writing back," adapting given class categories and creating their own senses of class traditions.

We follow the *OED* definition in the present volume to the degree that we draw our texts and topics from the past three centuries, the modern period, although we recognize that there were writers of lower class origin in the medieval and early modern period, notably in the socially wide range of political voices that welled up during the brief life of the Commonwealth. We have divided our study into three sections, broadly representing the past three centuries (the third section ends with some twenty-first century, forward-facing perspectives on our field of research). However, we adopt a broader sense of what "working class" writing might mean than the dictionary definition might suggest, purposely casting our net wide. Thus the writers discussed range from the unknown, almost anonymous women whose appeals to the Foundling Hospital are the topic of Jennie Batchelor's opening chapter, to figures like William Cobbett, famous and powerful enough to be caricatured and parodied, as closely examined by Ian Haywood in Chapter 11. The range of meanings in the floating signifier "working class," evident in the contrast between patrician perspectives and "writing back," is the central critical dynamic addressed by the volume.

A key issue in this dynamic is of course our own roles as readers, consumers, and mediators of this writing. The very act of assembling and critically discussing writers using a category such as "working class writing," necessary as it may be to the task of recovering a still neglected tradition, colors perceptions of it, and also, of course, affects the writers themselves. To take a well-known example, how does someone who has been patronized (in the original sense of receiving the patronage of a powerful figure), published and presented to the public as "The Northamptonshire Peasant," cope with the expectations and implications of such a role? The poet John Clare (discussed by Gary Harrison in Chapter 12), who was so-termed, found it very difficult to adapt to such a role. Clare was a gardener, a limeburner, and sometime militia-man who found it extremely difficult to settle to a role in life before he became a poet. He was rather well-educated by the standards of village culture in his time, taught to secondary level at a generally progressive "church porch" school; later he taught local children mathematics. His recent ancestors included a schoolmaster and several parish officials, literate individuals (Bate, *John Clare* 9–30; Clare, *By Himself* 2–8, 73–5, 79, 93–6, 185). The shoes, then, did not fit, but Clare still had to walk in them to reach his readership. There were many others like him: the "Database of British and Irish Labouring-Class Poets, 1700–1900" names over 2,000 published laboring class poets in the two centuries in which Clare lived (Goodridge, *Database*). How did he, how did they, cope?

Caedmon's hymn came to him, according to Bede, in a vision or a dream (248–50). Thirteen centuries later, the Leeds-born working class poet Tony Harrison (discussed by Jack Windle in Chapter 22) offered this short poem, "Heredity," on his own emergent "talent":

> *How you became a poet's a mystery!*
> *Wherever did you get your talent from?*
> *I say: I had two uncles, Joe and Harry–*
> *one was a stammerer, the other dumb.*
> (Harrison, *Selected* 111)

The amazed interlocutor in these lines may stand for all the ideological and psychological pressures that warn the poet that by writing poetry he is stepping out of his class role and regarded as a sort of freak. The "mystery" begins the familiar process of othering, restriction, and exoticization that routinely afflicts writers of lower class origin. Merely asking the question of where the poet's "talent" comes from implicitly reduces what has invariably been a long, painful acquisition of knowledge and skill, to a matter of genetics, sheer luck. "A poet is born, not made," John Clare's gravestone declares, regurgitating a debatable classical tag (Bate, *John Clare* 544). Harrison's poet-speaker's response is both defensive and defiant, matching mystification with paradox, puzzle for puzzle. Working class writing comes both from silence (dumbness), and from stammering, which Harrison in his poem "On Not being Milton," uses a medieval image to describe: "The stutter of the scold out of the branks of condescension." The *scald*, or poet, stutteringly struggles to escape the *scold's* bridle, breaking free of a device cruelly designed to silence women, here used as a metaphor for a mind-forged implement, an ideological restraint, a social silencing (Harrison, *Selected* 112). As Harrison's mordant lines suggest, working class writing is rarely received other than in partial or contingent ways, its mediators – patrons, publishers, consumers and scholars, even family and friends – repeating familiar patterns of limiting assumptions about what it is, and what its producers are and can be. Thus its recovery is not simply a matter of rediscovering and disseminating the materials in an accurate and accessible way (though this is certainly a vital task). It is equally important to seek nuanced understandings of the cultures, mechanisms, and ideologies of its production and reception.

The commonest modes of working class writing, poetry and lifewriting, evidence both patterns of limiting assumptions in their production, and modes of resistance. From the early eighteenth century onward, poets of humble origin were encouraged to write about their own working lives, and were presented to the reading public by their patrons and publishers in ways that foregrounded a class-based biographical context. The phenomenon of the "peasant-poet" was perceived as a species of natural genius, a kind of home-grown noble savage, whose poetry miraculously emerged from a rustic lifestyle, specifically without benefit of formal training and thus untainted with classicism or learned sophistry. Steve Van-Hagen in Chapter 4 offers a typology and case study of this ideology of "natural genius" and its variants, closely examining its development through the eighteenth-century period. The archetypal figure was the Wiltshire farm worker Stephen Duck (1705–56), who was prompted by his early patrons to write a poem "on his own situation," resulting in his famous poem, *The Thresher's Labour* (1730). Thus was born the limiting expectation that working class writers wrote about work, although Duck also included much else of interest in his debut volume, and later. His fame and success, led by the patronage of Queen Caroline, inspired many other writers as well as a slew of parodies and opportunistic imitations of various colors. In Chapter 2 Stephen Duck's biographer Jennifer Batt discusses these consequences, and the emergence of the "school" of Duck, while William J. Christmas in Chapter 3 puts Duck at the head of his analysis of genre and sociability.

To try and live out the fantasies of the reading classes was difficult, involving as it did a charade of unlearned innocence and a requirement never to cease being an unspoiled "peasant." Clare's patron Lord Exeter, for example, granted the poet a pension that was specifically designed to equal two days wages a week, with the implication that his "peasant" fieldwork would continue to balance and inform his poetic labors (Bate, *John Clare* 160). Merryn and Raymond Williams describe the cognitive dissonance involved in this, a "cultural model based on so deep a contradiction" (Williams and Williams, "Introduction" 5). Working class lifewriting emerged partly as a form of authentication for this poetical charade, though like the poetry that it often accompanied it also enabled self-expression, albeit of a sometimes cautious kind. Volumes of poems were often prefaced with brief autobiographical statements. Their focus on the simple, uneducated life the author had led signalled a further limiting assumption: that of the humble poet as a potentially deserving charity case. Jennie Batchelor in Chapter 1 and Scott McEathron in Chapter 10 consider what was involved in using written language to obtain such charity, in the areas, respectively, of child adoption and writerly financial support. Charity was very much the model Robert Southey used for the "uneducated poets," as he called them in his account of his selection of them in 1832 (Southey, *Lives*). His unfair description of Ann Yearsley (a poet discussed by Steve Van-Hagen in Chapter 4 and Kerri Andrews in Chapter 6) as an impoverished and mentally unbalanced failure in later life, a picture much at variance with recent scholarly accounts (Waldron, *Lactilla*; Andrews, *Ann Yearsley*), reflects his horror at her "ungrateful" rebellion against her patron Hannah More in 1785, and seems designed to punish her rebellion and damage her reputation.

By contrast Southey seems to admire the entrepreneurial spirit of the "Water Poet" and boatman John Taylor, a contemporary of Shakespeare and possibly the model for the garrulous, opportunistic boatman in *Shakespeare in Love* (1999; Southey, *Lives*; Norman and Stoppard, *Shakespeare* 67). At the time Southey was writing we can detect a general change in the limiting assumptions of working class writers, from the "peasant-poet" and the charity case, to the Victorian ideal of the enterprising and energetic self-made man (Winks, *Lives*; Smiles, *Self-Help*). The "heroic workers" of nineteenth- and twentieth-century radical culture further valorized and gave voice to the working class writer, but the idealization and the co-option of their writings for specific political purposes, especially in the official culture of the Russian and Eastern European pre-1989 states, led to pressures against and consequent neglect of other kinds of working class writing, such as spiritual poetry and aesthetic concerns. And if British postwar culture, educational reform, and the welfare state, made it easier for working class writers to find success, acceptance, and increased freedom in subject matter, still the exceptionalist view, Harrison's "condescension," and limited expectations predominated. The "peasant-poet" model, Williams and Williams wrote in 1986, "did not end in Clare's lifetime." It remained, even "as we write, and even in some of its original forms, unfinished" (6).

A recurrent tension in much of the work discussed in the collection is between whether working class writers felt and represented themselves to be part of a community, based on occupation, habitation, or other categories of affiliation, or as isolated and apart from their social or cultural milieu. The burgeoning labor movements of the nineteenth century, especially Chartism, often provided writers the opportunity for explicit articulations of a "class consciousness." We see in Mike Sanders's discussion of Thomas Cooper's *Purgatory of Suicides* (Chapter 14), that the best such writers saw their work as far from being simply propaganda. Indeed, if writers emphasized their affiliation with any occupational grouping, it was most often that of their fellow writers. The desire to understand themselves as part of a broader contemporary community or historical tradition of artists is a thread uniting many of the writers discussed in these chapters. While the myth of the isolated, impoverished genius has continued to be pervasive, our understanding of the many varieties of networks in which working class writers participated continues to grow and is widely reflected in the contributions to the volume. Kirstie Blair's chapter on newspaper culture evidences some of the new resources becoming available to working class writers in the nineteenth-century period.

One way in which working class authors affirmed their fellowship as writers was through the exercise of formal skills and expertise, as well as explicit literary addresses and intertextual allusions, paying homage to esteemed forebears and demonstrating their artistic *bona fides*. Focusing on eighteenth-century writers, William J. Christmas in Chapter 3 considers how the use of the verse epistle helped to create and represent links among laboring class poets, while Kerri Andrews (Chapter 6) shows how Ann Yearsley used the more "elevated" elegiacal mode both to connect with and to differentiate herself from an esteemed English tradition harkening back to John Milton. Gary Harrison (Chapter 12) explores John Clare's engagement with poetic modalities to represent rurality, in particular the idyll, a recurring challenge for working class writers, especially those who knew something of the real rural world like Clare. While shorter lyric forms were often preferred for very practical reasons by laboring class poets, laboring class writers did not shy away from experimentation with longer forms, even the epic (as explored by Mike Sanders in Chapter 14), and more commonly the novel, which begins to overtake poetry as a preferred form for capturing working class experience in the modern period. The modern working class novel is examined in several chapters devoted to twentieth-century literature, including H. Gustav Klaus's study on tramping (Chapter 18), Nicola Wilson's discussion of serial fiction by Ethel Carnie Holdsworth (Chapter 19), Anthony Cartwright's study of Alexander Baron and urban masculinity (Chapter 20) and Lisa Sheppard and Aidan Byrne's examination of postmodern experimentation in the contemporary Welsh working class novel (Chapter 23).

The question of form in working class literature extends beyond traditional genres, but may incorporate mixed media works such as song, discussed in Rod Hermeston's chapter on northeast music hall culture (Chapter 17), or film, which has profoundly influenced modern writing. Indeed, the role of film, and before that, of drama, in shaping working class identity could form the subject of an entirely separate collection of essays. Word limits precluded our ability to commission additional essays that would treat this area; nevertheless the essays in the volume begin to gesture toward the role of theater, film, radio, television, and new media.

One literary mode pervading both poetry and prose is lifewriting, especially autobiography of various kinds. Such writings often reflect the tensions and contradictions of writers whose writerly identity is always qualified by their class status and often other markers of social identity. This is especially prevalent for women writers, who navigate the triple stresses of an artistic calling along with inherited gender and class obligations. Mary Collier's elegant repartee to Stephen Duck's complaints about male worker's travails, *The Woman's Labour* (1739), vividly represents women workers' "triple shift" of caring for children, managing the home and housework, and laboring outside the family home. Men worked hard outside the home too, but could anticipate periods of rest and familial consolations that are, even today, unavailable to women who continue to be primary caregivers to children and perform the uncompensated work of cooking and cleaning for their families while men are "recovering" from a day in the fields or the factory. If it is remarkable that men who performed exhausting manual labor found the energy and inspiration to read and write, it is perhaps miraculous that women, who had to balance these further responsibilities, could do so, and did so with such skill and in such numbers. Kaye Kossick on the prodigiously talented, self-taught, tambour frame embroiderer Janet Hamilton (Chapter 13), Florence S. Boos on Victorian working class women's lifewriting (Chapter 15), Nicola Wilson on the achievements of Ethel Carnie Holdsworth (Chapter 19), and Sharon Ouditt on the lifewriting of Kathleen Dayus (Chapter 21), help to paint a fuller picture of the range of challenges that working class women writers powerfully overcame, vividly representing their realities and often building the groundwork for political change.

The expressions of identity generated from regional and national affiliations, and the linguistic manifestations of this variety, especially through dialect, are another unifying theme of the collection. The concept of "Britishness" may be as contested as that of "class" and, as we have discovered both through our own research and in working with the contributors, working class writing in Scotland, Ulster, and Wales could be regarded as traditions in their own right. While physical hardship and the "pursuit of knowledge under difficulties" might be common themes, the differences in history, economy, education, and language meant that the "transnational" Northern Irish writers considered by Jennifer Orr in Chapter 9, figures like Alexander Wilson (discussed by Gerard Carruthers in Chapter 5), Janet Hamilton (Chapter 13), and the modern Scottish writers of Corey Gibson's essay (Chapter 23), often forged very different paths from their English contemporaries. Our contributors on Welsh traditions are also strongly alert to both the separateness of Welsh working class writing (emphasized by Mary-Ann Constantine in her discussion of Iolo Morganwg and his contemporaries in Chapter 7), and the need to combat limiting stereotypes and to acknowledge the new realities of postindustrial, bilingual Welsh writing (Aidan Byrne and Lisa Sheppard in Chapter 24).

One stereotype of working class writing is that it is fixed in its location and local in outlook. This can of course be true: John Clare, describing a visit to Wisbech for a job interview, notes that he had "never been above 8 miles from home in my life" (*By Himself* 70). But many writers traveled widely, including shipbuilders like the Scottish poet John Macleay Peacock, who lived and worked on Tyneside and Merseyside, in Ireland, and in Spain, attending the First Chartist Convention in London for good measure (Goodridge, *Database*); or sailors and migrants, like the two poets discussed by Franca Dellarosa and by Gerard Carruthers in Chapters 8 and 5, Edward Rushton and Alexander Wilson, both notably cosmopolitan and "transnational" figures, the latter indeed a major figure in American as well as Scottish literary history. The global dimension of working class writing is also apparent when we examine the complex intersections of race and class, evident in Rushton's conversion from a sailor on a slave ship to a vociferous abolitionist, or the nuanced responses to race and society of the twentieth-century authors Sam Selvon and Tony Harrison, discussed by Jack Windle in Chapter 22.

The final chapter in this collection, by the young digital humanities scholar Cole Crawford, draws attention in its advocacy of new methods and opportunities to the question of theoretical approaches. On this subject we have no party line, the 25 essays each taking up their own position in order to offer what John Russo and Sherry Lee Linkon characterize, in their collection of essays on *New Working-class Studies*, as an "intellectual meeting ground" for different approaches (1). The research is often grounded in archival studies, based on the recovery of often rare and fragile work, but the state of the archive and its digitization has had considerable impact, and Crawford offers new ways of working that are both enriching to our knowledge of these writers and this tradition, and – in their integral interactivity – widely democratic in character.

The recovery and reappraisal of working class writing is a large, complex, and continuing task, involving archival work, editing and explication, scholarly presentation of various sorts, and a critical evaluation and re-evaluation both of the material itself and of our own roles as mediators, readers, and consumers of culture. It takes on a special critical urgency in a period in which traditional working class cultures in Britain and the industries that bred them are rapidly disappearing. It is a bitter irony that while the widespread nostalgia for such cultures has become increasingly commodified, especially as an element of heritage culture, the contemporary working class itself has grown ever more culturally and politically disparaged and unvalued (as scorchingly exposed in Owen Jones's book, *Chavs*). The first responsibility of any history of working class writing, then, must be to recover these writings with a keen alertness to the politics of class and of cultural appropriation. The search for "authenticity" should not eclipse such important critical topics as self-presentation, patronage, the relationships between fields of identity such as class, race, region, and gender, the growth of writing communities and new publishing outlets, and (not least), more formalistic question concerning literary and cultural value in the texts examined. While the present volume cannot cover more than a fraction of the rich mass of working class writing, it has been shaped and developed with these critical questions very much in mind.

NOTE

1. Contributors use the terms "working class" and "laboring class" writing/writers flexibly throughout the volume.

CHAPTER 1

When "Bread Depends on Her Character"
The Problem of Laboring Class Subjectivity in the Foundling Hospital Archive

Jennie Batchelor

> [Y]our humble Petitioner has had the Misfortune, like many of her Sex, [to get] with Child by a Person in whom I had the greatest confidence, but unhappely to my greatest Misfortune, I have never seen him since.... I am forced to implore your kindness to extend your charity so far as to admit it in to the Hospital, that I may be free'd again to go about & to get my Bread in an honest way, or else the Child and I must inevitably perish.
> – petition of Anne Wapshott, read in the General Committee, 13 March 1771[1]

Anne Wapshott's petition to the Foundling Hospital to admit her illegitimate infant is just one of the many hundreds of such documents preserved by the Thomas Coram Foundation and now held by the London Metropolitan Archive.[2] After the termination of the hospital's controversial period of General Reception (2 June 1756 to 31 March 1760), during which all infants meeting the charity's age requirements were admitted, mothers (or sometimes fathers and other encumbered individuals) were required to submit a written petition. These publicly read written petitions were intended to prove to the institution's General Committee that the petitioner's child was sufficiently deserving of a chance of admission. Testimony was never taken at face value, however, and a petitioner's story had to be verified before it was determined whether the petitioner could be admitted to the ballot, at which s/he then had to be fortunate enough to draw a white ball from a bag to secure a child's entry to the hospital. Wapshott's account of how her one "false step" had "reduced" her and her "innocent Baby" to "the greatest indigency[,] destitute of any Support either by Friends or Relations," engaged the Committee's attention. She drew a black ball in the ballot held on 1 June 1771 but a white one a year later on 11 January 1772. If, as Alysa Levene suspects, Wapshott's son was Richard Eyre, he would die five years later, on 2 February 1776 (*Narratives* 221, note 1).

Wapshott's account of the fatal consequences of misplaced confidence in men and of society's lack of compassion toward women who gave birth to illegitimate children would be repeated by "many of her Sex" in the Foundling Hospital's early decades. Hers was a proverbial tale, so familiar as to require little explanation and so common as to plead the necessity of the charitable institution from which she sought relief. Yet despite the fact that Wapshott knew she needed to conform to the generic model of charitable "Object" – one of "many" like herself – she also recognized that she needed to be viewed as an individual whose particular case merited support if she was to be successful. In navigating her way between these twin imperatives, Wapshott, like many of her fellow petitioners, steered a well-plotted course. For many women, such as Ann Smith, whose single-sentence petition was read in the General Committee on 11 April 1781, desperation was communicated most powerfully through brevity.[3] Others produced more elaborate and often rhetorically sophisticated testimonies that recalled sentiments and structures familiar from contemporary print and oral seduction narratives. Read collectively, this chapter will argue, these petitions provide a rich and still under-researched archive of laboring class literature that reveals significant insights into how working women, in particular, used narrative both to contest and to construct their lives.

A small but significant body of scholarship has illuminated the importance of the Foundling Hospital petitions to the histories of illegitimacy and bastardy (Levene, Nutt, and Williams), motherhood (Evans, *"Unfortunate Objects"*), breastfeeding and childhood (Levene, *Childhood*), and the charity movement (McClure; Outhwaite). More broadly, the petitions, along with sources such as depositions, pauper letters, and parish records, form part of the ever-growing archive from which we can retell "history from below" by reclaiming what Tim Hitchcock, Peter King, and Pamela Sharpe refer to in the subtitle of their 1997 essay collection as the "voices and strategies of the poor." Yet, the project of recovering the experiences of the poor on the level of the individual is fraught with pitfalls. The illiteracy of the majority of the laboring class in the period means that any written evidence of their lives must be viewed with an eye to its mediation by the hands who often transcribed it. Such forms of mediation include the institutional imperatives that the poor proved adept at internalizing in a bid to prove sufficiently deserving of relief (e.g., Hitchcock, King, and Sharpe 5).

Reading the Foundling petitions necessitates similar caution. Many of these documents are signed merely with the petitioner's cross, and some bear the hallmarks of professional letter writers. Furthermore, as we shall see, the petitioner's rhetoric can be suspiciously generic, injected as it is with a spirit of desperation actuated by the petitioner's realization that she likely had only one chance to put her case before the Committee (Levene, *Narratives* xv). The petitions' closeness to the conventions of seduction plots presents further and more intractable problems. Sentimental literary petitions by the likes of Elizabeth Brooks, a seduced and abandoned 30-year-old servant and carer for a desperately ill mother, or that of the well-educated but cruelly duped Mary Logdon, whose petition is discussed below, are unusually but not uniquely deft and arguably self-conscious in their literariness.[4] More commonly, petitions mirrored, and like Wapshott's relied on, the Committee's knowledge of the stock plots and well-rehearsed complaints against male infidelity and social injustice characteristic of the ballads that formed the soundtrack to eighteenth-century street life and to which, we assume, Foundling petitioners had more ready access. The sheer repetitiveness and disquieting familiarity of the petitioners' tales serve both to emphasize the appalling conditions in which many laboring class women lived and partly to blunt the intensity of the stories they document.

Modern scholars are much more troubled by the formulaic elements of the women's petitions than original Committee members were, in part because the latter required conformity to the charity's mission and because they could look to living sources to corroborate the personal claims amid the women's generic tales. In the absence of such supporting evidence, and confronted by the similarities between the petitions and contemporary imaginative accounts of seduction, it is hard to say what the petitions can reliably tell us about the reality of eighteenth-century laboring class experience. As Levene points out, although these documents can reveal "much about the strategies of the poor," their heavy mediation means that we can only "speculate" about how petitioners "genuinely felt" about their lives and children (*Narratives* xviii). Indeed, in the face of the unreliability of narrative, historians such as John Styles have turned instead to the material archive, specifically to the textile swatches and tokens left with foundlings so that they might be identified and reclaimed by their parents, to shed less ambiguous light on the affective lives of petitioners forced by circumstance to give up their offspring.

While acknowledging the challenges involved in text-based study of laboring experience in the eighteenth century, I want nonetheless in this chapter to assert the continuing usefulness of archives of the spoken and written word. Specifically, I want to focus on the slippage between many petitioners' stories and print and oral literature of the period. In the few pieces of historical scholarship in this area, most notably in the work of

Tanya Evans, seduction plots appear to confirm the cultural constraints within which eighteenth-century laboring women lived and worked. Thus, Evans claims, the literary, sentimental, and predominantly middling sort "concept of seduction" reified in eighteenth-century print was something that Foundling petitioners were well advised to accede to in order to generate sympathy and prove their worth (*"Unfortunate Objects"* 99). Ballads, on the other hand, with their tragic and often fantastic tales of revenge upon deceitful male lovers, are cast as offering up forms of poetic justice sadly unavailable to abandoned laboring women in real life (Evans, "'Blooming Virgins" 33). My interest here lies not in the extent to which literary texts reflected lived reality. Nor is it entirely in proving the reverse, that is, how the lived realities elucidated in the petitions severed the conventional connections between "sexual behavior" (for which read: chastity) and "virtue" that Ruth Perry and others have argued is paradigmatic of imaginative literature in this period (244–7). Instead, I want to ask what happens when the Foundling petitions are read not solely in dialogue with the texts with which they have so much in common but, additionally, in dialogue with each other and, most importantly, as laboring class literature in their own right.

Such moves seem both timely and provocative. Over the past two decades, the rise of the new formalism has had a marked impact on the study of historical laboring class literature, particularly on the poetry of so-called natural geniuses on which the majority of relevant work in eighteenth-century studies has focused. The renewed privileging of aesthetics over politics has certainly helped to redress an imbalance in scholarship in the area which, as Donna Landry and William J. Christmas argue, has tended to be "complicit in tying laboring-class writers... so tightly to their social difference from polite culture that their achievements cannot be appreciated artistically, but only sociologically" (414). A parallel move has been made in studies of eighteenth-century women's writing as we inch (arguably prematurely) toward a post-recovery moment in which it seems prescient to ask not merely which women wrote but which of them were good at writing. Susan Staves's 2006 women's literary history, for instance, takes impetus from her claim that "[i]t cannot be a sin against feminism to say that some women wrote well and others wrote badly" (4) or that many texts by female authors are of only sociological interest while only a significant minority are the "proper object of literary study" (5). To suggest otherwise, she claims, runs the risk of ghettoizing women's writing, of defining it by its difference or the mere fact of its existence rather than on its many artistic merits.

Of course, whether it is possible or desirable to disentangle politics from questions of aesthetics and value is a moot point, albeit one to which a number of eighteenth-century laboring class and women writers spoke with great clarity and conviction. It is perhaps sufficient to note here that, in this current scholarly climate, the Foundling petitions would seem to be decidedly less proper objects of literary study than their authors were of charitable benefaction. Nonfiction prose "authored" by non- or barely literate laboring class women, these documents seem to fit squarely into Staves's definition of texts of sociological interest. Indeed, some, like Ann Smith's aforementioned petition, offer little tangible evidence to attract any scholarly attention beyond the fragment of unglossed insight her petition provides into the desperation of an unknown woman from a largely unreconstructable past. Yet, this chapter will argue, the Foundling petition archive as a whole presents a rich seam of historical evidence and textual allusion that productively reframes our sense of eighteenth-century laboring class access to the literary world. The petitions of these women are invaluable for the important glimpses they provide into how literary texts enabled the laboring poor and illiterate to conceptualize, articulate, and wrest control of cultural narratives about their lived experience.

The potential richness of petitioners' claims is no better exemplified, perhaps, than by the case of Mary Logdon, whose petition was read on 6 November 1793. Logdon's story of relentless downward mobility in a mercenary world is immediately arresting. Although it opens with Logdon conventionally declaring herself "at a loss . . . to make herself in any degree an Object deserving the Benevolence she humbly petitions for," her show of embarrassment takes an unexpected turn when it becomes clear that it stems as much from her awareness that disclosing her situation will expose "the Depravity as well as cruelty of her near Relation" as much as publicize her own transgression. Having completed "a liberal Boarding School Education" financed by her aunt, Logdon explains, she left school to live with her relative, little expecting that her guardian "should plot her Ruin" by conniving her seduction by a "Man of Fashion," who would become the "unconscious . . . Instrument of her [Logdon's] Disgrace." Following her seduction and desertion by the unnamed man, Logdon was forced from her home. The family of Mr. John Woodyer, who provided a supporting letter for Logdon's case, provided "Comfort" for her, but "her Necessities" and fear of "the Horrors of a Jail" "for[c]ed Her into a second Prostitution," which resulted in the birth of the "beloved infant" for whom she sought relief from the hospital (359).

Logdon's disturbing tale of familial grooming, seduction, and whoredom bears a striking resemblance to Samuel Johnson's "The History of Misella" (essays 170 and 171 in *The Rambler* [2 and 5 November 1751]), a sentimentalized seduction-into-prostitution narrative that formed a prototype for the many that followed. Both Misella and Logdon are, disquietingly but importantly for their pleas, of "good famil[ies]" (82). For both, seduction leads inexorably to "a second Prostitution." And like Misella, who concludes her narrative by articulating her hope to be granted the "privilege of banishment" and restoration to "honesty and peace" (97), Logdon ends her plea with a wish to seek "the Discharge of her little Debts from a Plan for future Happiness and Reformation" in "the comfort of Retirement" (360).

"Misella," a fictional moral tale masquerading as a genuine letter from a periodical reader, and Logdon's factual yet nonetheless literary rendering of her descent from seduction into prostitution essentially share a plot. Although playing for very different stakes, both women lobby for their readers' sympathy and defend their right to think of themselves as "Object[s] deserving [of] Benevolence." Both point to the "desperation" attendant upon the corruption of the family unit, and both signal the disastrous consequences of society's unwillingness to forgive women whose "Caracter" is "blast[ed]" (359). Yet closer attention to the language and narrative trajectories of both texts reveals important differences between them.

The most obvious difference is that Logdon is a mother whereas Misella's apparent pregnancy – "Our crime had its usual consequence" (88) – is presented elliptically either as being an illusion or ending in miscarriage or abortion – "He . . . congratulated me upon my escape from the danger which we had both expected with so much anxiety" (91). The narrative convenience of the disposal of Misella's child serves, in part, as a hallmark of the essay's conservatism. Whether imagined or real, it forces Misella to understand her "Crime" – internalized as "our" rather than as her seducer's – for the first time. True to the Ovidian epigraph with which Misella's narrative begins, she "grants the charge" of her guilt even while requesting "forgive[ness]" for "the fault."[5]

Logdon, by contrast, presents her child as the source of her redemption. Had she not accepted the second relationship that resulted in her pregnancy, Logdon told Committee members, she would have killed herself and committed a greater sin than that of bringing a bastard into the world. Any regret Logdon feels for her "wretched" situation is not for herself, or for the absence of her child's father – "a worthless Caracter" with whom she endured a connection "not formed on regard"; instead she laments only that "her beloved infant" should be left with "so fruitless a Being as herself" (359). In stressing her child's innate innocence, despite its illegitimacy, Logdon subscribes to the Lockean logic of the institution from which she sought relief while simultaneously condemning its many critics who suggested that Foundling mothers were "*indifferen*[*t*]" to children (Hanway 27), who, in any case, "doubtless inherit[ed] their parents vices" (Purbeck II:192). Perhaps more importantly, and counter to Misella's logic, Logdon's pregnancy and love for her child confirm her sense of blamelessness. Expressing a sentiment that, as we shall see, reverberates throughout the petition archive, Logdon provocatively claims that, although her "Caracter" was ruined in the eyes of "every one who knew her" following her seduction, her virtue remained intact. Like her child, Logdon could not be held accountable for her misfortunes, for these were "Errors, to which her Will or inclination was never consenting" (360).

Logdon questions the sentimentalized literary rhetoric of seduction and its associations with female sexual passivity even as she relies upon it to articulate her worth as charitable object. She refuses to internalize the guilt articulated by Misella and upon which grounds readers' sympathetic identification with her plight was legitimized. She determinedly resists, even while demonstrating awareness of, a literary "concept of seduction" as victimization that Evans suggests Foundling petitioners were "forced to buy into" as "the only way their child could be admitted into the hospital by governors unsympathetic to their plight" (*"Unfortunate Objects"* 99).[6] Logdon, in common with most of her fellow petitioners, does not identify herself as a sexual agent: her first seduction seems to have been consensual, but "plott[ed]" by her aunt. Neither, however, does she deploy the discourse of victimization: her second seduction, she implies, was entered into knowingly and pragmatically even if her "Will" did not consent to it. Presenting herself as neither aggressor nor prey, Logdon problematizes a critical binary that, as Katherine Binhammer has elucidated, has distorted our understanding of eighteenth-century literary and historical accounts of seduction. Binhammer's interest in the vast if "murky, open and undefined territory" (2) beyond these dual possibilities lies in recovering forms of "affective agency" (4) for women that literary and social historians have traditionally denied.[7] If, and it seems unlikely, Logdon had the luxury of being able to act on her desire, she clearly could not articulate as much in this institutional context. Nonetheless, she carves out a space to argue for her personal integrity in the face both of the forms of objectification she had experienced in life and of the cultural discourses to which she was bound to appear to submit if her petition to the hospital were to be successful.

Although she casts herself as "an Object deserving [of] Benevolence," Logdon nonetheless quickly eschews the rhetoric of objectification to develop instead a more flexible and enabling understanding of "Caracter." As petitioners revealed with insistent clarity, "character" was everything to them. In large part because the a priori innocence of the foundlings was widely accepted by the hospital's administration, admission to the institution was largely predicated upon mothers proving themselves to be deserving objects of relief on the basis that they could prove their former, and therefore potential for a future life of, virtue. Yet if the woman's character was of vital importance within the hospital's walls, it was more crucial in the world beyond them. As the "unfortunate" Millicent King related to the Committee in a petition read on 10 January 1781[?], as a woman and as a servant, her "Bread" and very "livelihood" "depend[ed]" on her "Character," the integrity of which would be fatally jeopardized if she could no longer conceal her pregnancy by a lover who had been "impress'd into his Majesties Service" before being able to marry her (287). King's bid to persuade the Committee that "her tender Infant [was] a proper Object of [the] Charity" rested upon her conviction, corroborated by a witness statement provided by a Mrs. Jones, that her "Character . . . has been (and still is unexceptional[)]" despite her "Error" (287). In a typical move we have already seen in Logdon's petition, King plays with multiple concepts of "character" and reveals the potentially devastating fault lines upon which definitions of the term rested.[8]

Pressing on the distinction between a term that could connote both a "person with his assemblage of qualities" and a "representation of any man as to his personal qualities" (definitions 6 and 4 in Johnson's *Dictionary of the English Language* [1755]), King draws attention to the potential disjunction between a woman's private constitution and her public reputation as it was refracted through cultural conventions, sexual double standards that "prejudice[d] her in the eye of the world," and a labor market that offered negligible options to women who were forced to attempt to combine work and motherhood. Like Misella, King admits that she has committed a "fault," but, like Logdon, she maintains that her "inclination" was and remains post-seduction "far from being Vicious" (287). Nonetheless, she is all too aware that others' knowledge of her illicit sexual liaison will prevent her from obtaining, in yet another sense of the term, a "Character" (that is, a reference) or that any testimony she might conjure in her favor would be unwritten by the "unfit appearance" occasioned by her poverty

(287). (King had been forced to sell all but a few of her clothes "to support her lying-in.") Thus she is forced to author her own, competing character reference in the form of the petition for the hospital committee's consumption, one that goes beyond the institution's published requirement that potential objects of relief prove their "previous good character" (*Regulations for Managing the Hospital* 81). In her own mind, if not in those of her potential employers, King claims that her character would "bear enquiry" from anyone who seeks to question it despite her supposed deviation from the "Path of Honour" (287). Her case received a sympathetic hearing and her status as a proper object was accepted. The fate of her child, like Logdon's, is unknown.

Discourses of character also play an important part in testimonies by petitioners that superimpose their stories onto the seduction-and-abandonment plots and truisms about the competing worlds of affect and economics that characterized street literature, particularly ballads. Unlike sentimental seduction narratives, ballads, as Evans notes, presented "premarital sex... as commonplace and female sexual desire as given"; these were texts that were "rooted in the social, economic, and cultural context of eighteenth-century Britain and reflected the realities of the lives of English men and women" ("Blooming Virgins" 20). Like the Foundling petitions, seduction ballads are commonly structured around a set of gendered oppositions. Thus, as in the popular ballad "The Broken Contract; or, the Betrayed Virgin's Complaint," female constancy ("my love I plac'd most desperately") is pitted against male infidelity ("When I with child did prove, and him had told, / He call'd me twenty whores, brazen and bold"), while the great disparity between the choices available to unmarried mothers and the fathers of their illegitimate children (she "wander[s] to and fro" while he continues unencumbered in another town) is laid bare. Foundling petitioners relied heavily on the Committee's understanding of the unreliability of men and their "deluding tongue[s]." Petitioner after petitioner presents her one "false step" as part of a much wider pattern of male duplicity made proverbial in the ballad tradition; yet each begs the hospital to foreclose the narrative possibilities suggested by the comparison.

While considerable caution has to be exercised when talking about so heterogeneous and (since one text could have multiple and significantly different printed and oral variants) so slippery a body of work as ballads, broadly speaking two trajectories predominate in those tragic ballads (as Binhammer denotes them) dealing with seduction, abandonment, and illegitimate birth: those that culminate in the death of the mother, who either metaphorically returns from the grave to warn female readers of male perfidy (as in "The Broken Contract") or who reappears as a specter to haunt a perfidious lover (as in "The Yarmouth Tragedy; or, the Perjur'd Sailor"); and those that lead to the death of the child by cruelty, poverty, or murder (such as in "The Cruel Mother"). While the threat of infanticide is kept firmly at bay in the petitions (petitioners emphasized repeatedly that they were abandoning their children out of love and necessity, not neglect), women such as Wapshott, with whose petition this essay opened, were at pains to point out that their story would inevitably end in the same death that met so many ballad heroines and their children before them without the hospital's intervention.[9] Duped, "like many of [her] Sex" by a "Person in whom [she] had the greatest confidence" and who vanished after impregnating her, Wapshott pleaded for the hospital's help so that she could once again "get my Bread in an honest way," without which support "the Child and [she] must inevitably perish" (221). Although her strategy is different, like Logdon and King, Wapshott eschews the question of her own culpability by failing to concede any "crime" of the sort to which Misella admits. Wapshott took a "false step," but had her lover been worthy of the "Confidence" placed in him, she could have avoided the impossible "Misfortune" of having "no Friends or Relations to rear up [an] innocent baby" she had to labor to support but whose existence prevented her from undertaking any productive work at all (221).

That Wapshott is victimized not by seduction so much as by the lack of character in men for whom promises are cheap is as recurrent a refrain of Foundling petitions as it is of tragic seduction ballads. One example must suffice for many. The impassioned and eloquent plea of Dorothy Barnsley, a servant of Islington Road, London, to admit her five-month-old child to the ballot was read on 11 April 1781. In it, she looked to the hospital to be unto her "unhappy babe" the "father" her former lover had refused to be and thus to perform an act of charity for which "the great father of all" would surely "receive" committee members "into his blissful mansions, and crown you with eternal reward" (312). Barnsley much more emphatically casts herself in the role of sexual victim than the other petitioners I have examined thus far. In fact, all but one of the verbs she uses in her description of her seduction are passive: having had the "misfortune to place her affections" misguidedly, Barnsley describes how she was put under the power of an "undeserving man, who profiting of the weakness of her sex, and abusing of her tenderness for him, drew by degrees her mind from the paths of virtue" (312). Like Wapshott, Barnsley's plea relies on the Committee's acceptance of the cultural narratives of gender (in this instance, of male "perfidy" and female "weakness") out of which imaginative texts such as ballads made so much creative play. But like ballad heroines who wreak their revenge on their fickle lovers through literal hauntings or their metaphoric return through the repetition of their story of victimization in song, Foundling petitioners are far from the powerless agents Barnsley and others claimed to be. Indeed, unlike their imaginative counterparts, who could only achieve poetic justice, petitioners including Barnsley were well aware that the successful relation of their stories and defenses of their "good character" – matters of life and death for many of these women – could make a material difference to their and their children's future prospects, however circumscribed those possibilities might have been in reality. The stakes were high, as is made clear by the title of the satirical, misogynist ballad "Joyful News to Batchelors and Maids: Being a Song in Praise of the Fondling Hospital... Where young maids may safely take a Leap in the dark... get rid of their bantling, and pass for pure Virgins." The petitioners themselves, of course, painted a very different picture of the significance of the charity's intervention in which the rewards were not sexual but economic. If they were able to convince the charity of their deservingness, and if they were fortunate enough to get through the admission ballot, women might be able to attempt to return to the "manual labour" as Elizabeth Brooks promised to do, and earn a "subsistence" "without any injury being done to her Caracter with the wor[l]d" (277).[10]

In reading petitions such as Logdon's and King's alongside sentimental seduction narratives such as "The History of Misella," or Wapshott's and Barnsley's against the tragic ballad narratives toward which they elliptically gesture, my intention has not been to suggest a direct line of influence between the words of individual laboring women and specific texts, nor has it been to doubt through association the authenticity of these women's stories. Rather, this essay has argued through this necessarily small but characteristic selection of petitions from a vast archive that Foundling petitioners routinely exhibited a keen sense that their and their children's fate rested in their successful negotiation of a set of established cultural and literary narratives about gender, sex, and character. Seduced sentimental and ballad heroines plotted various configurations of these narratives and also ways of reading them, which could and surely did work in the petitioners' favor. Simultaneously, their plots must have seemed very remote from the "unfeeling[,] ungenerous world" Brooks described, in which self-pity and fantasies of revenge would have been mere indulgences (277). These narratives' inadequacy to account for the reality of the lives of laboring women petitioners, coupled with their need and the institutional demands of the hospital itself, produced a series of responses that were often both creative and critical. Most strikingly, in their repeated assertions of their "good character," these documents refute the presumed synonymy of virtue and chastity that has been taken to be paradigmatic of eighteenth-century literature from the mid-century onwards and which was ironically confirmed by the various virtue-in-distress plots mapped out in contemporary prostitution narratives, memoirs, and ballads. Indeed, a more detailed study of the Foundling petitions would add considerable weight to the rising tide of scholarship on gender and sexuality in eighteenth-century studies which has questioned, as Binhammer has so effectively, the presence of "a dominant ideology" of seduction in the period that was "punitive" and "constrict[ed] female desire" (2). Undertaking such a project is predicated, however, on an assumption that is far from a given: that the Foundling petitions can and should be studied as literary texts and as part of the imaginative literature of labor in the period.

This essay has argued for a more capacious definition of the literary and of laboring class writing that would accommodate documents such as the Foundling petitions and, by extension, other testimonies written by or transcribed from the laboring poor. Despite the fact that these are factual documents shaped by particular generic imperatives – surely similar, if different, imperatives are at work across all and even established textual genres – they provide us with invaluable insights into the lives of some of eighteenth-century society's poorest members. These insights can, of course, be excavated with little or no reference to the wider literary context that this essay has only begun to mobilize, but runs the risk of leaving unresolved the petitions' strategic, formulaic, and recognizably fictional elements. Considering these documents not solely as historical evidence but as laboring class life writing, for instance, provides other ways of theorizing this material which take as a given rather than as a methodological problem that writing, in Carolyn Steedman's words, "conceals as well as speaks" and "papers over the past with secrets" (259).

Such an approach invites us also to consider the self-conscious or otherwise allusions to narratives conjured by the words and plots to which the petitioners returned and allows us to reflect upon the archive's implications for our understanding of laboring class engagement with imaginative texts. As Catherine Richardson, writing of women's illiteracy in the early modern period, has argued: "knowing whether women could sign their names does not tell us the whole story" of their engagement with language and literature in the historical past. Given that men and women from the sixteenth century onwards "inhabited a world increasingly shaped by the printed word," we "need a much wider definition of literacy," she urges, "if we are to understand the nature of female practice" (91). Richardson's work focuses primarily on various forms of domestic writing such as wills and receipt books and also includes material objects such as textiles and verbally adorned household objects such as pots and walls. Like these documents and objects, the Foundling petitions, with their loud echoes of imaginative print and oral seduction narratives, suggest strongly that we need a more flexible and sophisticated understanding of the ways in which the literary and the non- or barely literate intersected in the eighteenth century beyond the examples of those few, exceptional unlettered laboring geniuses who have understandably, but perhaps unfairly, dominated scholarship in this area.

At a moment when the works of the likes of Stephen Duck, Mary Leapor, and Ann Yearsley are being required once more to justify their place in a new formalist canon – a demand they and their works can surely answer – the Foundling petitions offer a salutary reminder that, in privileging certain kinds of textual work above others, we risk privileging elite discourses of value around aesthetics or sexual politics or class. Our scholarly complicity in perpetuating these hierarchies, this essay has argued, merits careful reconsideration. Like the laboring poets that Christmas writes about in *The Lab'ring Muses*, Foundling petitioners, writing for their and their children's lives and in opposition to dominant cultural accounts of their gendered and social character, were "important interlocutors" in "ongoing cultural dialogue" about "work writing, ... social class" and gender in eighteenth-century England (35). The Foundling Hospital petitions are more than mere historical curiosities. They document the lives of laboring women and their children and relate personal tragedies that were all too real for those involved. They are also skillfully crafted documents that reveal the tellers' ability to manipulate language and narrative in order to secure the best chance of a successful hearing and to reimagine class-based and gendered understandings of seduction, maternity, and illegitimacy. If the relationship between the petitioners' lived experience and the printed and oral literature of the period in which the dialogue around sex and seduction took center stage was "symbiotic" as Evans has suggested, then the Foundling Hospital Archive suggests it was also a highly creative and contested one. That is a story, I think, that like each of the petitions in the archive, bears to be re-told.

NOTES

I would like to thank Chloe Wigston Smith for her comments on an earlier draft of this chapter.

1. All quotations from Foundling Hospital petitions are from Levene, *Narratives*.

2. The Foundling Hospital was granted a Royal Charter in 1739 and admitted its first charges in March 1741.
3. Smith's petition reads in full, "The Humble Petitioner has had the Misfortune of having a Child & that the Father is gone away & she knows not where & that she is incapable of providing for it, she therefore begs you will Admit her said Child into the said Hospital&your Petitioner as in Duty bound shall ever Pray" (316).
4. Brooks's petition was read on 30 December 1772 (278–9).
5. "*Confiteor; si quid prodest delicta fateri*" is from Ovid, *Amores*, 11.4.3 (*Rambler* 170: 82).
6. Many petitioners, such as Sarah Salt, whose petition was read on 16 November 1763, presented themselves as victims "Decoyed from [their] Virtue" (182). As we shall see, however, many more presented themselves as victims not of sex or their own passions but of the false promises of men, whose abandonment turns seduction into a crime. See, for instance, the petition of Ann Johnson, 19 December 1770, in which she describes being "seduced" not by her lover but "by false pretence of Marriage" (234).
7. See Rosenthal on how such conventional accounts have overdetermined how we have been able to read sexuality and desire in the period.
8. On the productive convergences between different notions of character in the second half of the eighteenth century, see Lynch.
9. On illegitimacy ballads and infanticide, see Freedman 3–18.
10. In emphasizing that her true value lies not in her virtue but in her economic and laboring potential, Brooks rehearses an argument utilized by many of her fellow petitioners. See, for instance, the petitions of Sarah Salt (182), Mary Griffiths (5 December 1770, 218), Anne Wapshott (221), Johnson (234), and Margaret Smith (23 September 1772, 259). Similar arguments were made about the women admitted to the Magdalen House, a charity for penitent prostitutes, founded in 1758, for which see Batchelor, "Industry in Distress."

CHAPTER 2

"Stirr'd up by Emulation of the Famous Mr. Duck"
Laboring Class Poetry in the 1730s

Jennifer Batt

In late 1730, the "Talk of the Town" (*Candidates* 4) – indeed, of the entire country – was an agricultural laborer from Wiltshire in whom had been discovered a talent for poetry. The title page of *Poems on Several Subjects by Stephen Duck* – a collection published without the poet's approbation in September – explained why. Duck was "Lately a poor Thresher in a Barn in the County of Wilts, at the Wages of Four Shillings and Six Pence Per Week" whose poems had been

> publickly read by The Right Honourable the Earl of Macclesfield, in the Drawing-Room at Windsor-Castle, on Friday the 11th of September, 1730, to Her MAJESTY. Who was thereupon most graciously pleased to take the Author into her Royal Protection, by allowing him a Salary of Thirty Pounds per Annum, and a small House at Richmond in Surrey, to live in, for the better Support of Himself and Family.[1]

As *Poems on Several Subjects* went through seven editions in less than a fortnight, the press erupted with panegyric and parody.[2] For every response that praised Queen Caroline for rescuing "Merit from Obscurity" (*British Journal* 10 October 1730), many more criticized her patronage of the poet. As well as mocking the want of taste which – so they argued – this act betrayed, many of the Queen's critics worried about the impact her beneficence might have on others who felt that they also deserved to be rescued from the obscurity in which they unfairly dwelt. If Horace Walpole's claim that "when the late Queen patronized Stephen Duck . . . twenty labourers and artisans turned poets, and starved" was alarmist hyperbole (Walpole to Hannah More, 13 November 1784, *Correspondence* 220), it was undoubtedly true that Duck's sudden fame was an encouragement to other writers. In November 1730, just months after the Queen's patronage of the thresher had been announced, reports circulated that "The ingenious Samuel Owens, Locksmith . . . having been stirr'd up by Emulation of the famous Mr. Duck, is now preparing some Poetical Works for the Press, which are not doubted to prove entertaining to the Publick" (*Universal Spectator* 21 November 1730).³ "Thy Fortune, Duck, affect[s] my kindred Mind," the one-time weaver John Bancks insisted a few weeks later (sig. A4ʳ); "A Miller Poet let a Thresher own," John Frizzle would urge;⁴ "If *Threshers, Millers*, entertain the Muse," countered Robert Tatersal, "Why may not *Bricklayers* too their Subjects chuse?" (*Bricklayer's Miscellany* 24).

As the eighteenth century's most high profile laboring class poet, Duck became the figurehead of a movement of writing; across the century, his example loomed large to poets, patrons, readers and reviewers. It has been long recognized that "The Thresher's Labour," the poem in which Duck depicted a year in the life of an agricultural laborer, offered an important example to other artisans who wished to depict something of their working lives in verse, resulting in Robert Tatersal's "The Bricklayer's Labour" and Mary Collier's "The Woman's Labour."⁵ This chapter seeks to explore what other lessons Duck's work – and Duck's fame – offered to his immediate contemporaries, both those who identified themselves as laboring class, and those who did not, who were stirred up in "Emulation of the famous Mr. Duck" in the months and years after *Poems on Several Subjects* was published. What those writers understood of Duck was mediated through the biographical texts by and about him in *Poems on Several Subjects*: the potted biography on the volume's title page; the short and somewhat error-strewn "Some Account of the Author" added to the collection's seventh edition; and the quasi-autobiographical "The Thresher's Labour." These biographical texts stressed both the practical difficulties which Duck had faced and the extraordinary rewards he had subsequently achieved; from them, some took instruction about how to obtain royal patronage while others found lessons in how to construct an identity as a laborer-poet. In the first group were authors, including Richard Savage, Mary Barber, and Catharine Cockburn, who, believing their superior merit languished in as much obscurity as Duck's had done, viewed his fate as a precedent which entitled them to appeal for equivalent royal support. The second, much larger, and much more visible group (also explored by William Christmas in his chapter in this volume) was formed by authors who saw in Duck a model they could use to craft their own poetic personas. This group included authors who labored for a living and authors who (probably) did not: some (Robert Dodsley) already had nascent careers as laborer-poets; some (Mary Collier) were inspired to pick up a pen by reading Duck's verse; some (John Frizzle and Robert Tatersal) for whom biographical details are so scant that it is impossible to tell how reliable their claims to be members of particular trades are; and some (John Bancks and John Lockman) who exaggerated, bent the truth, or simply lied in order to construct a poetic persona that was as novel as Duck's. Still others (Arthur Duck and Philip Goose) did not actually exist. Yet, despite varying motivations, this group of writers individually and collectively built on Duck's example to forge a set of conventions for describing the experience of being a laboring class poet in the 1730s.

From the eighteenth to the twentieth century, the laboring class response to the remarkable rise of Stephen Duck was typically viewed with hostility and cynicism; Rayner Unwin's dismissal of these writers as possessing "exceedingly little merit" and being "inspired more by ambition than skill" (68) was little better than the scorn Horace Walpole had directed at starving artisans and laborers nearly 200 years earlier. More recently, however, John Goodridge has proposed that writers such as John Bancks, Robert Dodsley, and Robert Tatersal were driven by much more than a basely rapacious desire to follow Duck in hitting the jackpot, since "the struggle that clearly went into the literary work these writers produced speaks of a genuine impulse to write, and to give meaning to their lives in doing so" ("Predecessors of Clare" 21). While agreeing on the importance of "taking them seriously as writers," William Christmas has insisted it is valuable to retain a sense of this group as "poets-as-opportunists," noting how adept many of them were in "us[ing] their laboring status to sell themselves and their writing" (*Lab'ring Muses* 96). This chapter offers a broader context for assessing the early development of laboring class writing by focusing on responses to Duck by authors who were laboring class and authors who were not, authors who were truth-tellers and authors who were liars, authors who were real and authors who were fictitious. If Bancks, Dodsley, and Tatersal sought to take opportunist advantage of the situation that Duck's extraordinary fame presented, then so too did Mary Barber, Richard Savage, Catharine Cockburn, and the booksellers who created the figures of Arthur Duck and Philip Goose. And if Bancks, Dodsley, and Tatersal drew on Duck's *Poems on Several Subjects* to sell themselves as writers, they did so as part of a larger movement which encompassed works by genuine poets, works by poets who were utterly spurious, and works by poets who were somewhere in between. This movement collectively established conventions that could be used – seriously, satirically, or opportunistically – to outline the challenges that a laborer-poet might tragically be restricted by or heroically overcome as they pursued their poetic ambitions.

For one observer writing late in 1730 in anticipation of the selection of a new Poet Laureate following the death of the previous incumbent,

Laurence Eusden, the example which Duck presented to his peers was an alarming one. The satirical scene "The Battle of the Poets" suggested that the Queen's generosity to Duck would encourage a cluster of "New Mushro[o]m-Poets of a Night" to aspire to this vacant position, prompting "Tinkers, Sow-gelders, Threshers, Footmen, Pimps, / Old punning Coblers, Taylors insolent, / And scribling snotty-nos'd Attorneys Clerks" to turn poet, "croud the Palace Gate," "bawl their Merit forth in hobling Verse," and "Put in their equal Claim" for royal patronage (*Bays Miscellany* 14). By the time this satire was published, the palace gates had already been rattled. In early October, Richard Love-Merit, a pseudonymous contributor to the *Grub-street Journal*, complained that one James Drake (currently "oblig'd to tug at the oar in a literal sense [being on board a little vessel]") was one of those whose claims equaled Duck's and yet he had "not once met with the least incouragement from Persons of the highest quality and figure" (*Grub-street Journal* 8 October 1730). Love-Merit's complaint on Drake's behalf did not contain an explicit appeal for royal patronage, but, a few weeks later, another poet in need, Arthur Duck, did make such a claim. "Now a poor Thresher in the County of Suffolk, at the Wages of Five Shillings and Six Pence per Week, though formerly an Eton-Scholar," Arthur had witnessed his cousin Stephen's sudden rise to fame and fortune and hoped to follow his example (*Thresher's Miscellany* title page). Arthur claimed he was more deserving because "I am double the Age of my Cousin Stephen Duck, and have therefore, you may rationally suppose, Ploughed, Harrowed, and Threshed, twice as long, and all to no Purpose" (*Thresher's Miscellany* sig. A3^{r-v}). Since it had been widely reported (including on the title page of *Poems on Several Subjects*) that the Queen's patronage of the thresher had immediately followed a public reading of his verse by the Earl of Macclesfield, Arthur dedicated his collection to that Earl, "in Order to be Read to Her Majesty, and in Hopes of Her most Gracious Favour" (*Thresher's Miscellany* title page). If "his Lordship will grant me this humble Boon," Arthur hoped "my kinsman and I may share one equal Fate" (*Thresher's Miscellany* sig. A3^{r-v}). Philip Goose, a Berkshire Thatcher, also appealed to well-placed courtiers to attract the attention of the Queen. His panegyric on her merits was, so the pamphlet in which it was published declared, "Presented to her Majesty by the Right Honourable the Lord *Townshend*, on *Thursday* the 29th of *October*, 1730" (*Duck drowned*). To onlookers, then, James Drake, Arthur Duck, and Philip Goose seemed to be at the head of an onslaught of laborer poets which gave truth to the *Grub-street Journal's* complaint that "the late extension of the Royal bounty to STEPHEN DUCK has given birth to new Poets, in a corner of the town, the most remote from the sun-shine of the Court" (21 January 1731). And yet, as their punning surnames suggest, all was not what it seemed. James Drake was a pseudonym briefly adopted by (or perhaps imposed upon) John Lockman; he was no sailor but an established writer and translator.[6] Meanwhile, neither Arthur Duck nor Philip Goose were real; the works that appeared in their names did so speciously, the absurdity of their claims designed to mock, rather than participate in, the scrabble for patronage which the Queen's bounty to the thresher was feared to have unleashed.

Not all claims for patronage were specious, however. Several genuine appeals were made which used, in all sincerity, the strategies spoofed through the characters of Arthur Duck and Philip Goose. One such appeal addressed Charlotte Clayton, the Queen's Woman of the Bedchamber. Clayton had been closely involved in bringing Duck to court (as "Some Account of the Author" described it, "happening to see" a manuscript containing Duck's verse which the Earl of Tankerville had brought to court, she "immediately presented it to the Queen" and, consequently, initiated the Queen's award to the poet [v]). Hoping that to address Clayton was to address the Queen, Patrick Delany paid tribute to how Clayton (and hence, Caroline) had "in a way very honourable, and very exemplary, eased one good mind of misery, relieved one good genius from the load of life, and placed improvement and happiness of every kind within his reach" (Thomson, *Memoirs* I: 70). Yet it was not possible to help Duck and no one else, Delany insisted:

> can one instance of this kind fill up the measure of your beneficence? Does the doing honour to one good genius do justice to your own? No, Madam, you think too justly and too largely to imagine it can. You know that every human creature that equally deserves, has an equal claim to your beneficence, and that nothing but want of merit in them, or ability in you, can acquit you of the claim. (Thomson, *Memoirs* I: 70–71)

Despite his rhetoric, Delany's appeal was not intended to persuade Clayton and the Queen of an obligation to support "every human creature that equally deserves"; rather, he hoped to win their aid for one writer in particular, the Dublin poet Mary Barber. Barber was then in the process of gathering subscriptions for a volume of her verse. Delany sketched in a brief biography of the poet ("on the verge of fifty, with an hereditary gout, cough, and asthma, with a load of four children, excellently educated, perfectly well disposed, and utterly unprovided for") and asserted – in echo of the claim spuriously made by Arthur Duck – that she was at least as deserving of support as Stephen Duck because she "hath laboured more years than Duck hath lived, in a course of upright, obliging, well-guided, and unwearied, though unsuccessful industry" (Thomson, *Memoirs* I: 71).

Another poet who considered – as Samuel Johnson would later note – that "his birth, his misfortune, and his genius gave him a fairer title [to royal support] than could be pleaded by him on whom it was conferred" was Richard Savage (Johnson, *Life of Savage* 103). The self-proclaimed Bastard had acquired a notoriety through his insistence that he was the illegitimate offspring of Richard Savage, Earl Rivers, and Ann Brett, Countess of Macclesfield.[7] Among Savage's many misfortunes was a conviction for murder from which only a royal pardon had spared his life. In November 1730, with the laureateship vacant, Lord Tyrconnel appealed to Charlotte Clayton to use her influence with the Queen to secure the position for Savage. Since providing assistance to "obscure merit, as in the case of Stephen Duck, has done you a great deal of honour," Tyrconnel hoped that Clayton would be "so good to favour Mr. Savage" for the Laureateship since he "stands as much in need of" royal patronage as Duck had (Thomson, *Memoirs* I: 242).

Catharine Cockburn also hoped Caroline would "once more descend, / The low to raise" when she recognized that her merit was languishing in obscurity (*Works* 2: 573). A noted playwright under her maiden name Catharine Trotter, by the 1730s, Cockburn was living in Aberdeen with her clergyman husband and devoting her energies to philosophical and theological controversies. Hoping to persuade the Queen, well-known for her interests in philosophy, to consent to be the dedicatee of her *Vindication of Mr. Locke's Christian Principles*, Cockburn argued that she was more deserving of support than Duck because of her gender:

> not the flail and sickle could retard,
> Or cares discourage, more, the rural bard,
> Than those restraints, which have our sex confin'd,
> By partial custom   (*Works* 2: 573)

Cockburn was unable to win a royal hearing for this petition: having unsuccessfully asked Lord Chancellor King to present her appeal to the Queen, she turned to the Duchess of Hamilton, but she was prevented by illness and family bereavement from completing the commission (*Works* 2: 271). Without the cachet the "royal stamp" of approval would bring (*Works* 2: 572), Cockburn's *Vindication of Locke* remained unpublished in her lifetime.

Though Cockburn regretted this missed opportunity, even those writers whose claims got as far as Charlotte Clayton had only mixed success. Savage did not gain laureateship for which Tyrconnel had petitioned, though Caroline did reward him with an annual pension two years later when he declared himself her Volunteer Laureat. Mary Barber's gains were much more modest. Delany's arguments seem to have convinced Clayton to purchase seven copies of her *Poems on Several Occasions* (1734), but Caroline herself was not persuaded to be among the work's subscribers. There was no all-male swarm of laborers and artisans rattling the palace gates, then; rather, those who sought to "share one equal Fate" with Duck were established writers who had fallen on hard times or who considered their merit to be unfairly neglected.

Duck's good fortune in being "enrich'd by Peers, advanc'd by Caroline" (Collier, *Woman's Labour* 5) was undoubtedly coveted by many writers who identified themselves as laboring class, yet despite expressions of envy, these writers recognized that obtaining royal patronage was not an achievable goal. Thus, when John Bancks dedicated his *Weaver's Miscellany* to Queen Caroline, he did so "without [her] Leave," and without expectation of any reward other than the hope that she would "forgive" him for this unsolicited "Tribute" (sig. A2^r). Robert Tatersal, meanwhile, considered the probability of such an act of royal patronage being repeated to be equivalent to that of one man metamorphosing into another:

> Oh! could my Trowel but that Shape [of a flail] assume!
> Could I a Wiltshire Thresher but become!
> Then might kind Fortune cast a Smile on me,
> And crown my Labours too with Lenity. (*Second Part* 2)

With royal patronage out of reach, the kind fortune which Tatersal – and many of his contemporaries – sought was to engage the curiosity and sympathy of the book-buying public. "Tho' She pretends not to the Genius of Mr. Duck," the advertisement prefacing Mary Collier's poems explained, "nor hopes to be taken Notice of by the Great, yet her Friends are of Opinion that the Novelty of a Washer-Woman's turning Poetess, will procure her some Readers" (*Woman's Labour* sig. A2^r). To declare affinity with Duck was not just to assert novelty; it also allowed one to claim an excuse for any defects a reader perceived in one's verse. Robert Dodsley urged "censorious" and "ill-judging Criticks" not to "seek for little Failings to accuse / A tender and uncultivated muse" (*Epistle* 4–5), and called upon the "Candour and Good-nature" of his readers in "recollect[ing] that the Author lies under all the Disadvantages of an uncultivated Mind; nay, even his natural

Genius depressed by the Sense of his low Condition" (*Footman's Miscellany* sig. A3^v–A4^r). John Bancks declared that his aim was to win favor with "the best-natur'd Readers" while "Criticks" were warned to "stand off, for you here is no Room; / Tho' nothing's sacred else, revere the Loom" (*Weaver's Miscellany* title page). "Look not for much Skill, / Nor yet for Smoothness from a Water-mill," John Frizzle cautioned his readers, while Robert Tatersal hoped that, by recognizing they were reading "the true and genuine Productions of a Mechanick Fancy and Genius," those who browsed his book would be induced to "put a more favourable Construction upon all Indecorums" (*Bricklayer's Miscellany* vi). To win the favor of readers, and perhaps also the support of local – if not royal – patrons, these writers drew on the model Duck presented in order to convey the afflictions by which their literary potential was constrained. If Tatersal and his trowel (or Dodsley and his silver salver, Bancks and his loom, Frizzle and his mill, and Collier and her washing tub) could not literally metamorphose into Duck and his flail, these writers could, at least, shape their biographies in such a way that they appeared to be as deserving of support – and readerly interest – as he had been.

To do so, several authors stressed a comparable – if a not more challenging – upbringing. Though with their claim that he had attended Eton and Cambridge the creators of Arthur Duck implied that his poetry would be more accomplished than his cousin's because of his superior schooling, most writers seeking to emulate Duck claimed an educational background at least as restricted as that he had experienced. Both Mary Collier and John Bancks alluded directly to the brief sketch of Duck's educational career given in the biographical "Some Account of the Author." According to this text, despite showing great promise as a student (taking "his Learning too fast, even faster than the Master could give it him"), when Duck "had some small share of Reading and Writing bestowed on him, with very little or no Grammar" his mother had removed him "from School to the Plow" (iii–iv). "Scarce had I learn'd my Concords out of Book, / When, from the Grammar, I to Plow was took" (sig. A3^r), John Bancks echoed in his account of his formative years – an account, which a later biography of the poet suggests, was at least partly invented.[8] While for Duck "the Seeds of Learning being once sowed . . . there was no possibility of weeding them out" (iv), Bancks explained that the young age at which his education was aborted meant that "There, in the Furrow, all . . . Was quickly bury'd, and for ever lost" (sig. A3^r). Mary Collier, meanwhile, missed out on even the rudimentary, interrupted schooling experienced by Duck and Bancks. "No Learning ever was bestow'd on me," she noted in "The Woman's Labour," echoing the language of "Some Account of the Author" (*Woman's Labour* 6). Collier's "Some Remarks of the Author's Life drawn by herself," published in 1762, filled in details: she had been "taught to read when very Young... but my Mother dying, I lost my Education, Never being put to School" (*Poems on Several Occasions* iii). For these writers, to claim a defective education was to encourage readerly admiration at what they had achieved and to offer mitigation for any poetic failings that a reader might perceive: as Robert Dodsley (who claimed to be as "unlearn'd as" Duck) protested, "Can he be learned who no Learning had?" (*Epistle* 3, 5).

Yet not all writers who identified themselves (or were identified) as laboring class claimed to be suffering from ongoing educational deficiencies. Richard Love-Merit argued that James Drake was at least as deserving of patronage as Duck because, despite having "had no better education than our celebrated Thresher," he had accomplished far greater things: "by dint of poring over books, fir'd by an insatiable thirst after learning, [Drake had] made no inconsiderable progress in the antient languages, and one or two of the modern; attain'd to some knowledge in the sciences; and distinguished himself a little in one branch of Literature" (*Grub-street Journal* 8 October 1730). Robert Tatersal had a different reason for refusing to dwell on the lasting disadvantages of his upbringing. The final leaf of the second part of his *Bricklayer's Miscellany* advertised his services as a teacher of "Writing, Arithmetick, Geometry, Dialling, &c.," alongside those of his schoolteacher father's (24). In using his poetic collection to promote himself and his father to prospective students, Tatersal could not afford to claim, as Dodsley (also the son of a schoolmaster) did, that "my Stock of Learning yet is low" (*Epistle* 6).

If a defective education was claimed by some as a significant obstacle to achieving literary success, so too was having to work for a living. One way in which poets – truthfully or otherwise – advertised their occupations was through the titles they gave to their collections of verse. Here, it was Arthur Duck's spurious collection *The Thresher's Miscellany* which headed the trend, inspiring the titles of John Bancks's *The Weaver's Miscellany* (1730); Robert Dodsley's *A Muse in Livery, or The Footman's Miscellany* (1732); and the two parts of Robert Tatersal's *The Bricklayer's Miscellany* (1734, 1735). Equally important were the brief biographies, citing occupation and location, which were used to introduce almost every poet who sought to emulate Duck. Duck had been announced to readers as "Lately a poor Thresher in a Barn in the County of Wilts"; this formula was copied for the spurious Arthur Duck ("now a poor Thresher in the County of

Suffolk"), Philip Goose ("the Berkshire Thatcher"), and James Drake ("a sailor, now on board a small English ship" (*Complaint* title page). Having formerly described himself as "a Footman" in his published work Robert Dodsley now took to identifying himself by his location as well as his occupation, signing one pamphlet "a Footman in London," and another collection "a Footman to a Person of Quality at Whitehall" (*Epistle, Muse in Livery* 2nd ed.). John Bancks was described as "now a Poor Weaver in Spittle-Fields," Robert Tatersal as "A poor Country Bricklayer of Kingston upon Thames," Mary Collier as "Now a Washer-woman, at Petersfield in Hampshire," and John Frizzle (by someone with a rather doubtful grasp of geography) as "*a Miller of* Corey's Mill, *near* Eniskillen, Dublin" (*Weekly Register* 17 February 1733). The recurrent adverb "now" that featured in so many of these brief biographies was an insistent reminder that, while Duck had "lately" left his laboring life behind, these writers were – at least, so they claimed – very much still embroiled within it.

"Think what could be expected from a barn," Robert Dodsley urged readers of Duck's work, insisting that "'Tis that exalts the merits of his cause" (*Epistle* 5). Though the engraved frontispiece of *Poems on Several Subjects* showed Duck reading Milton at work, and, though "Some Account of the Author" claimed that "the Labour of his Mind generally accompany'd that of his Body" with the works of Milton "his constant Companion in the Field and in the Barn" (iv), "The Thresher's Labour" told a different story. The threshing barns in which the agricultural laborer spent most of his working life were, Duck argued in his poem, incompatible with literary creativity, be that the sharing of stories with one's co-workers, the singing of songs, or higher muse-inspired pursuits:

> Nor yet the tedious Labour to beguile,
> And make the passing Minutes sweetly smile,
> Can we, like Shepherds, tell a merry Tale?
> The Voice is lost, drown'd by the noisy Flail.
> But we may think – Alas! what pleasing thing
> Here to the Mind can the dull Fancy bring?
> The Eye beholds no pleasant Object here:
> No chearful Sound diverts the list'ning Ear.
> The Shepherd well may tune his Voice to sing,
> Inspir'd by all the beauties of the Spring:
> No Fountains murmur here, no Lambkins play,
> No Linets warble, and no Fields look gay;
> 'Tis all a dull and melancholy Scene,
> Fit only to provoke the Muses spleen.   (17)

Though John Goodridge has rightly warned that "The Thresher's Labour" should not be read as "a statement of fact" (*Rural Life* 16), this evocative account of the incompatibility of work and writing was taken by Duck's peers as an autobiographical confession of the challenges he had faced. Writing in 1733, several years after Duck had left laboring behind, John Frizzle urged him to recall the conditions he had complained of in that poem: "Think when thy Flail rebounded from the Floor, / Was't then you made the Shunamite?" Frizzle was convinced it was not: "No sure," he answered emphatically on Duck's behalf. Echoing Frizzle's poem – which he might have read printed alongside Duck's work in the ninth edition of *Poems on Several Subjects* which had been published in 1733 – Robert Tatersal repeated this question and its answer as he drew on "The Thresher's Labour" to imagine how else Duck's life as a laborer might have clashed with his attempts to write poetry:

> Think what you was, when with a mighty Sound
> Your *Crab-tree Flail* did from the Floor rebound;
> When Hogs and Horses, Cows and Clowns did share
> With you in Toil, your chief Companions were;
> Or when to Field to cut the verdant Hay
> You chac'd with Sweat the sultry Hours away;
> Ah! on your Fate how often did you call,
> Alas! the Beer, the Bottle is so small:
> Were they fit places for thee to indite?
> Or didst thou there compose the *Shunamite?*
> No, sure some bless'd Retirement thou did'st find,
> Exempt from Labours to compose your Mind.
> (*Bricklayer's Miscellany* 24–5)

Significantly, the poem that Frizzle and Tatersal both agreed that Duck could not have written while at work is his Milton-influenced paraphrase of 2 *Kings* IV, "The Shunamite." The other pieces in *Poems on Several Subjects* – "The Thresher's Labour," "On Poverty," and the epistle "Honour'd Sir" – are all poems that connected with and drew upon Duck's own experiences as a laborer; if the field and the barn were not "fit places" to "indite" these poems, those verses did at least depend on, and seek to convey, Duck's experience of laboring life. But "The Shunamite," a poem much more obviously removed from his own experiences, could not have been written in a barn, Frizzle insisted; "some bless'd Retirement . . . / Exempt from Labours" was necessary for its composition, Tatersal agreed.

Seeking to insist that the conditions they faced were as challenging as those Duck had encountered, several writers echoed Duck's complaint that his workplace was "a dull and melancholy Scene, / Fit only to provoke the Muses spleen" (17). John Bancks claimed that as a weaver he experienced the same leadenness of thought that Duck was forced to endure. The scene with which the weaver was daily faced was as melancholy as that Duck encountered, and its effect on his creativity as crippling:

> Here tho' I think, my Thoughts will still be low;
> My Numbers still will move on dull and slow:
> Dull, as the Prospect which before me lies,
> Slow, as the Wages of the Weaver rise.
> No subject here that's worthy of a Song;
> All mean Ideas rise, a dusky Throng,
> Whilst thro' the opening Warp the Shuttle flies along.
> (sig. A3^v)

John Frizzle, meanwhile, claimed that the noise and the dust of his mill – equal to that suffered by Duck in his threshing barn – made the concentrated thought necessary to compose verse impossible:

> I near the Hopper stand with dusty Coat,
> And if my Mouth be open, dusty Throat.
> The Stones, the Wheels, the Water make a Din;
> Hogs grunt without, or squeeks [sic] a Rat within.
> To meditate sweet verse, is this a Place?
> Or will the Muses such a Mansion grace?

Robert Tatersal, alluding to Frizzle as well as Duck, also claimed that the dust and noise (a "horrid Din / Of Swearing, Chawing, and of drinking Gin") of the building site on which he worked had a detrimental impact on his capacity for focused contemplation, while its chaos hampered the physical act of writing, the putting of pen to paper:

> Clouds of Dust arise, and dark the Sky,
> And Bricks and Lime promiscuous scatter'd lie:
> In this Confusion can I use my Quill;
> And write with Pain reluctant to my Will?
> Are these dire Mansions fit to entertain
> The sacred Muse, to meditate with Pain?
> (*Bricklayer's Miscellany* 24)

This succession of melancholy scenes attempted to vie with Duck's "The Thresher's Labour" as comparable accounts of the challenges that each working environment posed to an engagement with the muses. John Frizzle explicitly encouraged readers (and potential patrons) to imagine what he would be capable of "Were I a while from Noise and Dust releas'd, /

And Sacks, and Horses, and the mooter Chest"; and Robert Tatersal similarly invited recognition of the potential that might be realized if only he "cou'd the Trowel leave" (*Bricklayer's Miscellany* 25). But without the "bless'd Retirement... / Exempt from Labours" which Duck now enjoyed, both poets argued that their ability to compose high-quality verse would always be compromised.

Yet there was a flaw in their argument: Duck had indeed managed to write "The Shunamite" – the poem which Frizzle and Tatersal viewed as the pinnacle of his achievement and insisted was incompatible with labor – while still a laborer. Indeed, some of it had actually been composed at work. The "sim[ile] of ye wolf" in "The Shunamite," Joseph Spence recorded in notes that went unpublished until the twentieth century, "came into his head as he was foll[owin]g ye Plough" (Osborn, "Spence" 127). For all that laborer poets stressed the incompatibility of work and writing, many of them found ways to combine the two. Robert Dodsley had time to write, he claimed, because he was fortunate in employers who supported his poetic inclinations; "few in my Station are able to find Leisure for Employments of this Nature," he noted in the dedication of *A Muse in Livery* as he thanked those employers for their indulgence and their support in sponsoring his volume's publication by subscription (*Footman's Miscellany* sig. A2^v). Even Robert Tatersal, who had insisted so strongly upon the incompatibility of the building trade and the muses, found ways to integrate work with poetry. In "The Bricklayers Labours" (a poem indebted to Duck's "The Thresher's Labour"), Tatersal depicted the building site as a place where "to divert the sult'ry Hours along / One tells a Tale, another sings a Song" (*Bricklayer's Miscellany* 29). In this account, even if those tales and songs were noisier, looser, more impromptu, and more communal than the verse Tatersal might wish to "write" or "meditate," the atmosphere on the building site did make possible a kind of poetic communication between workers, which enabled diversion for both the performer and his audience. Moreover, as Tatersal notes in "The Bricklayers Labours," the building trade was a seasonal business with a long winter period in which the bricklayer often "seek[s] for Work; but none, alas! Can find" (*Bricklayer's Miscellany* 30). Explaining that he chose to "employ" his "vacant Hours" in writing verse rather "than to be altogether idle," Tatersal presents his two collections of verse as the product of his "Winter Recreations, being the Production of those leisure Hours wherein I had not Employment to exercise the more material Business of my Calling" (*Second Part* i, iv). The natural rhythms of Tatersal's working life, then, did offer the kind of "bless'd Retirement... / Exempt from Labours" Tatersal argued was necessary to compose accomplished verse, but the temptation to echo Duck in complaining of the disabling effects of work proved too strong to resist.

A decade ago, reflecting on the "familiar double-act in eighteenth-century studies" that Duck's "The Thresher's Labour" and Collier's "The Woman's Labour" had become, John Goodridge rightly cautioned that to understand Duck's contribution to laboring class writing it was important to go beyond this well-established pairing to consider his impact on other laboring class writers ("Duck and Collier" 209). Building on Goodridge's astute observation, this chapter has argued that to understand the early evolution of laboring class writing it is now time to cast the net even wider. A miscellaneous group of writers – from a diverse selection of backgrounds and driven by a range of reasons – reacted to the fame that Stephen Duck achieved, and as they did so they shaped what it meant to be a laboring class writer in the 1730s. These writers wrote in response to Duck and in response to each other, echoing and amplifying tropes borrowed or adapted from Duck's biography as it was represented in *Poems on Several Subjects*: tropes about who was deserving of support and why, about the impact of a limited or interrupted education on poetic expression, and about the challenge of trying to pursue literary ambitions while also having to work for a living. For many writers, their attempt to emulate "the famous Mr. Duck" was a brief – and sometimes regretted – dalliance, but, as responses from Horace Walpole through to Rayner Unwin show, this surge of activity has had a lasting impact on the way that the early development of laboring class writing has been perceived. Undoubtedly, some of the earliest responses to Duck's success were opportunistic, and some were downright fraudulent, but these, together with responses that were truthful and sincere, were vital in shaping the early development of laboring class writing in the 1730s.

NOTES

1. All quotations from Duck's *Poems on Several Subjects* are taken from the seventh edition.
2. The first edition was advertised in the *Daily Post* on 28 September 1730; the seventh, in the *Daily Post* on 9 October 1730.
3. If Owens did produce such a collection, it does not appear to have survived.
4. Frizzle's poem was reprinted in *Flying Post* 13 February 1733, having first appeared in the *Dublin Journal*. It was subsequently reprinted in other newspapers and magazines as well as in the ninth edition of Duck's *Poems on Several Subjects* (1733). Unless otherwise stated, all quotations from this poem are taken from its appearance in the *Flying Post*.

5. Duck's influence on Collier's "The Woman's Labour" has been most widely covered, for example, by Ferguson, Thompson and Sugden, Landry (*Muses*), Goodridge (especially in *Rural Life*), and Christmas (*Lab'ring Muses*). More recently, Duck's influence on Dodsley, Bancks, and Tatersal has begun to be explored in more detail, for example, by Goodridge ("Predecessors of Clare" and "Duck and Collier") and Christmas (in this volume).
6. Lockman may at that time have already been enlisted as one of the team who would devote several years to translating *Bayle's General Dictionary, Historical and Critical*; see Osborn, "Thomas Birch," 30.
7. No relation, incidentally, to the Earl of Macclesfield who read Duck's verse at court.
8. For an alternative account of Bancks's formative years, see Shiells (1753) 5: 310–15. Christmas (2001) 96–97 sketches out some of Bancks's other possible untruths.

CHAPTER 3

The Verse Epistle and Laboring Class Literary Sociability from Duck to Burns

William J. Christmas

This chapter builds upon recent work in two related, sometimes overlapping, fields: "sociability studies" in the long eighteenth century, and studies concerned with "poetic communities," "literary networks," and laboring class writers in this same period. With regard to the latter, Kerri Andrews, John Goodridge, Jennifer Orr, Steve Van-Hagen, and Simon White have argued convincingly that Romantic-era laboring class poets such as Robert Bloomfield, John Clare, James Woodhouse, and Ann Yearsley in different ways forged literary communities with poets both past and present, and engaged in "sociable and communal models of poetic production" (Van-Hagen, "Patrons" 310). With regard to the former, I am most interested in what appears to be a developing subfield called "literary sociability" that concerns not only "sociable contexts in which literary production was discussed, circulated, and sometimes created" (Russell and Tuite 17), but also the role specific literary forms could play in either initiating or maintaining such sociable relations. For example, in *Literary Sociability in Early Modern England: The Epistolary Record*, Paul Trolander focuses on private letters written between 1620 and 1720 that contain evidence of "literary activity," and he argues that "small group networking" and sociability were central to literary production in both manuscript and print throughout this period (2, 1).

Given the importance of letters in tracing literary sociability, it is surprising that a related literary form – the verse epistle – has received comparatively little attention in terms of what we might call its "sociability quotient" in this context. David Fairer's concise definition of the verse epistle as a form of "sociable communication" that "entangles private and public, allowing a glimpse of the handwritten letter through the formalities of a printed page" is highly suggestive for considering this kind of poem in light of its social networking power (*English Poetry* 60). Practitioners of the form could exploit the sort of audience-oriented, private discourse that characterized the genre to address a wide array of people across class and gender lines. In his important study of this popular eighteenth-century poetic form, Bill Overton shows that the speaking postures adopted by epistolers could be quite varied, even antisocial, for example, in the satiric epistle (170–72). But verse epistles by and large reproduced the sociable conventions – such as the salutation – of the familiar letter, and likewise adhered to appropriate levels of politeness and decorum depending upon the addressee. Overton notes that laboring class poets "produced many epistles" throughout the eighteenth century, most of them addressed to patrons, potential benefactors, friends, or established literary figures like Alexander Pope (18). Though influenced by classical examples (Horace and Ovid), and governed by a range of conventions and practices – or perhaps even because of these features – the verse epistle turns out to be a wonderfully plastic form in which marginalized writers can speak their minds on the public stage. At the risk of reducing poems to mere discourse (just for a moment), my sense is that verse epistles addressed to specific persons often functioned (or attempted to function) as vehicles for social or literary networking in this period. As a form of "sociable communication" between epistoler, addressee, and – importantly – a wider audience of implied readers, the published verse epistle does not require a response to enable its sociability quotient to be measured. Perhaps more than any other poetic form, the verse epistle embodies the literary creation of sociability.

In what follows, I focus on three related forms of literary evidence – the published verse epistle, the private letter, and the unpublished verse letter – to locate examples of sociability, literary networking, and potential community building among laboring class writers in the period between the thresher-poet Stephen Duck's fabulous success in the early 1730s, and Robert Burns's similar experience in the late 1780s. First, I examine verse epistles by other laboring class poets addressed to Duck in the 1730s following his unprecedented rise to literary fame and royal patronage. The footman, Robert Dodsley, the Irish miller, John Frizzle, the London bricklayer, Robert Tatersal, and the Petersfield washerwoman, Mary Collier, all addressed Duck in verse epistles published in London between 1731 and 1739.[1] The range of sentiment delivered through these "familiar" epistles – including, as we shall see, friendship, compliment, competition, envy, and criticism – tells us something about potential forms of laboring class fellowship and literary community building at this time. Duck (apparently antisocial in this context) never responded to any of his fellow laboring class epistolers in print. However, by the early 1740s, Dodsley had become a successful bookseller/publisher, and Duck was connected to a growing social network at Dodsley's bookshop. That network would support the publication of literary works by several laboring class writers, including himself, Henry Jones, James Woodhouse, and the blind Scottish poet, Thomas Blacklock. Dodsley and Blacklock exchanged private letters in the late 1750s. These, combined with print history evidence from other laboring class writers in Dodsley's circle at this time, clearly document important features of the extensive social/literary network that characterized Dodsley's business at mid-century. Something of his experience exchanging letters with Dodsley seems to have stuck with Blacklock because several decades later, in the late 1780s, he would use both the private letter and, interestingly, the coterie verse letter to develop a genuinely friendly and, at times, collaborative relationship with Burns.[2]

By the time Duck's first poems appeared in London in the fall of 1730, Dodsley was already a published author. His *Servitude* – a didactic "advice" poem with introductory prose summaries of each section – had been published anonymously the previous year. In February 1730, the text was reissued under a new title, *The Footman's Friendly Advice to his Brethren of the Livery*, which essentially identified Dodsley as the author by adding his initials and current occupation to the title page. The popularity of Duck's poems no doubt influenced Dodsley's next publication: a formal verse epistle addressed to the thresher-poet. *An Epistle from a Footman in London to the Celebrated Stephen Duck* was first advertised on 27 February 1731 and sold by five booksellers, including James Roberts (the publisher of Duck's pirated *Poems on Several Subjects*). Three of these booksellers – Roberts, James Brindley, and Anne Dodd – had "direct publishing connections with Pope," circumstantial evidence that Dodsley's most recent biographer, Harry M. Solomon, uses to suggest Pope had a hand in the scheme (21). Whatever Pope's role may have been, Dodsley's *Epistle* was certainly designed to make a splash. As a large format folio publication, with elaborate ornaments for the headpiece and drop capital on the first page, this was a poem meant to be noticed.

In addressing Duck publicly with such a pretentious verse epistle, the footman-poet Dodsley no doubt hoped to further his own nascent career as a writer by linking himself to Duck primarily as a fellow "natural genius." The poem's opening salutation decorously alludes to Duck's recent success in self-deprecating fashion:

> To *Thee*, the happy Fav'rite of the Nine,
> On whom the *Great* and *Good* have deign'd to shine;
> Blushing, to *Thee*, these artless Lines I send,
> Ambitious for the *Title* of thy *Friend*;   (3)

By invoking the sentimental bonds of friendship, Dodsley effectively constructs his overall poetic purpose as altruistic, or, at least self-interested – "ambitious" – in the best of senses. As the poem continues, Dodsley marshals evidence of their shared laboring background, forging fellowship with Duck as "unlearn'd" poets, and then goes on to defend both Duck's royal patronage and his published verse against the criticism that flowed from the anti-Hanoverian press at this time:

> Cease then, censorious Criticks, to repine
> At *Virtues* which approach so near *Divine*!
> Nor seek for *little* Failings to accuse
> A tender and uncultivated *Muse*:
> In which, tho' you no *master Strokes* discern,
> Think what could be expected from a *Barn*
>
> (4–5)

Dodsley makes an important distinction here, celebrating Duck for his God-given poetic gift – his "natural genius" in Addisonian terms – while at once qualifying his published poetry based on his laboring life and lack of formal education ("Can he be learned, who no Learning had?") (5).

As a complimentary epistle, this turns out to be a deft performance as Dodsley both pays tribute to Duck and builds a more general case in favor of the natural, laboring class poet – a category that, of course, includes himself. In this respect, Duck represents a form of literary cultural capital that Dodsley presumably hopes might pay dividends for him as he describes *both* of them striving together for sublime heights in poetry: "On then, my Friend, nor doubt but that in Time, / Our tender Muses, learning now to climb, / May reach Perfection's Top, and grow sublime" (7). After an extended conceit figuring himself and Duck as birds about to fledge, Dodsley closes his epistle by imagining them together atop Parnassus singing "melodious[ly]" (8). That reads now as a prescient image. Both Duck and Dodsley would go on to have successful careers in letters, and a version of Dodsley's imagined literary fellowship between the men actually came to pass, as we shall see, in the 1740s and 1750s.

Following Dodsley's epistle, "An Irish Miller, to Mr. Stephen Duck" appeared in a number of London periodicals in 1733 (see Jennifer Batt's chapter in this collection for its publication history). The poem was published in the February number of *The Gentleman's Magazine* signed by "John Frizzle" of "Corry's Mill, near Enniskillen" – a town located in county Fermanagh in northern Ireland – the geographic details apparently establishing Frizzle's place of work, possibly in imitation of Duck's frequent association with Wiltshire at the time. Though no other traces of Frizzle have as yet been discovered, he appears to be an authentic correspondent based on the internal evidence of the poem: he claims to work in a "Watermill," which accords with the fact that Enniskillen is located on the River Erne, and he seems to have been a regular reader of London periodicals, perhaps including *The Gentleman's Magazine*, as he references Duck's poem "On the Queen's Grotto," which had been published in the December issue, two months prior to his own poem (232). Frizzle also knows Duck's early pirated poems (at least three Dublin editions had appeared by 1731) alluding to "The Thresher's Labour" and naming another of Duck's early poems, "the Shunamite," in one couplet (232). Frizzle's epistle was subsequently picked up by the publishers of Duck's *Poems on Several Subjects*, advertised on the title page, and included in the prefatory apparatus from the ninth edition on. Of course, none of these facts firmly places Frizzle in Enniskillen in the early 1730s, but unlike the vast majority of pseudonymous periodical poems about Duck in this period, Frizzle's stands out for, at the very least, its authentic potential.

Frizzle's poem reveals an entirely different motivation for sociable intralaboring class epistolary address: competition instead of friendship. He seems well enough acquainted with the genre to open with salutary verses that establish a familiar connection and project characteristic self-deprecation:

> O *Stephen*, *Stephen*, if thy gentler Ear
> Can yet a rustic Verse unruffled hear,
> Receive these Lines, but look not for much Skill,
> Nor yet for Smoothness, from a Water-mill.
> I near the Hopper stand with dusty Coat,
> And, if my Mouth be open, dusty Throat.
>   (232)

But instead of using the shared experience of writing "rustic Verse" amid the harsh conditions of labor either to compliment Duck or celebrate his achievement, Frizzle builds a case for himself as Duck's potential successor:

> And can I write? ah! make my Case your own,
> A Miller Poet let a Thresher own.
> ...
> Were I awhile from Noise and Dust releas'd,
> And Sacks, and Horses, and the mooter Chest;
> And could I see that Hermitage, even I,
> As well as you, my little Skill might try,
> The splendid Scene attempting to recite,
> Princes can build—and shall not Poets write?
>   (232)

Envious of Duck's newfound freedom from the travails of manual labor as Caroline's protégé, Frizzle references lines from Duck's "Grotto" poem describing the queen's hermitage (one of her recent, and indulgent, renovations) and suggests that, under similar circumstances, he would be more than up to the task himself. From this point, the final 11 lines of the poem – roughly one-third of the whole – launch into rather hyperbolic panegyric on Caroline, concluding with a rhetorical question the poem itself purports to answer: "The Grotto, *Stephen*, no hard Task has been, / But where's an equal Pen to such a Queen?" (232). This amounts to a decorous form of criticism appropriate for a familiar verse epistle, and also necessary because Frizzle's not-so-implicit audience for his poem is Caroline, whose attention and patronage he apparently hoped to gain.

A similar sense of purpose is evident in two epistles addressed to Duck by Robert Tatersal, a self-described London bricklayer who produced two thin, related volumes of poems both titled *The Bricklayer's Miscellany*, published in 1734 and 1735 respectively. In the 1734 poem, "To Stephen Duck, The famous Threshing Poet," Tatersal not only alludes to Frizzle explicitly – "If *Threshers, Millers,* entertain the Muse" – but also copies specific verbal and rhetorical features of Frizzle's poem as he expands on the same theme of promoting himself at Duck's expense (283). It would appear that some laboring class poets in the mid-1730s were reading each other's work, possibly through periodicals like *The Gentleman's Magazine*. Unlike Frizzle, however, Tatersal does not begin his epistle with salutary verses but instead launches into a ten-line account of the growth of his own poetic "Flame," which concludes with an implicit connection to Duck as a fellow natural genius laborer-poet:

> What, tho' the *Trowel* circumscribes my Muse,
> And *Bricks* and *Mortar* were my Fate to chuse;
> Beneath those servile Badges I display
> Some secret Sparks above a common Ray.
> (283)

Tatersal is more explicit than Frizzle in arguing that his "Art surmounts a *Country Thresher*'s," though he does add some wit to the proceedings by employing the dominant tools of their respective trades as metonyms for himself and Duck engaged in a pitched poetic battle:

> A *Flail*, a *Trowel*, Weapons very good,
> If fitly us'd and rightly understood;
> But close engag'd, beware the *useless Flail*;
> The *Trowel* then can terribly prevail:
> (283)

A good verse epistle should "entertain and surprise" its reader, and perhaps that is what Tatersal intends here, the form allowing for a bit of witty fun at Duck's expense (Fairer, *English Poetry* 60). Indeed, Tatersal continues in this vein by figuring his work site as an uncouth "*Phocian Mount*,"

> Where Bags and Bottles many you may count;
> Nine ragged Coats the dusty Mountain grace,
> To represent the Muses of that Place:
> And for *Apollo*, as their Chief and Guide,
> A growling Cur in Triumph doth preside
>
> (283–4)

This Parnassus is no place for poetry, and so Tatersal attempts in the lines that follow to elicit the empathy of both his addressee and the wider reading audience:

> In this Confusion can I use my Quill;
> And write with Pain reluctant to my Will?
> . . .
> Think what you was, when with a mighty Sound
> Your *Crab-tree Flail* did from the Floor rebound
>
> (284)

The poem then concludes in Frizzle-like fashion with an encomium to Caroline that leads to criticizing Duck for not producing enough royal panegyric verse since coming to court: "O, *Stephen, Stephen*! can you silent be? / Or cease to sing her grateful Clemency?" (284).

We may never know whether or not Duck appreciated Tatersal's rather jaunty and jocular effort to garner his support because Duck never responded in print. Perhaps that is why Tatersal opens the second part of his *Bricklayer's Miscellany* with another poem addressed to Duck. "The Introduction, to Mr. Stephen Duck" takes a different tack, however, to the problem of gaining Duck's attention. Here, because Tatersal opts for the more traditional approach, he concludes this complimentary poem with a panegyric on Duck and his poetic skills:

> But thou, auspicious Bard, so well canst write,
> To fit thy Subject for a QUEEN's Delight.
> Thy tuneful Strokes such Harmony inspire,
> That all Mankind thy wond'rous Flail admire.
> Stupendous Flail! what Virtues spring from thee!
> Thy Name shall sound to all Posterity.
> Oh! could my Trowel but that Shape assume!
> Could I a *Wiltshire* Thresher but become!

> Then might kind Fortune cast a Smile on me,
> And crown my Labours too with Lenity.
>
> (291–2)

Nevertheless, Tatersal's envy of Duck's success percolates just under the surface of these lines as he offers a curious rationale for his own lack of "Fortune": his status as an urban laboring class poet is holding him back. Hence, despite his celebration of Duck, there is no sense of a communal "we" evident in his address; rather, a feeling of separation and distinction prevails, illustrated in his consistent use of first- and second-person singular pronouns throughout the poem. Any sense of a shared literary community, or even a sense of intellectual fellowship, that might have been forged in these poems by both Frizzle and Tatersal – given Dodsley's model, for example – appears to have been undermined by self-interested ambition.

The last known verse epistle to be addressed to Duck in the 1730s, Mary Collier's *The Woman's Labour: An Epistle to Mr. Stephen Duck* (1739), is paradoxically the most critical of Duck as it also conveys a greater sense of communitarian understanding than any of the previous poems of this kind. For all of the critical attention that Collier's poem has received since its recovery in the 1970s, its self-described generic status as a verse epistle has largely escaped careful analysis. Perhaps because Collier's poem responds explicitly to Duck's earlier occupation-specific poem, "The Thresher's Labour," critics have tended to focus on their shared engagement with, and transformations of, georgic and pastoral modes (Goodridge, *Rural Life* 6–7; Landry, *Muses* 64, 76; Christmas, *Lab'ring Muses* 81, 122; Andrews "'Work' Poems"; Fairer, *English Poetry* 95–6). However, Collier's poem is a verse epistle while Duck's is not, and that difference is important in the contexts of laboring class literary sociability and community building.

The Woman's Labour participates in a poetic tradition, much in evidence throughout the eighteenth century, of critical epistolary verse essays by women poets addressed to specific male poets. Karina Williamson notes that such "openly feminist or at least counter-misogynist letters are common," particularly in the first half of the century, as female poets often used the verse epistle form to criticize poetical representations of women by their male counterparts (81). Overton classifies such poems under the umbrella term "discursive," linking them back to Horatian models, such as *The Art of Poetry*, which was originally addressed to the Roman nobleman Piso and his sons as *Epistula ad Pisones* (104). One of the examples Overton develops in his chapter on this discursive form is Lady Anne Irwin's "An Epistle to Mr. Pope... Occasion'd by his Characters of Women," a critical say-back poem to Pope's "Of the Characters of Women: An Epistle to a Lady" (1735) (112–15). Irwin's poem was first published in the December 1736 number of *The*

Gentleman's Magazine and, if Collier was perusing the poetry section of this popular periodical (as Frizzle and Tatersal possibly were several years earlier), it might have made an impression as a "judicious counter-argument" by a woman addressed to an established male poet (Overton 113).

Collier's negotiation of epistolary conventions to both engage her readers and establish a literary foundation for her critical voice is strikingly adroit. She begins her poem with an irreverent salutation:

> Immortal Bard! thou Fav'rite of the Nine!
> Enrich'd by Peers, advanc'd by CAROLINE!
> Deign to look down on One that's poor and low,
> Remembering you yourself was lately so;   (314)

The first couplet effectively rewrites the opening lines of Dodsley's earlier epistle seeking Duck's friendship and support. To address Duck as an "immortal Bard" in 1739 borders on the satiric; the phrase is certainly not meant as an earnest compliment, but neither is it of a piece with the worst sort of *ad hominem* attack Duck experienced throughout the early 1730s. The first line ends with a verbal echo of the same in Dodsley's poem, and I suspect Collier's readers are meant to notice the ironic but still familiar tone established here. Whereas Dodsley decorously finessed the issue of Duck's royal patronage – noting only that he was supported by "the *Great* and *Good*" – Collier goes so far as to name "Caroline" and clarify just how great ("Peers") some of Duck's supporters were (3). This description of class specificity serves pointedly to set up the next two lines in which Collier references her own laboring class status and reminds Duck of his similarly "poor and low" class origins. Because of their shared laboring class background, Collier is comfortable eschewing any formal third-person reference to her addressee here, sticking instead to the familiar second-person. In Collier's hands, then, the salutation becomes a carefully orchestrated set-piece that simultaneously connects and distances the epistoler to and from her addressee.

In the verse paragraph that follows, Collier also avoids the standard apology for the quality of her verses, noting only that "no Learning ever was bestowed on me," a statement that is immediately undermined by a short history lesson for Duck and her readers that juxtaposes women's fall into "Drudgery" against an idealized "Golden Age" past:

> When Men had us'd their utmost Care and Toil,
> Their Recompence was but a Female Smile;
> When they by Arts or Arms were render'd Great,
> They laid their Trophies at a Woman's Feet;
> They, in those Days, unto our Sex did bring

> Their Hearts, their All, a Free-will Offering;
> And as from us their Being they derive,
> They back again should all due Homage give.
>
> (314)

Grounded in the sort of pastoral imagery and ideal social relations that Collier might have found either in ancient sources (including certain Horatian epistles) or in contemporary poets' renderings of the classical "Golden Age," Collier imagines an ideal time when women were respected and valued by men. Collier's use of golden age rhetoric here typifies its use among English poets throughout the seventeenth century when a pre-lapsarian ideal of human interaction was often invoked nostalgically to cast critical light on a contemporary social issue or problem. For Collier, that problem is located in Duck's use of polarizing gender rhetoric throughout "The Thresher's Labour," which she references clearly in summarizing this section: "But now, alas! that Golden Age is past, / We are the Objects of your Scorn at last" (314).

Throughout the subsequent essay-response portion of her epistle, Collier certainly chides Duck for (mis)representing female agricultural laborers as gossipy and lazy; for erasing their essential contributions to carrying various harvests over the course of the year; and for forgetting the import of women's domestic or reproductive labor. Yet much of her counterargument is carefully presented using the same structural devices – the annual and diurnal cycles of rural labor – that Duck's poem employs. This imitative impulse often has the effect of *connecting* laboring class women with the men in this context. Examples of Collier's effort to align male and female rural labor experiences are rife throughout the poem. Collier notes that "When Harvest comes, into the Field we go, / And help to reap the Wheat as well as you"; "We cut the Peas, and always ready are / In ev'ry Work to take our proper Share"; "We oft change Work for Work as well as you"; and when brewing beer, "Like you, when threshing, we a Watch must keep, / Our Wort boils over if we dare to sleep" (316, 317, 319, 319). A strong sense of something like a community of the oppressed thus emanates from Collier's poem for, just as Duck's threshers are shown to be condemned to eternal toil, so too Collier's women: "Alas! our Labours never know an End" (319).

But I would argue Collier takes this idea of a community of the oppressed one step farther than Duck. Having established that women work as hard or harder than men, Collier nevertheless posits that "to rehearse all Labour is in vain" before playing her mythological trump card ("While you to *Sysiphus* yourselves compare, / With *Danaus' Daughters* we may claim a Share") (319). But whereas Duck concludes his poem resigned to that image of eternal labor, Collier adds a final verse paragraph, the shortest and perhaps most hard-hitting of her poem:

> So the industrious Bees do hourly strive
> To bring their Loads of Honey to the Hive;
> Their sordid Owners always reap the Gains,
> And poorly recompense their Toil and Pains.
>
> (320)

There are no analogous lines in Duck's poem to which Collier is offering a counterpoint here. Up to this juncture, Collier has presented carefully argued responses to specific passages, images, and allusions found in Duck's poem – often quoting relevant lines along the way. Now, with an air of summation, she seems to rise above the "you say / I say" fray to offer an inclusive conclusion that might be understood to apply to *both* of their poems. Collier's figure of the "industrious Bees" potentially represents both male and female agricultural laborers who are clearly exploited – their labor commodified – by a class of "sordid Owners." Collier may not have been happy with Duck's gender rhetoric, but she does seem to have read sympathetically those moments in "The Thresher's Labour" where he comes close to articulating a similar idea (141). Collier also turns Duck's sense of the breakdown of the traditional paternalist agricultural system – figured in the harvest-home feast that exposes the Master's "Cheat" to Duck's threshers – into a full-blown description of the capitalization of the countryside (146). One prominent purpose of her epistle, then, is to remind Duck of the ties that bind (see Goodridge, *Rural Life* 70). Unlike Frizzle or Tatersal, Collier is not addressing Duck either because she is envious of his spectacular good fortune or because she is trying to further her writing career. Instead, she acts the gadfly throughout much of her epistle, reminding him of his class roots early on and taking him to task for denigrating women workers but finally connecting their experiences as exploited laborers at the end. The flexibility of the verse epistle form makes all of this possible (as Collier well understands and exploits), and *The Woman's Labour* at least offers up the notion that laboring class community can and should be formed around the shared burdens felt by male and female agricultural laborers in this period.

Whereas Collier's poem leaves us with a clear sense of an imagined laboring class community, just a few years later a very real sociable literary community that included laboring class writers began to coalesce at Dodsley's bookshop. After the success of his play, *The Toy Shop*, in February 1735 and a timely £100 investment from Pope, Dodsley opened his publishing business at the sign of Tully's Head in Pall Mall two months later (Tierney 5; Solomon 44). From 1741 through the 1760s, as Dodsley's business grew, Tully's Head became the hub of an extensive social network that facilitated the creation and publication of literary works by laboring class writers. This network included patrons (Joseph Spence, Lord Chesterfield, William Shenstone, Lord Lyttelton), established authors (Pope, David Hume), and other booksellers (James Roberts, Mary Cooper, William Owen) who shepherded works by Duck, Jones, Woodhouse, and Blacklock into print. All four of Duck's pamphlet-style poems published between 1741 and 1755 on the title pages named Dodsley as either co-publisher or sole publisher.[3] Dodsley also included two of Duck's newly composed short poems in other formats under his imprint. "The Two Beavers" first appeared in 1746, without attribution, in *The Museum*, Dodsley's fortnightly literary periodical edited by Mark Akenside (1:295–7). That poem, along with "Contentment," were subsequently included in every edition of Dodsley's popular miscellany, *A Collection of Poems by Several Hands*, first published in 1748. The *Digital Miscellanies Index* reveals that both poems also appeared in cheaper miscellanies designed to target different audiences. For example, *The Sports of the Muses* (1752) and *The Comic Miscellany* (1756) were published in small duodecimo format by Mary Cooper, with Dodsley most likely hiding surreptitiously behind her imprint because these books did not measure up to his *belle lettres* reputation. Probably due to Chesterfield's influence, Dodsley published (with William Owen) the first London edition of the Irish bricklayer-poet Henry Jones's *Poems on Several Occasions* (1749) (to which Duck subscribed), and subsequently brought out two of Jones's pamphlet-style poems, *Merit: A Poem* (1753) and *Verses to His Grace the Duke of Newcastle* (1754), both of which listed Cooper acting as "seller." In 1753, Dodsley also paid Jones £100 for the copyright to his popular play, *The Earl of Essex* (Tierney 519). This must have been a bargain as it went to several editions before 1760 and Dodsley's brother James (who joined the firm in 1753 and took over after Dodsley's death in 1764) was still issuing the play under his own imprint in the 1770s and 1780s. Dodsley's literary collaborations with Shenstone in the early 1760s led to his issuing Woodhouse's first volume, *Poems on Sundry Occasions*, in 1764, thereby commencing a business relationship that would continue even after Dodsley's death as Woodhouse's expanded second volume, *Poems on Several Occasions*, appeared under James Dodsley's sole imprint in 1766.

Given all of this activity, remarkably little documentary evidence of Dodsley's interactions with Duck, Jones, or Woodhouse has survived. The only extant publishing agreement with any of them is that for Jones's *Earl of*

Essex, noted above, and Dodsley's surviving correspondence offers only one passing reference to Woodhouse in a letter to Shenstone (Tierney 431). Surprisingly, given the level of Dodsley's involvement in publishing their work, neither Duck nor Jones is ever mentioned. Perhaps because Blacklock lived in Scotland (therefore requiring regular epistolary communication, some of which has survived), his case offers considerably more detail with regard to how the Dodsley network functioned in the 1750s.

James E. Tierney's finely edited collection of Dodsley's correspondence contains a total of nine items that pertain to the publication of a London edition of Blacklock's *Poems*, which came to fruition in 1756 and ran to three editions in that year. These items include one of Hume's letters to Dodsley written in the midst of the planning stages; a letter from Spence to Dodsley regarding the publication of Spence's *Account* of Blacklock (which was published separately by Dodsley in 1754, and then prefixed to the 1756 *Poems*); six letters from Blacklock to Dodsley written between 1756 and 1760; and one partially dated letter from Dodsley to Blacklock that Tierney shows is a direct response to a letter from Blacklock dated 27 June 1757 (286). Taken together, these letters paint a rich portrait of the innerworkings and sociable relations that defined Dodsley's network, which I can summarize only briefly here. First, Hume's short note, dated 14 October 1754, reveals that he was well aware of the resources available through Dodsley that could help ensure a successful publication for a laboring class author. He refers to an enclosed letter to be forwarded to "Mr. Spence" (which would become the basis for Spence's *Account*, a marketing device he also had provided for Duck in 1731), and Hume names "Sir George Lyttelton" as "our Sheet Anchor" and hopes "to have him better acquainted with Mr. Blacklock's Care" (175). The letters from Blacklock to Dodsley largely concern the printing and distribution of the octavo third edition of Blacklock's poems, but are almost always personally revealing, which suggests that Blacklock and Dodsley developed a friendly relationship beyond their business dealings. Indeed, in one letter Blacklock engages in some light raillery warning of the "effects of presbyterian Air & Presbyterian eloquence" should Dodsley join Spence on a planned trip to Scotland and hear him preach (a visit that would take place in July 1758) (Tierney 354; Wright, *Joseph Spence* 160). Dodsley's one surviving letter to Blacklock shows that Blacklock's warm camaraderie was not one sided and, in response to Blacklock's concern about his account balance, Dodsley notes that the octavo edition "sell[s] but very slowly" and begs "you will not be in haste about it, I should be very sorry to send you an account without a ballance in your favour" which suggests that friendship supersedes business concerns here

(286). This letter also reveals that Dodsley could serve as an intermediary between laboring class poet and a potential patron, as he agrees to "mention" Blacklock's request that Lyttelton intercede with the Duke of Argyll regarding a vacant academic post at Edinburgh (286).

Though this and several other schemes proposed by Blacklock and his supporters to secure him a "place" in the late 1750s did not pan out, by the time he read Burns's Kilmarnock *Poems* and wrote him a (now famous) letter[4] in September 1786, Blacklock had already, with the help of James Beattie, embarked on "what was effectively a 'second career' ... as a literary journalist, scholarly essayist, translator, songwriter, and pedagogue" (Shuttleton 24). From about February 1787 through May 1788, Burns and Blacklock were both living in Edinburgh and collaborating on the second volume of James Johnson's *Scots Musical Museum*. Burns, however, left Edinburgh in June 1788 having leased the Ellisland farm and, one month later, gained a commission in the excise. Thus, the two private verse letters Blacklock wrote to Burns, in 1789 and 1790 respectively, were not about seeking out a relationship so much as furthering an existing one in specific ways.

Blacklock's first verse letter, dated 24 August 1789, opens with a warm address to his now absent friend and, somewhat oddly, continues with a semiformal celebration of Burns's poetic "art":

> Dear Burns, thou brother of my heart,
> Both for thy virtues and thy art;
> If art it may be call'd in thee,
> Which Nature's bounty large and free,
> With pleasure on thy breast diffuses,
> And warms thy soul with all the Muses.
> (Kinsley 489)

The full opening stanza should be read in the context of what David Shuttleton has recently shown to be Blacklock's "complex" relationship to the Scottish vernacular revival in this period (33). In addressing Burns as the "brother of [his] heart," Blacklock alludes to his own private, inner connection to this vernacular tradition now embodied by Burns. Though his poem is rendered in tetrameter couplets, a standard English form, and appears to eschew "broad Scots" vocabulary, the view of Burns's poetry expressed in the rest of the stanza – the emotional power of his "numbers" to elicit laughter, "softer passions," or "grief" from readers – implicitly declares Blacklock's support for his friend's vernacular poetry (489). The remaining stanzas take up quotidian matters as Blacklock inquires after Burns and his family in their new situation, and provides an account of his own activities and state of mind since they last were together.

Burns's response, dated from "Ellisland 21 October 1789," makes no acknowledgment of Blacklock's extended praise of his poetry – though Burns's use of standard habbie stanzas might be read in this context. The poem is, however, an enthusiastically genial and, at times, personally revealing reply to his "dear Friend['s]" verse letter (Kinsley 490). The anxieties Burns was feeling about his new career in the excise ("I'm turn'd a *Gauger* – Peace be here! / Parnassian *Quines* I fear, I fear, / Ye'll now disdain me,") and his venture into farming come through clearly:

I hae a wife and twa wee laddies,	
They maun hae brose and brats o' duddies;	[*must have porridge and tattered clothing*]
Ye ken yoursels my heart right proud is,	[*know*]
I need na vaunt;	[*brag*]
But I'll sned boosoms and thraw saugh-woodies	[*trim brooms and twist willow sticks (into rope)*]
Before they want.	– ("To Dr. Blacklock," Kinsley 490, 491)

Blacklock's second verse letter, composed in September 1790, is an attempt to convince Burns to contribute to a new periodical, *The Bee*, which was to commence in December under the stewardship of Dr. James Anderson. Reading this poem, one cannot help feeling that a regular prose letter might have sufficed in the business, but surely, Blacklock hopes that his playful verses will arouse his friend's dormant Muse: "The *Bee*, which sucks honey from every gay bloom, / With some rays of your genius her work may illume" (Chambers 3:145). Blacklock also sings Anderson's praises and apparently enclosed a full "plan" of the periodical for Burns to peruse. Yet Blacklock's efforts came to naught, as Burns wrote colorfully to Anderson that he was "worn to the marrow in the friction of holding the noses of the poor publicans to the grindstone of the Excise!" (Chambers 3:146). Despite the failure of this poem to achieve Blacklock's desired collaborative ends, the easy, informal sociability evident in this and the earlier coterie poems shows how the verse epistle form could be adapted for the maintenance of what seems to have been a real friendship (free of the envy and peevishness noted in poems by Frizzle and Tatersal addressed to Duck) between laboring class poets in the late-century period.

Verse epistles addressed between laboring class poets in the eighteenth century – of both the published and unpublished varieties – thus become important sources through which we can understand something not only about sociable communication between laboring class writers, but also, on occasion, their efforts to propose and forge literary community (imagined and real) in this period. It remains, then, to provide a more comprehensive view of all such poems of this kind, and perhaps also to re-evaluate the reams of epistolary poems laboring class writers also addressed to patrons and other established poets, as Van-Hagen suggests is necessary in the case of James Woodhouse ("Patrons" 319–20). There are, I suspect, more stories to tell of laboring class sociability and literary networking in the long eighteenth century.

NOTES

1. For a fuller account of the poetic response to Duck in the 1730s, see Jennifer Batt's chapter in this volume. The four poets discussed here represent apparently legitimate laboring class figures who addressed verse epistles to Duck in this period.
2. Following the success of Burns's *Poems, Chiefly in the Scottish Dialect* (1786), several circles of laboring class poets, based in Ulster and Scotland, addressed many verse epistles to Burns. It is well beyond the scope of this essay to include analysis of these poems. For discussions of some of them, see Orr, *Literary Networks*; Carruthers, "Robert Burns's Scots Poetry Contemporaries"; Andrews, "'Far Fam'd RAB'"; Andrews, *Genius* 94–103, 113–23.
3. *Every Man in his Own Way. An Epistle to a Friend* (1741) and *Hints to a School-Master. Address'd to the Revd. Dr. Turnbull* (1741) list Roberts and Dodsley as co-publishers; *An Ode on the Battle of Dettingen* (1743) and *Caesar's Camp: or, St. George's Hill* (1755) list Dodsley as the publisher and Cooper as the "seller." As the most prolific "trade publishers" in this period, Roberts and Thomas and Mary Cooper primarily distributed books for which they typically did not hold the copyright. Dodsley's evident shift in the early 1740s from Roberts to Mary Cooper (her husband, Thomas, died in 1743) accords with the decline of Roberts's business before his death in 1754 and the rise of Cooper's trade in this context (Treadwell, "James Roberts" 248–9).
4. Blacklock's letter, dated 4 September 1786, was sent through Rev. George Lawrie, from whom Blacklock had received a copy of Burns's Kilmarnock *Poems*. In it Blacklock encouraged Burns to come to Edinburgh to pursue the publication of a second edition. Later, Burns would write to Dr. John Moore that Blacklock's letter had "rous[ed] [his] poetic ambition" and so helped convince him not to emigrate to Jamaica (Ferguson and Roy I: 145). For a fuller discussion, see Shuttleton, esp. 25–9.

CHAPTER 4

"But Genius is the Special Gift of God!"
The Reclamation of *"Natural Genius"* in the Late-Eighteenth-Century Verses of Ann Yearsley and James Woodhouse

Steve Van-Hagen

Throughout the eighteenth century, patrons claimed that laboring class poets were worthy of readers' attention because the latter allegedly possessed "natural genius," an idea defined and debated by Joseph Addison, Joseph Spence, William Sharpe, Joseph Warton, Edward Young, Alexander Gerard, William Duff, and others.[1] "'Genius,'" as Tim Burke has observed, is a term "whose highly specialized sense in the eighteenth century has become diluted in our own."[2] There are two interrelated aspects of that sense that I wish to examine in this chapter, those of "natural" and "original genius" respectively. "Natural genius," in the earlier eighteenth century, may be defined within the context of poetry as the signifier for the means by which an uneducated poet, though capable of improvement through reading the Classics, was capable of writing poetry by imitating writers they had received no formal instruction in reading. As the century wore on, and although the two terms were sometimes used interchangeably, "natural" genius was increasingly supplanted by the more radical concept of "original genius." The aesthetic theory of "original genius" held that no reading of prior literature was desirable for the poets who possessed it, and even that reading earlier writers may harm their talent.[3] As Jonathan Bate neatly summarizes, after the publication of Edward Young's *Conjectures on Original Composition* in 1759, "The two very different concepts of poetry bequeathed to the modern world by the ancients, imitation and inspiration, are no longer viewed as complementary. The second is now pre-eminent" (180).

Typically, the result of being promoted as a "natural genius," both before and after Romanticism notionally glamorized its later, "original" variant, included publication of an introduction to a subscription volume of the poet's verses written by their middle or upper class patron apologizing for the poet's deficiencies. A modern critic such as Dustin Griffin, who clearly views "natural genius" as a positive rubric that allowed for the assimilation of laboring class poets into eighteenth-century culture, suggests that without such enabling patronage these poets would never have come to public notice.[4] Betty Rizzo suggests, alternatively, that such patronage was not as beneficent as Griffin suggests, and that writers patronized and promoted in this way were instead:

> ... so humble, so much less resourceful and independent, altogether more tractable, than such personages as Pope and Johnson. In fact, they made splendid household pets who could fawn in words. It was scarcely of consequence to their patrons that, confined to eternal gratitude, they were effectually muzzled, incapable of developing their own voices.... While better-known writers excoriated patronage, the natural poets exhausted their breath celebrating it. They upheld the ancient order: they knew their places – which were as low as the places of poets ought to be; and they kissed feet. (242)

Rizzo's view comes closer to the modern critical consensus. John Goodridge, although expressing himself in more measured terms than Rizzo, aptly summarizes this consensus by suggesting that "the prevailing model of 'natural genius' seemed to deny ... [labouring class poets] ... both agency and achievement, while praising their work for all the wrong reasons" ("General Editor's Introduction" to *Eighteenth-Century English Labouring-Class Poets* iv). Despite the scholarly attention given to these questions, as William J. Christmas has argued, "What has gone largely unexamined ... is the plebeian poets' counter-manipulation of the cultural tropes surrounding natural genius to serve their own interests" (*Lab'ring Muses* 27–8). No moderately experienced reader of criticism about poetry of the period could deny that Robert Burns's comparatively well-known "Epistle to J. L*****k, an old Scotch bard, 1 April 1785" has, for example, received consistent critical attention. However, while recent studies have discussed questions of "natural genius" as they affected late-century poets,[5] works by English laboring class poets of the period that specifically complicate and answer back to the limitations of "natural genius" as a trope have been relatively overlooked. This chapter, therefore, will attempt to redress this deficit by arguing for the reappropriation and reclamation of "natural genius" in the late-century poems of Ann Yearsley (1753–1806) and James Woodhouse (1735–1820).[6]

Yearsley and Woodhouse are prolific poets sometimes compared as perpetrators of the two most spectacular laboring class rebellions against polite patrons in the late 1780s. Yearsley's revolt against Hannah More is better known than Woodhouse's against Elizabeth Montagu. Since the former was the more public rupture of the two, it has attracted much critical discussion in recent decades.7 Yet the *works* of Yearsley and Woodhouse have been discussed directly alongside each other relatively infrequently.8 I will concentrate here on Yearsley's "To Mr ****, an Unlettered Poet, on Genius Unimproved" and "Addressed to Ignorance, Occasioned by a Gentleman's desiring the Author never to assume a Knowledge of the Ancients" and Woodhouse's pseudonymous autobiographical epic *The Life and Lucubrations of Crispinus Scriblerus*. By the century's end, these poems suggest, laboring class poets unhesitatingly manipulated and answered back to the conventions of "natural genius" for their own political, religious, aesthetic, and ethical ends. Both poets, in their different ways, also attempt their counter-manipulation of the discourse of "natural genius" as part of wider theological projects. Yet there are unavoidable dissimilarities in their methods. *The Life and Lucubrations of Crispinus Scriblerus* was a poem that Woodhouse did not publish, and perhaps never intended to publish in its entirety during his lifetime. Written sometime after 1788–9, following Woodhouse's final estrangement from Montagu, the poem's reclamation of "natural genius" is intertwined with the radical, evangelical philosophy he espoused by this point. Yearsley's two poems, by contrast, reflect her complex situation at the time of their publication in her second volume of poetry, *Poems on Various Subjects* (1787), after her public split from Hannah More. They seem squarely to contradict one another in the view they present of the poet's attitude toward "natural genius." At least one of the poems therefore must contradict More's established position on Yearsley's status as a "natural genius." Both Yearsley's and Woodhouse's reclamations of "natural genius" as a positive descriptor help us to understand their cultural, social, and ideological positions at the time they wrote these works. More than this, the poems encourage us to reconfigure our ideas about how laboring class poets interacted with the conventions of their promotion to the reading public and about how they responded to those conventions.

Yearsley was baptied Ann Cromartie on Clifton Hill, Bristol, in 1753. Her mother, though a milkseller, taught her daughter to read, borrowing books from traveling libraries to further the latter's education. In 1774, the poet married John Yearsley, a day laborer. She bore him six children over the next ten years, two of whom did not survive infancy. She helped to support them by selling milk from door to door, like her mother before her. In the winter of 1783–4, a number of disasters befell the Yearsleys and they became destitute. At a time of food shortages they stubbornly (and arguably foolishly) refused to take advantage of parish charity and, having lost their accommodation, took refuge in a disused farm on the outskirts of Bristol. Yearsley's mother died, and the poet was in danger of her own life, before the charitable Richard Vaughan inadvertently found and saved the family.[9] One of those to buy milk from Yearsley was Hannah More's cook, who showed her mistress some of Yearsley's work. Supported by the Bluestocking Elizabeth Montagu, More enlisted national support for a subscription of Yearsley's work, and *Poems on Several Occasions* was published by Thomas Cadell in June 1785. The volume was wildly successful, attracting more than a thousand subscribers, but public disagreement and schism followed. More and Yearsley quarrelled about the latter's access to the proceeds from the volume, and about Yearsley's intentions to embark upon a poetic career. Dropped by Cadell, with the aid of new patrons Yearsley found an alternative publisher in G. G. and J. Robinson. Yearsley's second volume was published two years later, though subscriptions were barely a third of those of her predecessor volume. Nonetheless, Yearsley went on to enjoy an extended publishing career, including another volume of verse, *The Rural Lyre* (1796), a novel and several plays. In later life she ran a circulating library.

There is a chapter devoted to Yearsley in probably the most comprehensive examination yet undertaken of the relation of laboring class poets to "natural genius," a PhD thesis by Jefferson Matthew Carter, *The Unletter'd Muse: The Uneducated Poets and the Concept of Natural Genius in Eighteenth-Century England*. Arguing that "[t]he Classical view of natural genius – that learning is essential to the innately gifted poet – dominates poetics from the time of Pindar to the age of Jonson," he suggests that "[t]he radical concept of natural genius – that learning impedes inborn genius – develops during the early eighteenth century and prevails in English critical thought after mid-century" (v). Carter associates this late-century "radical concept of natural genius" with the alternative term "original genius" and argues that More promoted Yearsley as a post-Young "original" genius, who was deliberately protected from Classical reading and learning so as not to ruin her "natural" gifts (see Carter, vi–vii).

Read alongside one another, Yearsley's poems on "natural genius" seem ambiguous and inconsistent. Carter's reading of More's promotion of Yearsley, however, makes possible the view that in "To Mr ****, an Unlettered Poet, on Genius Unimproved," Yearsley was satirically parroting her former patron in advancing "the radical view [of] the 1780s." This might imply that "Addressed to Ignorance," against our expectations of what might initially seem the more conservative poem of the two, was a rebellion against More, arguing that the more desirable identity was that of "natural" or "improved" genius. There are other impulses and influences at work in the poems, however, especially in "To Mr ****." Once laboring poets began to invoke religion to support their right to greater political and social equality,[10] and their right to write verse, reclaiming "natural genius" as a positive (self-) descriptor was a logical consequence. The obvious benefit of being a "natural" genius was that the term implied a gift given by a God of mercy whose worship entailed a doctrine that held potential for greater social and political equality for the laboring classes. In "To Mr ****," Yearsley advocates the supremacy of "natural" (or, within Carter's definitions, "original") genius over Classical learning:

> Ne'er hail the fabled Nine, or snatch rapt Thought
> From the Castalian spring; 'tis not for *thee*,
> From embers, where the Pagan's light expires,
> To catch a flame divine. From one bright spark
> Of never-erring Faith, more rapture beams
> Than wild Mythology could ever boast.
> . . . .
> What are the Muses, or Apollo's strains,
> But harmony of soul? Like thee, estrang'd
> From Science, and old Wisdom's classic lore,
> I've patient trod the wild entangled path
> Of unimprov'd Idea. Dauntless Thought
> I eager seiz'd, no formal Rule e'er aw'd;
> No Precedent controul'd; no Custom fix'd
> My independent spirit: on the wing
> She still shall guideless soar, nor shall the Fool,
> Wounding her pow'rs, e'er bring her to the ground.
>   (19–24, 33–42)[11]

While the poem is clear that Classical learning is not for the "natural genius," the speaker also explicitly identifies herself with the addressee ("Like Thee").[12] Both Christmas and Waldron[13] emphasize the Romantic privileging of inspiration and intuition over formal education, but it is surely important that the first verse paragraph (19–24) above emphasizes that Christian faith is the source of poetic inspiration. Likewise, the (unstated) implication of the subsequent verse paragraph (33–42) is that Yearsley is thus religiously inspired. If autodidacts could not compete on level terms with their educated counterparts in Classical learning, one solution was to shift the criteria one had to meet in order to be considered a poet. An emphasis on New Testament theology, with its worship of the servant king, offered an opportunity for the laboring classes to lay claim to the identity of "poet" – via "natural genius" – that was unavailable to writers from more privileged backgrounds.[14] Even scholars who have been interested primarily in the limitations upon women poets of the models provided by the "genius" debates have consistently seen "To Mr. ****" as establishing a resistant voice.[15]

Mindful that in an age in which presenting oneself to the public as a "natural genius" still invited condescension from the critics, Yearsley attacks the problem from a different perspective in "Addressed to Ignorance, Occasioned by a Gentleman's desiring the Author never to assume a Knowledge of the Ancients." Here, unlike in "To Mr. ****," she defiantly boasts her Classical learning. Waldron suggests that "Addressed to Ignorance" demonstrates that "To Mr ****" is ironic, since the former comes much closer to Yearsley's characteristically satirical, prickly tone. This impression is only strengthened if one accepts Waldron's reading that Yearsley's poetry and letters elsewhere generally suggest she expended no little effort in trying to dispel notions of herself as plebeian.[16]

"Addressed to Ignorance," like "To Mr. ****" a verse epistle, is written in a traditional, though elaborate meter of trochaic lines of either 11 or 12 syllables, alternating with eights or nines – the meter, like the learning, designed to refute the suggestion that the speaker and addressee were not competent to read and write "Classical" verse. Yearsley tells Ignorance that "Lactilla and thou must be friends" (8) and laments, with equal irony, that she is forbidden to "feed on the scraps of the Sage" (14) before listing everything that "Fancy" shows her. What follows is presumably intended as a virtuoso display of Classical learning, as she alludes to 33 different Classical figures or places within the space of 41 lines.[17] Via allusions to Voltaire and Wat Tyler, the poem ends with the feisty rejoinder:

> Here's Trojan, Athenian, Greek, Frenchman and I,
> Heav'n knows what I was long ago;
> No matter, thus shielded, this age I defy,
> And the next cannot wound me, I know.[18]

This seems very much like the confrontational tone frequently found in Yearsley's writing after her breach with More. The latter had first introduced Yearsley to the reading public in "A Prefatory Letter to Mrs. Montagu. By a Friend" from *Poems on Several Occasions* (1785) in which More claimed that Yearsley's reading had been very limited. "Addressed to Ignorance" also gives the lie to these claims (unless Yearsley acquired a great deal in a very short time). It is tempting to see the two poems, considered together, as Yearsley's attempts to experiment with or rehearse alternative counter-arguments to (different) assumptions that would deny her the status of poet. Free of More, Yearsley flirts with the identities of both "original genius" and the "natural genius" improved by Classical learning, trying on for size the advantages and disadvantages of both. Ultimately, however, the precise nature of the relation between the two poems remains difficult to resolve, all the more so because the theological content of "To Mr. ****" is in keeping with the wider theological concerns of Yearsley's second volume, also seen in poems such as "On Jephthah's Vow taken in a Literal Sense."[19] It is difficult, therefore, to see "To Mr. ****" as being straightforwardly satirical, or as only satire.

James Woodhouse experienced a rise to fame in some ways quite different from Yearsley's, given that his backstory lacked the latter's compelling hardships. Woodhouse began working life as an apprentice cordwainer, later becoming a carrier between Rowley Regis and London, and then a schoolteacher. In 1759 he addressed two elegies to his neighbor William Shenstone, the poet and landscape gardener. The two men became friends, and Shenstone initiated plans for a subscription volume of Woodhouse's verse that were seen to completion by publishers Robert and James Dodsley, after Shenstone's death in 1763. Woodhouse's *Poems on Sundry Occasions* appeared the following year, although it was the expanded *Poems on Several Occasions* in 1766 that marked the high point of Woodhouse's fame. Patronized now by Edward and Elizabeth Montagu, and by George, Lord Lyttelton, the volume was dedicated to the latter. As would be the case with Yearsley's *Poems on Several Occasions* nineteen years later, subscribers to Woodhouse's breakthrough volume included a range of noteworthy nobles and writers of the day.[20] At this point Woodhouse went to work for the Montagus, remaining in the employ of Elizabeth after Edward died in 1775. He published nothing new until a second (different) *Poems on Several Occasions* in 1788, after an acrimonious final break from his surviving patron. During his final decades, with the assistance of James Dodsley, Woodhouse became a successful stationer, bookseller, and printer. He subsequently published *Norbury Park, and Other Poems* (1803), *Love Letters to my Wife* (1804, though, like its predecessor volume, written in 1789), and at least one anonymous (brief) selection from a 28,013-line epic autobiography, *The Life and Lucubrations of Crispinus Scriblerus* (hereafter *Crispinus Scriblerus*) in 1814. Following Woodhouse's death from a street accident in 1820, his complete *The Life and Poetical Works* – containing the whole of *Crispinus Scriblerus* – was not published for another 76 years.[21]

While a number of commentators have touched on Woodhouse's life, work, and career in the light of contemporary conceptions of "natural genius," in passing at least,[22] Carter again provides arguably its most comprehensive examination. The latter argues for the view that Woodhouse's early publications present him as a "natural genius," whose talents were supplemented by Classical reading and learning (see Carter 184). The question of whether or not Carter is ultimately correct is a complex one that arguably extends beyond the remit of the present chapter;[23] but the view Carter advances of Woodhouse's early work and promotion to the public is, at the least, plausible. Carter contends that "The works which best illuminate the aesthetic background against which Woodhouse's contemporary reputation should be studied are Warton's essay, Young's *Conjectures*, and the writings of Duff" (164), maintaining that Woodhouse himself accepted that supposedly "natural genius" should be augmented by reading recommended by a patron. Carter further suggests that this was an absolutely conventional view in the 1760s, stemming from a not entirely consistent mixture of the writings of Addison and Warton (164). In Duff's *Critical Observations* (as Carter summarizes) "Original genius is the highest degree of innate genius; perhaps the inborn genius exhibited by a poet like Woodhouse was enough to guarantee his contemporary notoriety, if not a reputation for original genius" (169). It becomes significant, therefore, that "natural" (rather than the newer term, "original") genius continues to be ascribed to the laboring class poets after Duff's work, since the descriptor "natural genius" thereafter became associated with a lesser talent. Hence Carter suggests that Shenstone was safe to lend Woodhouse his books because, unlike an "original genius," a "natural genius" "would not be harmed by cultivating his (lesser) talents" (172).

Although Carter suggests that only "a few passages" of Woodhouse's work "verge[d] on the radical view of natural genius" (184), this is not true of late work such as *Crispinus Scriblerus*. In the latter, written while Woodhouse was inspired by the evangelical, egalitarian Methodism that seems to have been part of the reason for his final break from Elizabeth Montagu, Woodhouse claims, manipulates, and answers back to a number of the conventions surrounding "natural genius." He does so as part of a wider theological project that castigates the privileged and powerful as hypocrites who oppress the weak, neglected, and poor, suggesting that the former will deny themselves the Grace of a just and merciful God through their disregard for New Testament teachings. Peter Denney, not unaptly, states that *Crispinus Scriblerus* expresses "a strange form of radical Evangelicalism, which oscillated between righteous wrath and irreverent wit, being anti-clerical, anti-monarchical, solemn, pious, scornful and levelling" ("Popular Radicalism" 64). Woodhouse's late (re)appropriation of natural genius can only be fully understood not just within the contexts of eighteenth-century aesthetic theories, but within parallel foci upon both political and theological contexts.

Arguably one of the reasons why Carter concludes that "the Shoemaker-Poet's characteristic attitude toward himself was classical" is that the presentation of Woodhouse as a "natural genius" in the prefatory "Advertisement" to *Poems on Sundry Occasions* (1764) was conventional, and Woodhouse's 1760s poetical self-presentations (to some extent) reflect its content. Apart from attributing acquired learning to Woodhouse, otherwise "The Advertisement" contains all of the signifiers that motivate the modern critical suspicion of conventional eighteenth-century depictions of "natural genius" that Goodridge was quoted summarizing earlier. "The Advertisement" contains a four-and-a-half-page account of Shenstone's kindness and generosity to Woodhouse by helping him as much as he could, and of Woodhouse's apparent gratitude.[24] Woodhouse is constructed as a poet who believes in the desirability, and even the necessity of improvement, and yet the agency for this improvement is ascribed more to Shenstone than to Woodhouse. In *Poems on Several Occasions* (1766) two years later, Woodhouse even apparently contributes "The Author's Apology" himself, striking a series of similar-sounding notes.[25] "'The Author's Apology,' prefacing his second volume," Carter argues, "sets the tone for the autobiographical comments in his works ... Like previous uneducated poets, Woodhouse reveres learning and acquired art" (179).

By the 1790s, however, Woodhouse's works were making a very different kind of claim to the title of "natural genius." From the vantage point of Woodhouse's later, Methodist worldview, this "naturalness" implied a gift given directly, and purposely, by an Evangelical God of mercy whose worship entailed adherence to a doctrine that promoted the potential for laboring class social and political equality. A long passage in Chapter IV of *Crispinus Scriblerus* that has been reprinted in modern anthologies and editions on several occasions details Woodhouse / Crispinus's rise to fame in the early to mid-1760s, and characterizes the novelties, pressures, opportunities, and limitations of being a laboring class bard. It is during this extended passage that, while Woodhouse is careful to suggest that most of his patrons acted for the best of motives (the exception is Elizabeth Montagu), he first offers strident criticism of the kind of "improvement" that is possible through acquired learning. Critiquing the kind of verse that was fashionable in the 1760s, he bemoans the imitative style that was expected of a would-be bard:

> None could bind couplets – stanzas twist, and bend,
> Figures, and tropes, at tongue's and finger's end,
> But those that folios, learn'd, would frequent thumb,
> Whose titles strike rude, English, readers dumb.

> None without Latin stilts could stalk sublime,
> In bold blank Verse – or more elaborate Rhyme.[26]
>
> (IV: 197–202)

Woodhouse builds a two-part argument not just attacking what Carter terms "the classical view" of "natural genius," that geniuses could be made (or, at least, improved), but agitating in favor of what Carter calls "the radical view." The former comes first (IV: 257–84). Here the "proud Professors of cold Critic-Bands" (IV: 259) – Horace, Ben Jonson, Samuel Johnson, and perhaps Addison spring to mind – who maintain that genius could be acquired through learning and development are refuted through mockery, and the classical maxim most associated with natural genius, *poeta nascitur, non fit* ("poets are born, not made"), satirically inverted: "That Poesy's no more than trick and trade / Its first Proficients not born Bards but made" (IV: 271–2). To think this inversion could be so is, it is suggested, to deny Man his God-given place in the divine creation, and to reduce him to the stature of the animals (IV: 273–82). Typical of the characteristic complication and contradiction of Woodhouse's polemical argumentation is the fact that he suggests by satirical implication that Pope was as much of a (presumably "original" rather than "natural") genius as Homer or Milton, as the three of them mourn the pronouncements of the "proud Professors" (IV: 269–70). This was despite the fact that Young, whose ideas in the *Conjectures on Original Composition* Woodhouse seems partly to draw upon here, taxed Pope "with imitation in its most derogatory sense and [hence Young] sees imitation as a danger to genius" (Carter 167). Not for the only time in reading Woodhouse's oeuvre we become aware of a conflicted, ambivalent relationship toward the Catholic, conservative Pope on the part of the radical, Methodist poet, who nonetheless admired the radical power and ambition of Scriblerian satire.

In the second half of Woodhouse's argument (IV: 303–40), he unambiguously stakes his own claim to be thought of as a "natural genius." Neither the words "natural" nor "original" are used in the passage, which makes it difficult to know how much critical and theoretical reading about the subject Woodhouse had completed. Nonetheless, this passage advocates for the "radical view" of "natural genius," tempered only by an initial qualification:

> Knowledge, and Learning, may supply, in part,
> Their needful helps in true poetic Art –
> Like crutches, may assist mechanic skill
> To hobble round the base of Ida's hill
>
> (IV: 303–6)

Thereafter, however, if anything, Woodhouse describes what Duff would term "original" genius more than its "natural" predecessor. We are left in no doubt that "Genius" is innate, and granted directly, exclusively, from God: "Ev'n Common Sense may with pure Knowledge plod, / But Genius is the special Gift of God!" (331–2). Modern critics including Christmas, Keegan (*Nature Poetry*), and myself have all sought to build an understanding of the power and fervor of Woodhouse's radical late work. Yet the significance of his reappropriation of "natural genius" as part of that politico-theological project, not just in his authorial addresses to the public but in his late verse itself, has arguably still not yet been examined in the depth required.[27]

(Re)reading both Yearsley and Woodhouse, we are conscious that, to some degree, the poems discussed take opposite paths toward their ends; Yearsley answers back to More by claiming what was by the end of the century a venerable concept of an improved "natural genius," just as Woodhouse embraced the more contemporary, radical alternative of "original genius." Hence we are reminded, however, of the significance in the period of the stance of a poet from a marginalized background on questions of "natural genius" as a signifier of their complicated cultural, social, and ideological positions. We are reminded, ultimately, that there is still a need to respond positively to Christmas's call, quoted earlier, to attend to the laboring class poets' "counter-manipulation of the cultural tropes surrounding natural genius to serve their own interests." If we do not, we fall into the trap of merely perpetuating the myth that "natural genius" limited and confined them within straightforwardly damaging and undesirable identities, something that was far from the case by the eighteenth century's end.

NOTES

1. See, for instance, Joseph Addison in *The Spectator*, no. 160 (Monday 3 September 1711); William Sharpe, *Dissertation on Genius* (London: 1755); Joseph Warton, *Essay on the Genius and Writings of Pope* (London: M. Cooper, 1756); Edward Young, *Conjectures on Original Composition. In a Letter to the Author of Sir Charles Grandison* (London: A. Millar; and R. and J. Dodsley, 1759); Alexander Gerard, *An Essay on Taste . . . with Three Dissertations on the Same Subject* (Edinburgh: A. Millar, A. Kincaid and J. Bell, 1759) and *An Essay on Genius* (London and Edinburgh: W. Strahan, T. Cadell and W. Creech, 1774); William Duff, *An Essay on Original Genius; and its Various Modes of Exertion in Philosophy and the Fine Arts, Particularly in Poetry* (London: Edward and Charles Dilly, 1767) and *Critical Observations on the Writings of the most Celebrated Geniuses in Poetry. Being a Sequel to the Essay on Original Genius* (London: T. Becket and P. A. de Hondt, 1770).

2. Tim Burke, "Ann Yearsley and the Distribution of Genius in Early Romantic Culture," in *Early Romantics: Perspectives in British Poetry from Pope to Wordsworth*, edited by Thomas Woodman (Houndmills, Basingstoke: Macmillan, 1998), 216.
3. For useful overviews of eighteenth-century debates about "natural" (and "original") genius as they were applied to literary questions, see James M. Osborn, "Spence, Natural Genius and Pope," *Philological Quarterly* 45.1 (1966): 123–44; Christine Battersby, *Gender and Genius: Towards a Feminist Aesthetics* (London: The Women's Press, 1989), 4–7, 16–17, 33–4, 36–8, 43–7, 71–102; Drummond Bone, "The Emptiness of Genius: Aspects of Romanticism," in *Genius: The History of an Idea*, edited by Penelope Murray (Oxford: Basil Blackwell, 1989), 113–27; Andrew Elfenbein, *Romantic Genius: The Prehistory of a Homosexual Role* (New York: Columbia University Press, 1989); and Jonathan Bate, *The Genius of Shakespeare* (London: Picador, 2008), 161–86. See also Jefferson Matthew Carter, "The Unletter'd Muse: The Uneducated Poets and the Concept of Natural Genius in Eighteenth-Century England" (PhD Diss., The University of Arizona, 1972), 6–26; and Tim Burke, "Ann Yearsley and the Distribution of Genius in Early Romantic Culture," 215–30 (especially 217–23).
4. See Dustin Griffin, *Literary Patronage, 1650–1800* (Cambridge: Cambridge University Press, 1996), 189–95.
5. An indirect example of how a laboring-class bard may turn the conventions of "natural genius" to their advantage is discussed, for instance, by Simon White in *Robert Bloomfield, Romanticism and the Poetry of Community* (Aldershot, Hampshire and Burlington, VT: Ashgate, 2007), 126–7. See also Daniel Cook, *Thomas Chatterton and Neglected Genius, 1760–1830* (Houndmills, Basingstoke: Palgrave, 2013), 13–34.
6. One of the exceptions to this rule in addressing questions of how a laboring-class poet of the late-century period responds specifically to the available models of "genius" attends to some of Yearsley's own work; see Burke, "Ann Yearsley and the Distribution of Genius in Early Romantic Culture." Burke mostly examines poems other than those under discussion in the present chapter, such as "On Mrs. Montagu," "Clifton Hill," and "Night. To Stella." Burke's chapter considers how Yearsley responds to the "muting" that is caused for the female laboring-class poet by contemporary definitions of "genius" which seemingly define the concept as exclusively masculine. For a welcome recognition that "not all eighteenth-century laboring-class poets were content to fit the mold of the solitary, artless 'natural genius,' or worse, to impersonate the fashions of polite poetry, as many unsympathetic critics suppose," see Bridget Keegan, "Cobbling Verse: Shoemaker Poets of the Long Eighteenth Century," *The Eighteenth Century: Theory and Interpretation* 42.3 (2001): 196.
7. For influential accounts of Yearsley's life and career, and of the relationship and break with More, see Moira Ferguson, *Eighteenth-Century Women Poets: Nation, Class and Gender* (Albany, New York: SUNY Press, 1995), 45–90; Donna Landry, *The Muses of Resistance: Laboring-Class Women's Poetry*

in Britain, 1739–96 (Cambridge: Cambridge University Press, 1990), 120–87; Betty Rizzo, "The Patron as Poet-Maker," *Studies in Eighteenth-Century Culture* 20 (1991): 258–62; Annette Wheeler Cafarelli, "The Romantic 'Peasant' Poets and their Patrons," *The Wordsworth Circle* 26.2 (1995): 79–81; Mary Waldron, *Lactilla, Milkwoman of Clifton: The Life and Writings of Ann Yearsley, 1753–1806* (Athens, Georgia: University of Georgia Press, 1996); Christmas, *The Lab'ring Muses*, 235–66; Julie Cairnie, "The Ambivalence of Ann Yearsley: Laboring and Writing, Submission and Resistance," *Nineteenth-Century Contexts* 27.4 (2005): 353–64; and Kerri Andrews, *Ann Yearsley and Hannah More, Patronage and Poetry* (London: Pickering and Chatto, 2013).

8. An exception is H. Gustav Klaus, *The Literature of Labour: Two Hundred Years of Working-Class Writing* (Brighton: The Harvester Press, 1985), 5–6, 20–21. Klaus compares Yearsley's and Woodhouse's generic experimentations because both testify "to a greater confidence in their artistic abilities" than was evident in earlier works by laboring-class writers. Bridget Keegan provides another exception by discussing Yearsley at the end of her chapter "Return to the Garden: James Woodhouse and Polite Cultivations" in *British Laboring-Class Nature Poetry, 1730–1837* (Houndmills, Basingstoke and New York: Palgrave Macmillan, 2008), 62.

9. For the origin of this much retold account of Yearsley's "discovery," and many other stories about her early life, see Hannah More's "A Prefatory Letter to Mrs. Montagu. By a Friend" in Yearsley's *Poems on Several Occasions* (London: Thomas Cadell, 1785), iii–v.

10. For various discussions of these phenomena, see Bridget Keegan, "Mysticisms and Mystifications: The Demands of Laboring-Class Religious Poetry," *Criticism* 47.4 (2005): 471–91; Christmas, *The Lab'ring Muses*, 203–9; Steve Van-Hagen, "The Poetry of Physical Labour 1730–1800: The Duckian Tradition" (PhD Diss., University of Kent, 2006), 24–7, 97–116, 154–67, 240–55.

11. Ann Yearsley, "To Mr. ****, an Unlettered Poet, On Genius Unimproved," in Yearsley, *Poems on Various Subjects* (London: G. G. and J. Robinson, 1787), 78–80 (ll. 19–24, 33–42).

12. The addressee has not been definitively identified. Scholars have suggested possibilities such as the autodidact poets John Frederick Bryant (1753–91) and William Job (*fl.* 1785–90), both of whom hailed from Yearsley's native Bristol.

13. See Christmas, *The Lab'ring Muses*, 253; and Waldron, *Lactilla, Milkwoman of Clifton*, 152.

14. On Yearsley and religion, see Waldron, 18–19, 128–9. Waldron notes that "the power of dissent in Bristol" was strong, though is unaware of Yearsley's "allegiance to any particular group." Nonetheless, she asserts that Yearsley "was certainly firmly set against the idea of a vindictive God and to some extent anthropomorphism in general" (129).

15. See Elfenbein, *Romantic Genius*, 126; and Burke, "Ann Yearsley and the Distribution of Genius in Early Romantic Culture," 228.

16. See Waldron, 3–6, 16–17, 24–5, 46–78. For further discussion of such readings, see Frank Felsenstein, "Ann Yearsley and the Politics of Patronage: The Thorp

Arch Archive," parts 1 and 2, *Tulsa Studies in Women's Literature* 21.2 (2000): 346–92 and 22.1 (2003): 13–56; Cairnie, "The Ambivalence of Ann Yearsley."

17. These allusions are to Pythagoras, Homer, Ilium, Nestor, Achilles, Ulysses, Menelaus, Paris, the river Salmacis, Zeno, Tibullus, Socrates, Diogenes, Plato, Lycurgus, Tyburn, Longinus, Helicon, Virgil, Hesiod, Ovid, Horace, Penelope, Helen, Sparta, Democritus, Solon, Pliny, Clytemnestra, Agamemnon, Egysthus, Ajax, and Troy.

18. Ann Yearsley, "Addressed to Ignorance, Occasioned by a Gentleman's desiring the Author never to assume a Knowledge of the Ancients," in Yearsley, *Poems on Various Subjects*, 99 (ll. 69–72).

19. For "On Jephthah's Vow taken in a Literal Sense," see *Poems on Various Subjects*, 131–38. See also Waldron, 162–5.

20. See James Woodhouse, *Poems on Several Occasions* (London: Mills, 1766), which contains two pages listing Woodhouse's 109 "Benefactors," and a further six pages listing the nearly 300 "Subscribers."

21. *The Life and Poetical Works of James Woodhouse*, edited by Rev. Reginald Illingworth Woodhouse (London: The Leadenhall Press, 1896), 2 vols.

22. For critical treatments of Woodhouse and his work since the 1980s, see H. Gustav Klaus, *The Literature of Labour: Two Hundred Years of Working-Class Writing*, 1–21; Betty Rizzo, "The Patron as Poet-Maker," 254–58; Annette Wheeler Cafarelli, "The Romantic 'Peasant' Poets and their Patrons," 78–79; William J. Christmas, *The Labr'ing Muses*, 183–207; Bridget Keegan, "Cobbling Verse: Shoemaker Poets of the Long Eighteenth Century," 210–12; Keegan, *British Labouring-Class Nature Poetry, 1730–1837*, 37–64; Peter Denney, "'Unpleasant, tho' Arcadian Spots': Plebeian Poetry, Polite Culture, and the Sentimental Economy of the Landscape Park," *Criticism* 47.4 (2005): 505–10; Denney, "Popular Radicalism, Religious Parody and the Mock Sermon in the 1790s," *History Workshop* 74 (2012): 64; Van-Hagen, "The Life, Works and Reception of an Evangelical Radical: James Woodhouse (1735–1820), the 'Poetical Shoemaker,'" *Literature Compass* 6.2 (2009): 384–406; Van-Hagen, "Patrons, Influences, and Poetic Communities in James Woodhouse's *The Life and Lucubrations of Crispinus Scriblerus*," in *Social Networks in the Long Eighteenth Century: Clubs, Salons and Textual Coteries*, edited by Ileana Baird (Newcastle upon Tyne: Cambridge Scholars Press, 2014), 309–33; and Sandro Jung, "Shenstone, Woodhouse, and Mid-Eighteenth-Century Poetics: Genre and the Elegiac-Pastoral Landscape," *Philological Quarterly* 88.1–2 (2009): 127–49.

23. On the complexities of Woodhouse's identities in his early life and work, and on the importance of sociability in these questions, see Van-Hagen, "Patrons, Influences, and Poetic Communities in James Woodhouse's *The Life and Lucubrations of Crispinus Scriblerus*."

24. "The Advertisement," in James Woodhouse, *Poems on Sundry Occasions* (London: Richardson and Clark, 1764), iii–vii.

25. "The Author's Apology," in James Woodhouse, *Poems on Several Occasions* (1766), v–viii.

26. The text is taken from *The Life and Poetical Works of James Woodhouse*, vol. 1, 69. Obvious typographical errors have been corrected. Subsequent citations are from this edition, and line references are given after quotations in the main text.
27. See Christmas, *The Lab'ring Muses*, 196, for his reading of Woodhouse's "Address" in 1788's *Poems on Several Occasions*, which the former reads as "a plea for social mobility based on innate, God-given talent – Woodhouse's 'inclination.'" For Christmas, the "opportunity" to make such a plea is "Implicit within eighteenth-century conceptions of natural genius," the chance "to escape the condescending support that defines polite patronage of natural genius."

CHAPTER 5

Alexander Wilson
The Rise and Fall and Rise of a Laboring Class Writer

Gerard Carruthers

The writing career of Alexander Wilson (1766–1813) is pioneering, both as a beset laboring class poet in Paisley, Scotland during the turbulent 1790s, and as a pamphleteer, poet, and naturalist in the early American republic. Unsettled and adventurous as his life was, Wilson would likely be surprised at his posthumous positive fame: the recipient of respectable Victorian antiquarian endeavors; memorialized in a statue in his hometown, a short distance from where his poetry was once publicly burned; and the subject of a recent Harvard University Press biography hailing Wilson as "the Scot who founded American ornithology."[1] There are possibilities for reading Wilson as someone of multiple, disrupted careers and, at the same time, bringing a sense of cogency to his life and work by placing him as a man obviously marked by the Enlightenment, and – not unrelated to this mentalité – within the recent theoretical framework as a "Trans-Atlantic" individual. What his career most certainly demonstrates is the possibility in late-eighteenth-century Scotland for the rise of a laboring class writer and the danger of his downfall if he were to become too political. In America, Wilson continued to write poetry but in his work as a naturalist resorted to an area of interest that predated the political disintegration of his Scottish career. He makes for an interesting case study of the particular opportunities for and vicissitudes of the late-eighteenth-century aspiring laboring class writer. Regrettably, we remain far short of having all the necessary materials for a longer and much-needed cultural study of Wilson.[2]

In only a few short years following Wilson's death, the poet, who in 1794 had found his native country politically and personally so uncomfortable that he felt he had little option but to emigrate to America, was subject to a wave of renewed interest back in Scotland and also in Ulster. This "rehabilitation" occurred in the Renfrewshire publication *The Weaver's Magazine and Literary Companion* (featuring the two-part "Biographical Sketches of the Late Alexander Wilson" in May and July 1819). It is likewise seen in the *Paisley Magazine* (1828), edited by William Motherwell, the reactionary

Tory who encouraged the Orange Order in Scotland as well as the Burns Movement. Both gambits were designed in large part to head off the potentially more radical proclivities within the working classes of the West of Scotland.[3] A Belfast edition of Wilson's *Poetical Works* appeared in 1845, and the *Renfrewshire Magazine* of 1847 featured "The Life and Writings of Alexander Wilson." In 1876, the two-volume *Poems and Literary Prose of Alexander Wilson, the American Ornithologist* appeared "for the first time fully collected and compared with the original and early editions, MSS, etc" (title page). The editor of the latter was the Rev. Alexander B. Grosart, a wide-ranging literary historian whose studies, for instance, in both Elizabethan writing and in poetry in Scots might be read ideologically as following the Arnoldian agenda of shoring up British cultural identity in the nineteenth century.

Wilson's newfound respectability takes its most public shape in the aforementioned Paisley statue, unveiled in 1874. In its subject's pose, simultaneously sensitive and about to perform taxidermy on a bird, sentimental poetry and naturalism are equally registered. It belongs to a time of Paisley's reawakened cultural awareness, the same year seeing the erection in the town of a statue of Wilson's contemporary, poet and songwriter Robert Tannahill. The plaque for Wilson reads, "Remember Alexander Wilson 1766–1813. Here was his boyhood playground." Close to the River Cart, scene of the writer's youthful gambols, much more apparent to the modern viewer is that the memorial stands in the shadow of Paisley Abbey. The Abbey was also repurposed in the late nineteenth century – for douce, Presbyterian worship when it had stood in ruins from the Reformation until well beyond Wilson's lifetime. In this place of historic elision, speaking of newfound Victorian cultural solidity, Wilson's statue, referencing childhood, post-Romantic poetic sensibility, and the man as naturalist, erases the most difficult part of the writer's biography as a radical writer of the 1790s.

The career of Burns is a crucial lens through which to view that of Alexander Wilson, as it is with all poets writing in Scots during the several decades following the appearance of Scotland's "national poet." This is not only due to direct influence, but also because the biographical construction of Burns both during and especially after his lifetime forms a template which his contemporaries find difficult to escape. One instance of this pattern can be found in the textual memorials mentioned above where we witness the predominant "Burnsian" trope of depicting Wilson, the "weaver-poet," in the context of settled rural labor. It is important to note that Wilson felt the literary urge prior to Burns's first public appearance in 1786. During the late 1770s, Wilson penned a song in Scots celebrating the pleasant scenes around Castle Semple in Renfrewshire.

While *songs* in Scots might be seen as a stock-in-trade for any writer from the west of Scotland before Burns, *poetry* in Scots was not. In keeping with this pattern, Wilson's early poetry was in English. Both popular and academic accounts have failed to understand fully why Burns had such an electrifying effect when he first appeared as a published poet. Burns brought to his cradle-Presbyterian culture an Ayrshire stanza-form and a literary Scots, that if not entirely unknown in the west country of Scotland, were much more associated with Edinburgh and even more so the North East, especially Aberdeenshire. His great sleight of hand was to introduce to the Presbyterian west of Scotland a largely alien mode, poetry (as opposed to song) in Scots. Such poetry was previously associated with Episcopalianism and even Catholicism. Burns's great predecessors in Scots verse, Allan Ramsay and Robert Fergusson, were, in eighteenth-century Scottish political terms, Tories and crypto-Jacobites. They were convinced that Whiggish, Calvinist culture, including an often puritanical outlook on the arts, had culturally crippled the country. Part of this conceit promoted by a Scoto-Latinist group that operated throughout the eighteenth century was that a rich cocktail of literature including work in English, Latin, and Scots ought to be promoted to counter the crassness of Scottish Whig culture. These are the crucial ideological roots of eighteenth-century Scots poetry, forgotten subsequently, which culminated in the work of Burns. After Burns, the association of Scots literature with the hoi polloi and the laboring classes is seen as axiomatic. In fact, it originated with a higher social stratum: that of Tory, sometimes aristocratic, Jacobitism. The compass was only set toward a laboring class direction by Burns's virtuoso championing of Scots in his peasant-poet persona.

Burns's *Poems, Chiefly in the Scottish Dialect* (Kilmarnock, 1786; expanded, Edinburgh, 1787) gradually made him a literary celebrity for all classes. The "Kilmarnock" edition was largely the construction of the enlightened Ayrshire middle classes who advised him on the volume and provided the majority of its subscriptions. The "Edinburgh" edition was dedicated to the Caledonian Hunt (as their name suggests, drawn from the upper strata of Scottish society), a group that block-subscribed and confirmed Burns's portable appeal. The lower classes followed more slowly in their admiration of the "heaven-taught ploughman." The initial resistance to Burns came in the face of the poet's attack on the supposedly hypocritical Calvinist personality and even their democratic kirk politics, for instance, in "Holy Willie's Prayer" and "The Ordination." The latter poem objected to a congregation in Kilmarnock presuming to choose its own minister and showed Burns most clearly at loggerheads with the popular Presbyterianism of his day. In distinction from Burns's Scots-language medium and in keeping with their "Whiggish" heritage, Scottish Presbyterian poets, whether politically conservative or progressive, more often preferred English over Scots until well into the nineteenth century.[4] There were, however, also a substantial number of Burns imitators, the first wave including those from Burns's own circle to whom he had written verse epistles. Several dozen of these imitators copied the title, *Poems, Chiefly in the Scottish Dialect*. This title was also used in the posthumous naming of Alexander Wilson's 1816 collection.

Wilson himself partially adopts the Burnsian idiom following the "Kilmarnock" edition of 1786 and is one of the more commercially successful of Burns's followers. Following Burns's example, Wilson sought local patronage to enable publication of his work. In 1789 he showed Thomas Crichton, governor of Paisley's Town Hospital, his collection of poems in manuscript, newer ones in Scots, and older ones (but also some new texts) in English. Crichton was impressed and introduced Wilson to John Neilson, the finest printer in the town, who agreed to publication on the basis of Wilson obtaining a subscription list. Wilson's friend and fellow poet, James Kennedy, helped with the funding by supplying cash up front, and, after several months, around 400 subscriptions had been pledged. This was only about two-thirds of the quantity Neilson had prescribed, but the printer went ahead and in 1790 printed the volume with the simple title of *Poems*.

Prior to collecting subscriptions, Wilson had been a weaver, apprenticed at thirteen. He left weaving, though not finally, to become a packman, or pedlar, selling handkerchiefs, cloths for dressmaking, and also soliciting subscriptions for his putative volume. Wilson's peregrinations had taken him to the east of the country, and from these he compiled his "Journal as a Peddler, 1789–90," which formed the introduction to his first book. Like Burns's writing, whose prefaces to his 1786 and 1787 collections demonstrated an accomplished Augustan prose-style, Wilson's "Journal" is a highly fluent, self-assured performance discoursing self-reflexively on the "polite pedlar" (4). He is a character selling material wares and, retrospectively (in the "Journal"), abstract thoughts on poetry and natural observation. The "Journal" is also anthropological and political, with ironically understated anecdotes describing an unfeeling upper stratum of society. It is not coincidental that the "Journal" is begun in September 1789, in the new postrevolutionary atmosphere sprung from France. In this mood

Wilson tells of his attempts to importune the subscription of a Duchess for whom he leaves a note begging her attention:

> To Her Grace, the Duchess of —
>
> Madam, – The person who has the honour of presenting the inclosed poetical hand-bill, humbly begs your gracious acceptance and perusal. The goods which it enumerates, your humble servant carries along with him, that he may, by their means, have an easier opportunity of soliciting the favour of the literary world, for a volume of poems he has just now published. May it therefore please your Grace, to allow, for once, a young poet to spread his elegant assortment at your feet – to entreat your acceptance of a copy of his poetical performances, and your pardon for this intrusion, which will for ever bind him,
>
> Madam,
> Your, &c., &c. (22)

Wilson, or his persona, is here not one thing or the other, neither packman nor poet. He provides a kind of fantasy (though the episode seems altogether unlikely to have actually happened) which comments on the difficulty of supplying subscribed poetry from the bottom of society. Wilson may here be satirizing literary patronage, including Burns's success with the upper classes, his admiration of Scotland's most famous poet notwithstanding.

Wilson's *Poems* (1790) is a collection of texts largely devoid of explicit political commentary. Much of the contents, either in Scots or in English in fact, are consistent with an overall tone of good-humored observation of "everyday" life that is found in his greatest public success as a Scots poet, "Watty and Meg, or the Wife Reformed" (1792). Marketed through the country by chapmen, the poem was sold anonymously as a penny chapbook and mistaken for the work of Burns. "The crown of [Wilson's] achievement" and "inimitable" according to his Victorian biographer (Wilson, *Poems* xxxvi), this chapbook reputedly sold in excess of 100,000 copies (Cantwell 75). Such an extraordinary number helped clear his debts to Neilson, who had produced his undersubscribed *Poems* a year earlier.

"Watty and Meg" is a highly competent performance of 200 lines and a very gender-conservative homage to *The Taming of the Shrew*. Husband Watty, in the end, wins complete freedom to enjoy his favorite pastime of drinking in the pub by threatening to leave nagging Wife Meg and join the military. Watty's gambit exacts a promise from his spouse to stop her habitual scolding. It ends:

Down he threw his staff, victorious;
Aff gaed bonnet, claes and shoon; [shoes]
Syne below the blankets, glorious,
Held anither Hinnymoon! (10)

Wilson's text is soaked in the carousing phraseology of Robert Burns's great mock-epic, "Tam o' Shanter" (1790). However, if interpreted properly, the attentive reader understands, in spite of his frightening monitory encounter with witches one night, Burns's poem is a comedy on the recidivist nature of the male who will return inevitably to drinking and flirting with women. Wilson's text is straightforwardly didactic, which is to say simply sexist. It does not, perhaps, say much for its large reading public nor indeed for the Victorian editor Alexander Grosart, who in his 1876 edition places this text that he so admires at the beginning of "Part I – Scottish Poems."

In 1791, Wilson produced another long poem in Scots, "The Laurel Disputed; or the merits of Allan Ramsay and Robert Fergusson contrasted." This was written for a public competition held at the Parthenon in Edinburgh on 14 April 1791, to be decided by a voting audience. Among seven competitors, Wilson was alone in advocating Fergusson and placed second. It was discovered, however, that the winner had bought 40 tickets for his own supporters (Burtt and Davis 20). "The Laurel Disputed" was published in a handsome pamphlet publication along with another competition entry (by his friend and fellow Paisley poet Ebenezer Picken) and was also included in a second edition of Wilson's work *Poems: Humorous, Satirical and Serious* (1791). This book included much of the work of his first edition, with over half a dozen new texts, but enjoyed a more prestigious publication by Edinburgh bookseller, Peter Hill, who was for a period a close friend of Burns. What the Parthenon competition shows is part of the late-eighteenth-century negotiation of the heritage of Scots poetry. Burns's virtuoso ability to re-establish Scots poetry encompassed his popularization of Robert Fergusson, who had died in 1774 at the age of 24 in the Edinburgh Bedlam. Whereas successful businessman and cultural entrepreneur Allan Ramsay had a couple of decades of literary success from 1715 to the 1730s, Fergusson had died in penury and obscurity, having operated within a much smaller ambit as virtual house-poet for Jacobite sympathizer Walter Ruddiman's *Weekly Magazine*. Fergusson, who had shared Ruddiman's Tory and Jacobite mentality, was never going to be mainstream in the capital city in the way in which Ramsay had succeeded in becoming with his popular pastoral drama *The Gentle Shepherd* (1725). Burns took it upon himself to raise the money for a proper headstone at Fergusson's unmarked grave in the Canongate cemetery. He was assisted by the aforementioned Peter Hill, who acted effectively as banker. Burns referred to the University of St. Andrews-educated city legal clerk, Fergusson, as his "elder brother in Misfortune / . . . my elder Brother in the muse" (323). Here we see Burns's transformative role, already alluded to, as he brings to public notice in the wider (predominantly Whiggish) Scotland a dead poet of minority cultural credentials.

Burns was not the only poet to use his verse and cultural capital to promote fellow Scots poets, as we see in Robert Tannahill's poem lamenting his friend, Wilson's, departure to America:

Come let our tears thegither flow;
O join my mane!
For Wilson, worthiest of us a,
For ay is gane.   [*always*]

He bravely strave gainst Fortune's stream
While Hope held forth ae distant gleam,
'Till dasht and dasht, time after time,
On life's rough sea,
He weeped his thankless native clime,
And sail'd away.

The patriot bauld, the social brither,
In him war sweetly join'd thegither;
He knaves reprov'd, without a swither,
In keenest satire;
And taught what mankind owe each ither
As sons of Nature.   (Tannahill 78)

Tannahill here mirrors the Burnsian mode of lament for Fergusson whom Burns claimed had been neglected by his country. Similarly, the superlative Wilson in Tannahill's verse experiences Fergussonian struggles in his "thankless native clime." He is a "patriot" (presumably in his use of the Scots language), he is humanitarian in the manner of Burns, and reproves knaves without a swither (or second thought), a clear reference to Wilson's most politically radical work, which had appeared in neither of his 1790 and 1791 collections. In Tannahill's text, he registers the end of the working class Renfrewshire literary brotherhood of which Wilson and he had been a part. This fraternity had been enabled due to a combination of the Enlightenment cultural sociability engendered in Paisley by periodical and library culture as well as by the potent idea of the laboring class poet that Burns formulated. Wilson's encourager Thomas Crichton was part of this fraternal association and was himself a poet, as well as a schoolteacher and avid reader of periodicals who was also at the forefront of establishing the first public library in Paisley.

As already suggested in this essay, Victorian-period critics identified Wilson as a pleasant, pastoral Scots versifier. It is also true that the two collections published in Wilson's lifetime largely supported such an interpretation, demonstrating very little in the way of explicit political or cultural commentary aside from the most conventional moralizing. Instead, we have a series of texts with scenes of the common folk and of nature. No doubt representing a literary democratization in itself, this also comprised the respectable or official idiom of Scots-language poetry in the late eighteenth century. The pioneers of landscape and folk scenes in Scots, Allan Ramsay and Robert Fergusson, used such settings to register pleasure in the everyday occurrences of life. It functioned as part of their ideological arsenal to counterpoint what they witheringly saw as the predominantly blighted puritanical culture of Whiggish Scotland. In the hands of Wilson and others, representations of rural life become more neutral exercises in the scene-painting of eating, drinking, and music-making. From the late 1780s until the Victorian period, a de-politicized, safely affirmative Scots poetry predominated; Burns himself, though seldom guilty of lacking cultural or political trenchancy, helped inspire this safe terrain in collaborating with the manufacture of his image as the "heaven-taught ploughman." This was a guise, on the face of it, largely innocent of any kind of ideological guile or purpose. Many of Burns's own most outspoken political productions, especially involving the 1790s, had to wait – sometimes decades – for posthumous publication.

By contrast, Alexander Wilson was one of only a few Scots poets who, following the French Revolution, produced explicit political poems, albeit in anonymized, broadside form. This format operates as a kind of "unofficial" counterpoint to Wilson's other published oeuvre. By 1876 Grosart was quite happy to include this work in his edition, though these pieces are underplayed, presented as rather fool-hardy, reckless productions of the moment, out of kilter with their author's more responsible work. Their significance is only explicitly reclaimed in 1990 with Tom Leonard's selection of Wilson in *Radical Renfrew: Poetry from the French Revolution to the First World War*. While he also includes "Watty and Meg," Leonard spotlights Wilson's most explosive Scots poems, "The Hollander, or Light Weight" (1790), "The Shark, or Lang Mills Detected" (1792, unfortunately excerpted) and "The Insulted Peddlar" (c. 1792), which had resurfaced in an 1829 edition of Wilson's poems. Leonard's anthology also powerfully demonstrates that – contrary to a traditional line in Scottish criticism – the "Burnsian" mode in Scots poetry, most especially the usage of "Standard Habbie" and "Christ's Kirk" stanzas, deteriorated into a sentimental painting of manners devoid of political traction. Leonard refreshingly disinters several other political poets who follow Wilson and were directly influenced by his political poetry tracts: William Finlayson, James Yool, John Macgregor, and John Mitchell, are all powerful witnesses to a pungent polemical Scots poetic voice in Renfrewshire through the nineteenth century. Leonard also includes in his anthology the arch-Tory, William Motherwell, thereby counterbalancing the more revolutionary voices.

The circumstance surrounding "The Hollander" represents one of the most actively dramatic episodes in eighteenth-century Scots poetry. The text is a full frontal attack on a Paisley mill-owner, William Henry, who, in response, accused Wilson both of libel and even more seriously of inciting industrial unrest through his publication, which he produced anonymously in broadside form and without an acknowledged printer or publisher.[5] "The Hollander" has a prefatory quotation from Robert Blair's "The Grave" (1743) which hypothesizes uncommon tortures in hell for those whose conduct has been especially damned. Thereafter, the poem announces Wilson's particular skill in the "Christ's Kirk" stanza, one of the cultural signatures of the Scots poetry revival of the eighteenth century. This energetic four- and three-stress form was utilized by Allan Ramsay and his successors as implicitly, jauntily, cocking a snook at the joyless Calvinist culture of Scotland. Wilson transposes it to other purposes, in his opening essaying the brisk energy of the Paisley weaver on his machine and the concomitantly brusque way in which silk manufacturer, William Henry (who was well-known locally for having spent some time in Holland), is fleecing the workers:

Attend a' ye, wha on the loom,
Survey the shuttle jinking,
Whase purse has aft been sucket toom, [empty]
While Willie's scales war clinkin';
A' ye that for some luckless hole
Ha'e paid (though right unwillin')
To satisfy his hungry soul,
A sixpence or a shillin'
For fine some day. (Wilson 62)

This was highly shocking material. Here, and in fuller detail as the text proceeds, it explicitly excoriates William Henry, alleging he was "lightweight" in his payment to weavers by taking delivery of their goods and deliberately spoiling parts of these prior to payment so as to drive down that eventual payment:

> See! Cross his nose he lays the specks,
> And o'er the claith he glimmers;
> Ilk wee bit triflin' fau't detects,
> And cheeps, and to him yaummers,
> "Dear man! – that wark 'ill never do;
> See that: ye'll no tak tellin';
> Syne knavish chirts his fingers through,
> And libels down a shilling
> For holes that day.   (Wilson, *Poems* 63)

This portrait of self-righteous hypocrisy possibly owes something to Burns's "Holy Willie's Prayer," which until then had not been officially published but had circulated widely in chapbook form in 1789. The poem also provides an early glimpse of modern Irish emigration into the west of Scotland as Wilson's narrator hails the "brave Hibernian boy" who has threatened a measure of physical violence against Henry after finding the latter attempting to cheat him in his signature manner. If we are not yet into the period when the United Britons and United Scotsmen are formed and making common cause with the United Irishmen, we see something of the early burgeoning of class solidarity among the downtrodden of diffuse identity that was to become such a feature of popular political movements in the 1790s. Wilson's text implies that the church and civil authorities are complicit in the actions of Paisley's unjust businessmen, and ends with a bitter lament and an appeal to the people to pray to the devil to gather such folk into his bosom:

> What town can thrive wi' sic a crew
> Within its entrails crawlin,'
> Muck-worms, that must provoke a spew
> To see or hear them squallin'!
> Down on your knees, man, wife, and wean –
> For ance implore the devil,
> To haurl to himself his ain;
> And free us frae sic evil,
> This vera day.   (Wilson, *Poems* 66)

The threatened legal charges of libel fell into abeyance and Wilson, presumably feeling that he could get away with this kind of thing, in 1792 again dispensed poetic justice in another broadside, "The Shark, or Lang Mills Detected." This time things proceeded in a much darker direction. Wilson sent the printed broadside poem to "the shark" in question, or

William Sharp, whose name was obviously punned upon, saying that the text could be suppressed if its owner agreed to pay the author five guineas (see Leonard 8). When the case came to court, this fact unsurprisingly told against Wilson and, indeed, the claimed nobility of the weavers, which the poem begins setting out:

> Ye weaver blades! Ye noble chiels!
> Wha fill our land wi' plenty,
> And mak our vera barest fiels
> To waive with ilka dainty;
> Defend yoursels, tak sicker heed,
> I warn you as a brither;
> Or Shark's resolved, wi' hellish greed,
> To gorge us a' thegither,
> At ance this day.   (Wilson, *Poems* 57)

The "lang mills" in the title is a reference to the way in which it was alleged Sharp was fixing his machinery to make "returned weavers work seem smaller than it was" (Leonard 8). Wilson's text is a funny and satirically effective fantasy of the Shark versus the common man, but the attempted blackmail and the author's previous publication made Sharp enlist the full weight of the law against him. Wilson's arrest was sought; he was ordered to pay £60 in legal costs. Eventually, unable to pay, he was "incarcerated in Paisley's Tolbooth for fourteen days in February 1793" (Egerton 478).

Before imprisonment, and now in full-throttled political mode, Wilson produced perhaps his most dangerous poem, "The Address to the Synod of Glasgow and Ayr" (1792), yet another pamphlet-poem with a trenchant prose introduction. Produced under the pseudonym of "Lawrie Nettle," it lambasts the kirk for complicity with the state at a time of increasing "liberty" and "democracy." At its center is one of the most outspoken statements celebrating Thomas Paine to be found in 1790s Scottish literature:

The 'Rights of Man' is now weel kenned,
And read by mony a hunder;
For Tammy Paine the buik has penned,
And lent the Courts a lounder;   [*blow*]
It's like a keeking-glass to see
The craft of Kirk and statesmen;
And wi' a bauld and easy glee,
Guid faith the birky beats them   [*chap*]
Aff hand this day.   (Wilson, *Poems* 73)

The striking image of Paine's book as mirror showing up the behavior of church and state makes a bold statement amid the growing political turmoil in Britain. The text attacks "patronage," the rights of local land heritors to appoint Church of Scotland ministers, rather than congregations. Here we see an interesting contrast with Burns, who favored the democratic politics unleashed by the French Revolution, but was "moderate" in church affairs and repeatedly came down on the side of patronage. Had Burns produced a poem as outspoken in its radicalism as Wilson's "Address," the bard's subsequent lionization by the left down to the present day might have known no bounds. Wilson's text also threatens that King George is going to know about "rights and liberties" (Wilson, *Poems* 74), moving Wilson closer to espousing republicanism than any other Scottish poet during this period, with the exception of Alexander Geddes, who by the 1790s was largely operating out of London. Wilson's poem is dated 5 November 1792, flagrantly celebrating the attempt almost two centuries earlier to blow up the Houses of Parliament. Wilson could not have picked a more incendiary moment to publish his text. It was produced not long before the Scottish authorities moved to prosecute James Thomson Callender (who was declared an outlaw in December 1792), James "Balloon" Tytler (also declared an outlaw after he left the country prior to his trial for sedition in January 1793), and most famously Thomas Muir of Huntershill, who was tried and sentenced to fourteen years transportation to Botany Bay in the late summer of 1793. All of these were associated, rightly, with promulgating Paine's ideas; Callender and Tytler were, like Wilson, poets (though it was their actions and prose-writings that brought them into contention with the authorities). Interestingly both were Presbyterian republicans whose poetic language of choice was English rather than Scots. Like Callender and Tytler, Wilson was soon to make a cultural and political mark on the other side of the Atlantic, comparable to his achievements in Scotland. The three contributed to a rich "transatlantic radical" culture in Massachusetts, Pennsylvania, and elsewhere in America.[6]

The last of Wilson's radical texts in the same period is "The Insulted Pedlar" in which Wilson wields that other signature Scots stanza of the eighteenth-century Scots revival, the "Habbie Simson" or "Standard Habbie." The poem describes its pedlar-narrator defecating in a field, and has been seen sometimes as a rather crude performance; however, there is something more trenchant going on in the context of its political times. The enraged landowner threatens the narrator with jail and curses him, "Dem your blood" (Wilson, *Poems* 36), a critique of the often Anglicized Scottish propertied class (a feature we do not find in Burns). The defecating migrant turns out to be a man of enlightenment logic, as he responds to his detractor:

"Gin ye can prove, by pen or tongue,
That lan ne'er profited by dung,
That by its influence ne'er sprung,
Though I should lumple,   [*crumple*]
I'se thole a thump o' that hard rung,   [*put up with; wooden-stick*]
Out owre my rumple.   [*backside*]

"My order, sir, was Nature's laws,
That was the reason, and because
Necessity's demands and ca's
War very gleg,   [*clear*]
I hunkered down 'mang thir hard wa's
To lay my egg.   (Wilson, *Poems* 37)

In the challenge to debate, we find the Wilson who had been schooled in the Scottish enlightenment, reading (and contributing several poems to) James Anderson's politically reformist periodical *The Bee* (founded in 1791), which frequently featured discussion of agricultural matters and land use. Here again, we see Wilson on the political cusp, in tune with – perhaps reading – Thomas Spence's *The Real Rights of Man*. Spence's work, which had circulated in a number of forms since 1779, featured ideas about the land being held in common and argued against concentrated ownership. It was eventually published under its book title in 1793 (see Thompson, *Real Rights* 7). In a familiar trick of Wilson's, the landowner is seen as Satanic, but something additionally emerges as the narrator describes his detractor as "a speaking swine... [with] devilish feature [who dares] to curse a work o' Thine" (Wilson, *Poems* 39). Here the tables are turned on Edmund Burke, whose infamous epithet for some of the followers of the French Revolution was the "swinish multitude." As elsewhere in his 1790s poems that sit outside his official canon, Wilson is developing and showcasing his reformist credentials.

However, just as Wilson's Scots poetic voice was reaching a sustained political outspokenness surpassing anything Robert Burns felt able to say in the same period, it was to disappear from Scotland. In May 1794, mired in ongoing libel actions that he felt he could never escape, he left his native country, accompanied by a favorite nephew, first arriving in Belfast and then America. He stayed briefly in Shepherdstown, Virginia, before moving on to Milestown, 20 miles from Philadelphia. There, he resorted to his past professions as weaver and pedlar, also finding work as an engraver where he developed further his natural talents as an artist and draughtsman. In Milestown too, for five years until 1801, he was the local schoolmaster. A repeated pattern emerges, with Wilson writing political poetry and going on long walking trips. From 1802–6 Wilson took a different teaching job near Gray's Ferry, Pennsylvania and began the serious work of cataloging and illustrating American birds. This pursuit led to longer and longer walking excursions, including a journey as far as Niagara Falls in 1804. From 1806, Wilson took up editorship of the *New Cyclopaedia*, which also gave him the financial and logistical means to develop and publish by subscription his landmark *American Ornithology* (1808–14). As with his Scottish literary output, Wilson's early-nineteenth-century political poetry appeared in the popular press. Works memorializing George Washington and praising Thomas Jefferson are today in sore need of new bibliographical and editorial work. It is in America, near the end of his life too, that he achieved his most significant literary success, with the longest of all his works. At over 2,200 lines "The Foresters. Description of A Pedestrian Journey to the Falls of Niagara" (1809–10) was famous during the Romantic period although it is now regarded as of minor importance.[7] The text charts Wilson's extended pedestrian journey of 1804. Full of natural description, it is also a long paean to the political *plein air* that Wilson believed to be more possible in the new world, away from the hopeless *ancien régime* of Europe. For instance,

> The theme, Columbia, her sublime increase:
> 'Blest land of freedom, happiness and peace:
> Far, far removed from Europe's murderous scene,
> A wide, a friendly waste of waves between;
> Where strangers driven by tyranny to roam,
> Still find a nobler and a happier home
> Hail, blessed asylum! Happy country, hail!'
> (Wilson, *Poems* 159)

Utilizing the idea of sublimity, "The Foresters" essays the greatness and the clarity of nature, in contradistinction to the obfuscations of humanity in the reactionary Britain he had left behind him. Ironically, the aesthetic of the sublime had been developed during the eighteenth century by Edmund Burke, arch-opponent of the French Revolution. Frequently reprinted in the US through the nineteenth century until the 1920s, "The Foresters" is a another important element of Alexander Wilson's literary output that merits serious reappraisal in the twenty-first century.

NOTES

1. Edward H. Burtt, Jr. and William E. Davis, Jr., *Alexander Wilson: The Scot Who Founded American Ornithology* (Cambridge, MA: The Belknap Press of Harvard University Press, 2013).

2. The excellent biography by Burtt and Davis (2013) has a strong scientific focus. A monograph on Wilson's poetic and polemical career would strongly supplement our knowledge of the man, and such a work in turn might most profitably emerge from a proper modern edition of Wilson's poems and prose.
3. See Gerard Carruthers, "The Failure of Historicism in Scottish Literary Studies: A Case-Study Involving the Burns Movement and the Chair of Scottish History and Literature at the University of Glasgow," in K. P. Müller (ed.), *Scotland 2014 and Beyond* (Frankfurt am Main: Peter Lang, 2015), 291–92'.
4. See, for instance, the popular Presbyterian attack on Burns to be found in William Peebles, *Burnomania: The Celebrity of Robert Burns Considered: In a Discourse Addressed to All real Christians of Every Denomination* (Edinburgh, 1811).
5. See a copy of the original broadside version of "Hollander" along with "Papers relating to the legal actions surrounding 'The Hollander'" at the National Library of Scotland, MS 499.
6. See Michael Durey, *Transatlantic Radicals and the Early American Republic* (Lawrence: University Press of Kansas, 1997), a landmark study. The literary efforts of its numerous subjects after emigration, including Wilson, would repay further study.
7. The text might today have applied to it an eco-critical perspective, among other approaches. Among the best extended treatments of the text of rather sporadic secondary literature are Irving N. Rothman, "Alexander Wilson's forest adventure: the Sublime and the Satirical in Wilson's 'The Foresters' in *Journal of the Society for the Bibliography of Natural History* 6.4 (1973): 242–54, and Bridget Keegan, "*The Foresters*: Alexander Wilson's Transatlantic Labouring-Class Nature Poetry" in *Key Words* 8 (2010), 51–61.

CHAPTER 6

Neither Mute nor Inglorious
Ann Yearsley and Elegy

Kerri Andrews

In 2005 Donna Landry and William J. Christmas stated in their introduction to a special issue of *Criticism*, "Learning to Read in the Long Revolution: New Work on Laboring-Class Poets, Aesthetics, and Politics," that "[a]nalyzing laboring-class poetry according to strictly formal criteria without some obeisance to the ideological or political stakes involved has rarely been undertaken, if at all" (414), and appealed for more attention to be paid by critics to form, and less to biography. Matters have improved somewhat since then, as a result of interventions such as those made by Landry, Christmas, the contributors to their special issue, Bill Overton, and others,[1] with scholars now increasingly willing to consider laboring class poets as, first and foremost, *poets*, with aesthetic, intellectual, and professional ambitions which we ought to, indeed *need to*, take into account.

In this chapter I build in particular upon work done by Christmas and Overton, both of whose essays in a special issue of *Tulsa Studies in Women's Literature*, dedicated to the poetry of Mary Leapor and Ann Yearsley, document these poets' use of, and experimentation with, recognized genre forms in the eighteenth century. Overton's cataloging of the range of genres deployed (and adapted) by Leapor serves to reveal the surprising extent to which Leapor played with, subverted, or ignored generic conventions. Christmas's essay focuses on one genre – the soliloquy poem – as it was used by Leapor and Yearsley, and, in doing so, charts both the development of the two poets as users of a specific genre and the genre itself as a vehicle for particular kinds of poetic expression. I utilize elements of the approaches and methodologies of both Overton and Christmas in what follows in order to consider Yearsley's deployment of elegy. Over the course of her literary career she produced 113 known poems and wrote seventeen that are either explicitly titled "Elegy" or are otherwise on an evidently elegiac topic. The only types of poem utilized by Yearsley more often than the elegy were the "Address" (of which I count 55 – nearly half of all her poems), and miscellaneous poems (25), which are not easily classified as one thing or another. It should be acknowledged that there is some overlap between genres (some of Yearsley's elegies are described by the poet as an "Address," as in "Addressed by Mrs. Yearsley to a Recent Widower, with whom she had had a Disagreement"), and readers might disagree with some of my categorizations, but the broad point I am making with these figures – that a large and statistically significant proportion of Yearsley's poetic output was elegiac in nature – holds. It is also significant that Yearsley produced elegies throughout her career; they appear in all three of her published volumes, and a number of Yearsley's unpublished occasional poems were elegies (these poems were possibly sent by the poet directly to the family of the deceased).

Examining Yearsley's use of the elegy is productive, I think, because it enables an exploration of how some of the ways in which the conventions of this genre, as they were understood in the eighteenth century, might further, or threaten, Yearsley's professional and aesthetic ambitions. In particular I will explore the consequences of a female, laboring class writer taking on a form which has been described by Celeste M. Schenck as being "a resolutely patriarchal genre" which is, "above all a vocational poem" in which the younger (male) poet wrests "the pipes of pastoral poetry" from the "barely cold hands" of the deceased (male) mentor poet in a "gesture of aspiring careerism" (13, 14). While this essay seeks to avoid condemning Yearsley to the "biographical prison house" of which Landry and Christmas warned, and to which too many laboring class poets have been sentenced in the past, it will nonetheless be important to assess how far Yearsley's positions as a female writer and as a laboring class writer intersect with her experiments in a genre linked throughout its literary history with a particular type of poetic inheritance, of a certain way of claiming one's poetic place. Yearsley's generic innovations are suggestive of new possibilities for both the elegiac poet and the elegy as a different means of inheriting, a different way of demonstrating oneself to be a poet.

I Genre

One of the central claims in this essay is that Ann Yearsley adapts and experiments with the elegy form, and that these rewritings of the genre are significant. It is important to note at the beginning, however, that theorists of genre argue that some degree of modification, some degree of evolution, is both inevitable and inherent within systems of genre. As John Frow has suggested:

> Genre systems form a shifting hierarchy, made up of tensions between "higher" and "lower" genres, a constant alternation of the dominant form, and a constant renewal of genres through processes of specialisation or recombination. Genres, it follows, are neither self-identical nor self-contained. (114)

Frow posits a structure that is by its very nature in flux as a result of the "constant renewal" of genres as they are utilized by writers for specific purposes; there are no absolute or fixed categories, just shifting and contested distinctions that obtain only temporarily. As a result, Frow suggests, "Genre" becomes "the driving force of change in the literary field" (110).

Frow's description of the ways in which genres function would seem to be at odds with the rather more prescriptive view taken at the beginning of the eighteenth century. John Newbery, writing of the elegy in his enormously influential and foundational *The Art of Poetry on a New Plan* (1702), asserts that an elegy should contain:

> No *epigrammatic points* or conceits, none of those *fine things* which most people are so fond of in every sort of poem, can be allowed in this, but must give place to nobler beauties, those of *Nature* and the *Passions*. Elegy rejects whatever is facetious . . . or majestic, and is content to be plain, decent, and unaffected; yet in this humble state is the sweet and engaging, elegant and attractive. This poem is adorn'd with frequent *commiserations, complaints, exclamations, addresses to things or persons*, short and proper *digressions*, allusions, comparisons. . . . The diction ought to be free from any *harshness*; *neat, easy, perspicuous, expressive of the manners, tender* and *pathetic*: and the numbers should be *smooth* and flowing, and captivate the ear with their uniform sweetness and delicacy. (I: 70)

As my ellipses indicate, Newbery's instructions go on at even greater length than I have included here: Would-be eighteenth-century elegists received direction from him not only about what form the poem should take (its meter and poetic features), but also the effect the poet should be seeking to create and the means by which that effect was to be constructed. The poet is told explicitly what not to do, as well as what he or she should do, in order to conform to the expected standards of the genre. Yet Newbery himself indicates that the elegy is not a stable category when he allows that the elegy was "first invented to bewail the death of a friend, and afterwards us'd to express the complaints of lovers, or any other doleful and melancholy subject" (70). Such a dramatic shift in subject matter, and such a widening-out of topics considered appropriate for this mode, suggests the existence of, and potential for, considerable change and development in the form of the kind outlined by Frow.

While Newbery's instructions are very particular, and would seem to indicate a restrictive view of genre (a poem must do, or not do, certain things to qualify as elegy), the instability inherent in genre systems means that his directions would inevitably be contested, revised, or even disregarded. By 1777, for instance, the elegy had come to be defined (in this case by Samuel Johnson), as "1. A mournful song. 2. A funeral song. 3. A short poem without points or affected elegancies" (Curran 238). There are overlaps with Newbery's earlier injunctions (Johnson similarly insists that the elegy be unaffected in style), but Johnson's definition is so broad in its last point that it might be describing a whole writing style, not an individual genre. Therefore, as a result of these demonstrable shifts in the definition of what qualifies as "elegy" in the eighteenth century, it is reasonable for us as literary critics to expect some degree of generic experimentation from any writer working within this, or indeed any other, genre. I will argue here, though, that Yearsley's innovations in the elegy go beyond what might plausibly be considered changes inherent in the natural evolution of the genre's conventions. These innovations, I will suggest, are indicative of a more substantive challenge to ideas of what an elegy should be and by whom it can, or should, be written.

II Elegy

There are several useful definitions of what an elegy is, not least among them Samuel Johnson's, cited above. The current meaning of "elegy," according to the *Oxford English Dictionary*, is "A song or poem of lamentation, esp. for the dead; a memorial poem," and (perhaps or) "A piece of writing, drama, art, etc., imbued with a sense of mourning or melancholy affection for something. Chiefly with for, to" ("elegy, n."). While such definitions are helpful in understanding what an elegy might *be*, they give no indication of the genre's very particular literary history, a history which requires certain things not only of the poem, but also of the poet. As Schenck has noted, the origins of elegy lie (as with many genres) in classical literature, where the elegy was "a song sung over the bier of a friend-forbear in order . . . to lay the ancestor to rest" (13). This type of poem "is modelled on archaic initiation rituals of [a] younger man by an elder" (13). The elegy, then, has two main functions: to mourn or commemorate the dead, and to act as the public symbol of the passing on of the dead's work (and/or ideas) to a new generation, represented by the poet. As such it hinges on the delineation of a very particular relationship between the dead and the poem's speaker, and indeed between the dead and the poet himself (I use the gendered term deliberately). Joshua Scodel, writing about death rituals more broadly (but in which category he places the elegy), notes that these processes:

> seek to bring about or affirm the new status of the deceased. The person who has been violently torn from the living must be incorporated into the world of the dead, however conceived, so that he or she can be related in a new way to the community of the living. (89)

Peter Sacks argues that this new "relation" between living and death, as enacted through the elegy, must involve some separation between the two: "few elegies or acts of mourning succeed without seeming to place the dead, and death itself, at some cleared distance from the living" (19). The poet both creates and traverses this "cleared distance" between the living and the dead through his or her writing; their poetry records and commemorates the person who has died and outlines the shape and nature of his or her new relationship with the living s/he has left behind.

Through this process the poet comes to occupy a privileged position among the mourners, acting, effectively, as a speaker for the dead. The principal task in this role is to create the work that signifies the passing on of the "pipes of pastoral poetry" that marks the poet as the legitimate successor to the dead and the inheritor of their poetic tradition. As Eric Parisot has argued in relation to the most famous and commercially successful elegy of the eighteenth century, Thomas Gray's *Elegy Written in a Country Churchyard*, "What troubles the elegist is a dilemma . . . the choice between humble Christian resignation on one hand and secular (poetic) ambition on the other" (120). Typically, this "dilemma" is resolved by the poet in favor of ambition; Sacks observes that an elegist will need to draw attention, consolingly, to his own surviving powers (2). Or, as Parisot notes about Thomas Gray's decision:

> Resignation coupled with obscurity is not a fate that appeals to the ambitious young poet within the *Elegy*; being written into history is. This is precisely what the *Elegy* is: an attempt to inscribe the poetic self into social memory. It is an expression of the poet's desire for public recognition. (123)[2]

It is easy to see how these aspects of elegy writing might give rise to tensions between the immediate requirements of the form (to mourn a specific person now) and the ideas of literary inheritance (and poetic advancement or recognition) coded into its history, and it is not hard to see potential problems for poets navigating between these competing elements. Schenck observes that "in the masculine elegy" (which tends to be the only sort of elegy recognized by literary critics; Sacks, for instance, discusses only elegies by men in his field-leading study), "death is one's great occasion, one's opportunity to take the stage" (18). Taking up this "opportunity," Schenck argues, leads to the "substitution" of the faces of the dead – supposed to be at the fore – for the poet's own (18).

The elegy tradition most commonly recognized is, then, one that is written by men who commemorate people or things that will allow them to claim – more or less explicitly – their right to be publicly recognized as poets, as the inheritors of the tradition represented by the dead. This is because, as Schenck has argued, "The masculine elegy marks a rite of separation" as well as inheritance from the (usually male) poetic progenitor, "that culminates in ascension to stature" (15). For Schenck, "Eulogy and transcendence are the most salient features of the masculine elegy, and they arise directly from masculine patterns of competition, separation, and individuation" (18). What Schenck terms "the masculine elegy" is, as a result, therefore always at risk of becoming more about the chief mourner (the poet) than the mourned, and is at risk, also, of being more about the competition between the mourner and the mourned for poetic preeminence than the mourned himself.

III Ann Yearsley and Women's Elegy

Things seem to stand rather differently when women write elegies. As Schenck, Anne K. Mellor, and Stuart Curran have demonstrated,[3] there was (and indeed is) a parallel tradition in literary history of women's elegy which tends to have emphases distinct from those recognized as central to the masculine elegy. For instance, with no equivalent for the model of patrilineal inheritance encoded in male-authored elegies, "women writers," Schenck argues, "tend to mourn their personal dead rather than predecessor poets" (15). More fundamentally, she suggests, "a female elegist might feel that as yet nothing had been articulated" in earlier elegies written by men "that might speak to her case" (14), making it likely that female poets will use the elegy form for rather different purposes to male poets. Indeed, as Schenck suggests, women have turned to other women for their patterns in a way that has created "an elegiac mode of their own, an intertextually verifiable tradition of mourning their dead in a poetic form that calls the genre, as patriarchally codified, into question" (23).

The stakes, then, are high for a woman writer engaging with the elegy form: in addition to the traditional (masculine) conventions of the genre most commonly recognized, celebrated, and rewarded by readers and critics, a female poet must also negotiate the consequences of being, as a result of her gender, a disruptive presence within that genre. It might be argued, therefore, that the very act of writing an elegy, for a woman, has to involve some kind of change or challenge to the rules of that genre. And how much more might this obtain if that woman is also laboring class, if she belongs to the class of the "mute inglorious Miltons" both lamented and used by Gray in his *Elegy* as the means by which he was to be "written into history" (Parisot 123)? What kind of poetic inheritance might such a poet seek to claim through her elegies? What kind of challenge might she pose by availing herself of the elegy and its literary history in order to "ascend" to the "stature" of publicly recognized poet (Schenck 15)?

I would like to argue here that Ann Yearsley's use of elegy – which was both extensive and sustained – was strategic. It was not, however, consistent. It will be important here to consider Yearsley's writing of elegy as part of the female tradition of mourning which can be seen to stand in stark contrast to the male (as argued for by both Schenck and Mellor), but Yearsley also wrote elegies that at times seem to fit more squarely within the masculine tradition of lamentation. In my conclusion I will assess the significance of these contrasts.

Published in *Poems on Several Occasions*, Yearsley's first volume of poetry, "On the Sudden Death of a Friend" is Yearsley's earliest known elegy. In many ways it sits quite neatly within the elegiac tradition delineated by Newbery, and later Sacks and Joshua Scodel: It "bewails the death of a friend," as Newbery held elegies should, and, with its simple metrical structure (eight plain stanzas of iambic pentameter quatrains, ABAB rhyme scheme without variation) and simple diction (there are few poetic adornments or elaborate expressions), the poem succeeds in being "plain, decent, and unaffected" (Newbery 70). Yearsley figures Delia's soul flying to God, who has commanded her presence, thus "ensuring a sense of progress and egress" (Sacks 19), and, with Delia's imagined arrival in Heaven, she is firmly "incorporated into the world of the dead" (Scodel 89) by the end of the poem. In the final stanza, Delia's grieving widower, "Thyrsis," is commanded by the speaker to remember that Delia now "lives where boundless joys shall ever, ever flow" (Yearsley, *Collected* I: 18), which has all the hallmarks of proper Christian resignation before the power of God and death.

For all this apparent conventionality, there are hints of something else, a countercurrent that runs against recognized genre rules, from the very beginning of the poem when God speaks his will to his "sightless Minister of Death":

> 'Go seek the spot where guiltless joys reside,
> Seize DELIA's frame, suspend at once her breath,
> And from its long-lov'd home the wondr'ing soul divide.
>
> Be deaf to all, nor heed the plaintive moan
> Of weeping husband, parent, child, or friend,
> 'Tis my high will that she attend my throne
> Where flow those perfect joys which never shall have end.'
> (Yearsley, *Collected* I: 17, ll. 2–84)

The final line here, with its celebration of the consolations of death, cannot quite counterbalance the lingering sense of injustice, of wrongness, about the deity's decision to override all earthly claims for the satisfaction of his own selfish wishes. Delia's home, among her friends and family, is the "spot where guiltless joys reside" and, when the moment comes to take Delia away, the Minister of Death has been so moved by the simple goodness of the "seat of humble love" created by Delia and Thyrsis, where "[c]ontent and joy in every breast elate," that he mourns "his errand from above" so deeply that he does not "dare to look while he directs the dart" at Delia's "asonish'd" and "dismay'd" soul (ll. 17–18). It is difficult to avoid the conclusion that the act of taking Delia is fundamentally and profoundly unjust – the God of Yearsley's poem seems in his decision more like a capricious Greek or Roman god than the good, wise and benevolent God of the New Testament.

The poem's resolution is more conventional in that it seems to submit before the will of God (however unjust that will is suggested to be), but Yearsley's poem also subverts this submission and the conventional consolations offered by Christianity that death is the prelude to eternal life in the presence of God. While Delia is dispatched to Heaven (thus conforming to the requirements both of Christian belief and the elegy), she does not go there to await a new life to be given at the coming again of Christ, but is figured as being alive *now*: Thyrsis is commanded by the speaker to "[m]ourn not thy love, nor think thy DELIA dead; / She lives where boundless joys shall ever, ever flow" (ll. 31–2). While it could be argued that this description sits within the bounds of Christian ideas about the condition of the soul after death, the command given by the speaker to "Mourn not," given in an elegy – the dedicated poetic form for mourning – is curious. It is not necessarily, though, unique: John Milton's shepherd narrator in "Lycidas" (1638) offers a similar type of comfort, saying "Weep no more, woeful shepherds, weep no more, / For Lycidas, your sorrow, is not dead" (ll. 165–6) because the young man is now "mounted high" (l. 172). However, while Yearsley's poem mirrors Milton's in the type of consolation it offers, it differs in the use made of that consolation. For Milton's speaker, the ascension of Lycidas to some kind of heaven serves to complete the removal of the dead from the realm of the living, thereby enabling a satisfactory emotional and intellectual resolution to the elegy:

> Thus sang the uncouth swain to the oaks and rills,
> While the still morn went out with sandals gray;
> He touch'd the tender stops of various quills,
> With eager thought warbling his Dorick lay;
> And now the sun had stretch'd out all the hills,
> And now was dropt into the western bay;
> At last he rose, and twitch'd his mantle blue:
> To morrow to fresh woods, and pastures new.
> (ll. 186–93)

The speaker here completes the grieving process by finishing his song, then imaginatively and physically leaving Lycidas behind him as he continues with his nomadic existence. In contrast, the mourners of Yearsley's poem remain suspended between grief and consolation: while Delia may now "live where boundless joys shall ever, ever flow," the pervasive sense of injustice at her sudden death (an injustice felt by Delia as well as those mourning her) prevents a neat resolution.

Yearsley's next volume of poetry, *Poems on Various Subjects*, featured no fewer than five elegies out of a total of 30 poems: elegies (on her brother, her mother, and her son, the Dowager Duchess of Portland, and Thomas Chatterton) constituted a full sixth of the entire volume. Here is considerable variety and more sustained experimentation that builds on the innovations, or "revisions," explored in "On the Sudden Death of a Friend," with the exception of "On the Death of Her Grace, the Duchess Dowager of Portland." This, the first of the five elegies encountered by the reader of *Poems on Various Subjects*, is rather blandly efficient at accomplishing the task of mourning the death of Yearsley's one-time patron. In its description of the journey taken by Portland's "spirit" through the sky to Heaven, where she voyages with "angel troops" and is "hailed" by beautiful "Celestial beings" (Yearsley, *Collected* I: 53), the poem obediently includes all the required features of the elegy – the lamentation of the dead, the securing of the "distance" between the living and the dead that Sacks holds as "crucial to any successful mourning" (l. 19), and the inclusion of appropriate "allusions" in a poem with a "*smooth* and flowing" meter (Newbery 70) – but it never seems to really engage the reader's interest, or indeed the speaker's.

While technically the poem conforms to the generic conventions of the elegy, it does not satisfy them fully because the poet is unable to occupy the role as speaker for the dead, or intercessor between the mourners and the mourned, as required of the elegiac poet. Yearsley's failure here to occupy that role is perhaps attributable to problems with the genre itself, in its more commonly recognized male-oriented guise; Anne K. Mellor highlights a tradition of women attempting to conform to the expectations of the genre, but failing to convince with their performances because of the emphasis placed in traditional elegy on moving past grief in what Mellor terms an "instrumentalist" way (444). Describing Elizabeth Tollet's poem *Pastoral. In Memory of Mrs. Elizabeth Blackler* (1717), Mellor notes how it "dutifully follows ... conventions ... – nature mourns, shepherds and nymphs lament, the beauties, graces, and accomplishments of Blackler are listed ... in a poem that seems entirely detached from any real feeling" (444). Similar problems can be seen in Yearsley's poem lamenting the Duchess: in her first elegy, the speaker was included among the "we" suffering shock and considerable emotional distress at Delia's death. In the elegy to Portland, the speaker's only direct engagement with the Duchess as a person, rather than as an idea, comes in the final stanza, and the relationship is summed up and dispatched in two rather cursory lines: "Time ne'er my strong effusions shall alloy, / My soul exults that thou wert *once* her friend" (Yearsley, *Collected* I: 54, ll. 27–8). Otherwise, the poetic speaker remains obscured behind a series of allusions to angelic orders, who do the actual work of distancing the dead from the living by assisting in carrying Portland's "spirit" on its imagined flight to Heaven.

For Mellor, more success is to be found when women elegists do not attempt to distance the dead but keep them close: Mary Chudleigh, Katherine Phillips, and Elizabeth Rowe are suggested as examples (447–8). Yearsley could perhaps be offered as a further example in support of this pattern, with the contrast between the flatness of the elegy to the Duchess of Portland, and the much more emotionally involved elegy to Chatterton, illustrative of the possibilities of rejecting the "instrumentalist" convention of seeking a total separation of the living from the dead. While Yearsley, in her "Elegy, on Mr. Chatterton," makes explicit and deliberate use of one of the key conventions of the masculine genre, poetic inheritance, she does so in a way that does not require the predecessor poet's elimination from the realm of the living. This is perhaps, at least in part, because it is impossible that the inheritance be patrilineal in nature, both because Yearsley is female and because Chatterton died aged only seventeen: when Yearsley wrote this poem she was old enough to have a child of Chatterton's age. Inheritance must, therefore, take another form: it becomes co-operative rather than competitive. At the heart of the elegy is a speech made by Chatterton's ghost, in which he laments his neglect by the "patrons of the tuneful Nine" (Yearsley, *Collected* I: 95), who failed to save either the poet or his talents from the ravages of "cruel Mis'ry," "Insult," "Agony," and "Anguish" (ll. 27–32). But, rather than express anger at the failure of such people to properly recognize his poetic abilities, Yearsley's Chatterton seeks no acknowledgment. Instead, he offers his assistance to those who would follow him:

> 'I ask no laurel, claim no late-born sigh;
> Yet should some rustic Muse, in Nature drest,
> Strike her soft bosom with a tearful eye,
> While keen Emotion's in her strain confest,
> Resting on yon white cloud, I will be near.'
> (ll. 33–7)

Of course, it is Yearsley who is the "rustic Muse" to whom this imagined Chatterton "will be near," and, while Yearsley uses this construction to make an explicit claim to be Chatterton's poetic successor, there is no apparent contest for preeminence. Instead, Chatterton's presence will assist Yearsley, and Yearsley's speaker vows to give Chatterton new life – first in this poem, as she grants his "ghost" a "voice" – but also through her poetic career more generally:

> Now rest, too hapless Chatterton, whose strain
> My bosom warms while singing Bawdin's fate;
> Yet shalt thou live! nor shall my song be vain
> That dares not thine, but dares to imitate.
> (ll. 53–6)

Yearsley, in fact, gives "life" to Chatterton here, a symbolic act which makes separation impossible, and which invokes, to some degree, the female ability to give life from her body. In this case "life" comes from and through poetry – it is Yearsley's poetic body that enables Chatterton to "live." Though Yearsley undoubtedly positions herself unambiguously as Chatterton's successor – who, by "resting," leaves the field clear for her – she does not obscure Chatterton when she steps forward; rather, she steps along*side* her poetic "forbear." This is demonstrated through the reference to "Bawdin," which is a nod to the character of Sir Charles Bawdin, who featured in Chatterton's poetry,[4] but it is very likely also a reference to a play Yearsley is known to have written, but which has since been lost, on the same character. By writing about this same topic Yearsley keeps "warm"

Chatterton's own literary achievements by "imitation," without threatening to supersede him. As a result, we can see Yearsley doing something quite different to the traditional masculine elegy. As Schenck has observed:

> Built upon a different set of internalized relations with predecessors, the female elegy is a poem of connectedness; women inheritors seem to achieve poetic identity in relation to ancestresses, in connection to the dead, whereas male initiates need to eliminate the competition to come into their own. (15)

By refusing to "render up her dead," as Mellor has put it (449), Yearsley points, in her "Elegy to Mr. Chatterton," to the potential for a much greater accommodation of the lamented among the living in ways that allow for more meaningful and productive grieving.

Many of Yearsley's later elegies further this work, including the four elegies written between the appearance of *Poems on Various Subjects* in 1787 and her final volume of poetry, *The Rural Lyre* (1796). Two of these were published: "Elegy, On Visiting the Hermitage, near Bath" (1787; about the death of Anna Thicknesse) and "On the Death of Mr. Richard Smith, Surgeon" (1791); and two were unpublished: "Verses on the Death of Miss Scrafton, who Died Sept. 1, 1788 Aged Twenty Two Years" (1790) and "Addressed by Mrs. Yearsley to a recent Widower, with whom she had had a disagreement" (1791). All four poems are elegies about local people, all of whom, with the exception of Anna Thicknesse, were known personally to Yearsley. In these poems, Yearsley seeks to "deconstruct the valorization of separation . . . (by refusing resolution and the absolute rupture that is death)," and "imagining new or alternative elegiac scenarios that arise from a distinctly feminine" perspective (Schenck 18), thereby "invert[ing] or suspend[ing] the masculine" elegy (18), with the result that something quite different is constructed. There is, for instance, no final resolution offered for the grief of the bereaved; certainly, Yearsley's speakers articulate a recognizably Christian consolation, but it is only ever partial. Grief ends in Yearsley's elegies only with the death of the mourner, as can be seen in "Verses on the Death of Miss Scrafton":

> Pass a few years, and thou shall dare the way,
> That wearied millions, oft have gone before;
> Thy soul to slumbers wakes to endless day,
> And Harriots first to hail thee on the shore.
> (Yearsley, *Collected* I: 138, ll. 37–40)

As a result, the separation between the dead and the living, held by Sacks to be essential to a successful elegy, is incomplete; the bereaved in Yearsley's elegies live only to join their loved ones in death, and so there is no final "rupture," to borrow Schenck's phrasing, between the two states because both groups are imagined as existing in a space suspended between life and death. In this way Yearsley can again be seen to be working within a female tradition of grief-work, one which holds, Mellor argues, that "grief never ends," so that the "function of elegiac poetry" becomes the "naming" and "memorialization" of the dead (449), rather than the banishment of the dead.

It is unsurprising, then, that the four poems should imagine "alternative elegiac scenarios" to those typically seen in masculine elegies (Schenck 18). Thomas Gray's *Elegy Written in a Country Churchyard*, for example, moves from a generalized elegiac lament of the unrecorded lives and deaths of "mute inglorious Miltons" (59) toward a more particularized mourning of an unnamed individual (perhaps the poetic speaker himself, though readings of this part of the poem differ). As the poem shifts from mourning the many to lamenting the individual, the loss of the individual comes to overshadow the loss of the many. Yearsley's approach is subtly different: while her poems also feature individual speakers, their function is to support and legitimize the grief being felt by the more numerous bereaved: their grief is felt, shared, and understood by the speaker. This can be seen particularly in "Verses on the Death of Miss Scrafton":

> Thy deep distress surpassing human thought
> Dissolves my soul, bidding me touch the strings
> Attun'd to human woe ne'er touch'd by aught
> But sympathy, who trembles as she sings.
> I charge thee not with unavailing sighs,
> For ah! cold admonition is disguise,
> When nature shiv'ring views the ruthless bier.
> (Yearsley, *Collected* 1: 137, ll. 1–7)

The power of this poem comes not from the elegiac traditions celebrated by Sacks or Scodel, but from the connection between the bereaved Mrs. Scrafton and Yearsley's speaker who exhibits understanding of the pain of losing a child. There is no attempt here to construct "a point of view beyond" that of the mourner's which "affirms, with unequivocal finality, the new state of death" (Scodel 89). Such an attempt would be, in this poem's logic, "cold admonition in disguise." Rather, comfort is derived from the presence of a sympathetic speaker – from the presence of a woman – and the knowledge that life, and therefore grief, are temporary.

There are interesting variations of these techniques in "Addressed by Mrs. Yearsley to a recent Widower, with whom She had had a Disagreement." Here, Yearsley writes of the death of Anna Maria Eames, wife of Levi Eames, former mayor of Bristol. He and Yearsley had had a very bitter, and very public, dispute over the ill-treatment of two of Yearsley's sons at the hands of Eames's footman.[5] This is laid aside in Yearsley's poem, though, because of her "love" of "mankind" which prompts her to attempt to comfort him in his grief:

> I see Thee now,–not as a Man whose gold
> Renders him haughty insolent and bold
> But as a Victim at pale Sorrow's shrine
> Thy spirit wounded by her shafts like mine.
> (Yearsley, *Collected* I: 155, ll. 13–16)

As Yearsley herself notes, "no flatt'ry tunes my song" (l. 9), something which is abundantly clear from her list of Eames's faults. Yet, the wry amusement afforded by this moment does not detract from, but adds to, the poem's power; in the very next couplet, the speaker looks beyond these individual grievances to see, as a result of their common experience of mourning, a fellow human being. In turn, the opening wish expressed by the speaker seems more ardent, more heartfelt:

> By all the joys which yet my soul may know!
> And all thy pangs of complicated woe
> I would console Thee! – ev'ry wish is vain
> Thy heart *must mourn* nor can I heal thy pain.
> (ll. 1–4)

Yet, while this declaration is moving, it is also conditional. The speaker "*would* console" Eames (my emphasis), but is unable to because here, as in other elegies by Yearsley, consolation is represented as being unachievable: Eames's heart "*must mourn*," and there is no power available to the speaker that will enable her to "heal" his "pain." The only consolation is fellowship – one human being sympathizing with another in their distress.

IV Conclusions

This essay has, for reasons of space, covered only some of Yearsley's elegies. One of the omissions is any discussion of "Bristol Elegy," published in 1796 in *The Rural Lyre*, a deeply political poem and most curious elegy.

Nor have I looked at Yearsley's elegies about members of her family or her elegies about historical figures. All these poems would reward close analysis of the ways in which they align with, or adapt, the elegy form, and in particular the ways in which they speak to, and perhaps continue, a female tradition of elegiac poetry. It is to be hoped that such analyses will be forthcoming in future studies of Yearsley's poetry or the elegy genre. Even in a partial examination of Yearsley's deployment of elegy, though, some useful conclusions might be drawn about the ways in which Yearsley's utilizations of the form map onto, or challenge, the conventions and literary history associated with the genre.

Of particular interest is Yearsley's decision in "Elegy, on Mr. Chatterton" to engage with the kinds of poetic inheritance associated with the masculine elegy, despite there being, in general, a preference to eschew this mode in her poetry. That she does this without competing with, or separating herself from, the predecessor poet is especially intriguing as the more collaborative relationship between the dead and the living suggested by her poem offers powerful new possibilities for both: the dead's work will live on, while the living poet receives guidance and inspiration which will strengthen her writing.

Indeed, one of the hallmarks of Yearsley's elegy writing, and one which stands in contrast to the usual approaches to the genre associated with male writers, is the importance of maintaining connections with the dead. This happens throughout Yearsley's elegies (including those not discussed here), and with such force that the continued presence of the dead threatens to undermine the premise of the elegy itself, as in the early "On the Sudden Death of a Friend." In general, though, Yearsley's refusal to surrender the dead to the usual processes of separation, apotheosis, and distancing makes her elegies emotionally very powerful because, it is suggested, the grief being represented is too strong to allow the dead to pass. Mellor has noted of female elegists that grief in their writing tends to be a "never-ending emotion," and, because of this, it "serves to sustain the powerful emotional bonds felt by wife for husband, mother for child, daughter for parents, friend for close friend, even beyond the death of the beloved" (444–5). Arguing that women tend to grieve differently than men, Mellor makes a persuasive case that the writing of elegies that refuse to accept the usual consolations of the genre is borne out of that difference. If this is the case, then Yearsley's elegies deserve to be recognized as a significant contribution to a distinct and fascinating tradition of female-authored elegies.

NOTES

1. See, for examples of significant rereadings of laboring-class poetry, Steve Van-Hagen, "Literary Technique, the Aestheticization of Laboring Experience, and Generic Experimentation in Stephen Duck's *The Thresher's Labour*," *Criticism* 47.4 (2005): 421–50; Bridget Keegan, *British Labouring-Class Nature Poetry, 1730–1837* (Basingstoke: Palgrave Macmillan, 2008); John Goodridge, *John Clare and Community* (Cambridge: Cambridge University Press, 2012); Bill Overton, "Mary Leapor's Verse and Genre," *Tulsa Studies in Women's Literature* 34.1 (2015): 19–32; Sharon Young, "Visiting the Country House: Generic Innovation in Mary Leapor's 'Crumble-Hall,'" *Tulsa Studies in Women's Literature* 34.1 (2015): 51–64; William J. Christmas, "Lyric Modes: The Soliloquy Poems of Mary Leapor and Ann Yearsley," *Tulsa Studies in Women's Literature* 34.1 (2015): 65–87; David Fairer, "'Flying Atoms in the Sightless Air': Issues of Coherence and Scale in Leapor and Yearsley," *Tulsa Studies in Women's Literature* 34.1 (2015): 141–62.
2. It should be acknowledged that the ending of Gray's poem, and Parisot's reading of it, are at odds with Gray's documented attitudes toward fame and recognition (both of which he consistently eschewed).
3. See Anne K. Mellor, "'Anguish no Cessation Knows': Elegy and the British Woman Poet, 1660–1834," in *The Oxford Handbook of the Elegy*, ed. Karen Weisman (Oxford and New York: Oxford University Press, 2010), 442–62, and Stuart Curran, "Romantic Elegiac Hybridity," *The Oxford Handbook of the Elegy*, 238–50.
4. See introduction to Volume II, *Earl Goodwin*, in *The Collected Works of Ann Yearsley*, ed. Kerri Andrews (London: Pickering and Chatto, 2014).
5. For more details about this incident, see Mary Waldron, *Lactilla, Milkwoman of Clifton: The Life and Writings of Ann Yearsley, 1753–1806* (Athens and London: University of Georgia Press, 1996), 174–82.

CHAPTER 7

"British Bards"
The Concept of Laboring Class Poetry in Eighteenth-Century Wales

Mary-Ann Constantine

> In my road to this place, I was told by a blind Harper, whom I had asked if there were any Bards remaining in the Country, that there was only *One*, and that he lived near Llanroost. If this single spark be not out when I come there, I will send for Ellis Roberts the Cooper, who alone possess the poetical fire, which once animated your Countrymen to deeds of hardy enterprise.
> – "A Tour in North Wales" (1776), 62–3

This anonymous English gentleman, traveling through North Wales in 1776, knows exactly what an educated tourist should look out for: mountain scenery, fine salmon, Druidic monuments, and last bards – living fossils of the Ancient British past. It would, from a literary-historical point of view, have been a precious encounter, not because Ellis Roberts really was the last gasp of the Welsh poetic tradition (rumors of its death would enjoy a vigorous life for centuries to come), but because we have very few occasions like this when the two literary traditions, English and Welsh, actually collide. Alas, it was not to be. Our traveler, worn out by bad Welsh roads and weather, found himself on the return journey "too much fatigued to have any curiosity of seeing that *Remnant* of the Brittish Bards, Ellis Roberts the Cooper" (71).

His earlier comment that he plans to "send for," rather than visit or even wait upon, Ellis Roberts is significant. Like the purest-blooded descendants of her princes, frequently lampooned in earlier descriptions of the principality (e.g., Torbuck's *Collection of Welch Travels*), Wales's greatest poets have to be figured as comically rural, unsophisticated, and far lower down the social scale than their equivalents in England. The idea that a man who makes barrels for a living might be the modern correlative of the great vatic bards described by Caesar is both piquant and amusing – although not, perhaps, amusing enough to go that extra rainy mile. Even this non-encounter with Welsh poetry, then, cannot help but appear as another nice example of the enthusiastic primitivism of a period taught by Gray and

Macpherson to thrill to the thought of such "remnants" at the peripheries of the British Isles. "As there has been little or no communication between the English and the People of this part of Wales," notes our man sagely, of Meirionethshire, "one would suppose they still had preserved their originality of character" (53).

Yet there is more to all this than first appears. Elis Roberts ("Elis y Cowper," d. 1789) remains a well-known name in the eighteenth-century Welsh canon: the author of several popular interludes or folk-plays, as well as many surviving poems and ballads, he did indeed make his living at Llanddoged, near Llanrwst in Denbighshire, as a cooper. His possibly better-known contemporary Thomas Edwards ("Twm o'r Nant," 1738–1810) of nearby Llanefydd, was another writer of interludes, poet, and song-maker, who, when not flitting south to avoid debts, worked as a farm-laborer and a haulier (Jones, "The Interludes"). In fact, an initial trawl through two anthologies of eighteenth-century Welsh-language poetry (Millward's 1991 collections and Lake's from 1993) throws up a sizeable crowd of nonformally educated laboring class writers, holding their own among the schoolteachers and the ministers of religion with apparent unconcern. The editors' notes make relatively little of their social origins, though these can usually be found in the entries in the online *Dictionary of Welsh Biography*; among them we find professions including weaver, fuller, shoemaker, carpenter, glazier, farmer, itinerant schoolmaster, gardener, and mason.

The aim of this chapter is to explore how and why "laboring class poetry" in eighteenth-century Wales might differ from its counterparts in England, both materially and conceptually. It will also examine what happens when the two traditions meet – when Welsh poets writing in English choose to develop a distinctively "laboring class" persona modeled on English (or, indeed, Irish or Scottish) examples. This is a complex and exceptionally fluid period in Welsh literary history, a period responsive to social changes which included the growth of industry, Nonconformist religious revival, burgeoning popular literacy, linguistic change, and, toward the end of the century, a significant rise in tourism which contributed both to perceptions and the self-image of Wales as a whole (see Hughes, "Life and Thought"; Morgan, *Eighteenth-Century Renaissance* and "Death to a View"; H. Davies, "Wales").

Stonemasons and schoolteachers rubbing shoulders in literary anthologies look unusual and somehow heartening. But it should not be assumed that the cultural life of eighteenth-century Wales was more egalitarian than that of the rest of Britain, or that modern editors have been more enlightened. Laboring class poets may find themselves included relatively naturally within the canon, but the tradition had its own fierce internal hierarchies. The two anthologies discussed above actually represent the two main branches of poetic craft, *canu caeth* (usually translated as strict-meter poetry) and *canu rhydd* (free-meter poetry). The former encompasses examples of the complex, alliterative, and highly regulated poetry practiced by professional poets from the middle ages: mastery of this type, and an intricate understanding of its rules, was essential to attaining status within a poetic guild (Johnston, *The Literature of Wales* 40, 48–50). From the earliest middle ages such professional poets were valued members of the royal courts and the households of the nobility, and even well into the modern period the big gentry houses might employ or at least patronize a family bard, who would produce poems for occasions – births, marriages, deaths, and other less solemn events. Praise and elegy were the twin strands of such poetry, and the poets drew on a distinctive, high-register lexicon of archaic terms and phrases, displaying their skill in working within the confined complexities of the prescribed meter – *caeth* means bound, constrained, even imprisoned.

By the mid-eighteenth century the social structures which sustained professional Welsh poetry had all but crumbled. Many of the gentry were non-Welsh-speaking, either because they were English who had married into Welsh families or because their political and social focus was on London, Chester, Bath, or Bristol and they spent relatively little time in Wales (Howell, *Patriarchs*). The Anglican Church in Wales, which largely represented gentry interests, was also little concerned with the continuation of Welsh-language culture for its own sake. The intricacies of *canu caeth*, preserved in manuscript in various bardic grammars, and practiced by a dwindling number of individuals, passed largely into the hands of the amateurs and antiquarians who would, from the 1760s, respond with an anxious energy to a broader renewal of interest in the medieval and ancient British past. In effect, then, an elite, high-status poetry directly inherited from a flourishing medieval tradition becomes, over a relatively short period of time, fragmented and scattered, and subject to the randomness of oral, print, and manuscript transmission. The presence of a collector with a good library and a generous lending habit, like Sir John Philipps of Picton Castle (Howell 196) or Paul Panton at Plas Gwyn in Anglesey could affect the chances of knowledge passing beyond the circles of aristocratic scholars into society more widely; others were more jealous of, or indifferent to, the treasures they owned. A crucial difference with England, perhaps, is that the "medieval" is almost within arm's reach – it is less exotic, not such a foreign country, never completely lost.

So who, in this fluid literary landscape were the new "professional" poets? Among the 24 writers in the edition of *Canu Caeth* we find the major names of the Welsh revival, including the three Anglesey-born Morris brothers who worked in various capacities for the British state: Lewis, who became a Crown steward, based in Ceredigion; Richard, who worked for the Navy Office in London; and William, who remained in Holyhead and worked for the Customs; and some of their many protégés, including the Anglican clerics Evan Evans (Ieuan Prydydd Hir), Goronwy Owen, and Walter Davies (see Lewis, *School*; J. Davies, *Letters*; Owen, *Additional*; and Prescott). The volume also contains poems by Rhys Jones, Llanfachreth, and Huw Huws of Môn, both of independent means; and Edward Richard, a renowned Classicist and schoolmaster. Some of these men were financially far from secure, and many, including the Morrises themselves, were only one generation away from a laboring class life: Goronwy Owen, considered one of the finest and most "classical" poets of his era, was the son of a tinker (Jarvis, *Goronwy*). In among this group, however, we find gifted poets who are also manual laborers: Michael Prichard, a weaver's son who earned a living gardening the Bulkeley estate; John Jenkin (Ieuan Siencyn) who began life as a cobbler before becoming a schoolteacher; Edward Evan, the son of a cobbler, who became a carpenter and glazier working for Lewis Hopkin, the Glamorgan carpenter. These two latter would mentor a poet generously represented in this volume, the journeyman-mason Edward Williams (Iolo Morganwg) – to whom we shall return. The *canu caeth* tradition, then, though an elite type of poetry, was, by the mid- to late eighteenth century, by no means restricted to the gentry and professional classes: it was clearly possible for a wide range of people to gain access to the necessary knowledge. But before considering how this transfer of tradition actually happened, we need to look briefly at the *canu rhydd*.

The companion anthology (Millward) contains double the number of poets and an even broader social mix. The "free meters" are more song-like, often ballads or carols, with rhymes and metrical patterns more familiar to English ears (many are based on English folk tunes); poets may indulge in flights of alliteration and internal rhyme, but these are not bound by the same rules as in the strict-meter poems. The volume also includes a selection of anonymous folk verses, the *pennillion*, or free-floating stanzas often sung to the harp. Subject matter is much broader, and does indeed frequently reflect the lives and experiences of a rural, laboring society; poems can be funny, bawdy, satirical, religious, and elegiac in turn. More sophisticated writers like Goronwy Owen and Evan Evans had nothing but scorn for these "rhymesters," calling them "bumkins" and peddlers of "trash"

(Millward 15). Yet many of the high-minded practitioners of *canu caeth* also turn up – slumming it, as it were – in the companion volume, and someone like Lewis Morris, the century's most versatile poet, could and did turn his hand to pretty well anything, from finely crafted strict-meter elegy to knockabout ballads on his favorite prostitute. Absent from either volume are – unless the "anons" contain a few – the voices of women. Cathryn Charnell-White's anthology of Welsh women's poetry up to 1800 adds several eighteenth-century female poets to this mix. There is often frustratingly little to identify and locate them socially, but striking cases include, from early in the century, Angharad James of Dolwyddelan, who farmed and looked after four children and an ailing husband (Charnell-White 384–5); and two composers, printers and sellers of Welsh broadsheet ballads, Lowri Parry and Grace Roberts – as Siwan Rosser has pointed out, women seem to have been well integrated into the production of ballads at all stages (4–5).

The collapse of the old order, which took place over the seventeenth and eighteenth centuries, thus brought about an odd kind of poetic social mobility in Wales. Knowledge of the medieval strict-meter tradition seems to have passed down both orally – some of the century's poetic mentors were apparently unable to read or write (Lake xiv) – and through manuscript, with local poets compiling anthologies of medieval texts to use as patterns for their own poems; medieval bardic grammars, printed and in manuscript, were also copied and studied. Certain areas had particularly strong clusters of practicing poets – Bala, Trawsfynydd, parts of Glamorgan – but it appears that most counties in Wales were still producing poets capable of composing *canu caeth* into the eighteenth century. Occasional local *eisteddfodau* (poetic gatherings, usually held in taverns) helped to bring poets together; these would be more formally revived at the end of the 1780s by the London Welsh societies, which, by offering prizes, brought a new national focus to the craft. The London societies themselves played a large part in recovering and maintaining the poetic tradition: if the Cymmrodorion, established by the Morris brothers in 1751, had social pretensions, the Gwyneddigion Society was more inclusive, and, crucially, had a large number of corresponding members (see Jenkins and Ramage). Aspiring young poets from rural Wales could thus be part of a larger community of writers and gain advice and experience without having to leave home. Correspondence between poets was another important factor – poetic conversations, and sometimes deliberately provocative poetic contentions, could involve several writers, and provided another incentive to sharpen one's technique. Lewis Morris was a frequent instigator of these, and the

Morrises as a family were hugely important in spotting and encouraging local talent.

A further channel for poetic skill which cut across social divides was religion, especially as it developed in the nonconformist sects which grew rapidly in Wales from the middle of the century onwards. Religion is a key theme for poets of both *canu caeth* and *canu rhydd*, and Welsh-language broadsheet ballads, compared with their English counterparts, tend to offer a profoundly (not to say grimly) religious interpretation of current affairs from shipwrecks to the events of the French revolution (Jones *Welsh Ballads* and Jones "Welsh Balladry"). Indeed, the editor of the *Canu Rhydd* volumes points out interesting differences in poems by the English writer William Cowper and the Welsh Elis Roberts (our original "Ancient British Bard") on the 1782 sinking of the Royal George in Spithead harbor, with the loss of a thousand lives. Cowper's poem ("Toll for the brave – The brave! That are no more") focuses on the loss to Britain and the navy of her valiant fighting men, whereas Roberts also points out that there were 300 women and children aboard, wives and prostitutes – and sees the judgment of God in their drowning:

> Er ei fod E'yn hir ei amynedd, fed daw i daro o'r diwedd
> Heb un trugaredd gydag E':
> Daeth help o law puteindra i suddo'r llestr yma
>
> Though His patience is great, he will strike in the end
> There will be no mercy on his part
> Whoring helped to sink that vessel   (Millward 217, 331–2)

Revival meetings, besides their focus on literacy and Bible reading, provided opportunities for the likes of brothers John and Morgan Dafydd, both shoemakers who became hymn writers and had their work included in published collections, reaching wide audiences. Ann Griffiths, daughter of a tenant farmer from Llanfyllin, left a small but extraordinary corpus of visionary hymns and is acknowledged as one of greatest Welsh poets of any century (James, "Cushions"). The revival hymn of the eighteenth century went deep into the lives of large swathes of the population and remained a part of popular culture long after the decline in chapel attendance (James, "The Evolution").

Many of these poets offer glimpses of rural life lived at the sharp end: Huw Jones's "Dyrifau Digrifol" reveals a good ear for the decidedly unspiritual cadences of gossip and barter outside church on a Sunday, where members of the congregation are busy looking out for a new maidservant, comparing prices for cattle, or fighting over sheep-pasture and rent-hikes –

even the gravedigger is only there to speculate on who might be next to need his services.

> O hynny o gwmni gole a welswn oll yn yr unlle
> Ni ddaethai neb i deml Duw heb geisio rhyw negese
>
> Of all the fair company I saw gathered in that place
> not one had come to God's temple without some business or other.
> (Millward 64)

In "Cân y Tri Slave," the Cardiganshire poet and shoemaker, Evan Thomas Rhys, evokes the lives of three hardworking characters – the Laborer, the Cobbler, and the Dog. A vivid cameo describes the laborer struggling home at the end of a long day to his hungry family: like the world around him he is "grey" and oddly shapeless, not a proper man. The poem bears witness to the dehumanizing effects of unrelenting physical labor:

> Trwy'r dom, trwy'r dŵr, trwy'r llaca llwyd,
> Trwy'r gors hyd glwyd ei glun,
> Nes mynd i'w fwth yn llwyd ei big
> Heb wedd na diwyg dyn
>
> Ei wraig a fydd, pan ddêl i'r tŷ,
> Â'i lliw â'i llety'n llwyd;
> A'r plant yn crïo o ddeutu'r tân
> O fawr i fân, am fwyd:
> Heb ganddo rith yn mynd tua thre,'
> 'Gael llonni'i gartre llwm
> On'd dyna *Slave* – pwy dengys llai? –
> Dan lwyth o drai'n rhy drwm?
> (Millward, 98)

> Through dung and water, through the grey mud, through bog up to his knees, until he reaches his cottage, grey in the face, having scarcely the shape or form of a man. His wife, when he enters the house, will be as grey as her hospitality; the children around the hearth, from the biggest to the smallest, crying for food; heading back without a morsel to relieve his empty home – is this not a *Slave*? – who could deny it? – under a too-heavy burden of affliction.

Even this brief overview suggests that "laboring class" is unlikely to have signified the same things within the eighteenth-century Welsh poetic tradition as it did in the English; and many of the paradigms which have been the focus of literary criticism on this subject fit Welsh-language poets awkwardly, if at all. Ironically, given the bardic fog that surrounds the notion of "Celtic" poets in general, what emerges from Wales for the period is surprisingly down-to-earth: poetry is not so much a mystery as a craft, the techniques of which can be learned from others in the community, or by correspondence with an educated enthusiast or antiquary. It is primarily a social activity, addressing local people and events. Moreover, it was still possible to make a name for oneself without going into print. Although a handful of anthologies appeared over the century, and although the interludes and ballads were often printed, many poets, well-known in their day, remained in manuscript – to be copied, memorized, passed around. That alone constitutes a crucial difference from England, where laboring class writers could experience frustrating isolation within their communities, and where the act of getting into print sits so often at the heart of a narrative of aspiration and conflict involving patronage from a higher class. In this respect, Ireland and Irish-language poetry may offer more useful parallels with the Welsh.

This is why it is deeply fascinating to find a Welsh-speaking Glamorgan stonemason launching a career as an English-language writer in a pen-portrait which appeared in the *Gentleman's Magazine* in 1789:

> The pieces you herewith receive were written by *Edward Williams*, of Flimston, near Cowbridge. – he is absolutely self-taught, and was never at school; and it may be observed, that, in those parts, the Welsh is the general language of common conversation, the English being very little known, and very little understood. His first poetical productions were in the Welsh language. About the age of twenty he was admitted a Bard in the ancient manner; a custom still retained in Glamorgan, but, I believe, in no other part of Wales. (Williams, *Iolo* 464)

Having explained a little more about the "Mysteries" of the Bardic order, the piece goes on to assure its readers that Williams "is remarkably sober and temperate, very seldom drinks any strong liquors, and if he sometimes tastes them, it is in very small quantities, and was never seen in liquor. His food is almost entirely vegetables" (465). He lives, moreover,

> the life of a hermit, is very little known and knows very few; is never seen in any kind of company. He is naturally reserved, very bashful, and has been very unfortunate in his little concerns through life hitherto; yet he is cheerfully contented with his lot, diffident to a fault, and too inoffensive to thrive in such a world as we live in. (465)

The word "Genius" also slips in toward the end. The whole piece is, in brief, a master class in melding the fundamental elements of what one might term the "English" concept of the "laboring class poet" with a more exotic Welsh "bardic" persona. Writing in 1956, Williams's biographer, arguing that the piece was penned by the bard himself, noted with some amusement just how wide of the mark it really was (especially, perhaps, the "never seen in company" and "diffident to a fault" [Williams, *Iolo* 465–6]). He speculated that this was a bid for patronage on the part of a man deeply versed in a Welsh medieval poetic tradition which depended on the generosity of the nobility toward the bards. It was also, clearly, the work of a man who understood that the ideal object of aristocratic patronage in eighteenth-century literary England must be sober (not necessarily a bardic trait), hardworking, and "inoffensive," as well as talented – and that even talent was less essential than the quality of being "deserving."[1] And by 1789 there was no shortage of models on which to draw: in his unpublished manuscripts, Williams shows knowledge of the careers of Stephen Duck, Ann Yearsley, Robert Burns, and later (and more grudgingly) Robert Bloomfield (Constantine, *The Truth* 64–5). Of these, as Daniel Huws has suggested, the most important to Williams was doubtless Burns (337–40); but his work is haunted by another, more ghostly, presence – that of the volatile, provincial autodidact much discussed in literary circles in the 1780s, Bristol poet Thomas Chatterton. In the same year that the "absolutely self-taught" Williams introduced himself to a polite reading public, the London Gwyneddigion society would publish a volume of poetry by the fourteenth-century poet Dafydd ap Gwilym: it contained, unbeknown to its editors, a dozen or so pieces fabricated by Williams himself. Like Chatterton, but over decades rather than months, he would create worlds within worlds – poems, stories, law-codes, proverbs, which retrospectively reshaped the literary history of Wales (Constantine, *The Truth* 14–82).

Edward Williams was born in 1747 in the village of Pennon in Glamorgan; he was the eldest of four boys, who all learned the trade of their father, a talented stonemason and general craftsman with an interest in Welsh culture. Their mother, brought up after the death of her own mother by well-to-do English-speaking relatives at Boverton Hall, had been educated "in a manner that was rather disadvantageous to a woman of no fortune," and passed on her love of English literature and music to her eldest son (Williams, *Iolo* 91). Williams was, then (notwithstanding his comment about "the English" being "very little known"), heir to two literary traditions from the start. He was sickly and asthmatic and received very little formal schooling, but he had ready access to books and generous mentors in his neighbors, John Walters the Welsh lexicographer and the poets John Bradford (a weaver and fuller), Edward Evan, and Lewis Hopkin – all artisans, Dissenters, and members of a literary circle based in the Glamorgan uplands known as the Grammarians of Tir Iarll (*Gramadegyddion*), after the poetic grammars from which they derived much of their knowledge of the strict meters (Williams 1948). Williams was also, from the 1770s, in correspondence with members of the London Welsh Gwyneddigion, who encouraged his early attempts at poetry.

His twentieth-century biographer provides a striking geographical correlative to this dual inheritance, contrasting the markedly different communities of Glamorgan itself – the rough, Welsh-speaking, traditionally conservative uplands of Blaenau Gwent, and the rich pasture-lands of the Vale, the subject of much of Williams's lyric writing, engaged in constant traffic across the Severn and open to the busy mercantile and cultural worlds of Bath and Bristol – hardly, as Williams himself would later claim, a "very sequestered corner of Wales" (Jenkins, Jones, and Jones I: 439). Where Williams appears especially deft or manipulative is in being able to envisage these versions of a local normality – artisan poet; rich surviving medieval tradition – as something entrancingly strange.

Dualities – both contrasts and outright contradictions – mark his life and works. The dual persona of the humble laborer (inoffensive, useful to society) and Welsh bard (linked via Classical authors to a traditional independence of spirit and then via Gray to one of outright defiance to the English crown) proved difficult to sustain. The next five years would see Williams steer this uneasily melded authorial identity and his volume of *Poems, Lyric and Pastoral* (1794) through the process of publication by subscription in Bath, Bristol, and London – the strain of it would, ironically, turn him into something much closer to a "laboring class poet" than he had been at the outset. Although he seems to have enjoyed his acquaintance with the literary ladies of Bath and Bristol – Hannah More and Harriet Bowdler among them (Constantine "A Subject") – encounters with potential subscribers in London clearly introduced him to attitudes he had not previously experienced:

> I took the liberty of addressing a letter to you last week with proposals for publishing two small vols of poems, and I presumed to solicit the favour of your name, sir, without any money. I waited at your door in Downing Street this morning and was informed I could not expect any answer. Whenever I shall be so fortunate as to be convinced that I presumed too far, I shall be heartily sorry. Till then I cannot help complaining that a man of humble station in life, who endeavours to divest himself of the rust of ignorance, is generally treated with galling superciliousness, with a contempt that tells him he is a being of inferior nature and, as I cannot possibly believe any such thing, I do not feel myself under the least obligation to apologize for my conduct. (Jenkins, Jones, and Jones I: 438–9)

This draft, probably to William Pitt's private secretary, is unlikely to have been sent; no doubt fortunately, since it goes on to explain how much sympathy the writer has with the "main body of the nation" in revolutionary France, and adds, ominously: "I can venture to say that I am better acquainted with what passes in humbler walks of life than all the peers of the realm. I know how sore the great body of the people feel." The series of horribly tortured draft letters to George, Prince of Wales (to whom the volume was ultimately dedicated in a brief, tongue-biting sentence), shows how hard it was for this Welsh bard to praise his aristocratic patrons in the traditional fashion (Jenkins, Jones, and Jones I: 439–42, 491–4); Damian Walford Davies's neat formulation "bardic Jacobinism" captures much of the irony of this position (136–52).

London radicalized Williams, and the cumbersome, inefficient process of publication through subscription brought him, in the summer of 1792, to a kind of nervous breakdown (Constantine, "Wildernessed"). He appears to have contemplated suicide; letters home to his wife Peggy (herself struggling desperately to feed their four children) speak of miserable living conditions, cold, poor nutrition, laudanum, a delusion that all his children are dead – and Thomas Chatterton:

> tell me sincerely whether the little ones are alive. I cannot possibly put it for two minutes together out of my thoughts but that they are dead . . . I should not have been in this world now but from the hopes of still being of some help to them. . . . It was from this street, and within a door or two, that poor Chatterton was obliged to force his way out of this good-for-nothing world. (Jenkins, Jones, and Jones I: 516)

It is not the least strange fact in Williams's career that, living as a provincial "self-taught" poet in the metropolis, he should have found lodgings in Beauchamp street, so close to where Chatterton had died, supposedly by his own hand, in 1770 (Constantine, *The Truth* 43–8). The proximities are haunting.

Williams is now recognized as a key figure in Romantic-era Wales: a complex and brilliant mind, he exemplifies the "organic intelligentsia" seen by the historian Gwyn Alf Williams as the driving force behind a great deal of the period's social and cultural change. He was as widely read as anyone, and his literary output – whether in his own voice, or in the many borrowed voices of poets from other centuries – encompasses *canu caeth, canu rhydd*, odes, sonnets and ballads, political poems, essays, hundreds of letters, lyrical folksongs, and Unitarian hymns. Given his own artisan background, the professions of those who taught him the poetic craft, and the landscape of Welsh-language literature sketched out above, it is hard not to find a strong element of theatricality in his deployment of the tropes of laboring class authorship; these were further expanded in the introduction to *Poems, Lyric and Pastoral*, which is heavily indebted to the model established by Burns. It is a form of what Joep Leerssen, in an Irish context, has termed "auto-exoticism": "a mode of seeing, presenting, and representing oneself in one's otherness (in this case one's non-Englishness)" (37). Prys Morgan accuses him, perhaps not unjustly, of "playing the noble savage" (*Iolo* 12). Yet a similar element of staginess, consciously or otherwise, is embedded in the experiences of many if not all laboring class writers, for whom the manipulated public image (whether self-generated or produced by a patron) was often at odds with the private feelings, especially in matters of politics. One thing is quite clear, however: Williams was never financially secure. *Poems, Lyric and Pastoral* was generally favorably reviewed (one or two jibbed at its politics, and considered what Williams called his "kingflogging notes" ungracious), but it did not turn him into a Welsh Burns. Other literary opportunities came his way, but it was only when his frail health completely failed that he gave up practicing his original profession. He was still working as a mason in his late sixties, and the letters of his old age (he died in his eightieth year) are a depressing catalog of increasing frailty and frustrated reliance on his equally struggling children.

In that angry draft letter to Pitt's secretary, having sympathized with the French people, Williams warns: "There are now amongst the mountains of Wales, the dreary moors of Devonshire, the highlands of Scotland, persons to be met with in the very lowest station, who know more of human nature than all the kings in the world" (Jenkins, Jones, and Jones I: 439). The prerequisites of poetry – intelligence, insight, articulacy – are here radically decentered, and not merely in terms of a traditional oppositional paradigm of Country versus City, or rural honesty versus the sophisticated urbanity of court. Even within the context of a rural economy and mind-set these are extreme landscapes – uplands, moorlands, the uncivilized edges. Iolo Morganwg, Bard of Liberty, nurtured by the Grammarians of Tir Iarll, knew how productive such landscapes could be.

The notion of a brotherhood of provincial, peripheral British poets was also voiced by Williams's gentler northern counterpart, Richard Llwyd, the "Bard of Snowdon." In her recent anthology of Llwyd's work, Elizabeth Edwards astutely situates him within a number of current critical debates around the concept of laboring class poetry, noting "the new prominence of regional and national difference" as a topic of particular interest (Edwards 2016, xiii). She draws attention to the footnote in Llwyd's "Hymn to Temperance" referring to "our contemporary and humbly born Bards – Burns,

Dermody and Bloomfield... a tuneful trio composed of natives of each of the United Kingdoms" (xiii). Llwyd is clearly staking his claim to join them as the fourth (and, once again, explicitly sober) Welsh voice in a tuneful quartet; though, as Edwards points out, the phrasing of the poem may also "signal his painful exclusion from such a model" (xiii–xiv). She goes on to explore the ways in which moments like these, and Llwyd's poetry in general, speak to a recent focus on decentered "archipelagic" dialogues across the British Isles, where models of inspiration and fellowship may be both "reciprocal and rival" (xvi).

Richard Llwyd is something of a mystery, in that relatively little documentation survives which allows us to map crucial parts of his career in detail – in particular, we do not know enough about how he became an antiquarian scholar, or why, a native Welsh speaker, he wrote his poetry in English. He was born on Anglesey in 1752 into a relatively successful family – his father was a coastal trader and owned his own sloop. His father's death, the deaths of his brother and sister, and the subsequent illness of his mother left the family effectively destitute; Llwyd received some nine months of schooling at Beaumaris, but by the age of 11 he was working as a servant at the gentry house of Henblas near Llangefni. In 1780 he was a steward on the Caerhun estate in the Conwy valley, and in the subsequent decade his poems began appearing in the *Chester Chronicle*, one of two Chester papers serving the North Wales area. He published his best-known work, a lengthy, densely foot-noted topographical poem, *Beaumaris Bay*, in 1800. He wrote little after 1807; and, unlike Edward Williams, he seems by this point in his life to have attained a level of financial security.

As Edwards notes, Llwyd's relationship with the *Chester Chronicle* is one of the most distinctive aspects of his career as a writer; in a sense, the newspaper took on the role of the aristocratic patron he never had (xxi). During the 1790s he became a kind of "house bard" at the *Chronicle*, and his name was mentioned and his work praised even when he had nothing to contribute; John Fletcher, the paper's printer, also printed *Beaumaris Bay*. What success he had, then was very much down to their support. The vigorous growth of the Welsh press during the nineteenth century, with titles in both Welsh and English (and English-language papers often printing poetry in Welsh) would offer further opportunities for poets to take their work beyond their local communities. Another example of the available channels and mechanisms for supporting poetry would be Llwyd's later use of his own standing as a published poet to seek help from the Literary Fund on behalf of Welsh-language writers David Thomas (Dafydd Ddu Eryri) and Jonathan Hughes of Llangollen.

As literary recovery work brings more and more marginal and forgotten writers into view, critics have increasingly come to recognize the contingent nature of "laboring class poetry" as a category (Leask, "Was Burns" and Blair and Gorji, *Class and Canon*). For all the frequent similarities in authors' experiences (similarities which allow them to identify strongly with precursors or "contemporaries," and model their own narratives accordingly), there are the differences of individual circumstance, and in the modes of bringing their poetry to a wider audience. This is as it should be: it would be pointless to let the individuality of the writer become overwhelmed by the category itself. The different experiences of Edward Williams and Richard Llwyd, publishing at roughly the same time in English and working self-consciously within a laboring class tradition, demonstrate this well enough. This is not to suggest, however, that the concept has no value. Indeed, it is in testing the validity – the "fit" – of various models in new contexts that we refine and advance our understanding of the culture of the period as a whole.

This chapter has tried to show that eighteenth-century poetry from Wales in both languages has plenty to contribute to the study of laboring class writers, precisely because it forces us to pay very close attention to how concepts like class, patronage, and poetry itself might trail different cultural penumbrae of meaning and association. Tracking the stress points as these concepts move between cultures is especially illuminating. The word "bard" is a case in point, since its Welsh equivalent, "bardd," one of the usual words for "poet," does not necessarily come with any exotic or medieval frisson; and it is intriguing to say the least that the concept of the "bardd gwlad" or "peasant-poet," now used in Welsh literary criticism for uneducated poets, usually of the nineteenth and twentieth centuries, is not recorded in *Geiriadur Prifysgol Cymru* (the Welsh equivalent of the *OED*) before 1949.

As the critical field in this area expands, more and more comparative material emerges: one might, for example, examine laboring class women's writing in a four-nations context, or consider how the concept of "nature poetry" translates across languages and cultures (see Keegan, *Nature Poetry*); and, in the light of recent work by John Goodridge (*John Clare*), there is scope for mapping more precisely the processes by which networks of manuscript, print, and sociability sustained poetic communities in Wales. The history of literature in these islands will be richer and more interesting if we can find ways of bringing these voices into the conversation.

NOTES

My thanks to the editors for their patience, to Liz Edwards for generously sharing her work on Richard Llwyd, and to Dafydd Johnston, who looked over my Welsh translations and inadvertently found a new Welsh word for "affliction." All translations from Welsh are my own.

1. Three years later, in an impossibly fawning draft letter to George, Prince of Wales, Williams would write of those who gave him early encouragement: "My Poetry could not possibly be the object of their taste and judgement; it was rather their benevolence exerting itself in favour of one that hopes his conduct in life never incurred their disapprobation and who, with a weak constitution and bad state of health, had a family of eight persons to maintain on a very scanty income" (Jenkins, Jones, and Jones I: 441).

CHAPTER 8

"Behold in These Coromantees / The Fate of an Agonized World"
Edward Rushton's Transnational Radicalism

Franca Dellarosa

On 5 September 1782, the members of the Liverpool Philosophical and Literary Society met – "'precisely at seven o clock," as the invitation ticket scrupulously advised – to debate "The Influence of Climate on Human Nature," a paper delivered by the eminent associate of the Liverpool liberal intelligentsia and President of the Society itself, Dr. James Currie.[1] Interest in climate was common intellectual currency in the late eighteenth century, which historical geographer David N. Livingstone has described indeed as a crucial phase in the genealogy of *moral* climatology, i.e., the "persistent and widespread inclination to use climate as the vehicle for moralistic construals of global space" (159).[2] This tendency can be appreciated also in the title of a later talk, "The influence of Climate on national customs," which was delivered by another member of the Society, the Reverend Henry Barton, on 17 April 1783. On 9 June, the attendees' consideration was directed to "On the Colour of Negros," a lecture by yet another associate, Mr. Edward Rogers. The scanty records of this short-lived Society, which was terminated later in 1783, to resurface in the following years and finally to become the Liverpool Literary and Philosophical Society in 1812 (Wilson, *William Roscoe* 26–7), conjure up Liverpool as a particular center for discussing environmental explanations – not only of "human nature," but also, arguably, of human diversity, which is noteworthy to the extent that Liverpool was Europe's leading port in the transatlantic traffic of human beings. Liverpool's (and Liverpool-related) discourse of race may be connected, on the one hand, to the wider developing transnational debate, and, on the other, to the local specifics of a town that was at once a candidate for being the *heart of darkness* of the expanding Empire and an enthralling hub of radical politics and antislavery campaigning. Crucial to both sides of this intricacy of contrasting drives is laboring class poet and radical activist Edward Rushton (1756–1814).

The current process of *recovering* and *uncovering*[3] the intellectual patrimony and legacy of this long-silenced Liverpool writer,[4] whose writing career spanned the course of the three decades marking the height of the Age of Revolution, exemplifies the complexities of the task scholars face when tackling noncanonical literature, especially laboring class poetry. These include the loss of manuscript sources, and the evanescence, fragility, and fragmentation of printed sources, as well as the lack of personal correspondence and the seemingly sparse critical reception. At the same time, however, a variety of firsthand evidence establishes that Rushton was fully immersed in the most heated debates of his time. He gained an especially keen political awareness from the diverse vantage points he experienced in his assorted career.[5] He started off as a gifted apprenticed sailor getting on in the merchant navy along the transatlantic routes to the West Indies, up to the traumatic termination of his career in the mid-1770s, when he contracted trachoma while on a slaving voyage, apparently in the attempt to bring aid to the enslaved people below deck. In the following years, he had a brief experience as an innkeeper, trying to cope with his new condition as a blind person; it appears that his increasingly advanced political stances caused the failure of his business during the mid-1780s. He turned journalist at the end of that decade, working as coeditor of the radical-minded *Liverpool Weekly Herald* for about two years. Again, his political attacks on naval impressment in Liverpool forced him to quit the place. He then set up a new and eventually fairly successful business in the book trade, despite enduring political intimidation. As a *Jacobin* bookseller and a "friend of peace," he became a "marked man" (Shepherd xx) during the stormy 1790s and through the end of the century. In his final years, after various operations, he partially reacquired his sight, and continued his activity until his death in 1814.

This chapter examines Rushton's single explicit statement on race – an undated and unpublished essay first printed in Shepherd's posthumous collected edition – and attempts to locate it within local, national, and international debates. I will argue that Rushton's notion of human diversity, while at times awkward in its handling of the conceptual apparatus and current vocabulary of race, is still consistent with his radical poetic/political project, which is intended to construct, by the sheer energy of the poetic word, a potentially seditious and politically visionary transnational map of oppression. In the process, the categories of race and class – whose contiguity is often capitalized in contemporary pamphlet literature, under different agendas – are repositioned, to implicitly identify and connect *articulate* subjects. These subjects are envisioned as speaking for themselves in a collective, revolutionary act of self-empowerment. This is geographically located and historically grounded in – but not confined to – the "Revolutionary Atlantic" (Linebaugh and Rediker).

Indisputably, the transcontinental trafficking of human beings, euphemistically defined as the "African trade" in contemporary literature, played a central role in the late-eighteenth-century economy and in the communal life of Liverpool. At the close of the century, a local historian observed, in a significant and often quoted passage, that the "great annual return of wealth" deriving from the slave trade:

> may be said to pervade the whole town, increasing the fortunes of the principal adventurers, and contributing to the support of the majority of the inhabitants;... almost every order of people is interested in a Guinea cargo.... [M]any of the small vessels that import about an hundred slaves, are fitted out by attornies, drapers, ropers, grocers, tallow-chandlers, barbers, tailors, &c. some have one eighth, some a fifteenth, and some a thirty-second. (Wallace, *General and Descriptive* 229, note)

The passage, unequivocally devoid of any *ethical* preoccupation, despite its historical positioning well into the abolition debate, is a pertinent illustration of the wide range of printed matter – speeches and petitions, pamphlets and poems – produced during the late eighteenth century and intended to extol the glory of "the town and trade"[6] – while dreading its dissolution, which would certainly follow abolition. The Petition of Liverpool to the House of Commons against the abolition of the African Slave Trade, presented to Parliament by the Liverpool Common Council on 14 February 1788, evidences the intense and timely lobbying activity on behalf of Liverpool merchant interests at the onset of the abolition struggle in Parliament.[7]

It is hardly surprising that the "Liverpool Merchant" might be considered as the very embodiment of pitiless greed. The mask of the Liverpool trader was indeed used as a most effective rhetorical device for conveying abolitionist intent in *No Slaves – No Sugar*, a pamphlet ostensibly by an anonymous "Liverpool Merchant," which was published in London in 1804. Interestingly, a rather puzzled Robert Southey ultimately classified it as "an ironical defence of the slave trade" in an 1805 review article ("Art IV" 644).[8]

The transactions between European merchants and African leaders to "procure slaves" are unashamedly illustrated in the tract with the purpose of advocating their lawfulness and moral suitability. Accordingly, a rhetorical pattern is established early in the text, which is founded on a

"*Behold in These Coromantees*" 119

blunt, polygenetic standpoint, rejecting the "[philanthropists'] admission... which takes for granted, what is extremely problematical indeed–that the Negroes of Africa are of the same family with ourselves":

> Now, Lord Kaimes [*sic*], and many other eminent philosophers, are of an opinion directly contrary; and indeed, the black colour, the deformity and stupidity of Negroes, are convincing proofs of it; for, admitting that the sun, the climate, and other physical causes, may produce some slight effect on the complexion, they surely can never be supposed capable of making a white man black.... But, granting that the sun could produce the black colour, how could it possibly make a flat nose or thick lips? The thing is impossible – it is ridiculous to suppose it: and we may just as well believe, with Lord Monboddo, that we are connected with the Oran outangs, as that the Negro Savages are of the same race with ourselves. (*Addresssed to* 7)

A rejection of the climatological explanation of human diversity from a polygenetic stance is made in the passage, as the appeal to the authority of Lord Kames makes unquestionably clear. Leaving aside the wonderful historical irony entailed in the final part of the extract – in the conjuring up of Lord Monboddo, the eccentric Scottish intellectual who had argued that man and the orangutan shared the same species and that human beings had tails until recently (Wahrman 136–8) – the reference to Lord Kames's *Sketches of the History of Man* (1774) situates the assumed Liverpool Merchant within an intricate intellectual contest, of which the divergence between monogenetic and polygenetic hypotheses on the origin of mankind was only one component. Conflicting evaluations of the role of cultural and environmental change and an unstable vocabulary, where the notion of *race* was itself far from conveying a single and delimited meaning, mark the "transitional" nature of the debate in those critical decades. This would in time prepare a conceptual shift, as Dror Wahrman has observed, toward increasingly "rigid, essentialised, racialized... understandings of human difference" (Wahrman 87–126 (117); Hudson 247–74; Kitson 11–25). Edward Rushton contributed to this debate, probably at some point during the 1790s: an "unpublished Essay" (*List* 12) ascribed to him was read at a meeting of the Literary and Philosophical Society in Liverpool, on 7 April 1815 – only a few months after Rushton's death, in November 1814 (Shepherd xvii–xviii; *List* 12).

Included as the closing text in William Shepherd's 1824 posthumous edition of Rushton's *Poems and Other Writings*, the paper – under the title *An Attempt to Prove that Climate, Food and Manners, Are Not the Causes of the Dissimilarity of Colour in the Human Species* (Rushton, *Collected*

205–15)[9] – takes sides, too, against contemporary environmentalist theories of human diversity, as exemplified in the French naturalist the Comte de Buffon's *Natural History of Animals, Vegetables and Minerals* (1775–6) – but from an opposed stance, with respect to the "Liverpool Merchant." Buffon attributed human varieties to an alleged process of "degeneration," where climate and environment played a major role and Europe was considered as offering the optimal conditions. In Britain, both James Ramsay's *Essay on the Treatment and Conversion of African Slaves* (1784) and Thomas Clarkson's *Essay on the Slavery and Commerce of the Human Species* (1786) argued against polygenetic theories. Though from different standpoints (Wahrman 115–20), they both endorsed on balance the environmentalist explanation whereby, in Clarkson's words, "climate has a considerable share in producing a difference of colour" (198).

Placed as an epigraph to Rushton's article on race, a quote from Ecclesiasticus (13.23) establishes a recognizable, and distinctly class-oriented, rhetorical frame which significantly summons the relation between material wealth and social standing: "When a rich man speaketh, every man holdeth his tongue; and lo! what he says is extolled to the clouds: but if a poor man speak, they say, What fellow is this?" The meditation on money and status in the scriptural text would initially seem to support an apologetic stance, but soon reveals a challenging edge:

> When an important subject has been discussed by men eminent for abilities in the most polished nations of Europe, and the result has in general been uniform, it must have the appearance of great presumption in any one (particularly in an individual so humbly situated as myself) to endeavour to prove by arguments drawn from nature, that the hypothesis which they have founded is not quite so invulnerable as the learned fabricators may have fondly imagined. Yet, notwithstanding this, like the poor Greenlander, I here launch my little skiff to encounter a huge leviathan; and should I be so fortunate as to give him but a single wound, it may encourage some one, more expert and weighty than myself, to advance and transfix him in such a manner that he may be dragged from his profound depths, and deprived of that enormous strength which had been so long accumulating. (Rushton, *Collected* 205)

The passage displays an array of associations and references, which partly rely on a set of commonplace motifs that are presented, only to be questioned, and partly establish politically overdetermined intertextual connections *within* the writer's corpus. The overall effect is that of a multilayered, complex piece, despite its seemingly straightforward argument. The apologetic tone in the first place, as would suit an *uneducated* writer,[10] strikes the familiar keynote of the alleged intellectual inadequacy of the "humbly situated" individual, who is guilty of "great presumption" for even daring to enter a debate that is the preserve of the cultivated – "men eminent for abilities in the most polished nations of Europe" – the Frenchman Buffon, as it will turn out, but also Clarkson, and James Ramsay, in Britain. The challenge is soon identified as opposing culture to nature, where the holders of knowledge *fabricate* – literally, *construct*, make, but also *make up*[11] – an unnatural (we may infer) and certainly not "invulnerable" *edifice*. Significantly, the association of power with money and status in the epigraph is conflated into the notion of *culture*'s power in the text, to the point that they are made to coincide – the pen has always been in the hands of the rich, after all. It is in the second part of the passage, however, that the full political potentialities of the argument emerge, in the sustained imagery of the poor seaman – the "Greenlander" – epically making his way with his "little skiff" into the *body* of his enemy, the "huge leviathan," by "a single wound." That same image forms the symbolic core of a poem composed by Rushton during the same period:

> As when the huge Leviathan is seen
> Torpid and slumb'ring midst his native seas,
> The seamen ply the oar with anxious mien
> Quick every eye, and noiseless every voice–
> And now the keen harpoon its entrance makes,
> At first unfelt; till deeper grows the wound,
> When lo! the enormous animal awakes,
> And his broad tail spreads death and terror round–
> (Rushton, *Collected* 96)

Included in both of Rushton's principal early editions (1806, 1824) as "The Leviathan,"[12] this poem characteristically modulates the literal and the symbolic into a seascape that is marked by the experiential quality of the sea labor, both in its pure physicality – the seamen's watchful and nimble movements – and its psychological implications.[13] In the allegory proposed in the poem, however, the identification of victim and perpetrator is reversed, and it is the (political) *body* of a prospective rebellious Leviathan that rises up under the "shaft" of oppression, to turn the entire world upside down – as *the tail soon mounts on high*, crushing all embodiments and symbols of state and religious power:[14]

> So when a nation, cold and sluggish, lies,
> Silent and slow th' oppressor drives his steel;
> At first the wound's unfelt; again he tries,
> Deep sinks the shaft, and now the people feel–
> Pierc'd to the quick, the tail soon mounts on high,
> And kings, peers, bishops, all in one proud ruin lie.
>
> (96)

It appears clear that the symbolic instability of the Leviathan trope responds to the changing political agendas in the writings considered. Where in the poem the focus is on the potentialities of people's *collective* power for revolt as "a unitary 'body'" (Rushton, *Collected* 267), in the essay it is the heroic *individual* effort that is set in contrast with the "huge," oppressive supremacy of the leviathan of (mainstream) culture. It is indeed a singularly sharp image, that of the "poor Greenlander," struggling to inflict a "single wound" to the sea monster of a dominant cultural locus, and thus open a fissure in its monolithic *fabrication* for others to step in and continue dismantling. It strikes the reader as an image that establishes a concealed but discernible connecting line with the central political point that Rushton's essay "On the Colour of the Skin of the Negro"[15] ultimately intends to make.

The opening paragraph of Rushton's essay, discussed so far, precedes a descriptive explanation of the climatological hypothesis under scrutiny (Rushton, *Collected* 205–6). While immediately recognizing "benevolent warmth in behalf of the poor oppressed Africans" (206) in the "advocates of climate," Buffon[16] and Clarkson[17] – as if responding to a major ethical priority – the essay proposes to minutely discard their account of human difference. The method intended to "evince the fallacy" (206) of the climatological position may be described as rationalist and based on observation – where the object of observation is the climatological *fabrication* per se. Its evident aim is to expose the incongruities in the logic underlying the object of the writer's critique: "Facts are stubborn things, and will not easily yield to fanciful speculations, however bold, elegant, or ingenious" is the authorial comment on the growing number of contrary indications (210). No alternative cause, however, is suggested to account for "the various colours of the human race" (206). This, in a somewhat paradoxical sense, confirms Rushton's rationalist stance, as the "phenomenon" remains unexplained (215), and it is left to the will of "the great Author of Nature" (206) to allocate the "amazing difference of mankind" (215), with the consequent recognition of man's limited abilities to understand nature and its "incomprehensible" variety (208).

The essay engages in a detailed critique of a number of points, whose source is at times explicitly identified. For example:

> A celebrated naturalist [Buffon] has indeed asserted that the inhabitants of Quito, from their vicinity to the snowy Andes, are nearly white; but if boisterous regions, if frost or snow, can produce an effect of this kind, then the inhabitants of Canada, and the dreary Terra del Fuego, whose winters are remarkably long and severe, ought to be fairer than even those of Quito; yet the former are known to be as brown as any Indians on the continent. (209)

The passage, attacking one specific point in Buffon's account,[18] is one of many examples that substantiate Rushton's detailed, meticulous appraisal and warrant his concluding admonition that "[i]nstances like these should teach us... not servilely to conform to the opinions of any individuals, however eminent for wealth, titles, or understanding" (209). The keynote is heard again, implicitly advocating the intellectual independence of the *low*. Consistently, the same note resounds to call for human equality, regardless of skin pigmentation:

> And here it may be remarked, that though I object to the learned hypothesis, yet I cannot suppose that mankind are either exalted by their whiteness, or degraded by their receding from this supposed favourite colour of nature.... [T]o imagine that the wise Framer of the Universe is partial to this or that particular colour; or that he created a race of beings with sable complexions and woolly hair to be servile drudges to the rest, is, in my opinion, to degrade Omnipotence. Away then with this fancied superiority which the Europeans have vainly arrogated to themselves. Nature knows it not. (208)

As radical a move as any to be found in the most advanced contemporary thinking appears to be devised in the passage.[19] While the environmental/climatological model is disproven in that it endorses "misrepresentations" (208) of human variety[20] – whether explicitly positing a racial hierarchy, as was the case with Buffon, or accounting for blackness as a "universal freckle," as with Clarkson[21] – it is the mounting *fabrication* of essential racial difference that is bluntly exposed in its ethical and conceptual void. Whiteness or blackness per se – the "difference" conveyed in an individual's external traits – simply do not serve to define humankind. The (imaginary) ascription of an allegedly natural inequality of human "races" to abstract divine will, and its consequent partiality to a single "supposed favourite colour of nature," entails a *degradation* of Omnipotence to a mirror of the self-assumed *omnipotence* of one single human "race." Accordingly, white ascendancy is a fake, a "fancied superiority," and the product of Europe's *vain arrogance*: "However different in appearance, we are all the production of the same wonderful hand" (208).

The essay proceeds by accumulation of evidence, ranging geographically through the construction of an anticlimatological world map of human variety that touches all continents. On occasion, nevertheless, moral-climatological commonplaces insinuate themselves within this texture of progressive thinking, indicating its residual imbrication in the conceptual and ideological predicament that was inherent in late-eighteenth-century race discourse (Burke 245–8; Wahrman 117ff). An example is the allusion to the "stationary negroes [living 'on the southern banks of the Senegal'], who are remarkably indolent, and spend the hottest part of the day either reclining beneath their cane-built sheds or lolling under the umbrageous shelter of their spreading trees" (Rushton, *Collected* 207, 214). In another case, the argument moves to consider the "collateral assistants [to climate], food and manners," and a cursory descriptive survey of the diet and social habits of diverse populations is used to reinforce the anticlimatological case. That in Rushton's account the *food* for the "native of the New Zealand" might "not unfrequently" include "an horrid repast from the body of some slaughtered enemy" (213) conjures up "the unproblematic way" in which the *narrative* of cannibalism, as reported in James Cook's *Journals*, would be "taken as revealing a truth" (Hulme 22–3).[22]

Rushton's essay on race appears indeed to restage the conflict in action in *West Indian Eclogues* (1787), Rushton's four-poem *anti*-pastoral sequence that had marked a turning point in the writer's poetics and politics, pointing to an increasingly radical pledge, and in which an intricate, perplexing connection between the poetic text and the extensive apparatus of notes significantly complicates interpretation. The paratext of *West Indian Eclogues* as a whole, including the authorial Advertisement, establishes the apparently mainstream conceptual and ideological frame against which the poems' *actual* politics takes on an especially subversive edge. The appeal to "humanity" in the first place, and the dedication to the Bishop of Chester, Beilby Porteus – whose authority is conjured up and whose ameliorationist Sermon XVII is credited in the notes as suggesting "sound policy" (Rushton, *Collected* 59, n. *q*) – would seem to qualify the poems' radical significance. Instead, they end up magnifying, by contrast, the subversive drive prevailing in the realm of the *poetic word*, as contemporary responses did not fail to perceive (Dellarosa 150–54, 161–70). Remarkably, *West Indian Eclogues* appears to resolve its controversial ideology in its ultimate reliance on a radical call for black agency, where poetic form is both the instrument and the locus for performing an alternative narrative of plantation life. The eclogue's dramatic dialogue is acted out by black speakers only – which, in terms of the poetic stance, demands the acknowledgment of, and imaginative access to, an *unspeakable* territory. This embraces the vindication of the enslaved of their right to agency, no less than their talk of resistance per se, and their actual suffering bodies – "And shall we still endure the keenest pain, / And pay our butchers only with disdain?" (Rushton, *Collected* 46, ll. 75–6).

West Indian Eclogues sets the scene for Rushton's distinctive poetic experiment, which stands out as a transnational – and increasingly far-reaching and vocal – claim for the rights of the oppressed. Poetic form is vitally at stake, in shaping a world where the margin finds its way to the center. The Caribbean antipastoral of *West Indian Eclogues* is a pertinent example. Another one is the Gothic experiment in the "marine ballad" *Lucy's Ghost* (1800), where a forsaken woman's specter, i.e., a doubly silenced subject, is made to *speak*, and indict her lover on board a merchant vessel. Rushton's focus on *the wretched of the earth*, and of the sea, calls attention to the most glaring forms of injustice devastating the lives of individuals in the Age of Revolution. His use of poetic form is essential to his highly political act of choosing a subject unfit for poetry, to the extent that it very often results in a gesture of empowerment. This is true of Rushton's street ballad denouncing naval impressment and its impact on the destinies of men, women, and children, such as those of sailor Will Clewline and his family (*Will Clewline*, 1801; Rushton, *Collected* 108–9). This is most significantly true of the ballad whose protagonist *and* speaking voice is the leader of the Haitian Revolution, Toussaint L'Ouverture. "Toussaint to His Troops" (1802?, published 1806) carries out an act of paradoxical *meta*-ventriloquism, whereby the white metropolitan laboring class poet's rhetorical appropriation of the voice of the black leader from across the Atlantic effectively realizes a process of contestation of colonial domination, as it is itself the product of a marginal metropolitan subject (Scrivener 236, 244–7; Goodridge and Keegan 282–3; Dellarosa 171–85).

The plantation and the slave ship, as claimed by Linebaugh and Rediker, are two "sites of struggle" (327) in the early age of global capitalism, where actors from the "motley crew" of the revolutionary Atlantic carried out rebellion. Both *loci* are inscribed in Rushton's life and writing: enslaved Africans and British "tars" – whether subject to the violence of the press-gang or to the sheer toil of sea life, or both – inhabit this underworld of marginalized and subjugated individuals, communities, and nations (Pierrot 134–8), and are equally entitled to the right of resistance. Indeed, the mapping of transnational human rights violations that Rushton's poetic corpus knowingly delineates expands to embrace other "sites of struggle," oppression, and resistance. This is the case with Ireland, outraged by the "merciless doings" of the "soldiers of Britain" at the time of the 1798 rebellion ("Mary Le More," Rushton, *Collected* 97–8). In the same vein, the tragedy of "poor partition'd Poland," and the fields of Europe, "drench'd" with the blood of the countless dead, are conjured up to abhor the incalculable human cost of the Napoleonic wars ("Lines Addressed to Robt. Southey, Esq. Poet Laureat on the Publication of His *Carmen Triumphale*," Rushton, *Collected* 169, l. 62; 168, l. 21).

Edward Rushton's poetic and political insight proves most acute and far-reaching at the close of his career and life. The indictment of the new Poet Laureate Robert Southey in Rushton's powerful counternarrative of the Napoleonic wars, and the symbolic and no less than brutally *real* parable of "The Coromantees" (published 1824), provide the most coherent and radical evidence of Rushton's anti-war, anti-imperialist, and anti-slavery stance. A French act of privateering against a British slaving ship, with the involvement in the battle of the enslaved Africans, who are, in the end, "Again . . . to the deck-chains consign'd" (Rushton, *Collected* 176, l. 69), becomes the paradigm for the global dynamics of power and exploitation that sweep away the lives of "millions" – and the valiant Coromantees themselves, the synecdoche for those "millions" who are the casualties of *any* imperial power:

> Oh, Britons! behold in these Coromantees
> The fate of an agonized world,
> Where, in peace, a few lordlings hold millions in chains,
> Where, in war, for those lordlings men open their veins,
> ("The Coromontees," *Collected* 176, ll. 71–5)

In the section "Of the Varieties in the Human Species" in Buffon's *Natural History*, the "Greenlanders" appear at the very opening, alongside other peoples from the North, to exemplify a "race," "whose figure is uncouth, and whose physiognomy is as wild as their manners are unpolished. . . . Nor is it alone in deformity, in diminutiveness, and in the colour of the hair and eyes, that these nations resemble each other. . . . Incivility, superstition, and ignorance, are alike conspicuous in them all" (Buffon 171–3). Whether intended or not, in the light of Buffon's words, the imagery permeating the opening paragraph of Rushton's essay on race takes on new significance, conflating as it does the orthodox construction of the race and class categories into a single, revolutionary metaphor for his authorial stance. The "poor Greenlander's" epic struggle against the "huge leviathan" of established culture implies a double gesture – of self-recognition *and* acknowledgment of the "other" as equal subjects and agents, performing an act of (self)empowerment and self-liberation that is integral in the process:

> But the period approaches when poor prostrate man
> Shall enjoy what the Deity gave;
> When the oculist Reason shall touch his dim eyes,
> With a soul all abhorrence the sufferer shall rise,
> And undauntedly throw off the slave.
> ("The Coromantees," 176, ll. 76–80)

NOTES

I am grateful to editors John Goodridge and Bridget Keegan for inviting me to contribute to this volume, as the beginning of a new and exciting connection – as well as for their precious editorial work, and to Annamaria Sportelli, Alex Robinson, and Paul Baines, for reading this paper while it was still in the making and/or sharing their thoughts on the issues at stake.

1. The ephemera referred to are all included in the Holt & Gregson Papers, LRO (ff. 491, 547, 561, and 553).
2. The topic has been explored from a variety of disciplinary perspectives. See Wheeler, *Complexion* (21–33, 183–8, 260–79); Wahrman (83–126); and Whiters, especially Chapter 7.
3. John Goodridge points to the relevance of the enterprise of laboring class scholarship as a whole, as intended to "discover and recover . . . an important and extensive tradition that has been hidden or marginalised" ("Introduction to the Database"). A parallel reflection on the bearing of a process of *recovering* and *uncovering* Rushton's writing corpus and legacy shapes my article for Rushton's Bicentennial Conference's Proceedings, *La Questione Romantica* (forthcoming).
4. On the Bicentennial Anniversary of the poet's death in November 1814, Liverpool hosted a network of related initiatives. These included a two-day international academic conference at the University of Liverpool, three different exhibitions involving National Museums Liverpool and the Victoria Gallery and Museum, a Thanksgiving Service held at the Liverpool Cathedral on 22 November 2014, as well as the stage reading of the biographical play *Unsung*, whose premiere took place on 9 March 2016 at Liverpool's Everyman Theatre. Rushton's bicentenary saw also the publication of the first modern edition of his writings and monograph study. See Rushton, *Collected*; Dellarosa. Fully detailed reports of the initiatives and partnerships composing the *Unsung* project are available at www.uniba.it/ricerca/dipartimenti/lelia/ricerca/progetti/progetto-unsung and www.dadafest.co.uk/the-festival/unsung/.
5. The key biographical sources are Edward Rushton's, Jr.'s "Biographical Sketch" and William Shepherd's "Life of Edward Rushton," which introduces his 1824

edition of Rushton's *Poems and Other Writings*. See also Rushton, *Collected* (1–24); Dellarosa (1–19; 23–47).

6. As did diffusely *A Descriptive Poem on the Town and Trade of Liverpool, by John Walker, Shoemaker* (1789) – interestingly, another laboring class poet. See Burke (256–60); Dellarosa (25–42).

7. In the Petitioners' "judgement," the intended provision "must... tend to the prejudice of the British manufacturers, must ruin the property of the English merchants in the West Indies, diminish the public revenue and impair the maritime strength of Great Britain." Reported in Williams ("Petition of Liverpool" 609–10). The Privy Council Enquiry on the slave trade was established that very month. Eleven years later, in 1799, the Liverpool "African Merchants" would still appoint a delegate in London, Peter Whitfield Branker, Esq., to "obtain a Parliamentary Regulation and to oppose an abolition of the African Slave Trade." The Corporation of Liverpool would compensate him by "Two Pieces of Silver Plate," as "an Acknowledgment of his Repeated exertions," as testifies a handwritten note (*Mayer Papers*, LRO).

8. As he commented in a letter to Charles Watkin Williams Wynn, dated 14 January 1805, "if [the pamphlet] be not ironical is the most impudent defence of that xxxx accursed traffic that ever yet disgraced the English language. I really cannot tell whether it be serious or ironical... – however I shall treat it as irony" (Letter 1019).

9. All quotations from Rushton's texts are from Baines's edition. Page numbers are given in parentheses, lines are provided where available.

10. The obvious reference here is Robert Southey's 1831 foundational essay (Southey, *Lives*). See Goodridge and Keegan (284–7).

11. *OED* reports Johnson's 1755 *Dictionary* as the earliest record of the word in sense 2: "'When they [Scottish lawyers] suspect a paper to be forged, they say it is *fabricate*'" (Profitt, *Oxford*).

12. The poem is recorded as having been printed on 9 June 1797 in the New York paper *The Time-Piece and Literary Companion*, under the title "Remedy," and paired with "Hibernia," a companion poem on the state of Ireland (Rushton, *Collected* 266–7); in the later versions the apocalyptic final line is replaced by a less explicit image of "splendour, wealth and power" that are left to lie "in one sad ruin" (Rushton, *Poems* 1806, 147; *Poems* 1824, 54). The paper, whose editor was Philip Freneau, hosted a number of Rushton's poems, as well as his *Expostulatory Letter to George Washington* (26 May 1797, Rushton, *Collected* 185–90), especially over the stormy 1790s, when most of his writings would appear anonymous or overseas.

13. On the general significance of "labouring-class poetry at sea," including some pages devoted to Rushton, see Keegan (*Nature Poetry* 122–47); on Rushton's corpus of sea poetry, Dellarosa (48–74).

14. It is hardly necessary to call to mind the cover engraving for the first edition of Thomas Hobbes's *Leviathan* (1651), where the political body of the state, formed by the multitude of the subjects, upholds the sovereign's head, who carries a sword and a crosier, as symbols of his temporal and religious sway.

15. This is the title under which the piece was presented in Liverpool in 1815 (*List of Communications* 12).
16. Buffon comments in passing on slavery in the same extended session "Of the Varieties in the Human Species" (Buffon I. IX, 171–292), echoing the sentimental appeal to *humanity* that would become the hallmark of abolitionist discourse: "Their [Negroes'] sufferings demand a tear. Are they not sufficiently wretched in being reduced to a state of slavery; in being obliged always to work without reaping the smallest fruit of their labour, without being abused, buffeted, and treated like brutes? Humanity revolts at those oppressions, which nothing but the thirst of gold could ever have introduced" (244).
17. James Ramsay, too, is mentioned in passing at this stage, apparently less for his contribution to the debate than to the cause of enslaved Africans. Rushton recalls his own long residence in Jamaica to support the evidence of their testimonies. On this point, see his Advertisement to *West Indian Eclogues* (Dellarosa 150–4). Thomas Clarkson visited Rushton in Liverpool in 1787 during his fact-finding mission around the country and later acknowledged his role in the abolition struggle.
18. "The Indians of Peru are also ... copper-coloured; those especially who live near the sea, and in the low countries. The inhabitants, however, between the two ridges of the Cordillere-mountains, are almost as white as the Europeans" (Buffon 270). At the time, the Viceroyalty of New Granada, under the Spanish rule, included today's Ecuador and northern Peru – which explains Rushton's geography.
19. See Dror Warhman's discussion of James Dunbar's 1780 *Essays on the History of Mankind in Rude and Cultivated Ages* (Wahrman 121–2).
20. Much more relevant than climate factors in defining color mutability, in Rushton's view, is "the mixture of blood" deriving from interracial unions (Rushton, *Collected* 208), which is also described as "the admixture with the other families of mankind" (212). Rushton's use of the word *family* – here as elsewhere in the text – appears to correspond to the biological notion of *cline*, whereas in the *No Slaves – No Sugar* passage, quoted above, *family* evidently overlaps with *species*.
21. Clarkson 210–12. The expression is first found in Ramsay's *Essay*, 215–16 (Wahrman 119).
22. Peter Hulme cites James Boswell's response to Cook's direct relation of his assumed firsthand experience of man-eating in New Zealand, over dinner in April 1776, as evidence of such an attitude. The actual episode, which occurred on board the *Resolution* during Cook's second voyage to the South Seas in November 1773, and is reported in Cook's *Journals*, once cross-referenced to other sources, turns out to be much less straightforward, as it entailed "a fully interactive relationship between English sailors and the Maori" (Hulme 23). Captain Cook is summoned only a few paragraphs earlier in Rushton' text, in support of the anti-climatological argument.

CHAPTER 9

Transnational Ulster and Laboring Class Self-Fashioning
Jennifer Orr

Introduction

In its specific transnational identity, embedded in the very mythological roots of the region, and the well-known political turbulence that has dominated its history, Ulster provides a unique case study in Romantic writing. A notable rise in laboring class poetic activity was facilitated by Belfast's cosmopolitan print culture, at its height during the United Irish republican activity of the 1790s. This microcosm of European revolutionary activity provided the means for laboring class writers to publish and disseminate their works throughout the neighboring islands and across the Atlantic through dissenting contacts in Revolutionary America. Attached to such publications as the *Belfast News-Letter* (1737–), which claims to be Ireland's longest-running continuous newspaper, and the radical *Northern Star* (1792–7) were networks of rural poets, connected through political and economic activity to the capital. Prominent among these contributors, which ranged from Ascendancy salon members to Dissenting weavers, were tightly knit networks of laboring class poets, often bonded by radical confessional and political beliefs. Such poetic activity in Ireland emerged from a reading culture in which Scottish works were particularly popular[1] as well as a share in the general British literary interest in the primitive and the Celtic "margins."

Since the popularity of English poet Stephen Duck (1705–56), the phenomenon of the laboring class poet, though admittedly often problematic in terms of class identity, opened up the literary marketplace to the nonclassically educated. This self-taught, primitive figure was increasingly romanticized both in Thomas Gray's sympathetic benevolence toward the "mute inglorious Milton" in *Elegy Written in a Country Churchyard* (1751) and the eponymous and tragic "last of the race" subject of *The Bard, a Pindaric Ode* (1757). Furthermore, the public's appetite for undiscovered poet figures who embodied the remnants of an ancient "British" culture was only whetted further by a series of literary forgeries, notably James Macpherson's *Fragments of Ancient Poetry Collected in the Highlands of Scotland* (1760). With the celebrity of Robert Burns (1759–96), the "heaven-taught" figure and the Celtic bard found its contemporary embodiment. When compared with their middle class contemporaries William Wordsworth, Samuel Taylor Coleridge, and Percy Bysshe Shelley, laboring class figures like Burns and John Clare (1793–1864) have been less readily associated with intentional Romantic poetic theory; yet the prefatory, often "regional," poses of laboring class poets offer insight into poetic self-conception, albeit indirectly. In an article that examines Burns's use of language as a means of national self-construction, Jeremy Smith concludes that "Burns loved to pose" (73). Subsequent critics have since pointed to the "ploughman poet's masterful ability to adopt intricate and destabilising personae in his poems, code-switching between Standard English, Standard Scottish and broad vernacular Scots" (Broadhead, *Language* 20–29). Although it is more or less commonplace today to assert that Burns's image as a national bard was partly self-fashioned, his early critics and editors often accepted at face value his prefatory self-description as "[t]he simple Bard, rough at the rustic plough" (Burns, "Brigs of Ayr," l. 1, 226). More recent criticism, notably Gerard Carruthers (*Robert Burns*), Nigel Leask, Leith Davis, Murray Pittock (*Burns and Other Poets*), Tim Burke, and Fiona Stafford ("Scottish Poetry"), has argued forcefully that Burns, keenly aware of his own artistic mission, represents a Romantic incarnation of the self-fashioning laboring class figure as national bard. This figure of regional, and later national, significance not only paved the way for writers like Walter Scott (1771–1832), who would put Scotland on the international literary map, but also for other aspiring poets across the regions of Ireland and Britain who sought to create innovative poetry partly in their own vernacular dialects and languages, not least the Irish Romantic circle who form the subject of this chapter.

Class, Nation and Identity: Ulster's Bardic Tradition

From the start, Burns' birl and rhythm, *[traditional music note]*
That tongue the Ulster Scots brought wi' them
And stick to still in County Antrim
    Was in my ear.
From east of Bann it westered in
    On the *Derry air*. (Seamus Heaney, "A Birl for Burns," ll. 1–6)

The reader familiar with Scottish poetry will note that Seamus Heaney's "A Birl for Burns" (1998), written in the distinctive six-line Scottish "Habbie Simson" stanza, is immediately recognizable within the genre of Scottish mock elegy, typified by Allan Ramsay's "Elegy on Maggy Johnston." It is often known as the "Burns stanza" from its popularized form in some of Burns's most famous poems, "To a Mouse" (1785) and "To a Louse" (1786), in which he expanded the use of the form to examine more serious, Enlightenment subjects such as sympathy, self-awareness, and man's moral position in society. The flexibility of the form has been exploited by poets of various nationalities throughout the centuries, and though Heaney's poem has the essence of formal pioneering, he was by no means the first Irish poet to adopt the stanza. Heaney's poem is a personal celebration of shared linguistic and cultural origins, a newly discovered synergy of working class cultures that at first might seem foreign, even in direct opposition to one another. Both Burns and Heaney shared laboring class heritage as the sons of farmers, and both were influenced by Scots vocabulary spoken in their native communities, but, having felt the responsibility in his earlier career to speak on behalf of his own Roman Catholic minority whose native tongue was Irish Gaelic, it was all the more significant that Heaney chose to celebrate what he once might have viewed as the language and culture of his neighboring "colonizers." Nowhere is this tender, sympathetic appreciation more evident than in his depiction of the respectful Protestant neighbor in "The Other Side," a portrait of ecumenical goodwill that is reminiscent of Ulster laboring class poet James Orr's praise of the hospitality shown to him by his Gaelic-speaking "compatriots," presumably Roman Catholic, in "To Miss Owenson: the Authoress of *The Wild Irish Girl*," published in *The Belfast Commercial Chronicle* on 2 May 1807.

Both James Orr (1770–1816), writing shortly after the Irish Rebellion of 1798, and Heaney, writing during "the Troubles" of the 1970s, reflected on tense sectarian relations between Ulster's communities. Heaney's resistance of a rigid national paradigm reflects the re-categorization of literature in response to twentieth-century sociological theories of transnationalism. A "Birl for Burns" voices those minority cultures which do not fit neatly into nineteenth-century, ethno-nationalist paradigms based on majority self-determination. Likewise, a rigidly ethno-nationalist categorization of Irishness would have been foreign to Orr. Critics have long since recognized that the literature of "long" eighteenth-century Ulster, that which was contemporaneous with the Scottish writings of Allan Ramsay to Robert Burns, can be seen as a precursor to modern transnationalism, or what James Kelly has described as "the clearest example of [Romantic] transnational conversation" (444). Here, the theoretical term is employed in a positive sense to denote the particular cultural, confessional, and linguistic hybridity of Ulster's shared identity. The changing labels attached to these multifarious cultures testify to the continuing political contest that inhabits the idea of identity in this part of the world, ranging from Irish, Scots, Ulster Scots and, since the 1920s, Northern Irish down to more polarized descriptors such as "planters," "Gaels," and Anglo-Irish. As this chapter will elucidate, Irishness and Scottishness were neither cohesive identities in Romantic-period Ulster nor the only national influences at work; this is especially true as the province increasingly opened up during the eighteenth century as a result of global migration and considerable waves of emigration, mostly of Protestant Dissenters to America. Heaney's poetic recognition of Burns's cultural influence on his corner of Ireland might therefore be seen as an important stage in a long process of forgetting, rediscovery, and the eventual disinterment of Ulster's transnational culture.

This culture originates specifically in laboring class poetic movements where the Ulster variant of the Scottish vernacular was spoken, described as "the tongue the Ulster Scots brought with them" (Heaney 2). This linguistic culture, so strikingly similar to that of Burns's Ayrshire, existed alongside more deeply ingrained value-systems shared between Ulster and Lowland Scotland, such as Dissenting confessional identity and literary/folk tradition. Like Burns, Ulster Scots poets often wrote in Standard English, but made selective use of a literary form of Scots to serve the functional demands of intended audiences. Such linguistic "code-switching" allowed for different kinds of content to be mediated to different audiences, defying generic and class expectation and even deliberately upsetting received understandings of language. The odes "To a Hedgehog" (1799) and "To the Potatoe" (1804) of Samuel Thomson (1766–1816) and James Orr (1770–1816) respectively, overturn class and linguistic expectations to destabilize meaning and send coded political messages about Irish revolutionary politics to a knowing laboring class audience (Orr, *Literary Networks* 155–60). Such code-switching also occurs in Heaney's "Birl for Burns," which, consciously or unconsciously, invokes a shared working class cultural heritage that had been all but lost in the twentieth-century "teleology of partition" that afflicted Ireland. Written in the wake of the Good Friday (Belfast) Agreement (1998), which marked a halt to the decades of bitter conflict known as "the Troubles," Heaney's poem embodies a hybrid northern cultural inheritance both in its imagery and in its own position as part of an Ulster poetic tradition. The poem's inclusive imagery marries "planter" and "native" elements; "the tongue the Ulster Scots brought with them" floating in "on the *Derry air*" playing on a well-known Irish nationalist ballad tune, while its theme of shared identity echoes a long line of Protestant Irish poetic influence. These include John Hewitt (1907–87), the critic and broadcaster who helped return the radical Ulster Romantic poets to prominence, and W. B. Yeats (1865–1939), who was in turn influenced by the Ulster Romantic poet Sir Samuel Ferguson (1810–86).

Though Sir Samuel Ferguson was a landed gentleman and author, his own literary inheritance had its origins in a largely laboring class poetic movement of previous generations, including Dissenting republicans discussed in this chapter such as Samuel Thomson (1766–1816), James Orr, and Thomas Beggs (1789–1847). This laboring class circle intersected with the politically conservative salon coterie of antiquarian Bishop Thomas Percy (1729–1811), and although Percy's protégés were more prolific at the time, they are generally now less well known than their laboring class poetic contemporaries Orr and Thomson. Retrospectively, critics have defined this within an evolving "northern" Irish literary tradition with its origins in the late Enlightenment and Age of Revolution, starting with the vernacular, laboring class poets of the Thomson circle.[2] This tradition, as many previous studies have emphasized, represents a broad political and ideological spectrum that includes republicans, Unionists, liberals, conservatives, Marxists, plebeian writers, and aristocrats, and poets from a range of confessional identities, though primarily Dissenting.[3] Because of the quality of their poetry and, in part, because of their United Irish credentials, Orr and Thomson remain the most well-known Irish figures, with several individual studies dedicated to them. This rest of this chapter examines how they and other laboring class members of the Thomson circle envisaged their identities as translocal and transnational, including metropolitan and even cosmopolitan figures.

Rural schoolmaster and poet Samuel Thomson was the instigating figure of this coterie, arguably the "father" of Ulster's Romantic movement, and I have discussed his work and importance as a laboring class poet extensively elsewhere.[4] Just as Heaney would later explain Burns's poetic appeal for him in "A Birl for Burns," Thomson offered the following expression of hybrid national identity in his 1806 poem ("To Captain McDougall, Castle-Upton, with a copy of the author's poems"):

> Oft wild-wood Fancy restless roams,
>   Among her [Scotland's] well-sung, classic braes,
> Where our forefathers had their homes,
>   The hardy sons of other days.

> ...
> I love my native land, no doubt,
>   Attach'd to her thro' thick and thin;
> But tho' I'm IRISH all without,
>   I'm every item SCOTCH within.
>   (*Simple Poems*, ll. 1–4, 17–20)

For this Romantic-period poet, who identified as a bard speaking on behalf of his rural "compeers" (*Poems* "Dedication"), hybrid identity was no less problematic than it was for Heaney, prompting his longing to be part of an imagined ancestral community. Clearly, for these poets, the idea of nation and home was not confined to a geographical space but embedded in a collective ancestral imagination:

> And still when inspiration comes
>   To my night thoughts and mid day dreams,
> 'Tis from her breezy, willowy holms,
>   Romantic groves and winding streams.
>   (*Simple Poems* ll. 9–12)

A note of caution must be sounded when considering the poem out of context. The full title of the poem, "To Captain McDougall, Castle-Upton, with a copy of the author's poems," reveals that Thomson gifted the verses along with *New Poems* to a Scottish military patron. The reader ought therefore to remain mindful of the self-fashioning topos so frequently found in the prefatory material of published volumes by members of his laboring class circle. The poetic phrase that has come to be synonymous with the Ulster Scots identity –"But tho' I'm IRISH all without, / I'm ev'ry item SCOTCH within" – has been interpreted by some critics as a calculated literary pose in which Thomson seeks to reinforce the superiority of his Scottish ancestry over his birth in Ireland. This may, in part, explain Thomson's disappearance from literary prominence in the nineteenth century. In *Subverting Scotland's Past*, Colin Kidd has argued that Enlightenment thinkers in Scotland sought to disassociate a progressive modern Scotland from its barbaric Irish past; meanwhile, in Ireland, Anglo-Irish issues began to preoccupy the nationalist movements of the nineteenth century, leading to the indiscriminate conflation of Scottish cultural influence with colonialism. Reading within a transnational context, it is persuasive to interpret the identification as "IRISH all without . . . / 'ev'ry item SCOTCH within" as a *bona fide* expression of hybrid identity which has its roots as far back as Scotland's fourteenth-century iconic king, Robert the Bruce, who identified a common Irish/Scottish identity –

"one seed of birth" – born out of shared language and custom (Duffy 55–86). Thomson passed round his circle a copy of the Early Scots poem *The Brus* by John Barbour (c. 1320–95), a volume that remained popular in Ulster throughout the eighteenth century (Adams, *Printed Word* 72). By the time "To Captain McDougal" was published, Scotland was prospering economically under a contractual Union with England while Ireland had recently been subdued under force following the unsuccessful United Irish Rebellion of 1798, and subsequently consolidated by Acts of Parliament as part of the United Kingdom in 1800. For Thomson, Irish and Scottish history and culture remained intertwined, with the province of Ulster increasingly suspended between two nations whose political, economic, and religious differences had begun to drive them apart. That Thomson, a former United Irish sympathizer, expressed his faith in Ireland suggests stalwart national pride, while his celebration of Scottish cultural identity might also articulate faith in a nation's ability to retain its cultural autonomy under the attempted subjugation of their common enemy, England. The poem was published in Thomson's third volume *Simple Poems on a Few Subjects, Partly in the Scottish Dialect* (1806), a volume often considered to reflect both Thomson's waning political radicalism and his increasing concern with spiritual, rather than national, identity. In this context, it is significant that "To Captain McDougall" addresses the national question so directly, refusing to gloss over tensions in Irish national identity while addressing itself to a Scottish, or at least Scottish-descended, military figure.

Language and Identity in Irish Laboring Class Prefaces

The claim that Ulster boasts its own legitimate language remains contested in spite of the Council of Europe's recognition of the Ullans (Ulster Scots) language in the 1990s. The laboring class prefaces discussed here reveal that even in the 1840s the role of Scottishness in Irish literature was fraught and had taken on political significance. Such laboring class prefaces from the second generation of the Thomson circle consistently seek to justify the choice of Scots as a distinctive, native dialect, some arguing that the Scots language itself originated in the Irish nation. The Glenwherry poet Thomas Beggs, cousin of James Orr, attached a strongly worded addendum to his unusually brief preface to *The Minstrel's Offering* (1836). This volume followed on the heels of several poetic successes, so we may assume a degree of self-confidence in the poet's tone:

> Should the reader of the following effusions suppose, that in some parts the Author has imitated the Scottish dialect, – he would wish to correct the idea, by alledging that he has written in *his own* style – in the language of his native glen – not constrained, but spontaneous as the lispings of our first speech. (Beggs 3)

Wordsworth's marketing of *Lyrical Ballads* (1798–1803) as a collection which captured the "spontaneous overflow of powerful emotion" in "the real language of men" is alluded to here by Beggs to justify the literary use of his spoken vernacular. By 1844, it was evident that this transnational identity could not be taken for granted. The County Down poet and artisan weaver Robert Huddleston of Moneyreagh (1814–1889) prefaced his *Collection of Poems and Songs on Rural Subjects* (1844) with a strongly worded cultural defense of what he termed "Ulster Irish":

> Though hoarse and guttural, do me the honor to believe, that I am as willing as ever a bird in the Emerald Isle to sing; and, that my lays are original, if not harmonious. In Ulster Irish (which some in their unmeaning eccentricity may term Scotch, to tear even the credit of language from its mother home), I sing the most of my songs. Know, that until the 15th century, this was the ancient Scotia, and the now modern Scotland, only the minor plant; and it is a questionable point yet by some, but given in by all men of profound knowledge and erudition, that the inhabitants of Scotland are the descendants of the people of Erin. Then Erin must be the mother land. (ix)

In asserting the Irish genealogy of the Scots people, Huddleston put forth a counterargument to the accusation leveled at the Ulster Scots that they were a mere "planter" tradition. Huddleston drew on the historical mythology of the sixth-century Gaelic kingdom of Dalriada, a transnational cross-channel territory that encompassed what is now County Antrim in Ulster and Argyll to Lochaber in Scotland. His Preface also plays into the recent, almost 50-year cultural war that had occurred between scholars over the legitimacy of James Macpherson's Ossianic "fragments," mentioned above, and the subsequent Irish and Scottish debate over the "ownership" of the Ossianic mythological and literary tradition. Huddleston followed both the Thomson circle's practice of writing partly in dense Ulster Scots, and of publishing the volumes by subscription, a method by which community members and fellow poets could publicly pledge their willingness to purchase the volume upon its release. This method, favored by working class poets in 1790s Belfast's atmosphere of democratic potential, was evidently much less successful in nineteenth-century Belfast, as noted by the weaver and poet Andrew M'Kenzie (1780–1839) who voiced his frustration as a laboring class poet in a growing middle class, mercantile Belfast:

> Belfast is not the place where a man compelled to work for a living will be admitted into the company of those who possess literary attainments. They generally move in a higher sphere of society and would think themselves disgraced by noticing a poor serf though gifted with genius.... When I think on some young men in your own neighbourhood – namely [Jack] Williamson, [Samuel] Walker, Crowe and yourself, I cannot refrain [from] drawing a comparison rather disgraceful to the Northern Athens.[5]

In Huddleston's Victorian Irish context, the topos of affected self-consciousness generally adopted in laboring class poet's prefaces gives way to the confident assertion of Irish cultural superiority. Huddleston evidently did not share Thomson's view that Irishness and Scottishness could be counterpoints in Ulster identity. Instead, he betrays anxiety that northern Irish writing, which reflected the vernacular elements of the Ulster culture, was increasingly mistaken for an affected Scottish dialect. Huddleston presents the Scots as a foreign and distinct nation, echoing the more extreme portrayal of the Scots as barbaric colonizers by his contemporary, the epic poet and religious controversialist William Hamilton Drummond (1778–1865):

> From Albin oft, when darkness veiled the pole,
> Swift o'er the surge the tartaned plunderers stole,
> And Erin's vales with purple torrents ran,
> Beneath the claymores of the murd'rous clan;
> Till Cumhal's son, to Dalriada's coast,
> Led the tall squadrons of the Finnian host,
> Where his bold thought the wondrous plan designed,
> The proud conception of a giant mind,
> To bridge the ocean for the march of war,
> And wheel round Albin's shores his conquering car.
>   (Drummond, *Giant's Causeway* I: 9)

In comparison to the cultural displacement described by Thomson in the hybrid identity "IRISH all without... ev'ry item SCOTCH within," Drummond and Huddleston each present Scotland as a culture to be kept at bay, subdued even, by the Irish. In short, both seek to colonize, or re-colonize, Scottish culture and literary achievement as an Irish export rather than a product of diaspora. Thomson's sensitive appreciation of hybridity would rarely be expressed again until the time of John Hewitt and Seamus Heaney.

One danger inherent in the critical fixation on the Scottish-Irish dimension of Ulster poetry is that it has tended to overshadow, even obscure, many other influences, not least the laboring class links between weaver poets of Ulster and their contemporaries across the British Isles and in Revolutionary America. It is beyond the scope of this article to discuss the connections between Ulster poets and Revolutionary America; indeed, a detailed work on the subject is in progress, but I shall discuss one poem that points to the conception of America as a pantisocratic haven amid an Irish industrial and political crisis. As the most widely published poet in the United Irish *Northern Star* newspaper, Samuel Thomson appears to have felt a bardic responsibility to represent the economic interests of his local community of textile weavers. Thomson was an exact contemporary to Renfewshire weaver-poet and naturalist Alexander Wilson (1766–1813), discussed in Gerard Carruthers's chapter. Wilson published a number of controversial attacks on linen owners, such as "The Shark" (1792), and, by further coincidence, both Wilson and Thomson published in newspapers under the pseudonym "Lowrie Nettle" (Orr, *Literary Networks* 100). Thomson's poem "The Bard's Farewell!" (1792) remains one of his best-known, outspoken protest poems against English protectionist legislation and the repression of free speech, urging his compatriots to emigrate to "Columbia," leaving the "vile Ascendancy" "ravagers... the unpeopl'd plain" (*Poems* 49). The poem was significant not only because it was adopted as anti-Ascendancy and anti-English propaganda by the United Irishmen, but also because it advocated a pacifist solution to the Irish question by encouraging proactive emigration, depriving the British state of exploitable Irish labor and colonial income. America, described as "the land of light" (Thomson, *Poems* 49), is afforded a Promised Land status which offers sanctuary to the persecuted Irish Dissenter, described in Rousseauvian terms as "ye *free-born souls* who *feel* and feel *aright*" (49). To traverse the Atlantic, then, severs Rousseau's social "chains," freeing the individual from his contractarian obligation to serve the state. Instead, the bard calls the people to follow a unifying divine will which solidifies them within a contractarian *religious* identity beyond national boundaries, enabling them to flourish across the Atlantic where "far-extending, boundless prospects lie / [and] sweet peace and liberty await us there" (49). By warning the population not to linger where they are "in voluntary fetters," they are exhorted to recognize their universal right to freedom and to rid themselves of oppression. Thomson's "voluntary fetters" suggest that Ireland's freedom will not be won by physical struggle, but by a process of emancipation from mental slavery, drawing on Rousseau's suggestion that "man is born free; and everywhere he is in chains" (430). The language is immediately recognizable alongside other Rousseauvian poems of the revolutionary period, such as William Blake's "London," a poem published two years later in which "mind-forg'd manacles" symbolize the people's indoctrination by the social and religious hierarchy. Likewise, the soaring rhetoric of the poem seems to foreshadow Percy Shelley's *pièce de résistance* of radical pacifism *The Mask of Anarchy* (1819) – "Rise like lions after slumber / In unvanquishable number! / Shake your chains to earth like dew / Ye are many, they are few!" (151–4). It is significant, then, that the poetry Thomson wrote in the traumatic aftermath of the Irish Rebellion which rejected political action anticipates the visionary genre so beloved by Blake and Shelley.

Thomson's suggestion of proactive emigration, in tandem with his faith in a transnational community based on Enlightenment and contractarian Presbyterian values, could be seen as political retreat from the Irish national cause. Alternatively, the poem can be read as offering a practical, transnational political solution which, when enacted, will eventually occasion "songs of freedom" which will "cheer [his] native Isle" (l. 56) and will enable a return to the homeland. Certainly the dissenting religious diction echoes the millenarian exodus imagery found in visionary poems of fellow Dissenters such as Anna Letitia Barbauld's *Eighteen Hundred and Eleven, A Poem*. For Thomson's bard, this is a half-hearted *peregrination*; the bard refuses to relinquish the hope of return to a much-loved nation. The speaker's struggle is clear; while Thomson's poem retains the hope that Ireland's hills will once again be "wreath'd in Shamrock" (49), an unmistakable United Irish image, nationalism must be aligned with the principles of religious freedom enjoyed in a New World. It is a spirit of the people, a *volkgeist*, then, and not the specific geographical space, that creates community.

Weaving Community in Migrant Circles: Robert Anderson, the Cumberland Bard

Although exacerbated by the preponderant national question, difficult economic circumstances, and exploitative practices facing Ireland linked laboring circles such as Thomson's to other radical groups of Dissenting poets in Scotland and northwest England. The connection between Ulster radical artisan movements and Lancashire cotton weavers, Yorkshire croppers, and Nottingham framework knitters was identified by one of the earliest critics of John Hewitt's *Rhyming Weavers* (1974), the anthology which first returned Thomson *et al* to prominence. The correspondent drew a comparison between the Ulster "rhyming weavers" and their dialect-speaking counterparts in northwest England, whose nonconformist education "gave rise to a fine [political] radicalism, deepened by the economic hardness of their lives" (Ronald M[?] to John Hewitt, 28 November 1950, quoted in Orr, *Literary Networks* 100). The "Cumberland balladeer" Robert Anderson (1770–1830), a calico weaver from Carlisle who settled for a time in Carnmoney, near Belfast, was the most prominent connection between the Thomson circle and the North West England weaving trade. The literary and linguistic interchange between northern dialects, particularly those of Lowland Scotland and the north of England, created an affinity among northern English poets with Burns's Scots language, the longevity of which is evidenced by several nineteenth- and twentieth-century song collections which published Anderson's lyrics alongside those of Scottish and Irish contemporaries. W. Stewart of Grainger Street, Newcastle upon Tyne, published a joint edition of *Burns' Songs and Anderson's Cumberland Ballads* (*c.* 1838–40), while Anthony Soulby of Penrith collected songs by Charles Dibdin, Robert Burns, Thomas Campbell, Robert Anderson, and Robert Southey for *The Harmonist; or, Musical Olio, A choice Selection of new and much-approved songs; Also, several Cumberland Ballads, By Mr Anderson* (*c.* 1803–*c.* 1811). Ironically, the content of the songs chosen suggests that Soulby's criterion for a "much-approved" collection appeared to be strong conservative, or anti-Napoleonic, sentiment.

Anderson, an aspiring poet and immigrant within the textile community of County Antrim, was a subscriber to Thomson's *Poems on Different Subjects* (1793), and shared with Thomson in the contemporary fascination with Burns's regional expression and ability to capture human emotion. In fact, Fiona Stafford's conclusion that Burns was a key literary inspiration for writers living outside the wealthy urban centers ("Scottish Poetry" 359) follows her examination of Anderson's "Epistle to Burns" (1796) and his subsequent pilgrimage to the recently deceased poet's tomb. The Burns pilgrimage was an experience that Anderson shared with other poets, not least Thomson and United Irish poet Luke Mullan, and like his Ulster contemporaries, Anderson's fame as a poet is strongly tied to the ethnographic interest of his readership. Like Wordsworth, Anderson introduced Cumbrian dialect words into his poetry, supplying his readers with a series of helpful notes, particularly to benefit regional readerships outside of England. His fellow Cumbrian predecessor Susanna Blamire (1747–1794), a poet featured prominently in Johnson's *Scots Musical Museum* (1787–1803), had incorporated both Scots and Cumbrian vocabulary into her verses and her poetry, like Anderson's, featured on several occasions in the Belfast newspapers between 1800 and 1812, testifying to the Ulster readership's wider interest in dialect poetry beyond Lowland Scots.

With the exception of the transatlantic radical James Orr, Anderson is arguably the most transnational laboring class figure of the Thomson circle, having spent time in London and Scotland before eventually settling in Carnmoney, County Antrim. His entry into the Thomson circle in the first decade of the nineteenth century had far-reaching consequences for the circle's position in British Romanticism. By the time he published in the Belfast press in 1807, Anderson had already enjoyed a literary reputation in his native England as author of *Poems on Various Subjects* (1798), a collection of poems in English, Scots, and Cumbrian; and *Ballads in the Cumberland Dialect* (published in Carlisle in 1805), the publication that propelled him to fame as the "Cumberland Balladeer." The latter publication was reprinted a number of times, including in the form of the two-volume *Poetical Works* (1820), which included an autobiography and numbered William Wordsworth and Robert Southey among its subscribers. Anderson's role within the Thomson circle helped to define the movement as a working class coterie. The single letter that survives from Anderson of 1812 refers to Samuel Thomson "toiling at the 'Loom of Posey'" (Orr, *Correspondence* 184), strikingly foreshadowing John Hewitt's grouping of the Ulster vernacular poets as the "rhyming weavers."

Anderson's collected poems of 1820 share some of the characteristics of his laboring class predecessors in the Thomson circle, demonstrating the typical modesty topos expected of the laboring class poet, in addition to the assertion of a popular mandate behind the republishing of his works:

> I have not the vanity to imagine the contents will amuse an enlightened reader; yet, should a few feel gratified on perusing the effusions of an unlettered Author, it will be a simple, but sufficient proof, that his time hath not been altogether misspent.... Never was it my intention to publish the work about to be offered to the public; but such was the wish of my numerous friends, merely to serve an Author, whose highest ambition has been to paint the simple scenery of nature, and describe truly the manners and customs of his native country. To the will of such, my pride shall ever be to bow with chearfulness. (Anderson, "Dedication" x)

The circumstances of Anderson's 1820 edition offer insight into the changes undergone by laboring class print culture since the confident, radical days of 1790s Belfast. In contrast to the self-authored prefaces of earlier poets such as Orr and Thomson, an "Address to the Reader" was added by editor Thomas Sanderson. Sanderson was eager to emphasize Anderson's own admission that the edition was produced solely by the subscription of the "friends" in order to "save from distress, a poor Bard, now in the decline of life" (Anderson, "Dedication" v). Furthermore, Sanderson claimed that his contact with Anderson originated purely in order to provide detail about the nature of the Cumberland peasantry and biographical details of the poet himself, demonstrating an overarching ethnographic market that governed the reprinting of Anderson's poetry. The lengthy prefatory biography, penned by the poet himself, offered a retrospective account of the poet's formative moments in the Cumberland region, further emphasizing Sanderson's role as editor, particularly his addition of the extensive "Notes to the Cumberland Ballads," which reinterpreted Anderson's ballads as genuine artifacts of Cumberland folk culture. Later editions of Anderson's work, such as the 1933 Centenary volume, which emphasized his Cumberland regional credentials, would completely efface the importance of Anderson's experiences in both London and Ireland. Here, his verses were chiefly celebrated for preserving the nostalgic state of the Cumberland countryside in the early nineteenth century:

> We watch his efforts to make up for his defective education, and his eager pursuit of that real knowledge of his country and people that was to stand him in better stead than any learning acquired from books.... Thanks to Anderson we see once more the life of a Cumbrian village . . . [and] the whole life of the Cumbrian peasant[.] (Anderson, *Centenary* 5)

Needless to say, Brown's assertion of Anderson's bardic relationship to his native Cumberland serves to completely obscure his early career in Ulster, the details of which are passed over with a simple reference to "Ireland . . . where he became addicted to intemperance" (Anderson, *Centenary* 10). It was perhaps against a growing sense of this "folk" reception that James Orr expressed to Samuel Thomson that he "wish[ed] 'B[ally]carry Fair,' in particular, had never been written" (Orr, *Correspondence* 155), as the song was frequently cited as a means to locate him, and his Ulster contemporaries, within an imitative tradition of Burnsian folk revelry.

Indeed, Anderson's London years detail the poet's formative clashes with a contemporary metropolitan fashion for Celtic song and poetry, which he describes as "a mock pastoral Scottish style":

> We felt equally disgusted with many of the songs . . . and supposing myself capable of producing what might by the public be considered equal, or perhaps, on the following day I wrote four, viz. 'Lucy Gray of Allendale,' 'I Sigh for the Girl I adore,' 'The lovely brown Maid' and 'Ellen and I.' 'Lucy Gray' was my first attempt at poetical composition; and was suggested by

> hearing a Northumbrian rustic relate the story of the unfortunate lovers. She was the toast of the neighbourhood; and to use the simple language of my Northumbrian friend, 'Monie a smart canny lad wad hae gane far efter dark, aye through fire and water, just to get a luik at her.' ... These songs I offered to my friend, Mr Hook, a composer of celebrity. They were set to music by him; and my first poetic effusion was sung by Master Phelps, at Vauxhall, in 1794. (Anderson, "Dedication" xxv)

Anderson obviously regarded his London years as the high point of his career, where he was given the opportunity to mix with members of the opposite sex and enjoy the arts but, crucially, he frames his metropolitan experience as the catalyst to his appreciation of "the manners of the Cumbrian peasantry" which "was now greater than ever" (xxviii). This is closely followed with thanks to the poet's "respectable and learned friend, Mr. THOMAS SANDERSON [who] encouraged me to other attempts in the same species of poetry" (xxviii). Though Sanderson's editorial concern with local culture might appear to offset the poet's artistic agency, Anderson's sense of his own exceptionality is clear within his memoir; his account of formative childhood experiences echo Wordsworth's *Prelude*, emphasizing the artistic value of childhood play during "Summer excursions, [where] an attachment to rural scenery first stole over my youthful mind" (xv). At other times, he reflected on his experiences of laboring class education and socialization, refracted through a sense of his own exceptionalism: "Oft did I get the halfpenny to spend, that could ill be spent, besides experiencing indulgences unknown to my brothers and sisters" (xiii). While weighing up the moral rectitude of parental favoritism, Anderson applied his personal experience to a wider social question: whether the encouraging behavior of his parents toward his education, which stimulated him to aspire to greater pursuits, contrasts favorably with the "harsh treatment... [which] drive[s] many to wretchedness, prostitution and the gallows" (xiv). Notably his education at a Charity School which was supported by the Dean of Carlisle, culminated in his praise for "encouragers... who place the offspring of the labouring-classes in the true road to knowledge and to happiness in a future state!" (xiv). Thus, Anderson concludes, parental indulgence of individual talent is the microcosmic expression of public, regional philanthropic beneficence.

These implicit political leanings strengthen toward the end of the Preface where Anderson dwells heavily on his financial losses as a result of the subscription process, supposedly a "democratic" means of allowing working class poets to publish without an advance. His narrative presents this as the experience that necessitated his relocation to Ireland in 1796, but not before his famous pilgrimage to the tomb of Robert Burns, which afforded him the opportunity to lament Burns's supposed neglect at the hands of critics. According to Anderson's narrative, this fraternal empathy from beyond the grave inspired him to write two new songs which were published "immediately on... arrival in Belfast" (xxx) as if the seemingly ghostly inspiration experienced at the tomb of Burns effectively enabled Anderson's admission into Ulster's literary circles. Again, Anderson is at pains to stress his exceptionality: while he "enjoy[ed] the society of some literary characters" (xxxi), he also endured "too many pretenders to merit" (xxxi), an accusation later leveled by Ulster poet Andrew M'Kenzie at the privileged poets of Thomas Percy's salon, jockeying for the Bishop's attention and patronage:

> Some to the top with straining step ascend,
> Frowning defiance on their peers below;
> Some deftly round the spiral pathway wend,
> Jostling and gibing onward as they go,
> Striving by turns each other down to throw,
> And glorying at the hapless struggler's fall,
> Who rolling headlong to the nether moat,
> Vents on the laughing victor words of gall,
> And vows revenge – for lo! His fine new coat
> Is so defiled with dirt, at home he dares not shew't.
> ("The Mount of Dromore," *Belfast News Letter*
> 8 November 1814)

M'Kenzie's dissatisfaction reflects the fact that few of Ulster's Romantic working class poets made a reliable profit from the subscription process, with the exception of James Orr who described his satisfaction to Samuel Thomson in a letter of 1804: "In reply to your question [of] how I succeeded with my publication – you have read the subscription list, and the printers were not immoderate in their demands" (Orr, *Correspondence* 155). Although Thomson's volume of 1799 had been successful, the assistance provided by local gentleman Samuel Thompson of Muckamore acting as a literary agent for him in London (Orr, *Correspondence* 138) had proved disappointing, and he continued to experience frustration at the hands of correspondents who failed to meet their promise to distribute his 1806 volume (Orr, *Correspondence* 181). And so the trajectory traceable from Thomson's prefaces of the 1790s to Anderson's Preface of 1820 is one of growing necessity of middle and upper class patronage and decline of influence of the working class coterie generally.

The mutual dependence of the laboring class poet and local community was highlighted too by Anderson who placed great emphasis on the social impact of his poetry, but highlights equally the risks of collecting subscriptions:

> Duty soon led me to share my income, with the wretched and helpless.... Subscriptions were liberally attended to at the print works, whenever they were deemed necessary; not only for the wretched families employed there, but for the helpless throughout the neighbourhood.... Notwithstanding my continual anxiety to serve my brethren in a strange country, I frequently experienced the most base acts of ingratitude; even my life, indeed, has been threatened by those whom I never offended! (Anderson, "Dedication" xxxii).

The subtext of Anderson's complaint strongly suggests that he met with hostility on account of his Englishness, offering evidence of the difficulty that transnational poets encountered when operating in a highly localized print market, affected by economic, and perceived colonial, injustices. While his transnational experiences in London and Cumbria offered Anderson a sense of superiority over his lesser-traveled contemporaries, it also had the potential to place him at odds with his subscribers.

Ulster as Transnational Space: Toward a Culture of Fluidity and Inclusiveness

Anderson's candid personal account, with its absence of a nostalgic view of laboring class print culture, cautions us against the approximation of individual laboring class poets to mechanical elements within cohesive national movements. The tendency of postindustrial critics to group laboring class poets together under the broad category of "northern," focusing on the vernacular and folk culture elements, may account in part for the double blow suffered by Ulster working class literature in the literary canon. The literary importance of poets such as Anderson, Orr and Thomson was often weighed in terms of their role in preserving a dying rural culture and, in the case of the Thomson circle, a defeated, Dissenting Protestant, form of Irish republicanism. For some, their decision to write some of their poetry in the vernacular, a mark of class, occasioned a deeper political problem; Ulster Scots, being associated by some with the cultural invention of a colonial, and predominantly Unionist, Scottish planter tradition, a "slavish...imitat[ion] [of] Burns" (O'Donoghue 20–22). The legitimacy of Ulster Scots within a broader working class Irish culture, though suggested in the poetry of John Hewitt, was not popularly promoted until the later writings of Seamus Heaney. Yet, from the examination of nineteenth-century laboring class prefaces of the Thomson circle, such cultural and class tensions are evident early in the poets' conception of themselves as a tradition or, at the least, a multigenerational circle.

In short, in order to fully appreciate Ireland's poetic traditions, it is necessary to think beyond the interlinked, sectarian concepts of class and "the nation." Though by no means a perfect classification, studies of laboring class poetry have recognized Ulster's poets' important literary role beyond the national paradigm, acknowledging their contribution to a longer tradition of working class literature. Ulster's cultural hybridity has more often been understood as an experience of middle class University students who, like their English Romantic contemporaries, felt connected to an "eighteenth-century [Enlightenment] ideological community," which comprised "a common ground of ideas and assumptions, firmly anchored in religion, culture and politics" (McFarland 1). Yet, although Ulster Romantic poetry was formed from this sense of shared "ideological community" with Scotland, it was also solidified in the firsthand experiences of economic and political migrants, particularly laboring class poets such as Anderson and Orr. Such writers, whose minority confessional and linguistic identities resulted in their being penalized or patronized by literary hierarchies, have much to teach us about Romantic-era Irish writing. If nothing else, their survival stands against the reductive categorization of Irish writers into "planter" and "native," within a canon which has been constructed largely on the back of an essentialist national paradigm. Attention to the transnational aspects of laboring class writing might, therefore, offer a particularly helpful theoretical framework, a "third way" even, by which to assess Irish literature of the Romantic period. Laboring class poets' prerogative to fashion themselves and to choose their own identity allowed Irish Romantic poets to cross physical, cultural, and ideological boundaries in a manner which, in a post-Agreement era, seems ahead of its time.

NOTES

1. For a full account, see J. R. R. Adams, *The Printed Word and the Common Man: Popular Culture in Ulster 1700–1900* (Belfast: The Queen's University of Belfast, 1987).
2. See Carol Baraniuk, "'things tragic and bitter': Samuel Ferguson, *Congal* and the northern Romantic tradition" in *Forging the Anchor: Samuel Ferguson and His Legacy*, ed. Frank Ferguson and Jan Jedrzejewski (Dublin: Four Courts, forthcoming).

3. Jennifer Orr, *Literary Networks and Dissenting Print Culture* (Basingstoke: Palgrave Macmillan, 2015); C. Baraniuk, *James Orr, Poet and Irish Radical* (London: Pickering and Chatto, 2014); F. Ferguson and A. Holmes, eds., *Revising Robert Burns and Ulster: Literature, Religion and Politics c. 1770–1920* (Dublin: Four Courts, 2009), F. Ferguson and J. McConnel, *Ireland and Scotland in the Nineteenth Century* (Dublin: Four Courts, 2009); Tim Burke, "'Yet tho' I'm Irish all without, I'm ev'ry item Scotch within': Poetry and Self-fashioning in 1790s Ulster," *John Clare Society Journal* 22 (2003), 35–49.
4. Jennifer Orr, "Constructing the Ulster Labouring-class Poet," in *Class and the Canon*, eds. Kirstie Blair and Mina Gorji, (Basingstoke: Palgrave 2012), 34–54. See also Chapter 2 of *Literary Networks*.
5. Andrew M'Kenzie to J. R. Semple, Moilena Turnpike, Antrim, 9 July 1832, transcript kept in John Hewitt papers, 16–17, University of Ulster, MS D 3838/3/18/Acc/7015, f. 19).

CHAPTER 10

Working Class Poetry and the Royal Literary Fund
Two Case Studies in Patronage

Scott McEathron

Founded in 1788 by the Reverend David Williams, the Literary Fund Society (later, the Royal Literary Fund) was an institutional experiment in the sponsorship of underprivileged writers, making moderate, lump-sum gifts to authors perceived as morally upstanding and in true financial need. The Fund aided writers from a variety of socioeconomic backgrounds, soliciting contributions at an annual Subscribers' Dinner and, in some cases, giving multiple grants to individual writers or their survivors over a period of years. Its basic administrative workings and putative mission – to "support deserving Authors in Sickness, Distress, Old Age, and at the Termination of life; and to give temporary relief to the Widows and Orphans of those who have any claims to the Publick from having written any useful book" (Cross, *Catalogue* 5) – stayed the same for several decades. Yet the detailed records maintained in the Fund's Archives reveal that, in practice, it was constantly struggling with basic definitional questions regarding good-faith processes of charity: what did it mean to earn, or to deserve, money for literary work? The Literary Fund was a patron neither in the ancient sense of offering lifetime annuities nor in the modern, grant-giving sense of backing a specific project. Its compromises suggest that the Fund was an institution typical of the historical moment – existing somewhere between familial and welfare-state models of giving, and closer to an alms-giving than an investment enterprise.

In his defensive early history of the Fund, *Claims of Literature* (1802), Williams sought to explicate several of the basic terms – Genius, Learning, Philosophy, Utility – that lay behind the Fund's formation and subsequent operation. Refuting criticisms that the Fund had been chartered as an implicit rebuke to governmental neglect of the arts, and that its mode of philanthropy – small awards recognizing past achievement, rather than substantial grants enabling future production – was ineffectual, Williams argues that the Fund was meant to promote the broad-based national good that only literature could provide. To tie this civic ideal too tightly to social utility, commercial viability, or even work ethic was to risk conflicts of interest associated with old-style, self-serving patronage, a mode of support Williams calls "despotic sovereignty over an abject dependent" (*Claims* 85). Instead, he sees the Fund's subsistence-level giving as working disinterestedly in the service of "genius," which, in "free governments... takes the lead, and always forms the spirit of the nation" (33). While many of Williams's observations have been read as rejections of Adam Smith's ideas in *Wealth of Nations*,[1] his most heated rhetoric is reserved for writers engaged in gossip or partisan warfare: "Calumnies, commanded by political factions, and expressions of esteem, inspired by fear and venality, are the dregs of literature," he writes, and "tend, of their own accord, to the filthy gulph of everlasting oblivion" (50). Such vehemence suggests a private history of hurt feelings on Williams's part, but he is also thinking of disenfranchised writers, including past Fund recipients, as especially vulnerable to co-optation "by factions as advocates" or "by jobbers as amusing literary gladiators" (70). So while proclaiming the bedrock cultural necessity of "THE LIBERTY OF THE PRESS," he argues that a private foundation can best justify its existence alongside public benefactors (the Church, charity schools, and universities) by declining to support the "endless tribe" of writers, "swarming like locusts" (40), who have a history of aggressive partisanship – or even, he implies, of political satire (51).

One lengthy strain of argumentation in *Claims of Literature* had especially important implications for working class writers. Williams was anxious to dispel the belief that Fund grants were "increasing the number and misery of authors, by holding out encouragement to the choice of Literary Employments" (8). In dismissing this notion, Williams emphasizes that the Fund provides emergency charity, not the temptation of salaried literary work, and argues laboriously that "the evils of literature generally spring from negligence and injustice towards men of letters" (55). Thus re-routing the charge of false hope into a broader account of authorial debasement, he does later admit to worries over the increasing numbers of claimants on the Fund, a development he blames on "the enervating Influence" of the country's educational system, through which the "the sons and daughters of farmers and Tradesmen... by the perusal of tales for children, and the adventures of imaginary heroes and heroines, acquire a taste for romances" (97). Judging from other documents, this last point may have been a sop from Williams to the more conservative members of the Fund Committee,[2] but its public rehearsal was nonetheless a concern for those working class authors whose applications were going to be judged partly on the realism of their professional expectations. For while the Literary Fund's emphasis on humane charity was meant to simplify the system of giving, in actual practice it would spend several decades trying to thread a tiny needle, acknowledging writers for past work without implicitly promising payment for future work. Indeed, though dedicated to the cultural value of Literature, trustees shunned any annuitizing investment model for its practical continuance. Further, Williams's fear of the Borgia-like control that he saw as latent in patronage relationships meant that – in theory – the Fund's gifts were to be understood by the grantees neither as public endorsements nor as private literary directives.

These paradoxes were necessarily obtrusive for working class writers, many of whom applied to the Fund over the years, including the poets John Clare, James Hogg, and John Nicholson, as well as the survivors of Robert Burns, Joseph Blacket, James Bird, and others. This chapter is concerned with this group of applicants, examining the ways in which their "claims" – on the Committee, and on Literature in the abstract – illuminate tensions in literary culture that surrounded the category of working class writing in the early nineteenth century. In doing so, it draws on correspondence held in the Fund archives, with a specific focus on the cases of Robert Bloomfield, author of the popular poem *The Farmer's Boy* (1800), and the lesser-known Robert Millhouse (1788–1839), a writer of sonnets and religiously inflected philosophical verse. These two cases were very different in character, with Bloomfield representing a sort of ideal transaction from the perspective of the Fund and Millhouse exposing the numerous stress points that underlay its seemingly unobjectionable mission. It is important to remember that, although one might assume that imaginative writers were the Literary Fund's main focus, its purposefully capacious definition of Literature encompassed "any useful book." And, not only did the Fund receive applications from writers in diverse fields – engineers, historians, archeologists, inventors, theologians, cosmologists and self-proclaimed sooth-sayers – it often seemed skeptical of writers of imaginative literature, possibly because the majority of committee members were "reputable writers of non-fiction" (Cross, *Common* 36). Poets were perhaps not viewed as doubtfully as novelists, that entire genre still seeming, to many, an embodiment of feminized bad taste and nonutility.[3] Even so, it is no surprise, given the context I have outlined above, that the Fund showed particular discomfort with those working class poets who embodied what Brian Maidment has called the "Parnassian" impulse: the desire to "step beyond the cultural constraints of working-class life into a more ambitious, even universal and trans-historical, poetic discourse" (*Poorhouse* 97). To judge from correspondence held in the Literary Fund's archives, few applicants voiced this Parnassian desire more irksomely than did Millhouse, a Nottingham weaver. Millhouse's frankly expressed intellectual ambitions – and his rumored reluctance to "perform the slightest office that he considered menial or degrading to a man of talent" ("Biography" 268) – focused the Fund's discomfort with a model of exchange or paid labor. His correspondence shows, in direct terms, that both applicant and donor parties had strong opinions about the extent to which literary production should be deemed legitimate "work."

I begin, however, with the less contentious case of Robert Bloomfield (1766–1823), which in many ways typifies what the Literary Fund stood for and how it was meant to operate. In 1818, when the Fund was first approached on his behalf, Bloomfield was 54 years old and in declining health. Though he had published several volumes of poetry since the turn of the century, Bloomfield's literary fame still rested upon his first work, *The Farmer's Boy* (1800), a 1,500-line verse narrative of rural life in Suffolk. *The Farmer's Boy* had sold extraordinarily, indeed historically well, and had been through thirteen editions by 1815, but several factors, including unfavorable contractual arrangements with publishers and a slew of family travails, had rendered Bloomfield nearly destitute.[4] He was presented to the Committee by an outside advocate as "in circumstances of the greatest embarrassment, having lost the sight of one eye.... [He is] so much affected, that he can neither see to read nor write, from which most unfortunate event he is rendered totally unable to support himself & family."[5] This rhetoric targeted the Fund's established tendency to view writers first as familial providers, second as producers of a saleable commodity.

Regardless of any literary aspirations Bloomfield might still have entertained, funds were vital for basic sustenance, and the Committee promptly made him a £40 grant.[6] And, when his case reappeared four years later, they again acted quickly, with Fund vice-president W. T. Fitzgerald suggesting a special meeting during the annual summer recess as "certainly we have seldom stronger claims upon The Fund than what Bloomfield may make" (1/382/5; 26 May 1822).[7] Bloomfield's "strong" claims were of a nature the Committee was willing to corroborate virtually in-house, as, in both instances, it effectively solicited its own ranks for letters of sponsorship. In 1818, the interlocutors were Anne and Walter Pye – the sister and brother of Henry James Pye, a former member of the Committee best remembered by literary history as a painfully mechanical Poet Laureate ridiculed by Byron.[8] In 1822, the correspondence similarly traced a triangle of insiders, running from Sir William Pepys, another Vice-President of the Fund, to Fitzgerald, to Richard Yates, the Fund's Treasurer from 1804–34.[9]

In citing these elements, I mean less to imply a culture of cronyism (though these charges surfaced at several points in the Fund's history) than to indicate the striking degree of goodwill that the Committee demonstrated toward Bloomfield – a goodwill which would be extended to his widow, who received a £30 grant after his death in 1823. Politics, both internal and external, worked in Bloomfield's favor. Although the Fund's roots had been firmly in the Dissenting tradition, by the middle 1810s it began being criticized for being too lordly in the way it gathered and dispersed its capital. Administrative costs were high, the Annual Subscribers' Dinner was seen as embarrassingly self-regarding, and there was a view, most aggressively voiced by Robert Southey, that the Fund practiced a faux liberality that was "as useless to the cause of literature as it is pitiful itself":

> The Literary Fund provides no present employment for the hungry and willing labourer, and holds out no hope for the future; a first donation operates against a second claim; a second or third becomes a bar to any further bounty, and the teamed mendicant who leans upon the broken reed is abandoned by it in prison, or turned over to the parish or the hospital at last. (Southey, "Disraeli's" 113)

The evidence suggests that the Fund was not especially responsive to such reproaches: it was not until four decades later that they were forced seriously to confront a challenge to their practices when Charles Dickens staged a failed internal revolt intended to force an expansion of the Fund's services to writers. (I discuss this incident further below.) But trustees in 1818 were well aware of the criticism that the Fund tended to "humiliat[e] ... the receiver" (Southey, "Disraeli's" 113), while providing little actual support. The poet Bloomfield – fondly remembered by the reading public but now manifestly suffering – presented them an easy opportunity to act.

It cannot have hurt Bloomfield's cause that he was viewed as politically uncontroversial, a situation owing partly to his career-long commitment to being publically "nutral in Politicks and Religion" (29 May 1804; *LRBC* Letter 129). Bloomfield's personal politics were, in fact, a complex blend of patriotism, radical sentiment, piety, and working class advocacy, with recent critics sifting the balance of these various impulses in markedly different ways.[10] But *The Farmer's Boy* itself, a poem which was essentially contiguous in the public imagination with the person of Bloomfield, was mostly read as a hearth-and-home celebration of English country life, despite references to social isolation, animal cruelty, and creeping luxurianism.[11] The Committee members prominently involved in the Bloomfield petitions – Pye, the clergyman Yates, and Fitzgerald, whose own politicized verses positioned him "a Homer to the House of Hanover" (Cross, *Common* 17) – were on the Tory side of the Committee's internal ledger, and, thus, a superficial reading of this situation would suggest that the Fund could readily support writers who, like Bloomfield, were politically safe.[12] There is plainly some truth to this. But putting it more broadly, we should see the Bloomfield case as one that did not force any kind of soul-searching about the more complicated theoretical questions that the Committee tended implicitly to be engaged with, even when they would have preferred not to be. Bloomfield was in immediate need, he was broadly respected as a writer, and he was declining. The grants were, in essence, valedictions.

Robert Millhouse, born the same year as the Fund and first brought to its attention in 1822, the year of its second grant to Bloomfield, kept these theoretical questions disturbingly alive for Committee members. If Bloomfield is useful as a brief opening example because he was so centrally in the Fund's wheelhouse, I would argue that Millhouse's quite different case, spooling out through much contentious correspondence over the last 20 years of his life, actually reveals more about the Fund's goals and policies. His Fund file, a cache of materials which represents his only known manuscript material, shows Committee members growing dismayed over a period of decades by Millhouse's continued penury and failure to improve his family's lot, despite the Fund's repeated gifts and despite help from patrons in securing him regular work as a bank clerk. Contra both Southey's sarcastic formula and David Williams's abhorrence of patronage relationships, each "one-time" grant seemed to draw Millhouse and the Committee further into a shared narrative of obligation, whereby the gifts carried expectation (on both sides) of future improved performance.

One of ten children, Millhouse was, by the age of ten, put to work at "that starving business, weaver of stockings" (quoted in Wylie 162). Formally educated only in Sunday school, in 1810 he joined the Nottinghamshire Militia, later called the Royal Sherwood Foresters, in which he eventually rose to the rank of corporal. When his regiment was temporarily disbanded, he returned to the stocking-frame, and, after marrying in 1818, began, according to his brother, "seriously to consider his future prospects in life; and perceiv[ed] that he had no other chance of bettering his position than by a publication" (Millhouse, *Blossoms* 17). Millhouse's first volume of poetry, *Vicissitude*, appeared in 1821 and was followed by further volumes in 1823, 1826, 1827, 1832, and 1836. There is some ambition to the poetry – the final two volumes, *The Destinies of Man*, parts 1 and 2, are presented as quasi-continuations of Milton's epics – but Millhouse was not especially prolific: all of the volumes are fairly slender, and the first four contain some significant overlaps in material. Millhouse was enterprising enough in generating and, occasionally, re-packaging literary ideas; the problem was that he became caught in a cycle of ill health and debility, and kept believing that he had more to gain from the gamble of producing a book – for always, in this, he enjoyed one or more patrons' support – than from the piecework he could manage physically, and alone, as a weaver. At his artistic best, he was a trenchant writer of sonnets, and I will reference several of these in what follows.

Millhouse viewed poetry as a vehicle for the promulgation of proper religious belief, noting in his sonnet "The Bard" that the poet is blest "if he teach (on Truth's eternal plan) / That Virtue only dignifies the Man" (ll. 13–14).[13] His early patron the Reverend Luke Booker, Vicar of Dudley, described him as "friendly to the Religion and Laws of the country" (*Blossoms* 21). Even so, one of the most striking aspects of Millhouse's verse is the tension between a proud, dignified orthodoxy and an angry populism. While his poems urge obedience and rectitude within the hierarchy of God's creation, they also feature regular complaints regarding social hierarchies, with Millhouse railing against greed, snobbery, and the false distinctions that wealth creates. Running through the disparate topics addressed by the poems "Antiquity," "The Herb Chickweed," "A Bird Affrighted by the Author," and "A Debilitated and Sickly Son" are repeated references to the binaries of wealth and poverty, status and true worth. In the sonnet "The Insolent in Office," he writes,

> I despise the slave
> Who could with fawning look, and pliant knee,
> Cringe to the state-proud shackle-binding knave,
> Because, forsooth, he holds the glittering fee:
> As if an honest man, of meanest birth,
> Did not outvie the greatest knave on earth!
>
> (ll. 9–14)

Though the sobriquet attached to Millhouse – "The Burns of Sherwood Forest" – was in many ways inapt, these lines do strongly recall Burns's polemical rallying-cry, "A Man's A Man For A' That." Similarly, in "The Proud Man's Contumely," which, like "The Insolent in Office," takes its title from a phrase in *Hamlet*'s "To be or not to be" soliloquy, Millhouse seethes at the arrogance of a rich toff:

> Imperious Mortal! can thy pigmy soul
> Treat thus the poor man for a good design?
> Know, that thy ill-judg'd mandate of control
> Moves but the censure of the Power Divine.
>
> (ll. 1–4)

Money itself is described ambivalently. Gold, in the sonnet of the same name, is called a "thing of Good or Guile" (l. 1), and Millhouse wishes for its power so he can "teach sad poverty to smile" (l. 14). He says this even having opened the poem by calling it a "Fee for the knave, in every age and clime! / Thou shield to gilded Ideots! slave to Kings! / Pander to War and other horrid things" (ll. 1–3). The aggregate message, then, is somewhat unsettled: the poor are honest and worthy – perhaps even, by virtue of their situation, noble. But the notion of contented poverty is, for Millhouse, a poisonous one, especially if voiced by the rich.

Turning this problem inward, he renders poverty as a curse that has been visited upon him, one that the frustratingly poor sales of his poetry are never able to lift. Poverty's repercussions are especially trying for enlightened aspirants like himself, for whom it is "base taunting humbler of the noble mind" ("To Poverty," l. 1). While Millhouse regularly denounces elitism as a rampant social disease, then, he also believes the "varied strain" of his "Harp" (*Blossoms* 23)[14] marks him as distinct, lifting him above what, in the sonnet "To Genius," he calls "the blockhead throng" (l. 5). Similarly, he believes a world that was more truly meritocratic would help the worthy poor, asking rhetorically in "The Proud Man's Contumely": "shall not Poverty the licence have / With Merit and with conscious Truth, to dare / To climb one fathom on this side the grave?" (ll. 10–12). Yet his own worth sometimes seems a more pressing concern. A second poem called "The Lot of Genius" has the speaker attempting "[t]o feel a conscious dignity within" while being "despised amidst a crowd of fools" (ll. 1–2). It is also Genius's lot to

> trust to after-ages to repeal
> A nation's apathy, and critic's ban;
> Ages–which rear base piles to mock the dead,
> And shame the sons whose sires denied them bread
> (ll. 11–14)

"The Lot of Genius" concisely presents Millhouse's view of his own professional situation, and his repeated success in attracting friendly patronage suggests that his self-concept was also convincing to others. The pleadings of advocates appear throughout his Fund file and universally proceed from arguments for his personal rectitude and the moral value of his poetry. Millhouse received his first gift of £20 in 1822, his application endorsed by the Reverend Booker, who would be his primary patron until around 1830.[15] (In the 1830s his sponsors grew to include Thomas Wakefield and the brothers Richard and William Howitt.) This first grant set off a chain reaction that I describe in some detail below, as it reveals the Fund's particular sensitivities regarding the implied meaning of its donations.

Initially, the exchange functioned according to convention. Millhouse responded to the Fund's gift with the letter of thanks that the Committee required, and, whatever his bubbling well of anger about the tyrannies of social status, showed himself a master of the syntax of gratitude:

> I take the earliest opportunity of thus manifesting my most unfeigned and heartfelt Thanks for your most salutary Bounty, which has turned my Despondency into Joy: and if a steady Perseverance in the Paths of Truth and Virtue may be deemed a further Token of my Gratitude, it shall be my study, my Lords and Gentlemen, to prove to your generous and noble Minds, that your valuable Donation has not been bestowed upon one, who is either ungrateful or unworthy. (1/462/2; 12 May 1822)

But gratitude aside, immediately Millhouse and Booker went to work to leverage this gift, conceiving of a volume of old and new poems headed by the new sonnet "To Beneficence" (*Blossoms* 35), a poem explicitly dedicated to the Fund. Booker put out feelers to the Committee as to the propriety of this plan and, apparently not receiving an immediate response, went ahead with the publication. But when later Booker sent the Committee a longer communiqué offering them first dibs on the copies, "by means of which," he said nakedly, "I presume to solicit your additional small bounty," the plan exploded in his face. The Committee was always fiercely protective of the names of applicants, whether or not they received grants, and this attempt to parlay their initial gift into both a public literary endorsement and a further gift represented a serious breach in protocol. In a meeting of December 1822, two resolutions concerning the case were passed, the first demanding that all references to the Literary Fund be removed from Millhouse's volume, since they promoted "a belief that the Society approves of, and patronises the Work" (1/462/7; 11 December 1822). The second operated on a larger scale, setting an official Fund policy that Millhouse had, frustratingly, made necessary:

> Resolved also, that no applications to the individual members of the Committee for subscriptions to works published, or to be published, can make any part of the business to be brought under the consideration of the said Committee. (1/462/7; 11 December 1822)

Individual Committee members were not to be approached regarding subscriptions, nor was the Fund, even tacitly, to be presented as an arbiter of literary value. Unsurprisingly, Booker was defensive, backing and filling in a long, argumentative letter in which he described himself as only spreading the word about the Fund's good work: "I did think that an Institution whose very 'Being, End, and Aim' is avowedly to do Good, – & which I firmly believe really does accomplish all the Good that is practicable with its present Means – must feel an ardent Desire to have those Means increased, that the Sphere of its Beneficence might be enlarged." Finally, and perhaps too fulsomely, Booker apologized: "far be it from me to set up my unimportant & isolated opinion against the united Wisdom of a learned Committee" (1/462/8; 8 January 1823).[16]

The Booker strategy had been both backward- and forward-looking, offering a public thanks for a past gift and then presenting that very commemoration as grounds for a future one: thus the chain of patronage might extend to infinity. But as spectacularly awry as this opening exchange had gone, in the years that followed, Millhouse was, in fact, able to achieve a lesser version of perpetual Fund support. For 12 consecutive years starting in 1824, Millhouse or his patrons made a successful annual appeal to the Fund, his plaintive requests following a regular format: acknowledgment of the committee's past generosity; discussion of the ill health and impoverishment of his ever-growing family; complaints about the difficult economy for stocking-weavers; and citations of favorable recent reviews of his poetry – poetry which, nonetheless, had brought him little or no financial gain. Millhouse, writing in 1828, was certainly aware of the pattern.

> Honourable Gentlemen,
>
> I am again compelled by the chilling and depressing influence of my fortunes to solicit a further repetition of your beneficence. I had hopes at one time that instead of year after year being under the necessity of craving your bounty I should by a continuance of well doing have been enabled at some future period to add to the fountain of that Charity from which I have so often been supplied. That period has not yet arrived, and that it ever will arrive, if I may judge of the future by the past, I have many doubts. For the last four months past I have been without employment owing to the depression of my branch of trade; and how to bear up against the rigours of approaching Winter with a wife and four small children, is petrifying to contemplate, when it is considered that we have already been long in a state of positive starvation. (1/462/26; 6 November 1828)

Millhouse never seemed to have enough cash: "I am growing old, alike, in fame and poverty," he told the Committee in 1833 (1/462/39;

Table 10.1 *Robert Millhouse: Literary Fund Chronology of Grant Applications*

Application Date	Grant Date	Amount	Notes
Unknown	May 1822	£20	
2 December 1822		None	Failed plan for Fund endorsement of new volume
4 May 1824	May 1824	£10	
5 June 1825	June 1825	£10	"I have nothing... except your beneficent Society, to secure myself and family from a Workhouse"
10 August 1826	November 1826	£10	
7 November 1827	November 1827	£5	
6 November 1828	November 1828	£5	
7 November 1829	November 1829	£5	Application by Richard Howitt
26 October 1830	November 1830	£5	
4 November 1831	November 1831	£5	
21 October 1832	November 1832	£5	Application by Wakefield of *Nottingham Mercury*
8 November 1833	November 1833	£5	
7 November 1834	November 1834	£5	
9 November 1835	November 1835	£10	As part of request, Millhouse declares he will enter the "field of prose," provoking Committee ultimatum
20 June 1837	July 1837	£10	Application by William Howitt
23 February 1838	November 1838	£10	Application by Richard Howitt
May 1839	June 1839	£25	Grant to widow after Millhouse's death

13 November). Since the Fund's usual monthly meetings were not convened between late May and mid-October, the timing of requests and gifts was partly a function of the organization's schedule. Table 10.1 lays out the chronology.

Looking at Table 10.1, it is almost painfully easy to reconstruct Millhouse's thinking. Limited to one application per year by the Fund's rules, he makes it in the month he describes in his poem "To November" as "bring[ing] redoubled gloom upon my soul" (l. 2). The Committee, meanwhile, is caught between recognition of Millhouse's need and a reluctance to offer the kind of encouragement, or endorsement, that would be implicit in a larger gift. Their move to the paltry £5 is significant – not quite the smallest gift they ever awarded, but still pointedly low. R. H. Super has described the grant range in the mid-nineteenth century as being from about £10 to a maximum of £100 (316).[17] Nigel Cross, the Fund's archivist, puts the average grant at £16 in 1835, adding that "a persistent applicant or one whose authorship was negligible might receive as little as one or two guineas, while a more distinguished author might get as much as twenty guineas" (Cross, *Common* 20). (Notable here, beyond the numbers, is Cross's sense that "persistence" and "negligibility" were linked in the Fund's mind-set as evidence of applicants' poor comportment.)

Two things, then, stand out about Millhouse's history of support: by the Fund's own standards, the individual gift amounts were small, but the number of individual gifts he received was unusually large. Indeed, having reviewed dozens of Fund files, I can find no other figure from this era who received as many individual gifts.[18] His success can be attributed to the effectiveness of his determined patrons, to the Fund's certainty of his moral standing, and to the centrality of charity as the Fund's core motive. But even as the charitable rationale for supporting Millhouse remained a consistent drumbeat in the various letters concerning him, comments by Fund administrators in the 1830s indicate a growing sense of frustration with the situation – a frustration assuredly fed by the very marks of ambition and self-certainty that are apparent in Millhouse's verse.

The souring of the Committee toward Millhouse is given full voice in archival materials from 1835, the year of the poet's thirteenth petition. Writing on 9 November to Joseph Snow, clerk of the Fund, Millhouse observes that, despite the excellent reviews afforded his latest volume, *The Destinies of Man*, sales have "not mended my condition so much as would enable me to purchase a single dinner" (1/462/42). Then, and before going on to ask for the committee's "further consideration of my necessities," Millhouse dramatically announces that "I have determined to abandon the walks of poetry forever" (1/462/42). For a moment, Committee readers must have caught their breath in relief. Yet Millhouse blunders on with an addendum revealing his total failure to internalize the lessons of the prior fourteen years:

> [I have] already commenced the study of that style of composition (prose) by which alone genius now stands any chance of obtaining remuneration for its labour ... I hope this field of prose, which I am now entering, will render me more independent, and consequently less troublesome to the Society in future. (1/462/42; 9 November 1835)

Knowing by now that Millhouse's dream of ceasing to solicit the Fund "in future" was entirely hollow, the Committee must also have been galled by Millhouse's proposing an alternate investment scheme of just the sort they had tried to avoid – and in terms, no less, implying that his savvy about current market conditions and earnings projections would somehow ingratiate himself with them.

Not only would this tactic do Millhouse no good, it brought to the surface the Committee's ire. Nine days later, Millhouse's patron Thomas Wakefield, then serving as Mayor of Nottingham, wrote to Snow, evidently having received an unhappy message from Snow concerning Millhouse's new intentions.[19] It is clear from Wakefield's long letter that the Committee was about to deliver Millhouse an ultimatum regarding his vocational aspirations: get out of the literary business entirely or forget further support from the Literary Fund. Approving this plan, Wakefield never suggests that the Fund's position is out of line; indeed, he admits having been at a similar pass with Millhouse himself. "I had no idea that Millhouse had so long been a pensioner on the Literary Fund or that he had received to the amount you mention," Wakefield begins. "I also fully agree with you that it is useless for him to expect to maintain himself by poetry and that he must look to something else for a means of living" (1/462/43; 18 November 1835). As Wakefield continues, it emerges that he himself has been offering Millhouse private aid for some time:

> I told him some months since that it was useless following poetry and that I would not assist him any further to that purpose, and he then begged that he might try prose composition... I told him that I should withdraw my assistance unless he was ready to seek other employment[.] (1/462/43; 18 November 1835)

Wakefield describes arranging a job for Millhouse at a Savings Bank – "in consequence he has been learning accounts" – but his feelings of futility are apparent: "[Millhouse] has already been a very heavy expense to me, much more than I ought to have allowed, but I did not like to let Millhouse starve which otherwise he must have done" (1/462/43; 18 November 1835). Perhaps "the kindest plan," Wakefield tells Snow, "would be ... to inform him that he must not expect any further assistance" (1/462/43; 18 November 1835).

Snow's follow-up dictate to Millhouse is lost and its precise terms unknown, but when Millhouse replied a month later he appeared duly chastened: "I assure you I shall ever feel the fullest sense of gratitude for [the Committee's] numerous donations, and I hope Providence will, for the future, enable me to rely more on my own exertions" (1/462/45; 14 December 1835). In actuality, however, the grand ultimatum turned out not quite to be, since two and three years later, after Millhouse had begun at the Bank, the Committee again acceded to applications on his behalf – in the process actually returning to the £10 level. After so much internal angst, their willingness to do so is remarkable, and signals a kind of institutional loyalty that Millhouse had managed to generate – a loyalty that the Literary Fund usually exhibited when they made late-in-life grants to individuals who had been, in flusher days, contributors to the Fund rather than applicants. It was as if Millhouse could neither do fully right nor fully wrong by the Committee; one wonders what would have happened had he lived another ten years and made another ten requests. But by the time of the second of these late gifts in 1838, Millhouse's health was failing badly, and he died in April 1839. A letter written during his decline by his doctor Godfrey Howitt, another Howitt brother, diagnosed his disease as "continued fever – , induced by poverty – and the latter now is I am persuaded the principle hinderance [sic] to his recovery" (1/462/49; 23 February 1838).

The Fund's tortured pattern of giving to Millhouse reveals the Committee as, in some sense, working against its better judgment. Within Wakefield's November 1835 "ultimatum" letter, a closing reference to another Nottingham poet, the basketmaker Thomas Miller (1807–74), suggests a ruefulness that the Fund itself had inadvertently made Millhouse into a special case. Earlier that year Miller had received £15 from the Literary Fund, and Wakefield was determined not to embark on redundant local charity: "Miller was a basket maker here and I would him to continue one, but his dreams of fame and literary success were too sanguine to allow him to continue at his work. [I]f he has become sobered I hope he will do well" (1/462/43; 18 November 1835).[20] Wakefield here seems to conflate Millhouse's story with Miller's, but whoever was uppermost in his mind it is worth noting that his predicative analog of doomed ambition was mistaken: over the next 40 years Miller would write "more prolifically and persistently than any other working-class writer," publishing "about fifty titles" in a wide variety of genres between 1833 and 1874 (Cross, *Common* 134).[21]

Nigel Cross sees Thomas Miller as an almost unique case among working class writers in terms of this versatility across forms, but also as a sadly typical case in terms of his overall career arc; despite decades of publishing, and the intervention of Samuel Rogers, who in 1841 provided him £300 to secure his copyrights. "[Miller's] life illustrates the several themes of working-class authorship: from achieving local celebrity as a poet, through aristocratic patronage and bestsellerdom, to a slow decline as a disappointed hack living on a penny-a-line and charitable hand-outs" (*Common* 134). Respecting Literary Fund support, however, Miller's case was almost as anomalous as Millhouse's: The archives show that he and family "received a total of £415 over 40 years, more than any other applicant of the same period."[22] Miller's 1842 autobiographical novel *Godfrey Malvern* refers to the Fund as "that little Lighthouse on the gloomy sea of Literature" (106); three years later the Fund came to Miller's rescue when "bailiffs stripped him of everything but a bed and chair" (James, "Thomas Miller" *ODNB*).

In Cross's view, the main historical lesson that emerges from the files of Miller and other mid-century writers – perhaps most especially the files of working class writers – is how untenable literature was as a profession in the nineteenth century. And, he notes, while the Fund was a vital stopgap for many writers, it was almost never more than that, especially in the early years: "[t]he author who applied to the Literary Fund... might, if he was very lucky, receive an amount equal to the yearly wages of the poorest members of English society, to which class he clearly belonged" (*Catalogue* 16). Was the Fund more discouraging of working class literary aspirants than they were of middle class literary aspirants? The answer to that is almost certainly yes – but it may well be that this was at least as much a matter of pragmatic skepticism as of social engineering or repression. S. D. Mumm's study of female applicants to the Fund between 1840 and 1880 suggests that 90 percent of them came from middle class backgrounds (3), and the Fund's core bias seems to have been doubt of authorship as a viable professional pathway, regardless of socioeconomic background. Certainly the most famous single incident in the Fund's history – Charles Dickens's failed revolt of 1855–8 – suggests that the Fund rightly or wrongly perceived itself as the advocate of the economically disenfranchised author more than the economically privileged one.

Dickens and his reformist allies, long bothered by the Fund's high administrative overhead and annoyed that the Fund "tended to reduce the bona-fide man of letters to the same level of the begging-letter writer" (Cross, *Common* 32), sought a new Fund charter that would allow the diversion of some of the Fund's considerable reserves to the establishment of a literary club and Institute, offering free lodging to authors. Though the intent of this approach was to make the Fund a more effective tool for literary good, and though David Williams himself had initially envisioned this sort of mission expansion, Dickens's proposals were repeatedly voted down, partly because the "idea of providing club facilities for some of the richest authors in London appalled the conservatives on the committee" (Cross, *Common* 33).

The reformers were almost certainly right that, by the 1850s, "all the usual signs of a corporate body, in its easy, indolent, and self-satisfied stage" had "fully manifested themselves" and that the Fund's numbingly layered bureaucracy, which included a Managing Committee and a Council, was being used in "opposition to inquiry" ("Literary Fund" 250). Nonetheless, much of the Fund's resistance to reform seems to have been grounded in an instinctive resentment of critique itself; Cross also argues that Dickens's tactless style made him enemies and doomed the enterprise. In any case, the Fund's differing treatments of Millhouse and Miller, fellow townsmen of similar economic backgrounds, resist easy ideological classification. Each man had well-connected advocates, received private support beyond the Fund, and viewed authorship as a profession to which he had legitimate claim. Even though the two men received comparable numbers of individual gifts, Miller received almost triple the sum. The best explanation for this is that Miller, as the saying goes, prayed to God but rowed to shore: he moved to London and managed for many years to maintain a series of publishing contracts without ever making a killing. Thus there was an extramural consensus that he was being sufficiently vetted by the publishing industry on an ongoing basis, even as he was still demonstrably in need. His "claims," it seemed, were perceived by the Committee as more conceptually limited and more manageable than Millhouse's, even though, in raw monetary terms, Miller was by far the greater drain. Surely it cannot be a coincidence that the most prolific and versatile working class writer of the era was also the writer best supported by the Royal Literary Fund.

If Millhouse too had a significant publishing résumé, his narrower talent and slimmer body of work were interpreted by the Committee as indicating that his dreams were incongruent with reality. More than this, his ambition at once meshed and collided with the Fund's raison d'être. David Williams had wanted his charitable foundation to encourage the proliferation of genius, and to do it in a depersonalized way that was removed from the politics of "gratitude and ingratitude" (*Claims* 124). The goal was anonymous alleviation of the "absolute INDIGENCE of ingenious and learned men" (125), without the aggrandizement of either side or the taint of economic influence. Millhouse assuredly thought of himself as possessing such genius – a fact the Committee was able to perceive despite Dickens's conviction that it suffered from a fatal lack of "literary men" ("Literary Fund" 256) who could discern the stylistic and thematic tendencies of claimants. Then again, it did not require deep reading, or close analytical skills, to identify Millhouse's belief that his genius was being constrained by the gross inequities of mortal existence. Appealing to the Fund on that basis, he was funded for so long because the Committee finally focused on charity instead: the parallel tracks of charity and genius as intuitional priorities in the Fund's mission were constantly at play, but in proportions that Millhouse was inclined to misperceive. Arguably this mistake was only natural, for despite his philosophic reliance on the hereafter, Millhouse's goal was to make his name as a writer in the here and now. At the same time, despite his early debacle with the sonnet "To Beneficence," he seemed to perceive the Fund's approach to charity as morally just. That, at least, is the evidence of his "To Charity," which makes a virtue of the anonymity that he so often struggled to reconcile himself to. Taking a page out of both the Bible and the book of David Williams, he writes:

> the Redeemer, fraught with heavenly fire,
> Knowing man's pride, bade hide the giving hand,
> With him didst thou sojourn, and o'er the land,
> Made boasting Pharisees in shame retire; –
> And taught, that alms, *the most in secret given*,
> Are deem'd *most worthy* in the Eye of Heaven.
> (ll. 9–14)

NOTES

1. Interestingly, Williams had tried to get Smith involved in the Fund at its formative stage. For an account of Smith as an implied argumentative foil in Williams's *Claims*, see Batchelor's "'The Claims of Literature': Women Applicants to the Royal Literary Fund, 1790–1810."
2. *Claims of Literature* was criticized for its radical flavor, and Williams was forced to answer the charges of one Committee member, Sir James Bland Burges, who disparaged it as a "radical polemic" (Cross, *Common* 21). In his later memoir, Williams said Burges had always sought to "pervert" the mission of the Fund "by mingling religion and political enquiries with the cases of the unfortunate claimants" (Williams, *Incidents* 51–2).
3. Relatedly, Batchelor argues that Williams's language in *Claims* was "unequivocally masculine" and denigrated "female literary endeavour (particularly that of novel writing)" ("Claims" 506).
4. For an extended discussion of Bloomfield's situation in these years, see Sangster 124–9.
5. Ann Pye to the Royal Literary Fund. 14 November 1818. "The Letters of Robert Bloomfield and his Circle," eds. Tim Fulford and Lynda Pratt, *Romantic Circles* Electronic Editions, 2009. Letter 328. Hereafter *LRBC*. I thank the editors for permission to quote from this edition. www.rc.umd.edu/editions/bloomfield_letters/HTML/letterlist.htm.
6. My citations of the Royal Literary Fund Archives, which are held at the British Library, omit the Loan number (96), listing series, case, and item numbers, followed by item date, all of which are recorded in the BL online catalogue.

These materials are also available on microfilm: *Archives of the Royal Literary Fund: 1790–1918*, 145 reels (London: World Microfilms Publications, 1981–4). After Bloomfield received this first grant, one of his Fund contacts indicated it had provided him a sprig of hope: "I believe I may predict that it will greatly facilitate the work poor Bloomfield has in hand – at least he expresses himself quite in spirits to proceed" (1/382/4; 3 December 1818). It may also have contributed, at least indirectly, to his being able to compile a final volume of original poetry, *May Day with the Muses*, which would appear four years later. But it is also true that, as early as March 1819, Bloomfield was writing Samuel Rogers asking for money (*LRBC* Letter 332), and, a month later, Bloomfield was asking Baldwin, his publisher, for an advance of £20; "however my affairs stand with you," he wrote, he was desperate to give money to his suffering brother, "who is in danger of trouble for a small debt leading to the ruin of his business and distress of his Children" (*LRBC* Letter 333; 11 April 1819).

7. William T. Fitzgerald to Richard Yates.
8. For Pye family genealogy, see Noble, *Memoirs* 110. Pye's fulsome verses celebrating the work of the Literary Fund can be found in Williams, *Claims* 165–8 and 224–5.
9. Fitzgerald also had a long tenure, serving on the Committee from 1791–7 and 1804–6, on the Council from 1798–1803 and 1806–16, as Visitor from 1809–16, and as Vice-President from 1817–29. When he died in 1829, the Fund granted his wife Maria £100, to that date the highest amount in its history; see Cases 661 and 1109 in Cross's unpaged Index to his *Selected Catalogue of Applicants to the Royal Literary Fund*.
10. See, for example, Sales (*English Literature in History*), Christmas ("*The Farmer's Boy* and Contemporary Politics"), and White (*Robert Bloomfield*). Peter Denney ("The Talk of the Tap-Room") argues that, even in his own day, Bloomfield was not always read as politically benign.
11. For two excellent extended discussions, see Christmas, "*The Farmer's Boy* and Contemporary Politics," and White, *Robert Bloomfield, Romanticism, and the Poetry of Community*, esp. 7–30.
12. For a sense of Yates's keen interest in the relationship between Church and State, see his *The Church in Danger* (London, 1815).
13. Because Millhouse's volumes often included both new and reprinted works, individual poems can be found in multiple places, even when the volume titles might suggest otherwise. The texts I use here are drawn from the earliest available publication of each poem. For "The Bard," "To Genius," "To Gold," "The Proud Man's Contumely," and "To Poverty," see *Blossoms* (1823). For "To Charity," "To November," and "The Insolent in Office," see *Song of the Patriot* (1826). For "The Lot of Genius," see *Sonnets and Songs* (1881).
14. The phrase is originally from Millhouse's earlier poem "Vicissitude."
15. The Fund records are not complete regarding this first grant, but the meeting probably occurred in late April 1822, and the make-up of the Committee was likely identical to the one that heard the Bloomfield case the following month.

16. Despite the Committee's express wishes, surviving copies of *Blossoms* (1823) nonetheless feature "To Beneficence" ("Inscribed, With These Pages, To the Society of the Literary Fund") as the lead poem. Perhaps publication went forward because it was, in fact, too late to stop the presses, and not because of Booker's reluctance to "mutilate" the volume (1/462/8; 8 January 1823). Such an explanation does not square, however, with Millhouse's decision to include "To Beneficence" in his subsequent volume, *The Song of the Patriot, Sonnets, and Songs* (1826). Though the poem no longer had a place of prominence in the collection, and, though its subtitle referencing the Fund was slightly truncated, its inclusion indicates a strong strain of self-righteousness in Millhouse's thinking.
17. For more on the complex question of average Fund grants, see Mumm, "Writing for Their Lives" (1990).
18. Millhouse and his survivors received sixteen gifts. The only comparable figure I have identified is Thomas Miller (1807–74), recipient of fifteen gifts, who is discussed later in this essay. John Saunders (1810–95) received nine gifts. John Watkins, a historian, petitioned the committee eighteen times and may have received more grants than Millhouse; a comprehensive survey of the Fund's entire archive might well yield additional examples of frequent grantees.
19. Wakefield served two one-year terms as mayor, one beginning in 1835 and the other in 1842.
20. Miller is Case 816 in the Fund Files.
21. For Cross's full account of Miller, see 132–41.
22. Addendum to File 816 coversheet, RLF Archives, Loan 96, British Library.

James Gillray, *Life of William Cobbett*, 29 September 1809. Courtesy of the Lewis Walpole Library.

The Life of WILLIAM-COBBETT. _written by himself._

2.d Plate.

— as I shot up into a hobble-dehoy, I took to driving the Plow for the benefit of mankind, which was always my prime object;— hearing that the Church-Wardens were after me, I determined to become a Hero, and secretly quitting my agricultural pursuits, and Sukey Stubbs, Voluntered as a Private-Soldier, into the 51.st Regiment, commanded by that tried Patriot and Martyre Lord.Edw.d Fitzgerald, and embarked for the Plantations.

Vide, my own Memoirs
in the Political Register for 1809.

The Life of WILLIAM COBBETT, written by himself.

3.d Plate.

arrived in safety (according to the proverb), being a Scholard, (for all the world knows that I can Read and Write,) I was promoted to the rank of a Corporal, and soon after appointed to teach the Officers their duty.— found them all so damnably stupid, that 'though I took the pains to draw up my instructions on Cards, I could not with all my Caning and Kicking, drive one manual movement into their thick heads!

—N.B: These Cards were so much admired by Gen.l Dundas, that he made them the foundation of his New Military Systema.

— Vide, my Own Memoirs in the Political Register of 1809 —

The Life of WILLIAM-COBBETT, — written by himself.

4th Plate.

— I was now made Sarjeant-Major and Clerk to the Regiment, and there being only One Man in it, besides myself, who could read or keep himself sober, (viz.— poor little Corporal-Bestland). I constituted him my Deputy;— being intrusted with the care of the Regimental Books, the Corporal and myself (tho' both of us blastedly afraid of a pair of Bloody Shoulders,) — purloined and Copied by night such Documents as promised to be serviceable in the great National Object which I had in view; — namely, to Disorganize the Army, preparatory to the Revolutionizing it altogether!

Vide — my Own Memoirs in the Political Register of 1809.

The Life of WILLIAM COBBETT,— written by himself.

5th Plate —
— my next step was to procure a Discharge from my ever lamented associate the Lord Edwd. Fitzgerald; — with this I returned to England, and directly set about writing "the Soldier's Friend" which I nightly "dropt about the Horse-Guards; and drank "Damnation to the House of Brunswick!" — moreover I wrote 27 Letters to my Royal Master to Mr. Pitt and the Judge Advocate, against my Officers, 23 of which Letters were stolen by the public Robbers, and never came to hand, so that, I had no means of obtaining Credit for my Charges, & procuring a Court-Martial — but — by solemnly Pledging my precious Soul to the Devil in the presence of Judge Gould for the Truth of my alegations, and my ability to support them by evidence !!!' —
Vide my own Memoirs in the Political Register 1809.

The Life of WILLIAM-COBBETT, written by himself.

Plate 6th

— the Court-Martial was assembled at Chelsea as I requested, and Capt.n Powell and the other accused Persons were placed at the Bar; — when — blast-my-Eyes! — I saw, the whole of that damn'd 51st Regiment Drummers, Fifers and all, marching boldly into the Hall to bear Testimony against Me!! — on this, I instantly ran to a boat which I had Providentialy secured, and crossed the Thames. —
— damn'd infernal-Ideots! — did the Judge-Advocate and his Gang of Publick Robbers think that I would stay to witness my own Exposure and condemnation?

— Vide, my own Memoirs in the Political Register — 1809

The Life of WILLIAM COBBETT,—written by himself.

Plate 7th.—

I did not look behind me till I got to St Omers; but this being still too near the scene of my detection, I fled to America. Here, I offered to become a Spy for my most gracious Sovereign; this being scornfully rejected, I contented myself with Plundering & Libelling the Yankees, for which I was fined 5000 dollars, and kicked out of the Country!— Seven years had elapsed since I absconded from England, so I thought that my exploits there might be forgotten, and ventured to return.— I set up the Crown and Mitre, under cover of which, I abused the Church and State, very comfortably,— my Loyalty being thus established, I accepted from the Doctor (so I always call the Right Honble Henry Ld. Visct. Sidmouth) £4000, which was to be expended in printing & dispersing a pamphlet against the "Hell-Fire Yell of Reform!"— with this money I paid my debts, I purchased a pretty bit of Land at Botley, and sat quietly down to enjoy the the fruits of my honest Industry.— A thousand applications have been made to me, to refund or account for some part of this enormous Sum; but, blast my Eyes! I will see the Doctor damned, and all such Fools as the Doctor, before I open my mouth on the Subject!—— At Botley my natural-bent returned, but upon a larger scale, for being now Lord of the Manor of Botley, & in the receipt of Five Thousand pounds a year from the sale of my Weekly Register, therefore not caring a single God-damn for Public Opinion, I reacted the peccadilloes of my youth, & with maturer mischief, began by sowing dissentions thro' the whole County, I kicked the Sick & the Infirm Labourer into the Street.— I oppress'd the poor; I sent the Aged to hell!— damned the Eyes of my Parish Apprentices before they were opened in a morning, and being nobly supported by a loyal band of Reformers, I renewed in our Orgies, my old-favourite Toast of "Damnation to the House of Brunswick"—,— thus exalted in glory & popularity I found myself on the point of becoming the greatest Man in the World, except that Idol of my thoughts, that object of my Adorations, his Royal & Imperial Majesty NAPOLEONE.—

The Life of WILLIAM-COBBETT, _written by himself_.

Plate 8th.

_ but alas, in the midst of my towering prospects, while I was yet hesitating between a Radical-Reform and a Revolution, & doubtful whether to assume the Character of Old-Noll or Jack-Cade, _ down came my Political Register, & the fabrick of my visionary greatness vanish'd_ my Schemes for my Country's good perish'd by the blaze of my own Candles! _ The Ghost! _ slid? _ Lord forgive me for swearing! _ the Ghost of Capt:n Powell utter'd a scream of Joy _ little Jesey's brandy-faced-bitch of a Mother _ Lord pardon me! _ called out for Justice! _ the Bats and Harpies of Revolution hid their heads in the gloom of night, _ and to compleat the horrible scene, the rigid Pawnbr*k*r of Hell, Old-Beelzebub, enter'd and demanded his property, the Forfeit Soul, which I had pledged! _ Lord have mercy upon me! _ _ Our Father! _ to the Truth of my accusation's! oh! oh! _ oh! _ Hell-Flames.

Vide. My own Memoirs in the Political Register. 1809.

CHAPTER II

The Life of William Cobbett
Caricature, Hauntology, and the Impossibility of Radical Life Writing in the Romantic Period

Ian Haywood

I

In September 1809 James Gillray published the last original caricature of his long and illustrious career (Hill 114, 117). In an eight-plate series entitled *The Life of William Cobbett*, given here, Gillray mercilessly lampooned the career of the Romantic period's most prolific radical journalist, accusing Cobbett of (among other things) dishonesty and disloyalty. These images are well known to Cobbett scholars but they have never been studied.[1] This chapter will provide the first detailed discussion of the meaning and significance of this intriguing cultural encounter between two towering figures of Romantic popular print culture.[2] Far from dismissing Gillray's satirical series as the last gasp of an embittered reactionary, I argue that the caricature provides both an insight into and an alternative aesthetic model for the fractured and inchoate cultural condition of radical and working class life writing at this formative time in its development. Gillray's emphasis on radical spectrality challenges the predominantly realist and psychological paradigms that govern the ways in which autobiography is conventionally conceived and assessed; it also helps us to understand the transformative pressures which an era of revolutionary politics exerted on both the radical ego and the self-presentation of a radical life.

Gillray's extraordinary attack on Cobbett was by no means an isolated or maverick incident. In fact it was part of a sustained loyalist counter-offensive against what Peter Spence has called the "rise of Romantic radicalism." Spence argues that a new type of popular reformist politics emerged in the wake of the "Broad Bottom" coalition ministry of 1806–7. Although the essential goals of political reform remained unchanged, the new generation of democratic leaders presented a very different public image from their rakish, dissolute Foxite forebears. The new stars – Francis Burdett in parliament, Cobbett and Leigh Hunt in journalism, and "Orator" Henry

Hunt on the podium – all prided themselves on respectability, moral rectitude, and virtue. In this "new era" of politics (a phrase Cobbett used for the ascendancy of Burdett), personal integrity was a defense against slander (Spater 188). An unimpeachable character and purity of purpose was the personification of the true character of the reform movement and the antithesis of the corruption of the ruling classes. But the elevation of personal integrity also made it an easy target and it had to be constantly defended against both political and personal smears. This was particularly the case for lower class radicals like Cobbett who lacked genteel social credentials.

The year 1809 was a difficult time for the government as it tried to cope with several overlapping cases of what Spence calls "military, moral and political corruption" (117).[3] Public support for the war against Napoleonic France was fragile. In Spain, the only theater of war where the British military were fully active, initial gains in 1808 had been offset by the much-criticized Convention of Cintra and the death of Sir John Moore at La Coruña in early 1809. Meanwhile the British invasion of Walcheren in the Netherlands had been a disaster, resulting in massive casualties from disease. If this incompetence was not enough to dent public confidence in the government, a further blow was struck when the Duke of York was forced to resign as commander-in-chief of the army. Caricaturists had a field day when it was discovered that his mistress Mary Anne Clarke had been selling commissions for the army with the Duke's knowledge. Cobbett not only reported these events with glee but launched his own campaign against flogging in the army, presenting it as a barbaric throwback (*PR* 1 July 1809, 993–4). The criticism clearly struck home as the government retaliated with a lawsuit, and the following year Cobbett was imprisoned for two years, though he carried on publishing from his jail cell. Finally, in September 1809 the "Old Price" riots erupted in London in protest at a rise in the price of tickets at Covent Garden Theatre. The disturbances quickly acquired political overtones and raised the "jacobin" temperature of antiestablishment protest even further (Spence 180–81). This was the same month that Gillray's *Life of William Cobbett* was published.

Mired in "scandal upon scandal" (Cox 102–3), the Tory government decided to hit back. Its counteroffensive, reminiscent of the 1790s, utilized both the repressive and ideological state apparatus. Before it opted for direct action, prosecuting and imprisoning Cobbett, Burdett, and Leigh Hunt over the next three years, the state launched a propaganda offensive of pamphlets and caricatures designed to blacken the reputations of the leading reformers: "Reformers without merit were merely Jacobins in disguise" (Spence 102). The campaign against Cobbett was particularly well planned as it targeted one of his most formative experiences and a bedrock of his steadfastness, his military career. Cobbett had volunteered for the British army in 1783 and spent six years in Nova Scotia; he rose to become the regiment's amanuensis and only returned to England to attempt to court-martial his superiors for embezzlement. Labeling himself the "Soldier's Friend" (the title of his first published work which appeared just after the court-martial incident in 1792), Cobbett was peculiarly vulnerable to aspersions about this aspect of his past. As in the 1790s, satire and caricature were powerful tools in the government's armory (Spater 622; Reitzel 246; Grande and Stevenson 5). Gillray's satirical "Life" was actually the visual accompaniment to a widely distributed pamphlet alleging that Cobbett had fabricated the charges against his regimental officers in 1792 and had fled the country to avoid exposure. The pamphlet was a brilliant piece of muck-raking propaganda as it eschewed narrative or declamation and simply reprinted original correspondence between Cobbett and the authorities that had lain in War Office files for almost 20 years. The quotations from Cobbett on the cover are particularly effective in seeming to clinch his guilt (Figure 11.1). The first is from a letter to Judge-Advocate Charles Gould: "If my accusation is without foundation, the authors of cruelty have not yet devised the tortures I ought to endure. Hell itself, as painted by the most fiery bigot, is too mild a punishment for me." The second is the verdict of the court-martial, acquitting the officers. This witty intertextual exchange, carefully staged by the pamphlet's compiler, gave Gillray one of his most spectacular tableaux.

Cobbett was rattled by these long-forgotten revelations and accusations. He tried to clear his name by publishing a lengthy, "unmutilated" account of his army career in the *Political Register*, including (for the first time in print) the incident of the court-martial ("To the Independent People of Hampshire," *PR* 17 June 1809, 897–920, 903). Gillray used this autobiographical fragment and Cobbett's earlier memoir the *Life of Peter Porcupine* (1796) as the basis for his pictorial narrative. Yet neither of these sources could be described as conventional life writing, as their main purpose was defensive and tactical, providing experiential evidence to counter hostile propaganda: in the case of *Porcupine*, to convince the American public that he was not a British spy, and in 1809 to refute accusations of unpatriotic and cowardly insubordination. The veracity of Cobbett's narrative of the court-martial, about which critics still disagree,[4] is less important than the resort to personal experience to clear his name: what Kevin Gilmartin has called Cobbett's "radical egotism" (166–7) was a form of self-defense in a

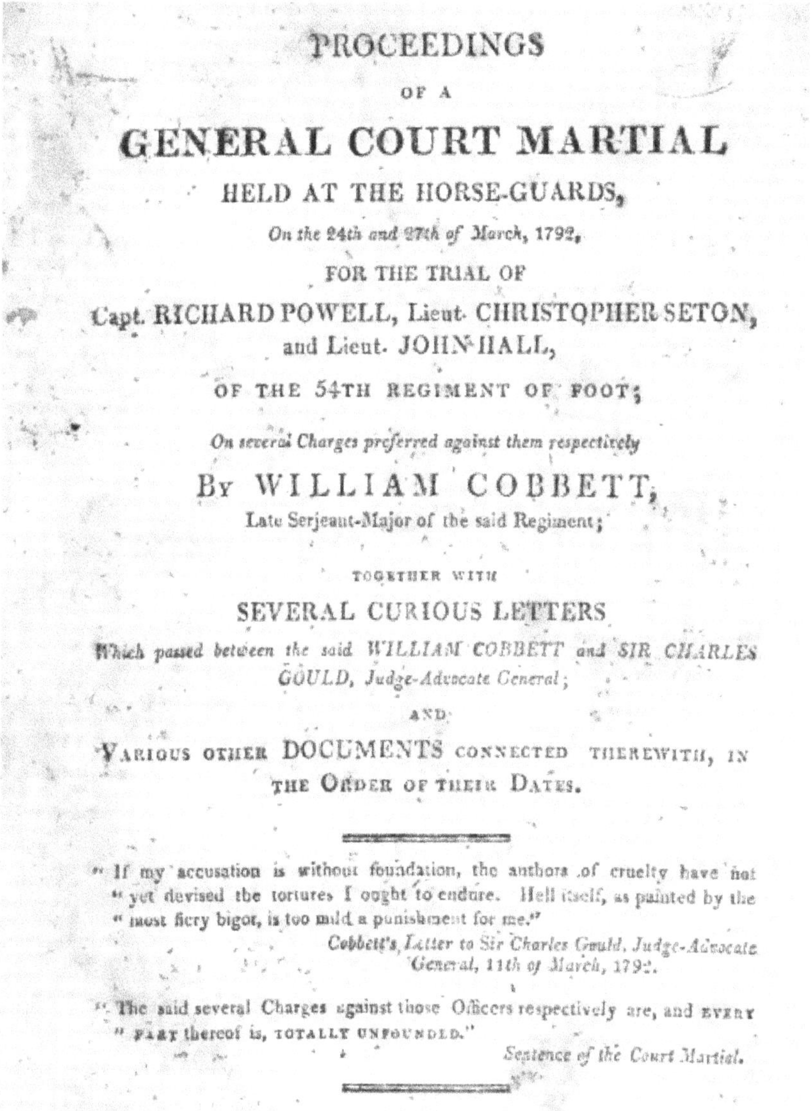

PROCEEDINGS

OF A

GENERAL COURT MARTIAL

HELD AT THE HORSE-GUARDS,

On the 24th and 27th of March, 1792,

FOR THE TRIAL OF

Capt. RICHARD POWELL, Lieut. CHRISTOPHER SETON, and Lieut. JOHN HALL,

OF THE 54TH REGIMENT OF FOOT;

On several Charges preferred against them respectively

By WILLIAM COBBETT,

Late Serjeant-Major of the said Regiment;

TOGETHER WITH

SEVERAL CURIOUS LETTERS

Which passed between the said WILLIAM COBBETT and SIR CHARLES GOULD, Judge-Advocate General;

AND

VARIOUS OTHER DOCUMENTS CONNECTED THEREWITH, IN THE ORDER OF THEIR DATES.

" If my accusation is without foundation, the authors of cruelty have not
" yet devised the tortures I ought to endure. Hell itself, as painted by the
" most fiery bigot, is too mild a punishment for me."

Cobbett's Letter to Sir Charles Gould, Judge-Advocate General, 11th of March, 1792.

" The said several Charges against those Officers respectively are, and EVERY
" PART thereof is, TOTALLY UNFOUNDED."

Sentence of the Court Martial.

Figure 11.1 Front page of *Proceedings of a General Court Martial*, 1809. Courtesy of Toronto Public Library.

hostile political environment. Gillray's parodic response to Cobbett's virtuous self-fashioning was to present the court-martial debacle as the natural or logical outcome of a plebeian upbringing. In this counternarrative of a radical life, Cobbett's progress is dominated from the outset by violence, self-interest, and mischief-making. The eight plates are witty and engaging: although not vintage Gillray, they bring the controversy to life in ways that only caricature could do, transforming current events into vivid, extrovert, and fantastical dramas (Haywood 5–9). But like all caricatures, they are also hermeneutically unstable. The next section of this chapter will read the prints dialectically – in both "loyal" and "disloyal" ways – in order to elicit their importance for rethinking Cobbett's "life." The final section of the essay extrapolates from Cobbett's example to explore the "impossibility" of radical and working class autobiography in an era of persecution and highly charged print politics.

II

Gillray's series is modeled on Hogarth's influential narrative sequences which chart the moral progress or regress of social types (the rake, the harlot, the apprentice, the impoverished aristocrat). In this genre, each scene represents a significant stage in the biographical journey and displays the visual clues for the course of the hero's or heroine's destiny. The closest parallel to Gillray's *Cobbett* is probably Hogarth's *Industry and Idleness* (1747) which features a hero from humble origins who lapses into a dissolute and criminal life and meets his end on the gallows, unlike his "industrious" and conformist brother who rises socially to become mayor of London. Gillray first used the format in a mock life of Napoleon in 1798, where the violent career of the Corsican upstart is foreshadowed by his rude upbringing.[5] Gillray's breakthrough was to take the Hogarthian genre and adapt it for real rather than fictional characters. In the case of *Cobbett*, the images also act as illustrations to a bogus or parodic autobiographical text. The epigraph used beneath the first plate establishes the complex ironies of Gillray's satirical appropriation of life writing. The quotation, which is taken from Shakespeare's *Henry IV Part 1* ("Now you lying varlets you shall see how a plain tale shall put you down") is another example of Cobbett's own paratexts being deployed against him, as it originally appeared on the cover of *Life of Peter Porcupine* (see Figure 11.1). The original intention of using personal history to set the political record straight is inverted: Gillray's "plain tale" – a composite of Cobbett's own words and Gillray's fabrications – exposes Cobbett as the "lying varlet" both in his actions (the court-martial) and his unreliable narration. Yet the viewer of the prints would know and relish the fact that caricature operates through excess and hyperbole. Far from being "plain" fare, the images translate the text into an alternative mode of representation in which the normal rules of spatiotemporal reality can be violated with aplomb. In the process, intriguing new cultural and ideological conjunctions can emerge, not all of which are under the control of the artist.

Plate 1 debunks Cobbett's nostalgic and idealized account of his origins in what he called "Old England," a rural idyll of artisanal independence, industriousness, and community. Instead of a pastoral scene reminiscent of Constable or Morland, we are presented with a feral seven-year old Cobbett running amuck and showing clear signs of a penchant for inciting violence and disorder. The obscured church in the background, the father lounging in the door of the pub and the Bewickian washing line of ragged clothes are damning visual motifs that imply negative social determinism: even at this tender age Cobbett's life is controlled by his lowly origin's worst aspects: deprivation and brutality. So much for the "loyal" reading. But a focus on what Roland Barthes calls the "punctum" or neglected detail in an image allows us to read against the grain (26–7). In this case our eye is drawn by the fault line that runs along the front of the ale-house and which separates background and foreground, community and Cobbett. This partition can be interpreted as an expression of the traumatic socioeconomic destruction of a traditional way of life which for Cobbett functioned as a kind of primal scene. In other words the formal organization of the print shifts ideological agency away from Cobbett the individual to the (as yet) unseen forces of history which lie outside the frame of the image and which are driving this village Hampden into the jaws of military and political conflict. In addition, it is hard not to see the inflamed bull-dog as an allusion to John Bull, suggesting that Gillray's Cobbett is exhibiting signs of aggressive jingoism rather than plebeian unruliness.

Plate 2 mocks Cobbett's decision to enlist in the army in 1783 by recycling gossip that he abandoned a pregnant lover; the text also refers sardonically to "that tried patriot and martyr" Lord Edward Fitzgerald, the United Irish leader who secured Cobbett's honorable discharge in 1791, implying that Cobbett was a crypto-republican agitator and proto-Jacobin sympathizer, or at the very least that his hatred of the British state knew no bounds. But once again there are countervailing ways to read the image. To begin with, the diminutive drummer is clearly a ludicrous figure and hardly an advertisement for military grandeur. There is also another fault line corresponding to the diagonal shoreline. As Cobbett leaves behind his beloved plow (a prized emblem of his humble origins which formed part of the title of his planned autobiography, an issue discussed below), his trajectory is toward the anchored ship which will transport him to the "plantations," a jarring word which suggests slavery and injustice. Furthermore, the church in Plate 1 has been replaced by a gallows, an ominous symbol of the bloody British penal code. Finally, there is a significant absence in the scene: the leap of chronology between the first two Plates omits Cobbett's education, the crucial development which enabled him to "conspire" against his superiors in the first place and which transformed him (and other laboring class writers and leaders) into a new cultural phenomenon: the plebeian intellectual (Krishnamurthy 1–24). This lacuna undermines the constant reminder that the text is "written by himself," as if Cobbett's literacy has no origins or legitimacy. However, the next group of plates puts books, reading, and writing center stage.

Plates 3–6 represent the main theme of the series in which Cobbett becomes (in modern parlance) a whistle-blower. Gillray replaces Cobbett's righteous account of exposing regimental corruption with an anti-Jacobin narrative of botched seditious conspiracy; stereotypically, radicalism is presented as simultaneously threatening and ludicrous. However, the illustrations are also a testimony to the staying power of radical discourse and radical textuality. One of the most conspicuous features of these scenes is the presence of large numbers of contested texts. The episodes are strewn with malevolent and imperiled documents that dramatize Cobbett's mission to "register" the truth: and like the "life" on display, these "necrobibliographical" texts are uncanny, simultaneously real and fantastical (Wolfreys xii).

Plate 3 satirizes Cobbett's account of writing instructions on cards for his illiterate officers. In this reimagined version, Cobbett is physically bullying the officers and he has indoctrinated the regiment to the extent that they are flying a tricolor flag. The documents spilling out of the casket signify Cobbett's usurping of authority, but they can also be read as evidence of the productiveness of radical print culture. Another "disloyal" punctum is the ineptitude of the officers: the "Aristocracy of the Army" are ostensibly victims of Cobbett's arrogant domineering, but there is no disputing that they are illiterate.[6]

In Plate 4 we see Cobbett and his nocturnal co-conspirator Corporal Bestland stealing evidence from the regimental accounts. Gillray's text ventriloquizes Cobbett's declared intention of "revolutionizing" the army by stirring up discontent against officers, and although this is clearly a distortion and exaggeration of what happened, the scene does stage a symbolic

Figure 11.2 James Gillray, *Smelling Out a Rat, or, The Atheistical Revolutionist Disturbed in His Midnight Calculations*, 3 December 1790. Courtesy of the Library of Congress.

coup d'etat in which radical print culture appropriates official discourse. Cobbett's own account of the incident is freighted with emblematic connotations: as the "keeper of the books," his aim was to "collect materials for an exposure" (and even the name of his co-conspirator Bestland seems allegorical). In effect, therefore, this episode does indeed represent a revolutionary threat: the transfer of political and cultural power to the new "keepers" and "registers" of truth and virtue, the subaltern classes. Furthermore, the displacement of the conflicts of 1809 onto 1791–2 begins to take on some intriguing new resonances once we appreciate that Gillray is reworking some of his most famous antiradical caricatures of the 1790s in which the authorities uncover seditious nocturnal meetings. Prominent examples are *Smelling out a Rat* (1790), in which a giant emanation of Edmund Burke appears to a startled Richard Price, and *Search Night* (1798) which shows Pitt and other watchmen bursting in on a group of Foxite Whigs (Figures 11.2 and 11.3). The visual echoes reinforce the idea that the Jacobin genie was once more out of the bottle, but this "exposure" always ran the risk of enhancing rather than exorcizing Cobbett's spectral presence in Romantic print culture.

Figure 11.3 James Gillray, *Search Night – or – State Watchmen Mistaking Honest Men for Conspirators*, 20 March 1798. Courtesy of the Lewis Walpole Library.

By reawakening the ghosts of that revolutionary decade, and by resurrecting a pivotal moment in the fortunes of Cobbett's career in particular and radicalism more generally, Gillray unintentionally released a new, hauntological narrative.[7] In Cobbett's account of the court-martial controversy (the one he published in the *Political Register* and which Gillray simultaneously subverts and plunders) he describes the political mood of early 1792 in prescient terms: "glorious 'Jacobinical' times were just then beginning." This seems to support Gillray's portrayal of the lurking republican, but the plot thickens when we discover from another autobiographical fragment that it was precisely in early 1792 that Cobbett read Thomas Paine's *Rights of Man* for the first time and admired the text. Moreover, Cobbett had seemed to anticipate Paine's notoriety by fleeing to France as Britain descended into counterrevolution (*PR* 17 June 1809, 907; Reitzel 53).[8] As shown below, there are further ramifications to this intriguing textual and spectral overlap of Cobbett's and Paine's careers, as one aspect of *Rights of Man* that may have impressed Cobbett was Paine's own, high-minded autobiographical snapshot of his disinterested pursuit of truth and justice. By presenting Cobbett as the reincarnation of Jacobinism,

Gillray offered an alternative, hauntological model for the disrupted textual shaping of a radical life in this period. This becomes even clearer in Plates 5 and 8.

Plate 5 shows Cobbett pleading his case before the reluctant Judge-Advocate Gould, who did in fact accede to Cobbett's ardent requests to move the court-martial from Portsmouth to London, though the raised hand suggests the opposite. Cobbett's words in the speech bubble are (as noted earlier) the epigraph from *Life of Peter Porcupine* coming back (literally) to haunt him. Gillray takes Cobbett at his word and delivers a suitably infernal punishment. Cobbett is now a civilian (his soldier's uniform lies discarded) but he has no place in civil society as he is already morphing into a monstrous emanation, a phantasmagorical intrusion into judicial processes which are represented once again by formidable tomes stacked on the bookcase shelves. At one level the scene is enjoyable grand guignol: the drapery, the stage effects, and the pantomime devil are all suggestive of popular culture. Yet intervisual allusion suggests a different reading, as the scene is a conspicuous inversion of a caricature print already mentioned, Gillray's *Smelling Out a Rat*. Gould now occupies Price's treacherous seat while Cobbett substitutes for the spectral Burke. It is hard to believe that these ironies were not intentional. Moreover, Gillray must have known that turning the iconographic tables in this way was a classic maneuver of radical culture: indeed, the revival of the reform movement was accompanied by numerous caricatures in which the state was depicted as the monstrous enemy of the virtuous radical hero. Examples include Burdett as *The Modern St George Attacking the Monster of Despotism* (1810) and Sheridan as *The Champion of Liberty* (1810) (British Museum Satires 11538, 11531).⁹

Gillray tries to correct this ideological instability in the final Plate 8 where Cobbett is reassigned to Price's sedentary position as a Faustian, self-inflicted catastrophe erupts around him. Once again the scene is bursting with print culture. We finally see Cobbett the eminent journalist at his desk but only at the moment of judgment. The scene literalizes the idea of inflammatory radical discourse as his works are catching fire. Gillray first used this trope in *A Peep into the Cave of Jacobinism* (1798), his frontispiece for the *Anti-Jacobin Review*. In this print, the skulking, demonic Jacobin author is no match for the searing light of Truth's torch whose fierce rays ignite the funereal pyre of seditious pamphlets (Figure 11.4). By 1809 the motif had been revived in *The Porcupine's Den*, one of the many attacks on Cobbett launched from the pages of the *Satirist* magazine (British Museum Satires 11049; Spater 228). In this image the darkened "den" is inhabited by

Figure 11.4 James Gillray, *A Peep into the Cave of Jacobinism*. Published in the *Anti-Jacobin Review*, 1 September 1798. Courtesy of the Firestone Library, Princeton University.

monstrous versions of Cobbett, Horne Tooke, and Burdett who are composing disloyal tracts (Figure 11.5). Radical discourse is simply not allowed to exist except as a malevolent infestation. Similarly, Gillray imagines the "real" Cobbett as a spectral doppelganger, an uncanny emanation of radical print culture. Yet this transformation is ideologically unstable, as it gives Cobbett a perverse, carnivalesque immortality. Cobbett was more than ready to embrace the role of tribune and prophet, and Gillray's mock apotheosis is an ironic confirmation of this elevated role. Like other radical authors, Cobbett claimed that he was doing the exact opposite of the smears against him; he was leading his readers out of Platonic darkness into light: "what might be expected to be produced on the eyes of one bred up in the dark, and brought out, all of a sudden, into broad daylight" (Reitzel 143).

This appeal to Enlightenment rationality is in stark contrast to Plates 6 and 7 which present Cobbett as a coward and Napoleonic sympathizer. Plate 6 shows Cobbett fleeing from the court-martial in a boat to avoid "exposure and condemnation," words that apply as much to 1809 as 1792.

The Life of William Cobbett 187

Figure 11.5 Samuel De Wilde, *The Porcupine's Den*. Published in *The Satirist*, 1 November 1808. Courtesy of the Library of Congress.

His guilt seems indisputable, but with the hindsight of his full career (which Gillray failed to halt), the scene becomes an eerie anticipation of his flight to America in 1817 to avoid prosecution and victimization. Moreover, in 1817 he was evading the repressive Two Acts, antidemocratic legislation which was first passed in 1795. Its revival in the postwar period shows how strongly the decade of the Terror defined subsequent political culture and debates, and radical lives (both lived and textualized) had to negotiate this legacy. The anti-Jacobin mythology of disloyalty – atheism, republicanism (particularly in its Paineite, antimonarchical guise), anarchy, feminism – proved to be very durable.

Gillray's absurd accusation that Cobbett was a Paineite republican reaches its climax in Plate 7 where he is shown in the company of drunken radical leaders toasting Napoleon and cursing the "House of Brunswick." The latter offense was not Gillray's invention as it was one of the charges leveled at Cobbett in 1792 and which he feared would secure his conviction. Gillray may also have calculated that Cobbett was vulnerable to such aspersions, having refused to support plans for the King's fiftieth jubilee celebrations. Cobbett savaged the proposed junket as both a distraction from the war and as having "the more malignant purpose of reviving the distinction of *Jacobins* and *Anti-Jacobins* by imputing disaffection, and antiroyalty principles, to those who refuse to join in a celebration *professed* to be in honour of the king" (*PR* 23 September 1809). Gillray's scene reminds the viewer of the chilling consequences of "anti-royalty principles" as one of the busts on the back wall is of Colonel Despard, executed for treason in 1803. Gillray conveys the idea that radical conviviality is inherently dangerous by transplanting Cobbett and his peers into what Iain McCalman calls the "radical underworld" of seditious toasts and sentiments. The omnipresent "Botley ale" is also a reminder that Cobbett has regressed back to his publican roots depicted in Plate 1. Read against the grain, however, Plate 7 can be interpreted as a rather desperate attempt to undermine the new culture of radical banquets which combined fund-raising with inspirational oratory and morale-boosting toasts. At the first major new political dinner on 1 May 1809, Burdett toasted that "decrepit, bed-ridden old gentleman, whom we had long lost sight of, called *Magna Carta*, whom we yet hope to see again walking abroad" (cited in Spence 127). The resurrection of liberty is the spectral antidote to menacing Jacobin revenance. Radical lives were pulled between these two hauntological extremes with little option, opportunity, or resources to settle in the middle ground.

III

The final part of this chapter will use Gillray's fake biography of Cobbett as the basis for a brief, theoretical reexamination of the fractured condition of life writing by plebeian radicals in the Romantic period. Against the grain of most commentary and (almost certainly) the intentions of the writers themselves, I will propose that Gillray's phantasmal model of cultural agency offers a new paradigm for our understanding of the political efficacy of working class autobiographical discourse at this formative moment.

Though Asa Briggs points out that "Cobbett's own biography is inextricably bound up with the social and political biography of his country," Briggs is not referring to a coherent autobiographical text written (as Kevin Binfield puts it) "with the primary intent to tell or reflect upon the author's life story unrelated to other purposes" but a dispersal of fragments or sketches throughout Cobbett's writings (Briggs 1: ix; Binfield 161–78, 162). These pieces were eventually stitched together by William Reitzel in his seminal *Autobiography of William Cobbett* (1933). But Cobbett is not unique. Of the few examples of radical political autobiography that were published in the Romantic period, none live up to the conventional expectations of life writing: in essence, there is either too little or too much ego (Thelwall; Holcroft; Hunt; Hardy). Such was the pressure to avoid accusations of egotism and self-interest (misdemeanors that were seen as over-compensations for the persistent stigma of lowly origins) that both Thomas Hardy and John Thelwall wrote their pioneering memoirs in the third person, a mode they regarded as more suitable for their status as "historical figures" (Vincent, *Bread* 26). This was a drastic aesthetic response to the adverse ideological climate: to guard against malicious personal attacks, confessional revelations, the "rare moment of self-reflection" (Higgins 69) and intimate details of private life are subordinated to the more pressing business of public politics and the collective achievements of radical print culture. The prioritizing of public service (rather than plebeian callowness) could explain why Paine and Cobbett, two key intellectual players in the "making" of the working class, never got beyond what Leonara Nattrass calls "snapshots" (124–6).[10] Only Henry Hunt's forgotten prison-autobiography goes some way to redressing this imbalance, though Hunt's modern biographer dismisses the work as "notoriously immodest and unreliable" due to Hunt "accentuat[ing] his egotism for political purpose" (Belchem 8, 144–5).[11]

Leading critics in this field tend to explain the fragmented and elliptical nature of laboring class political life writing not as a generic or aesthetic deficiency so much as a compelling class signifier: working class autobiography must not be judged by the standards of the bildungsroman, a form built on the bourgeois ideology of a fully constituted, individualized subjectivity. Regenia Gagnier is the most outspoken advocate of this collectivist and public-spirited reading of radical working class lives. She argues that these texts reject "bourgeois individuation" in favor of class "epic" and "revelations [not] of self, but of class," however jarring this might seem to the modern reader (Gagnier 169, 160, 139). Gagnier draws on the pioneering work of David Vincent, for whom working class autobiographies are indeed epic, functioning as "fragments of the single mosaic of the developing working class as it made itself and its own history in its struggles for economic and political freedom" and also as "weapons" against misrepresentation by those who preferred the lives of "cabinet minister rather than the cabinet maker" (Vincent, *Testaments* 2, 13, 12). John Burnett, on the other hand, sees a tension between the cultural and ideological pressures placed on the "clearly exceptional" radical autobiographer to speak for a whole social class, and the fact that, by definition, the same writer was not a "strictly representative figure" (Burnett, *Destiny* 10; Burnett, *Useful* 10). For Bernard Sharratt, the answer to this problem is poststructuralist Marxism: textual fragmentation is merely "a *displaced* response to the problems of organising at the social or political level" and hence the deep structure of reform is always "imputed" and imminent beneath the surface (315–18).

Class solidarity (between critic and author, and author and imagined community of readers) is therefore one way to recuperate Cobbett's "snapshots." Cobbett's textual voice, in the words of Jon Klancher, is "both idiomatically personal and the very sign of an emerging social class" (121). Like its antecedent the spiritual autobiography, the ultimate point of a radical plebeian life – in other words the reason for writing it down at all – was to impel the higher goal of collective redemption: as Emma Griffin notes, such writing was "indelibly linked with achievement" (222). But we can penetrate yet further into the genre if we focus on what critics have overlooked or under-estimated: the fact that these radicals, lives were forged in extremely defensive ideological and cultural conditions. For radicals, personal experience was not only a past to be retrieved and explored but a live political issue to be defended and contested in the present. To its enemies, the radical ego was an overblown monster of pride, impudence, and malevolent trespass, an emanation of what Georgina Green calls the "spectral invincibility of popular opinion," but for radicals it was a tactical resource (51). As Cobbett declaimed in 1820: "This is the '*egotism*,' '*disgusting egotism*,' the ruffians of the press will exclaim! They first assail me with atrocious falsehoods, and then, when I defend myself, they call it *egotism*" (*PR* 19 February 1820).[12] Reconfiguring radical subjectivity as consistently combative, polemical, and agitational is the first step toward rethinking and re-appreciating the disrupted narrative of working class political life writing.

The second step is to recast the "spirit of the age" as spectral and traumatic. Gillray both understood and visualized the tortured relationship between political past and present in the Romantic period.[13] His version of Cobbett's life offers a hauntology of trauma, repetition, and revenance which (however factually distorted) animates the dramatic historical conflicts behind the evolution of Cobbett's "egotism." In Gillray's spectropolitical narrative, 1792 figures as an epistemological break or primal scene which permanently disfigured or predestined Cobbett's later career. Interestingly, Cobbett's recollection of the 1809 controversy is similarly full of apocalyptic overtones:

> Some time in 1809 I had brought me a copy of the *ex officio* information. I was leaning over a gate, and looking at the turnips in the field. I saw at once the hell-born intention, and I saw the consequences. The beautiful field disappeared, and, in my imagination, I saw the walls of a prison. My blood boiled with resentment and, cramming the paper into my pocket, I

made an oath never to cease to oppose, never cease to annoy, as far as I legally could, [this] body of men. (Reitzel 232–3)

The signature vignette of the rural farmer gazing at his beloved (probably Swedish) turnips is dramatically transformed – in the manner of caricature – into a visionary pledge to oppose the "Thing" whose malevolent publication is "crammed" into his pocket like a fetish. Like all foundation-myths, this recollection may be unreliable, but it evokes revenance and revisitation.

Such tipping-points were a mainstay of radical autobiography. As in the slave narrative, there were obligatory *rites de passages* on the voyage to freedom, and though these were usually structured as staging posts on a linear progression to civilization and emancipation, they could also be reconceived as restagings of and reengagements with earlier crises. The first step was usually the quasi-religious discovery of the book: in Cobbett's case this was reading Swift's *Tale of a Tub* while working as a laborer in Kew Gardens (Reitzel 18). The second step was initiation into politics. Gillray has a particularly illuminating role to play here as he filled a gap in Cobbett's autobiography by anchoring Cobbett's radicalism to the moment when "glorious 'Jacobinical' times were just then beginning." It was also the point (though this event is buried beneath Gillray's narrative) when Cobbett first read Paine's *Rights of Man*. Given that Gillray presents Cobbett as Paine's successor, the spectral significance of this textual encounter is retrospectively heightened. Furthermore, in Part Two of *Rights of Man* Paine constructed his own political foundation myth in an intriguing autobiographical sketch that crystallizes both the necessity and impossibility of the radical life:

At an early period – little more than sixteen years of age, raw and adventurous, and heated with the false heroism of a master who had served in a man-of-war – I began the carver of my own fortune, and entered on board the Terrible Privateer, Captain Death. From this adventure I was happily prevented by the affectionate and moral remonstrance of a good father, who, from his own habits of life, being of the Quaker profession, must begin to look upon me as lost. But the impression, much as it effected at the time, began to wear away, and I entered afterwards in the King of Prussia Privateer, Captain Mendez, and went with her to sea. Yet, from such a beginning, and with all the inconvenience of early life against me, I am proud to say, that with a perseverance undismayed by difficulties, a disinterestedness that compelled respect, I have not only contributed to raise a new empire in the world, founded on a new system of government, but I have arrived at an eminence in political literature, the most difficult of all lines to succeed and excel in, which aristocracy with all its aids has not been able to reach or to rival. (Paine 218–19)

Some of these details seem barely credible, most notably the allegorical-sounding name of the first ship "Captain Death," though modern scholars have confirmed the authenticity of the account (Keane 31–6). The echo of the early pages of *Robinson Crusoe*, including a role for the quasi-Oedipal father, further enhances the symbolic, proleptic tone of Paine's break with England. As the "carver of my own fortune," Paine becomes the prodigal son of revolutionary politics. This new heroism, in which the goal of national liberation is achieved by the pen rather than arms, is the complete antithesis of the anti-Jacobin, rabble-rouser stereotype. Paine's self-fashioned radical egotism replaces aristocratic hauteur with self-made "eminence" and republican disinterestedness.

This democratic persona was far more threatening to the political establishment than the well-worn trope of the unruly agitator, hence the determination to snuff it out with, among other things, fake biographies.[14] The idea that the lower classes could become bona fide members of the political public sphere, and even rise to the status of national figures, was simply unthinkable. Note that Paine does not claim any special talents behind his remarkable success; his modesty is also a tactic to defuse the smears of his detractors. It is as if he has to over-compensate for his stardom by cleansing himself of any personal gratification other than a devotion to Liberty, a trope repeated in most radical life writing. The result is a new ideal of the English Jacobin ego: an elevated political consciousness without the darker associations of Robespierreian Terror. Paine's legacy for radical life writing was to democratize the persona of republican virtue, untainted ambition, and intellectual power; he replaced the romance of empire and capitalism with the romance of politics. But he did this against overwhelming odds. When Gillray gave Cobbett Paine's mantle, the caricature revealed graphically what was at stake.

Bizarrely, or perhaps tellingly, the 1809 episode anticipated another spectral intertwining of Cobbett's and Paine's lives ten years later, at the height of the Peterloo crisis. By 1809 Cobbett had become a devotee of Paine, not for his republicanism but for his withering analysis of paper money. Cobbett's hero-worship became a literal pilgrimage when he fled to America for a second time in 1817 to avoid persecution and embarked on an eccentric plan to bring Paine's bones back to Britain and deposit them in a new radical shrine. Whether this stunt was a cynical ploy to re-ingratiate himself with the reform movement after fleeing the country is open to question, but predictably the caricaturists had a field day. Amid a rash of prints, another mock-biography of Cobbett appeared under the title *Sketches of the Life of Billy Cobb* (1820). The illustration "B stands for Bones" shows

Cobbett extracting Paine's remains from his coffin like a furtive resurrection man. In this reactionary cartoon apostolic succession becomes graveyard humor, and the final irony is that Paine's corpus becomes Cobbett's "interest" (British Museum Satires 13523–30). However, the image of Paine as a bag of bones is a suitably grotesque reminder of the fragmented and vulnerable nature of the radical "life" and the fact that Cobbett also penned an unpublished biography of Paine at this time is simply further irony (Claeys 6).

With these controversies in mind, it is perhaps understandable that as Cobbett approached the end of his life he planned to write a complete autobiography which would emphasize triumphal social and political mobility rather than the ghosts of the past.[15] He intended to dedicate *The Progress of a Ploughboy to a Seat in Parliament* to that lost organic community of his rural origins, "the race of English labouring people, amongst whom I was born and bred" (*PR* 15 February 1834). In the spectral mode of remembering mobilized by Gillray, however, the unfinished Jacobin past haunts the present: in Derrida's words, spectrality is "the furtive and ungraspable visibility of the invisible" (7). With the stakes this high, perhaps it is no surprise that radical plebeian life writing in the Romantic period remained inchoate and tactical, unable to break free from journalistic and polemical necessity, but nevertheless expressing an important if maligned notion of a radical ego, the great "I am not." Ironically, it was Gillray and the caricaturists who provided a spectral solution to this problem: revenance is a powerful way to bridge absence. But perhaps this was too radical for most plebeian radicals to consider.

NOTES

1. Like many Cobbett scholars I first saw the series in Spater. In the most recent biography, Richard Ingrams simply calls the images an artistic "*tour de force*" (Ingram 91). For Dorothy George they are "cruel and amusing" (George 124).
2. Cobbett called Gillray a "base hireling" (*Cobbett's Weekly Political Register* [*PR*] 23 June 1832).
3. Francis Place referred to 1809 as "a year of considerable agitation" (cited in Baer 240).
4. For David A. Wilson, Cobbett "was quite prepared to distort his past" to win an argument, so we should be "sceptical" of his accounts (xiv–xv). But for Craig Calhoun, Cobbett's "constant self-presentation" was his "certificate of authenticity ... embedded in an ongoing narrative of his independence, from his childhood to his struggle with abusive authority in the present" (148).
5. See *Democracy: or A Sketch of the Life of Buonaparte* (1800); British Museum Satires 9534.

6. See *The Soldier's Friend* (1792) in Butler 134.
7. The term "hauntology" derives from Derrida.
8. *The Soldier's Friend* was published just weeks before the Royal Proclamation of May 1792 and there is evidence that a prosecution against its publisher James Ridgway was being planned. This makes the parallels between Cobbett and Paine even more marked. See Grande 18–26.
9. Marc Baer notes that "Burdett's popularity peaked visually in 1810" (227).
10. Francis Place's autobiography was not published until 1972.
11. Belchem is unimpressed by Hunt's claim that he was correcting "the malignant slanders, base assertions, and foul attacks of the public press" (1: 70–71). Gregory Claeys remarks on the "overweening egotism" of Cobbett and Paine though he concedes that Paine's "vanity" was "quite justifiable" considering his role in "three revolutions or near revolutions" (10).
12. James Treadwell notes that "the proper management of the figure of egotism" was a source of "ubiquitous autobiographical anxiety" for all writers (65), though I argue that laboring-class political figures faced unique pressures.
13. It is the explicit political engagement which makes the themes I am discussing distinct from Gothic fiction, the other predominantly spectral mode in Romantic culture.
14. An early attack on Paine was a fake autobiography by Francis Oldys (George Chalmers) published in 1793. See Claeys 5.
15. Cobbett regarded his social mobility as a class signifier and the obverse of the Pitt "system" of promoting cronies "from dunghill to a coach and four" (Reitzel 93).

CHAPTER 12

John Clare's Agrarian Idyll
A Confluence of Pastoral and Georgic

Gary Harrison

In this chapter, I examine how John Clare's poetry participates in what Jeremy Burchardt in *Paradise Lost: Rural Idyll and Social Change since 1800* describes as the progressive idealization of rural life in Britain from the mid-eighteenth through the early twentieth centuries. Simplifying the complex shift in ways of seeing and feeling that covers ground visited by Raymond Williams in *The Country and the City*, Burchardt adduces a few representative examples to show that, on the one hand, poets such as Thomas Gray, Oliver Goldsmith, and William Wordsworth, along with novelists, such as George Eliot and Elizabeth Gaskell, fashioned the rural countryside as space – if sometimes a remembered space – of personal renewal, self-realization, and relative harmony in contrast to the city (30, 34). On the other hand, Burchardt observes, agrarian radicals such as Thomas Spence, William Cobbett, and Richard Carlile saw the rural countryside as a contested space, the site of political conflict between landowners and farmers, on one side, and the increasingly wage-dependent rural work force, on the other. Both the writers and the radicals, Burchardt shows, held in common the antithesis between the country and the city, and both relied in their works upon the strategic deployment of "powerful ruralist imagery" (44). As I will show, in poems from "Helpstone" through *The Shepherd's Calendar*, Clare's work participates in the literary production of that "powerful ruralist imagery" and its appropriation for a socio-political critique using the "*rural* idyll" in a way that presents us with two competing but sometimes complementary attitudes toward rural life mapped along the lines of georgic and pastoral (50). Given the political resonances of this idyll in Clare's work, as I explain below, I invoke the "*agrarian* idyll" as a fitting rubric that conveys a sense of Clare's antipathy to the erosion of customary rural values and practices and captures his celebration of what he calls in "Recollections After a Ramble" "rurallity" (l. 265, *Early Poems* II: 196). In the double register of the agrarian idyll, Clare's protest intersects with, but troubles, the idealized, nostalgic visions of the rural past implicit in eighteenth-century versions of pastoral and georgic. I will begin by discussing the doublings of pastoral-georgic and then move to consider more fully the agrarian idyll.

The Doublings of Pastoral-Georgic

From its beginnings, pastoral entails a critical as well as an idealizing perspective and, like its cousin the georgic, alludes to questions of society, politics, labor, and poetic practice. Historians of pastoral, including Paul Alpers and Annabel Patterson, remind us that the tranquil demesnes of Virgil's eclogues are unsettled by georgic concerns about property, the politics of the country and the city, and the social function of poetic labor. Recall the contrast in Virgil's *Eclogue* 1, for example, between the fortunate Tityrus, granted free tenure of his land, and his interlocutor Meliboeus, dispossessed of his lands and moving into exile. As Leo Marx points out in *The Machine in the Garden*, Meliboeus's alienation "brings a countervailing force to bear upon the pastoral ideal," which already in Virgil appears as a "rural myth" (21). In *What is Pastoral*, Alpers points to georgic allusions in Meliboeus's tribute to Tityrus, where Meliboeus creates a picture of "normal country life," replete with the sounds of bees, doves, and a woodman pruning trees; this picture incorporates "something of [Meliboeus's] 'agrarian' version of pastoral into his own" (167). In light of the concerns about agriculture, expropriation, and politics in Virgil's *Eclogues*, Patterson concludes that "Virgilian pastoral would have indicated its liminal status on the borders of georgic even if the *Georgics* had never been written" (*Pastoral and Ideology* 134).

This cross-fertilization between pastoral and georgic becomes particularly acute in eighteenth-century and early-nineteenth-century British poetry. David Fairer claims that, after Stephen Duck's challenge to conventional representations of labor in georgic poetry in *The Thresher's Labour* (1730), "it became increasingly difficult to show pastoral figures 'simply chatting in a rustic row'" without rolling up their sleeves and getting to work ("Persistence" 274). If, as Fairer suggests, "All things pastoral holds at bay – heroism, politics, money, war, time, and death–are there to haunt it from an echo's distance" (266), sometimes that echo reverberates loud and long. Critics such as Fairer, Corey Andrews, John Goodridge, Bridget Keegan, and Donna Landry, among others, have invoked the pastoral and georgic to frame in particular the generic tendencies of laboring class poetry and poetics.[1] "Tracking georgics," in Anne Wallace's phrase ("Farming"), as it brushes shoulders with pastoral in Stephen Duck, Mary Collier, Robert

Bloomfield, and John Clare has enhanced our understanding of the interrelationship between these two modes in plebeian poetry and tightened our purchase on these poets' transformations of pastoral and georgic inherited from Alexander Pope, George Dyer, and James Thomson, among others. Inevitably, these frames are troubled with generic dissonance, for, although we can define theoretically pastoral and georgic as particular formal modes with distinctive features, in actual poetic practice georgic and pastoral – especially in the work of rural laboring class writers – inevitably confound and collapse into one another. As John Murdoch puts it in "The Landscape of Labor," by the mid-eighteenth century, transformations in land, labor, politics, and aesthetics reached a point where "the Georgic is assimilated to the Pastoral, so that in literature and painting they are often almost indistinguishable" (190).

John Clare's "Last of March, Written at Lolham Brigs" exemplifies the crosscurrents of pastoral and georgic. This poem, an idyll offering a dynamic series of "little pictures" – not just visual, but auditory – portrays a chilly day in late March. The poem leads us through a sequence of scenes where we "watch the creeping spring" (l. 16, *Early Years* II: 471) break up the remnant snows and dark skies of "ambush'd winter" (l. 2, *Early Years* II: 471). Each of the fourteen stanzas, unified by an intricate rhyme scheme (ababbcdc) and related to each other paratactically, presents us with one or more things – a daisy, a marsh marigold, robins, lowing bullocks, fen-sparrows, bleating lambs, and more – busy with springtime labors. Integral to this glad day, alert to "Spring's opening promise," is the "hardy seedsman spread[ing] the grain," performing "his hopfull toil" (ll. 60, 51–2; *Early Years* II: 473). The poem exemplifies what John Barrell describes in *The Idea of Landscape and the Sense of Place* as Clare's "sense of the landscape as a manifold of simultaneous impressions" (169). Labor here is not objectified from the panoramic perspective of conventional georgic; rather, individual laborers take their appointed places in a network of productive, but joyful, activities shared by birds, flowers, cattle, and sheep.

"Last of March" illustrates the absence of the "aristocratic biases" and gentrified representation of labor that Rachel Crawford's *Poetry, Enclosure and the Vernacular Landscape* identifies with mainstream georgic. The poem does not display the larger "didactic concerns, generally impersonal point of view, encyclopedic procedures, and (when all flourishes are allowed for) turgid and euphemistic style" Johanne Clare rightly associates with the georgic in *John Clare and the Bounds of Circumstance* (165). With its emphasis upon the interrelationship, even reciprocity, between human labor and the workings of nature, the poem instead reflects what Johanne Clare calls the "tactful, unpossessive attitudes Clare brought to the act of natural observation" (165). Thus the poem does not valorize labor as a mode of national improvement but as an integral part of nature's rhythms, advancing Clare's sense of empathy with living things, fellow laborers, and the land itself all taking part in an organic community.

While we do not find the formal elements of pastoral or georgic in "Last of March," this thoroughly "rural" poem has affinities to both of these modes. If Clare's poetry does not advance what Clifford Siskin calls the "conjunction of life, labor, and productivity" (122) in the service of a comprehensive vision of national or imperial expansion and improvement that we associate with georgic, neither does it offer a highly stylized and artificial sense of ease and simplicity in shepherd's lives typical of the pastoral. Clare's impatience with conventional pastoral poets who substituted fancied universal ideals for experienced local realities is worth remembering here. While Clare can praise Alexander Pope, he dismisses the artificiality of Pope's rural descriptions, especially as gleaned and recycled by Pope's followers. As early as 1819, Clare complains that William Shenstone's pastoral verse comprises an empty catalog of pastoral ornaments: "Shenstone is a Good Poet but his pastorals (as I think) are improperly call'd so the rural Names of Damons Delia Phillis &c rural Objects Sheep Sheepfolds &c &c are the only things that give one the slight glimps of the Species of Poetry which the Title claims" (*Letters* 12). In his journal of 25 October 1824, Clare comments that Pope's pastorals are so "nick[n]amed for daffodils breathing flutes beachen bowls silver crooks and purling brooks and such like everlasting sing song does not make pastorals" (189). From these early interventions in reading pastoral, Clare displays a sense that pastoral is not a formal arrangement of conventional tropes but an integrative vision.

Clare gives the term "pastoral" a highly positive valence when applauding the poetry of his beloved Robert Bloomfield, whose rural vision, as John Lucas observes, shares less with pastoral than it does with georgic ("Bloomfield and Clare" 61). With some degree of hyperbole, in a 10 August 1824 letter to Thomas Inskip, Clare praised Bloomfield as "the most original poet of the age & the greatest Pastoral Poet England ever gave birth too" (*Letters* 300). Writing to Allan Cunningham just a month later (9 September 1824), Clare bestowed further accolades upon Bloomfield, setting him, "our English Theocritus," above Crabbe, whose depictions of the rural poor for Clare fell short of capturing their "pleasures and pastoral feelings" (*Letters* 302). Clare praises Bloomfield, as he does the painters Peter DeWint and Edward Rippingille, for creating what Clare understands as unmediated pictures of the rural countryside. In an April 1828 letter to Cunningham,

Clare praises Rippingille's "pastoral poesy of painting," characterized by a "true English consception of real [english]? pastoral [of real]? life & reality of english manners & english beauty" (*Letters* 423). Perhaps Clare expresses his idea of pastoral best when describing in his journal of 8 September 1824 Isaac Walton's *The Compleat Angler*:

> what a delightful book   it is the best English Pastoral that can be written   the descriptions are nature unsullied by fashionable tastes of the time   they are simply true and like the Pastoral Ballads of Bloomfield breath of the common air and grass and the sky   one may almost hear the water of the river Lea ripple along and the grass and flags grow and rustle in the pages that speak of it   I have never read a happier Poem in my time. (171)

Clare's version of pastoral, then, blends with a particularized and localized *sense* of georgic effected, as we have seen in "The Last of March," by means of poignant descriptions of rural life drawn from Clare's direct experience of the place and people in and around Helpston.

The Agrarian Idyll

From pastoral-georgic conventions, *topoi*, and strategies, Clare fashioned a distinctive poetics in a voice that closed the distance between poet and place with a unique intimacy and immediacy absent from conventional georgic and pastoral. The confluence of these perspectives amplifies Clare's position as a man, in Jonathan Bate's neat encapsulation, "not only torn from his own world of rural labour, but also torn between the very different assumptions and manners of the aristocracy and the middle classes" (203). Marked as the "peasant-poet" – an epithet Clare embraced with reluctance – Clare occupies an in-between space, where pastoral and georgic mingle and play, and where competing senses of social, political, and literary affiliation enter into a space of ongoing negotiation. In this sense, the agrarian idyll may be read apropos to what Anne Janowitz calls Clare's position at a "crossroads between . . . the kind of collective agrarian poetics" she finds in Shelley's "Mask of Anarchy" and the poems of Allen Davenport, on the one hand, and the "transcendent lyricism of Wordsworth in his post-Jacobin period," on the other (*Lyric and Labour* 108). John Goodridge and Bridget Keegan similarly describe what they call "John Clare's cross-cultural trespassing, his refusal to be confined by his class to a particular idiom and his appropriation of the refined poetic discourse of the age on his own terms" ("Clare and the Traditions of Labouring-Class Verse" 282). Clare's agrarian idyll, I believe, captures these doubled registers stemming from his in-betweenness, particularly as they are voiced in a dialectic of rural protest and praise.

In *Wordsworth's Vagrant Muse*, I described what M. M. Bakhtin in *The Dialogic Imagination* calls the "idyll with a focus on agricultural labor" (224) as a *topos* in late-eighteenth- and early-nineteenth-century poetry that reflects and fuels a cultural imaginary seeking in utopian images of rustic life signs of national prosperity, civic virtue, and personal integrity (40–42). For Bakhtin, the agricultural idyll presents rural labor as a transformative agency that "creates a real link and common bond between the phenomena of nature and the events of human life" (227). That is, un-alienated agricultural work presents itself as the organic means of bonding generations within the family, families within the local community, the human community within the natural community. Clare's vision of un-alienated agricultural labor serves as a foil to the forms of alienated wage labor that were fast overtaking the customary relations of agricultural production. Thus, in Clare, the idyll functions critically, emphasizing his antipathy to the mechanisms of agricultural improvement and the technologies of moral control eroding common customs. Clare thus deploys the idyll as a critical, even utopian, ideal against which to plumb the negative impact of the new agricultural regime – accompanied by enclosure, engrossment, and the erosion of customary relations – in Helpston and its environs. While Bakhtin uses the term "*agricultural* idyll" as the sign of this formation, because Clare's work emphasizes the precariousness of that ideal and often uses it in the context of overt protest against the dire consequences of enclosure, I adopt the phrase "*agrarian* idyll" to stress the critical aspect of this chronotope.

How far Clare was radical in his politics and what he and we might mean by "radical" has been the subject of ongoing debate, with critics such as Johanne Clare, P. M. S. Dawson, John Lucas, James McKusick, Eric Robinson, and Alan Vardy, among others, taking up different positions on the question.[2] Each of these critics agrees that while Clare was not and did not see himself as a card-carrying radical along the lines of a Thomas Spence or William Cobbett, the positions he takes up in his poetry and prose against the abuses of institutional privilege and power that contributed to the distress of the rural poor align in various degrees with the criticism that self-identified agrarian radicals levied against the state. Clare did not, as they did, endorse a practical politics of reform or rebellion; nor did he, like the Spenceans, advocate a leveling that would restore a "people's farm." Explaining what he dubs Clare's "political lubricity," Simon Kövesi nicely sums up the issue this way: "It is true that Clare hones sharp resentments against the corruption of entrenched social hierarchies, capitalist greed, self-righteous elitism and individualist self-promotion. But equally he was nervous about 'radical' movements which peppered – and sometimes disrupted – rural and national affairs" ("John Clare &" 78, 75). Indeed, Clare criticized the ideas of the relatively moderate William Cobbett, opposed the sometimes violent tactics of the Spencean radicals, and abhorred the incendiarism, mob actions, and violence associated with the Swing riots. Whatever Clare's actual political position, as Sam Ward argues in "'This is Radical Slang,'" the politically charged climate of the early 1820s led certain of Clare's readers to construe statements in his early poems as echoes of the discourse of agrarian radicalism. Clare's patrons, friends, and editors – specifically Lord Radstock, Eliza Emmerson, and John Taylor – endeavored, with however good intentions and however reluctantly in the case of Emmerson and Taylor respectively, to suppress or soften passages that rang in Lord Radstock's ears as "radical slang."³ While John Lucas claims that "Radstock was in a very good position to understand Clare's radicalism" and "[took] it seriously" ("Clare's Politics" 156), Sam Ward argues persuasively that it is "highly unlikely" Radstock would "have suspected Clare of harbouring radical sympathies" (197). As Ward notes, in a letter to Emmerson (quoted in hers to Clare of 11 May 1820), Radstock attributes what he calls Clare's "error" and "injustice" to his "depressed state," not to any political position (Ward 195; Storey, *Critical Heritage* 61). Even so, Ward observes, Radstock "clearly detected close thematic and tonal parallels between Clare's protests about inequalities in the countryside and the discourse of contemporary radicalism" (197). If, as Ward suggests, Radstock and Emmerson were concerned less about Clare's politics and more about how his statements would be "misinterpreted" by readers (197), it seems clear that at its highest pitch Clare's voice of indignation could equal that of the agrarian radicals.

In addition to verbal parallels, congruences between Clare and the agrarian radicals include his well-known opposition to enclosure; his public witness to the injury and loss that the expropriation of land and the demise of the commons wrought upon his fellow agricultural laborers; his criticism of greedy landowners, opportunistic farmers, and the collusion between the clergy and politicians to suppress and/or refashion customary rural festivities; and his longing for independence and support, albeit sometimes qualified, for the dignity of rural life. In light of these tacit affinities, Clare's agrarian idylls advance a dialectic of rural protest and praise, as we see in "Helpstone" and *The Shepherd's Calendar*, to which I will now turn.

As is well known, in "Helpstone" Clare attributes the cause of rural privation and "wretchedness" to the large landowners, personified as "wealth," who benefited from enclosure: "Accursed wealth oer bounding human law... / Thou art the bar that keeps from being fed / & thine our loss of labour & of bread" (ll. 127, 130–31; *Early Poems* I: 161). Also in "Helpstone" Clare celebrates agricultural laborers, personified as "Industry," a typical georgic trope that here collapses under the poem's critical pressure. In language that would remind readers of the discourse of the agrarian radicals, Clare insists that laborers have lost the dignity and level of compensation – both in wages and in custom and commons – they once enjoyed at the hands of the very productive forces that georgic celebrates:

> Sweet rest & peace ye dear departed Charms
> Which once Industry cherish'd in her arms
> When peace & plenty known but now to few
> Where know to all & labour had his due
> (ll. 135–8; *Early Poems* I: 161)

In these lines, we see what Johanne Clare describes as Clare's "moral opposition" to enclosure, whereby he saw the "rural labouring poor as innocent victims" of "the acquisitive values of the master class" (37).

As we have seen, Clare's discursive affinities with the language of agrarian protest often appear in poems charged with intensive feeling evoked from closely observed vignettes of rural life in and around Helpston. Clare brings to, and derives from, these scenes a palpable sense of affective engagement with the ordinary stuff of his world, which the poems – in Wordsworthian fashion – make extraordinary. In "Helpstone," for example, Clare creates a scene of little birds hopping upon a "snow cloth'd bough" fruitlessly seeking for food in a "f[r]ozen plain" (l. 32; *Early Poems* I: 157). Imagining the birds' anticipation of spring, the speaker's self-identification with the birds' distress leads him into a landscape of memory, fleshed out in a sequence of detailed images: a brook running over "pebbles dimpling sweet" and crossed by an "oaken plank"; beetles "With getty jackets glittering in the sun"; "golden kingcups" opening; "silver dazies.../ tottering" in the silver grass dotted with lilacs; cowslips seeming to bend from the hand that would pick them; and amid these images the sound of oxen lowing and shepherds calling to their "woolly charge" (ll. 75–107; *Early Poems* I: 159–60). The idyll here invokes a half-remembered, half-imagined picture of a more golden past when "No calls of hunger pitys feelings wound / Twas wanton plenty rais'd the joyful sound" (ll. 109–10; *Early Poems* I: 160). In an imagined present, these lines construct the picture of past felicity suffused with the critical force of nostalgia that works in tandem with Clare's more strident attack upon the privileged agents of agricultural "improvement." In *John Clare and Community*, John Goodridge explains how "Helpstone" draws upon eighteenth-century traditions of sensibility and satire – from Goldsmith and Pope, respectively – to effect a powerful attack upon enclosure and to articulate an emphatic sense of personal loss and outrage. Goodridge notes how the poem advances "a tone of political indignation ('Accursed Wealth'), an appeal to natural justice ('human laws'), and the presence of a 'feeling heart' and a tearfulness that are characteristic of sensibility poetry" (106). In contrast to Goldsmith's *The Deserted Village*, itself a "poetical lament for a lost rural idyll," Goodridge rightly sees that Clare's poem is "more personal" and "more able to exemplify the observer's implicated position" (106). "Helpstone" thus presents an agrarian idyll where the competing but complementary ways of thinking – praise for rural life, explicit protest over its transformations – combine forces to enhance the critical import and emotional resonance of the poem; and it does so with a compelling intensity of personal affect.

As in "Last of March" and "Helpstone," the poems of *The Shepherd's Calendar* exploit the oxymoronic character of the agrarian idyll, advancing what James McKusick calls Clare's "radical conservativism" ("John Clare's Version of Pastoral" 82), or perhaps in more nuanced terms what Katey Castellano explores as Clare's version of Romantic conservatism – "intergenerational responsibility and continuity in land use," in which Clare visualizes "a radically bioegalitarian community without human authority and tyranny" (*The Ecology of Romantic Conservatism* 4, 162). In "Pastoral Elegy in the 1820s," Fiona Stafford rightly marks Clare's *The Shepherd's Calendar* as a work taking part in a renewal of pastoral elegy – from Goldsmith, Gray and Burns and Wordsworth, Hogg, and Clare – that brought together an elegiac engagement with loss, a celebration of rural virtues, and a recuperative sense of the possibilities for a future recalibration of the relations of production. In these elegies, Stafford writes, the poet would as likely "be grieving over the inexorable retreat of the rural world as to be lamenting the death of a friend through pastoral motifs" (107), but through those lamentations he or she would also likely be demonstrating "the recuperative capacities of pastoral and its tendency towards new life" (107). Comparing Clare's *Shepherd's Calendar* to James Hogg's prose stories of the same title, Stafford finds "the energy, variety and sheer plenitude of the descriptions suggests that the shepherds are part of a vigorous, self-sustaining community. However, in both texts, there are also signs of threatening external forces and a pervasive sense of irreversible change" (119). Rather than see here, as Stafford does, an erasure of the "rural idyll" – that idyllic moment set in a past felicity that has given way to dystopic forces in the present –

I suggest that we see the signature doubleness of the agrarian idyll wherein the tension between past felicity and present pain serves a critical poetics aimed to a new future.

The critical voice of the poems in *The Shepherd's Calendar* is unquestionably more muted than in "Helpstone" and other enclosure elegies. Nonetheless, many Clare scholars have noted the shifting tones, "both celebratory and elegiac" (Lucas, *John Clare* 51); the contrast between visions of past and present forms of rural life and social relations; the tension between cyclical and linear modes of time;[4] and the modulations of pastoral and georgic in the poem as a whole. John Goodridge writes that Clare, like Robert Bloomfield, worked "to describe physical comfort and discomfort in labour" and sets this poem within the "georgic descriptive tradition" stemming from John Philips's *Cyder* and James Thomson's *Seasons* (*John Clare and Community* 94). On the other hand, in *John Clare and the Place of Poetry*, Mina Gorji describes the pastoral of Clare's *The Shepherd's Calendar* in terms that suggest its debt not just to the British pastoral tradition, but to georgic:

> Clare refused to gloss over what he called the 'dirty reality' of rural life; the broken, blotched and stained, the harsh and the inharmonious are all described in exacting detail. He describes a countryside of battered fences where whistling ploughmen blunder along, herons swing heavily across grey skies and men loiter with tattered hats slouched down. (83)

Again we see critics sounding the confluence of pastoral and georgic in Clare's poetry in order to emphasize the different tones, moods, and themes in the work, which Hugh Haughton and Adam Phillips describe in their introduction to *John Clare in Context* as "a latter-day English book of hours and robust illuminated diary of the agricultural year written from the standpoint of a village labourer" (5).

The sequence of twelve poems, written in a variety of verse forms, that compose *The Shepherd's Calendar* "present us," in Edward Storey's opinion, "with a history and scenario of village life that has rarely been equalled" (*Right to Song* 192). The poem bustles with scenes of work – happy laborers busy about their herding, hedging, chopping, sewing, plowing, reaping, gleaning, milking, spinning – all synchronized to the cyclical and seasonal rhythms of country life. In "February," the ploughmen "go whistling to their toils," and the milkmaid awakens in song, leaving "her bed / As glad as happy thoughts can be" (ll. 33, 25–6; *Middle Period* I: 27). As the plowmen and sowers prepare the fields in "March," we find them stopping their songs only "to clean their ploughs" (l. 62; *Middle Period* I: 40), while in

"May" the village square and fields are filled with the "merry minstrelsy" of the cuckoos, swallows, crickets, and children in whose "humming joys" we find music (ll. 2, 11; *Middle Period* I: 58). Lest we mistake these figures for the happy swains of eighteenth-century patrician georgic, in "June" Clare supplements the personified "Labour pursu[ing] its toil in weary mood" with sketches of the sweating plowman seeking shade (l. 41; *Middle Period* I: 77); in July, the shepherd "long with heat opprest / Betakes him to his cottage rest, " and the mower bends his way home "wi weary strides" (ll. 369–70, 474; *Middle Period* I: 97, 100). Clare depicts both the celebratory spirit with which workers awaken to the fields in late winter/early spring and the weariness they experience after a season of toil by the end of summer and fall.

Throughout the *Shepherd's Calendar*, we also glimpse the subsidence of traditional rural customs, as the speaker in "May," for example, asks "Old may day weres thy glorys gone" (l. 429; *Middle Period* I: 73) and when in June, Cobbett-like, Clare reminds us of the social posturing of the uppity new farmers of the postenclosure era, whose pride and acquisitiveness have opened a gulf between themselves and their laborers:

> ... ale & songs & healths & merry ways
> Keeps up a shadow of old farmers days
> But the old beachen bowl that once supplyd
> Its feast of frumity is thrown aside
> & the old freedom that was living then
> When masters made merry wi their men
> ...
> All this is past–& soon may pass away
> The time torn remnant of the holiday
> As proud distinction makes a wider space
> Between the genteel & the vulgar race
>   (ll. 153–8, 163–6; *Middle Period* I: 83)

Comparing Clare's *The Shepherd's Calendar* to Robert Bloomfield's *The Farmer's Boy*, John Lucas captures well the spirit of these lines, writing that "Both poets are keenly aware of the hurts and insults of the newer arrangements, which break what Alun Howkins and Ian Dyck call 'the old order,' where social harmony was achieved because 'men were bound together by their "words" into a society of mutuality'" ("Bloomfield and Clare" 62).[5] Clare strikes this note of belatedness throughout *The Shepherd's Calendar*, lamenting the loss of commons and customs, while, as in "May," targeting "enclosure" – used as a kind of shorthand for multiple forces at work in the countryside – as the primary cause: "& were inclosure has its birth / It spreads a mildew oer her mirth" (ll. 460–61; *Middle Period* I: 74).

As in "Last of March," *The Shepherd's Calendar* is structured as a series of vignettes. While I have emphasized the laborers depicted in the poems, these figures appear as part of a cascade of images pointing to other elements in the scenes – barking dogs chasing after crows ("February"), daisies peeping up from the grass ("March"), humming wood flies and bees buzzing around hedges ("June"), horses grazing on "moisting grass" at the day's end ("July"), and more. The paratactic flow of these little pictures of rural life and local ecology exemplify what John Barrell calls Clare's economy of description – Clare's desire not just to capture the particularity of each object, but also to grasp the "the multiplicity of objects in his field of experience" (*Idea of Landscape* 151). As the eye and ear move from, say, "gad flyes" and a horse bee, to a grazing horse, to the cowboys plodding home and playing at soldiers, we feel that "tendency towards disorder" in the arrangement of objects in the rural scene that Barrell finds typical of Clare's sense of place (*Idea of Landscape* 152). Patrick Bresnihan elaborates upon Barrell's assessment of Clare's technique, describing in "John Clare and the Manifold Commons," the poet's "attentiveness to things in their singular presence, to the ways in which they form and radiate and intervene in ways we might ignore" – or, we might add, in ways that exceed our persistent efforts to organize experience hierarchically – "as a relational, material process through which self and world unfold together" (78). Of *The Shepherd's Calendar*, Bresnihan argues that Clare "did not discriminate between things in their concrete singularity. His imagery is not ordered by any particular aesthetic in which certain images are counted above others according to their relative qualities" (82). Thus, Clare's agrarian idyll offers us moving pictures of rural life replete with close up, if fleeting, shots of a rich variety of persons, animals, flora, fauna, and objects organized horizontally into a "community of equals," to adapt Theresa Adams's observation about *The Village Minstrel* – including human and nonhuman beings (372).

The Shepherd's Calendar presents, in sum, a comprehensive picture of rural life that held for Clare a model for, if not the promise of, a better, more just, rural community and a productive reciprocity between human beings and the land. In the poems discussed here, the agrarian idyll aligns his work with the discourse of agrarian protest against the threats to rural life posed by enclosure, engrossment, and social change, even as it renders a celebratory, but not unqualified, vision of rural life with affinities to both pastoral and georgic. Making strategic use of the long-standing interanimation of pastoral and georgic, Clare's agrarian idyll invokes versions of pastoral-georgic in a dynamic verbal space of ambivalent filiation and affiliation impelled by a set of rural vignettes weighted with a powerful critique of what he sees as the *destructive* forces of agricultural improvement. In its doublings, Clare's agrarian idyll captures what it means to respect and treat with care the land that one reveres, while acknowledging the land as a resource for both rural leisure and labor. In John Clare's work, then, the rural countryside was a site of antinomies – both a place of personal renewal and relative harmony, as well as a contested space of conflict. In this idyllic realism, Clare's poetry speaks to us powerfully today, when our own agricultural and recreational practices place demands upon the land and call for a rethinking of our agrarian and environmental future.

NOTES

1. See Fairer, "'Fuming Trees"; Andrews, "Work Poems"; Landry, "Georgic Ecology"; Keegan, "Georgic Transformations"; Goodridge, *John Clare*.
2. See Clare, *Bounds of Circumstance*, 18–22; Dawson, "Common Sense or Radicalism"; Lucas, *John Clare*, 15–18 and "Clare's Politics"; McKusick, "William Cobbett, John Clare and the agrarian politics of the English Revolution" 178–80; Robinson, "Introduction" to *John Clare: Champion for the Poor*, passim.; and Vardy, *John Clare, Politics and Poetry*, 167–87.
3. Ward and Zachary Leader remind us that Taylor capitulated "reluctantly" and "belatedly" to Radstock's efforts to censor the purportedly radical passages and poems (Ward 190; Leader 243). For Eliza Emmerson's somewhat delicate and reluctant role in being tasked with conveying Radstock's censure to Clare, see Trehane 75–6.
4. See, e.g., Richard Lessa 61 and Paul Chirico 129–30, 160–61.
5. The quote is from Alun Howkins and Ian Dyck 23.

CHAPTER 13

"And aft Thy Dear Doric aside I Hae Flung, to Busk oot My Sang wi' the Prood Southron Tongue"
The Antiphonal Muse in Janet Hamilton's Poetics*

Kaye Kossick

That Scots-born Janet Thomson Hamilton (1795–1873) has secured a place in the pantheon of Victorian women poets, working class or otherwise, is beyond dispute. That she was passionate in pursuing knowledge under exigencies of deprivation that would have destroyed creative ambition in a lesser being is equally sure. Despite having subaltern status in terms of national cultural identity and bearing the additional stigmata of gender and poverty, Hamilton succeeded against all odds in an era subject to rigidly policed social and aesthetic apartheid, when the "gush" of the heart's affections might sustain the genteel poetess, but could rarely be the business of a laboring woman's life.[1]

Hamilton's stated pride in being the "daughter, wife and mother of working men" (*Poems, Essays, and Sketches* 389) exemplifies the "embedded identity" with "commoners," the men and women of the laboring classes that Anne Janowitz finds in Robert Burns (67). Inevitably, however, both Hamilton and her "hero," Burns, were subject to pressures, insidious and patent, that complicated their linguistic and political allegiances. This chapter will address the historical and cultural politics informing Hamilton's life and work and consider whether her divergences from the "excessively univocal" Anglocentric mode of speech described by Murray Pittock (*Edinburgh* 10) serve to challenge the prevailing formal and ideological boundaries in Victorian literature.

From her earliest years, Hamilton was an omnivorous reader who "mused and sang" to "please herself," yet made no attempt to publish until she was 53 (Wright, *Janet Hamilton* 25). But, barely into her teens, she and her father's journeyman, a shoemaker with only a "dollar in his breek pocket," "started on foot early for Glasgow, on a cold February morning" to be married (Hamilton, *Poems and Ballads* xxii). Their union proved enduringly affectionate. Hamilton's "*fell*" passion for self-culture was nurtured by "armfuls of books" cheerfully sourced by her devoted husband from more distant villages after she had "used up" the local supply (Hamilton, *Poems, Essays, and Sketches* 32–3). The extreme vulnerability of their existence – haunted by the specter of destitution and the poorhouse – is nevertheless made plain in the compact that she and John, her "ain gudeman," agreed on when they married: "To be warkrife [industrious], an' honest, an' haud [keep] oot o' debt" (Hamilton, *Poems, Essays, and Sketches* 315). Hamilton descended from strict Calvinist forbears who exalted labor and thrift as moral virtues. As Weber identifies, the congruence of "innerworldly asceticism" and internalization of the work ethic, exemplified in the lives of Hamilton's antecedents, forms the core of Protestantism's instrumentality in forging the "iron cage" of present-day bondage to the economic conditions of machine production: "The Puritan wanted to work . . . we are forced to do so" (Weber 181). Doubly driven by brute economic necessity and moral conviction Hamilton entered the "cage" at the age of seven to begin homeworking as a yarn spinner, taking up her occupation at the tambour frame some two years later.[2] With the Bible as her primer, she was taught to read at her mother's knee while she "plied her spinning-wheel." This was the sole form of education that Hamilton, her mother, and foremothers, were ever given. The intensity of the connective cord of orality between generations of women is lovingly recalled in Hamilton's historiographical writings where, for instance, she describes her childhood delight in listening to her grandmother's "tales of eld" with "bated breath and rapt attention" (Boos, *Working-Class Women Poets* 36, 52–3). Religious sensibility and respect for the role of women as educators, moral tutors, and communicants of local lore became ingrained and ineradicable.

Hamilton had composed "about twenty pieces in rhyme, all of a strictly religious character" while still in her teens (Hamilton, *Poems, Essays, and Sketches* 27), but the birth of five children before she was 20, and five more after, had an overwhelming impact on her life. The inescapable demands of childcare and daily labor subsumed literary ambition until she was 50, when Hamilton taught herself to write, devising an idiosyncratic "pseudo-oriental script" to "preserve my compositions till I gave them to be written by my husband or son" (Hamilton, *Poems of Purpose* 6). Hamilton's creative *volta* from domestic care to "composition" initiated a stunningly prolific late-life renaissance. In the years between 1850 and 1870, Hamilton produced and published four substantial volumes of poems and essays, together with prose sketches of "Scottish Peasant Life and Character."[3]

Contemporary critical reaction to the force of her writing and implicit testament to the embeddedness of gendered assumptions surrounding literary production are manifest in her seeming elevation into honorary maleness by Scots critic George Gilfillan: "Manhood was her great quality. She wrote a manly style. She had a manly mode of looking at all subjects" (Black and Wallace 1). A comparably phallocentric approach is taken by a reviewer who notes that Hamilton was "at home in her native Doric," and yet equally capable of "wield[ing] with power the polished shaft of correct English" (Hamilton, *Poems, Essays, and Sketches* 509). This encomium delivers more than an acknowledgment of Hamilton's linguistic competence; it reveals a grounding assumption of cultural hierarchy. The "homely" tongue of the "native," domestic, and subaltern is implicitly lesser than the sanctioned discourse of "correct" English – "polished," civilized, predominant.

Hamilton is fluent in the Anglophone, monoglot language of colonial governance – Liz Lochhead's "English-male-posh-grown-up-dead-speech" – that is regarded "as being the norm, voiceless, neutral," yet such vocalizations are by no means "neutral" (quoted in Kidd, "Writing" 97). Language is loaded, words are weapons: the "real difference between a language and a dialect is that one has the armed might of the state behind it, the other does not" (Joyce 194). "Scottish cringe" is Billy Kay's indicator of the anxious embarrassment induced in speakers of Scots – a "disadvantaged," "deposed" language – by their cultural colonization (39). Robert Burns's editor, James Currie, locates the political genesis of the "cringe" in the arranged "marriage" of Scotland and England: "since the Union the manners and language of the people of Scotland have no longer a standard among themselves, but are tried by a nation to which they are united" (quoted in Pittock, *Burns* 92). The debilitating effects of metropolitan elitism and the "Pinkerton Syndrome," engendered by John Pinkerton, an eighteenth-century Scots historian, who denounced the "barbarisms" of the Scots dialect, became systemic and internalized. Even Robert Burns feared seeming like an uncouth rustic when writing in Scots, feeling compelled to "look over his shoulder to see the reaction of his aristocratic patrons and polite society" (Kay 118, 109).

Hamilton shared Burns's sensitivity to the notion of linguistic propriety but was similarly gifted with a chameleonic talent for verbal shape-shifting, adopting native and "polite" registers according to context. Recollections of her early years are delivered in Burns's "plain, braid Lallans" (broad lowland Scots) to one interlocutor, Joseph Wright, a lifelong friend and fellow poet with whom she is entirely at ease (Wright, *Janet Hamilton* 25). Standard English is reserved for Alexander Wallace, a Doctor of Divinity, who expressed surprise that Hamilton "could write so grammatically without having formally learned any rules." The Reverend George Gilfillan wrote a memoir of Hamilton's "life and poetical character" in which he describes her "clear and correct enunciation as if (to use [Sir Walter] Scott's expression) she 'spoke from a prent [printed] book.'" Gilfillan nevertheless goes on to note that "of course" Hamilton exhibited "some of the drawbacks of the self-taught," namely "opinionativeness" and the want of "that polish and correctness which only a classical education can bestow" (Hamilton, *Poems, Essays, and Sketches* 33, 25, 22).

Despite Gilfillan's elitist cavils, Hamilton's skill in writing "correct" English assuredly led her to success. She gained imprimatur by winning an essay competition promoted by John Cassell, a "liberal publisher," committed to the "use and improvement of the working-classes" (Boos, "The Homely Muse" 263). This entrée freed her for a time from the humiliation of begging for patronage that beset working class writers – "dancing a jig to the humours of a foolish patron," as Aberdonian weaver-poet William Thom remarked disgustedly.[4] Having relocated his provincial publishing hub to London in the 1840s, Cassell was in one sense ironically akin to the "big men o' print," derided in "A Plea for the Doric" for deserting their native ground to be "nearer the [money-making] mint" in London. Despite her contempt of "mammon-seeking" disloyalty, Hamilton offers a penitential apostrophe to "mither Scotland" in "A Plea for the Doric," acknowledging that her defection to the "proud" English tongue also constitutes betrayal:

Forgi'e, oh, forgi'e me, auld Scotlan,' my mither!
Like an ill-deedie bairn I've ta'en up wie anither;
And aft thy dear Doric aside I hae flung
To busk oot my sang wi' the prood Southron tongue.   *[busk oot = to adorn, decorate]*
(*Poems, Essays, and Sketches* 177–8, ll. 1–4)

Brian Maidment's assessment of Hamilton's work, including her winning essay, "The Uses of Poetry to the Working Classes" (Hamilton, *Poems, Essays, and Sketches* 365–9), acknowledges the difficulties surrounding its production yet deplores her capitulation to hegemonic values: "Despite [her] career of exemplary literary hardship, Mrs Hamilton's writings remain a compendium of ferociously conservative attitudes, which include this utterly untroubled celebration of the pleasures of reading" (*Poorhouse* 188). Few took greater delight in reading than Hamilton, but there is more at stake here than the anodyne detailing of a pleasurable pastime. As John Barrell points out,

> whenever we speak or write we are adopting... a specific discourse, one that we feel is more or less appropriate to the topic we are addressing and the situation in which our utterance is being made.... All our utterances are therefore political utterances, in the widest sense of being attempts to claim for ourselves particular positions in language. (*Poetry, Language and Politics* 9)

As an autodidact, and therefore devoid of educational credentials, Hamilton was no more than a pauper when assessed according to Bourdieu's concept of *institutionalized* cultural capital.[5] But her meticulously constructed text displayed sufficient *embodied* cultural capital to gain entry to the cultivated enclave of literature, a symbolic patriarchal space in which even Virginia Woolf felt *persona non grata*. Hamilton's price of admittance is that she must unsex and "unscotch" herself by adopting what Burns deplored as the "thoroughly and entirely English" style of *The Spectator* (which she read) and in a form which functioned as a "univocal instrument for instilling sensibility... divorced... from the heteroglossia of the periodical press" (Pittock, *Edinburgh* 10). Audre Lorde contends that "the master's tools will never dismantle the master's house."[6] Hamilton could well have countered that "nothing will come of nothing," and proceeds to set forth an argument that in form and content firmly refutes Burkean notions of *innate* intellectual inferiority in the "swinish" poor.

She begins by expressing her "deep regret that working-men and women" are debarred from the "high advantages of a liberal and finished education," but then affirms that they are equally capable of "appreciating... the best poets," as if they *had* been given access to the "patrician halls of Oxford or Cambridge" (*Poems, Essays, and Sketches* 365). To this clear assertion of intellectual equality between "patrician" and proletarian readers, she adds an endorsement of similar parity between poets of major canonical stature – Shakespeare, Milton, Gray, Cowper, and those of "humbler" provenance like Robert Burns and the radical, self-taught "Corn-Law Rhymer," Ebenezer Elliott. Hamilton's inclusion of Thomas Campbell's "The Battle of Maciejowice" reveals a powerful empathic engagement with peoples, however distant, subjected to the "leagued oppression" of powerful neighbors. The "wrongs and sufferings of the Magyars" under Russian dominance arouse "sorrow and indignation": "Oh! Bloodiest picture in the book of Time / Hungary fell, unwept, without a crime." Hamilton's political picture of Britain is equally brutal, highlighting the institutionalized nature of gross injustice by quoting Ebenezer Elliott's "words that burn" on the plight of "poor o'er-laboured wights," abject and starving, while their rich "brothers" fare "sumptuously every day." Her essay concludes with a deflective swerve toward conciliation via the cathartic power of poetry to "cleanse the charged bosom of that perilous stuff / That weighs upon the heart" (*Macbeth*, Act V, iii). But the root causes of radical anger exposed in Elliott's attack are explicit and – despite a dusting of palliatives on the "uses of adversity"– remain resonant. Hamilton's first venture into print presents a palimpsest of deference and assertion that prefigures later works of intense engagement with national and world politics. Pittock has devised the term "fratriotism" to signify "the espousal of the rights of other countries as displaced versions of one's own." By engaging in what might also be termed insurgence by proxy, Hamilton's subaltern status is displaced and acted out on a larger geographical and political stage. Through sympathetic identification with oppressed peoples and powerful combatants in the cause of liberty and political autonomy, notably her lifelong "twinned" heroes, Giuseppe Garibaldi and William Wallace, Hamilton is able to see herself "in the other," and read "the other as the unachievable self." Her fratriotic embracement of "cultural alterity" and the heroic past, may thus function as an oblique means of expressing discontent at her own situation and Scotland's political defeat (Pittock, *Scottish* 29).

Despite the global reach of her political sympathies, Hamilton never ventured more than 20 miles from her marital home in Langloan, Coatbridge, originally a moorland *clachan* (small settlement) of modest thatched cottages. Hamilton's childhood recollections are of a ruralized communitarian enclave, rich in birdsong and artisanal craft. In "A Wheen aul' Memories," she describes her rapturous discovery of copies of *Paradise Lost* and Ramsay's poems casually laid down on the frame of a neighbor's handloom:

> It was there my young fancy first took to wing;
> It was there I first tasted the Helicon spring;
> It was there wi' the poets I wad revel and dream,
> For Milton an' Ramsay lay on the breast beam.
> (*Poems, Essays, and Sketches* 180–82)

Remembrance may enchant the view, yet Hamilton's literary epiphany at the age of eight is grounded in circumstances that enabled an organic congruence of productive labor and inner contemplation. These workers are readers – reasoning, meditative beings who cannot be subjected to synecdochic reductionism, figuratively stripped down to their base functionality as mere "hands." Significantly, the authors of choice here are fervent naysayers: Milton, a passionate republican and defender of the belief that "all men were naturally born free, being made in the... image of God Himself," and Allan Ramsay "father-figure of the [Scots] vernacular revival," who despised "culturally colonised fops" for aping neoclassical models of high, *ergo* English, culture (Kay 106–7). Ramsay's disdain for Anglocentric mimicry sheds ironic light on Hamilton's key-change from Doric to Standard English and neoclassical allusion when she describes her momentous first connection with poetry, an "elevated" literary form regarded by Bourdieu as foundational in the acquisition of "cultural capital," and *habitus*.[7] Hamilton's rhapsodic "revelling and dreaming" figures the symbolic maiden flight of unfettered imagination and "spontaneity of consciousness" associated by Matthew Arnold with Hellenism. But Hamilton's immersive delight in "the wondrous pages" of Shakespeare raised the Presbyterian ire and anti-English hackles of her disapproving mother. To avoid a second "bonfire of the vanities" and local gossip, she learned to "stappit Wull Shakespeare" and *Blackwood's* magazine into "the hole in the wa" when she heard anyone approach (Wright, *Janet Hamilton* 25). A fusion of Hebraism and Hellenism was Arnold's prerequisite for a "full" life, but the code of conduct instilled and imposed on Hamilton was Hebraic, its essence "strictness of conscience."[8]

The discovery of Blackband ironstone in the area, which included Coatbridge, Langloan, and other villages, in 1801, destroyed the rural isolation of Hamilton's youth irrevocably.[9] In Heideggerian terms, Lanarkshire was "revealed" as a mining district and the landscape became a thing to be used, reduced to a "standing reserve" of "energy" (320), there to be ruthlessly exploited and commodified: "get[ing] gowd [*gold*] oot the ironstane, an' siller frae coal" (*Poems, Essays, and Sketches*, "Rhymes for the Times III" 235–6, l. 11).

Hamilton was immured in a cacophonous hell: "a sink of stench and pollution," its "flaming furnaces and great mounds of slag, turning the green fields... into a very pandemonium" (*Poems, Songs, and Sketches* 30). Her moments of reading and meditation, stolen from sleep, were invaded by "the thud of the ponderous hammers smashing the molten metal in the works close by... the shrill screaming of whistles, and the never-ending rattle of machinery" (Wright, *Janet Hamilton* 278).

It has been argued that the notable absence of poetry describing "*la vraie verite*," the "fret" of working class life in industrialized Scotland, was because its horrors defied the "scope of realism" (Findlay 359). For conventional poetic purposes, as *Blackwood's* magazine dictates, it was beyond representation, unspeakable:

> It is not the province of the poet to depict things as they are, but so to refine and purify as to purge out the grosser matter; and this he cannot do if he attempts to give a faithful picture of his own times . . . all poetical characters, all poetical situations must be idealized. The language [cannot] be that of common life.[10]

Hamilton's "location" was at the epicenter of a unique historical phenomenon. The ineluctable blasting of all that was familiar into a ghastly simulacrum of Matthew Arnold's "darkling plain" rendered polite versifying wholly inadequate to the moment. Only poets on the front line, enduring the seismic shocks of quotidian reality, as Hamilton did, could fully articulate its effects. Like Burns, in "Our Local Scenery," she turned to the Doric when she most needed to "attack with vigorous directness all the ills in [her] society" (Kay 109):

Smoorin' wi reek and blacken'd wi' soot,
Lowin' like Etna an' Hecla to boot,
Ought o' our malleables [*malleables* = materials shaped by hammering]
want ye to learn?–
There's chappin' an' clippin' an' sawin' o' airn; [*airn* = iron]
Burnin' an' sotterin,' reengin' an' knockin'; [*sotterin'* = soldering]
Scores o' puir mortals roastin' an' chokin'
Gizzen'd an' dry ilka thrapple and mouth, [*Gizzen'd* = dry, parched]
Like cracks in the yird in a het simmer drouth;
They're prayin,' puir chiels, for what do ye think?
It's no daily bread, it's drink, 'Gie us drink!'

(*Poems, Essays, and Sketches* 173–4)

The caustic mockery implied in Hamilton's title is prelude to a perverse "educational" tour of the locale, in which the speaker acts as guide and sardonic interpreter of indigenous culture. If Dante's *Inferno* is a "drama of the soul's choice" (Sayers 11), this is Hamilton's satirical burlesque of the genre. Mimicking Virgil's role as spirit guide to the underworld, the speaker challenges our willingness to engage with what we are shown: "want ye to learn?" "what do you think?" (ll. 3, 9). Dante offered the opportunity to "look down upon the agonies of the damned" (see Hill, *Ovid*) as a somewhat dubious reward for the "saved" in the afterlife, here we are invited to view an "underclass" condemned to "roast" in a contemporaneous hell of human manufacture. Hamilton's dense acoustic texture, the poem's insistent backbeat, concatenation of transitive verbs, and conjunctional conveyor-belt, evoke a stunning phonic mimesis of the fever and "fret" of industrialism and Marxian dehumanization. Forcibly calibrated to the unresting rhythms of the machine, subjected to intolerable heat, laborers *are* "malleables," expendable products of Thomas Carlyle's detested "Mammon-worshipping" modernity (*Past and Present* 234). Their condition portends the actualization of Heideggers's "extreme danger" – technology's conversion of humanity itself to an "available resource" (334). Yet these vitiated "puir" souls are doubly damned by their blasphemous inversion of "The Lord's Prayer"; they plead for the opiate of alcohol, not, as Marx – and Hamilton – would have it, religion. Though famed as the "apostle of temperance," Hamilton is fired by more than abstract religiosity in her furious condemnation of the human wreckage caused by alcoholism. Her sympathy for victims of abuse is intense, seemingly rooted in intimate knowledge and most trenchantly vocalized in the "mither tongue" (Boos, *Working-Class Women Poets* 55).

Inverting the primal order of maternal nurturance, "The Drunkard's Wife" inscribes the gross self-absorption of a drink-sodden husband, a "bairn wi' a beard," vampirically draining the life spirit out of a wife so malnourished that she can no longer suckle their child: "For he draws the red bluid frae yer hert an' yer face" (*Poems, Essays, and Sketches* 353, ll. 11–12). "Blows and shrieks and curses mingle" with the "sobbing" of children in "the drunkard's dwelling" (*Poems, Essays, and Sketches* 357; "The Contrast," ll. 24, 31); elsewhere "the wife of a summer" lies cold, beaten to death, her "bright hair all clotted with blood" (*Poems, Essays, and Sketches* 358, "The Plague of Our Isle" l. 25). The brutalizing effects of parental neglect, amid an "accumulated mass of squalid wretchedness" unequaled elsewhere in the British dominions,[11] erupt in the learned aggressive behaviors and verbal obscenity even of the youngest children, as she describes in "Our Local Scenery":

> ... oh, siccan weans! [*siccan weans* = such wee ones]
> Rantin,' an' playin' an' castin' o stanes.
> Hearken, thae toddlin' bit things hoo they swear;
> Had I wings like a doo I wadna be here –
> I wad flee far awa' an seek oot a rest
> Whaur drinkin' an' swearin' nae mair wad molest.
> (*Poems, Essays, and Sketches* 174, ll. 29–34)

Hamilton's stay against the feral chaos of the urban ghetto is the "guid mither." Her insistence on the centrality of woman's role as moral guardian appears to endorse the essentialist tenets of Letitia Landon's head/heart dichotomy between male intellect and female affect – a woman's sphere "must be in the affections... which it is her peculiar province to refine, spiritualise, and exalt" (*Poetical Works* v–vii). Hamilton's poem "Woman," for example, appears to ventriloquize Landon's adjurations on the maternal "holy mission":

> ... A guiding star, to shed and shine
> Soft radiance on the household shrine
> And from her sphere – a span of earth –
> Pour light and love on home and hearth
>
> And such should woman ever prove –
> The pole-star of domestic love,
> To which the youthful circle tend,
> A mother, guardian, teacher, friend.
> (*Poems, Essays, and Sketches* 91–2, ll. 17–20)

Tropes of softness and celestial light, overtly affective and suffused by unexpectedly Marian numinosity, conform to the modality of "idealization" approved by Landon and by *Blackwood's*. But there are indicators here of power beyond "the empire of the gentle heart." The pole-star is a fixed point of reference, signifying emotional stability, and an inviolable, safe domestic haven (a "shrine") in which the moral and intellectual training of the young can be securely undertaken. Symbolic structures of "order, boundary and control" such as this are rooted in the compelling need "to manage and bring meaning to the experience of poverty, endemic economic insecurity and ordered industrial production" (Joyce 151). Hamilton's holistic concept of the maternal vocation as "teacher" and protective "guardian" against vice demands an intellectual component and strenuous "on-site" vigilance that is born of intrinsic social urgency beyond Landon's ken: "until I visited the wynds of Glasgow I did not believe that so much crime, misery and disease could exist in any civilised country... theft and prostitution form the chief means of subsistence of this population."[12]

Fired by a hunger for justice, Hamilton breaches the bounds of Landon's "woman's sphere" by demolishing the gendered demarcation between politics and morality, action and restraint. For Hamilton, the personal and the political are of the same root, of the same family. Thus, in "A Lay of the Tambour Frame," a trenchant, explicit advance on Thomas Hood's "Song of the Shirt" (1843), Hamilton berates her "brothers" as "selfish, unfeeling men!" (l. 33) for refusing to act in support of the complaints of their grievously exploited "sisters, cousins, aunts" (l. 41):

> She who tambours – tambours
> For fifteen hours a day –
> Would have shoes on her feet, and a dress for church,
> Had she a third of your pay.
>
> (*Poems, Essays, and Sketches* 249–5, ll. 37–40)

The desperate, voiceless plight ("no union speaks for you," l. 25) of women employed as seamstresses at home or in unregulated sweatshops – "slaves in all but name" (l. 4) – is targeted for vituperative attack. Hood speaks compassionately *of* the working class predicament *to* the middle classes. Hamilton's gaze may be leveled directly at her working "kin," but by voicing her critique in Standard English, she enables a connection with the consumers of "fine linen," who are – wittingly or not – complicit in the circle of exploitation. Subsequent to this appeal for workers' solidarity, however, Hamilton's "Rhymes for the Times, II" (*Poems, Essays, and Sketches* 70–73) demonstrates her even-handedness in dealing out censure when she berates female workers – *blacknebs*[13] – for seeking to take over men's jobs in the printing industry: to "sort the teeps [*type*]" and "wield the pen" (ll. 81–2). "Glib" middle class orators – "speechifyin' women"(l. 105) – like Bessie Rayner Parkes,[14] who encourage such ambition are pragmatically directed *first* to the moral training of "lassies" within a far less protected social context in a bid to prepare for a "warl' baith caul an' stern" (that is, a cold and cruel world) (l. 113).

Hamilton and Rayner Parkes approach the "woman question" from different levels of the caste structure but are conjoint in resistance to culturally ingrained misogyny. Hamilton herself is a "speechifying" woman, and in her incisively feminist "Address to Working Women" attacks the hegemonic inculcation worked by "that spirit of predominance and exclusiveness which . . . has met us at every turn, [so that] we are lowered in our own estimation, so far as to acquiesce in our own *implied* inferiority"(*Poems, Essays, and Sketches* 389–96, my emphasis). Submission to internalized self-doubt can be conquered only by assiduous cultivation of the intellect, without which women function at the level of farmyard animals: The "most affectionate mother" will find that "a hen with a brood of chickens will perform as effectually as she can herself."[15]

Laggards in Hamilton's "March of the mind" get decidedly short shrift. "Crinoline" mocks frivolous women who worship the "fause gods" of fashion: "fule hizzies [hussies] – blawn oot like balloons." The narcissism of the "exquisite slave" is countered by Hamilton's insistence on rational dress: "aff wi' the whalebone, the cane, an' the steel!" (*Poems, Essays, and Sketches* 88, ll. 4, 29). But men who prefer "dress, complexion and figure; silly, pretty things; matter over mind" (*Poems, Essays, and Sketches* 394) are sternly censured for encouraging women to learn the demeaning arts of coquetry decried by Mary Wollstonecraft. Hamilton's disgust at human depravity is vented most forcibly in "Oor Location":

Oh, the dreadful curse o' drinkin'!
Men are ill, but tae my thinkin,'
Leukin' through the drucken fock,   [*fock* = folk]
There's a Jenny for ilk Jock.
Oh, the dool an' desolation,   [*dool* = sorrow]
An' the havoc in the nation,
Wrocht by dirty, drucken wives!
Oh, hoo many bairnies' lives
Lost ilk year through their neglec'!   (*Poems, Essays, and Sketches* 75–6, ll. 25–30)

Alcohol abuse is common to both sexes, but Hamilton reserves her harshest invective for "dirty, drucken" wives and "unwed mithers," whose children die of neglect.[16] "Local" difficulties become symptomatic of post-Darwinian ontological anxieties, as the "unnatural" ("animal") behaviors of the female are indicted as the root cause of national disaster, creating "havoc" in the body politic. A "dirty" woman's "habits and dangerous morals . . . threaten the nation's offspring" and endanger the "very basis of civilized society" (McDonagh 125). More terrible still are those "vile" mothers described in "Rhymes for the Times III," who murder by design:

O heavy the bluid o' the innocent hings   [*hings* = hangs]
On the skirts o' vile hizzies: my auld heart it wrings
to hear that sae mony puir babies fin' death
at the mither's ain han,' as sune's they draw breath.

Self-murder, an' a' kin' o' murders are rife,
Wife-beatin,' garottin,' an' usin' the knife.
                                                  (*Poems and Ballads* 189–91, ll. 33–42)

In part these poems function as apocalyptic narratives, exposing the ramifications of the Industrial Revolution, in which the "sanctified" domestic sphere is breached and defiled by alien necessity. Exploitation is endemic – "We're 'herry't wi' taxes, and racket wi' toil" (l. 31). Grief for the murder of "sae mony puir babies" (l. 35) is a cry of the human against Malthusian theories of population "surplus" within an "all-consuming and autonomous" system (McDonagh 116–17). The term "wife-beating" entered "the language in the eighteen-fifties and marital violence – assumed (dubiously) to be confined to the working classes" – became a national concern (Howarth

181). Hamilton's reportage derives *Grand Guignol* impact from sensationalized accounts in the national press of the "epidemic" of infanticide in mid-Victorian Britain. But her presentiment of anarchic collapse shares the profound unease manifested in Dickens's signs and portents of murderous chaos "lurking just below the surface of London life and the gory, nightmarish urban wasteland of James Thomson's 'City of Dreadful Night'" (Pordzik 168). After her evocation of a pathologically dysfunctional culture, Hamilton's conclusionary *volte face* is jarring. "Bless'd" Victoria's place in the people's affections is affirmed and Britain's global stature – its "place" in the world – is given a somewhat ambiguous "salute." Hamilton's express horror of rampant materialism becomes surprisingly quiescent in "Rhymes for the Times II," as her *envoi* assumes, however implausibly, that the cerebral "van of progression" will outstrip the Juggernaut of Capitalism:

> We hae muckle that's ill, but mair that is gude
> Oor place 'mang the nations is weel unnerstude –
> Improvement in knowledge, in science, an' art –
> The van of progression, oor post, an' oor part.
> (*Poems and Ballads* 189, ll. 49–52)

A far cooler assessment of England's political dealings is tabled in "Auld Mither Scotland," Hamilton's damning audit of the power balance between the two nations:

I like the English tongue fu' weel
In writin' an' in readin';
But 'tween the English an' the Scotch
There's lack o' truth an' breedin.'
It's England's meteor flag that burns
Abune oor battle plains;
Oor victories, baith by sea an' lan,'
It's England aye that gains.

It's England mak's an' signs the peace
Whan nations tire o' fechtin';
Whan Europe's balance gangs agee,   [*gangs agee* = becomes disordered]
She trims the scales for wechtin.'   [*trims the scales for wechtin'* = adjusts the scales]
An' England lauchs, as weel she may,
The Wallace touir at Stirlin'   [*touir* = tower]
Maun tapless staun, like pillar'd saut,
Until the maiks are birlin.'   [*maiks are birlin* = more coins roll in]
(*Poems, Essays, and Sketches* 159–60, ll. 25–40)

Burns spoke bitterly of Scotland's debasement as a commodified "province," "bought and sold for English gold."[17] In her jaundiced summation of the state of the Union, Hamilton concedes that the scales of power are "weighted" inexorably in favor of the metropolitan "mint." England will appropriate the advantage in every arena: battlefields and bloody casualties may be "oors," but the "glory" and the spoils will be forever England's.

The "touir" at Stirling, historic capital of the Kingdom of Scots, was raised to honor William Wallace – revered by Wordsworth as the embodiment of "independence and stern liberty"[18] and immortalized in Burns's blood-rousing call to arms: "Scots wha hae wi' Wallace bled." In an earlier poem Hamilton marks the laying of the foundation stone by blazoning the "lowe o' freedom" that has burned "het an' clear / In Scotland's hert this mony hunner year" (*Poems, Essays, and Sketches* 84–5). The taxonomy of "immortal" glory fueling the libertarian flame is "For ever – Wallace, Bruce, an' Bannockburn."[19] But even the "lyric cry" of "Red Bannockburn" (l. 22) is mute as the headless tower – "consecrated as a memorial of the nation's victories"[20] – comes to symbolize all that is wrong in the post-Enlightenment, post-Culloden reality of Scotland's subaltern status.[21] Rendered as a subject state, Scotland is emasculated and punished – like Lot's wife – by becoming a "pillar" of salt, a thing of tears, impotent and retrogressive, its true "crown" lost in the myths of history. England, its powerful colonizer, looks on and laughs – "as weel she may" (*Poems, Essays, and Sketches* 159–60). To this humiliation is added the implied betrayal of Scotland by her own people and of Scotland's heroic past as it fades in the light of fiscal expediency.

Hamilton engages passionately with national, global, and historic events, yet the awareness inscribed by a lifetime of unremitting labor, latterly beset by blindness and infirmity, is that "heroism" is a protean concept, manifesting in locations and identities that could have no place in *Blackwood's* Valhalla. It seems fitting to conclude with Hamilton's encomium to her sisters in spirit and in deed, women who pit their lives against the cold realities of penury, "the given and raw, the almost implacable material from which a living has to be carved" (Richard Hoggart, quoted in Joyce 159). In "The Feast of the 'Mutches,' Verses Commemorative of the Annual Supper given to the Poor Old Women, in the City Hall, Glasgow," she salutes the indigent women of Glasgow in a poem that is radical in its apotheosis of those most often rendered invisible and redacted from history – the poor, the aged, the female. Metonymically "signed" as morally spotless by the pristine "mutches" (linen caps) that modestly cover their heads – caps and hair both "white as the sna" – these women are valorized as survivors who may assert: "Look! We have come through."[22] Hamilton's persona – "the aul' blin' grannie that sings to ye noo!" – is dauntless in response to the tatters and ravages of the body's decay: "The speerit inside, that's the gist o' the matter." They have all endured "dolour an' din in the battle o' life" but "rise hopefu' again" (*Poems and Ballads* 243–5, ll. 17–20):

There's ane wi' a face that nae glunches nor girns,	[*nae glunches nor girns* = neither sulks nor snarls]
Though she wins her bit bread by fillin o' pirns:	[*fillin o' pirns* = winding yarn onto spindles]
She never was wed. Keepit clear o' the men,	
A canny auld maiden, o' threescore an' ten	[*canny* = knowing, wise]
An' there's a puir heid that's been cutit and clour'd	[*cutit and clour'd* = cut and battered]
But Heaven an' hersel' kens what she endured	
Lang years frae a drucken ill-deedie gudeman:	[*ill-deedie gudeman* = badly behaved husband]
He's yirded, an' sae are the sorrows o' Nan.	[*yirded* = dead and buried in the churchyard] (ll. 21–8)

Hamilton subjects the patriarchal ideologies that inscribe women's economic and emotional dependence on the "protection" of men to sardonic reappraisal. Her "speerit" and epigrammatic style anticipates Oscar Wilde's mode of challenging orthodoxy by turning received assumptions on their head. The status of conventional objects of misogynistic contempt and pity within the Victorian domestic economy – the embittered "old maid," the grieving widow – is here revisioned and recalibrated. The "wise" single woman who has actively chosen to "keep clear" of heterosexual relationships and be her own "bread-winner," is – despite poverty – manifestly content. Conversely, the "puir" widow is only pitiable because of the violent abuse she endured (silently) within the supposedly safe marital "haven" of domesticity. Hamilton's pithy use of zeugma within the sealed "casket" of a rhyming couplet emphatically makes the point that Nan's grief is *ended*, not caused, by her husband's "yirding." Her "sorrows" are dead and buried with him.

Hamilton's pragmatic deconstruction of societal axioms clearly disturbs the assumption of "untroubled" conservatism in her work. Nor, despite Parnassian excursions, does she conform to the modality of etherealized, disembodied falsity to lived experience, demanded by *Blackwood's*. Undoubtedly there are conventional thematic and ideological cells in her work. Her "Sacred Pieces," in Standard English, for example, hold minimal interest for the secular reader. More contentious are the antiphonal juxtapositions of political censure and seeming approbation, genuflections to the colonial status quo that complicate our sense of an "authentic" voice in poems such as "Rhymes for the Times II," which seems to turn on its own heel. Nevertheless, it remains clear that Hamilton cannot be relegated to the *Whistle-Binkie* genre of "milk and water vernacular verse" that limply serves a "sentimental, complacent, and utterly trivialised notion of what poetry might be" (Watson, *Literature* 28).

Her combative Doric utterances, bloody, and unbowdlerized, as, for example, when she threatens to "cuff the lugs" of "ill-deedie" women, confront the "living, throbbing" age as Elizabeth Barrett Browning demanded poets should do, but with matchless vigor. In a decidedly stratified, misogynist and subaltern culture, she dares to be "a woman moved" to bardic rage: "I'll speak my min' – an' whatfor no?" (*Poems, Essays, and Sketches*, "Oor Location" 76, l. 41). Most significantly, and rarely for one of her time, gender, and class, Hamilton interrogates the industrial revolution from within. Her "war bulletins" activate the kinaesthetic "slam" of physical specificity, clamor, and "fret" of working class existence. She succeeds in exposing the savage material conditions of life after the coming of the machine, by employing vernacular language of such "heft" that her words embody the materiality they condemn.

Hamilton's work manifests the spirit of the *thrawn* (twisted, wry, crossgrained), the "contraire," of Scots "antisyzygy,"[23] and thus resists confinement within a totalizing aesthetic. She has been described as a poet of "social progress," a poet of "liberty," a "doughty Nemesis," and a "female Burns" (*Poems and Ballads* 316–20). In all her guises she was *smeddum fou* (full of spirit, mettlesome) and irreducibly extraordinary.

NOTES

* Title excerpt: *Doric* – traditionally the language of rustic pastoral. Here a dialect of lowland Scots, or *Lallans*. *Busk oot* – to dress up, to adorn. From "A Plea for the Doric" (Hamilton, *Poems, Essays, and Sketches* 177–8, l. 3).

1. "Subaltern" literally denotes an officer of inferior rank. Antonio Gramsci uses the term to denote subordinate social groups who are subject to the hegemonic dominance of the ruling classes. I argue, in agreement with Douglas Mack, that the Scots and Irish were subject to English imperial aspirations (*Scottish Fiction* 1–14).

2. Embroidery work and prodigious reading may have contributed to the onset of blindness in the last eighteen years of Hamilton's life.

3. For a comprehensive bibliography of Hamilton's publications, see Florence S. Boos, "The Homely Muse."
4. From a letter written by Thom, to his poet friend, David Vedder, in 1845. See Robert Bruce, *William Thom: The Inverurie Poet – A New Look* (Aberdeen: Reid & Son, 1970), 91.
5. Pierre Bourdieu defines Institutionalized cultural capital as learning that is sanctioned by academic qualifications or credentials. See *The Forms of Capital*, 1986, available online at www.marxists.org/reference/subject/philosophy/works/fr/bourdieu-forms-capital.htm.
6. See Audre Lorde, "The Master's Tools Will Never Dismantle the Master's House," in *Sister Outsider: Essays and Speeches* (New York: Ten Speed Press, 2007), 110–13.
7. Bourdieu (1986) refers to *Habitus* as the physical embodiment of cultural capital, a set of values and practices learned early in life. Habitus extends to our "taste" for cultural objects such as poetry and art. He insists that aesthetic sensibilities are not "innate," but culturally acquired by habitual exposure to literature, art, etc. Hamilton argues for this point in her essay above.
8. Matthew Arnold, Chapter IV, *Culture and Anarchy*, 1869. Available online at www.victorianweb.org/authors/arnold/writings/4.html.
9. At least 16 blast furnaces and additional engineering works were built, and workers surged into what became known as "the Iron Burgh." Glasgow's population increased from 77,000 to 275,000 during the period 1801–41.
10. *Blackwood's Edinburgh Magazine*, January 1857, 34. Available online at www.forgottenbooks.com/books/Blackwoods_Magazine_1857_1000389315.
11. See W. W. Knox, *A History of the Scottish People: Urban Housing in Scotland 1840–1940*. Available online at www.scran.ac.uk/scotland/pdf/SP2_4Housing.pdf.
12. From Frederick Engels, *Condition of the Working Class in England* (1845). Available online at www.marxists.org/archive/marx/works/1845/condition-working-class/ch04.htm.
13. *Blacknebs* were similar to *blacklegs*, strike breakers or those who will take the jobs of striking workers.
14. For examples of Rayner Parkes's lectures and articles on women and work from the *English Woman's Journal*, see Carol Bauer and Lawrence Ritt, eds., *Free and Ennobled: Source Readings in the Development of Victorian Feminism* (Oxford: Pergamon, 1979).
15. Hamilton took care to ensure that her children, boys and girls alike, were trained in performing the "duties of the housemaid" (*Poems, Essays, and Sketches* 27).
16. For details on child mortality, often from diseases associated with desperate overcrowding and appallingly insanitary conditions, see *A History of the Scottish People: Health in Scotland*: www.scran.ac.uk/scotland/pdf/SP2_3Health.pdf.
17. From Burns's poem, "Such a Parcel of Rogues in a Nation" (Burns, 178–9).
18. *The Prelude*, Book 1, l. 220.

19. The Scots victory at "Red Bannockburn" effectively won the war of independence against the English in 1314.
20. From the Rev. Charles Rogers, "The National Wallace Monument," 1860, p. 5. Available at http://my.stirling.gov.uk/services/libraries-and-archives/archives/archives-document-of-the-month/archive-document-of-the-month-2014/archives-document-of-the-month-sept-14.
21. Completion of the Wallace memorial stalled for lack of money from public subscription. It was completed in 1869 after eight years in construction. The tower is "topped" by a huge crown spire.
22. The title of a poem by D. H. Lawrence.
23. Gregory Smith used the phrase to denote a spirit of contrariness in the Scottish national character in his work *Scottish Literature: Character and Influence* (1919).

CHAPTER 14

"The Guilty Game of Human Subjugation"
Religion as Ideology in Thomas Cooper's The Purgatory of Suicides

Mike Sanders

Apart from a brief period in the 1840s when he was unquestionably Chartism's first "Labour Laureate" (to use Anne Janowitz's phrase), Thomas Cooper has always occupied an uncertain position within the literary, and political, traditions of the laboring classes. Born in 1805 into an artisanal family of dyers, Cooper was, arguably, *the* quintessential working class autodidact of the early nineteenth century, teaching himself Latin, Hebrew, and Greek while working as a shoemaker. However, in his early twenties, a combination of physical and mental over-exertion caused something akin to a nervous breakdown, and Cooper exchanged shoemaking for a career as a schoolmaster, subsequently becoming a Methodist preacher in 1829. In 1835, following disagreements with two Methodist Superintendents, Cooper abandoned preaching and became a journalist for a number of provincial papers, most notably the *Leicestershire Mercury*. It was this paper which was indirectly responsible for Cooper's "conversion" to Chartism, by sending him to report on a Chartist meeting in 1840.

After joining the Chartist movement, Cooper quickly established himself as an important regional leader, firmly associated with the "physical force" current within Chartism, and a staunch supporter of Feargus O'Connor. Cooper was arrested in the aftermath of the mass strikes of 1842. Following conviction on charges of sedition and conspiracy, he was sentenced to two years in Stafford Gaol. Ironically, imprisonment gave Cooper the freedom to write *The Purgatory of Suicides*, an epic poem comprising 963 Spenserean stanzas, or 8,667 lines of poetry, arranged in ten books. In 1845, after his release from prison, *The Purgatory of Suicides* was published by Jeremiah How (a commercial publisher) to widespread critical acclaim, and Cooper became a figure of national importance both within and beyond the Chartist movement. However, his period as Chartism's poet laureate was short-lived and, after a serious disagreement with Feargus O'Connor, Cooper was expelled from the movement in August 1846.

Following his expulsion, Cooper combined the roles of radical journalist, writer, and lecturer, and enjoyed a reputation as one of the most effective advocates of free-thought. In 1859, he became a Baptist and thereafter combined preaching with lecturing and writing.

As this thumbnail biographical sketch suggests, Cooper was a somewhat protean character whose life can be seen as a series of abrupt, even contradictory, "conversions" – with the teenage Primitive Methodist becoming firstly a "physical force" and then a "moral force" Chartist, a religious skeptic, then a theist, before finally embracing the Baptist faith. Indeed, the only consistent aspects of Cooper's intellectual career were his commitment to intellectual enquiry and his readiness to promulgate the outcomes of those same enquiries regardless of their popularity. In similar fashion, in addition to his journalism, Cooper wrote poetry, novels, shorter prose fiction, autobiography, and works on religious questions. He was also a prolific lecturer and preacher, who once calculated that between 1858 and 1866 he had preached on 1,169 occasions and given 2,204 lectures – after 1867 he had a self-imposed limit of two sermons and four lectures per week!

Despite this prodigious output, Cooper's literary reputation largely rests upon *The Purgatory of Suicides*. This poem is organized around a series of dream visions in which Cooper observes various figures (all suicides) from world history discussing a wide range of political, philosophical, and religious topics. The work attests not only to Cooper's cultural and intellectual ambitions, but also to those of the overwhelmingly working class activists who constituted the Chartist movement. Indeed, for Cooper's fellow Chartist poet John Skelton, the existence of *The Purgatory of Suicides* served as "living proof of the greatness of mind to be found in the ranks of the people" (*Northern Star* 27 September 1845 5). In similar fashion, the leading Chartist newspaper, the *Northern Star*, identified Cooper's poem as a challenge for cultural and political leadership by the wider working classes (6 September 1845 3). This claim was recognized by opponents of Chartism. The *Britannia*, for example, simultaneously acknowledges the aesthetic qualities of *The Purgatory of Suicides* ("full of eloquence, full of grand detached passages. . . . [Cooper] is master of his verse") while lamenting its politics and its political significance; the *Britannia*'s reviewer concludes by arguing that there is "more danger in the spirit [*The Purgatory of Suicides*] breathes, than in a thousand Chartist meetings by torchlight."[1]

Post-Chartist critics have on the whole been less persuaded of either the aesthetic value or the political significance of *The Purgatory of Suicides*. In 1910, Hugh Walker described the poem as "inartistic and bad,"

Yuri Kovalev's pioneering *Anthology of Chartist Literature* (1956) makes no reference at all to *The Purgatory of Suicides*, while Martha Vicinus in *The Industrial Muse* (1974) describes Cooper's epic as "virtually unreadable."[2] In passing, it is interesting to note how all three critics disapprove (for varying reasons) of Cooper's political stance and compare him unfavorably with other radical writers of whom they approve both politically and aesthetically. More recently, there have been signs of a more positive reappraisal of Cooper's work. Isobel Armstrong in her *Victorian Poetry: Poetry, Poetics and Politics* describes *The Purgatory of Suicides* as "one of the major achievements of Chartist poetry" (214). Stephanie Kuduk's "Sedition, Chartism, and Epic Poetry in Thomas Cooper's *The Purgatory of Suicides*" calls the poem a "philosophical epic" and offers a detailed analysis of "Cooper's appropriation of epic forms" (165–6).[3]

In her illuminating summary of *The Purgatory of Suicides*, Isobel Armstrong identifies the reasons why the poem should command critical attention. She describes the poem as:

> a vast modern myth, a new working-class cosmogony, challenging classical and Christian orthodoxies by appropriating the epic form... fusing, epic with a Danteseque visit to Purgatory, and rewriting history and political relations in a 'historical romance,' as Cooper calls it, which is an attempt to reconstruct knowledge. (*Victorian Poetry* 214)

Furthermore, Armstrong notes that the poem is also "shaped" by Cooper's political struggles. In this chapter, I argue that Cooper's epic is not merely shaped by his political struggles but rather that it needs to be understood as constituting a political challenge in its own right. The dual focus of this challenge, classicism and Christianity, are key components of the cultural (which is to say hegemonic) sources of ruling class legitimacy in the early Victorian period.

A brief glance at the book summaries provided by Cooper in later editions of *The Purgatory of Suicides* demonstrates the extent to which the poem draws on classical history and literature, for example. Oedipus, Nauplius, Aegeus, Ajax Telamon, Lycurgus, Appius Claudius, Mark Antony, and Nero are just a few of the participants in the debate which occurs in Book One. The inclusion of so many classical references has a number of different political resonances. For example, Martha Vicinus in *The Industrial Muse* regards it as a self-promoting, possibly even a self-aggrandizing, display of classical knowledge by Cooper (110). Yet it might also be read as an attempt to democratize "elite" knowledge, as Cooper takes and demystifies forms of knowledge which had previously been the preserve of the privileged. The fact that Cooper provides explanatory footnotes for a number of his protagonists increases the educational value of the poem.

Furthermore, Cooper's invocation of classical knowledge is strategic as well as tactical, as the first of the dream debates within his poem makes clear. In Book 1, the first dream debate takes place in the hall of the suicide Kings, where a variety of historical figures argue as to what form of government is most conducive to human well-being and social order. Those readers steeped in classical literature will recognize the antecedents of Cooper's debate in the "Constitutional debate" which occurs in Book Three of Herodotus's *The Histories* and in Cicero's *The Dream of Scipio*.[4] Thus Cooper goes back to the very origins of recorded European political debate. However, unlike his classical predecessors, Cooper declares for democracy. From the outset then, *The Purgatory of Suicides* offers a fundamental challenge to the use of classical knowledge to legitimize "tyrannical" (i.e., nondemocratic) societies.

The second hegemonic basis of ruling class legitimacy challenged by *The Purgatory of Suicides* is religion. To date, the scholarly debate around the poem has remained generally silent on this topic, preferring instead to focus on its political rather than its religious concerns. However, this de-coupling of the "political" from the "religious" produces an incomplete account of Cooper's politics. Hence, this chapter is concerned with tracing the interplay between religion and politics in *The Purgatory of Suicides*. The template for this analysis draws on E. P. Thompson's discussion of Methodism in *The Making of The English Working Class*. In the chapter entitled "The Transforming Power of the Cross," Thompson observes that the challenge facing historians of working class culture is to understand "Why so many working people were willing to submit to this form of psychic exploitation [Methodism]" (*Making* 411). Thompson himself adduces three reasons, "direct indoctrination, the Methodist community-sense, and the psychic consequences of the counter-revolution [against 'Jacobinism']" (*Making* 412). In other words, any analysis must give due weight to the positive attractions of religion (community-sense) as well as its broader "ideological" functions. The reading of *The Purgatory of Suicides* which follows is guided by this Thompsonian schema and begins by examining Cooper's analysis of "priestcraft" as a block on the development of human freedom, that is religion as direct indoctrination on behalf of the prevailing powers. However, as will be shown, while the poem offers a clear rejection of priestcraft, it is simultaneously troubled by the prospect of a thorough-going nihilism which might follow from abandoning religious belief. Accordingly, a number of the poem's suicides entertain the possibility that religion might be harnessed to serve the cause of human freedom. Ultimately, this possibility is rejected by the poem which instead affirms the final triumph of "Reason" or "Mind" as both the means and the end of the struggle for human freedom. Yet as part of that same irenic triumph of Reason, certain religious figures are understood as playing an important role in the fight for human freedom. The focus here falls on religion as a mystified form of freedom which serves as an analog to Thompson's notion of "psychic consequences." Finally, the chapter considers the positive attractions of belief which, for Cooper, are centered on notions of the afterlife and on the figure of Christ rather than the wider religious community.

From the very beginning of the poem, Cooper identifies priests as key agents in the work of oppression. In stanza five, he describes the defense of social inequality as "the game / Long practised by sleek priests in old Religion's name" (Book 1, 5:8–9). In the very next stanza, Cooper accuses priests of fomenting civil disorder, describing them as:

> ... surpliced things
> Who, through all time, have thirsted to embroil
> Man with his neighbour, and pollute the soil
> Of holiest mother Earth with brother's gore, –
> (Book 1, 6:3–6)

In short, Cooper's speech invokes the idea of "priestcraft" in order to explain the role played by organized religion in support of unequal and unjust societies. Later in the poem, Cooper elaborates on the role which religious institutions have played in creating and maintaining the slave consciousness necessary to preserve class society, noting the:

> ... specious arts, whereby the bees beguiled,
> Yield to the sable drones their sweet repast,
> And creep, themselves, the path to heaven by pious fast;
> (Book 3, 11:7–9)

Cooper identifies religious belief as the key terrain on which the ideological struggle for hegemony has taken place across human history.

In the specific historical moment of the poem's composition, Cooper also recognizes that the Anglican church is thoroughly imbricated in the exercise of State power. From the confines of his cell, the Church's complicity with the repressive state apparatus is made clear by its role in the grotesque spectacle of the gallows which casts a literal as well as a figurative shadow across the pages of *The Purgatory of Suicides*. As Cooper's first note to Book Six records, "Six human beings underwent capital punishment in front of Stafford Gaol, during the two years I remained in it" (225). Cooper views capital punishment as a concentrated example of the oppressive violence which necessarily accompanies and underpins an unjust social order and Book Six begins with the impassioned question:

> Blood! blood! – Ye human hell-hounds, – when, oh! when
> Will ye have had your fill?   (Book 6, 1:1–2)

The imminent execution confirms Cooper's view of the prison as a "grisly den / Of demon Power" (Book 6, 1:3–4), but he reserves his strongest criticism for the presiding minister:

> Hah! curse upon thee, priest! – is it well done,
> That thou, a peace-robed herald pattering prayers,
> Dost head the dead-march?   (Book 6, 2:3–5)

Cooper reads priestly involvement as signifying approval and argues that this clearly contradicts the ideas of "Peace and Goodwill to Man" (Book 6, 2:7) and of "mercy" (Book 6, 2:8) which are central to Christianity.

Cooper's initial responses to "the bloody cavalcade" (Book 6, 3:1) are pity (for the condemned man) and anger at the "hireling butchers" (Book 6, 3:9) who uphold and enforce the law. However, in a move which characterizes *The Purgatory of Suicides* as a whole, Cooper reminds himself of the need to master his emotional responses in order to become "a calm adept / In tracing errors to their spring" (Book 6, 4:7–8). Only analytical reason is capable of uncovering the "errors" which for Cooper fuel "the fire / Of that real Hell that burns on earth" (Book 6, 4:8–9). No less typically, this insistence on reason re-opens the questions of individual agency and responsibility, as Cooper asks if he is right in cursing a priest who is obeying his "patched creed's dogma?" (Book 6, 5:2).

Cooper's answer is to tease out the wider implications of the description of Christianity as a "patched" creed. In particular, Cooper points to what he considers the contradiction between Mosaic law which permits proportionate revenge, "Blood for blood" (Book 6, 5:2), and the gospel of mercy and forgiveness preached by "the Nazarene – the Good!" (Book 6, 6:3–4). Furthermore, he argues that this contradiction is a "conscious inconsistency" (Book 6, 6:2), a deliberate policy on the part of the Church. For Cooper, priest and hangman are "yokefellow[s]" who together "prop the stern / Sway of brute Kings" (Book 6, 7:8–9). Priests are assigned a particular role in what Cooper memorably describes as "the guilty game /

Of human subjugation!" (Book 6, 8:4–5). It is their job to exercise ideological domination by preaching "peace... To slaves" (Book 6, 8:1–2) and thereby "tame / Man's spirit" (Book 6, 8:5–6), and through a process of mystification, "To wield o'er prostrate Reason subtler empire still!" (Book 6, 8:9). Finally, if all else fails, the priesthood both legitimates the use of lethal force by the state and threatens eternal punishment to cow popular resistance (Book 6, 9).

However, the rejection of priestcraft is not experienced solely in terms of ideological liberation in Cooper's poem. The rejection of religious authority also brings with it the worrying prospect of nihilism, as Cooper struggles to find a way of grounding morality in the absence of the divine.[5] At various points in *The Purgatory of Suicides*, Cooper struggles with the question of nihilism. Book Five opens in a particularly bleak vein with Cooper wondering if it might have been better had "Night" continued to rule uninterrupted:

> Would that o'er Chaos thy wide rule had been
> Perpetual, and reptile Man's birth-wail
> Had ne'er been heard, –   (Book 5, 2:2–4)

Having raised the possibility that humankind is merely a cosmic mistake, Cooper engages in an extended *contemptus mundi* sequence, cataloging human vice across a series of stanzas.[6] The sequence ends with a misanthropic rewriting of Jaques's famous speech from *As You Like It*:

> Is not the world known
> Unto itself to be a stage of cheats, –
> (Book 5, 7:5–6)

Similarly, in Book Seven Apicius traces a number of apparent contradictions across a variety of religious belief systems. Firstly, he notes the apparent irony of positing a Creator who "doth add / To being merely to destroy by th' myriad" (Book 7, 54:8–9). In a similar vein, he questions whether a world in which "All things... prey upon each other" can really be the product of "Benevolent design" (Book 7, 55:3–5). Small wonder then, remarks Apicius, that humans who have this as "their model of perfection" worship "human slaughter-shapes" as their gods (Book 7, 56:4). However, Apicius's debunking of religious systems leaves him only "the joys of sense / And appetite" (Book 7, 56:6–7). His life becomes one of carnal sensuality with no higher purpose.

In response to the suicide Lumley offers an even bleaker view of the universe declaring, "It is a universe designed for sorrow – / Designed if't be" (Book 7, 62:1–2). He sees a universe dominated by pain, and this fact renders "Worthless" all "thought, sense, motion" (Book 7, 62:6). For Lumley, "Annihilation" is the only thing to be desired and he rejects all notions of a blessed afterlife as the product of feeble minds (Book 7, 63). Vatel responds that Lumley's doctrine is so monstrously false that it has actually reawakened his sense of "reverence for the good in life" (Book 7, 64:8). In addition, Vatel declares a newfound hope that they will eventually discover their condition to be caused by their own folly rather than by Fate (Book 7, 65). Once they have discovered and acknowledged their errors, Vatel believes that they will enjoy "deliverance.... For Mind was formed all Evil to subdue" (Book 7, 66:5–6).

One alternative to nihilism explored within the poem is the possibility of harnessing religious authority to promote the goal of human freedom. A variety of speakers consider this possibility, beginning in Book One with Lacon who accuses himself of seeking "to engraft, / Mystery with Truth," in his own teachings (Book 1, 135:3–4). Lacon claims his intention was to harness the grandeur and authority of religion in the service of Freedom. However, experience has taught him that Freedom's "own native grace, / Alone, could charm men, lastingly, to her embrace" (Book 1, 135:8–9).

In Book Two, Empedocles reinforces Lacon's warning of the dangers of attempting a "short-cut" to freedom. Empedocles both acknowledges, and regrets, that in his desire to raise the moral and intellectual condition of his fellow humans, he allowed "Some tinge of mystery . . . [to] be allied / With moral lessons" (Book 2, 36:6–7). The example of Empedocles highlights two dilemmas with which Cooper grappled throughout his political career. The first is a version of the universal problem of the relationship of ends to means. Here it is brought into particular focus by the question of the extent to which it is permissible to compromise the purity of the message in pursuit of popular support. As has been shown, privileged speakers within *The Purgatory of Suicides* consistently reject such compromises. Later in Book Two, the Indian philosopher Calanus argues that it is impossible for the truth to be nurtured by lies and articulates what might be called an "ultramoral force" position in which the means absolutely determine the ends:

> Falsehood and ignorance will ever bow
> The human soul; and urge it, base and low,
> To grovel in the dust. Falsehood and sooth
> Breed no amalgam. Flame from flood shall flow, –
> The summer's sun shed drops congealed, – and youth
> Be sire unto Old Age, – ere Lies shall nurture Truth!
> (Book 2, 57:4–9)

The second and related dilemma is that of the proper relationship between leaders and followers. Calanus criticizes Empedocles' "pride," his belief that he was entitled to attempt "a false controul / To forge for Virtue o'er the human soul!" (Book 2, 68:4–5). Empedocles tries again to defend his actions by describing them as a "harmless fraud" designed to "save / The sons of degradation" (Book 2, 65:3–4). To use an anachronistic term, Empedocles falls prey to vanguardist thinking; he believes that an enlightened leader is both entitled and able to manipulate the "masses." Calanus insists that such an approach is self-defeating because even the smallest "Tinct, grain of falsehood" corrupts the entire project. Instead, Calanus argues for the necessity of, what Raymond Williams described as, the "long revolution" – a lengthy process of ideological struggle and suasion which sees the masses slowly acquire the same level of understanding and consciousness as their leaders: "Knowledge must win, / By toilsome steps and slow, her widening way" (Book 2, 70:2–3). Calanus predicts the eventual victory of knowledge and even suggests that it is occurring in the present time of the poem's composition. Calanus declares that the torch of knowledge "Now beams on Thule's shore" where the slogan "'Knowledge is Power!'" adorns her banners (Book 2, 73:1, 9). By citing the masthead of the radical *Poor Man's Guardian*, Cooper clearly identifies the Chartist and radical press as key agents in the dissemination of knowledge. This emphasis on the consumption of the *written* word also suggests a rather more individualized approach to political change, and in the stanzas which follow Calanus envisages an entirely pacific revolution (Book 2, 74, and 75).

Calanus's anxieties regarding the ability of a leader to mislead his/her followers is in part a recognition of the dangers of that staple of antidemocratic writers, the demagogue. The ability of a charismatic leader to mislead a movement would shortly become a practical as well as a theoretical problem for Cooper as he locked horns with Feargus O'Connor over the Chartist Land Plan. However, if we focus on Cooper's own speech in Book One, a rather different concern emerges. Cooper tells us that his spoken words produced the opposite effect to that intended:

> For that I boldly spake these words of truth,
> And the starved multitude, – to fury wrought
> By sense of injury, and void of ruth, –
> Rushed forth to deeds of recklessness, – but nought
> Achieved of freedom, – since, nor plan, nor thought
> Their might directed: (Book 1, 8:1–6)

Cooper's worry here is not that the different levels of knowledge and understanding enjoyed by leaders and followers produces a situation in which the

"The Guilty Game of Human Subjugation" 235

leader misleads his followers (Calanus's anxiety), but rather that the leader is betrayed by his less enlightened followers.[7]

Cooper revisits the question of a potentially positive role for religion, more specifically for Christianity, in Book Five. This time Cooper finds himself amid the spirits of the suicide patriots from the French Revolution. Buzot speaks first and, contemplating the wreck of the Revolution's hopes, asks Condorcet if they were right to reject Christianity.

> ... tell me, did we err –
> Deeming the Palestinian story fraud
> Or dreams, while we ourselves the dreamers were [?]
> (Book 5, 35:1–3)

Buzot also wonders to what extent their dreams of human liberation are justified. Condorcet is far more certain than Buzot; he thinks human freedom is imminent and the days of priestcraft numbered. Moreover, for Condorcet, these two phenomena are clearly interrelated; he tells Buzot:

> The spirit of Prometheus doth but sleep: –
> The Mind's tornado wakes, through earth, e'en now!
> And soon it will to nought the fabric sweep,
> Of age-reared Priestcraft, and its shapes of woe, –
> Its Hell, Wrath-God, and Fear – that foulest foe
> Of human freedom!   (Book 5, 39:1–6)

In effect, Condorcet argues that it is necessary to reject the claims of religion because it provides the ideological underpinnings of tyranny. Condorcet observes that the threat of eternal damnation acts as a brake on rebellious energies; he also denounces a God who effectively tyrannizes his creation:

> ... a God
> Who forms without their will His creatures, – graves
> Their natures on them, rules by his own nod
> Of providence, their lives, – and, then, beneath his rod –
> ...
> His scourge eternal, tortures them, without
> Surcease or intermission!   (Book 5, 40:6–9 and 41:1–2)

It is clear from his account that the worship of such a God is merely a masochistic or mystified response to the sadistic exercise of power.

In response, Roland argues that the "universe her Architect / All-wise proclaims" (Book 5, 44:4–5). However, due to the limits of human reason – what he terms our "finite, frail, / And borrowed being," – we are unable to perceive "His wisdom's goodness questionless!" (Book 5, 46:9).

Consciousness of these limits, suggests Roland, requires us to show reverence toward the Godhead. Condorcet rejects this argument as priestcraft's "master-trick" which throughout history has been used to subdue "primal thought" and prevent humankind from questioning the rule of kings and priests (Book 5, 47 and 48). Next Pétion and Valazé join the fray. The former is simply impatient with the debate and argues for the rejection of priestcraft without thought of the consequences. Valazé is equally dismissive of Roland and his arguments, but introduces a new, misogynistic tone into the debate with his description of Roland as a "Weak, fickle spirit, – on old Earth, mis-sexed!" and possessed of a "woman's soul" (Book 5, 60: 1, 3). Valazé contrasts the "manly thought" of the free-thinking revolutionaries with Roland's "bondage unto weakness" and proposes his expulsion as a "slave of wrong" (Book 5, 59:4, 60:7, 61:5).

At this point, the Jacobin Le Bas invites Valazé to contemplate his own shortcomings before castigating others and then, in a grim parody of the French Revolution, Jacobins and Girondists resume their fratricidal struggle. This fighting only ceases following the sudden appearance of "A Shape – threat'ning as spectre," who calls on the "Dark atheist brood!" to stop maligning the Almighty (Book 5, 64:3 and 65:1). The specter argues that their behavior both on earth and in Purgatory proves God's judgment. Accusing them of a willful pride which prevents them from acknowledging God, the specter warns them that they will not know peace until "Ye bow to the Most High" (Book 5, 67:6).

This elicits a furious response from Condorcet who recognizes the specter as the shade of Samson. Condorcet persists in his unbelief even to the extent of claiming that Samson is simply the product of their own arguments and over-heated imaginations and has no more independent, real existence than the God whom he invokes:

> Phantasm avaunt! – no real shape thou art; –
> But gendered of our insane rage and broils; –
> Or, with a myriad other mists athwart
> Our thoughts that flit, – thou and thy god are foils
> Of truth, which, when her strength she overtoils
> The purblind Mind creates –   (Book 5, 70:1–6)

Condorcet also argues that Samson's "murderous life" could be celebrated only by a homicidal "Blood-God" (Book 5, 69:3 and 68:9). This accusation incenses Samson who observes that the sanguinary careers of the revolutionaries left the "Earth, with headless corses strown / And drenched with gore" (Book 5, 73:7–8). Indeed, Samson goes further and argues that he slew in self-defense, restricting his wrath to "haughty tyrants" (Book 5, 74:4). Thus, having justified his actions, Samson invites the patriot suicides to join the great debate and advises them to "purge" their spirits of "the foul stain of atheistic doubt" (Book 5, 77:3–4).

Following Samson's departure, the patriot suicides continue their discussion in a far less confrontational manner. Baboeuf affirms his rejection of the Judeo-Christian God and maintains the critique of priestcraft as the handmaiden of tyranny. However, he also urges a gentler tone in debate:

> . . . let us desist
> From unfraternal gibes whereby our woe
> Is deepened, – soul to soul antagonist
> Rendered   (Book 5, 80:6–9)

In response, Condorcet observes that neither humility nor self-criticism necessarily promotes the growth of wisdom. Both, he writes, can be irrational – as is understood by priests who encourage such behavior as "the true / Discipline for the soul" (Book 5, 82:6–7). Rather, it is necessary to maintain the "calm, firm, steady toil to emancipate / Mind from its frailties" (Book 5, 83:1–2). Condorcet predicts that once humans are capable of moderating their emotions "By Reason's rule – not monkish rigour strict –" it will be possible to move society forward, albeit slowly, to "Elysian height serene" (Book 5, 83:3 and 84:2).

This theme of the eventual triumph of Mind is taken up by Robert Le Diable in Book Seven. Indeed, Le Diable predicts imminent victory on earth, pointing to the development of science, and improvements in maritime technology as clear evidence of "the power of Mind" (Book 7, 71:5). Even the peasants, Le Diable notes, are exercising their capacity for independent thought and both "the crosier and the crown" are losing their power to command (Book 7, 72:3). These events have found their counterparts in the Hall of the Suicide Kings where thrones are beginning to disappear. Le Diable argues that they were wrong to commit suicide in despair at the apparent triumph of Evil and now recognizes that the struggle against Evil is a necessary aspect in the full development of humanity:

> . . . [On earth] Evil was blent
> With Good through Being with th' all-wise intent
> T'ennoble human thought by healthful toil
> That should have issue in magnificent
> And universal triumph.   (Book 7, 74:4–6)

Le Diable concludes with a triumphant prediction:

> Come, listen the inspiring theme of Good
> And Right, – of Wisdom and Equality!
> Spirits, – the universe one brotherhood
> Of Knowledge, Truth, and Love, full soon shall be!
> (Book 7, 75:1–4)

Le Diable's words offer a view of history which is simultaneously dialectical, divinely inspired, and teleological; later in the poem, Cooper removes divine intent from this triad to generate an account of history that is both dialectical and teleological.[8]

Book Eight opens with Cooper recalling his experience of listening to the "Old Hundredth" while in prison. Cooper associates this hymn with Luther and this, in turn, gives rise to a meditation on Luther's historical role and significance. Cooper hails Luther as a champion of intellectual freedom, describing him as a "True warrior / For all men's right to think unawed by man" (Book 8, 5:6–7). However, Cooper also historicizes Luther's project arguing that Luther himself was unaware of its final outcome: "I care not that thou didst not comprehend / Its ultimate" (Book 8, 6:2–3). Thus Cooper's sense of history here (and elsewhere in the poem) is quasi-Hegelian insofar as Luther's career offers an example of the ruse of reason. Historical actors are never fully conscious of their purposes and intentions, and Reason inheres in the historical process as a whole:

> What though these words, like oracles of old,
> Were sealed, in their full meaning, to the seer
> Who uttered them? – The future shall behold
> Their splendid verity: (Book 8, 9:1–4)

This allows Cooper to posit a gradual, progressive (almost evolutionary) unfolding of Reason as the central dynamic of History:

> And Reason's heroes with Mind's foes contend
> From step to step, – yea victory for Thought
> By years of struggling toil be stably, fully wrought.
> (Book 8, 6:7–9)

Cooper's insistence on a future which is not a restoration of a lost golden age is unusual in Chartist writing. As many commentators have noted, the predominant trend within Chartism conceived of the movement as a quest for rights which had been lost, but very few Chartists thought with Cooper in terms of rights which had never previously been won.

Cooper strives to imagine that future perspective, thereby historicizing his own position as well as that of Luther. He imagines the construction of a pantheon, "Truth's great temple" in which "each dazzling portraiture" will be appropriately placed (Book 8, 10:4–8). From this future vantage point, Cooper contemplates the eclipse of faith by knowledge and wisdom:

> When later Faiths, like older Phantasies,
> Are reckoned with the Past;
> ...
> When wisdom hath outgrown the childish guise
> Of mythic story   (Book 8, 11:2–8)

The imagined future is irenic; the perspective offered by the end of history allows apparent opponents to be reinterpreted as different aspects of, or moments in, the progress toward a fuller truth. Thus, for Cooper, it is possible that Thomas Paine and the most devout believer:

> May stand, as right co-workers, equal, true,
> *For* Truth; – although the world's old bigot-story
> Of Man's mind-infancy did long misview
> The scope of their twin-toil: scope that themselves scarce ever knew!
>   (Book 8, 12:6–9)

Indeed, in the book's closing vision it is precisely this Pantheon that is built.

Throughout *The Purgatory of Suicides* the critique of religion and priestcraft is accompanied by a deep reverence for, and emotional attachment to, the figure of Christ. Indeed, Christ operates within the poem as a kind of Derridean "supplement" continually threatening to overwhelm the established logic of the text. The logic of the text tries to provide an anthropological explanation for religious belief. In Book Three, for example, Cooper speculates that it is a fear of death which has caused humankind in all ages to develop ideas of resurrection and an afterlife (Book 3, 14–16). All of these beliefs, Cooper argues, were originally inspired by observing the daily "death" and "rebirth" of the sun, and are, therefore, essentially solar myths. Stanzas seventeen to nineteen identify a wide range of world religions, "from Babel to Stonehenge... Guebre or Parsee... Osiris... Mithras... Thammuz... Titan... Apollo." Even the God "claimed by regal Incas," is a variant of a universal solar myth (Book 3, 17–19). Cooper then explains that as a result of his studies, he has reluctantly come to the conclusion that Christ is another version of the sun god:[9]

> I hesitate, demur, surmise, and glean,
> Daily, new grounds to doubt the Mythic dress!
> Phoenician woof, once more! – through which is seen,
> I fear, thy ancient face,
> ...
> The good, – the toiling one, – the Crucified, –
> ... Is he not,–
> Magnific beam! – thy power personified, –
> (Book 3, 20:5–8 and 21:2–7)

What is striking in Cooper's account is the depth of his emotional attachment to the figure of Christ. "I love the Galilean," Cooper declares at the opening of stanza 22 and continues by acknowledging that, even if human, Christ would be worthy of worship. Indeed, Cooper goes further and identifies the presence of Christ as necessary for any sense of Paradise:

> ... no Eden I could find
> Restored, – though all the good of humankind
> Were there, and not that yearning One, – the Poor
> Who healed, and fed, and blest! Nay to my mind
> Hell would be Heaven with him!   (Book 3, 22:4–8)

Cooper experiences his skepticism as loss: "I would the tale were true," he writes of the four Gospels (Book 3, 23:4). However, the most keenly felt loss for Cooper is not that of belief in Christ's divinity. As we have seen, this loss is recuperable to a certain extent insofar as Cooper can still conceive of Christ as worthy of worship ("Such goodness I could own; and though entwined / In flesh, could worship" [Book 3, 22:2–3]). Rather, it is the loss of a belief in an afterlife which troubles Cooper most:

> I would the tale were true: – that heritage
> Of immortality it doth presage
> Would make me glad indeed: – but doubts becloud
> Truth's fountains as their depths I seek to gauge, –
> Till with this trustless reck'ning I am bowed –
> Man's heritage is but a cradle and a shroud!
> (Book 3, 23:4–9)

For Cooper then it is having to acknowledge the reality of death as oblivion, as nothingness, which is the greatest loss sustained in his loss of faith. The real cost of this loss is a near fissuring of Cooper's psyche. Unbelief is the product of an unflinching intellectual enquiry into the grounds of faith. Belief commands Cooper's emotional consent. Ironically, Cooper can only sustain his unbelief by allowing his reason to tyrannize his emotions.

The psychic cost of Cooper's unbelief (and as his subsequent career as a Baptist preacher shows, it was a cost which was ultimately unsupportable) is suggested by the dream vision which follows these waking thoughts. Cooper finds himself on the shore of a lake in the middle of a storm.

> ... On the shore
> I wandered, while my thoughts, amid the roar
> Of winds and waters, dwelt on One who stilled
> The waves, and fed the hungry; and the more
> My spiritual sense with hunger thrilled
> And cold, – the more that Form my inward vision filled.
> (Book 3, 26:4–9)

Cooper figures his own splitting, his body wanders while his mind contemplates the events recorded in *Matthew* 14:15–33, the feeding of the 5,000 and Christ's walking on the water.[10] This is accompanied by a form of perceptual dissonance in which somatic sensations are experienced by his "spiritual sense [which] with hunger thrilled / And cold" and as these sensations intensify so does his meditation on Christ. Tellingly, Cooper imagines the emotional responses of the disciples, how "joy succeeded fear" (Book 3, 27:2) and once more declares his (conditional) willingness to worship Christ:

> ... 'Who'– I cried – 'would not revere
> Such power and love? – worship I, on this strand
> Would give the Nazarene – did He these waves command.'
> (Book 3, 27:7–9)

It is precisely at this moment that Cooper encounters the most tormented of all the spirits encountered thus far in Purgatory. A spirit whose gaze proclaims "'My being's ceaseless heritance / Is agony!'" (Book 3, 27:7–8), and who Cooper recognizes as Judas Iscariot. Thus far in the poem, Cooper has only been a silent witness to the debates and disputes of the suicides; he has, in essence, been an eavesdropper. This changes with the appearance of Judas, who addresses Cooper directly with a singularly disturbing question: "How know'st thou my soul's deed more criminal than thine?" Judas reproaches Cooper for the latter's conditional willingness to believe and he cautions Cooper against attempting to justify his skepticism:

> Worship to Him my treason brought to shame
> Thou talk'st of rendering, – did he here display
> His power and love, – feigning to shift the blame
> Of thy foul unbelief –
> ...

> Avaunt – dissembler! – distant age and clime
> Excuse not unbelief; – 'tis the soul's self-spawned crime!
> (Book 3, 32:1–9)

Indeed, Judas refuses Cooper as a possible companion, "No sceptic spy / Shall bide with me" (Book 3, 33:5–6). Cooper is unable to respond to Judas's denunciation, despite "yearning" (always a positive term within the poem) to communicate with him:

> ... to tell
> My heart unto the fallen one, with ache
> Unutterable, I yearned! (Book 3, 34:7–9)

Judas interprets Cooper's unwillingness to leave as stemming from fear, and he offers to supply Cooper with a companion, another suicide who is unable to face "the fierce scorn . . . / Of all he meets in Hell!" (Book 3, 35:5–6). Who, the implied reader wonders, is this figure whom even Judas affects to despise? Cooper follows Judas deep into a labyrinthine cave composed of "Crowds of huge snakes" (Book 3, 37:5) and at its center discovers Castlereagh (Book 3, 39).

There then follows a grimly comic debate between Judas and Castlereagh as to which is the more generally despised figure. Each rehearses the crimes of the other, until Judas declares that it is now Castlereagh's name which has become a "synonym / Of Villany!" which all new arrivals in Purgatory avoid uttering (Book 3, 49). Castlereagh ignores Judas and continues to defend his career. At length Judas interrupts this apologia and performs a kind of ideological unmasking, arguing that what Castlereagh regards as his greatness has really been a career of cowardice, bloodshed, guilt, pride and madness (Book 3, 67–9). In the stanzas which follow, Judas takes an almost sadistic pleasure in enumerating and describing in detail the "deep, dark debt / Of woe" Castlereagh must pay (Book 3, 76:4–5). First, Judas argues, Castlereagh must atone for his repeated denials of popular suffering:

> ... Hah! how aloof
> Thou stood'st from mercy, while on earth! Disproof
> That millions starved and suffered, thy false tongue
> Forged, daily: (Book 3, 79:4–7)

Judas also accuses Castlereagh of bearing some responsibility for the ongoing suffering of the working classes, those:

> ... starveling sons
> And famished daughters, – who still pine and moil
> By law: mere skin-and-bone automatons!

>   . . .
>   What breathe ye for, on earth, – such slime-born things?
>   To suck your brethren's blood; and, while ye gorge,
>   Mock your poor victims!   (Book 3, 81:1–3, 82:1–3)

With his descriptions of economic degradation and use of vampiric imagery, Judas here sounds very like a Chartist orator or poet. Indeed, there is a sense in which Judas can be seen as a surrogate for Cooper. As has been shown earlier, Judas (like Cooper) performs acts of ideological unmasking in order to delegitimize existing forms of class rule. Again, the figure of Judas demonstrates the complexity of *The Purgatory of Suicides*. On one level it is a daring, if not outrageous, move on Cooper's part to challenge the Christian cultural orthodoxy which, from Dante onwards, has consigned Judas to the very lowest circle of Hell. This is an ideological shock tactic, akin to that practiced by Blake in *The Marriage of Heaven and Hell*, an attempt to unsettle the most deeply held assumptions of readers, as a prelude to the radical reconstruction of their consciousness. However, there is another and, for Cooper at least, a more troubling sense in which Judas serves as his double. For if the skeptic Cooper experiences his skepticism as in part a "betrayal" of Christ, then Judas serves as a very powerful (if rather self-aggrandizing) point of identification.[11]

When Judas describes Christ, he does so using the negative sublime:

>   Goodness unmeasured, undescribed, untold:
>   . . . Goodness unfelt,
>   Unwitnessed, unconceived, in mortal mould,
>   Before:
>   . . .
>   . . . as if it would the wide world melt
>   Into a sea of bliss, and deluge heart
>   Of man with joy!
>   (Book 3, 105:2–9 and 106:1–2)

Judas argues that Christ represented a "Goodness that glowed with inexhaustless zeal / To spread, enhance, perfect, eternize human weal!" (Book 3, 106:8–9). In short, Christ is represented as a revolutionary force capable of remaking the entire world. Later in *The Purgatory of Suicides*, Cooper uses similar terms to describe Christ. For example, when Cooper contemplates the example of Christ, he draws attention to his dying prayer, "Forgive them, – for they know not what they do! –" (Book 6:10, 1). Cooper regards this prayer as more remarkable for its rejection of what Cooper sees as an ingrained desire for proportionate revenge within Judaism ("From rule of blood for blood ne'er to depart, –" (Book 6, 10:7). For Cooper, the almost incredible nature of Christ's example keeps alive the possibility of his Divine origins and, if not divine in being, Christ's actions certainly belong to the category of the miraculous:

> ... if not Divine
> Thou wert, – thy self-born light and love is more
> Miraculous than aught by all the line
> Of the heart's precept-makers writ in page benign.
> (Book 6, 11:6–9)

Cooper continues to pursue the significance of the final actions of a human (rather than a divine) Christ, and concludes that his willingness to forgive his torturers "doth prove / A glorious nobility in Man enwove!" (Book 6, 12: 8–9). Indeed Cooper infers Christ's humanity from his dying words, arguing that Christ's prayer is infused with a form of "High reason" (Book 6, 13: 2). Cooper's Christ forgives his torturers because their deeds are the result of ignorance not "natural vice." This allows Cooper to posit the possibility of peaceful social and political change brought about by the workings of "Reason":

> ... By Reason brought
> Thus to regard our brother, inner might
> Of love fraternal springs, and Pity's calm delight.
> (Book 6, 13: 7–9)

Of interest here is the tension between love and reason in Cooper's own account. Stripped of its supernatural/theological significance, Christ's death can no longer be seen as a redemptive sacrifice – as a gift, an act of radical love which frees humankind. Instead, for Cooper, the focus shifts to Christ's dying words which are seen as exemplifying the transformative nature of "Reason." This "Reason" requires us to forgive injuries that result from ignorance and are, therefore, "errors accidental" (and in Cooper's account, ultimately, all errors are accidental). Similarly, this "Reason" requires us to regard all human beings with compassion and thereby institute "love fraternal" as the wellspring of all human relations. Paradoxically, "Reason" is charged with the task of unleashing the redemptive power of "love."

The stanzas which follow oscillate between rapturous praise for the "moral beauty" of Christ which is punctured every time Cooper remembers that Christ too invoked Hell. Cooper's respect for Christ is unmistakable. Stanza 17 begins, "Thine, Galilean, is of all earth's creeds / The greatest marvel!" Cooper acknowledges the intensity of his desire for Christ, referring to his "yearning heart" (Book 6, 17:6) and his "tempestuous wish to love thee" (Book 6, 17:8). Similarly, in stanza eighteen he describes the chief attraction of the Christian afterlife as "the bliss / Of knowing such a heart as thine" (Book 6, 18:5–6). The same stanza also registers Cooper's regret at losing this consolation:

> And still I wish thy heaven were not a dream, –
> And, to my latest hour shall doat upon that theme!
> (Book 6, 18:8–9)

The only thing preventing Cooper's complete identification with Christ is the latter's "repetition of that most / Enslaving of all slavish thoughts – a Hell" (Book 6, 19:1–2). For Cooper, the threat of Hell as the punishment for disobedience is something which "doth outlive / All tyrannies in horribleness of wrath" (Book 6, 16:7–8). Once again for Cooper, theology and politics are intimately connected; the threat of Hell is simultaneously obnoxious to both. Thus, Christ's insistence on Hell both prevents Cooper's total identification with him and also reveals the historically imposed limits on Christ's thought:

> [Christ's repetition of Hell] . . . restrains the heart's love-swell
> Rushing to centre in thee, and reveals
> To Reason that thou couldst not burst the spell
> Of Circumstance – which ev'n the mightiest seals
> In Impotence: we do but act as she impels. (Book 6, 19:5–9)

The introduction of an historical perspective enables Cooper to present Christianity as a progressive advance for human civilization. While Christ's "penal Hell" connects him to "The age of error, force, and punishment," the great bulk of his teaching, his "themes of mercy vast, / Of love and brotherhood," point the way to the future (Book 6, 21:1–4).

It seems fitting that Cooper should identify so strongly with a Christ whom he represents as a figure who is simultaneously inspirational, transitional, and historically conditioned, for this would also serve as a description of Cooper himself. It is tempting to see Thomas Cooper as an idiosyncratic, if not irascible, individualist whose uncertain place within the working class literary tradition reflects his uneasy position within the wider working class movement. However, I would argue that it is more helpful to consider the contours of Cooper's career in relation to the particular historical conjuncture in which he wrote. Such an analysis reveals Cooper to be an intriguing amalgam of residual and emergent forms (to use Raymond Williams's terms). Politically speaking, Cooper is a transitional and paradoxical figure insofar as he sought to deploy elite forms of knowledge in the service of working class emancipation. In a somewhat ungainly metaphor which nonetheless captures the messy complexities of the historical moment, Cooper attempted to pour the old wine of the "traditional" intellectual into the new wineskins of the "organic" intellectual. If Cooper had been born a generation or two earlier, his obvious intellectual and literary abilities might well have attracted the attentions of a higher class patron. Yet, in one sense Cooper's literary career depended, in part, on the assistance he received from a collective patron in the shape of the Chartist movement. For it was the support of that movement which offered some protection (however limited) from the vagaries of the literary marketplace. Cooper's literary career is an unusual one insofar as he offers an example of a working class writer living by virtue of his intellectual labor while largely avoiding the compromises associated with either patronage or Grub Street.

NOTES

1. The *Britannia* review was quoted extensively in the *Northern Star* (13 September 1845, 3).
2. For a survey of the post-Chartist critical debate, including the critics cited here, see Mike Sanders, *The Poetry of Chartism: Aesthetics, Politics, History* (Cambridge: Cambridge University Press, 2009), 40–45.
3. The relationship of Cooper's poem to the epic tradition is also the subject of a brief discussion in Herbert Tucker, *Epic: Britain's Heroic Muse 1790–1910* (Oxford: Oxford University Press, 2008).
4. I am grateful to my colleague Professor Alison Sharrock for drawing my attention to this aspect of Cooper's poem.
5. As Timothy Larsen observes, it was precisely Cooper's inability to find a secular grounding for morality that ultimately led to his reconversion to Christianity (*Crisis of Doubt* 84–5).
6. The vices dealt with by Cooper are lechery (4), adultery (5), murder (6), and hypocrisy (7).
7. The Christian resonances which attend this idea of a good leader betrayed by a follower are unmistakable.
8. Pamela K. Gilbert comments that Cooper's view of history in the poem is a combination of Hegelian and Carlylean impulses ("History" 32).
9. See Larsen (96) for details of the likely sources for Cooper's (then) belief in the sun god theory.
10. Mark 6 also records these events but omits the details of Peter's role, which Cooper refers to in stanza 27.

11. The Judas/Castlereagh colloquy also marks an important turning point in Cooper's own journey. At its conclusion, Cooper awakes and finds himself "from soul-quelling dread / Set free" and, for the first time since his imprisonment able to reconnect with life, "I blessed the morn, upon my prison-bed" (Book 3, 125:8–9).

CHAPTER 15

At the Margins of Print
Life Narratives of Victorian Working Class Women

Florence S. Boos

Introduction

In recent decades, a number of scholars and critics have turned their attention to the study of nineteenth-century working class autobiography. David Vincent's *Bread, Knowledge, and Freedom* (1982), for example, interpreted working men's autobiographies as works of witness, reflection, and self-definition, but noted with regret that fewer than five percent of the works he had found were written by women (8). John Burnett, Vincent, and David Mayall observed in the introduction to their comprehensive bibliography, *The Autobiography of the Working Class, 1790–1940*, that "[t]he most obvious distortion in the body of autobiographies is the small number written by women. Of the main group, just seventy, less than one in ten, record the lives of daughters, wives and mothers from their own point of view" (vii). More recently, however, Jane Rendall and Barbara Kanner have identified other memoirs by Victorian working class women, and I have been fortunate to locate further examples. Uncertainties of attribution and identification have made it difficult to estimate how many more memoirs of Victorian working class women may be found, but those we have offer poignant and at times eloquent testimonies to the situation of women in working class culture. To borrow a phrase from Jane Carlyle, "they too [were] there."

The great number of Victorian autobiographies and the vast differences between them have prompted efforts to tame their exuberance into categories. In *Traditions of Victorian Women's Autobiography*, Linda Peterson has characterized nineteenth-century *middle class* women's autobiographies as forming "a hybrid genre [which] drew on many genres of life writing" (x), in particular, the spiritual autobiography, domestic memoir, and narratives of familial authorship (as with the Brontës). In *Subjectivities: Self-Representation in Britain 1832–1920* Regenia Gagnier identifies several patterns in *working class* (mostly male) autobiography: personal memoirs, sensational confessions, political and polemical vindications, conversion and gallows narratives, and accounts centering on self-analysis and -examination (151). Jane Rendall's account of slightly earlier memoirs by *working class women* (1775–1845) suggests categories of "spiritual autobiography, the repentance narrative, the world of oral story, the petition, the genre of romantic fiction, the language of middle-class womanhood, and the life-cycle of the family economy" (35).

Although such paradigms remain useful, most working class women's memoirs fail to fit readily into a single category. For a working class woman, family, work, and even religion were inevitably interdependent, so that a farm worker's life story may include the account of a religious conversion in addition to familial events and political commentary (*The Autobiography of Elizabeth Oakley*); even memoirs ostensibly intended for one's immediate circle (*Aunt Janet's Legacy*) may consider wider issues, such as educational reform or women's roles; and narratives composed later in the century are more likely to address political issues, such as domestic violence protection or an expanded suffrage (Mary Smith's *Autobiography*).

It also makes obvious sense to view memoirs in the context of the occupations and relative social class of their respective authors. The life narratives of rural workers (Oakley, Elizabeth Campbell, Christian Watt) seem quite different from those of autobiographers from urban settings (Ellen Johnston) and/or with more educational access (Mary Smith); only the latter could aspire to a not always attained upward mobility, and their accounts show relatively greater awareness of national issues and identification with reform movements.

Another means of arranging these autobiographies is by the circumstances of their publication, since few working class women could command the resources to self-publish or the name recognition needed for sales. Not surprisingly, therefore, several of the memoirs which have come down to us were sponsored by a reformist organization (e.g., the Anti-Slavery Society, who published *The History of Mary Prince*), a religious society (The Religious Tract Society, who issued *A Brief Sketch of the Late Sarah Martin*), or a group of patrons sympathetic to an aggrieved victim (advance subscribers to *The Autobiography of Elizabeth Storie*). Several autobiographical sketches were attached as prefaces to poetic works published by reformist editors (e.g., Campbell's *Songs of My Pilgrimage* and Ellen Johnston's *Autobiography*); only Janet Hamilton (a temperance poet), Janet Bathgate (a beloved local teacher), and Smith (an influential schoolmistress and reformer) had attained sufficient regional prominence to attract a ready publisher. Also interesting are oral narratives (*The History of Mary Prince*,

The Autobiography of a Charwoman), which enabled the voices of those without formal education to be preserved, but also required the collaborative efforts of a transcriber/editor.

Yet a further approach might be *teleological* – identification of the writer's apparent purposes in recording her life. Here again, of course, motives may be mixed; one might seek to pay tribute to a past way of life as well as enunciate grievances or argue for reform. In what follows, I would like to present three memoirs, reflecting the different social backgrounds, occupations, literary styles, and purposes of their respective authors. Mary Ann Ashford's *The Life of a Licensed Victualler's Daughter* provides a rare example of unmediated self-publication; Bathgate's *Aunt Janet's Legacy* is distinctive for its artful presentation of the writer's life in a third-person narrative; and Mary Smith's *Autobiography* testifies to an earnest life of activism, intellectual effort, and self-reflection. These three memoirs reflect different regions (southern England, southern Scotland, and northern England) and different familial circumstances: Ashford was a twice-married mother of six, Bathgate a widow who had remarried, and Smith remained single and independent by choice. Most important, however, are the differences in tone and purpose, as Ashgate relates the grievances of her past work life with asperity and distaste; Bathgate remembers her youthful struggles with good-humored nostalgia; and Smith employs her *Autobiography* as a means of analysis and self-scrutiny, identifying the guiding principles of her life and honestly confronting what she believes had been its failures.

Mary Ann Ashford (1787 to after 1861)

The 91-page *Life of a Licensed Victualler's Daughter, Written by Herself* (1844) was carelessly printed with several pages out of order by Saunders and Otley, a well-known publishing house which had issued the work of better-known authors such as Edward Bulwer-Lytton. All that is known about Mary Ann Ashford, in addition to what she has told us, is what can be derived from census records, which provide the names of her siblings, husbands, and children, all in accord with her account.[1] There seems little reason to doubt the authenticity of her tale, for it lacks the elements of romance, sudden fortune, or melodramatic adventure which might signal a fictional account.

Ashford's preface pointedly raises questions of class and the extent to which stereotypes dominate the representation of ordinary women workers:

> In the month of July, 1842, as I was passing the site of the Royal Exchange, ... my attention was caught by one of the very numerous bills with which the boards ... were covered: it ran thus – "Susan Hopley, or the Life of a Maid Servant." This book, I thought to myself, must be a novelty; for although female servants form a large class of Her Majesty's subjects, I have seen but little of them or their affairs in print: sometimes, indeed, a few stray delinquents, from their vast numbers, find their way into the police reports of the newspapers; and in penny tracts, now and then, a "Mary Smith," or "Susan Jones," is introduced, in the last stage of consumption, or some other lingering disease, of which they die, in a heavenly frame of mind, and are duly interred. (iii–iv)

Not everyone of the literate lower classes, it seems, identified with penny tracts. When she learned that *Susan Hopley* was a work of fiction (a popular novel published in 1841), Ashford decided to write down her experiences, an unusual ambition for someone of her position. Clearly defensive about her class status, Ashford firmly tells her reader that she was not a "servant," for "seventeen years of my life have been spent in service; ... [but] that is not the third part of fifty-seven." Her father had been briefly an innkeeper, though not a successful one, and she preferred to style herself "a Licensed Victualler's Daughter," even though the "licensed victualler" had played only a brief part in her life.

Born in 1787 to Joseph Ashford, a London glove and leather worker, and Jane Gadderer, an orphan who inherited a public house, Mary Ann was given over as an infant into the care of a woman in the country who neglected her ("I used to take an egg and a small bit of bread, which was to last me the day" [12]). Her mother died when she was about 12, and her father, weakened by asthma and bloodletting, followed a few months later. Nonetheless, she paused in her narrative to express a rare moment of gratitude ("I have frequently been very poor, yet I never felt any of the real evils of poverty; and health, the best of all Heaven's blessings, I have enjoyed almost continually" [18–19]).

Her surviving relatives offered to apprentice her to a milliner, but despite her cousin's warning that she would "not be introduced into society by her or any of my respectable friends if I was a servant" (21), she entered service instead. As with other important decisions in her life, Ashford later felt some ambivalence about this choice; on the one hand, "respectable" milliners could make little money (20), and on the other hand, as a young person none too fond of her unhelpful relatives she might have made a rash judgment.

In thirteen positions over the next seventeen years, Ashford slowly climbed the ladder from housemaid to general servant to cook. The tales of her different employers give a rare servant's eye view of conditions in this form of unregulated labor. She offers an unpleasant and unforgiving retrospect of false accusations, deceitful fellow servants, withheld wages, and relegation to winter quarters in a flooded cellar. One of her more miserly mistresses – the daughter of a Scottish earl who fed a large menagerie of pets – begrudged her food:

> One day, after looking at me earnestly, she said, "Mary, child, you would be very handsome were it not that your cheeks are too large; if you would eat less, they would soon be thinner." ... I thought about it, and soon after went to a looking glass and examined my face more than I had ever done before, and thought my cheeks, which were very rosy then, would do very well: at any rate, I would not quite starve myself to make them thinner. (30)

She later ate some of a lodger's cheese; when he remarked that "if the girl had been properly fed, ... she would have [not] taken his cheese" (32), a storm ensued, and she resigned. In one of her other positions, she "had very bad living; very little meat, and the bread kept till it was mouldy before it was cut" (37).

In her last post as a servant, her best, she worked for a clergyman's family in an institution she called "Fairyland" (in actuality, the Duke of York Military Asylum in Chelsea), an orphanage for the children of dead soldiers. Even here, she suffered disappointment when her mistress replaced her, for she was "now near thirty years old, seventeen years of that time I had spent in service, and never had warning given to me before; and if I had served one mistress better than another, it was my present one" (56).

Now an "old maid" by nineteenth-century standards, Ashford had rejected two earlier proposals of marriage. After she had been released from her post at the orphanage, however, she accepted an offer of marriage from an older widower (James Dallison, whom she married in 1817), who worked as the institution's shoemaker. When a "respectable Quaker gentleman" named Isaac proposed to her shortly thereafter, though "He was very well-looking, and about my own age," she felt obliged to decline his offer for she could "not break my word upon any account, unless my intended husband gave me some just cause" (61). Clearly, this was a decision she would have preferred not to make. Her husband suffered from arthritis, and the heavy demands of his occupation made him ill-tempered: "it was no easy matter to keep nearly thirteen hundred children in shoes, and the boys in caps. ... [H]e was very rough, [but] he generally had truth and justice on his side.... [Still] it made me think – 'Dear me! I have rejected Isaac and taken Ishmael'" (63).

As she tells it, a fortunate coincidence attended her daughter's birth. The Duke and Duchess of Kent (Queen Victoria's parents) visited the Asylum shortly thereafter and were much taken by the shoemaker's new child and his tidy shop, and the Duchess sent a gift with a message that "I was to name the baby Victoria Louisa Maria, after Her Royal Highness." The couple readily complied, and Ashford took the child to Kensington Palace annually thereafter, in the hope that "the Duchess [might] remember her... at some future time, [and] take her into her service, or put her forward" (70). The Duchess did in fact arrange for little Victoria Louisa Maria to receive a modest annual sum and increased it after the shoemaker's death. Sincerely grateful for patronage, years later when Ashford learned of the Duke's funeral, she "could not help crying bitterly, [for] I thought of the only time I ever saw him, when his extreme condescension was enough to inspire respect and gratitude in any mind" (69).

The marriage with "Ishmael" was a good one in one important respect, for "my husband and I were thoroughly agreed in everything that was essential" (71), and during his last illness, "very few men would, while suffering almost continually from a most painful complaint, have exerted themselves as my husband did for the sake of his wife and children" (70). After his death shortly after the birth of their sixth child, Ashford faced bureaucratic intransigence when the Institution rejected her plea for a pension for her husband's sixteen years of work. Without income, Ashford eked out a temporary living selling fruits and cakes to the Institution's children, "crush[ing] all the pride I had, which was very little" (74–5).

At this point her husband's close friend, the Institution's thrice widowed merchant tailor (Edward Green), a man in his sixties, offered marriage on the grounds that "he knew I should do my duty by him, and he could assist me in rearing his old comrade's children" (76). They married in 1830, but she soon rued the consequences of this arrangement when the Asylum refused to let her lodge her children on its grounds. Forced to send her infant to a nurse and her daughter to a boarding school, she remarked bitterly that "I had, for the sake of my children, entered what might almost be termed a sepulchre; for I had seen three women, all of whom I knew well, carried dead out of it; and it was hard indeed [for me] to be parted from my children, or my husband to give up his situation" (77).

Several years later, her second husband, no longer able to use his right arm after many years cutting cloth, was given six days notice and fired without the expected "superannuation allowance" of half his annual salary.

This left him and his family with only his military pension – thirteen pence a day after 28 years of service – and no place to live. Ashford was

> quite thunderstruck at this wind up of affairs; for the consequences bid fair to be most serious to me: my husband, who was now seventy-six years old, was quite unable to do anything beyond dressing and undressing himself; and my hands were in a manner tied; for I could not leave him long together; and I saw no other prospect than that of my own remnant of property being melted away, together with his own, in sustaining me, if it should please God to spare his life long [he died in 1842 aged 82]: and I might be left at an advanced age to encounter the poverty I had always endeavoured to avert. (83–4)

Hurt and depressed but apprehensive that an appeal might lose him his military pension, her husband refused to petition the authorities for restitution of his "allowance" and forbade her to do so. Undeterred, the decisive Mary Ann drafted a letter in a neighbor's house to "her Most Gracious Majesty Queen Adelaide, . . . humbly begging that she would cause an inquiry to be made" into the cause of her husband's denial (84). Quite remarkably, her appeal was successful, and her husband's pension was restored with a few months of back pay.

This was perhaps Ashford's greatest triumph, and she concluded her brief memoir's last paragraph with an unattributed quotation from Longfellow, prefaced by her claim that "the many struggles I have met with in my journey through life, may be likened to some lines I saw in a newspaper, of which the following is a copy:

> A beacon that, perhaps, another,
> Sailing on life's stormy main –
> A forlorn and shipwreck'd brother –
> Seeing, may take heart again.
> ("The Psalm of Life")

Ashford's autobiography thus recorded a life of lost gentility, economic precariousness, wounded pride, and considerable assertiveness, lightened by anomalous flashes of Dickensian good fortune. Aided by a quick mind and primary education, she composed her memories in standard English and enlivened them with anecdotes, dialogue, and a bit of caustic humor. Almost certainly, aristocratic "condescension" and restoration of her second husband's hard-won pension made it possible for her to bring it into print.

Pragmatic, unsentimental, and sometimes more upright than she wished to be, Ashford was restless, *déclassée*, in early life a rolling stone, and independent to a fault. No radical egalitarian, she was quick to praise those of a higher class who had singled her out for notice and grateful for the interventions which helped her keep her family together. She had also known fear and injustice and had worked doggedly to care for her four surviving children and two elderly husbands in their final travails. For her at least, her memoir's modest celebration in print of her eventual relative successes was indeed "its own reward," and the only form of "transcendence" she had ever sought.

Janet Greenfield Bathgate (1804? to 1898)

Janet Greenfield Bathgate's *Aunt Janet's Legacy to Her Nieces: Recollections of Humble Life in Yarrow in the Beginning of the Century* employs fictional and dramatic techniques to present the emotions of an outwardly unremarkable and contented life. Relatively unpolemical and attentive to childhood psychology, *Aunt Janet's Legacy* was published in Selkirk, Scotland in 1892. Although written for her relatives and friends, "to whom she thought they might be interesting and helpful" (iii), the *Legacy* was sufficiently successful so that George Lewis (b. 1848), a lifelong friend and admirer as well as her publisher, later published a 177-page book of reminiscences, *The Life Story of Aunt Janet*, with a frontispiece photograph of the dignified, tastefully dressed Bathgate at 88.

An unusual feature of *Aunt Janet's Legacy* is that its events are recorded in semifictional form, with "Janet" presented in the third person. The book's informality may reflect its intended audience, Bathgate's nieces, as well as its author's lifelong occupation as a teacher of young children. Bathgate's account shows considerable dramatic and narrative gifts, as she arranged her memories as a series of crises or surprises as seen by the mind of a bright and earnest girl and young woman. The third-person technique adds a tone of dispassion, for though the author empathizes with the distresses and perturbations of her 75-years-past self, she also brings humor and detachment to the account of a childhood ruled by a righteous and industrious but at times stern father, a fervently Calvinist if affectionate mother, and the need for all family members to work at farm labor from an early age.

Typical early events include the family's forced departure to a new, much less comfortable and more remote farmstead; the attendance at severe

"Cameronian" church services; and Janet's first, very unpleasant job at the age of seven, as a maid of all work for an ill-tempered old woman on a yet more remote farm. Bathgate's desire for her account to illustrate the development of a child's sense of religion is relieved by her memories of the pangs and anxieties of childhood, and her relatively nonjudgmental account of family and neighborly interaction is rendered with the appropriate degrees of regional dialect. Short quotations are inadequate to convey the building of tone, as when the mistress who had so often berated and overworked the seven-year-old child becomes frightened in a windstorm, as told in the present tense:

> As the storm increases in fury, Katie trembles from head to foot; she leaves her spinning, and draws close to Janet, and says – "Lassie, are ye no afear'd?"
> "No," says Janet, "I'm no fear'ed; for my mother says that God walks on the wings of the wind and rises on the storm.... But did yer mother never tell ye hoo God gae the de'il leave to raise the wund, and let it blaw doon the hoose on Job's bairns?"
> "Yes, my mother told me that the de'il said to God that Job was a selfish man ... but God knew that Job loved Him, so he said to the de'il, I will allow you to take all these things from Job, but I will not allow you to kill him. So you see that the deil canna hurt us, and if he should knock down the house, God can spare our lives, and give us another. . . .
> "O lassie, ye are ower wice; but div 'e no hear hoo the hoose is creekin'? Oh, I never heard sic a wund as that."
> A great blast comes and carries away part of the roof. Katie clung to Janet and exclaimed, "Oh, preserve us, the hoose is doon!"
> "No," says Janet, "it's just the theekin' blawn off, and you see we are no deid."
> The old woman trembled, and Janet commenced to cry. "Aye," says Katie, "I thocht you wad get fear'd if the hoose fell."
> "I am no fear'd," says Janet; "but I'm vexed to see you so frichtened, and I canna help greeting for you." (77–8)

After this her mistress became very attached to Janet, grieved to see her depart, and welcomed her eagerly on her occasional visits.

Bathgate portrayed her heroine as an imaginative and dreamy child, given to reveries and fantasies, and with an introspective devoutness unusual even in her religious family. The final chapters of the book narrate at length her courtship and idyllically happy four-year marriage to James Kemp, a saddler of frugal habits, an interest in astronomy, and similar religious views. Bathgate reenacts in moving detail the couple's shared dismay and grief as James becomes increasingly ill with tuberculosis, his final attempts to cheer her and prepare for his end, and his quiet and resigned death after bidding his wife a loving farewell. Characteristically Bathgate notes the psychology of grief, as the bereaved Janet, alone with her husband's corpse, becomes terrified that his soul may not yet have reached heaven, then becomes anxious over how she will pay for her husband's coffin.

The autobiography's final scenes, though, celebrate the young widow's survival and commencement of an independent occupation. One day a friend suggests that Janet keep a school, and though at first she demurs from a sense of unworthiness – "I never was six weeks at a regular school at one time, and I feel that it would be the very height of presumption for me to pretend or attempt to teach any one" (186) – she is excited at the idea and tells an old neighbor. The neighbor's publicity in Janet's former village of Lugton (East Ayrshire) brings her eighteen pupils the next week, and the narrator describes her first eager attempts to organize and teach her flock. The school prospers, and the narrator reflects with manifest relief and pride on her new situation:

> Janet is filled with wonder at the wisdom and goodness of God, by which all her earthly wants are supplied. Now she has six shillings a week for her brother's board, the fees from her eighteen scholars, and a sum [for tutoring]; and though she has her hands full, she is gathering strength of body . . . her heart is eased, and her eyes enlightened. (189)

After a lapse of 60 years, the narrative here glows with happiness at its author's achievement of a congenial occupation, well-suited to the sociable, child-loving, and didactically minded Janet. Nothing is said about her later remarriage to Robert Bathgate, and her attainment of the role of child's religious schoolteacher remains the climax of her life story.

Bathgate's account is an impressive achievement for an elderly woman who had only a year or so of formal schooling. Some of the book's mellowness of tone may derive from its author's advanced age and long view back, juxtaposing an acute memory of her youthful troubles and gratifications with a pleasure in the simple, representative quality of her remembered past. The third-person narration also enables Bathgate to take pride in the quickness and resilience of her youthful self without seeming immodest. Modeled on family storytelling, and with its unusual formal resemblance to autobiographical fiction, Bathgate's informal and lively *Legacy* shows how its author employed the ideologies and opportunities available to the rural poor of her time and place to create a life which brought her many satisfactions and a sense of self-worth.

Mary Smith (1822 to 1889)

Possibly the most successful, intellectually minded, and broadly reformist of Victorian working class women autobiographers was Mary Smith, whose *Autobiography of Mary Smith, Schoolmistress and Nonconformist. A Fragment of a Life*, was published in 1892 with an editorial afterword three years after her death in 1889. In its attention to religious and political ideas, and its extended introspection and careful chronicling of its author's intellectual development, Smith's account resembles the better-known middle class intellectual autobiographies of its day, such as that of Harriet Martineau. Though Smith led an active life of many accomplishments, she records with some bitterness the many years of unpaid labor which delayed her attainment of financial and personal independence, and her sorrow that she could not devote more of her life to her beloved pastime of writing poetry.

Like most other Victorian women memoirists born to relative poverty, Smith felt pride rather than regret at her origins: "I was born in an English nonconformist household, of simple country habits, of the order of the common people, without any pretension whatever to wealth or rank" (1). Her father, William Smith, was a boot and shoemaker of Cropredy, Oxfordshire, and her mother, Ann Pride, an energetic woman who kept a grocery shop in their home. When Ann died in Mary's infancy, William married his housekeeper, a woman Mary generally esteemed but found unsympathetic to her desire for education. William was a devout Independent (in this context I think Baptist) of kindly and mild personal traits and a love of education, and he encouraged his brightest child's passion for books, at one point bringing home a cartload of volumes he had bought cheaply, including Shakespeare's plays and Kirke White's [Poetic] *Remains* (39–40).

Even at an early age, this future teacher was a stern critic of the education she received, and feminist indignity rises in her critique of the denial to girls of academic learning, as she criticizes her third school: "Thus I did an endless quantity of embroidery and flowering, children's caps, muslin aprons, and many other things;... What long months I worked at it – and how I hated it – but it was all in vain! For long years Englishwomen's souls were almost as sorely crippled and cramped by the devices of the school room, as the Chinese women's feet by their shoes" (32). But she read voraciously in the school's small library and devoured every book in her locality she was able to borrow, including legends, romances, handbooks of logic, and theological treatises.

Formal education ended when her father became town registrar, and for a time she and her brother minded the boot shop. When her brother's marriage left her stranded with no source of income, however, she was quick to note the marginality of a woman's labor: "But for myself, as is often the case with women, even the most capable and energetic, the one small event of my brother's marriage had stranded me without occupation" (65). Mary had already rejected one suitor urged by her father, declaring firmly, "I did not want him, and could work for myself" (57), and now, resolved not to burden her beloved parent, she made the determining decision of her life. She accepted the offer of a nonconformist minister, Mr. John Jones Osborn, to move north with his family to Cumberland as their servant. Thus, in mid-winter 1842, she left without other family members for what to her was an alien land of harsh climate, rough but intriguing dialect, and unaccustomed religious habits.

The remainder of her *Autobiography* is largely the story of her many adjustments, her steady efforts at intellectual self-improvement, and her unhappiness at her exploitation by the Osborns – who broke promises, borrowed shamelessly from their indigent servant, and repeatedly demanded her services after she had escaped to be well employed elsewhere. In addition, for some years, the Osborns virtually supported themselves on her labor as a teacher in a school run by the ineffectual and erratic Mr. Osborn. Though disappointing, the experience with Osborn's school had brought Smith a local reputation for painstaking and successful tutelage, and when she at last opened a school of her own designed to appeal to the children of regional farmers, it became an immediate and lasting success. Self-denying, frugal, and debt-averse, Smith gradually gained a modest competency, eroded only by taking a friend's advice to invest in local bank stocks which lost their value, and by her inability to work during her final illnesses. In her last years, she was sufficiently prosperous to assist younger relatives and other needy persons, and at her death she left more than £1,400 for charitable causes, a remarkable amount for someone of her initial disabilities.

The form Smith's faith took was nonsectarian for her time, as she affirms: "Indeed, as I have grown older, I have come to see and feel that creeds are less than life. The latter may be true, when the former is far from it" (122); or more simply, "What we believe is not of so much importance as what we are" (237). She records many favorable impressions of Quakers, Baptists, and Roman Catholics of her acquaintance, and when an employer asked her whether they should attempt to persuade her fellow servant Ann to change her religion, Smith quickly replied, "Do you think we can make

Ann a better girl by doing so?" whereat the mistress desisted. Avowing that she had been "a decided mystic... all my life" (199), Smith spent many years enraptured with the transcendental philosophy of Emerson, recalling that her first reading of "Nature" "woke in my soul a thousand new and wonderful thoughts. I could not forget it... whenever I could get a chance I read it over and over again, till I knew it by heart as I knew the Psalms of David..." (95). In later life, Smith worshipped in a Unitarian Church (though careful to note that she was not a Unitarian), and in outlook she came to embody the sort of catholic and civic-minded reformist associated with Quaker and other nonconformist philanthropists and former Unitarians such as Martineau.

Smith's secret love was the writing of poetry, managed while doing housework or on Sundays. As a girl, she had written verses, and during her days as a servant she kept a verse book by her to "pursue my own thoughts, with great zeal and delight" (140), though it could lead her to such deep reveries that she failed to hear her employer calling: "Poetry, in fact, grew into a passion with me. I soon found I must be on my guard against it" (142). Her stylistic ideal was unpretentious simplicity, traits more often associated with prose: "My great aim was to use simple, natural language, avoiding metaphors as Wordsworth did, and never to write without a feeling of help and inspiration" (144). Though literary endeavors were always "a solace and joy" (144), her gratitude for the consolations of poetry are tinged with regret that she could not devote her life to literature:

> Poetry indeed was through all the hard periods of my life, my joy and strength, the uplifter of my soul in trouble. Now it was that every prospect of a literary career – always the cherished ideal of my soul – seemed forever blocked out of my prospects and hopes. (242)

Interestingly, she attributes her want of greater success, not to the absence of connections or a relatively limited education, but to her sex:

> I had higher visions than matrimony; literature, poetry, and religion gleamed fair before me. Had I been a young man, how gladly should I have gone into the Non-conformist ministry, and should probably have been accepted. But as a woman I had to struggle with all sorts of difficulties, hardships, and insults.... (196)

> My object has been to show the inner cravings of my soul after literary pursuits, which, being a woman, I failed to attain, despite of all my self-denial and persistent endeavours. (192)

Her most ambitious ventures were two volumes of poetry published at her own expense, the 1860 *Poems* and the 1863 *Progress, and Other Poems; The*

Latter Including Poems on the Social Affections and Poems on Life and Labour, dedicated by permission to Thomas Carlyle and issued both in London and Carlisle. Used to facing unpleasant truths, however, Smith acknowledged the limitations of her cherished efforts: "Like all second rate poets, I lacked imagination, and believed too much in the lower powers of will and continuous study, [though s]ome few of the minor poems attained a more poetic height" (289). In fact, her poetic "tales of the affections" were somewhat better than her didactic poems, but ultimately her distaste for metaphor blinded her to some of the imaginative ranges of poetry. Her poems reached her primary audience, however, "I was pleased to know they were read by working men, in reading rooms, news rooms, etc." (289).

Smith probably chose singleness and independence for reasons of temperament. Though by her own account, she was plain and unfashionable, four men sought to marry her, and of these three were shy men of considerable means who probably hoped the earnest and unfriended Smith might desire security. Nonetheless, she rejected all with similar alacrity: "Riches were the reverse of attraction to me. I had too independent a mind to allow anyone to say that they had made me rich." She noted: "Had I been a duke's daughter, I could not have been more careful of keeping clear of any matrimonial liaison than I was. I did not want matrimony; it was congenial labour I wanted. For this I prayed, and waited, and suffered" (122). Her comments on marriage also show a feminist contempt for women's economic subordination: "women, in reality, [are] bought and sold in the marriage market as in any other" (101).

She was also a lifelong activist and campaigner. Her "leisure" time was spent, among other things, in reporting speeches and sermons for Carlisle newspapers, supporting local reform candidates, organizing and performing at public readings, and teaching and recruiting for the adult education movement, for which she organized the first classes for women given in Carlisle. She wrote and campaigned against slavery, standing armies, public executions, denial of burial to non-Anglicans, slanderous election campaigns, and other forms of what she believed to be abuse, injustice, or intolerance. She notably departed from general sentiment in opposing the Crimean War on populist grounds, seeing it as "a great quarrel among kings, fought out for their good, at the expense of the common people" (203).

As her remarks on the disabilities of nineteenth-century women might suggest, Smith's most protracted allegiances were with the woman's movement, and she participated vigorously in its education, suffrage, and sexual-reform sectors. She recorded that during the 1860s, "I began to take an interest in the circumstances and conditions of woman's life" (256), because her efforts to educate poor women had taught her "[t]he helplessness of women in the great battle of life... especially in large towns..." (257). Soon after its inception, she became a member of the Carlisle Woman's Suffrage Society founded by Lydia Becker, and more remarkably, she threw herself into the campaigns against married women's disabilities and the Contagious Diseases Acts.

> I worked and wrote whenever I could in favour of the Married Woman's Property Bill, and against that disgrace to humanity, the "C. D. Acts," which, thanks to the exertions of women, and Mr. Stansfield, are not what they were. I lectured on this subject to women to full audiences, and helped Mrs. Hudson Scott, who worked heartily in the cause, to get up petitions to Parliament against them. (258)

The retrospective view brought no regrets over her choices:

> I feel great satisfaction, in looking back, that in the midst of a busy life, wherein my own head and hands had to supply every need, I tried to take a humble part in this cause, and still try to help with the helpers of women. (258)

Indeed, Smith was even more radical for her time, perhaps, on women's issues than on issues of religious equality and other reformist causes.

The *Autobiography* was issued with an editorial afterword by George Coward, a local bookseller and publisher, who had brought out her *Progress, and Other Poems* 29 years earlier. Coward recalls Smith's "unceasing craving for intellectual intercourse," "her intense love for the higher class of literature," "her warm sympathy" (301–2), and above all, that "She was one of the most truthful spoken of Adam's race it has been my fortune to know, with any kind of intimacy" (302). He also notes somewhat wryly that "Your clever or intellectual woman is invariably a woman with a will of her own, and Miss Smith was no exception to this rule" (302). Smith was indeed a woman who lived by her principles to the end.

Conclusion

The three memoirs we have examined all center on their writers' lives as workers and record their unceasing efforts to achieve higher status, financial security, or vocation. Here they part company, however, with the earliest, Ashford, finding her greatest triumph in her family's mere survival, whereas both Bathgate and Smith were able to find intrinsic satisfactions in the relatively respected occupation of teacher, and the more educated and intellectual Smith found greatest fulfillment as a poet and feminist campaigner. As we have seen, Ashford's blunt, unvarnished account of her experiences was prompted by the desire to assert her existence against an expectation of silence, whereas Bathgate's genial vignettes and Smith's earnest confessions evince a greater sense of potential audiences. The more self-consciously crafted autobiographies of Bathgate and Smith also share a recognizably Victorian moralistic and self-disciplined tone, offering a more socially conscious version of Samuel Smiles's self-help ethic. All three of our autobiographers place a high value on personal independence, and in the cases of Bathgate and Smith, their interests in the inner life is expressed through religion or its variants – mysticism, skepticism, or a belief in spiritual presence. And although Ashford, Bathgate, and Smith all chafed against some aspects of their fate, all expressed at least qualified satisfaction in what they had managed to achieve or witness and in their ability to record their arduous lives for posterity.

NOTE

1. For census details I am indebted to the researches of Sharon Knapp of Burnaby, British Columbia, who has traced Ashford's family line and marital history.

CHAPTER 16

The Newspaper Press and the Victorian Working Class Poet

Kirstie Blair

In October 1863, a poem by "John Stargazer," "My First Attempt," appeared in the correspondents' column of the Dundee, Perth, and Forfar *People's Journal*, a newspaper that had rapidly and deliberately established itself as a major venue for working class literature. It opened:

> I lingered in the shady nook, beneath the spreading trees,
> I wandered by the babbling brook and listened to the breeze;
> I dreamed away the broad daylight, I "burned the midnight taper,"
> In the high hope that I might write a poem for your paper.   (2)

As the aspiring poet wastes away in his efforts at composition, he is finally driven to confess to his mother:

> I knew her watchfulness would pry and worm my secret out.
> So telling her my hopes I bade her let none other know it,
> She shook her head, "Ah, John," she said, "I doot ye're nae a poet."
>   (2)

Undaunted by his family's pragmatic diagnosis of an upset stomach, Stargazer completes his masterpiece and fantasizes about its rapturous reception in the press, eagerly awaiting its publication:

> I bought the paper, inside out I laid its columns bare;
> I looked – could I my optics doubt? – my poem is not there!
> The reason why is told me soon, although I didn't ask it:
> "Stargazer's 'Ode unto the Moon' has gone to the waste basket."
>   (2)

The correspondents' column, as I have examined in detail elsewhere, was the primary medium for discussing, with either mockery or encouragement, poems rejected as unsuitable for publication (see Blair, "Let the Nightingales Alone"). This unidentified poem is a comic, self-reflexive study of the likely fate of a newspaper poem. It is one of a great many poems and prose pieces that satirize the intense desire of young working men (and, less commonly, women) to see their poems in print in their local newspaper. Such poems themselves conform to generic norms. The would-be poet will have a comically inflated sense of his own self-importance, modeling himself on the literary image of the poet as a frail, delicate individual entirely dedicated to his craft: an image popularized a decade prior to Stargazer's poem by another Scottish working class writer and newspaper poet, Alexander Smith, in his notorious 1853 "spasmodic" poem *A Life-Drama*. The aspiring poet also attempts – not always successfully, in such poems – high-class standard English ("optics" rather than "eyes," for instance), providing a humorous contrast with the homely Scots of his family.

"My First Attempt" is an example both of the "literariness, the linguistic and formal self-consciousness" that Brian Maidment sees as characteristic of "writing by self-taught working men," and, in its publication context, of what Michael Sanders calls the "dialectical interplay between readership and editor in the creation of the poetry column's editorial policy" (Maidment, *Poorhouse* 13; Sanders 71). It assumes readers' existing knowledge of the contexts of the *People's Journal*, of contemporary poetic norms, and of the usual standards and topics of newspaper poetry. Such "original" newspaper verse, as opposed to reprinted poems by established poets, has attracted little sustained critical attention.[1] As Maidment rightly notes in an important 1985 article on the verse culture of Victorian Manchester:

> Newspaper poems have to appeal to a wide variety of readers and cannot be too controversial in their views. They have to be easily understood at first reading, and cannot afford to be formally or intellectually complex. They must be musical and melodious. Consistent and competent use of simple verse forms is a necessary adjunct to this need for immediate accessibility.... Such constraints imposed by the newspaper locale suggests that most poems written in this genre will be little more than occasional verses using, without much thought about form or tone, the simple and conservative conventions of banal public utterance. ("Class and Cultural Production" 158)

No one could deny that newspaper verse leans toward the generic, embracing cliché and familiarity, nor that it is difficult to make a case for the significance of most newspaper verse on aesthetic grounds. But, as I suggest in this chapter, even the most standard or seemingly "occasional" poetry column provides valuable insights into why and how editors supported particular kinds of working class verse culture. Newspaper poets wrote to order. Their ambition, like John Stargazer's, was to see their poetry in print, and those who succeeded possessed a very clear and often cynical understanding about the best means to achieve this. The fact that the poems they tended to produce are lacking in formal and linguistic experimentation and aesthetically conservative does not indicate an absence of talent. It shows their understanding of the marketplace: a marketplace that we must also understand if we hope to revalue Victorian working class poetics.

The relationship between the aspiring working class poet and the newspaper press has always been crucial. Indeed, it is possible to argue that at least from the late eighteenth century onward, every laboring class or working class poet had a significant relationship with the press. In the case of many, like Robert Burns, the relationship was vexed. As Lucyle Werkmeister's detailed studies indicate, Burns sent a number of poems to London and local newspapers in the late 1780s and 1790s, both pseudonymously and under his own name, and developed relationships with editors like Peter Stuart of the London *Star*. "I would scorn to put my name to a Newspaper Poem," he wrote to one friend; yet, in a letter to Stuart in the same week, he observed that "I am charmed with your paper. I wish it was more in my power to contribute to it" and gave Stuart license to do what he wished with the poems Burns sent him, short of publishing Burns's name with them (Burns I: 405, 407). Burns valued the press for its publication of political poems, though as a government employee, he had to be cautious, running into trouble when satirical poems on Establishment figures were wrongly attributed to him, or when editors were unable to resist adding his name to his own satires (see Werkmeister). John Clare, as Eric Robinson has shown, was also an avid reader of and contributor to the newspaper press, local and national, though the extent of his contributions has still not been fully traced. Burns and Clare, who was supported and championed by the London *Morning Post*, had a status that entitled them to consideration by the London papers. As the press expanded and expanded again in the course of the nineteenth century, however, and as the rise of literacy and the prior reputation of poets like Burns increased the number of would-be working class poets, the primary relationship tended to be between a working class poet and one or more of their local newspapers.

The Victorian provincial press offered, as Laura Mandell notes, "unexampled opportunities for publication by local writers who remained isolated from metropolitan literary circles" (314). As David Vincent comments, it "constituted at once a nursery and a shop window for literary talent," enabling those with little education, and little leisure for composition, to produce short pieces that were readily publishable (*Literacy* 214). It is an extraordinarily rich, and surprisingly under-examined, resource for the study of working class verse cultures.[2] Andrew Hobbs has begun to reassess poetry in the Northern and English provincial press, as well as more broadly, and his recent article with Claire Januszewski argues that the local paper "was the type of publication in which most Victorian poetry was published and – from the 1860s – in which most Victorian poetry was read" (65). Hobbs and Januszewski's statistical analysis estimates that around 4 million poems appeared in the local press in England, of which "between a third and a half" were "original and locally produced" (65), which demonstrates the scale of this issue. For scholars of working class literature, Sanders's excellent work on the Chartist press has substantially established the importance of newspaper poetry in constituting and commenting upon a radical political movement. Yet, while most researchers in this field are doubtless aware of the existence of newspaper poetry, the scope of its importance for studies of working class literature and culture has not always been acknowledged. The majority of poems we read in volume form by working class poets from this period were first published in newspapers, and thus shaped, mediated, and indeed altered by the literary editors of those papers. Because it is rare for a poet to state where and when poems first appeared, however, this relationship is frequently rendered invisible – unless, of course, as is true for many volumes by working class writers, the local newspaper was also the publisher of the volume. Of a small but lively group of mid-Victorian working class poets in Airdrie, North Lanarkshire, for instance, at least four – David H. Morrison (miner and millworker), William McHutchison (stonemason), Frank Henrietta (hairdresser), and James Stewart (profession untraced, but presents himself as a railway worker) – had collections published at the office of the *Airdrie Advertiser* with the help of the editor, John Baird. All had contributed substantively to its active poetry column. In addition, we need to be aware of what we are *not* reading, when we pick up a volume by any named Victorian working class poet; we are not reading the newspaper publications that were deemed unsuitable for inclusion. In rare cases where scholars have compared the newspaper output of a poet to poems published in book form, as in Ed Cohen, Anne Fertig, and Linda Fleming's recent edition of Marion Bernstein's poems, it is evident both that substantial numbers of newspaper poems were left out, either deliberately or because they postdated volume publications, and that newspaper poems can be more radical than the contents of a published volume would suggest.[3]

Moreover, newspaper publication was vital for drumming up patronage and subscriptions. A poet in a small rural community might, perhaps, be able to marshal enough support from friends and acquaintances to form a suitable subscription list, as Burns had done. In the larger, diverse communities of the industrial city, though, newspaper publication was a far easier way to acquire a fanbase of potential subscribers and admirers. For mid-Victorian working class poets, the most desirable patron was a local newspaper editor, who would, for the right poet, advertise their forthcoming volume, publish other poems and letters in support, encourage subscribers, publish extracts from the book, and then review it in glowing terms on publication. They might even give the aspiring poet a job. A substantial number of newspaper employees started out as newspaper poets, like John Mitchell, assistant editor of the *Dundee Advertiser*, who began his career "in a mercantile office" and "first made his mark as a contributor of poetry to the "Advertiser" columns" as "P.D.G."; the editor, William Leng, was impressed enough to offer him a staff post (Millar 30; also cited Blair, "A Very Poetical Town" 91). Newspapers and working class poets had a mutually profitable understanding. Unlike periodical contributions, newspaper contributions were unpaid. The *People's Friend*, founded in 1869 as a spin-off from the highly successful Dundee *People's Journal*, and with an explicit mission to "foster and encourage the literary talent which we know exists among the people," grandly announced that "all manuscripts of Stories, Essays, and other Literary Articles which are accepted for publication *will be paid for at a fixed rate*" ("Our Design and Purpose," 5 January 1870, 1). Yet just over a month later, the editor clarified that this did not include poetry, except in the unlikely case that it was of "*very superior merit*" (his italics) (23 February 1870, 128). The assumption was that newspaper poets would be satisfied simply by seeing their works in print: publication supplied cultural capital, an enhanced reputation among peers (and potentially employers), and free publicity for future publishing ventures.

Studying working class writers in the Victorian newspaper press can be problematic, both because of the vast scale of such an enterprise, and because of the practice of publishing under a pseudonym. Although diligent research can unearth the relationship between a named working class poet and particular newspapers, such as Ellen Johnston and the *Penny Post*, Janet Hamilton and the *Hamilton Advertiser* and *Airdrie Advertiser*, Alexander Anderson or "Surfaceman" and the *People's Friend*, or Marion Bernstein and the *Glasgow Weekly Mail*, this ignores the thousands of other working class poets who published only occasionally or whose pseudonyms were never publicly linked to their real-life identity.[4] And even in the case of these relatively well-known poets, it would be extremely difficult to state with authority that all their newspaper publications (and republications) had been traced. It is also impossible to identify how many anonymous or pseudonymous newspaper poets were "working class." Even with detective work and the assistance of the tireless local anthologizers of the late

Victorian period, working class newspaper poetry poses a significant challenge to the traditional identification of working class writers through details from their biography.

The great benefit of this, however, is that newspaper poetry offers an opportunity to study the *self-identification* of poets as "workers," whether through signatures such as "A Voice from the Factory," through the use of dialect and other forms of nonstandard English, or through content reflecting working class life. From this perspective, the key question is not whether "Tina, Blairgowrie," author of "The Slatternly Wife" in the *Weekly News* (2 November 1874, 4) might be the real-life Tina Galbraith, a domestic servant later located in Lanarkshire, who "thought in verse, spoke in verse, and wrote in verse" and was a very frequent newspaper contributor around this period (Knox 228). The question is, rather, what the selected authorial persona of "Tina, Blairgowrie" tells us about the language, themes, and form considered appropriate for working women's newspaper verse. Many pseudonyms, as in Anderson's "Surfaceman," identified the poet as a worker in a particular field, and some poets identified themselves by name and trade, like McHutchison, whose poetic signature was "William McHutchison, stonemason." This was also, of course, a useful means for poets to advertise the other services they might offer to local readers. Hugh Miller recalled that when he traveled to Inverness to find work as a stone-engraver in 1828, his first move was to write a poem on the Ness and send it to the local press:

> My verses, thought I, are at least tolerably correct: could I not get one or two copies introduced into the poet's corner of the *Inverness Courier* or *Journal*, and thus show that I have literature enough to be trusted with the cutting of an epigraph on a gravestone? (*Schools* 398)

The practice of identifying *where* the poet lived or worked equally served as a means for readers to assess the authenticity of claims to working class status: hence Colin Sievwright, a well-known figure in the poetry columns of the *Weekly News*, wrote in April 1867 that he had changed his profession from the "rural joys" of weaving to factory work "And now he courts the muse amid / The factory's whirling noise." His signature, distinct from his earlier and later poems in the paper signed "Kirremuir'" or "Forfar," includes his new address "Don's Factory, Forfar" ("Colin's Reply to 'J.G.,' Arbroath," 6 April 1867, 4).

Poets like Sievwright were personalities in the newspaper press, and the sense that readers knew their real name and address was part of their celebrity status. Whether everyone who wrote as "A Factory Lassie," "A

Herd Laddie," or "A Barber's Apprentice" genuinely pursued these occupations is, however, doubtful. Cross-class as well as cross-gender representations were common. John Fullerton, for instance, a poet local to Aberdeen who left school at ten to work in a mill (he eventually became a lawyer's clerk and factor after attending night school) and began contributing to papers in his teens, was known best by the pseudonym "Wild Rose." He also published verse and prose, however, under the names "Alice Douglas," "Robin Goodfellow," "Rob Gibb," "The Vicar of Deepdale," or "J. F." (Fullerton xi). The posthumous selection of his work is devoted to preserving a small selection of his most aesthetically pleasing compositions as "Wild Rose." What he published under his other pseudonyms and whether his poems varied to suit the selected persona would be a fascinating study but virtually impossible to conduct. Many if not most of the newspapers patronized by poets such as Fullerton are not digitized (and thus not readily searchable). Some only exist in limited runs of hard copy, and some are entirely lost.

For this reason, studies of newspaper poetry, such as Hobbs's excellent recent work or my own current research, tend to rely on either sampling from a range of papers or an in-depth study of one paper (see Blair "Let the Nightingales Alone"; Hobbs "Five Million"). My conclusions here, for example, are extrapolated almost exclusively from the English-language Scottish press in the mid-Victorian period. Scotland had a certain advantage over other contemporary working class verse cultures in its education system and in the possession of Burns as a model, and for these and other reasons, a high proportion of Victorian Britain's working class poets were Scottish by birth or adoption.[5] It also possessed a particularly vibrant cheap newspaper culture, especially after the abolition of Stamp Duty in 1855 and the repeal of paper duties in 1861. But similar verse cultures centered around local newspapers existed in the industrial cities and regions of England, Ireland, and Wales, in colonial cities such as Delhi, and in the US, Canada, Australia, and New Zealand. Studying any set of Victorian newspapers will uncover not only the presence of local verse cultures, but also evidence that poems that were originally "local" were freely circulated and reprinted on a global scale.

In many papers, poems appeared wherever there was a small space that needed to be filled. The standard position, though, tended to be either on the top left-hand corner of the front page, beside the classified advertisements, or on the second or fourth page in an identified column. Correspondence columns, as noted above, would also sometimes contain poems, often with editorial commentary. Most newspapers published both reprinted poetry taken from other papers, or, more rarely, from new volumes by established authors like Tennyson, Longfellow, or the Brownings, and poetry written specifically for the newspaper in question. The latter category of poems usually appeared under the heading "Original Poetry": while reprints of "original" poems from other Scottish, British, and international newspapers were common, these were generally identified as such. Papers also occasionally carried advertising poems, both from local companies and in advertisements syndicated across the British press, and frequently published poems in the form of word-games – acrostics, riddles, enigmas, and other short verses centered on puns and wordplay. Local newspapers would, in addition, review volumes of verse published by local writers, often with copious extracts. And they reported on the presence of verse culture in everyday life by reprinting verses recited at and allegedly specially composed for celebrations, dinners, and assorted significant occasions in the region associated with the paper. In this way, the press remained, as Raymond Williams noted, "significantly interactive with a predominately oral culture, which in the development of the cities was itself assuming new forms" ("Press and Popular Culture" 45).

Generically, it is possible to classify a huge mass of "original" newspaper poems as pastoral, elegy, or love poems, predominately lyrical, and, with few exceptions, written in easily recognizable verse forms with predictable patterns of rhyme and meter. These stock poems should not be lightly dismissed, since uncovering the topics that were the surest hits with newspaper editors and readers is vital to understanding what Victorian working class poets wrote and why they wrote it. A typical example of editorial opinion on the function and subject matter of newspaper poetry can be found in a September 1855 celebration of "Our Local Poets" from the *Airdrie and Coatbridge Advertiser*, a provincial newspaper serving one of the most heavily industrialized areas of Scotland and thus an excellent source for examining regional working class verse culture. The author begins by acknowledging that "The cold and barren soil of a mineral district may at first seem uncongenial" to poetic composition, yet nonetheless, "there are poets among us." These local poets are firmly counseled "to fulfil their divine mission":

> [L]et them consecrate their verses to the social and moral elevation of their fellowmen, and they may rest assured that those who make the people's songs have more power for good than those who make the people's laws. (22 September 1855, 2)

This is a high – though by no means exceptionally high – valuation of the "people's" poetry, referencing in its final clause a very popular and oft-quoted saying.⁶ Victorian newspaper editors and reviewers throughout Britain strongly agreed: poetry by working men and women had substantial power to "elevate" the thoughts of readers, inspiring them toward more moral lives and encouraging educational and cultural aspiration. This aim is both politically conservative – poetry helps working class readers and writers to be more contented with their lot – and radical. In the hands of editors such as John Leng and William Latto of the *People's Journal*, for instance, there was a direct correlation between the ability of working class writers to produce high-quality literary works and their fitness for the franchise. Promoting the "people's" writings, in the Scottish press at least, was strongly associated with support for Liberal, reformist, or radical causes.

In the *Airdrie Advertiser's* "Our Local Poets" selection, the four poems highlighted are George Tennant's "To the Patriots of Italy – an Ode" and "The Wee Beggar Wean," A. McDougall's "Farewell to Bute," and "Lines by a Sentimentalist" by "Aliquis." Only the first of these poets is identifiable. Tennant was the lesser-known brother of Robert Tennant, the "postman poet," whose works appeared regularly in the Glasgow press in later decades, and thus part of a local working class family of weavers with shared poetic interests. Several of Robert Tennant's poems are epistles to his brother (Tennant 11, 23). George Tennant was a regular contributor to the *Airdrie Advertiser* and is a good example of a typical newspaper poet because his topics invariably embrace the most popular themes of the poetry columns from these decades. "The Wee Beggar Wean," written in Scots, is one of many newspaper poems designed to provoke charitable thoughts in the reader by a focus on poor and helpless street children. Tennant's poem opens:

O, ance to our door cam a wee beggar wean,
    A' wearit an' lorn leuk't the laddie,
An sair the thing grat, whan I speirt 'im his name,   [*grat* = *cried; speirt* = *asked*]
    An what was the name o' his daddie.   (2)

Dialect is characteristically used by Scottish poets in this period for scenes from working class life and culture and in poems spoken by the poet in the first person, whether humorous or pathetic. Poems like this one, in which the object of the reader's pity is unnamed, homeless, and without family, do speak obliquely of the injustices of mid-Victorian society, but their primary aim is less to criticize the rich for neglecting the poor than to invoke a sense of working class community and solidarity. The weeping child finds a sympathetic listener and financial aid from the home of a working family.

Tennant's second selected poem, now in standard English, "Rouse! Italian patriots brace! / High your martial banners wave!" reflects the strong Scottish interest in Italian political affairs in the 1850s and 1860s. Janet Hamilton, whose political poems were a staple of the *Airdrie Advertiser* and were republished throughout the Scottish press, is perhaps the best example of a poet deeply and passionately engaged with European political struggles in Italy, with Garibaldi as hero, and in Poland, where Kossuth is the deliverer. But in adopting these topics, she was one of thousands of other minor poets. The author of "Our Local Poets" suggests that many of Tennant's lines are "not unworthy of a place beside 'Scots wha hae wi' Wallace bled,'" thus tying Tennant's poem to an existing tradition of laboring class martial and patriotic verse and linking Scottish patriotism to the growing European nationalism. As indicated by very frequent comparisons between Garibaldi and William Wallace in newspaper verse, this was a commonly felt link. Connecting "Scotland's historical fight for freedom with the contemporary Italian liberation struggles," as H. Gustav Klaus comments on Johnston's Garibaldi poems, "postulates a nation's right to self-determination as a universal goal," and is thus significant in fostering Scottish national identity (*Factory Girl* 51). Tennant's poems, here, are formally and linguistically undistinguished; in themselves easy to pass over, yet, as representative of two major themes in working class newspaper verse, they are highly significant.

Even more representative is the third poem highlighted in this column, "Farewell to Bute." With six stanzas in the most popular measure and rhyme scheme (four-beat, alternately rhymed lines), the poem in its entirety runs:

> Adieu, thou green and fairest isle
>   Arising on the western main,
> Long may your flowers in beauty smile
>   For me they ne'er may smile again.
>
> The lofty mountains far away,
>   With misty summits rising hoar,
> Look on the billows, at their play,
>   That wash thy sweetly bending shore.
>
> Farewell the cool and calm retreat;
>   Ye fragrant, leafy bowers farewell,
> Where I have listened to the beat
>   And music of old ocean's swell.

> I've seen along thy pebbly strand
>   The sons of labour rest awhile;
> I've thought upon the better land,
>   Where men shall rest from sin and toil.
>
> The autumn sunbeams linger yet,
>   But soon her leaves shall fade and die;
> The summer scene I may forget,
>   When winter chills the cloudy sky.
>
> But till my memory departs,
>   I'll cherish still, where'er I roam,
> The warm and living, loving hearts
>   I met within your island home. (2)

The opening, particularly in "For me they ne'er may smile again," suggests that this could be an emigrant poem, in which the speaker laments a lost childhood home, either from his or her position within an industrial city or from the colonies. But as the poem progresses it becomes clear that its genre is the tourist poem. Only when we appreciate the date on which the poem was published, the end of September, does its seasonal topicality become evident. Poetry columns favored works, like this poem, in which the speaker celebrates a specific British or Scottish location but in highly standardized tropes of towering mist-covered mountains, rugged glens, crystal streams, billowing ocean waves, and "fragrant, leafy bowers" filled with wild flowers. Such poems are write-by-numbers and entirely, reassuringly, predictable. There is no possibility, for instance, that "roam" will not rhyme with "home." Whether A. McDougall identifies with the holidaying "sons of labour" mentioned in stanza 4 is unclear. But the presence of these working men, their labor a contrast to the "play" of nature, disturbs the poem, emphasizing that the ability to access the beauties of nature and the pleasures of community is temporary and limited (readers of the *Advertiser* would, of course, know that Bute was easily reached from the major industrial city of Glasgow by steamer and was thus a popular tourist destination). The poet's immediate turn to the pleasures of heaven recognizes that on earth, leisure is a rare commodity. Poems in the "Farewell to Bute" genre have a strong tendency to acknowledge that rural delights are at best a brief respite from the standard working lives of poet and reader, just as the poem itself is a respite from the news and factual reports on the same page.

    The final poem selected in this column is the most interesting, because "Lines from a Sentimentalist" acknowledges and parodies the sentimental style of many newspaper love poems. After several stanzas celebrating the touching beauty of a weeping girl, the speaker begs her to "Unfold then, fairest maid, I pray, / The care thy troubled looks betray":

Softened, then, she spake thus free –
"Last nicht I was on the spree,
I'm seedy noo, and no mistake –
I say man, chappie, lend's a make." [*halfpenny*] (2)

That the object of the speaker's high-flown rhetoric (emphasized by the archaic "spake") is a coarsely spoken, hungover woman asking for a loan brings realism into sharp contrast with poetic flights of fantasy. This poem by "Aliquis" nicely indicates how very self-aware newspaper poets were of the difference between poetic rhetoric and reality. The author of "Our Local Poets," however, seemingly does not approve. "Aliquis must purge and purify," he concludes, commenting that the Scots lines are "too vulgar" compared to the "above tolerable" rhetoric of the rest of the poem. Given that the poem obviously *parodies* such rhetoric, it is possible that this commentary should be read as ironic, though it may also reflect the author's assumption that if poetry is not improving, it is worthless.

Dwelling on this one column in some detail highlights the diversity of newspaper poetry and the ways in which even the most clichéd poem speaks to issues relevant to the predominately working class readership of the cheap weekly press. All four poems selected for notice here are "political," in the sense of dealing with issues of social concern to working people, and they are good instances of the way in which poetry columns negotiate between local, national, and international concerns, and, in the Scottish context, between differing linguistic registers. Much newspaper verse, and indeed Scottish Victorian verse in general, has been heavily criticized for "distortion and avoidance of the real social and political conditions and issues," in favor instead of escapism and romanticism (Gifford 324–5). Close study of poetry columns, however, indicates that this is not the case, and supports Andrew Nash's revisionist claim that Scottish Victorian writers "addressed contemporary urban life more directly in poetry than they did in fiction" ("Victorian Scottish Literature" 145). Every provincial paper included numbers of poems that served as immediate commentary on topical local issues, though these are, of course, precisely the kind of poems that would never be republished should an author attain success, because their purpose was entirely context-dependent.

A good example of this is found in a poem on "The Udny Case," by "Kenna Fa, Corbie Heugh," dated 29 March 1850 and printed on 13 April 1850 by the *Aberdeen Herald* with a note that it had previously appeared in the *Banffshire Journal*. The "Udny Case" concerned Mr. John Leslie and an appeal that had been lodged against him becoming a Presbyterian minister in the small village of Udny in Aberdeenshire. The evidence, heard by the Established Church Synod and reported verbatim in the same issue as the poem, centered on whether Leslie was unfit to be a minister due to his association with the lower classes and their labor. It was thus a potent combination of religious and class issues. Servants testified, for instance, that Leslie had helped them with hoeing the turnips and working in harvest: "We addressed him 'Johnny'"; that he had been seen "ploughing" and "driving a cart at laying down the dung," and that he dressed like a working man (2). To the author of "The Udny Case" and presumably the readers of the *Herald*, which had moderate radical sympathies in this period, the appeal was an example of the wealthy persecuting a man for his friendly relations with the poor and an attack on the dignity of labor:

> We a' hae heard in ancient time
> That labour wasna thocht nae crime
> In them that brocht the truth sublime
>   Frae Heaven to man;
> But, wiser now, we've chang'd our rhyme
>   For newer plan.   (13 April 1850, 4)

The poet satirically notes the artificial distinction between approved upper class leisure and rural pursuits such as hunting and shooting, and meaningful labor, and between the pleasures of the wealthy and the needs of the poor:

Or ye may spen' half days at dinner,
An' bandy jokes wi' foul-mou'd sinner,
Or stap your painch wi' flesh an' finner,
   Till near hand bokin';   [*to vomit*]
But help in hairst a weary bin'er,   [*harvest, binder*]
   Na, that's nae jokin'   (13 April 1850, 4)

"Gin ye shak a corn-riddle / Fareweel the manse," "Kenna Fa" notes with grim humor, concluding by hoping that in the modern world "The proud may yet to them be cringin' / They noo ca 'vermin'" (13 April 1850, 4). The fact that the poem is written in Scots, and in the habbie stanza, which was strongly associated with Burns's satirical poems, helps to locate the author as one of the working people implicitly maligned by this case and aligns the poem with a tradition of satirizing the hypocrisy of the clergy, most famously seen in Burns's "Holy Willie's Prayer." The use of this stanza also shows that he will not change his rhyme "for newer plan." Like most topical newspaper poems, the author does not mention the key players by name and presumes readers' familiarity with the fine details of the case. Every action referenced in the poem features in the *Herald*'s report of the hearing. In the absence of editorial commentary on the case, the republication of this biting satirical poem indicates the *Aberdeen Herald*'s stance. The poetry column, as is not infrequently the case, is where the paper's politics come through most clearly and are presented in a more radical light than overt editorial statements might suggest.

Poetry columns supported political action from those whose voices might otherwise get a limited hearing, including working class women. In an example of a series of poems on the same issue, as opposed to the stand-alone poem on "The Udny Case," poetry played a significant role in an ongoing dispute over female servants' working hours in the 1860s. As Jan Merchant has discussed, the "insurrection of maids" in the early 1870s, leading to the formation of the Dundee and District Domestic Servants' Association, was a key moment in fostering a radical working class women's movement and was largely supported by the *People's Journal*. Poetry had, however, been deployed to protest about servants' working conditions for at least a decade prior to this. A. M. B.'s "Song of the Servant Maid" was widely reprinted in spring 1860, appearing a week apart, for instance, in the *Aberdeen Herald* and the *Dundee Advertiser*. With a title deliberately recalling Thomas Hood's enormously influential "The Song of the Shirt," it opens:

> Close the office, and shut the shop
> And let the human machinery stop;
> Toil is wearing, and life is sweet,
> Toil and rest make life complete;
>   Stop the wheels of labour and trade –
>   But oh for the weary servant maid!
>   (12 August 1860, *Aberdeen Herald* 2;
>   17 August 1860, *Dundee Advertiser* 2)

Female servants, A. M. B.'s poem points out, do not even have access to the hours of leisure afforded to working men (and women) in industrial employment. Five years later, "The Grubses," by "Betty Martin" in Glasgow's *Penny Post*, is a scornful discussion of a proposal to set up a training institution for maidservants in the form of a conversation between maids in Glasgow's West End.[7] The mistresses' "real wish," one reports, is "that such as you and me / Be made still greater slaves for oor / Bit paltry penny fee." She concludes:

> And let us hear nae mair aboot
>   Their filanthrofick cry
> For institutions to train us –
>   For that's all in my eye.
>   (25 February 1865, 1)

Like many political Scots poems, this is humorous and self-mocking in its misspelling of "philanthropic," but also angry. By 1866, agitation for better holidays and working hours for female servants spread through the poems and letters pages of the *People's Journal* and other Scottish papers, as a definite movement got under way to form a trades union. J. C., Elie, responding to a letter from "A Servant Maid" asking men to join this cause, wrote:

> Ye fathers, brothers, lovers all
>   Oh! Hasten to their aid
> And brave the system that enthralls
>   The Scottish Servant Maid.
>
> And when we have our nine hours gain'd
>   It never shall be said
> That we have left in slavery
>   The Scottish Servant Maid.
>   (17 March 1866, *People's Journal* 2)

This directly links the causes of working women and men. On 19 May "A Scottish Servant Maid" cited these verses and gratefully thanked J. C. "our noble poetic friend," "whose name is immortalized in the memory of many of us," for his support. In the same issue, A. L. B., Craigellachie, joined the cause with his poem "A Scottish Servant Maid," in which "we" are working men, glad that women workers are joining their cause:

> Come – for we thought that thou hadst slept
>   In ignorance, nor wished to raise
> Thy voice o'er slavery, and protect
>   Sweet freedom's sunny days.
>
> But no, it is not so, for we
>   A Scottish Servant Maid can find,
> To bear the palm of liberty
>   And lead fair womankind.
>   (17 March 1866, 4)

A. L. B.'s poem was similarly greeted with enthusiasm by "An Aberdeenshire Lassie" in her letter of 2 June, "Cheer up my sisters, and let us all unite hands and hearts together. We are no longer to be mere walking machines, with no higher aim than to eat and sleep. . . . I am much obliged to the Craigellachie Bard, who last week cheered our hearts with his beautiful lines." Poetry, here, is key both because it promotes affective investment in a political cause and also because the act of producing poems in itself demonstrates that workers are more than "human machinery," displaying a level of cultural literacy that serves to advocate for better treatment.

This brief example also shows the regular level of interaction between poets and correspondents to newspapers, with new poems and poets subjects of praise and commentary by readers and other poets. Sometimes these responses, as in Ellen Johnston's long-running correspondence with a number of other poets in the *Penny Post*, could run over months and years (see Boos, "Queen of the Far-Famed Penny Post" and Rosen, "Class and Poetic Communities"). At the same time as the maidservant's debate, to take only one further example, "A Factory Lassie's Sang" by "Jessie Jimpwaist, Kenmisel Crescent, Aberdeen" – a poem which defends the author's work in the mill and celebrates her unnamed young man – attracted an immediate response, "The Factory Lassie," by "Jessie's Sweetheart," with the final line "Dear Jessie, in a week or twa I'll tak ye frae the mill" (21 April 1866 and 5 May 1866, *People's Journal* 2). Readers understood that such poetic romances and friendships were almost certainly fictional, but this did not hinder enjoyment of the pleasures of serial reading and the sense of community that the poetry columns could produce.

Local newspapers did not simply support existing working class poets. They *created* them by providing an aspirational venue for publishing their works. They made the practice of writing poems, in the intervals of highly demanding labor, seem both exceptional, something to be lauded and celebrated, and unexceptional, in that everyone was doing it. And they profoundly influenced what working class people wrote, as well as what they read. In Victorian studies, book collections are the tip of the iceberg when it comes to assessing the influence of working class poetics. Working class readers were not, on the whole, reading these books. They were reading and discussing the poetry columns and then cutting their favorite poems out of newspaper columns and pasting them into scrapbooks or on the walls of their workplace. William Donaldson observes in his groundbreaking study of popular prose literature in Victorian Scotland that the writers who operated "through the medium of the popular press" created "a cultural achievement of massive proportions; and it is still largely unexplored" (148). Only by undertaking the substantial labor of tracing both named and unnamed working class writers through the columns of the newspaper press can we understand the relationship between their writings, their readership, and the print culture of their period.

NOTES

I am grateful to the Research Society for Victorian Periodicals for a Curran Fellowship and to the Carnegie Trust for the Universities of Scotland for funding in support of this research.

1. On Tennyson, *The Times*, and the circulation of poems by established poets in the newspaper press, see Houston. Recent work on newspapers and literary culture, especially Rubery's, has concentrated on fiction.
2. Working class poets also published frequently in the periodical press, and their presence in this medium also requires further research. While the distinction between periodical, magazine, and newspaper is blurred in the nineteenth century, for the purposes of this chapter I consider only "newspapers," defining such as daily or weekly publications primarily focused on reporting current affairs.
3. For example, Cohen, Fertig, and Fleming note that poems such as Bernstein's "Oh! I Wish That All Women Had Power to Vote" and "The Govan Riveter's Strike" appeared in the *Glasgow Weekly Mail* but have not since been republished (239, 247).
4. See Boos, Rosen, and Klaus on Johnston and Cohen and Fertig on Bernstein. Hamilton is discussed in this volume by Kaye Kossick.
5. Goodridge's "Laboring-Class Poets Online" identifies "well over half" of the named poets in the database as "of Scottish origin or acculturation" ("Statistical Notes," https://lcpoets.wordpress.com/introtobibliography/, consulted 29 July 2015).
6. This quotation or misquotation appears throughout the Victorian press. It is originally attributed to the seventeenth-century Scottish writer and politician Andrew Fletcher.
7. "Betty Martin" is a Cockney slang term. In the 1830s and 1840s there was a running joke that it was short for "Harriet Martineau." It is not impossible that the author of this poem intends an in-joke about Martineau's study of political economy. See Pegge, 66 on the origins of the phrase and Maidment, "Imagining the Cockney University" 35, for a poetic example of a working-class speaker referring to Martineau by this nickname.

CHAPTER 17

Tensions, Transformations, and Local Identity
The Evolving Meanings of Nineteenth-Century Tyneside Dialect Songs

Rod Hermeston

Tyneside, an area on both banks of the river Tyne in northeast England, is the site of a blossoming of local dialect songs in the nineteenth century – songs abound about pitmen (coalminers) and keelmen (who carry coal down the river Tyne in boats known as keels). They also take as their subject matter local eccentrics of Newcastle, Tyneside's main town, as well as sporting events and sporting heroes, local pride, drinking, and love. Written as it is in Tyneside dialect, this material has led recent scholars to interpret it as a focus of regional and laboring class identity and solidarity. Tyneside dialect is indeed central to the meaning of the material and some songs enhance solidarity from the outset. There can be no doubt of the sentiment expressed in the chorus of Joe Wilson's (*c.* 1860s–70s) piece, "Aw'll Sing Ye a Tyneside Sang":

> An' oh, me lads, it myeks me heart se glad,
> Te sing or hear a lokil sang...
> (*Tyneside Songs* 141)

The local loyalty, linked to dialect, is clear in this piece. Frequently, however, other songs reveal tensions and hostilities between social groups in the area alongside local identity. The present chapter shows that meaning and the significance of dialect are part of an ongoing process negotiated with the audience or reader and new meanings can evolve over time. It is this that allows connotations of local identity to become dominant in the nineteenth century and beyond.

The concept known among sociolinguists as indexicality is central to my argument. According to Mary Bucholtz and Kira Hall this "involves the creation of semiotic links between linguistic forms and social meanings" (594). This occurs through repeated social action (Eckert 456–7). Speech styles, and individual features of language, can index group membership and identity related to concepts such as social class, local or regional belonging, ethnicity, gender, or to specific groups such as urban teenagers, but they can also index character trait, behavior, and particular attitudes.[1] The social meanings are not restricted to any one of these. Indexicality can be related to the work of Mikhail Bakhtin. Bakhtin argues that the meaning of an utterance arises from a dialogue with a background of other utterances, frequently offering contradictory value judgments and points of view (281). Bakhtin's ideas, as Elinor Ochs notes, imply that the "voices of [the] speaker/writer and others may be blended in the course of the message and become part of the social meanings indexed within the message" (338). Social meaning, therefore, is not fixed but instead emerges in ongoing social and cultural practices or activities, and through dialogue with other utterances.[2] This implies that utterances, including those in song, can have different social meanings to different people, and these social meanings may change over time.[3]

Modern scholars often oversimplify explanations of song. Recent dominant interpretations view northern dialect literature of the nineteenth century (including Tyneside song) and the nonstandard dialect within it as promoting solidarity and representing people at the levels of some or all of the following identity categories: the locality or region, the laboring class, and the community. They also see it as promoting largely positive values such as self-help, common sense, the communal, the family and the domestic, temperance, decency, and populism.[4]

In the case of Tyneside, I complicate such interpretations in relation to the time period when songs are written and differences in audience composition. I categorize songs into two broad time periods in the nineteenth century: an early period in the first half of the century and a later period beginning approximately at mid-century with the onset of music hall. Divisions in audience composition will become apparent. These points need to be taken into account even before examining changes in meaning.

Acknowledging an earlier debate between social historians Dave Harker and Robert Colls, I have shown elsewhere that attitudes toward the speech styles and behavior of pitmen and keelmen in early nineteenth-century song, and that of the pitman figure "Bob Cranky" in particular, are dependent on audience response ("Indexing"). In John Selkirk's song "Bob Cranky's 'Size Sunday" ([1812] 1971), the irrepressible Bob, bound for a day in Newcastle, boasts "Nyen' them aw cut a dash like Bob Cranky." However, having quite proudly engaged in a drunken fight he dismisses the ruin of his "breeks and ... fine jacket" (in Bell, *Rhymes* 25–7). Harker, a Marxist, claims that at the time of this song's composition pitmen and keelmen are being satirized in a petit-bourgeois song culture and cannot enjoy such material ("John Bell" xliv–v; "The making" 41–3; "The original" 74–5). However, Colls argues that they derive a self-celebration from the songs (*Collier's Rant* 51). Tyneside song of the early nineteenth century is written and performed by clerks, artisans, and shopkeepers for friends in pub singing rooms.[5] Unlike Harker ("Thomas Allan" iii), I do not make strict class demarcations or deny that such writers and performers belong to a rigidly defined laboring class. Nevertheless, these writers and their primary audiences appear to be receptive to nineteenth-century discourses of "respectability." This concept might include belief in the value of a range of the following: education, self-help, self-improvement, "correct" speech, prudent domestic economy, morality, religion, and abstinence or moderation in drinking.[6] While it is true that awareness of these discourses spreads only gradually as the century progresses, Jenny Uglow refers to the "respectable atmosphere that settled like a cloud during the Napoleonic wars" (314). To the early authors of Tyneside song and their audiences, songs and the linguistic styles attributed to semiliterate, drunken, and rough pitmen and keelmen can foster satirical meanings of mockery when in dialogue with discourses of "respectability" (Hermeston "Indexing"). Yet dialogue with such, frequently intrusive, discourses of "respectability" also underlies much of the pleasure taken in the same songs by pitmen and keelmen as respite, resistance, or simple exuberance, and this also impacts on the social meaning of speech style perceived by these groups (Hermeston "Indexing").

Songs arising in music hall from the middle of the century have a clearer provenance within Tyneside's industrial laboring class, or at least, as Russell notes (*Popular Music* 122), their primary audience is drawn from this group. While it is tempting to conclude that this signals a convergence toward strongly laboring class identities and values, it is important to understand the controversial position of music hall in the nineteenth century. Modern commentators tend to view the venues as resistant to pressure, usually from the middle classes, to impose "respectability" on the laboring class.[7] In particular, social reformers of the period object to the sale of alcohol within the halls.[8] Colls has argued, however, that as the nineteenth century progresses the drive toward "respectability" is led in the northeast by primitive methodists (particularly in the mining communities) allied to the teetotal movement, and that both are dominated by the laboring class (*Pitmen* 151, 158; *Collier's Rant* 58, 73–7, 153). Much of the opposition to music hall, then, comes from within the laboring class. The linguistic style within the halls (including dialect and swearing) indexes and celebrates a particular mode of laboring class life and culture, at odds with a more "respectable," religious, and self-improving laboring class lifestyle. Ned Corvan encapsulates these tensions in "The Shades Saloon":

> Aw winna jaw nor preach a sarmin,
> Nor freetin' folks wiv ought alarmin'
> (*Random* 14)

Corvan goes on to praise the music hall/public house mentioned in the song title (*Random* 14).

Nineteenth-century Tyneside dialect song, particularly in initial performances or publications, can reflect tensions and conflicts within and across social groups on Tyneside, and the social meaning of the dialect is affected by that. Yet, at the time of initial performances or publication, and even more so with the further passage of time, these songs have great potential to be perceived as representative of Tyneside and to foster local patriotism. By this, I mean a sometimes strong loyalty to and pride in the locality, its people, and speech. As we shall see, some songs are overtly locally patriotic. However, others may need to be subject to and in dialogue with additional discourses, or their reception may need to be transformed over time, for them to realize their locally patriotic potential. A variety of processes are involved in the enhancement of local patriotism in song. It will become apparent that, despite dialect being implicated in tensions, beliefs about dialect are of great importance in several of these processes. Perceptions of the existence of a Tyneside dialect, and that particular features belong to it, are in a state of formation in the nineteenth century (Beal, "Enregisterment" 142–6). Nevertheless, discourses revealing an emerging belief that a Tyneside dialect exists and that songs are written or performed in that dialect play a central role in enhancing locally patriotic meaning.[9]

The processes involved in enhancing local patriotism include the naming of the locality in some songs and the use of locally patriotic statements. Also important are overt and proud references in particular songs to a local dialect or genre of Tyneside song. More generally, the use in the material of particular, often iconic, words that enhance solidarity is crucial, as is the use and growing awareness of pronunciations and spellings that enhance a sense of local belonging. A process of change in meaning related to repeated publication and the passage of time is also important. This is linked to discourses about songs particularly on song books (titles, prefaces) that identify the locality, and identify the songs and the dialect within them as local. Finally, other discourses, spoken or in print, about the songs and the dialect as local enhance their potential to be perceived as locally patriotic.

These processes will be discussed in varying detail below. However, in order to show that they are necessary for meanings to be narrowed, I will also consider, especially in my discussion of language, specific examples of tension revealed in Tyneside song. In most cases, in the analysis of song that follows, dates correspond to the publication from which the song is taken rather than the date of composition.

The first point to consider is the naming of places in song. This creates a sense of locality and there is repeated naming of Newcastle and its surrounding area. Also important is a tradition in the songs of praising Tyneside or Newcastle. This is frequently accompanied by hostility to London. One example, famous in its time, will suffice. In the chorus of Tommy Thompson's early-nineteenth-century song, "Canny Newcassel" ([1812] 1971), the narrator answers Cockney boasts: "For a' the fine things ye are gobbin about, / We can marra iv canny Newcassel" (in Bell, *Rhymes* 314). The Newcastle man is confident that his town can "marra" (equal) or better anything the capital may offer.

There is also an overt linguistic dimension to this rivalry, and this relates to the second process I have outlined, of referring to local dialect in song. The narrator in "Canny Newcassel" (in Bell, *Rhymes* 316) accuses Cockneys of mocking the Northumbrian burr, a pronunciation of *r*.[10] Ned Corvan in "Wor Tyneside Champions" (1860s) too is scathing of Cockneys who "chaff" about the "tawk" of keelmen (in Allan, *Illustrated* 430). Also, as seen already, Joe Wilson (*Tyneside Songs* 141–2) offers the piece "Aw'll Sing Ye a Tyneside Sang" (c. 1860s–70s). Such songs, especially when they demonstrate awareness of language alongside locally patriotic statements, constitute a discourse which may raise audience awareness of dialect in other songs. The latter songs may then be all the more likely to be perceived as locally patriotic simply by virtue of the language used within them.

A more detailed discussion of language in song is now appropriate. As indicated in the outline of processes that influence and transform meaning, perceptions that features of language belong to a specific Tyneside dialect enhance the sense of locality in song. However, this language can itself be bound up with initial tensions revealed in the material. First, I consider lexis and, in particular, the words *canny* and *hinny*. The word *canny* has a range of values in Scotland and the north of England, ranging from the negative such as "frugal," "shrewd," "sparing," "careful," or "knowing," to far more positive meanings such as "pleasant," "nice," and "good."[11] But, by the nineteenth century, commentators also note a special place for the positive meanings of the word on Tyneside and in the northeast. John Trotter Brockett, in his 1825 dictionary, *A Glossary of North Country Words*, says *canny* is "applied to any thing superior or of the best kind... 'Canny Newcassel,' *par excellence*, is proverbial" (37). Richard Oliver Heslop in his dictionary of 1892, *Northumberland Words*, says *canny* is "an embodiment of all that is kindly, good, and gentle. The highest compliment that can be paid to any person is to say that he or she is *canny*" (130). In our own era, both Katie Wales (*Northern English* 132–3) and Patrick Joyce (284) have linked or equated the function of the word *canny* to the role of pitmen or keelmen in nineteenth-century song, suggesting that both are involved in the construction of community. Positive core meanings of the word are cherished in the northeast in the nineteenth century.[12] However, in song these positive meanings can be used for ironic effect too. This implies additional layers of meaning for the audience, related to genre, when applied in situations in which characters behave in noncommunal, "nonrespectable," or "vulgar" ways.

In William Midford's "The Royal Arch Dukes" (1818) the Standard English narrator refers to pitmen as "canny," but the pitmen are extremely uncouth as they swear and insult an interpreter (44). In Robert Emery's "Paganini" (1842) a pitman and his "neighbours se canny" are depicted as boorish and lacking in sophistication (in Fordyce and Fordyce 256–7). These are songs by early writers who pen satirical pieces about pitmen and keelmen. The word *canny* is here bound up, as so often in the early songs, in satirical mockery of the industrial laboring class, related to a supposed lack of sophistication.

Among the later writers, Ned Corvan's music hall song, "O, maw bonnie Nannie O" (1850), is narrated by a keelman, who beats his wife and is given the same treatment in return (*Random* 19). Nevertheless, the keelman recounts that when Nannie comes to coax him from the pub, "It's then aw treat her wiv a drop, what a canny man, folks cry." This is comedy, but the audience is undoubtedly invited to see ironies surrounding the word *canny* even as part of its enjoyment of rough, "non-respectable" behavior. Something very similar occurs in the Corvan song, "Ha'e ye seen wor Jimmy" (1850s). A mother recounts her son's faults (not least that he assaults policemen) and says "marcy, he's a bad un, / O, maw canny Jim!" (*Corvan's Song Book 3*, 22). It must be emphasized that this is humor, but it requires a very particular appreciation of the word *canny*. Here the word is ironically suitable for a comic rogue, its use resistant to respectable ideals.

The word *canny* is not always steeped in ironies or controversies. From the early nineteenth century there are fairly straightforward uses extolling communal or domestic virtue. However, in the work of Wilson among the later writers, the unironic meanings of *canny* are most clearly promoted. This reflects the greater emphasis that Wilson places on the communal, the domestic, and "respectability," whether as a music hall singer or later as a temperance campaigner.

Wilson at various points offers definitions or character types that fit his understanding of the word *canny*, and at the same time, attribution of the word to some characters is problematized. In his song, "Aw Wish Yor Fethur wes Here" (c. 1865), old Mary storms at her wayward son: "Are ye me canny lad?" (*Joe Wilson's* 11). In the song "Vary [very] Canny" (c. 1865), Wilson lists characteristics that fit the phrase of the title. Such characteristics encompass self-control, moderation, modest achievement, and communal spirit, and *canny* can apply to those who engage in convivial drinking, or even a state of mild drunkenness (*Joe Wilson's* 66–7).

Wilson later becomes teetotal, and it may be that this is reflected in the song "Canny Man" (1860s–70s). The man in question is fond "ov enjoymint," "likes a joke," "lens a helping hand te them he thinks 'ill need it," and, thinking of "hyem . . . minds the cumforts weel o' them that's roond aboot him" (Wilson, *Tyneside Songs* 180). However, there is no mention of drinking.

The word *canny* is also applied to place names in highly affectionate ways. Of particular relevance are the combinations "canny Toon" and "canny Newcassel." We should recall Brockett's comments above regarding the latter phrase, and also the use of the phrase in Thompson's song ([1812] 1971) "Canny Newcassel" (in Bell, *Rhymes* 314–16). Half a century later, a dewy-eyed local patriotism is invoked in Wilson's song "Tyneside Lads for Me" (c. 1865): "Noo a' ye lads that's Tyneside born, just cock yor lugs an' lissen, / Aw'll gie yor canny toon a turn, an' myek yor goggles glissen" *(Joe Wilson's* 51). The word *canny* in the nineteenth century clearly has cherished associations with local loyalty.

Much of what I have said about *canny* can also be applied to the word *hinny*. Brockett in 1825 calls *hinny* "a favourite term of endearment" (96). For Heslop, in his dictionary of 1892, the word is "a term of kindly regard, generally applied to women and children. Like the word *canny*, this is one of the choicest of our local terms, and they are often used together. . . . It is applied in the purest and most lovable sense to sweet-heart, wife or bairn" (376–7). Heslop seems to ignore or downplay the use of *hinny* to men and between men here, though such uses certainly occur in nineteenth-century song.[13] For Joyce, writing in the 1990s, *hinny*, like *canny*, is involved in the rhetorical creation of communal values in the songs (284). Just like *canny* it is important to see the tensions and ironies within which *hinny* is implicated and the way these can clash with more "respectable" communal and domestic ideals.

It is instructive to return to the character Bob Cranky in the often satirical early songs. Thus, in John Selkirk's "Bob Cranky's 'Size Sunday" ([1812] 1971), Bob proves himself to be a violent drunkard before his sweetheart uses the fond endearment: "My hinny, thou's fuddled, / Ho'way hyem now, my bonny Bob Cranky" (in Bell, *Rhymes* 27). The audience can detect the songwriter's ironic mockery. In William Armstrong's song, "The Skipper in the Mist" (1842), the skipper of a keel roars, becomes enraged, curses and swears. It is in that context that we hear him say: "Now hinnies, my marrows! come tell's what's to dee" (in Fordyce and Fordyce 320). Here the word *hinny*, associated as it is with (potentially feminized) ideals of affection noted by Heslop above, becomes laughable, bound up with satire and irony when in the mouth of the stereotypically rough and aggressive skipper.

In the later songs ironies can be wide-ranging, though often celebratory, and we can consider *hinny* premodified by *canny*. In the chorus of Corvan's "Lads o' Tyneside" (1850s), a lass describes the courting practices of the "Tyne laddies." They will coax her to go with them "doon the burn Jinny, maw canny hinny," and she adds: "then they'll caress ye, an' so cosey they'll press ye" (*Corvan's Song Book 2* 16). This is risqué. Use of the term *canny hinny* is imbued with nuances of resistance to notions of moral "respectability."

Wilson, as with his treatment of *canny*, narrows the attribution of the word *hinny* aligning it more with positive core meanings. In the song, "Pride" (c. 1865), a man talking to his sweetheart or wife says "Cum an' give us yor cumfort, maw hinny, / An' ease a poor mind that's distrest" (*Joe Wilson's* 45). The distress has been caused by the pride of those in the outside world. The wife in "Ungrateful Bill" (c. 1865) comforts her "hinny" in the face of the unreliable and ungrateful friends in "this world" (*Joe Wilson's* 69–71). The domestic, with its associations with the word *hinny*, at least from this masculine perspective, provides a shelter from the outside world.

Whatever the ironies or contested nature of attributions of the words *canny* and *hinny* in the nineteenth century, these two words are iconic. By describing them as *iconic* I mean speakers are aware of the words and even proud of them as symbolic of local or regional identity and culture.[14] Wilson, after all, celebrates the phrase *vary canny* and makes the word *canny* the subject of songs (*Joe Wilson's* 66–7; *Tyneside* 180–81). Also, we have seen the use of the word *canny* in the description of Newcastle. The iconic status of the word *hinny* is undoubtedly aided by Wilson's song "Keep Yor Feet Still!" (c. 1865). This is among those pieces still remembered by Tynesiders today, with its memorable chorus including the words "Keep yor feet still! Geordey, hinny" (*Joe Wilson's* 89–90). The discussion of lexical features indicates that, while they might be bound up with contemporary controversies during initial performances in the nineteenth century, cherished and iconic words may assist in the evolving meaning of songs, narrowing those meanings to the locally patriotic.

Nonstandard spellings too are a central feature of the songs in print and, like the words just discussed, play a role in those processes gradually solidifying Tyneside identity through song. I have used an electronic corpus to identify a range of spellings regularly occurring in nineteenth-century Tyneside song ("Linguistic" 90–99). Not all of the spellings are listed here, but those listed correspond to well-known phonological contexts of variation.

By convention, spellings are given in angled brackets. Words are added as examples. The spellings include:

<aw>: <aw> *I*, <maw> *my*[15]
<aw>: <knaw> *know*, <blaw> *blow*
<ee>: <neet> *night*, <reet> *right*
<ee>: <deed> *dead*, <weel> *well*
<oo>: <noo> *now*, <doon> *down*, <oot> *out*
<ye>: <myek> *make*, <tyek> *take*

Some of these spellings correspond to those highlighted by Beal in her studies involving nonstandard features that are found in Tyneside dialect literature ("From Geordie" 348–50; "Enregisterment" 145). As noted in the discussion of indexicality, speech styles, and individual features of language can carry social meaning. These nonstandard spellings inevitably convey such meaning because they differ obviously from the standard "norm": they are bound up with linguistic identity for groups of people, and signal difference from other groups, as do the sounds they may represent.[16] Clearly, the expression of regional or more local identities is possible, but I again wish to give examples to show there can be more problematic meanings. I focus on the use of just one feature, the spelling <oo>, conveying a sound represented phonetically as [u:], a pronunciation still heard on Tyneside. I track the tensions and transformations in which it can be involved.

In John Shield's "Bob Cranky's Adieu" ([1812] 1971), Bob, set for a spell of soldiering, bids farewell to his "pet," telling her that he is "doon for *parm'ent duty*"; he intends to be "prood" and "swagg'ring" and reminds her to "cloot" his pit "claes" while he is away (in Bell, *Rhymes* 31–2). This song satirizes pitmen, mocking an imputed lack of sophistication and gentility. The schoolmaster, songwriter, and editor of a large collection of songs, Joseph Philip Robson, writing in c. 1849, disingenuously apologizes for presenting songs in his collection that are "vulgar and decidedly ungenteel," yet he singles out "Bob Cranky's Adieu" as the "perfection" of local songs at which he has "laughed to tears," identifying as he does Bob's boorish attributes (v–vii). Through repeated performances and readings, and by association, the spelling <oo> and corresponding pronunciation [u:] are linked indexically to Bob's "vulgarity" and lack of gentility.

In the early music hall at mid-century, Ned Corvan clearly implies and indexes resistance to respectability in "The Shades Saloon" (1850), a piece about a local hall:

> Whe wad think't but smash it's truth man,
> It bangs them aw byeth north and south man,
> The landlord tee desarves a crown man,
> For bringin' concerts to wor toon man.
>
> (*Random* 15)

In performance the song clearly celebrates the sound [u:], which is indicated in "south" and "crown" even if not reflected in spelling here. However, the corresponding spelling <oo> is not found just in the word "toon," it also occurs elsewhere in <doon> and <aboot> (Corvan, *Random* 14). Also, in Corvan's "The Happy Keelman" (1850), the boatman in question hates teetotallers "That runs doon guid whisky" (*Random* 12). Both songs link the linguistic features [u:] and <oo> with alcohol-fueled conviviality and, thus, "non-respectable" behavior and identities.

The same might be said of George Ridley's piece "Johnny Luik-Up" (1860s), simply by virtue of its being a music hall song:

> Johnny luik up! Johnny luik doon,
> Johnny gans wandrin roond the toon,
> He'll find yor kid for half-a-croon
>
> (19)

This song is, nevertheless, a celebration of what is, by the middle of the nineteenth century, clearly an iconic feature of Tyneside pronunciation, strongly associated with the locality by Tynesiders. Ridley draws maximum effect from that pronunciation and the spelling <oo>.

By the late nineteenth century, Richard Oliver Heslop, the author of the dictionary *Northumberland Words*, could also contribute his own song to the tradition, celebrating the spelling <oo> and the corresponding pronunciation in the song "Newcastle Toon Nee Mair" ([1891] 1972). The song is a lament at Newcastle becoming a city: "We like the soon' o' 'Canny Toon.' / We like wor aad Toon sair" (in Allan, *Illustrated* 532). In Heslop's song the sound [uː] and the spelling <oo> are again iconic, central to an overt expression of linguistic identity on Tyneside and local experience, especially with the use of the latter in <toon>.[17] The examples given demonstrate acute awareness among Tynesiders of features of the dialect and can feed into awareness of dialect in other songs.

Meanings of song and dialect might be comic, satirical, resistant to respectability, or exuberant, when represented in the mouths of pitmen and keelmen in the early nineteenth century. They might convey a specific cultural identity somewhat distanced from the "respectable" laboring class when emerging from the frequently comic song of music hall after the mid-century. Such meanings may co-exist with a sense of local linguistic belonging when a song is first written or sung. However, with the passage of time in the nineteenth century, satire and controversies can be forgotten, and so can indexical meanings arising from them as songs are repeatedly published in collections. This loss of satirical and controversial meaning is aided by increased awareness of the dialect as a signal of local belonging. Such awareness arises especially from printed songs that use nonstandard spellings and words, and that are accompanied by statements about the local provenance of the songs and the dialect. The increased awareness of the local nature of songs and dialect alters the meaning of those songs as they appear in one collection after another and feeds back into newer songs. Many of the original songs will remain humorous. Nevertheless, with the passage of time the meanings of dialect in songs may be narrowed with a more simplified emphasis on local patriotism.

It is worth considering in greater detail, now, the role of printed statements about songs on title pages and in prefaces. Gérard Genette has called these, along with certain other textual elements, "paratexts." By examining such "paratexts" one may track the existence not just of ideas about Tyneside dialect but also Tyneside song itself, and also how these ideas co-occur with other meanings or change as the nineteenth century progresses. From the beginning to the end of the century, songs appear repeatedly on broadsides, in song books by individual authors, and in anthologies of varying size. Decisions by authors or publishers whether or not to describe songs as satirical, and decisions about the attested geographical origin of songs and their language may reflect but also strongly influence the way readers interpret songs and the social meaning of nonstandard dialect within them.[18]

A consideration of the attested provenance of songs on the title pages of edited collections is helpful. Wider northeastern county names carry as much weight as Newcastle on the title pages of Ritson's *The Northumberland Garland; Or, Newcastle Nightingale: A Matchless Collection of Famous Songs* ([1793] 1810) and Bell's *Rhymes of Northern Bards: Being a Curious Collection of Old and New Songs and Poems, Peculiar to the Counties of Newcastle Upon Tyne, Northumberland, and Durham* ([1812] 1971). Among collections by most subsequent editors in the nineteenth century this changes. Apart from Bruce and Stokoe's edition, *Northumbrian Minstrelsy* ([1882] 1965), editors, despite sometimes including wider content, focus on Newcastle, Tyneside, and the nearby surrounding area on their title pages. Thus Marshall publishes *A Collection of Songs, Comic, Satirical, and Descriptive, Chiefly in the Newcastle Dialect, And illustrative of the Language and Manners of the Common People on the Banks of the Tyne and Neighbourhood. By T. Thompson, J. Shield, W. Midford, H. Robson, and others* (1827). Fordyce and Fordyce publish *The Newcastle Song Book; Or, Tyne-side Songster. Being a Collection of Comic and Satirical Songs, Descriptive of Eccentric Characters, and the Manners and Customs of a Portion of the Labouring Population of Newcastle and the Neighbourhood. Chiefly in the Newcastle Dialect* (1842). Robson offers *Songs of the Bards of the Tyne; Or, a Choice Selection of Original Songs, Chiefly in the Newcastle Dialect. With a Glossary of 800 Words* (c. 1849). Finally, at the end of the nineteenth century, Allan, after publishing numerous smaller editions, issues *Allan's Illustrated Edition of Tyneside Songs and Readings. With Lives, Portraits, and Autographs of the Writers, and Notes on the Songs* ([1891] 1972).

A local genre, indeed a canon, of "Tyneside" song overtly said to be in the local dialect, therefore develops over the century with certain authors appearing repeatedly, and new writers being added. Harker has accused Allan of attempting to create a single tradition out of two separate strands of songs, one belonging to the "middle class" and the other emerging from "working communities" ("Thomas Allan" iii, xxi–xxiii). Although he admits that the two traditions are closely linked, Harker is ideologically committed to maintaining the distinction ("Thomas Allan" iii). I agree with Harker that early songs (written by tradesmen, artisans, and clerks) have a somewhat different provenance from the music hall material, and often satirize pitmen and keelmen.[19] Additional information about genre is revealed in some of the titles arising in the early nineteenth century. Hence Midford's volume mainly of his own songs is *"Comic and Satirical"* (1818). Marshall's edition is *"Comic, Satirical, and Descriptive"* (1827). Fordyce and Fordyce's edition is also *"Comic and Satirical"* (1842).

Parallel to satire, nevertheless, the process of constructing a Tyneside canon through genre attribution based on local qualities of songs is also well under way even from the early nineteenth century. Across social groups we see a desire to create or belong to a local canon of Tyneside dialect song, even if the initial performances indicate sometimes very particular perspectives on local identity, which set it alongside antagonisms within the same local area. This easily predates Allan's collections. Bell, despite the use of the word *northern* on the title page of his 1812 edition, and the inclusion in his anthology of songs from the northeast in general, expresses the desire in his preface to "rescue from the yawning jaws of oblivion the productions of The Bards of the Tyne" (3). Marshall in a small collection of 1806 (cited in Harker, "John Bell" xli), and in the preface to his large edition (1827) expresses the desire to give "a local habitation and a name" (i) to songs and writers some might dismiss as insignificant.

Marshall (1827) can see the commercial benefit of offering songs in the "language" of the "common People of Newcastle Upon Tyne" (i). Nevertheless, the emphasis on songs and their language being from Tyneside or Newcastle is not, as Harker would have it, simply part of a "middle class" chauvinist tradition ("Thomas Allan" xiii, xvii, xxvi). Marshall in 1827 says small local song books are read by the "labouring classes" in the early century (i). At the middle of the century, Corvan calls a small book of his own material *Random Rhymes, Being a Collection of Local Songs and Ballads, Illustrative of the Habits and Character of the "Sons of Coaly Tyne"* (1850). In addition, while Allan's editions steadily grow over a 30-year period to include many early writers, a point noted disapprovingly by Harker ("Thomas Allan" xx–xxii), Allan's initial editions which are dominated by Corvan and Ridley are labeled "Tyneside Songs." Also, Wilson's (c. 1865) book containing his own material is billed as "Tyneside Songs . . . Drawn i' wor awn awd canny toon style" (*Joe Wilson's*). Corvan, Ridley, and Wilson are well-known music hall performers and these collections are bought by members of the laboring class who, like the middle class, are keen to read Tyneside songs.

Parallel, also, to the emergent sense of a Tyneside canon can be seen explicit references to the strengthening concept of the local dialect. On their title pages Ritson ([1793] 1810) and Bell ([1812] 1971) do not refer to the dialect, whereas this is a prominent feature on title pages of several later edited collections. Thus Marshall (1827), the Fordyces (1842), and Robson (c. 1849) all carry the wording *"Chiefly in the Newcastle Dialect"* on their title pages. Wilson (c. 1865), as noted, says his own songs are "Drawn i' wor awn awd canny toon style" (*Joe Wilson's*). There is a desire to recognize both the dialect and local song written in the dialect.

Title pages and other paratexts contribute strongly to discourses which reflect and influence meaning in the books themselves, and therefore the social meaning of the nonstandard dialect within those books. Early in the century the emphasis is not on Tyneside or its dialect. Very quickly the emphasis switches to these alongside satire. But later the emphasis is on Tyneside and its dialect with satire not prominently mentioned. Tyneside song and the dialect begin to seem far more straightforward in meanings related to local identity.

A sense of locality in song as a highly prominent or dominant meaning, however, is not facilitated through information printed on song collections alone. Discourses of locality run parallel to the production of material. This is the final process influencing local meanings, mentioned in the introductory pages of the present chapter. Conversations occur. The engraver Thomas Bewick in 1791 sends a letter containing a dialect song to his brother in London for his "collection" (cited in Beal, "Enregisterment" 149). Newspaper articles mention dialect song, as Allan notes (*Illustrated* 43, 484). All of these activities contribute to discourses emphasizing the locally patriotic nature of song and its dialect.

Songs that may be implicated in social tensions on Tyneside can at the same time have, or subsequently come to have, narrower locally patriotic meanings. This all impacts upon the social meaning of the local dialect and linguistic styles depicted in performance or print. Language, even some of the most iconic features of the Tyneside dialect, is subject to these tensions and yet, along with discourses of locality whether in song or external to it, also aids the transformations that I have described. To ignore such issues is to miss the rich, complex and evolving meanings of songs.

NOTES

1. See Swann et al. (143), Eckert (453–7).
2. See Bucholtz and Hall (587–8, 593–7), Ochs (338); cf. Mannheim and Tedlock (15).
3. Cf. Eckert.
4. See Beal ("From Geordie" 353–4; "Enregisterment" 149), Wales ("'North of Watford'" 61; *Northern English* 132; "Northern English in Writing" 67), Joyce (329–31), Russell (*Looking North* 120, 123, 125); Goodridge ("Introduction," *Nineteenth Century Labouring-Class Poets*, vol. III, xvi, xx–xxi).
5. For details of these authors and audiences see Allan, *Illustrated* (esp. v. 230).
6. See, for instance, Bailey (*Popular* 31–33); see also Agha (249–59) on the spread of ideas linking accent, character, and social advancement.
7. See Kift (176, 182), Bailey ("Conspiracies" 155), Gregson and Huggins (91), Medhurst (67).

8. See Russell (*Popular Music* 25); cf. Kift (177).
9. Dialects often occupy larger geographical areas than those to which they can become popularly assigned. The process by which they can become associated with more restricted areas is called "enregisterment" and is aided by "talk about talk" in, for instance, dialect dictionaries and songs (Beal, "Enregisterment" 142–6; cf. Johnstone et al. 93–6). Perceptions of the existence of Tyneside dialect and of Tyneside dialect song are mutually reinforcing in the nineteenth century.
10. This uvular *r* is represented phonetically as [ʁ].
11. See Heslop (130–31) and *English Dialect Dictionary*. Cf. Wales (*Northern English* 133).
12. This has led Michael Pearce to conclude recently that *canny* holds "cultural saliency" in the north east during that era (568).
13. Cf. Griffiths (*Dictionary* 84).
14. See Beal ("Geordie Nation" 43) for her account of the iconicity of the spelling <oo>.
15. This particular spelling is conventional across much northern material.
16. Cf. Sebba ("Spelling" 7, 32, 56, 160–61; "Sociolinguistic approaches" 39; "Orthography" 3–4), Honeybone and Watson (312, 315).
17. See Beal ("Geordie Nation" 43) on the iconicity of these features.
18. See Jaworski et al. (3) on the way that "metalanguage," or communication about language, influences the meaning of the language commented upon. See also Macksey (xviii) on the way that "paratexts" mediate texts to the reader. Also, see Genette's comments on the way "paratextual" information about texts, including genre attribution, can change over time as texts are republished (6, 94, 101).
19. See Harker ("John Bell" xliv–v; "The Making" 41–3; "The Original" 74–5).

CHAPTER 18

On the Road
All Manner of Tramps in English and Scottish Writing from the 1880s to the 1920s

H. Gustav Klaus

> Walking is the condition of the poor.
> – Frédéric Gros

I

In a famous novel published in 1847, a solitary female vagrant is plodding the country lanes of what is presumed to be the Peak District in search of work. Penniless, she offers her handkerchief in exchange for a crust of bread, but has it refused. She sleeps rough, on damp ground. The next day, she continues to seek work, but "as before, I was repulsed; as before, I starved." Only once is she lucky, when she notices a little girl emptying a pot of porridge into a pig-trough. She begs for a portion of the leftovers and overhears the girl's mother say: "'give it her if she's a beggar. T'pig doesn't want it'" (Brontë 329).

Less than two years later, in a forgotten serialized fiction an "emaciated and haggard-eyed" man is tramping the streets of the metropolis, "seeking bread but finding none; exploring, with ardent gaze, the very pavement of the streets in the vain hope of finding something that would procure a meal's victuals" (Wheeler 161). Month after month he has looked for work, in vain. The narrative traces in great physical and psychological detail the degradation and despondency that has come over a once proud, honest, and energetic character, down to a desperate act of mugging. In empathy with his creation, the author hails his audience: "Reader, hast thou ever known the pangs of hunger... in the literal sense of the word?" (Wheeler 165).

In *Jane Eyre*, the heroine's fate, resulting from a courageous moral choice but exacerbated by the ill luck of losing her purse, occupies one brief chapter. It is a link in the chain of trials and tribulations of Charlotte Brontë's character. In the more extensive treatment of "Sunshine and Shadow" by

Thomas Martin Wheeler, Arthur Morton is the victim of forces beyond his control; a trade depression has put his employer out of business. A small but significant detail reveals another difference. Jane, who as a governess is a cut above Arthur, a mechanic, feels that her refined appearance might arouse suspicion; Arthur to the last, after everything else in the family's possession has been sold, holds on to his respectable apparel hoping to find an opening.

The "Hungry Forties" does not bear that name for nothing. But in subtitling his work "A Tale of the Nineteenth Century," Wheeler accords it wider relevance, just as he reminds his readers that "Arthur Morton is a type, a representative of his class" (124). Looking out from the middle of the century, the author turns his gaze to the trajectory the working class has traversed; the story itself covers the whole history of Chartism. At the same time, writing as he does in the light of the movement's defeat and the failure of the European revolutions, peering ahead he appears under no illusion about the long road still to travel to the emancipation of that class.

Certainly, when several decades later, in Margaret Harkness's *Out of Work* (1888), we accompany the principal character on his "weary tramp" through London, "which he had accomplished every day lately," calling at all the buildings where a carpenter might be wanted, walking "miles and miles, hour after hour, resting sometimes for a few minutes, then tramping on again" (89), and then follow the downturn of his life to its bitter end, this is a déjà vu. But it comes with a vengeance; for, in contrast to both Jane and Arthur whose good fortunes are restored, Jos goes under, naturalism having left its stamp on Harkness's novel.

This is also true of a serial that was in progress in the socialist weekly *Justice* at the time *Out of Work* appeared, "A Working Class Tragedy" (1888–9). Signed by H. J. Bramsbury, a pseudonym, it presented another bleak and depressing picture of a tramp, newly arrived in the metropolis, footsore, weary, and penniless, after vainly having "visited all the engineers' shops he could find, in search of a job" (120).[1] He is different from Jos in that he has not only been victimized by his employer and blacklisted thereafter, but is also a hunted man, accused of murder. But at least he is spared the experience of the casual ward by being befriended and put up by a socialist, whom he has met in one of those appalling Darwinian battles for a day's work at the dock gates. While losing itself in intrigue, romance, crime, and highly improbable chance encounters, this fiction is littered with destitution-related deaths, making it more than one working class tragedy.

A contemporary of Harkness and Bramsbury, Allen Clarke begins rather than concludes his novel *The Knobstick* (1893) with a haggard tramp at the end of his strength. The man carries a little boy through a desolate wintry landscape. An unemployed engineer, he is acutely aware of his shabby appearance. His thoughts echo Arthur Morton's: "No doubt he would have great difficulty in getting a hearing at any works, much more a place. His whole appearance was against him. His clothes were his condemnation" (15). The boy's innocent musings over the sight of barefooted sandwichmen advertising "Stickman's Boots" wonderfully encapsulate the contradictions of the capitalist order, and prompt Clarke to take, like Wheeler, a long view of the Victorian era: "Truly, a strange spectacle in a Christian land and a civilized century" (30).

Taken together, these dramatizations carry the message that poverty and starvation, and the consequent bodily, psychic, and moral decline, with crime lurking on the way, were constant hazards of working class lives throughout the nineteenth century, settling upon the unfortunate victims with the same inexorable regularity as the cyclical crises of capitalism. Once on the road, chances were that such tramps, instead of finding a new situation, might end up as vagrants, as "casuals of the city," paupers, and candidates for the workhouse. Such tramps were a common sight in working class towns. And so they are in the working class fiction of the period. A last case in point is the female tramp who makes only the briefest of appearances in Ethel Carnie Holdsworth's *This Slavery* (1925). At first hardly recognizable as a woman, to the startled spectator in the novel (and the reader) she turns out to be in labor, dragging herself to the maternity ward of the workhouse. And the figure who witnesses this spectacle will himself shortly be acquainted with "trampdom," becoming part of the "flotsam and jetsam" in a doss-house (*This Slavery* 26). When told, the lives of these tramps are part of a wider narrative of poverty and unemployment.

II

There is a world of difference between those tramps, eager in their search for work and desperate to return to a life of respectability, and the outcasts we encounter in what might be called the golden age of tramp literature, that is the period from the 1890s to the 1920s. Driven not by dire necessity, but a "fever of restlessness" (Davies, *Autobiography* 144), a wish to be released from social constraints, a spirit of adventure, a deliberate setting out into the unknown, the tramp that surfaces here was never enthusiastic about work. He delights in male bonding and comradeship, and may have a penchant for tales and yarns. His next of kin is the sailor, and it comes as no surprise that so many seamen were, at one time or another, tramps, and that to them we owe so many accounts of "trampdom." As if to affirm the natural affinity between the two travelers, the title of one of several books about the subject by Bart Kennedy, *A Sailor Tramp* (1902), joins them together. While the sailor may choose his ship and destination, he lacks, for the duration of his voyage, the opportunity of the tramp to pick his company. Instead of enjoying the freedom of the open air, he works and lives in sequestered conditions – all of which may, in independent spirits, only increase the desire for freedom.

More striking than the fact that Kennedy, Jim Phelan, Liam O'Flaherty, George Garrett, and James Hanley, the last four all authors of tramp stories in the interwar period, went to sea is the circumstance that, without exception, they have Irish roots. So has Patrick MacGill, whose novel *Children of the Dead End* (1914) is a blend of navvy and tramp life. Commercially the most successful book of them all, promoted by a preface from Bernard Shaw, W. H. Davies's *Autobiography of a Super-Tramp* (1908), comes from a fellow Celt.

The title *A Sailor Tramp* reminds us of another renowned member of the tribe, once known by the nickname of Sailor Kid. Like Kennedy a one-time oyster fisher, Jack London chose the opposite route across the Atlantic, and explored incognito the East End of London in the year Kennedy's book came out, publishing his findings, *The People of the Abyss*, twelve months later. On his rounds through the British capital, London was sometimes actually taken for "'a seafaring man,' who had spent his money in riotous living [and] lost his clothes" (*People* 37). His rich experience of life on the beat stood him in good stead as he effortlessly mingled with the flotsam of the metropolis, "carrying the banner" (*People* 51) like his fictional predecessor Jos (that is, shuffling along all night), spending time in doss- and workhouses, looking for work at the docks, and several times hitting upon vagrants who had been to the US and cursed themselves for having returned to Britain. North America indeed proved the greatest attraction. Kennedy, Davies, Garrett, Phelan, and Alfred Holdsworth all tramped there, and it was there too that Charlie Chaplin created his figure of the tramp in the mid-1910s.

Although these book-length works are, without exception, based on personal experience and episodic in structure, they display some generic differences, ranging from straightforward autobiography (Davies) to fictionalized autobiography with the ingredients of a proletarian *Bildungsroman* (MacGill), to plotless semidocumentary fiction (Kennedy) to reportage characterized by close attention to the single revelatory detail (London).

While none of the authors enjoyed a formal education beyond the age of fourteen, their backgrounds and motivations were different, too. Davies, from South Wales, had served an apprenticeship as a picture-framer before the wanderlust seized him. MacGill escaped to try his luck in Scotland, fleeing from the claustrophobic conditions of an ever-growing poor Donegal peasant family, which kept pestering him for years after with demands for money. Jack London alone was already a well-established writer when he sank himself as an undercover reporter into the lower depths of the East End. He was also the only one who, after several years of toiling, tramping, and boozing, had returned to school and even enrolled for a term at university. Kennedy, bred in Leeds and Manchester, worked in factories before becoming a sailor and tramping in many places, experiences that were transmuted into the books in which the author extolled the virtues of life on the road. It is also worth mentioning that Davies and London had a safety net: the former a share in his grandmother's estate, which left him with ten shillings a week (never touched during his wanderings, but a nicely accumulating amount over his five years on the beat); the latter a rented room in the East End (where to change garb, rest, and take notes) and a sovereign sewn into his jacket, in case things came to the worst.

Davies and MacGill are exceptional figures by any account, not only as voracious readers, but also by answering the vocation to become authors themselves. No room of one's own here. MacGill pens his first poems in a navvy's hut, surrounded by noisy drinkers, gamblers, and boxing experts discussing the latest bout; Davies's first efforts, also poems, were composed in common lodging houses. Their two narratives thus take a teleological direction; the books ending with their breakthrough as writers, despite MacGill's claim that "in my story there is no train of events or sequence of incidents leading up to a desired end" (111). While not "rags-to-riches" accounts, they are, nevertheless, success stories, with social exclusion overcome or, at least, suspended. The means by which the authors achieve this is, again, by taking the road and hawking their first volume of poems from door to door and, also, in Davies's case, by mailing copies to magazines and illustrious people.

Kennedy's book, the least known of the three, stands out not only because it is free from such conceits or ambitions – its only near-closure being the eponymous figure's return to Britain – but also through its attempt at objectivity achieved by avoiding a first-person narrative and refusing to give the tramps proper names. What names there are derive from former occupations (Sailor), origins or places (the Cockney, the Norwegian, the Man of the Swamp), or physical features (One-eyed Kelly). Of course, this is in keeping with the custom among tramps and can also be found in Davies and MacGill. But Kennedy goes further by reflecting on that "curious sense of impersonality that comes upon men who are bereft of ties and of people who know them" (1). This statement comes very close to what, a hundred years later, a philosopher would couch in the following terms: "By walking, you escape from the very idea of identity, the temptation to be someone, to have a name and a history" (Gros 6).

Yet, despite such individual shades between the authors and their books, reading them together for an insight into the world of tramp life in the Edwardian period seems more profitable than considering them separately. One of the first things to notice is how much emphasis the authors put on the manly attributes required on the beat. Tramping in Britain means what it says, and only in North America does it also imply jumping trains. Tough, great walkers they all are, Davies even after having lost a foot by trying and failing to leap onto a running train. Moleskin Joe, the narrator's long-time partner in *Children of the Dead End*, is a giant of more than six foot, the Sailor is "a big, strapping man" (*Sailor* 10), Davies has the body of "an athlete" (*Autobiography* 164). Jack London towers over his two stunted companions and is almost ashamed of his more than twelve stone (29). Whether Davies or MacGill's alter ego Dermot Flynn, Moleskin Joe, or the Sailor, none shies away from a fight when the occasion arises. Danger, violence, brutality, and the prospect of prison are never far away. The Sailor and his mate, the Cockney, survive a death march through the desert and a swamp, after having been evicted from Galveston; others who set out with them do not survive.

Companionship helps. The tramps often stay together in pairs, or threes at the most, but these are temporary arrangements; for everything is in the here and now. For the Sailor and the Cockney, "two weeks meant the far away, almost the eternal" (Kennedy, *Sailor* 110). "Let us live to-day, if we can, and the morrow can go be damned!" (MacGill, *Children* 103) is Moleskin's motto. Money earned or won today is gambled or drunk away tomorrow. But when they strike out together, luck and misfortune are shared as are whatever little possessions they have or happen upon. In this male preserve, male bonding and homosocial camaraderie go hand in hand with the glorification of the naked body in fistic arguments or exacting toil. Masculinity asserts itself in the constant testing of strength and courage, in taking risks and proving oneself in dangerous situations, and in dodging laws and authorities.

Women are either invisible or kept at a safe distance, as if seen through the wrong end of a telescope, or, if briefly present, romanticized.[2] Even when desired, as in MacGill and Kennedy, the erotic impulse is pure and chaste.[3] George Orwell would later consider the absence of women as one of the three evils of a tramp's life, the other two being hunger and enforced idleness (*Down and Out* 180–81). It may well be asked whether the idealization of the absent female in Kennedy or MacGill is not the rationalization of a badly felt want. For a tramp or a navvy there can be no lasting attachment to a woman, and yet the heterosexual urge cannot be totally repressed and may seek an outlet in flights of romantic fantasy.

The one exception to this silence on women is Allen Clarke's novel *The Red Flag* (1907), which considers the plight of homeless females, often insulted as sluts or street-walkers and regarded "with eyes of lust" (174) by other tramps and workhouse wardens alike. However, the author's compassionate account is not based on firsthand experience, as he freely acknowledges. Clarke used the evidence collected by the social reformer Mary Higgs (recast in the text as "Mrs. Wilkinson"), who in disguise had spent several nights in lodging houses or the tramp wards of workhouses. Thus the focus is less on actual tramping than on an assortment of the inmates of the lodgings, among them a learned, poetry-reciting cobbler who argues "Christ Himself was a tramp, for He had nowhere to lay His head" (*Red Flag* 152).[4]

"He who knows but one class of tramps can no more understand that class of tramps than he who knows but one language can understand that language" ("Rods and Gunnels" 89), writes Jack London. He proceeds not only to differentiate between various parts of the US but also to establish a hierarchy among the outcasts, which reveals his Social Darwinist inclination. It is not easy to find evidence of such a hierarchy in the works under consideration, but there is no doubt about a particular type of tramp held in awe by all the writers. This is the man who has made it his business never to work, and who does astonishingly well by ingenious ways of begging. Invariably called the "Profesh" (London, "The Road" 71), the "downrighter" (Davies, *Autobiography* 215), or the "boss-hobo" (Kennedy, *Sailor* 293), they would all own the proud resolve of O'Flaherty's tramp:

> I said to myself that it was a foolish game trying to do anything in this world but sleep and eat and enjoy the sun and the earth and the sea and the rain. That was twenty-two years ago. And I'm proud to say that I never did a day's work since and never did a fellow-man an injury. That's my religion and it's a good one. ("The Tramp" 23)

While realistically seeing themselves as belonging to the downtrodden, the footloose men at the center of these works display a fierce sense of independence, autonomy, and human dignity. Some of them are, at heart, anarchists. Dermot holds that "no man is good enough to be another man's master" (MacGill, *Children* 46). Moleskin compares himself to "one of them sort of fellows as throws bombs at kings" (MacGill, *Children* 245). Kennedy's Sailor, much like Arthur in "Sunshine and Shadow," justifies to himself an act of robbery:

> Was he to lie down and die of hunger like a dog? . . . Robbery! Everything was based upon it. Nations plundered nations with no other licence than the licence of might; ruling cliques plundered people of their liberties; employers plundered labourers of their bread. And so on. It was a case of plunder all round. (28)[5]

The narrator distances himself from this kind of reasoning by having the Sailor being robbed, in turn, and thereby gesturing toward some higher justice. But, again like Wheeler, Kennedy does not wholeheartedly condemn his action. Nor does Jack London when he reports his Carpenter's remark: "'Actually make a man a criminal against 'is will'" (37). "Belly-thieving"[6] is, along with begging, hawking, and casual work, an accepted means of survival. Moleskin milks cows, steals fowl, and poaches with not a shadow of remorse. In Galveston or London, though, there is no hen or rabbit to catch.

The Carter and the Carpenter whom Jack London meets talk "of bloody revolution . . . as anarchists, fanatics, and madmen would talk" (*People* 37). The Carpenter might have stepped out of Eliza Lynn Lynton's novel *The True History of Joshua Davidson* (1872) or be a descendant of Harkness's Jos, both carpenters and named after their Biblical ancestor.[7]

Dermot Flynn goes through a brief phase of socialism to the point of organizing a strike among railway navvies, but, let down by his fellow workers, soon resigns himself to the fact "that in the grip of the great industrial machine I was powerless; I was a mere spoke in the wheel of the car of progress, and would be taken out if I did not perform my functions there" (MacGill, *Children* 144). Coming across a tramp immersed in Schopenhauer on the roadside, he sympathetically describes him as "an anarchist, a man with great courage, strength and love of justice" who "said that all property was theft, all religion was fraud, and a life lacking adventure was a life for a pig" (MacGill, *Children* 115).[8] In a scene uncannily reminiscent of the one in *Jane Eyre* described above, Dermot stops at a cottage and asks for a slice of bread. The woman of the house sends him off, but the daughter remonstrates: "'Poor thing! he must eat just like ourselves.' . . . Once I heard one of the servant girls on Braxey Farm use the same words when feeding a pig. . . . I felt that I was a man classed among swine" (MacGill,

Children 154). Indignant, he walks on. An avid reader, MacGill/Dermot has devoured all kinds of books, from Victor Hugo to Carlyle and Ruskin, to Marx and Henry George, but it is very improbable that he had read Brontë. Yet the legacy of the Chartist period, its rebellious affirmation of human dignity, of the right not to live like pigs, persists, and no less so in the fragment of a utopian song which is often on Moleskin's lips: "'There's a good time comin,' though we may never live to see it'" (100, 102, 106, 146, 149). This is from a poem of 1846, whose author, Charles Mackay, if only tangentially connected to Chartism, was a regular presence in the *Northern Star*.[9]

Most surprisingly perhaps, there is the odd flickering of an environmental consciousness. Moleskin, who has thrashed many an opponent in a boxing contest, has never knowingly killed an insect: "If we think evil of insects, what will they think of us? . . . My house for so long has been the wide world, that I can afford to look leniently on all other inmates, animal or human. Four walls coffin the human sympathies" (MacGill, *Children* 166).[10] The Sailor cannot bear the sound of trees being felled: "The slaying hand of man was upon them. They would fall and fall. Their death-cries would be taken up and echoed sadly through the forest" (Kennedy 206). In the chapter entitled "The Haven," he has a temporary job as a gardener, which fills him with marvel: "The mother of mothers, the earth, calmed him and brought him back to normalness. The earth. Man must go back to the earth if his race is not to become extinct in the world" (Kennedy 143–4).[11] Davies flies into a hot white rage when he reads of cases of vivisection and pictures himself "routing the doctors with a bar of iron, cutting the cords and freeing the animals" (*Autobiography* 70).

A less engaging feature occasionally surfacing in these works is the racism or Anglo-Saxon elitism. It is most pronounced in Davies's depiction of the Blacks, for example in the scene of a lynching, or aboard ship, the contempt for "the disgusting, filthy habits of the great majority [of passengers], who were the low class of Jews and peasantry from the interior of Russia" (*Autobiography* 147). In Kennedy it is more of an unease, which sits ill with his more prevalent validation of tolerance and fraternity. In a subliminal way, it colors the depiction of a boxing bout in a sugar-cane field between the Sailor and a "big Negro" who has provoked him. As if to atone for the scene, which ends with the black man defeated and dismissed by the overseer, Kennedy ends the chapter in his more generous mood. Returning home from the day's work, while walking in separate columns, blacks and whites "were all at one with each other. Just workers together. Forgotten even was the feeling of the difference of race in the common wide feeling of being workers together." And so on, in Whitmanesque manner, "All singing. All going peacefully together" (328).

In Jack London there is no cross-racial encounter, but his assumption of a white supremacy over other lesser races must have been given a check as he was confronted with the poor of the abyss, Anglo-Saxon though they were. He was shocked and feared that their children would "grow up into rotten adults, without virility or stamina, a weak-kneed, narrow-chested, listless breed, that crumples up and goes down in the brute struggle for life" (*People* 26). The paupers with whom London (and, in his footsteps, Eric Blair, another tall, part-time drifter, in the late 1920s) queued up outside casual wards, only to be refused entry when the maximum number of inmates had been reached, were, in the main, not of the kind that populate the pages of Davies, Kennedy, or MacGill. They had not chosen this way of life but had been engulfed in it because they were without work, without shelter, without luck. These unfortunates are distant relatives of Jos, the protagonist of *Out of Work*. When admitted into the "Spike," they must not have a penny or an ounce of tobacco on them, which is why Jack London spends his last change on food and Blair/Orwell buries his under a hedge. Orwell gets involved in an argument with a fellow tramp who has so completely internalized this harsh Victorian logic that he fully endorses it.[12] When, in Harkness's novel, a thin and worn-out Jos, having failed to procure work after more than a year's search in London, in despair tramps back to his native village and, rather melodramatically, dies on his mother's grave, the jury reaches the verdict that he died not of starvation "because a penny was found in his waistcoat pocket" (279).

III

In *A Sailor Tramp*, Kennedy gives us this paean to his tribe:

> Tramps and outcasts. Be easy with them. For it may come to pass that they will be held up to honour as the brave rebels and pioneers, who guided men up the tortuous path to the plane of intelligence and happiness. (138)[13]

But should that laurel not, rather, go to yet another category of tramp, the itinerant activist? Wheeler's "Sunshine and Shadow," once more, provides an early example; Arthur is, like his author, an active Chartist, who, prior to his marriage, had fled his homeland to escape persecution during the Government's crackdown on Chartist leaders in the aftermath of the Bull Ring riots in Birmingham in 1839. His wanderings had led him not only to the West Indies but also to the US, "that refuge for the world's criminals and the world's unfortunates, receiving daily the very refuse of Europe – all who are discontented – all who are in debt – those who cannot, and who will not accept the laws of their native land – mingled with a few of the noblest spirits" (97).

Nationally known leaders of Chartism traveled the country, in coaches, (later) by train or on foot, to address mass rallies. The undisguised appearance of such venerated figures is a feature of working class fiction from the start. Feargus O'Connor is referred to in "Sunshine and Shadow"; Félix Pyat and Charles Delescluze, leaders of the Paris Commune, in *The True History of Joshua Davidson*; Keir Hardie and Bob Smillie in James C. Welsh's *The Underworld* and Edward Hunter's *The Road the Men Came Home*, both published in 1920. These figures have no role in the plot, but, in contrast to the demonized agitator in the middle class social-problem novel, they are not depicted as irresponsible, alien elements, intruding out of nowhere upon a working class community, causing mischief and disappearing thereafter. Rather, they awaken or inspire the rebel at the center of those fictions. Joshua, who had hurried to Paris in support of the Commune, keeps defending its ideals after its defeat, "as he took up again the hungry trade of political lecturer" and "went about the country explaining the Communistic doctrines, and showing their apostolic origin" (Linton 263). This did not save him from being battered to death by a hostile audience instigated by a bigoted pastor, thus becoming a martyr for the Cause like his hero Delescluze.

In the fiction of the 1880s, the most powerful representation of the tramp with a mission is Etienne in Emile Zola's *Germinal* (1885), a work of paramount influence not only on the yet-to-be-written mining novel in Britain.[14] The man, as he is simply called at first, has, for a week, been tramping in search of work. In this respect, he resembles Jos in *Out of Work* or Belton in *The Knobstick*. But, only a couple of pages into the novel, we can already fathom his instinctive rebelliousness, as we learn that he has boxed his last boss's ears. One work, which is so closely modeled on *Germinal* as to raise the suspicion of plagiarism, is Welsh's *The Morlocks* (1924), which also starts with an initially anonymous solitary traveler who reaches a colliery in the middle of the night, is received into a miner's family, and falls in love with the daughter of the house. Like Etienne, Sydney has no previous experience of coalmining, and he also bears a grudge, in part, of a personal nature, but still with a class tinge. His secret is not disclosed until much later: he is the illegitimate son of a minister who had seduced a domestic servant and fobbed her off with a payment. Both Etienne and Sydney will, in due time, become leaders in an industrial conflict with dramatic consequences. Both share this role with other radicals, among them a fiery anarchist. Both novels end with the fervent belief in the rebirth of working class militancy out of the ashes of the present disaster (the miscarriage of the uprising, the division among its leaders, the grinding of the "iron heel" [Welsh 316]).[15] However, where the endings of *Germinal* and *The Morlocks* differ is in the paths the two leaders take. Etienne is, once again, on the road, heading for Paris, headquarters of the (First) International, "as a philosophical soldier of the revolution" (Zola 521),[16] ready to plunge back into the struggle of which he (and the narrator) already perceive the seeds. By contrast, Sydney, with the rival for his sweetheart removed, enters the haven of marriage, if similarly invigorated by the advent of spring "after the long winter of suffering and death" (Welsh 316). The very titles of the two novels encapsulate a threat to the established order: Germinal, the month of buds, harks back to the French revolutionary calendar of 1792; the Morlocks are the underground toilers in H. G. Wells's dystopia *The Time Machine* (1895), who in the darkness of the night creep up to the surface to prey on the lazy and effete Eloi, though in Welsh's usage the term refers only to the extremists among the miners.[17]

It tells us something about the longevity of Victorian plot devices that, in a work of the 1920s, the gifted working class leader can still be discovered to descend from a genteel parent, with all the questions of illegitimacy, inheritance, and heredity involved. In the 1890s, there had been several such exemplars, among them the strike-leader (and, later, parliamentary candidate) in Clementina Black's novel *The Agitator* (1894), who, blacklisted after a previous industrial conflict, had "tramped miles" before being re-employed (14), losing wife and child as a result of the deprivation; or the protagonist of Alfred H. Fletcher's *Lost in the Mine* (1895), actually the dispossessed son of the mine-owner, in whose colliery he works incognito.

It comes, thus, as a relief to notice that Edward Hunter's rebel in *The Road the Men Went Home* (1920) deviates from this pattern. Robin Laidlaw is a "thoroughbred" Scottish miner, who emigrates to New Zealand in the hope of finding better working and living conditions. Hardly arrived, he is thrown into the turmoil of industrial conflict, culminating in nothing less than a class war, "a fight between the Red Feds [the trade unionists who want to build a national federation of miners] and the Well Feds" (Hunter 74),[18] in which the latter are determined that "those hell-hounds are to be exterminated – *exterminated*" (62) once and for all. Robin resists all attempts by the employers, who recognize his talent as a leader of the men, to buy him off: "'I'll die before I leave my ain folk'" (39). Given that the mining camps in New Zealand have something rough and ready about them, with the workers shifting about a good deal, it is not unusual that Robin also drifts, but his peripatetic life is more due to his tireless work for the union and his having been blacklisted. An "agitator" and an "undesirable," he now addresses a crowd from the rostrum, now stands in the dock, next lingers in jail, but, indomitable fighter that he is, even when "foot-sore, hungry, and weary," "Robin plodded, ever plodded, with his bluey over his shoulders, o'er hill, gully, spur" (Hunter 112–13) to preach the gospel of socialism, often enough to indifferent or even hostile workers, until he succumbs to phthisis, the miner's disease. To the end, he is unbroken in spirit and always guided by a vision of internationalism and the inalienable human rights of men, women, and children. A combination of autobiography and historiography, the storyline, insofar as there is one in this descriptive work, closely follows the labor struggles down-under in the years up to the First World War. So strong is the documentary basis and political impulse behind the work that the unfolding drama (strikes, lockouts, divisions within the movement, victimization, evictions, imprisonment, blacklisting, the bitterness of defeat) appears more controlled by the sequence of re-enacted industrial struggles than by the author's hand.

IV

The tramps in the centerpiece of this chapter lead not only a nomadic but also a monadic life. They may temporarily congregate in work-camps or doss-houses, but when on the move – always on foot, never on horseback, in coaches or railway carriages (except for the hobos on the freight trains) – they rely on themselves and a few, ever-changing companions. They may get caught up in a demonstration or industrial dispute, but, in the end, they remain solitary travelers, defiantly independent.

This marks them off from the marchers, not considered here, who take to the road in a collective effort, under a banner and in large columns. By virtue of their social class, the overwhelming majority of the British hunger marchers of the interwar period,[19] the Indian salt marchers led by Gandhi in 1930, the American Civil Rights marchers, the huge processions forming the Egyptian Marches of the Millions are distant cousins of the tramps. But, united in the devoted pursuit of a social or political cause, these protesters – in the main workless or exploited, dispossessed or disenfranchised, in short "the wretched of the earth" – have more in common with the working class heroes we encountered in the last section. At the same time, the latter idealists, despite serving, and, in some cases, giving their lives for a cause, display much of the independent habit of mind and solitary state of the tramps by choice.

NOTES

1. Deborah Mutch thinks that "H. J. Bramsbury" may be the pseudonym of Henry Myers Hyndman; see vol. 1, 317–18, note 13. Whatever the case, it is likely that "Bramsbury" was aware of *Out of Work* and knew the identity of its author. In 1888 Harkness wrote for *To-Day*, in which Hyndman had a hand, as "John Law," and had an exchange with him in *Justice*.
2. For a detailed discussion of the homosocial community of the navvies and the rejection of the female in *Children of the Dead End*, see Peter Drexler, "Labour and Gender: Ford Maddox Brown's *Work* and Victorian Navvy Stories," in Dietmar Böhnke et al., eds., *Victorian Highways and Byways: New Approaches to Nineteenth-Century British Literature and Culture* (Berlin: trafo Wissenschaftsverlag, 2010), 67–101, especially 87–97. Drexler goes as far as suggesting that masculinity has entered the plot-making of this fictionalized autobiography.
3. The Sailor's highly romantic encounter with a sixteen-year-old in what is the longest chapter in the book ("The Girl") has a structural relevance in that it gives him "faith and strength and a new courage" (270), and thus eventually steers him back to England.
4. The novel was first serialized in the author's journal *Teddy Ashton's Fellowship* (1907), in the same year published in book form and reprinted in *Justice* (1908). *The Red Flag* is here quoted from vol. 4 (1907–10) of Deborah Mutch's *British Socialist Fiction*. An excerpt from Mary Higgs's *Glimpses into the Abyss* (1906) based on her "five days and five nights" undercover research, can be found in Peter Keating, ed., *Into Unknown England 1866–1913: Selections from the Social Explorers* (Glasgow: Collins, 1976), 273–84. Another, later female incognito exploration of what life on the beat meant for a woman can be found in (Mrs.) Cecil Chesterton's *In Darkest London* (London: Stanley Paul, 1926).
5. Note that the parallel with a dog will be taken up in Chaplin's *A Dog's Life* (1918).
6. A term used and explained by MacGill, *Children of the Dead End*, 159. All the works under discussion testify to the rich argot of the tramps; Davies's work in particular has been well mined by Eric Partridge for his *Dictionary of Slang and Unconventional English*. See also Chapter 32 in *Down and Out in Paris and London*.
7. Later editions of Linton's novel had *Christian and Communist* added to the title.
8. In view of the many hints at Individual Anarchism in *Children of the Dead End*, Jack Mitchell's criticism in an otherwise interesting discussion of the novel that "there is no lead on to participation in the organized class struggle and so the book entirely lacks a practical revolutionary perspective" is beside the point; see his essay "Early Harvest: Three Anti-capitalist Novels published in 1914," in H. Gustav Klaus, ed., *The Socialist Novel in Britain: Towards the Recovery of a Tradition* 79.
9. The poem was first published under the title "Wait a Little Longer" in Mackay's *Voices from the Town; and Other Poems* (1846) and reprinted several

times throughout the author's life (1814–89). The original opening lines run: "There's a good time coming, boys, / A good time coming; / We may not live to see the day, / But earth shall glisten in the ray / Of the good time coming."

10. The one exception is the black crow which Moleskin associates with death, after having seen them fall upon corpses.
11. A few years later Emma Goldman would entitle her Anarchist journal *Mother Earth*.
12. Eric Blair, "The Spike," written 1929, first published in *The Adelphi* of April 1931. Orwell knew his Jack London. The sketch is reprinted in *The Collected Essays, Journalism and Letters of George Orwell*. A revised version of the piece became Chapter 35 of *Down and Out in Paris and London*.
13. I should perhaps point out that the writers discussed in the previous section were not alone in their interest for tramps by choice. For some more material, see the pieces by R. M. Fox and Alfred Holdsworth in my *Tramps, Workmates and Revolutionaries*; and, as his title announces, Fox's *Drifting Men* (1930) in its entirety.
14. Its influence can, for example, be detected in two novels written under the impact of the sixteen-week long lockout of 1893 opposing the Miners' Federation of Great Britain and the colliery owners, W. E. Tirebuck's *Miss Grace of All Souls'* (1895) and Alfred H. Fletcher's *Lost in the Mine: A Tale of the Great Coal Strike* (1895). Havelock Ellis's translation of *Germinal* had appeared in 1894.
15. Welsh uses Jack London's image for the deployment of troops to quell the rebellion.
16. The belligerent language used will find its real historical equivalent in the British "Coal War," as the lockout of 1893 is sometimes referred to, during which in one incident troops opened fire on the strikers.
17. *The Time Machine* is another work composed under the shadow of the lockout. Historians have seen Welsh's depiction of the Morlocks as a thinly disguised attack on the Minority Movement within the trade unions. The work is set in the early 1920s; Zola's novel looked back at the 1860s.
18. Hunter was Welsh's brother-in-law; in 1904 the two had emigrated together to New Zealand.
19. The hunger marches are documented in several Scottish novels of the 1930s, among them from a middle class perspective Dot Allan's *Hunger March* (1934), and from a proletarian one Lewis Grassic Gibbon's *Grey Granite* (1934) and James Barke's *Major Operation* (1936).

CHAPTER 19

Ethel Carnie Holdsworth
Genre, Serial Fiction, and Popular Reading Patterns

Nicola Wilson

In November 1913, the monthly journal of the Co-operative Society, *The Wheatsheaf*, introduced Lancashire mill woman Ethel Carnie Holdsworth (then Miss Ethel Carnie) and her first novel published in book form to its readers. Partly biographical portrait and partly review, the article was prefaced by a critique of working class women's reading habits. The opening sketch, based upon a private conversation between two women in a railway carriage, makes interesting reading on many levels:

> In a Lancashire railway train not long ago two typical wives and mothers of the better-paid working class were talking of another woman who read books. One of the matrons declared that she herself had not done ten minutes' reading in the past year. Her companion replied, confessing that she, too, had not read a book for years. "There's too much to do in a house, wi' so many of 'em." ("'Miss Nobody' – and its Author" 85)

Whether this account is fictive or grounded in reality, the eavesdropper's attitude toward the women is fairly clear. The loaded commentary continues in the following manner:

> Although it would be as hard upon oneself not to go outdoors for ten minutes in a year, or never to ride in any railway carriage or other vehicle for years, this attitude towards books and papers is still shared by great numbers of married women. Owing to the pressure of housework, not to read becomes a habit, and by-and-by the habit is half boasted as a virtue. It is not always because the housework itself is so heavy, but because there is ever some homely duty, perhaps a trifling duty, which nevertheless will claim precedence if it is allowed. (85)

The reviewer's dismissal of women's talk and working class culture here reverberates throughout my discussion in the rest of this chapter. The invocation of a supposedly typical incident and the appeal to recognizable character types is surely meant to encourage the readers of *The Wheatsheaf* to dis-identify with the gossiping matrons. The tone, though perhaps not meant to be offensive, is dismissive of "trifling" domestic duties and harsh toward what is presented as the deliberately obtuse: "no reading means less thinking outside the little homely round of life and less expression of thoughts" (85). Whether or not readers would have seen themselves reflected in the attitudes of the women in the railway carriage or sided more readily with the opinions of the reviewer, the scene is introduced to juxtapose the subsequent portrait of Carnie Holdsworth, "herself a working woman" it is noted, "a writer possessing an instinctive sympathy with her sisters" who might, by dint of her apparent rarity in literary and publishing circles, begin to "exert... a due influence upon the opinions and life of the world" (85).

The disinclination toward reading apparent in *The Wheatsheaf*'s female railway characters is a typical feature in conceptualizations of working class women's history and social attitudes. In her study of Middlesbrough, *At the Works*, published in 1907 for instance, social explorer Lady Florence Bell found that "the workman reads, as a rule, more than his wife" precisely because of such difficulties for women in finding "more definitive times of leisure" and the long association of reading and "sitting down with a book" with guilt and unjustified rest (145). But there is another side to this picture. As contemporary historians of gender and leisure suggest, there was a complex, ambiguous relationship for working class women with activities categorized as "leisure" as well as between "work" and "home" (Langhamer 2). Reading – Carnie Holdsworth knew well – was not necessarily a solitary nor a domestic pursuit. There were different types of informal reading experiences and publishing venues that sidestepped the kind of private, unhurried time involved in "sitting down with a book." In an early article for Robert Blatchford's newspaper *The Woman Worker* for instance, Carnie Holdsworth takes evident delight in exposing the stolen culture of reading in the mills:

> If you took a stroll through a cotton mill whilst the "hands" were away in their homes having dinner, and were inquisitive enough to poke into the square, tin boxes that are for the purpose of holding weft, you would find a varied assortment of literature. You might find, deftly hidden (lest the eagle eye of the overlooker pop on them), Conan Doyle, Rider Haggard, Silas Hocking, Dickens, "Daily Mail," "Comic Cuts," and (sometimes) the "Clarion." ("Factory Intelligence" 10 March 1909, 219)

"Perhaps you will say that factory workers ought not to read in their masters' time?" she continues before answering: "Why should factory toilers spend more than half their lives in the service of others and never have time to live?"

Throughout her writing career, Carnie Holdsworth adopted a number of different forms – poetry, short stories, journalism, serial fiction, children's stories, and book-length novels – in order to reach a wide reading audience and to address those men and women unable to spend long periods of time sitting down reading at home. As a working class woman and socialist-feminist committed to the Labor movement in its many guises, Carnie Holdsworth adopted an eclectic and pragmatic approach to writing that made the most of different publishing formats and capitalized upon the great expansion in reading and print culture in the early decades of the twentieth century. The full extent of Carnie Holdsworth's literary and journalistic output is still unknown. With no diaries, only a handful of letters, and few records of her writing life preserved – as is often the case with writers from a working class background – the rare surviving copies of her novels that were published in book form are important literary evidence. Ongoing research into her voluminous shorter pieces and sketches for periodicals – national, provincial, and foreign – has so far only scratched the surface of what was clearly an important market for her work. By 1932 at least, the "Ex-Mill Girl Who Became a Literary Celebrity" had, according to *The Yorkshire Observer*, written a total of "ten novels, 15 serials, two films, and a host of short stories, essays and poems" (5 April 1932, 11). This chapter explores three key dimensions to Carnie Holdsworth's work and literary oeuvre: the attitudes to literature and popular reading patterns in her work; her writing as a newspaper and serial novelist; and how these combined to produce a purposively eclectic and radical approach to form and genre.

I

Born into a Lancashire weaving family in 1886, Carnie Holdsworth was immersed in a rich autodidact and literary culture. Her published work shows she was extremely well read and her knowledge of literature was extensive. As a child and half-timer, she borrowed books from Great Harwood's Co-operative Lending Library and as a teenager was supported by the Blackburn Authors' Society. Her first published poem, "A Bookworm," with its rapturous depiction of "The world of books," is a testament to the imaginative possibilities of creative writing and the power of the printed word to enact change. This is something Carnie Holdsworth would champion throughout her career and work toward through various means: by journalism and creative writing, education and teaching, and a passionate advocacy of public lending libraries and the work of the Co-operative Education Movement. In July 1923, with a radical penny monthly at her disposal (she ran *The Clear Light* with her husband from their home near Hebden Bridge between 1923 and 1925), Carnie Holdsworth sought donations from her readers for a scheme to distribute books freely among the people, starting with the agricultural workers in Norfolk who were on strike (Smalley 105). As a former factory worker, she was equally concerned with the human labor involved in the book making, printing, binding, and paper trades. In her first published novel, *Miss Nobody* (1913), the protagonist works briefly in a Christmas card factory, where the "grinding" of the printing press "seemed to shake the hot, gaslit room" and the girls folding paper insets are exploited and run down (139). In the summer of 1914, she announced her support for the Esher bookbinders' strike in a poem "Bookmakers and Bookbinders," which was printed in the *Daily Herald* (16 June 1914).[1]

In many of Carnie Holdsworth's novels and short stories, reading and print culture help to define the protagonists' sense of self and to offer powerful leitmotifs of change and possibility. The reading matter enjoyed by her characters is eclectic. While Carrie Brown, the heroine of *Miss Nobody*, reads yellow-backed novelettes, Rachel Martin, the political agitator of industrial novel *This Slavery* (1925) plows through Marx and Edward Clodd's popularizations of evolutionary theory. William Morris's socialist utopia *News from Nowhere, or an Epoch of Rest: Being Some Chapters from a Utopian Romance* (1890) underpins *This Slavery*'s scenes of domestic harmony and filial love. In *General Belinda* (1924), the eponymous heroine has "followed the poets ever from being a child, and her father has 'poeted' in his lifetime... but never got nothing published" (121, 97). Over the course of this novel and its heroine's "long Odyssey of domestic service" (back cover blurb), we are told that Belinda "knew and loved Omar Khayyam" (28) and has read H. G. Wells, Charles Lamb, Shakespeare, and John Ruskin. At one point, she owns only "a change of clothes, Napoleon's *Book of Fate* and Hugo's *First French Course*, and a little copy of *Silas Marner* which she had found wet with rain in the street when she was on an errand" (102). While in the employ of a "literary man" who lectures on Robert Burns and William Blake, Belinda "dip[s] into Plato's *Republic*, [and] wept over *Les Miserables*," which she reads from a "badly-printed page" (125). As Roger Smalley has pointed out, "[t]he writers Ethel valued for their fictional support of her political vision" (105) are most obvious in the many intertextual references in this book.

Though throughout her working life Carnie Holdsworth would campaign to improve working class education and for greater material access to literary and print culture, she had none of the scorn for working class reading habits typical of many social commentators. Imaginative freedom, creative and aesthetic pleasure – what she called, in early material for *The Woman Worker*, "colour" – could as she well knew take a variety of forms ("How Colour Is Introduced" 7 April 1909, 323). As Pamela Fox has pointed out, Carnie Holdsworth was well aware of the pleasures of popular mass entertainment like the new "cinematograph" and its power to transport viewers away from home and mill ("Introduction" *Helen of Four Gates*, xiv). It was this recognition of the necessity for human pleasure and imaginative escape – "We are not tin men and women: we have blood in our veins and eyes in our head, and want some sunshine and blue sky and bird-songs" – that characterized Carnie Holdsworth's lifelong disdain for the categories of high and low culture ("How Colour is Introduced" 7 April 1909, 323). As she points out in an early article about reading and "Factory Intelligence," it needed perseverance and patience, not to mention perspicacity, to attempt reading in the busy working conditions of a mill: "In some six hours, with good luck, you may manage two pages of pretty open print" (219). Read furtively "between the breaking of the threads and the throwing of the shuttle" (219), adventure stories, thrillers, melodrama, and romance were popular, entertaining genres to sustain interest and memorability.

Growing up as a factory girl, Carnie Holdsworth was well aware that literary taste and the form that print is bound up in – in addition to the means used to acquire it – were intimately related to class. In *General Belinda*, an interesting exchange on the politics of reading takes place when Belinda inadvertently burns the patties for a particularly tyrannical employer (she has been sent out on an *affaire de coeur* for her employer's daughter, Cora):

> "Do you mean to say you have allowed the patties to burn, Higgins?" almost shrieked Mrs. Riddings. "Good gracious! I can't take a needed rest but everything goes wrong. I suppose you were reading some trashy romance." (75)

Belinda is rightly annoyed by the intrusive and judgmental disparagement of her reading habits: "'If I like a bit o' luv,' she said, indignantly, 'I don't see that it matters to you'" (75). Mrs. Riddings, we are told, "herself read every novel, in its expensive edition" (75), meaning that she belonged to a fee-paying circulating library where newly published ("expensive") editions were stocked. Though Mrs. Riddings is snobbish about cheaper, "trashy" romances produced for working class budgets, the "expensive editions" of novels in circulating libraries were just as likely to be "trashy" in tone.[2]

The pleasures and values involved in the reading of "trashy romance" are also explored in *Miss Nobody*. This was first serialized in *The Christian Commonwealth* (The Organ of the Progressive Movement in Religion and Social Ethics) between June and September 1913, prior to being published in book form by Methuen in their "Popular Novels" series in autumn 1913. *Miss Nobody* is the story of the resourceful Carrie Brown, "an oyster-girl from the city" (61) who decides to sell up and leave Manchester when she receives an offer of marriage from a country farmer, Robert Gibson. Carrie is schooled in the popular romances of cheap yellowbacks: novels bound with glazed colored papers over strawboards and boasting attractive pictorial covers, often associated with railway reading and sold at one or two pence. On her train journey out to visit her sister in Greenmeads, we first meet Carrie transported by "colour":

> [S]he drew from her coat-pocket a yellow-backed "Tulip Novelette" entitled "The Duchess of Digglemore's Diamonds." It was written by a poor pot-boiler who had once cherished dreams of rising to the heights of the immortal ones, joining the choir invisible, but who had found the road too hard, and writing for posterity a thankless task.
>
> When he received the cheque for that impossible story he had broken his fast with a mutton chop, sighing a little, too, and telling the children not to make so much noise, as the flat wasn't all theirs.
>
> Carrie thought that the author must have been a personal friend of the Duchess to know the exact shade of her eyes. Perhaps he had been a former lover, and had sat in that exquisite room to be able to describe it so minutely.
>
> Instead of the gritty floor of the oyster-shop she [Carrie] trod soft Persian carpets upon which lovers knelt to propose in long-winded poetical sentences as sweet as barley-sugar, and not half as wholesome...
>
> Carrie herself was the Duchess for the time being. (9–10)

Like Austen's *Northanger Abbey* (1817), *Miss Nobody* highlights the gap between popular fiction and economic and social reality – part of Carrie's own *Bildungsroman* is to adapt to the "mixed up" realities of love and marriage (60). There is clearly a distinction set up for the reader here between the knowing voice of the narrator – aware of the economic reality of authorship, for instance – and Carrie's imaginative naiveté, supposing, as she does, that the author must be a friend or lover of the imaginary Duchess. But even if this gap in knowledge is set up for the reader, we are not invited to sneer. What wins out in the description of Carrie's imaginative freedom here are the visceral pleasures to be gained from reading "yellow rubbish," as Carrie's scornful elder sister-in-law calls it (77).

II

Following a visit from Robert Blatchford to her home in Great Harwood in July 1908 and an invitation to join the staff on his London-based newspaper, *The Woman Worker*, Carnie Holdsworth left the mills (she would go back for a time during 1910–11) and developed connections with a number of periodicals. In addition to writing short stories, articles, and poems for *The Woman Worker* (which she also edited between July and December 1909), she wrote for other newspapers and magazines, including *Woman's World, The Red Letter, Horner's Weekly, English Illustrated Magazine, Woman, Co-operative News, The Millgate Monthly, The Clarion*, and the two Blackburn weeklies, *The Weekly Telegraph* and *Blackburn Times* (Frow and Frow, "Ethel Carnie" 258). She also contributed a variety of work – travel articles, sketches, poems, and serial fiction – for the Co-operative movement's free publication *The Wheatsheaf*, as well as *The Christian Commonwealth*, and *The Sunday Worker*. The expansion of the popular press in the late nineteenth century and the development of mass-market penny papers and magazines aimed at working class readers (the most successful, George Newnes's *Tit-Bits*, was selling more than 600,000 copies a week by 1893) created an important new reading market for an aspiring writer from a working class background (Nash, "Production" 9). While for many social commentators, the "New Journalism" (so called by Matthew Arnold) was a source of some anxiety (Nash, "Production" 9), for a politically committed working class writer like Carnie Holdsworth the great expansion in the newspaper and magazine market meant increased opportunities both to publish and to reach a mass reading audience.

Carnie Holdsworth's remuneration for her piecework in periodicals is difficult to quantify. As Walter Besant, head of the Society of Authors, advised in *The Pen and The Book* (1899) – a well-known manual aimed at "those who are thinking of the Literary Life" (v) – there was no fixed rate of pay for writers with many journals. "[A] guinea a page," wrote Besant, "the page varying from 500 to 1,000 words, is a common sum to offer. . . . For a short story of two or three columns in a weekly, the author may expect as many guineas and sometimes will have to take less" (229). In terms of what we know of Carnie Holdsworth's career overall, her efforts to live by her pen were clearly precarious. When she lost her regular salary at *The Woman Worker* at the end of 1909, for instance, she "took the line of least resistance and went back into the factory again" ("Ex-Mill Girl" 11). She completed *Miss Nobody* slowly while "working on 'bread-and-butter' work," including short story work for magazines and newspapers in addition to shop work with her mother in Ancoats ("The Authoress of Our New Serial Story" *The Co-operative News*, 21 July 1915, 999; Smalley 49). Just over a decade later, even after the best-selling success of *Helen of Four Gates* (1917) which enabled her to buy a former inn between Todmorden and Hebden Bridge and offered a brief period of financial stability (Smalley 70), Carnie Holdsworth could write that: "as one who was half-starving in the richest city in the world only three years ago, with husband and two kids, I can see nothing in dry crusts but – dry crusts" (*Sunday Worker* 26 July 1925, 6).

One of the most profitable areas for the aspiring writer of the early twentieth century to exploit was the rapidly growing market for serial fiction. This was both an important income stream and a popular source of working class reading material and entertainment. The average serialized story appearing in a weekly newspaper format closely approximated the "two pages of pretty open print" that Carnie Holdsworth had estimated was possible to read during "some six hours, with good luck" at the mill ("Factory Intelligence" 219). It is more likely that the "factory toilers" who Carnie Holdsworth first worked among would have read her novels in weekly serial format than in their later iterations in hard-back.[3] Many of the novels were first published as serials. This includes *Miss Nobody, General Belinda, The Marriage of Elizabeth* (1920), *The House that Jill Built* (1920), and *This Slavery*, while other serial fictions that were not later published in book form are still being discovered.[4] Weekly newspapers like *The Christian Commonwealth* and *The Co-operative News* which contained two of Carnie Holdsworth's earliest serial fictions – "Miss Nobody: A Working Girl's Love Story" (June–September 1913) and "The Iron Horses" (July–December 1915) respectively – were sold at one penny and could easily be passed around, circulated, and shared. The advertisement of serial fiction – long regarded as an intimate, interactive form of communication – was widely used by newspaper publishers and socialist periodicals to attract working class readers and create a sense of community (Mutch I: xxiii). In a postcard addressed to "(Mrs or Miss) W. Hardisty" on 10 September 1924, thanking her for her appreciation of "This Slavery," Carnie Holdsworth wrote "'This Slavery' is not yet out in book form – truth to tell I have not had time to paste out all the serial cuttings completely yet." (E. Holdsworth to W. Hardisty, 10 September 1924. Hebden Bridge Local History Society archive, MISC 8/4).[5] But she included a free copy of *The Clear Light*, the one-penny monthly of the National Union for Combating Fascism that she published with her husband Alfred. This, she pointed out, included "another serial of mine, which some readers have thought better than 'This Slavery'" (E. Holdsworth to W. Hardisty, 10 September 1924. Hebden Bridge Local History Society archive, MISC 8/4).

There only were meager profits for the writer of the average first novel published in hard-back. As the authors of *How to Write Serial Fiction* pointed out, the novel was likely to "yield a gross return of about £40 . . . barely enough to cover the author's typing expenses" (Joseph and Cumberland 9). The demand for serial fiction on the other hand was great, the market potentially easier to penetrate, and the "payment is good compared to other forms of work" (16). Average payment for a serial was similar to that of a short story – namely two to three guineas per 1,000 words. But with the average serial story in a newspaper running to 60,000 words, this could add up, Joseph and Cumberland calculated, to £240 a story: "So, it will be seen that a young writer who can manage to sell only two serials a year can provide himself with a respectable income" (30). In addition to first British serial rights, there were other saleable rights involved, including book rights, "the second British serial rights, foreign serials rights, colonial serial rights, and film rights" (31). Carnie Holdsworth experimented with the latter and was successful in selling the rights to *Helen of Four Gates* in addition, apparently, to *The Taming of Nan* (though there is no evidence that a film was ever made of the latter) (Smalley 72, 75, note 47). Despite her enthusiasm for the "Living Pictures," however, she was clearly not as successful in exploiting the new world of the cinematograph as some of her more popular female contemporaries like Elinor Glyn or Ethel M. Dell ("Living Pictures" 416). The radical political content of Carnie Holdsworth's writing is one obvious reason for this. The scenes of domestic violence in the film version of *Helen of Four Gates* (Director Cecil Hepworth, Hepworth Picture Plays, 1921), for instance, raised concerns that viewers would be off put (Smalley 72).

We do not know how Carnie Holdsworth placed her earliest serial fictions, "Miss Nobody: A Working Girl's Love Story" and "The Iron Horses" with national periodicals. Possibly, this was through personal contacts she made during her early years as a journalist and freelance writer living in London. But there is evidence from one of her rare surviving letters that after she signed a contract with the publisher, Herbert Jenkins, in May 1915 for *Helen O' Four Gates* (in addition to her next six novels), there was some initial confusion about the placing of serial rights. In July 1917, she wrote in clarification to the Authors' Syndicate Ltd, which had been set up by William Morris Colles around 1890 to handle the business of members of the Society of Authors, that "Mr Jenkins . . . is quite agreeable for me to have my novels – prior to publication as books – serialised. Do you think you could approach some of the better kind of magazines re my next novel being serialised?"⁶ Following evident disappointment with a newspaper serial that had been started but not completed, she wrote in this letter that she planned to prioritize the novels over short story work for the time being. During World War One she worked on several novels in addition to campaigning for the British Citizen Party (see Smalley 63–7). Three of these were published by Herbert Jenkins in 1920.

But Carnie Holdsworth remained a "newspaper novelist" (Law, *Serializing* xi) and clearly continued – presumably with the aid of a different newspaper syndicate or literary agent after the Authors' Syndicate folded in 1926 – to sell the foreign and colonial serial rights to her work. The latest serial story that we know of to date, "The Beggar Prince," discovered by historian Chris Lynch in a recently digitized version, appeared in *The Age* (Melbourne, Victoria) over a period of five weeks daily from the end of November to the end of December 1932. In one earlier 12-part serial, "The Great Experiment," published weekly in *The Queenslander* (Brisbane) between December 1922 and March 1923, working class authorship is a key theme. Cora Drummond, "beautiful author of the underworld" ("A Great Experiment" *The Queenslander*, 6 January 1923, 42) turns to writing to counter her husband's "slumming" and the noxious attitudes of the upper class family she marries into. In some ways the story is Carnie Holdsworth's riposte to George Bernard Shaw's *Pygmalion* (1913). Taken out of her native home, Cora wants to write about the lives of her family and friends in Fiddle-Row and is encouraged to publish by a sympathetic Professor who advises her to study Flaubert's short story form for construction and literary technique (24 February 1923, 42). At the end of the story, again perhaps in a rebuttal to the conclusion of Shaw's famous play, Cora's writing serves to unite estranged husband and wife as they decide to "work together," with Cora's "little sketches of live people" guaranteeing the success of her husband Henry's plays (17 March 1923, 42).

III

In critical assessments, Carnie Holdsworth has long been regarded as a writer difficult to pin down. While her poetry and early fiction was compared to the work of Longfellow, the Brontë sisters, and Thomas Hardy, for others there was a confusion of genre in her writing, particularly revolving around her use of melodrama and romance. In a review of *This Slavery* for *The Plebs* for instance, we find that "[*This Slavery*] strikes the real, proletarian note; and this makes one regret all the more certain melodramatic passages and incidents which really detract from its strength. 'Penny plain' is always more effective than 'twopence coloured'" (H. O. B. "A Propaganda Novel" *The Plebs*, October 1925, XVII, 408–9). Questions about the comparative value of different style, genre, and reading patterns continue to affect interpretation of her work. As David Malcolm points out in a review of the centenary republication of *Miss Nobody*: "Like much of Carnie's fiction, *Miss Nobody* is a complex mixture of social realism and melodrama, of the kind of popular women's romance that Carrie herself reads, and gritty observation of poverty and exploitation.... In her oeuvre, the balance of these elements varies from book to book" (28).

Carnie Holdsworth's willingness to adapt across literary forms and to experiment with genre was clearly challenging. The form of *This Slavery*, for instance, is effusively polyphonic, littered with quotations (often offset) from songs, poetry, the Bible, socialist, music hall, and popular culture, as well as from canonical literary works. At the start of Book II, after mill girl Hester Martin has attempted to "sail out of it [*This Slavery*] in the barque of Matrimony" (117), "Time–Imp Sings the Prologue" in two stanzas of 22-line verse, disrupting both the page and the progress of the plot. In broad sympathy with the formal experimentation characteristic to other socialist novels of the time, including Robert Tressell's earlier *The Ragged Trousered Philanthropists* (1914), the narrator of *This Slavery* seeks to challenge readers' assumptions about form and plot from a consciously political and socially realistic standpoint:

> I am sorry if you had expected the curtain to ring down on a beginning which is traditionally the ending of a tale. I am sorry if sometimes you lose sight entirely of the hero and heroine – or rather the two heroines and heroes – or see them jammed at times, helpless units in the mass. Such is life. (122)

But re-reading Carnie Holdsworth as a serial or "newspaper novelist" also sheds light on the balance in some of her longer novel-length fictions. In "The Great Experiment," Cora Drummond is inspired to represent Fiddle-row and its varied characters as follows:

> Great things had happened in Fiddle-row – to her memory. Sad things, sweet things, comical things had been enacted in those huddled houses. There was the woman who stole the six spoons of the Apostles, and went to gaol for six months though fancying them! And the tin-whistle player, and Mrs. Casey, who had buried all her children but one, and Dan Crowther, who had had his water-tap cut off because he would not pay water rates, and Sanders Winters, who drank himself to death after his wife died. (3 February 1923, 42)

The short, episodic nature of the serial story enabled the introduction of fleeting though sharply drawn characters like this, alongside more fully drawn protagonists to accompany the reader through the narrative. Well-practiced in the art of rapid characterization through her serial and short story work, Carnie Holdsworth's novels, as Belinda Webb has pointed out, "giv[e] regular 'walk-on' space to many characters" ("Introduction" xxi) who then disappear from view. The high level of incidents, dramatic opening scenes, and immediately sympathetic protagonists in Carnie Holdsworth's plots help to distinguish her first and foremost as a serial novelist. As Joseph and Cumberland note in *How to Write Serial Fiction*:

> These readers demand a swiftly-moving story, that starts with a 'kick,' and ends with a stronger 'kick,' the story must start straight away, dramatically, with the principal characters introduced deftly, and a strong, interesting, puzzling 'curtain' arrived at – a 'curtain' that so stimulates curiosity that the reader must go on with the tale.... For the purposes of most serial plots, at least three principal characters must be introduced in the first instalment, and five, or an even greater number of characters, is more usual. It follows then, that the greatest economy of words, and the highest technical skill must be used to introduce, say, five characters, their environment and circumstance in the space of five or six thousand words. (79, 83)

The opening installment of *This Slavery*, first published in *The Daily Herald* (October 1923), closely follows this advice. The story begins *in medias res* – "Mrs. Martin was out" – with concise scene setting and characterization of the central protagonists (sisters Hester and Rachel Martin, their mother and grandmother, romantic hero Jack Baines). Short passages of dialogue, as Joseph and Cumberland advised, are broken up by descriptions of the character's mannerisms and actions. The first chapter is full of dramatic and romantic incidents, with scenes of domestic poverty, hunger, Jack and Hester's declaration of love for each other followed by Mary's dramatic rebuttal, and street scenes with brawls and domestic violence. It concludes with the most devastating of neighborhood and personal dramas, fire at the mill:

> Was it Barstocks or Ben Bridge? That was the great question. With anxious hearts and faces they rushed on through the night. It meant semi-starvation if it was Barstocks. From every direction came the sound of those anxious thousands, shawled figures, men, and even children running to the scene of the fire. (19)

If Carnie Holdsworth was well studied in the craft and techniques of serial fiction, she was more cavalier in her approach to literary genre. Over the course of her career, Carnie Holdsworth tried her hand at several different genres, including the industrial novel, romance, detective fiction, slum fiction, the gothic, the New Woman novel, and the crime novel. The extent of her eclecticism was ill advised on some fronts: in general, publishers and readers liked to know what to expect from their authors. As Margaret Irwin wrote to her publisher, Harold Raymond, in May 1930: "you know what a help it is to the library reader to be able to tack some definite quality, if not subject, on to a writer" (University of Reading, Special Collections. Chatto & Windus archive, CW 35/11).[7] Contemporary manuals, as Peter Keating points out, advised young authors to establish "a reputation in the magazines for a special kind of story": "Mr Kipling is identified with Indian life, Mrs Stannard ('John Strange Winter') with cavalry life, Mr G. R. Sims with London life (of a sort), while Mr Anthony Hope, Mr Machen, and others are all *specialists* in fiction" (Keating 340–41). According to Keating, the stratification of print culture at the end of the nineteenth and beginning of the twentieth centuries "encouraged novelists either to specialise in one particular kind of fiction, or, if the writer was exceptionally talented (or facile) to move between different kinds, thus profiting from (or taking advantage of) several sectors of the fragmenting market" (340).

We cannot know why Carnie Holdsworth chose to experiment so radically across so many different literary genres. Partly, it may have been a sense of the relative freedom afforded by writing for serial publication first rather than book form; partly, it may have reflected the generic eclecticism of her own tastes and reading patterns, education, and enjoyment of popular texts. Roger Smalley argues that Carnie Holdsworth was a propagandist who sought to promote socialist values and "use imaginative writing on behalf of the people" (50). It is likely that writing across different popular genres enabled her to reach a wide audience. There was a long cultural tradition, as Smalley and Deborah Mutch have pointed out, of socially committed writers incorporating popular forms into their fiction as both a democratic gesture and so as to educate and entertain.

Carnie Holdsworth continued this tradition on two fronts, both writing for and revising the structures of popular fiction. The plot of *This Slavery* is a classic example of this, with its combination of Marxist-feminist rhetoric and adaptation of the popular rags-to-riches romance. Hester and Rachel Martin are immediately recognizable as headstrong mill girl heroines, but in contrast to typical romances written for working class women readers like those in the twopenny weekly *Peg's Paper* (1919–40), Hester's rags-to-riches marriage involves her in another form of slavery: "I have reduced my Slavery from being a slave of many to being a slave of one" (138). Carnie

Holdsworth also wrote "inside" such publishing structures. In 1929, she published a romantic novelette, "All On Her Own," in *Ivy Stories*, a fourpenny paperback magazine of complete stories, published every fortnight. Though working within the familiar structure of the popular romance – the last subheading of the story, for instance, reads "Love at Last" – themes of failed marriage, land ownership, and the death of an impoverished child bring in a prominent feminist and socialist perspective. Significantly, the "fair" protagonist Estelle Gardiner (1), a foundling, does not discover herself to be of noble birth as would often happen in popular narratives. If we concede to linguists and genre theory that genres are "central to human meaning-making and to the social struggle over meanings" (Frow 10), we might also read Carnie Holdsworth's formal and generic experimentation as an aesthetic working-out of her political principles. The literary manipulation of genre, as critic John Frow explains, is indicative of a radical desire to re-make the world:

> [W]hat we learn, in 'doing' genre (in performing and transforming it), is the values we share or don't share with others and the means with which to challenge or defend them. Through the use of genres we learn who we are, and encounter the limits of our world. (144)

Carnie Holdsworth is an important but much-neglected working class writer of the Left. If we assume that it is not helpful to categorize her legacy in terms of either firsts (though she was probably one of the earliest published British working class woman novelists) or apparent rarity, what is important to readers and literary history is the powerful body of writing that remains. More of this is to be discovered. While my own work and that of others has so far gravitated toward the rare surviving copies of Carnie Holdsworth's novels in book form, changes in critical practice and methodology, with an increased interest in periodical culture coinciding with the technological benefits of digitization, may facilitate a much wider study of Carnie Holdsworth's serializations and short stories. The majority of these are still largely concealed in the vast archives of the periodical press (where these have survived, and this is less often the case with provincial titles). Working class periodicals and socialist newspapers have yet to benefit from the kind of critical and financial investment in digital initiatives, of course, that have recently transformed research and teaching in modernist studies of a similar historical period (Latham 411–12).

As a writer, Carnie Holdsworth has often faced censure and criticism: too radical for some and not radical enough for others, distracted supposedly by her eclectic use of genre from where the place of narrative and historical interest *ought* to be. Following the initial wave of recovery spearheaded in the 1970s and early 1980s by H. Gustav Klaus, Ruth and Edmund Frow, and Mary Ashcroft, Carnie Holdsworth has recently been reclaimed by feminist critics. She has still to be discovered by ecocritics who might find her sensuous and powerful writing about nature a purposeful bringing together of the "Red and the Green" (Rignall and Klaus 1). I conclude with these comments because the way we write about working class writing – in collections like this as well as outside of them – continues to affect how we read and teach the texts of working class writers and how often or not they are read. Writing critical assessments about writers within the modest forms of power at our disposal is a form of patronage or, what Pierre Bourdieu might have dubbed, the "power to consecrate" (42). Ethel Carnie Holdsworth would no doubt have scoffed at any latter-day academic patronage – she reported leaving a WEA summer school in Oxford early as she disliked the form of education on offer and felt like a "duck in pattens" ("The Authoress of Our New Serial Story" 999). But obscurity sits uncomfortably with such a powerful and prolific writer keen to address a mass reading audience through a variety of genres, forms, and means. Perhaps she would find it wryly amusing to be included in this volume from Cambridge University Press.

NOTES

With many thanks to Chris Lynch, who shared his extensive knowledge of rare sources on Ethel Carnie Holdsworth as well as his ongoing research into her publication history.

1. I am grateful to Roger Smalley's pioneering research for locating this poem (Smalley, 59). British Library Jaffray Collection, 168/31.
2. For some of the debates about the reading of fiction in this period, see the work of Mary Hammond.
3. Most of Carnie Holdsworth's novels, published by Herbert Jenkins, sold at the average retail price for hardback fiction of either six shillings, or seven shillings and sixpence, before going into a two-shilling "Popular" edition. *This Slavery*, published by The Labour Publishing Company rather than Herbert Jenkins, was an exception in being published in a first edition at two shillings and sixpence.
4. In an interview for *Woman's Outlook* we learn that "The Marriage of Elizabeth" and "The House that Jill Built" are now appearing in book form "after running as serials in current periodicals" ("Ethel Carnie Holdsworth: A Notable Lancashire Woman Novelist" 295). Three stories about "General Belinda" first appeared in *The Wheatsheaf* (July 1920, 101–2; September 1921, 133–4; April 1922, 53–4) (Smalley, 114, note 3). Both Roger Smalley and Chris Lynch have

carried out extensive bibliographical research on Carnie Holdsworth's serialization history.
5. Postcard from E. Holdsworth to W. Hardisty, 10 September 1924. Hebden Bridge Local History Society archive, MISC 8/4.
6. Ethel C. Holdsworth to the Authors' Syndicate. Rec. 4 July 1917. Wigan Records Office. I am grateful to Chris Lynch for alerting me to this letter.
7. University of Reading, Special Collections, Chatto & Windus archive, CW 35/11.

CHAPTER 20

"The Young Men of the Nation"
Alexander Baron and Urban Working Class Masculinity

Anthony Cartwright

I

> After the war, the first novels to get published were all by officers or people who'd come through Penguin New Writing.... Stories were by the kind of intellectuals to whom the army was an agony. They wrote about it as an awful experience, sleeping with thirty-five ruffians....
>
> I read those books and I thought that nobody was writing about the ordinary soldiers. Soldiers were the nation in arms, they were the whole people. They were the young men of the nation.
>
> – Worpole, introduction to *King Dido* 8

The fiction of Alexander Baron, written in the immediate aftermath of World War II, dealing with the experience of working class Londoners in war and peacetime, is, on the one hand, a kind of writing back to the "officers or people who'd come through Penguin New Writing," or certainly to their social class. Baron's work is also the work of a writer "on the inside looking in," to borrow Anthony West's phrase about another postwar working class novelist, Alan Sillitoe, with whom Baron's work bears some comparison (West 99–100).

Baron's depiction of the "young men of the nation," initially takes the form of a series of journeys (literal, temporal, and metaphorical) across London and wartime Europe. We move through time, from the postwar era back through the war and the years of the Depression to the Edwardian era and the "Darkest London" of the 1890s slum novel, and further, to mid-nineteenth-century depictions of the urban working classes. We move from the 1940s to the 1960s. We move across London, from the streets of Hackney and Islington back toward an east end, which represents the past, and outer suburbs, such as Finchley, which represent one kind of future. We move across Europe with the Allied armies in the final years of the war, across Normandy and the Low Countries, elsewhere into Catania in Sicily (the occupation of Catania by the British Army in 1943 is the subject of Baron's novel *There's No Home*). We also move between a sense of solidarity and collectivism engendered by war, and the political optimism of the postwar years, toward an individualism and marginalization, and ultimately, from a sense of energy and movement to stasis.

The sequence of novels that Baron wrote between the end of the war and the late 1960s, the war fiction *From the City, From the Plough*, *There's No Home*, and *The Human Kind* (subtitled *A Sequence*, a book of related short stories), and the London novels principally discussed in this chapter, *Rosie Hogarth*, *The Lowlife*, and *King Dido*, provide sharp portraits of London working class life and achieved popular and critical success, most notably his first novel, *From the City, From the Plough*, which sold more than 1 million copies and was called by V. S. Pritchett (ironically, one of those writers who had "come through Penguin New Writing") "the only war book that has conveyed any sense of reality to me" (Worpole 94). Baron's novels subsequently fell out of print from the 1970s onwards before a revival of interest in the twenty-first century, leading to the republication of the books discussed in this chapter by independent publishers.[1]

Baron was born Alec Bernstein, into a Jewish family in East London in 1917. His parents had grown up in Bethnal Green and Spitalfields. His father was a fur-cutter, who had arrived in London at age eight following his family's migration from Eastern Europe. His mother worked at a factory near the docks until the family settled in Foulden Road, Stoke Newington (fictionalized as Ingram's Terrace in *The Lowlife*). This movement follows a typical arc of migration for Jewish families leaving the Russian Empire, settling in the East End, and then moving further north and west, through Hackney, toward suburbs such as Golders Green and Finchley, where in *The Lowlife*, Harryboy Boas's sister Debbie settles with her bookmaker husband, Gus. Indeed, Baron's fiction, although he was at pains to declare himself a realist, a London novelist, and a working class writer before being categorized as a Jewish one, in some ways maps out this arc of migration. Baron "always had a personal rebellion against the idea of a 'separate Jewish identity. My father and both my grandfathers were freethinkers and so am I'" (Worpole 10–11). Baron died in 1999, having lived in retirement in Golders Green.

The Lowlife opens in Finchley, "the smart part," with Harryboy returning home to Hackney from a meal at Debbie's (6). As the novel progresses, we also look back, "to the other side of Commercial Road" (39), and the East End his parents arrived in. One of the great sources of pain in this novel is the death of Harryboy's mother in an air raid. Another is the fate of a Jewish girl, Nicole, Harryboy had known in prewar Paris, whom he assumes to have been sent to the camps by the Nazis. The past, for the male characters in Baron's fiction, is both painful and fixed geographically in the east.

II

Baron's initial challenge was to make the "young men of the nation" visible, certainly as individuals. In his essay, "The Welsh Industrial Novel," Raymond Williams sought to explain some of the reasons "the situation of the working class novelist is exceptionally difficult"(217) by analyzing some of the "ways of seeing" (215) that developed to describe the new industrial landscapes of the nineteenth century. Williams cites George Borrow evoking Hieronymus Bosch in a description of Merthyr Tydfil, and the autobiography of James Nasymth, inventor of the steam hammer, in a description of the Black Country, where "workmen covered with smut, and with fierce white eyes, are seen moving about amongst the glowing iron and dull thud of forge hammers" ("Welsh" 214).

The anonymity of working class people is essential to this way of seeing. Thus, even in sympathetic representations of nineteenth-century working class urban life, such as in the novels of Dickens or George Gissing, both formative writers for Baron, working people are initially dehumanized by the imagery used, in order to accentuate the dehumanizing nature of the conditions in which they live and work, so that in the first description of Clerkenwell in *The Nether World*, we read:

> It was the hour of the unyoking of men.... Great numbers were still bent over their labour, and would be for hours to come, but the majority had leave to wend stablewards....
>
> ... The energy, the ingenuity daily put forth in these grimy burrows task the brain's power of wondering... that these do it all without prospect or hope of reward save the permission to eat and sleep and bring into the world other creatures to strive with them for bread, surely that thought is yet more marvellous. (Gissing 10)

In a fictionalized vision of Preston, Lancashire, described in Dickens's *Hard Times*, live "the multitude of Coketown, generically called 'the Hands,' – a race who would have found more favour with some people, if Providence had seen fit to make them only hands, or, like the lower creatures of the seashore, only hands and stomachs" (59). This extract is, of course, highly selective and comes just before the novel focuses on Stephen Blackpool, a very specific individual. Dickens uses the dehumanizing language, this "external, incorporating perspective" ("Welsh" 215) as Williams calls it, as an ironic contrast to his acute characterization, "Dickensian people very unlike one another" ("Welsh" 215). This is a pattern that Baron follows and adapts in his own work. In a story in *The Human Kind*, the men find a copy of *David Copperfield:* "it showed me what a novel ought to be" (32), says the unnamed narrator, a proxy for Baron. *David Copperfield* is described as a novel which can "reach across time even to the unlettered, and who can bring them into communion with each other and him" (32). Dickens casts the longest shadow across Baron's work.

His "young men of the nation" emerge from the (literal and metaphoric) shadows and fog of nineteenth-century realism and also the more sinister dehumanizing imagery that grew out of it. Baron uses the apparatus of the nineteenth-century novel and, to an extent, subverts it. The soldiers come blinking into the Mediterranean sun in the opening of *There's No Home*:

> always struggling in single file. Their boots and garters were white with dust. Their khaki drill jackets showed black patches of sweat and their faces, scarlet or glistening brown with heat, were ugly with stubble and sores. They were bowed and weary beneath their packs and weapons. The rays of sun fell on them like hammer blows from above and bounced back at them from walls and pavements in dry gusts of furnace-like heat. (7)

The language used here borrows from Victorian descriptions of urban working class life. These men are anonymous, "ugly," "bowed and weary," with industrial imagery used to describe the environment they find themselves in: "hammer blows" and "furnace-like heat." These "ugly," "bowed," and anonymous troops have carried archetypal working class identities with them (from the cities and from the countryside, as the title of his first novel suggests), along with the imagery of industry (the "hammer blows," the "furnace") and this reworking of some of the "ways of seeing" evident in nineteenth-century realism – the anonymous working men, the imagery of dirt, industry, heat and hell – is a key feature of Baron's work. This darkness is extremely important, a darkness that comes to equate with the past, with a struggle to survive, with Victorian slums, the Depression years, the Blitz, and (in the case of *The Lowlife*) the Holocaust.

Raymond Williams identifies a particular anonymity in descriptions of working class life in the early to mid-nineteenth-century novel. By the 1890s an even darker vision (which some of those equations of industry and hell had paved the way for) prevails, foreshadowed by Dickens's reference to the working classes as "creatures." Williams identifies Gissing as writing of "the crisis of the city" ("Welsh" 216), in *The Nether World*, which he also applies to the "slum novels" of the 1890s. The slum novel developed during the late Victorian era, indebted to the novels of Dickens and Gissing, among others, but "consciously sensational and melodramatic modes which appealed to the 'new' middle class as another disreputable amusement" (Diniejko www.victorianweb.org/history/slums.html); "slum novels were not written by slum dwellers. However authentic and convincing they might seem, they necessarily conveyed an outside view" (Diniejko).

Williams identifies a "sour distancing" (216) between social classes in depictions of late Victorian London, a "crisis of the city"

> – of course the industrial city which London's East End had become, but also that East End against West End; an area of darkness – 'Darkest London' – physically contiguous but socially in another world from the luxurious and powerful Imperial capital. ("Welsh" 216)

The working classes of this great industrial city are submerged in the language of the time into Jack London's "people of the abyss," the title of his 1903 study of life in the East End, or in passages such as this by William Booth, the founder of the Salvation Army:

> Is anything to be done with them? Can anything be done for them? Or is this million-headed mass to be regarded as offering a problem as insoluble as that of the London sewage, which, feculent and festering, swings heavily up and down the basin of the Thames with the ebb and flow of the tide? (23)

This passage uses the language of homogenization and dehumanization that had developed to describe the urban working classes, people given a "collective self-consistency" as identified by Edward Said in *Orientalisms* (229). Indeed Said's description of the language used by nineteenth-century Western sources to *create* the Orient could be applied to *creations* of nineteenth-century industrial working class life, "as something one judges (as in a court of law), something one studies and depicts (as in a curriculum), something one disciplines (as in a school or prison), something one illustrates (as in a zoological manual)" (40).

The opening to *King Dido* exemplifies what Williams also terms the "sour distancing" between West and East, between middle class aesthetics and working class reality. The novel itself is an ironic response to Arthur Morrison's novel *A Child of the Jago*. This is an archetypal slum novel, sensational and moralistic in tone, to which King Dido, set on the same streets, offers a revision. In *King Dido*'s opening sweep from west to east on the day of the coronation of King George V in June of 1911, we move from the "coloured lights that streamed like a continuous firework display" and "the Imperium on which the sun never set" to Rabbit Marsh in Bethnal Green where "there were no fairy lamps. No bonfire blazed... darkness had thickened between its walls" (22–3). Indeed, "from time to time a few dark-clad figures scurried (seen from above, like so many rats) down the street and vanished into a doorway" (22–3). This image of the "dark-clad figures... like so many rats" is a very clear echo of the "creatures" of the depictions of the nineteenth-century poor and a specific reference to *A Child of the Jago*, Arthur Morrison's novel, published in 1896, where the parish priest refers to the people of the Jago as "breeding like rats" (77).

Baron's descriptions come within a tradition of London fiction represented by Dickens, Gissing, Margaret Harkness, Israel Zangwill, and Arthur Morrison. Where he develops this tradition, certainly in relation to the Victorian era, is as a specifically working class writer. The characters that emerge from the London darkness (even when in the Sicilian sun), from the literal or symbolic "east," are not the "Hands," or "creatures," or "vermin," or "sewage" of previous descriptions but fully formed "young men of the nation."

The characters that come forth are often complex and contradictory: Charlie Venable in *From the City, From the Plough*, who deserts his battalion to go home to Bow, only to return for the invasion of Normandy; Craddock, who dreams of better postwar world, who sets up house with a Sicilian woman in the occupation of Catania; Harryboy, gambler, lowlife, driven by the bell that signals that the dogs are running, who stays in Hackney and mourns the life on "the other side of Commercial Road" (39), who dreams at one point of becoming a slum landlord, clumsily offering his own eyes to save his neighbor's child; and Dido, who becomes "king of a scrap of Bethnal Green" (Worpole, Introduction to *King Dido* 15). The characters Baron depicts are very far from "a collective self-consistency" (Said 229), from "creatures," "Hands," "vermin," and so on, but complex and contradictory "young men of the nation."

III

As with *There's No Home*, Baron's novels typically begin with entrances into or journeys across a city. The opening to *From the City, From the Plough* describes Allied troop movements across Normandy in August 1944, before moving back in time to the start of the year, to "the bleak flank hills looking down on the English Channel... wrapped up in winter mists" (13), also an echo of *Bleak House*. The opening story of *The Human Kind* describes a boy's return to London by bike after a day out with friends along the Lea Valley, riding through Tottenham, where "on each side were brilliantly lit shops, neon-lit cinemas, pavements overflowing with crowds, people darting across in our path, great red buses" (15) – movements which owe as much perhaps to cinema as to Dickens, and to the expressionism of novelists such as Alfred Doblin and John Dos Passos, and London writers of the 1930s, such as Ashley Smith and John Sommerfield. Sommerfield's 1936 novel *May Day* begins with a similar movement across the city:

> Then there are the shining tarred roads, glistening shop windows, arc lamps nightly flowering into electric buds, geometries of telephone wires and tramlines, traffic lights flinging continuous coloured fireworks into the air, a hundred thousand motorcars and buses. (25)

These passages seek to capture the energy of the city and the excitement of life lived among "brilliantly lit shops" and "continuous coloured fireworks."

"I have always loved London," is a sentiment attributed to Baron by Andrew Whitehead in his introduction to the 2010 edition of *Rosie Hogarth* (5). This is an attitude in great contrast to the ambivalence, or outright antipathy toward the city, certainly the industrial city that London had become, of much nineteenth-century fiction, exemplified, perhaps instigated, by Cobbett's description of London as "the Great Wen."[2] Baron's idea of the city as "accumulated memory" (Worpole, Introduction to *King Dido* 12) informs all of his fiction. The voice of the fiction is also the voice of an insider, a Londoner, and a sense of insidership (and the fear of what happens if you become an outsider) becomes increasingly important to the men in Baron's novels and the key feature of the two novels written in the 1960s discussed here, *The Lowlife* and *King Dido*.

Baron's first London novel, *Rosie Hogarth*, begins with the return of Jack Agass four years after the war's end, and the pilgrimage he makes to Lamb Street, Islington, where he grew up and where most of the subsequent novel is set. In *The Lowlife*, Harryboy journeys back from his sister's in Finchley to his house in Stoke Newington. In *King Dido*, we are given a great sweep of London on Coronation Day 1911, from the lights of the West End to the darkness of Rabbit Marsh, Bethnal Green. The reader is led to these places, with the authorial voice as guide, or with Harryboy's distinctive Yiddish-inflected first-person narrative in *The Lowlife*, or that of the nameless narrator in the opening of *The Human Kind*. This is much the same way that innocents to the city (and the reader) are guided in Victorian fiction, as Oliver is led by the Dodger into the rookeries of Dickens's London. Again, Dickens provides a model for Baron, both in the apparatus of the leader and the led, the figure of authority and of naivety, and in the imagery, which is either replicated, in the case of *King Dido*, or inverted, as in *Rosie Hogarth*, so we are led into havens of working class community.

The sense of movement and energy that begin these novels are in some ways a false start, used as a counterpoint to the more fixed lives of the majority of the characters. After the grand opening panoramas and sense of movement, the novels focus on a highly specific geography. This is true of the war books, the claustrophobia of the camp for the bulk of *From the City, From the Plough* (which serves to contrast the action of the last section, the invasion and fighting in Normandy, where most of the novel's protagonists are killed) and the streets of Catania in *There's No Home*, and is even more the case with the London settings. Jack Agass returns to Lamb Street, just off Chapel Market in Islington, in *Rosie Hogarth*; Harryboy Boas walks the streets around Foulden Road, off Stoke Newington High Street in *The Lowlife*; *King Dido* is set in a few streets of Bethnal Green.

Indeed, these islands in the "archipelago" (Baron 20), as he describes them in *Rosie Hogarth*, "gathered round some centre, perhaps a street, perhaps a block of buildings, perhaps a market, perhaps a public house or a working men's club.... Within each of these little hives people live for each other as for themselves, and life generates a considerable warmth" (20–21), are the true terrain of Baron's novels. As with Oliver being led by the Dodger, the reader is both led toward and instructed about these "little hives": another echo of the nineteenth-century imagery, subverted here to something of "considerable warmth." But there is a sense of warning too:

> The man or woman who tries to settle in London without gaining admission to one of these little communities ... is on his own, and he can go mad or die for all anybody cares. (*Rosie Hogarth* 21)

A sense of insidership is crucial to Baron's "young men of the nation."

"Don't call Hackney the East End. That's the mark of an outsider" (20), Harryboy warns the reader early in *the Lowlife*. This need for insidership, belonging, becomes more acute when the characters suffer some kind of existential crisis, which come to the fore in the later novels in particular. The most dangerous thing for a man to be, in much of Baron's London, is an outsider. In Baron's novels *The Lowlife* and *King Dido*, outsidership, for all their apparent rootedness in place, becomes the defining feature of the main characters.

IV

Baron is meticulous in establishing a sense of place. One Sunday morning Jack Agass sets out and walks "the back streets of Islington and Stoke Newington, down to the banks of the Lea, along the river, and back homewards through Dalston and Highbury" (*Rosie Hogarth* 156), circumscribing the territory in which he lives and of which Baron writes. Harryboy takes a "half-hour walk around the houses" (21) early in *The Lowlife*. He talks of "small areas in front that used to have hedges or fancy iron railings but since the war have wooden fences or nothing at all; neglected gardens at the back, trampled and heaped with rubbish" (*Lowlife* 20). There is a constant taking stock of the local area and of the people who live there in the London novels, a consciousness of the gradations within working class life and of the flux of the city. Though most of the houses are now "tenements," Harryboy is at pains to tell us that "[t]he street is clean. All the people are in work. Their cars jam the kerbs on both sides. All is quiet and decent" (*Lowlife* 20).

In *King Dido*, a few streets east of Commercial Street preoccupy the novel. For a while, when things are going well for him, Dido spends afternoons visiting a tea shop in Great Eastern Street: "only fifty yards outside Bethnal Green in location, it was a hundred miles away in status" (*Dido* 78). *King Dido* centers on Rabbit Marsh, a corner of Bethnal Green, with a carefully established Huguenot past prior to the growth of the docks. The residents are "law-abiding," unlike their neighbors in Jaggs Place. Tough as the street Dido Peach grows up on, "it was a paradise compared with the sinister back alleys of Spitalfields" (*Dido* 26). Every street, every corner, is measured against neighbors, categorized, and judged. It is the same, of course, with the people. The "traders and artisans of Rabbit Marsh were its upper crust," followed by "regular labourers," and then by its "drifters," "sellers of matches and bootlaces," and its "flotsam" (*Dido* 26). These subtleties, of classes within classes, are something that Baron writes of with great care – a symbol of his own "insidership" – and form an antithesis of Dickens's ironic "large streets all very like one another, and many small streets still more like one another, inhabited by people equally like one another" (*Hard Times* 20).

How to live, and where to live, preoccupy his "young men of the nation." Dido daydreams of a move to Walthamstow or Clapton; Harryboy's sister tries to persuade him to move to Finchley, or, at least, to leave Hackney, and for a while, a scheme whereby he will become a man of property, but wins and then loses a row of houses in a game of dice. Bombsites proliferate in *Rosie Hogarth* and *The Lowlife*. A bomb destroyed the house Jack Agass grew up in: "Now, where it and a half-a-dozen other houses had stood, there stretched a rough expanse of waste ground, bound by ragged ends of wall" (*Rosie Hogarth* 24). Harryboy visits Cable Street: "I stopped at a gap in the decaying shops, and I cried. In the rain I stood and cried. This bomb crater, patches of diseased weeds, black puddles, rusty bedsteads, sodden newspapers, old prams, smashed packing-cases and the turds of tramps – this is where my mother died" (*Lowlife* 39).

For all the characters' rootedness, there is a sense of provisionality, an awareness that life can change very quickly for the worse. As Iain Sinclair observes in his introduction to *The Lowlife*, Baron is acutely aware of "the minute particulars of a ravished landscape, the scams, the hustles, the culture shifts" (vii). There is always the hope that change will be for the better, although this feels less likely in the later novels, and characters, as with the nineteenth-century realist novel, are always on their way up or down the social ladder. "It doesn't seem like London, does it?" Joyce Wakerell, Jack's fiancée, says of her sister's new council flat in Hackney, "it must be like living in fairyland" (*Rosie Hogarth* 172). The Deaners, the family that move into the flat beneath Harryboy's in *The Lowlife*, explain that "[w]e had a flat in Ilford. Only they put up the rent" (46).

The contrast between *The Lowlife* and *King Dido* and the earlier novels is clear. We move from men as part of a community, soldiers in wartime, to men as individuals. In the books written in the late 1940s and 1950s there is a palpable sense of hope among all the difficulty, of surviving the war, of finding new ways of living as part of a community. The later novels offer a change of tone, a creeping pessimism, which is informed perhaps by Baron's own political disenchantment over the period,[3] perhaps by keen observation of the wider rising tide of individualism and materialism through the 1960s. "A writer's job is to be the spectator who hopes he can see more of the game and try to make sense of it" (Sinclair vi), Baron told an interviewer in the 1980s, and it is possible to see a kind of proto-Thatcherism in the preoccupations of both Harryboy and Dido (this is complicated, of course, by *King Dido* being set in the Edwardian era, albeit that there are echoes of his rise and fall and that of the Kray twins, who came to notoriety on exactly the same streets at the time Baron was writing the novel). Dido measures his increased status (as he overcomes Ginger Murchison, the local gangster) with patent shoes and new shirts. He has his eye on "a bright new wallpaper and best quality lino...a nice bit of carpet to go by the bed" (*Dido* 166). When his fortunes ebb, "in desperation he had bought himself new clothes" (*Dido* 129). Both Dido and Harryboy are poised between an older world of community and ritual, narrow and comforting in equal measure, and a more individualistic, materialistic society. However, the competing tendencies of community and the individual are present for all of Baron's characters.

Charlie Venable admonishes a praying corporal in *From the City, From the Plough*:

> People 'ave been prayin' for a million years an' it didn't do 'em no good. It didn't stop the last war an' it didn't stop this one. It didn't stop the bombs comin' down on Bow, neither. No offence to you Corp. Put your trust in God; an' I don't think! Put your trust in Charlie Venable; that's my motto. (28)

A few pages later Charlie deserts, goes on the run back to Bow, only to then return to camp on the eve of the invasion of Normandy. He is loyal to his friends and family and the area he comes from. As with all Baron's "young men of the nation," any more abstract or grander concepts – religion, patriotism, politics – are given short shrift.

V

Ken Worpole writes of *From the City, From the Plough*:

> All of Baron's characters are working-class men, fully developed as individuals with inner lives of their own. . . . In Baron's male community there are no heroics, no great manly virtues, but rather we are shown a group of men thrown together, learning to live with each other, many of them frightened, trying to make the best out of a situation which they no longer control. They comfort each other, sort out squabbles, try to learn to live communally – and wait. (94–5)

This camaraderie is certainly true of the war novels, and waiting plays an important part in the later works too. Often there are great periods of inertia, followed by frenzied activity, a waiting that perhaps symbolizes the relative powerlessness of much of working class life: waiting to be told what to do from those in power, waiting for housing, waiting for work. This waiting is played out on macro and micro levels. The troops wait for orders. The majority of both *From the City, From the Plough* and *There's No Home* are taken up by what happens in these periods of waiting. "At the beginning of nineteen forty-one the long wait set in" (28), begins the third story of *The Human Kind*, the same story where the soldiers pass round and discuss *David Copperfield*. Indeed, reading and waiting become synonymous, Harryboy lies on his bed on "great reading jags" (*Lowlife* 18) before the frenzy of the dogs running, or a game of dice, or a brief sexual encounter on a factory break or with Marcia, his prostitute friend, who suggests the idea of becoming a slum landlord: "'What do you do, Mr. Boas?'" Evelyn Deaner asks Harryboy, "'Me? I'm in property,'" (*Lowlife* 35) he answers.

The creation, the making visible, of working class characters "fully developed as individuals with inner lives of their own" (Worpole 95) is Baron's achievement as a novelist. The tensions between the dominant ways of seeing, established ways of describing working class life, and the actual lived experiences of working class life are something with which his fiction grapples. A kind of waiting is what we are left with in several of the novels, and a sense of endurance, both individual and collective: "'So here I am, Harryboy Boas, back where I started from... Never mind'" (*Lowlife* 223). Jack Agass closes the curtains against the world at the conclusion of *Rosie Hogarth* and tells himself, "they would always be able to make the best of a bad job" (367). We are told about Dido that, destitute, waiting to die, "In silence he would endure anything" (354).

Baron's work brings young male working class characters into focus through an initial use of the apparatus of nineteenth-century realism. His work follows a tradition of the London novel but is also something distinct, a genuine attempt to portray working class lives, from the inside, with close observation of all their complications and contradictions. His "young men of the nation" set themselves collectively and increasingly individually, to borrow a phrase from Raymond Williams describing working class experiences in the nineteenth century, against "the fierce and dynamic trajectories of social and economic transformation and conflict" ("Welsh" 216).

NOTES

1. *From the City, From the Plough*, first published by Jonathan Cape, 1948, most recent edition Black Spring Press, 2010; *There's No Home*, first published by Jonathan Cape, 1951, most recent edition Sort of Books, 2011; *Rosie Hogarth*, first published by Jonathan Cape, 1952, most recent edition Five Leaves, 2010; *The Human Kind*, first published by Jonathan Cape, 1953, most recent edition Black Spring Press, 2011; *The Lowlife*, first published by Collins, 1963, most recent edition Black Spring Press, 2011 (a 2001 edition by Harvill Panther in their discontinued "The London Fiction Series," with an introduction by Iain Sinclair. Alongside the work of Ken Worpole, this edition did much to revive contemporary interest in Baron's work); *King Dido*, first published 1969 by MacMillan, most recent edition Five Leaves, 2009.
2. William Cobbett used this term in *Rural Rides*, outraged by the rapid expansion of the city: "But what is to be the fate of the great wen of all? The monster, called, by the silly coxcombs of the press, 'the metropolis of the empire?'" (I: 43).
3. Baron had been a Communist Party member and Youth League organizer before the war. As with many contemporaries, he became distanced from the party during the 1950s, although he did not renounce his views.

CHAPTER 21

Kathleen Dayus
The Girl from Hockley

Sharon Ouditt

"*Yes, this was where I was born . . . and the poor people who struggled to live until that struggle killed them were my people.*"
– Her People 1

This chapter will focus on the autobiographical writings of Kathleen Dayus. Born into the industrial slums of Birmingham in 1903, Dayus was one of six children (out of the thirteen born to her parents) scrabbling for attention in a dilapidated back-to-back house. Her mother, a gargantuan figure, was at best dismissive of her, at worst cruel: Dayus found protection and affection elsewhere in her family and her community more broadly. Her books recover for the reader the voices and stories of that community and cover Dayus's childhood, her working life in munitions factories and in the enameling trade, her marriage, widowhood, the loss of her children, and her slow recovery against the backdrop of the Depression and the Second World War. Having been nothing but a "little drudge, always in the way" (*Her People* 6), by the end of her life she had published nine books, had been awarded an honorary MA, and had a square named after her in Birmingham's jewelry quarter. But, unlike the more conventional narrative trajectories of working class autobiographies, her story is neither a tale of heroic social ascent, nor the story of a literary artist who made her living by her pen against the odds. She wrote her story late in life and tells it in vivid, life-affirming detail, insisting that she was no worse off than the thousands of others who, like her, were immobilized by poverty and ignorance. This chapter will situate her work in the context of its publication by a feminist press and will then focus on the "communal function" of the narrative and its dispersed narrative trajectory, which describes Dayus's difficult relationship with her mother, and then the impossible decisions she had to make as a mother herself. The tensions and ironies that emerge make for a compelling story of suffering endured and independence achieved, albeit at a cost.

In their respective studies of working class autobiography, Linda Peterson and Regenia Gagnier outline (tentative) typologies of the form (Peterson 1–42; Gagnier 152–67). It is, nevertheless, striking that Dayus's work does not fit into them. This could be because of the eras from which Peterson's and Gagnier's texts were drawn (from the Victorian period to the 1920s), but it might also be because those accounts, whether written by women or men, followed a design based on a certain class and an expected narrative trajectory. Dayus's writing suggests that working class women's lives do not necessarily lend themselves to standard narratives implying character development, religious conversion, political success, or scandalous confessions. Furthermore, editors or publishing houses would have taken a view of what would sell and what would be acceptable to the reading public and, in the wake of the second wave of the feminist movement, a distinct new model of publishing emerged. Virago Press, the Women's Press, Pandora in the UK, and numerous others, particularly in the US and Canada, sought to celebrate women's stories and histories, told in their own voices and in their own forms.

Virago published the first volume of Dayus's autobiography in 1982. At this point, inspired by Sheila Rowbotham's *Hidden from History* (1973), the Press was beginning to build what was to become a game-changing list of books. A new edition of Margaret Llewelyn Davies's *Life as We Have Known It* (1977) was already out; Amrit Wilson's *Finding a Voice* (1978) was proving popular; Barbara Taylor's *Eve and the New Jerusalem* (1983) was on its way. Along with Kathleen Woodward's *Jipping Street* (1928; reprinted 1983), set in the slums of London, Dayus's tales from the slums of Birmingham began to bring women's working class voices into the public domain. The early to mid-1980s saw the rise of a particular, if oddly nuanced, ideological curve. On the one hand Women's Studies courses were beginning to appear in universities and the feminist movement saw an increasing demand for the writing of working class women, black and Asian women, lesbians, and older women, in order to fracture middle class ideological dominance. On the other, in the commercial sphere, aided (ironically) by the Conservative Government's reduction of taxes and backing of small businesses, there was growing encouragement for the small entrepreneur to break free from unionized industry in a bid to prove that hard work and individualism would lead to prosperity. These circumstances provided opportunities for the growth of feminist presses, women's book clubs and bookshops, feminist magazines and academic journals, all of which confirmed that there were markets hungry for material. Dayus's autobiographies suited these markets perfectly: the unmediated voice of a working class woman with memories of a nearly forgotten world, who pulled herself out of poverty in order to make a home for her family, became part of a vibrant feminist archive, validating the diversity of women's voices and proving that the recovery of women's histories was a saleable project.

How the first volume came to be published is explained in John Rudd's Introduction to *Her People* and then, in Dayus's own words, in the Preface to the second volume of her autobiography, *Where There's Life* (1985). Dayus had been asked about her childhood by one of her grandchildren and, encouraged by the girl's astonishment that her grandmother had spent part of her childhood begging for food outside factories, she began recording her recollections. The grandchild passed these on to her teacher, who showed them to Rudd, a local historian, who brought them to the attention of Virago. Rudd's Introduction sets the account in the context of Birmingham's industrial development, housing, and social policy. But, while these issues are central to the tales Dayus has to tell, her perspective is not that of a social investigator, but of someone who sincerely believes "her people" have been forgotten in a postwar world of council housing, the NHS, and color television. This absence from cultural memory is what she sets out to address. Her books (there are four volumes of autobiography, plus an additional volume of recollections, an omnibus edition, and an edited recension of her writings) have been reviewed across a wide spectrum of the press, by the *Sunday Telegraph, Good Housekeeping*, and *Time Out*, have been reduced to fit the format of Radio 4's *Book of the Week* (21–5 August 2006), and have been cited in numerous academic studies. The latter tend to mine them for "evidence" of the social realities of working class life below the poverty line before the Welfare State was created as a "thank you" to working class people after the Second World War (Todd 119–48). There is, however, relatively little attention paid to the books' literary qualities, to their structure and narrative devices, or to the repetitions, résumés, and later additions. Also neglected are the social and ideological tensions that underpin this sort of *Decameron* that celebrates the good humor, rowdiness, nosiness, and supportiveness of a community while demonstrating the urgent need on the part of the writer to escape the infestations, decay, and general social misery, if she were not to see her own children beg for food as she had done.

If working class autobiographies are typically written by those who have led or represented their peers as part of a political or labor movement, then Dayus's is atypical. This is not the story of a heroine like Ada Nield Chew or Hannah Mitchell, nor is it a misery memoir or a piece of poverty porn, although there is misery here, and poverty, too. The author is not an aspiring writer, like Kathleen Woodward, seeking escape through literature. Dayus was not reading Milton in failing light. Dayus's memoirs do meet some of the other criteria for working class autobiography established by Peterson and Gagnier: they deal with multiple childbirths and infant mortality; they speak of domestic violence (although meted out by the protagonist's mother rather than by a male relative); Dayus succeeds through self-help, although not through religious or educational routes, and there is a clear awareness of social injustice, even if its exposure is not the principal motivation for writing. The writings here are apparently driven by a simpler, less political desire: to recall to public memory those people who had nothing; the disenfranchised who lived in the "rabbit warrens" of industrial Birmingham, who were left to "sink or swim, rise or fall as best we could" (*Her People* 1). She was lucky enough to be among those who (eventually) swam, but her story is not a linear narrative of success.

Even though across the five volumes there is a clear trajectory out of the slums and into a more pleasant environment, ultimately Dayus does not leave Birmingham, does not go to university or lead a union or a women's group. By the end of her story, she remains within walking distance of Camden Court, where she began her life. The "yard" where she grew up no longer exists, having been bombed in the war, and maybe its very invisibility is the point here: it is the historical vacuum between her prospects as a young child and the living standards enjoyed by her grandchildren that draws the stories from her. And at the center of this story is her mother, killed by the bombs that flattened the yard, a woman for whom the narrator has painfully mixed feelings. There is nothing sentimental about these memories. The past is hidden, obscured by postwar building projects and by the safety net provided by the Welfare State. Dayus does not regret this, but she wants to shed light on that other world, which she approaches head-on in *Her People* (1982), continues in *Where There's Life* (1985), almost completes in *All My Days* (1988), then revisits from other angles in *The Best of Times* (1991) and *The Ghosts of Yesteryear* (2000). The result is a repetitive, fragmented, incident-driven set of narratives that tells a vigorous life story in a way that continually probes her anxieties and, in particular, the near-crushing influence of her domineering mother. Dayus appears here under her childhood name, Katie: innocent and easily wounded. The underlying narrative concerns her reconciling herself to how much her mother disliked her, before escaping and finally building a life of her own. It is a fragmented, dispersed tale, in which her community – or communities – becomes just as important as her family, and in which, ironically, the price she paid for freedom was to lose her own children.

In *Subjectivities* Gagnier talks about the "communal function" of some kinds of autobiography, and in *Women's Life Writing* (1997), Linda S. Coleman notes the construction of an empowering and sympathetic community of readers as a principal strategy in women's autobiography (Gagnier 5; Coleman 1). The "communal function" is concerned with binding together a body of people with shared experiences and articulating to the general reader what those experiences meant. We can see this happening through Dayus's volumes. She focuses on her family, her friends, and the community that surrounds them. Her parents, five siblings, neighbors – the Buckleys, the Huggetts, Maggie and shell-shocked Billie Bumpton, Mrs. Jones, and Mrs. Taylor with her seven children and at least as many cats – are the main characters. These she describes as "my people": "the poor people who struggled to live until that struggle killed them" (*Her People* 1). Most of the houses are pullulating with adults, children, cats, dogs, and vermin. There is a general sense of claustrophobia and threat.

The scenario she describes is both simple and complex, centering on the yard: five houses back-to-back with five more, ash cans, lavatories (non-flushing), and wash-houses at the end of the yard, and a shared stand-pipe for water. There are rows about keeping the lavatories clean, rotas for using the wash-house. The children all play together out in the yard with whatever they can find when they are not running errands or doing chores. If an old orange-box is left outside a shop, the children sneak it away for firewood, sharing any moldy fruit with their friends. There is little work for the men, and the women keep things going by charring, taking in washing, carding buttons, or sewing. Most need parish relief (in the form of vouchers, not money, which the po-faced administrators of this meager bounty feared would be spent on beer or tobacco), and most do odd, undeclared, jobs to try to keep themselves and their families fed. Nobody snitches; everybody helps, and, even when there are flaming rows, they are usually forgotten over a pint of beer. There is no privacy; many sleep three to a bed; everyone knows everyone else's business. There is gossip, and there are showdowns: Katie's mother being among the loudest and most dominant in these. It is, then, a mixed picture: neither nostalgically warm nor alienating in its picture of deprivation. There are tensions, certainly: between parents, siblings, and neighbors (who get blamed for the wrongs of others; who are always borrowing and never paying back), but also between more abstract ideas such as privacy and community, justice and strength. Katie is caught between these tensions, intent on valuing her people while revealing the conditions in which they all lived. If that means exposing their drinking habits, their selfishness, and general rowdiness, then that behavior has to be set in the context of their struggle. So they are not admired, not perceived as role models, not even loved very much (with some exceptions), but we see them as clearly drawn individuals, always on the edge of extinction, whose quirks, streaks of kindness, and hints of slyness are attractive and threatening by turns. They are neither patronized nor idolized.

One of the striking elements of these narratives is that there is no middle class filter, no assumption of "embourgeoisement" shadowing Katie's early life, and this is in line with the communal function that the texts seem to offer. Those of higher social rank, the teachers and doctors, figure only slightly and seem no better behaved than those in their charge (one doctor is a groper); a pleasant, middle class young man offers to teach Katie to "speak nicely" so that he might introduce her to his parents: insulted, she slaps him and sees no more of him. Katie's older sister Mary marries into a slightly higher social class and is mortified that the wedding celebrations are to take place in the communal yard. This is a perfect example of the casual carnival that typifies Katie's people. Everyone helps out: there are trestle tables and benches borrowed from the local hall; the neighbors lend cutlery, crockery, cups, and mugs, the windows are cleaned, the clothes lines put away – "Everyone was singing a different song out of tune and taking no notice where they were throwing the water. Several people ended up with wet feet and all the cats vanished and even the kids who were trying to help got the odd clout for 'getting under our feet'" (*Where There's Life* 31). But the chaos is entirely cheerful, even if Mary remains embarrassed and entirely understands her new in-laws slipping away before things get too out of hand. And they do get out of hand: there is plenty of gin, whiskey, and stout to go round; someone insults the prime minister, another defends him, and what had been looking like a knees-up descends into a fight which is broken up only when the police cart away those not quick enough to run back into their houses. Just out of the main picture, we observe the (slightly) more genteel folks quietly leaving with a kind word for Mary. But we are not invited to see things from their point of view. This is not their scene, and, happily, they are gone before Mrs. Taylor's young twins are discovered, drunk, in the privy at the very end of the evening.

In a more macabre but no less carnivalesque scene, the vicar, presumably the very same who has continually chased the children out of his churchyard with a stick rather than welcoming them in with Christian charity, sighs to himself that he has "never come across such a disgraceful congregation in all the years I have given burial services" (*Life* 17). The occasion is the otherwise solemn burial of Katie's granny. But it is disrupted by the chirpy intervention of young Jonesy, who, after the intonation of "Ashes to ashes, dust to dust" chips in with "An' if God don't 'ave yer, the devil must" (*Life* 17). On receiving the inevitable parental clout, he lands in the muddy, freshly dug grave behind him. This is slapstick comedy, really, but Katie doesn't take offense. We see the point of view of the socially superior vicar but are not invited to share it. He is not one of Katie's "people," her "community," and it was not him that John Rudd had in mind when speaking of the book's capacity to "touch many hearts" (*Her People* viii). Dayus's own comments on the number of people who have contacted her to share recollections of the "bad old days" is a testament to the readership that she was successful in building up.

As the volumes proceed, it becomes clear that there is a complex narrative trajectory underpinning her tale, concerning motherhood. Her own mother's cruel disparagement verges on abuse. Katie wants to give her children a different kind of upbringing, but must make some heart-rending decisions in order to do so. From the outset, Polly, Katie's mother, is clearly going to be a "character." Sixteen stone, tall, with flowing black hair wound into a bun and speared with a hatpin known as a "weapon," she is a Valkyrie. When she claps her husband's cap on her head and sets forth to bully others in order to keep her family in shape, she is formidable. She is loud, demanding, "hard," the gaffer of the yard. Few dare to stand up to her as she bellows at nosey neighbors, slams doors, and strikes children. Katie tries her best to love her (*Her People* 6), but is more often than not terrified of a telling off, a beating, or some other random act of cruelty. In other working class women's autobiographies, there are similar tales of redoubtable mothers: Kathleen Woodward's mother in *Jipping Street* "had that strength and poise that comes to those who live without hope and without fear" (4). Her favorite phrase is "Life kicks you downstairs and then it kicks you upstairs" (5). But Woodward, who is in awe of her mother, is able to understand these characteristics in someone who has lived through a violent childhood, an impoverished adulthood, and has come to accept life's adversities with grim resolution. Dayus tries these routes toward comprehension, but they are blocked. She fears her mother's violent temper, often focused on Katie rather than on the outside world, in protection of the child. As she matures, Katie can imagine the fatigue felt by a woman who has given birth to thirteen children, with only six surviving, who has to use and reuse every single resource until it is utterly exhausted, who has to work against the odds to keep a verminous, dilapidated house clean and to keep her children healthy and at least clothed and free from lice. Nevertheless, Katie does not experience the love and warmth she craves from her mother. She gets something of this elsewhere – her father is kind and protective, her older sister Mary will explain things her mother will not, even her neighbor Mrs. Taylor offers advice when her mother refuses. Later, through her sister, Dayus comes to understand that she was the thirteenth child and was unwanted. Her mother tried to abort her and, for that reason, never took kindly to her. Hints that there is an underlying reason for Polly's antipathy are dropped into the narrative, but they merely confirm her irrational distaste for her daughter. So Katie spends much of her childhood dodging blows, doing the foulest jobs around the house, trying to please, and trying to make sense of acts of spite.

These vignettes make for painful reading. At Christmas 1911, for instance, when Katie is just eight years old, the other children receive modest but cheering Christmas gifts, while Katie is given a darning needle and a tiny ball of thread to repair a hole in her stocking. Her brother Frankie and sister Mary rally round to share with her what they have, but this sadistic trend toward always disappointing her expectations is broken only when Katie develops her own bargaining position.

This happens following a hop-picking expedition, the climax to *Her People*, which has resonances for the rest of Dayus's volumes. Hop-picking in the Kent countryside provided extra income and something of a holiday for city folk, who would otherwise rarely taste fresh air. On this occasion the women and children of the "yard" set off in high spirits. Katie, immediately, is alarmed by the raucous behavior of her mother and her cronies and begs to go home. Her fearfulness comes to a head one night, when, during a threatening scene involving a fight between the womenfolk and a group of men who have been "treating" them to drinks at the pub, Jack, her brother, turns up in a van to retrieve his family and steals the farm's pet, a small, lame pig. Polly, in fending off one of her suitors, sustains a black eye and, of course, back in Birmingham, the pig has to be disposed of before Katie's father finds out about it – and about the cause of his wife's injury. Unknown to Polly and Jack, Katie has heard them plotting and works out exactly what has happened. Distraught by the theft itself (she was fond of the pig), by her mother's and brother's duplicity, and by the rowdiness of all concerned in the court case that follows (the judge dismisses the case), Katie finds her nerve, rejects the bribes offered by her brother and blurts out to her mother what she knows. They make a pact: Katie won't tell her father or anyone else about the pig, and Polly promises that "I'll never 'it yer again" (*Her People* 186). This marks the beginning of a developing resolve on Katie's part. She is no less frightened of her mother, but now she has the means to fight back.

Where Katie really feels the need for maternal understanding and affection, though, is in the area of love, sex, and relationships with men generally. Nobody, not her mother, sister, or even Mrs. Taylor, would explain procreation, the sexual act, or the significance of menstruation to her. "Now yow keep away from the lads an' never let 'em kiss yer or the next thing yer know yer'll be 'avin' a baby," is the best her mother can offer, and "when yer grow older you'll find out" is Mrs. Taylor's advice (*Life* 95–6). Some years later, her sister Mary spots Katie and her boyfriend together in an alleyway and rapidly tries to warn her not to go too far, but it is too late: she is in love, and, when she becomes pregnant and her sister responds harshly to her confession, Katie retaliates by asking why on earth she hadn't told her earlier – "I was always asking you an' Mum to explain things to me... but you never did!" (*Life* 137).[1] There is a brief moment of reconciliation with her mother when Katie's first child is born, and, when the second arrives and there is no chance of Katie, her husband Charlie, and their two children finding lodgings anywhere, they have no choice but to move back into her parents' house and live in the attic, where she had slept with her two sisters and brother as a child. It is humiliating, a huge step backward, but it is at least some kind of shelter.

She pays her mother rent and some money to look after the children while she goes out to work, but relations are sour, and, as her mother begins to drink more and sometimes disappears for days, Katie finds herself despising her (*Life* 155). After Katie finally leaves, a decade passes in which there is no contact. Mary tries to persuade Katie to relent, but she can't forgive her mother. There is a frosty reconciliation and a final few unsatisfactory meetings. Then, Polly and Mary are killed in the air raid that demolishes Camden Court in 1941. Katie feels angry that her mother and sister have died "like rats without a chance" (*Life* 239), but her comment is not reserved for her relations alone; it extends to all those who were exterminated, like vermin, having struggled through the Depression and caught a glimmer of hope as factories started taking on labor again at the outbreak of war. The irony of the situation is not lost on her. Even so, she struggles to find kind words in memory of her mother. The reader is left to assume that this sadness is for the manner of her death, rather than the manner of her life: in emotional terms, Katie had lost her mother many years before.

As a young, married woman, Katie's fondest wish was not to replicate for her children the upbringing that she had experienced: lacking maternal affection and always hungry. So it is with dismay that she returns to the "hovel," paying her mother eight and sixpence a week for the room and, following the birth of her second son, doing press work all day at the factory, then office-cleaning at night after feeding the boys and putting them to bed. Two more children follow as she is variously in and out of work, in factories and enameling workshops, in order to bring in enough to keep the children fed. There are good times: her father and husband enjoy playing with the younger ones, and, when Charlie is in work, Katie (now "Kate") can relax a little. One of her better employers allows her to bring her baby in with her so that she can breast feed, and the women she works with arrive with treats for her children and even change the baby's diapers. Here, the sense of community spirit revives, although it is the community of the workplace rather than of the yard. But her narrative refrain is that "it was too good to last" (*Life* 159) and a series of disasters befalls her: her father has a stroke and is taken into the workhouse, where he dies a diminished man, her oldest son is killed in a road accident, and her friendly employer has to close down his business owing to lack of orders. This is in the late 1920s, deep into the Depression. At 24, as she buries her father, she reflects that "I'd seen nothing of life, only poverty and hardship, and it seemed to me then that I'd been born simply to breed" (*Life* 154). Having had four children and two miscarriages – brought on by heavy press work – she is near to despair and, in retrospect, amazed at her class's lack of knowledge about sex. She knew nothing of contraception: "the subject of sex was completely surrounded by ignorance, myth and misunderstanding throughout the working-class community"; educated people might have been better informed, but "in our neighbourhood these things were never spoken of" (*Life* 151). Abortions were illegal, of course, and, although there was some folk-wisdom surrounding them and local women claimed expertise in this area, she had known of too many women dying in the process to want to risk it. Although she is aware that the cycle of "pregnancy, hard work, poverty and grief" had made her life hard by the standards of the Welfare State in the late twentieth century, she insists that "it was no rougher than it was for thousands of other people like us in Birmingham in the 1920s" (*Life* 157). She is not asking for the reader's pity.

Her story departs from the "ordinary" tales of impoverished folk in a further sequence of disasters and decisions. Both she and her husband have work, but, pregnant with her fifth child and with Charlie increasingly ill, she comes home early one day to find him unconscious and being packed into an ambulance. Kate goes into premature labor and, with the help of capable neighbors, gives birth to another daughter. Charlie does not survive to see her. So in 1931, aged 28, Kate finds herself a widow with four young children. At various times she has had to rely on charity or on parish relief. At this point, unable to leave her new-born baby for long enough to return to factory work and having been turned down for a widow's pension as her husband had not paid enough insurance stamps, she has to return to the parish for support. The process is mortifying. As she prepares to "make [her]self humble" in order to answer the intrusive questions asked by these cold inquisitors, she feels sure that she will do "something desperate" if she is refused help and resolves that, once she has her strength back, she would "do something better for [her] children than sitting here being humiliated" (*Life* 174). After being interrogated about her marriage, her mother, and her children, and being told that she would be subjected to a means test, she hears one of these imperious ladies whisper to another: "Some of these women shouldn't have children" (*Life* 174). Dayus does not comment on this directly, but it erupts from the text as a judgment on the middle class, do-gooder approach to the working classes. There is no empathy here, only ignorance of the real conditions under which the poor must live. In the other vignettes in which the better-off have passed judgment (the judge closing the pig-theft case; the vicar admonishing the funeral congregation; Mary's in-laws hoping they can do something better for their daughter-in-law), the mood has been carnivalesque: there have been no material consequences and nobody is hurt. Here we have, for the first time, a sense of anger as Kate feels herself condemned as one of the undeserving poor, the vermin.

The means test provides her with a ration allowance that is insufficient even to feed her, let alone her children. She has no choice but to take on undeclared work, selling firewood for a few pennies. Her son is found begging outside the factory (just as she once did) and is brought home, terrified, by a policeman. When her extra income is discovered, she has to face the inquisitors again. This time her patience snaps, and we hear the voice she would herself have used at that time. In an act of rage, feeling "utterly humiliated and ashamed and defeated" (*Life* 181), she lets rip at her accusers, her Brummie defiance pitted against the pious disapproval of the Christian ladies on the Board: "You stand back there an' beg for crumbs an' see 'ow yow feel! Anybody'd think it was your money that paid for our chickenfeed!" (*Life* 182). This is her lowest point. With no income and no food, no sympathy from her mother, and no support from her siblings, the only thing she can think to do is to send her children away somewhere where they will be looked after, until she has the means to bring them back again. So she gives them up to a Barnardo's home. It is the only way out of the "web of penury and squalor" that she can see (*Life* 189), and, although her mother and her drinking companions deride her in the street (she's "the wust woman in the district"), she stands firm: "As far as they were concerned any kind of inadequate dragging up was better than allowing your children to be taken care of in an institution" (*Life* 190).

The matron she meets at Barnardo's is kindly. But it would be eight years before Katie got her children back – and even then only her daughters: her son had been enlisted in the Navy, without her consent, and she suspects that the Navy used such institutions to ensure a supply of cannon fodder (*Life* 208). All her children, and again without her consent, were moved from the home in Birmingham to one in Essex, and the two younger girls were fostered out from there. On one ill-judged occasion, Katie, egged on by her feckless sister Liza, attempts to snatch her youngest daughter away, is caught doing so and banned from visiting until further notice. Only at the beginning of the Second World War are her children returned to her, and they come back estranged, confused, unsure who this woman is who claims to be their mother. Again, we witness a bitter encounter with an institution. Although Kate has given up her brood for their protection while she restores her financial position, she is made to feel like a criminal, an inadequate mother justly deprived of the right even to see them and reassure them of her love. And, beneath all this, there is the unacknowledged subtext of Dayus's own regret. She knows that she has broken a cardinal rule: never to abandon your children. Polly, for all her faults, had always provided a home. Nagging away behind this narrative is the fearful anxiety that Dayus had set her own craving for respectability above the needs of others. Their need is constructed as dependent on her financial success, her independence, and, at face value, this is hard to deny: she had no support and had been denied the pittance that the parish might have offered. Nevertheless, the book, in part, reads like an inarticulate apology to them, struggling to find a voice beneath a narrative of self-justification.

In the intervening eight years, Dayus takes on a range of jobs purposely selected to teach her all the stages of the enameling process and the business end of running an operation. Relations with her own class, with employers, colleagues, and, eventually, employees usually run smoothly – and, when they do not, she never submits to humiliation or defeat. With employment for skilled workers, at the rate paid to women, being reasonably plentiful, she can simply walk out and find another job whenever she feels ill-treated, and, ultimately, her skills-base becomes sufficiently broad so that she can start her own business. She rents premises, buys equipment, and employs staff. Later, she rents a house with a garden, even buys a car. Steadfast, she does not suffer fools, but has enough experience of being a hired hand to know how to treat her employees with dignity: "[W]e'd been downtrodden, starving even, ourselves, and there was little chance that we would forget that in our dealings with our people" (*Life* 225). In wartime she is sympathetic to the effects of her workers' sleepless nights during air raids and is always the first to arrive and the last to leave. They even cook communally, each bringing something for the pot, which bubbles away as they work. Her employees effectively become her surrogate family.

If this is a narrative of escape, then, it is one that commits to the shared experience of thousands like her in working class Britain. She "escapes" only as far as Handsworth, keeping in touch with a few old friends, maintaining her distance from others. Winnie and Maggie reemerge, although Winnie, still impoverished, is forced to do a "midnight flit" and disappears, and Maggie dies, active and independent to the last. Writing as an old woman, Dayus has a large family of four children, twelve grandchildren, and ten great-grandchildren. She owns her own home and has married again. Her only regret (expressed at the end of *Where There's Life* and of *The Girl from Hockley*) is "the loss of those years half a century ago when my children needed a mother's love and care so much" (*Life* 241; *Hockley* 432). The irony is that, unwittingly, she has visited on her own offspring the very experience she wanted them most to avoid.

Ultimately, then, Dayus is not defeated by a bullying mother, desolate poverty, or by the humiliating operations of an inadequate welfare system. Unflinching hard work, in combination with the chaos of the war, restores her children to her. In the meantime, she relies on friendships and the support of her brother to keep her eye on the prize. It would be easy to read this as a straightforward "triumph over adversity" narrative in which the individualist spirit releases its heroine into a new and better life. Rather, it is a tale of compromise. The persistence with which Dayus returns to her childhood, carves out further memories, revisits the relationships with her mother, father, siblings, neighbors, and friends, suggests the anxieties of loss and guilt. In some ways, the book is an elegy for community spirit; in others, it unsentimentally depicts the material conditions inimical to human happiness. At the very least, it paints and repaints pictures of life from the Birmingham slums and ensures that those cultural memories, with all their ambiguities, are not erased.

NOTE

1. See Kate Fisher, *Birth Control, Marriage and Sex in Britain 1918–1960* (2006), on the prevalence of sexual ignorance in the early decades of the twentieth century despite the apparent availability of information and the existence of early Marie Stopes clinics from 1921 (37–54).

CHAPTER 22

"It Have a Kind of Communal Feeling with the Working Class and the Spades"
Sam Selvon, Tony Harrison, and "Colonization in Reverse"

Jack Windle

> What a devilment a Englan!
> Dem face war an brave de worse;
> But ah wonderin how dem gwine stan
> Colonizin in reverse.
>   – Bennett 17

Louise Bennet's 1966 poem "Colonization in Reverse" celebrates the postwar immigration that saw thousands of people from her native Jamaica and across the Caribbean "pack dem bag and baggage" and "tun history upside dung!" The dialect, humor, and critique of colonialism in Bennett's poem – and her assessment of the war as a catalyst for an epochal shift in the relationship between Britain and its former colonies – raise many of the themes central to this chapter and to British working class literature of the postwar era. The arrival of (post)colonial migrants in the working class inner cities of "de motherlan" heralded the beginning of a new chapter in the long and complex relationship between the British working class and their (post)colonial counterparts. This chapter aims to revisit and reclaim these interwoven histories through readings of Sam Selvon and Tony Harrison, two writers whose lives were shaped by the processes of postwar decolonization and whose work emerges from – and tackles directly – the legacy of British colonialism. These readings are contextualized through brief examinations of twentieth-century responses to immigration and racism in working class literature and of contemporary interdisciplinary and mainstream debates about racism and class in Britain. By historicizing their respective formations as working class writers and offering new readings of critically misrepresented elements of their work, the discussion aims to reposition Selvon as an important figure in the postwar history of British working class literature and to argue that Harrison is a working class writer whose work can be fully appreciated only with the aid of a postcolonial perspective. The discussion will suggest ways in which criticism of working class literature might productively engage with other critical discourses and, in doing so, resist the division and vilification of the working class in contemporary society.

The roots of the "communal feeling" that Selvon describes in his 1955 novel *The Lonely Londoners* run deep in British working class literature: many early working class writers were committed abolitionists, such as the file cutter and radical balladeer Joseph Mather and the domestic servant and poet Susannah Pearson (both active in the 1790s; Basker, *Amazing Grace* 412–14). The most important and influential text of British working class literature in the twentieth century, Robert Tressell's *The Ragged Trousered Philanthropists* (1914; unabridged 1955), describes and attacks the way in which the right-wing press – then, as now, owned and controlled by powerful vested interests – sought to provoke working class racism as a means of distracting the public from the hypocrisy and greed of its paymasters and political allies:

> The papers they read were full of vague and alarming accounts of the quantities of foreign merchandise imported into this country. The enormous number of aliens constantly arriving, and their destitute conditions, how they lived, the crimes they committed, and the injury they did to British trade. These were the seeds which, cunningly sown in their minds, caused to grow up within them a bitter and undiscriminating hatred of foreigners. (15)

Although this is a depressingly familiar dynamic in our own time, the hero of Tressell's novel responds by channeling the internationalism of the working class tradition, suggesting that his racist colleagues call a meeting and pass a resolution criticizing "the action of the Supreme Being in having created so many foreigners" (16).

This kind of debunking satirical riposte is characteristic, too, of postwar responses to immigration and racism by working class writers. Shelagh Delaney, whose *A Taste of Honey* (1958) was described by Colin MacInnes as the first play to portray black and gay characters "without a nudge or shudder," deftly deflates the racist anxieties of one of her central characters and challenges exclusive notions of British identity by having the unnamed black sailor come from Cardiff (205). In *A Kind of Loving* (1960), Stan Barstow's narrator Vic reacts to his mother-in-law saying of immigrants that she would "pack the lot off home" by telling the reader that "she could hardly open her mouth without showing everybody what a stupid, bigoted, ignorant old cow she is" (222–3). Alan Sillitoe makes a soldier from the Gold Coast (present-day Ghana) the only character whose speech is rendered in Standard English in *Saturday Night and Sunday Morning* (1958) in order to invert and critique racist assumptions and use a figure from outside the rigid hierarchy of the British class system to highlight the ignorant small-mindedness of some of his characters (191–9). These episodes – and many more besides – demonstrate that working class writers in the 1950s and 1960s were able and eager to react to their rapidly changing society and that they consistently did so in a progressive manner.

The importance of acknowledging and celebrating this internationalist heritage is all the more urgent when it is increasingly in danger of being marginalized and overwritten in the present day. As Stephen Garner points out, recent "academic and journalistic practice has been to characterise working-class communities either as the sole source of racism, or as the most stubbornly racist section of an increasingly tolerant society" (55). Beverly Skeggs argues that this phenomenon is part of a wider trend in Britain whereby the "white working class" is being repositioned as a kind of "constitutive outsider 'at home'" along the lines of the racialized "other" of the colonial past (26). As the BBC's "White Season" and recent political discourse has shown, the racialization of class has penetrated mainstream discourse to an alarming degree (Martin, "BBC"; Mason, "Liz Kendall"). This worrying trend obscures the internationalist working class tradition and effaces the important history of what Paul Gilroy calls "demotic multiculturalism" or the "ordinary multiculture of the postcolonial metropolis" (99, 124). Taking a cue from these developments in sociology and social theory, it is important to ensure that critical practice in the study of working class literature is not complicit in the cynical racialization of the working class by the establishment and its outriders. With this in mind, these texts can become useful resources for resistance to attempts to divide and demonize the working class and help to advance an alternative narrative and seek a more nuanced and sophisticated understanding of the complexly interwoven histories of class and racism in Britain.

It is testament to the prescient power of Tony Harrison's work that these contemporary cultural and critical contexts are anticipated in the first poem of his sequence of sixteen-line sonnets, *From the School of Eloquence*. The sequence takes its title from a ticket used as a "cover" for the London Corresponding Society – an early movement for working class representation – and Harrison uses the passage about its prohibition from E. P. Thompson's classic study *The Making of the English Working Class* (1963) as an epigraph. The opening poem, "On Not Being Milton," is dedicated to Sergio Vieira and Armando Guebuza – poet founder-members of the Mozambican liberation movement Frelimo – and Harrison calls his chosen verse form both his *"Cahier d'un retour au pays natal,"* after Aimé Césaire's founding text of the *Négritude* movement, and his "growing black enough to fit [his] boots" (112). The phrase, characteristically, is packed with multiple meanings: Harrison shows admiration for the poets of black emancipation and declares his intention to honor the British mining tradition of radical independence and internationalism, at once recalling the line "Damn it man, aren't we all black down that pit!" from the Paul Robeson film *The Proud Valley* (1940) and the custom of miners passing on their pit boots to their children. As Lee Jenkins suggests, in "On Not Being Milton," Harrison plays on the idea of "corresponding societies" set up by his epigram: there is "a correspondence between working class and black – for Harrison, 'growing black' is a way of recovering his 'roots'" (74). The poem closes with the lines:

> Articulation is the tongue-tied's fighting.
> In the silence round all poetry we quote
> Tidd the Cato Street conspirator who wrote:
>
> *Sir, I Ham a very Bad Hand at Righting.*
>
> (112)

The two lines bolted on to the conventional fourteen of the most canonical poetic form invoke the long and related histories of nonracial working class struggle and the fight for education and literacy. Tidd was hanged along with the African-Caribbean radical William Davidson and three others after having been drawn by an *agent provocateur* into a plot to assassinate the Cabinet in 1820. Along with the "nomination of blackness" in the allusion to Ham (son of Noah and "supposed progenitor of the world's black races"), this embeds the radical, internationalist working class tradition into the basis from which *From the School of Eloquence* develops (Jenkins, "On Not Being" 76).[1]

The formative early years of Harrison's poetic career provide insights into how he came to see working class and colonial history as so inextricably bound up. In 1962 Harrison left doctoral study in England to take up a position at the recently founded Ahmadu Bello University in northern Nigeria, where he collaborated with the Irish poet James Simmons on *Aikin Mata*, a play written for a Nigerian company tackling the ethnic and cultural divisions that would soon erupt into the Biafran (or Nigerian Civil) War (Nicholson 65). Asked by John Haffenden what he had learned from working in Nigeria, Harrison said that he "found the drama of [his] own education dramatically posed in black and white: people coming from illiterate backgrounds and reading about Wordsworth's daffodils . . . when they didn't know what a fucking daffodil was" (Astley 236). The Nigerian education system echoed the way Harrison had been bullied and browbeaten for his working class background at school and similarly foisted upon students a narrow conception of culture that bore little, if any, relevance to their own lives. Harrison's reaction was to introduce African literature courses, and, when he returned to England in 1967, he took with him a "collection of the literature of colonialism and ideas for a study of the subject," along with a deeper understanding of the relationship between "external and internal colonialism" and the experience of living through decolonization and the early years of independence (fully declared in 1963; Astley 19–20, 236). The dramatic reappropriation of agency and history that Harrison witnessed and took part in – and the resonance of his experience as a working class "scholarship boy" with the outdated imperialist education system in Nigeria – inspired his vision of "corresponding societies" and fueled the "communal feeling" so integral to "On Not Being Milton."

The reason for Harrison's deracinating and deeply ambivalent experience as a "scholarship boy" was the 1944 Education Act, which paved the way for many academically able working class students to attend grammar schools and universities for the first time. The increased literacy and social mobility the Act brought about were largely responsible for the boom in representations of working class life in the middle of the twentieth century, indeed David Lodge has described its effect as "a seismic shift in the English literary landscape" (3). Then, in 1948, the British Nationality Act extended to "British subjects" – whom it re-categorized as "Citizens of the United Kingdom and Colonies" – an invitation to move to the "Mother Country" and aid its postwar recovery. These two pieces of legislation passed on either side of a period that saw the end of the Second World War and British rule in India as well as the foundation of the National Health Service and the modern Welfare State, together placed the working class and citizens of the (former) empire at the center of British society's reconstruction. While the first Act set Harrison on a trajectory that would ultimately lead him to "occupy" poetry and wend his way from working class Leeds to the New York Metropolitan Opera, via Nigeria at the historical moment of decolonization, the second opened the way for Sam Selvon to set sail for England in 1950 (Harrison 123).

Selvon was born in Trinidad in 1923 and brought up in San Fernando, near the cane plantations and oilfields that were the twin pillars of its economy and the primary employers of the descendants of Indians and Africans respectively. Selvon's formal education ended at the age of 15 "because things were brown and [he] had to hustle a work" (Selvon qtd. in Nasta and Rutherford 76). He joined the Trinidad Royal Navy Volunteers during the war before moving to the outskirts of the capital, Port of Spain, and starting work as a writer. Selvon sailed to England on the same boat as his friend George Lamming, who describes him as an "essentially peasant" writer:

> That's a great difference between the West Indian novelist and his contemporary in England. For peasants simply don't respond and see like middle-class people. The peasant tongue has its own rhythms which are Selvon's and [Vic] Reid's rhythms; and no artifice of technique, no sophisticated gimmicks . . . can achieve the specific taste and sound of Selvon's prose. (45)

Lamming's formulation tellingly equates "West Indian" with "peasant" and "England" with "middle-class" and, in doing so, obscures the striking similarities between the work of Selvon and some of his British working class contemporaries, many of whom were either beneficiaries of the 1944 Education Act or emboldened by the opportunities it opened up for working class voices. In almost all of Selvon's prose about Trinidad, his skill for representing dialect is confined entirely to the dialogue; in his London-based work and a couple of transitional stories in *Ways of Sunlight*, this distinction breaks down and the narrative voice, too, takes on the cadences and the "taste and sound" of Trinidadian and Caribbean English. Selvon's use of dialect for the narrative voice "obliterate[d] the (class) difference between the narrator and fictional character" and was such an important development in the early 1950s that E. A. Markham labeled this radically experimental period "The Selvon Phase" in the history of the Caribbean short story (xxi–xxii).

Selvon's achievement in inscribing the "peasant tongue" in the novel builds on earlier experiments with "nation language" and the Trinidadian tradition of working class writing in the kind of "yard" literature of which C. L. R. James's 1929 story "Triumph" is a prime example (Markham xxii, 108–25). At the same time in Britain, Alan Sillitoe was building on the foundations laid by Walter Greenwood in *Love on the Dole* (1933) – where dialect speakers deliver the decisive dialogue – by similarly bringing working class dialect into his narration (Windle 41–2). The parallels between Selvon and Sillitoe are remarkable: both left school as young teenagers with no qualifications, both were wireless operators during the Second World War, and both had a strong writerly vocation from an early age. Both also brought a working class perspective to the era of decolonization following the Second World War: Into the very fabric of their groundbreaking works of the 1950s – *The Lonely Londoners* (1956), *Ways of Sunlight* (1957), *Saturday Night and Sunday Morning* (1958), and *The Loneliness of the Long Distance Runner* (1959) – are woven the threads of their respective oral cultures and the rapid shifts from rural to urban ways of life that characterize working class and immigrant experience. From completely separate traditions of working class literature, they arrived at the same point in terms of their intentions to make the novel speak – and speak in – the language of working class people. Far from there being a "great difference" between Selvon and some of his English contemporaries, the breaking down of the distinction between Standard English and dialect – and the literary representation of those historically marginalized in and by literature – are accomplishments they hold in common.

Lamming's diagnosis of "difference," though, set the tone for much more recent criticism of Selvon's work; rather than highlighting the extraordinary similarities between immigrant and working class writers, critics have instead echoed the divisive rhetoric of difference that characterizes wider contemporary debate. In his study of Britain's postcolonial populations, *Mongrel Nation* (2007), Ashley Dawson argues that "in contrast with the relentlessly misogynistic writing of the so-called Angry Young Men, Selvon . . . prepares the ground for a critique of black men's complicity with structures of patriarchal subordination in Britain and its colonies" (31). By way of negative comparison, Dawson seeks to differentiate between Selvon and his British contemporaries and, oddly, to argue that Selvon's treatment of gender was somehow ahead of its time. Selvon may have "prepared the ground," but he did not pursue this critique himself; indeed he was physically attacked by a Guianese feminist at a conference on Caribbean writing in London in 1986 for what she perceived to be his misogynistic portrayal of black women (Nasta and Rutherford 128–9). Dawson also misrepresents the Angry Young Men: the working class writers to whom this label is applied are certainly not "relentlessly misogynistic" but, rather, wrestle with the same suffocating social expectation of early marriage that is a recurring theme of Selvon's Trinidadian fiction (e.g., "Wartime Activities" in Selvon, *Ways* 72–83). Selvon, Harrison, and the Angry Young Men all emerge from a pre-feminist consciousness, and it is unhelpful anachronistically to read back into their work the critical orthodoxies of our own time.[2] The treatment of the changing nature of relations between the sexes is, rather, another site of convergence between Selvon's work and that of his contemporary working class novelists.[3]

Dawson also overemphasizes difference by framing his discussion of *The Lonely Londoners* with an account of the racist Notting Hill riots, which occurred two years after the novel's publication (27–30). Dawson rightly points out that Selvon depicts "the impact not only of racism in housing and the workplace but of racial fetishism in the sexual arena"; however he does not examine how this is bound up with issues of class (30). In the stream-of-consciousness summer section of the novel, the narrative voice says that "the cruder you are the more the girls like you . . . they want you to live up to the films and stories they hear about black people living primitive in the jungles of the world" and that Moses is paid to attend an exclusive party in Knightsbridge because "the high and the mighty . . . can't get big thrills unless they have a black man in the company" (100–101). In connecting the "films and stories" with the way Moses is treated, Selvon demonstrates his awareness of how racist ideology is transmitted through the commercialized culture of cinema and establishment-backed literature; in depicting landlords, employers, and wealthy thrill-seekers as racists, he also suggests that racism and the dynamics of class and power are thoroughly intertwined. Nowhere is this more forcefully conveyed than in Selvon's depiction of the British media. At the beginning of the novel, Moses goes to Waterloo to meet Galahad from the boat-train, and two encounters with journalists ensue before they leave.[4] First, a journalist approaches Moses and asks, "tell me, sir, why are so many Jamaicans immigrating to England?" (7). Moses's native Trinidad "is a thousand miles from Jamaica," and, in exasperation, he lies and says he is Jamaican, complains briefly about the hardship facing immigrants and then is overcome by "the infant feel that he get" and abruptly hurries away (7). Then, when his newly arrived aunt is approached by another reporter, his friend Tolroy intervenes to "growl" at her, "'Don't tell that man nothing'" (10). Although the reporters are ignorant about the Caribbean, it is not immediately clear why Moses and Tolroy are so distrustful of them. Once they are back at his basement room, though, Moses tells Galahad that "every shipload [of immigrants] is big news, and the English people don't like the boys coming to England to work and live" because "they frighten that we get job in front of them, though that does never happen" (20). Galahad, having formed his own view through his experiences as a Londoner, revisits the subject later in the novel and makes explicit what Moses earlier implied: that it "is the impression [made] on the English people [by] the papers always talking about fellars coming up here to work and creating problem" (129). The fragmentary treatment of the media adds up to a recapitulation of the message Tressell conveyed forty years previously; Dawson's critique ignores the fact that Moses and "the boys" understand that the press is responsible for stirring up racist sentiment and concludes that, for Selvon, "discourses of difference apparently seemed insuperable during the 1950s" (43).

Dawson's downbeat assessment of Selvon's attitudes toward difference overlooks the fact that there is also space in *The Lonely Londoners* for a countervailing narrative of class solidarity. Early on the narrator captures the ambivalence of life on the dole, describing the Ministry of Labour as a place "where hate and disgust and avarice and malice and sympathy and sorrow all mix up [and] everyone is your friend and your enemy" (27). Later, the narrative voice highlights a truth that is largely overlooked in contemporary debates about class and racism: that the working class was the author and originator of modern multiculturalism in Britain because postwar immigration was almost exclusively into working class areas. The narrator comments:

> The place where Tolroy and the family living was off the Harrow Road, and the people in that area called the Working Class. Wherever in London that it have Working Class, there you will find a lot of spades. This is the real world, where men know what it is to hustle a pound to pay the rent when Friday come. (59)

As well as living side by side in the "real world" of London's working class neighborhoods, Moses and his friends align themselves with the working class at the ballot box: Galahad says West Indians "had better chances when the Socialists was in power," and Moses replies, "I always go and put my X [and] I always canvassing for Labour when is elections" (129). Moses resents middle class students from the Caribbean who "have their bread buttered from home" and says of an acquaintance who "plays ladeda" by speaking in Received Pronunciation and adopting the accessories of an archetypal British bourgeois ("bowler and umbrella, and briefcase tuck under the arm, with *The Times* fold up in the pocket so the name would show"), "I suspect Harris, you know... I have a mind he is a Tory at heart" (103–4, 129–30). The clear implication is that Harris's allegiance to the party of the rich would be a betrayal of his fellow immigrants and of the working class, with whom the new arrivals live day by day and share a position on the margins of British society.

The sense of solidarity that Moses describes is fostered by the kind of working class life that the narrator evocatively sketches, detailing how the tightly packed terraced houses are so old that many "still had gas light" and how "little children playing in the road, because they ain't have no other place" (59–60). This description segues into a contemplation of how class works: "The rich people who does live in Belgravia and Knightsbridge [and] them other plush places [would] never believe what it like in grim place like Harrow Road or Notting Hill" (60). The inequality and lack of empathy across class boundaries are sharply contrasted to the solidarity and fellow-feeling within working class communities:

> It have a kind of communal feeling with the Working Class and the spades, because when you poor things does level out, it don't have much up and down. A lot of men get kill in the war and leave widow behind, and it have bags of these old geezers who does be pottering about the Harrow Road like if they lost, a look in their eye as if the war happen unexpected and they still can't realise what happen to the old Brit'n. (61)

The passage also points toward the epochal significance of the war and its lasting impact in terms of a collective experience of trauma and cultural and social change. This acknowledgment of the difficulty, particularly for the older generation, of adapting to a radically transforming world is a site of convergence with Harrison's work, especially his treatment of his father in the "Next Door" sequence of *From the School of Eloquence* and a late passage of *v.*, his 1984 poem written during the Miners' Strike. A later poem in *From the School of Eloquence* conveys the significance of decolonization and the end of the war to this phase in Harrison's oeuvre. "Old Soldiers" uses the CAMP coffee label – an icon of wartime branding that included a recursive image of a Sikh "chuprassy" serving a colonial officer – to articulate the centrality of Empire to the British collective consciousness forged through its long and much-mythologized past (159). On "the label in the label in the label," through "all infinity and down to almost zero," the faithful Sikh servant and "the breakfasting Scots hero" represent the perceived permanence and unshakable natural order of British superiority. The poem ends:

> But since those two high summer days
> The US dropped the World's first A-bombs on,
> From that child's forever what returns to my gaze
> Is a last chuprassy with all essence gone. (159)

The outdated prewar certainties represented by the infinitely repeating image on the label are shattered by the war and the A-bombs that so brutally brought it to an end. As with so many elements of *From the School of Eloquence*, this reflects back on earlier passages: in the "Next Door" sequence, this history of imperialist indoctrination haunts Harrison senior's reaction to his changing community. The first of the four sonnets goes back to Harrison's childhood, when his neighbor, Ethel Jowett, "gave [his] library its auspicious start" with a gift of *The Kipling Treasury* for "being her 'male escort'" to a light opera (129). Jowett's conservative cultural tastes and outdated moral fastidiousness make her representative of the "respectable" working class of the prewar years and her gift to the young Harrison, a book by the man George Orwell called "the prophet of British imperialism in its expansionist phase," evokes the ubiquity of Empire ideology in the first half of the twentieth century (*Essays* 186).⁵ The deaths of Harrison's mother and their neighbor leave his father isolated and anxious about the passing of the "old lot" and his rapidly changing area: "*It won't be long before Ah'm t'only white!*" (129). In the second poem, the unambiguously Anglo-Saxon Sharpes move in, and disturbing domestic violence signals social disintegration. In the third, Harrison worries from afar about his father falling in cold weather – "our street one skidding slide of ice" – and gives voice to his father's attempt to understand why the newcomers do not clear the snow from the sidewalk in front of their houses:

> You *try* to understand: *Their sort don't know.*
> *They're from the sun. But wait till they're old men.*
> (131)

It is in the fourth and final poem of the "Next Door" sequence, though, that there are clear echoes of Harrison's radical reimagining of working class history from "On Not Being Milton." His father bemoans the fact that "*turbans*" have replaced "*flat caps*" and that traditional pork-based working class foodstuffs are no longer available "*if it's a Moslem owns t'new shop*": "*t' Off Licence, that's gone Paki in t'same way . . . Ah can't get over it*" (132). In the third stanza, Harrison senior complains that "[n]*ext door but one*" there is "*some sort o' sweatshop*" with sewing machines going "*hell for leather all day long*" to produce "*them dresses . . . them . . . sarongs*" (132). The four lines that close the poem combine Harrison's unsentimental acknowledgment of the changing face of his community with his father's nostalgia and insecurity:

> Last of the 'old lot' still left on your block.
> Those times, they're gone. The 'old lot' can't come back.
>
> Both doors I notice now you double lock–
> he's already in your shoes, your next-door black.   (132)

Luke Spencer argues that Harrison fundamentally acquiesces in his father's fear and suspicion of "otherness," writing that this conclusion is "worryingly noncommittal" and that "the reading most forcefully suggested by the poem" is "that of black people as a collective threat, even if the 'next-door black' is himself threatened by the changes that are taking place" (81). There is another reading of this poem more in keeping with the work of someone inspired by the poets of black emancipation and firsthand experience of the dynamics of class and colonialism. Recalling the CAMP coffee label in "Old Soldiers," Harrison constructs his own poetic recursive image, with the "sweatshop" of the third stanza recalling the Luddite handloom weavers so integral to the opening poems of *From the School of Eloquence* and the history of working class radicalism the title invokes. This echo raises the new and complex ways in which postwar immigrants inherit, inhabit, and transform the long-established working class traditions of British inner cities. Harrison is able to empathize with his father's sense of insecurity and isolation but deploys double meaning to turn the final line into a radical assertion of commonality. As is so often the case in *From the School of Eloquence*, the line recalls an earlier one – the already quoted "growing black enough to fit my boots" of "On Not Being Milton" – and, in doing so, suggests that the "next-door black" is already uprooted from their past in the same way as Harrison's father. The message here, one that is repeatedly suggested throughout the sequence, is that capitalism strips people of agency and places them at the mercy of uncontrollable market forces. The "next-door black" experiences this as the necessity to migrate for work, while the "old lot" in working class Leeds see the decline and disappearance of long-established industries and the traditions and communities they sustained. Harrison sees their positions as two sides of the same coin: They are all in the same shoes.

Spencer makes a similar argument about race and racism in *v.*, in which Harrison's poetic voice is angered by graffiti – some of it viciously racist and some of it purely soccer-focused – daubed on gravestones in a Leeds cemetery, including that of his parents. Reworking Thomas Gray's *Elegy Written in a Country Churchyard* (1751), the first 160 lines ponder the adversarial nature of history through a discussion of its "versuses" in heroic quatrains and attempt to attach greater significance to the graffiti by making "the thoughtless spraying of his team / apply to higher things, and to the nation" (240). A skinhead – who turns out to be Harrison's "*alter ego*" (248) – wielding a spray can then interjects with a brutal stream of invective, lambasting Harrison's high-minded liberal response, saying that "*poet*" is "*a crude four-letter word*" and telling Harrison not to treat him like he is "*dumb*" (242). Spencer says this "is a scorching indictment of well-meaning ineffectuality; but, like the position of Harrison himself, it is uncomfortably problematical. For the skinhead is shown not as a lumpen-proletarian racist but as a tough-minded class warrior" (95). Following a prolonged exchange that dramatizes the fraught relationship between Harrison's strained class allegiance and his acquired liberal values, he leaves the graveyard and, on his way to the station, returns to the theme, addressed already in the "Next

Door" sonnets, of how immigration changes working class areas. Harrison recounts his father's "fear / of foreign food and faces" and how he had felt "squeezed by the unfamiliar"; "growing frailer," he had to undertake "longer tiring treks" to find familiar food in shops where "check-out girls [were] too harassed / to smile or swap a joke":

> But when he bought his cigs he'd have a chat,
> his week's one conversation, truth to tell,
> but time also came and put a stop to that
> when old Wattsy got bought out by M. Patel.
> (246–7)

Spencer argues that the final line suggests "ruthless commercial and cultural aggrandisement" that might make readers question Harrison's "fairness" (96), when, in fact, the following line reveals – by quoting "Our God, Our Help in Ages Past" – that Wattsy is both the old local shopkeeper and Isaac Watts, the father of English hymnody. Harrison goes on to rhyme "local souls" with the "cut-price toilet rolls" that are for sale from the pews of old "Methodist and C of E" churches now turned into cash-and-carries (247), making the passage an elaborate, bittersweet joke about the disappearance of religion as a source of working class organization and tradition. The crux of Spencer's argument is "that Harrison, having silenced the skinhead's racism, might allow it back into the poem by underwriting his father's attitudes" (96). In fact, the "skinhead's racism" is not "silenced" because it does not exist: Nowhere in the 58 lines that the skinhead "speaks" are there any racist sentiments expressed and his spray can only adds "a middle slit to one daubed V" and signs "the UNITED where [Harrison's] mam and dad were buried" with the poet's own name (244). While his father is preoccupied by the disappearance of familiar white faces, Harrison's younger alter ego shows the real tragedy when he wonders what occupation will go on his generation's headstones:

> what'll t'mason carve up for their jobs?
> The cunts who lieth 'ere wor unemployed?
> (242)

The pride in work of his forebears has been replaced by chronic unemployment and social disintegration in Thatcher's Britain. The racist graffiti is a shocking symptom of social and economic tragedy and of centuries of colonial ideology. Harrison senior's attitudes are a product of the same troubling history that Harrison certainly does not condone or "underwrite": indeed, in "Clearing II," he seeks reconciliation by asking his dead father to "[b]less this house's new black owners" (145).

The American Labor historian Theodore W. Allen "emphasized the centrality of the fight against white supremacy to struggles for democracy, progress and socialism" and urged white people to whom these ideals were important to "resign from the white race": Harrison prefigured exactly this when he described his exploration of working class history as "growing black enough to fit [his] boots"; Selvon asserted his Creole identity over his Indian roots and passionately believed that "a mixing of traditions makes for a more harmonious world" (Perry, "Theodore W. Allen"; Selvon qtd. in Nasta 70). Selvon and Harrison radically envision a world beyond "race thinking" and enact a "colonization in reverse" of the imperialist British culture whose fragmentation was such a defining element of the postwar era. In the texts examined here, they are centrally concerned with the changes wrought in British society by decolonization and immigration; and their lucid, balanced, and nuanced representations of the rapid diversification of Britain's working class are vital contributions to the literature of the period. In grasping the thorny subject of racism, they seek thoroughly to historicize and understand it, and their integrity in this endeavor provides invaluable insights into attitudes and dynamics that can be difficult to reach through the clamor of contemporary discourse. Having felt firsthand or witnessed up close the complex, age-old forces that prop up Britain's class system and continue to discriminate against immigrants and the poor, Harrison and Selvon write against such forces with compassion, commitment, and wit. In doing so they uphold a long tradition in British working class literature that demands a criticism which celebrates "communal feeling," rather than being complicit in the divisive racialization of the working class.

NOTES

1. Jenkins asserts that Harrison does not "intend us to read" Ham in this way (76), but the biblical figure is used precisely in this way in the earlier short poem "Voortrekker" (Harrison 101).
2. As Edith Hall points out, "Harrison has come in for a good deal of criticism . . . for the way that his poetry talks about women," although in his later poetry his appeal to a "universal human corporeality" through coprology is "neither sexed" nor "gendered" (104–5).
3. There is also a Jamaican landlord there "hustling tenants" whom he exploits because "[w]hen it come to making money, it ain't have anything like 'ease me up' or 'both of we is countrymen together' in the old London" (6). This signals

the emphasis on class over national allegiance that is a prominent feature of the text.
4. In "Come Back to Grenada," a short story written for the *Caribbean Voices* BBC radio series in which Selvon rehearses sections of *The Lonely Londoners*, the narrator says that "all the newspapers writing about how these West Indians coming and like nothing could stop them, and how the Government best hads do something or else plenty trouble would cause in London" (Selvon 174).
5. Orwell's friend and contemporary, the working class writer Jack Hilton, pithily describes his education in Rochdale as "1st: Heaps of God; 2nd: England first – the world nowhere; 3rd: Blatant swagger; one good honest Christian blue-eyed English schoolboy equalled twenty infidel Japs" – note again the debunking response to bigotry (6).

CHAPTER 23

Clannish Confines
The Folk, the Proletariat, and the People in Modern Scottish Literature

Corey Gibson

The title of this chapter derives from a song-poem, or "ballad pastiche," by the poet and folk revivalist Hamish Henderson (1919–2002). Titled "Glasclune and Drumlochy," its speaker describes an elevated view of the Lornty burn (stream) "that marked the clannish confine" (*Poems* 139–40): the border between the eponymous historical estates whose blood-feud was, according to Henderson, part of the local lore of his early childhood in Blairgowrie and Glenshee. In the stanzas that follow, the enmity between these families is described in language that variously flits between the aristocratic detachment of the ballad register ("There were two castles, / two battled keeps"), and the playful vernacular of a skipping rhyme ("the dowdy, duddy Lornty"). Glasclune's eventual victory is attributed to his use of the cannon: a breaking with traditional methods that invites disgrace in the eyes of "ceevilised folk." In the closing lines, Henderson provokes a sudden and quite startling shift in perspective. In the present inhabited by the poetic voice, all that is left of this historical blood-feud is "Twa herts on ae shiv / An' a shitten larach" (Two hearts on one blade, and a contemptible ruin) (*Poems* 139–40). In his notes, Henderson suggests that this might be understood as a monument to the "millennial internecine conflict of human kind." Its national dimension, expressed in its form and language, is further affirmed as these "confines" are said to lie in "jagged outline" across Scottish history (*Poems* 163). This local model of the universal – the common inhumanity that is our historical inheritance – is perpetuated, if not caused, by "clannish confines." These arbitrary lines of exclusion (and inclusion) can only be reimagined and reaffirmed; they seem always to resist resolution.

In a chapter on working class writers and representations of the working class in modern Scottish literature, the relevance of this turn of phrase, "clannish confines," and its source, is twofold. First, this effort to reconcile the local with the universal through the intermediary of the *national* speaks directly to a well-established strain of literary experimentation in Scotland founded in the 1920s. Second, it appeals to a conception of history as conflict. In this case, the clash is between landed families, one representing tradition and the other progress. It is a familiar dialectic, and one that acknowledges the conflict along "clan" lines as one capable of taking on the symbolic burden of universal transhistorical suffering. If history is to see any kind of advancement of the class interests of the unpropertied, the implication reads, we must break with the false consciousness that allows for such "inter-clan" violence. In other words, class conflict is the only permissible kind. Through its form – its lexicon and its prosody, in particular – "Glasclune and Drumlochy" appeals to a common *oral* culture that is, or might be supposed to be, protected from the mediation of a singular "artist" or the condescension of an editor. It speaks with the immediacy and intimacy of a children's rhyme and with the timeless authority of Scotland's own "lays," the ballads. As a product of the postwar Scottish folk revival, and a particular effort to graft that movement to the perceived cultural political achievements of the modernist "renaissance," this poem was conceived in conjunction with a radical national tradition that put great store in the culture of "the people."

This chapter will describe the relationship between working class identity and national identity in modern Scottish writing. It will scrutinize both the elisions that have been allowed to proliferate in representing this relationship, and the tensions and contradictions that are innate to it. Class is a designation that cuts across national boundaries and historical epochs, but it is lived, and carries its cultural signifiers, more locally, and more transiently. In his conception of world-systems theory, Immanuel Wallerstein elaborates on this nexus, insisting that "class" and "nation" are "two sets of clothing for the same basic reality": the former is global and economic, the latter is local, social, and most importantly, it is the setting and context for both "class consciousness" and "ethno-national" consciousness – states of being which can, though perhaps ought not to, overlap (Wallerstein 224–5; McCrone 56). The nation state, though born out of class conflict, is, therefore, at once too narrow and too broad a conception to be neatly reconcilable with lived working class experience. Nevertheless, since the interwar Scottish literary renaissance, the nation's literary traditions have been periodically characterized, by authors and critics alike, as distinctly *democratic* as compared to the English literary canon (see Lindsay; Wittig; Watson, *Poetry*; Crawford, *Scotland's Books*). This conception is perpetuated, as one might expect, by its notional appeal, the anecdotal evidence proffered by Burns's symbolic onus, and by confirmation bias. But it also rests on discrete models of authorship – and on prescribed notions of the relationship between artist and society. In recent years critics have come to interrogate the ways in which these claims to exceptionalism in the Scottish literary tradition have developed over time (see Bell, *Questioning*; Hames, *Unstated*; and Thomson, "'You Can't'").

This conception of the nation's literary heritage was, especially between the 1920s and 1960s, inspired and sustained by an effort among some writers to synthesize residual forms of romantic nationalism with emergent notions of socialist internationalism. After this period, this tension was variously compounded, broken down, or ironized by writers, if not completely circumvented. Meanwhile critics sought out ever more sophisticated articulations of the same dynamic, to absorb and account for shifting literary landscapes. The shape and direction of this development might be most concisely expressed using some predominant constructions for the "collective" *of* whom, *for* whom, or (at the very least) *from* among whom, the author speaks. From the "folk" and the "proletariat," which reach out respectively from the romantic and socialist traditions, to more nebulous conceptions such as "the people," and finally, to disaggregated "people" themselves (freed from the definite article), these constructs provide us with a useful shorthand for the development of literary intersections between nation and class.

Scottish Culture, Working Class Culture, and Folk Culture

In his contribution to Scott Hames's edited collection *Unstated: Writers on Scottish Independence* (2012), James Kelman explains:

> Being 'too indigenous' is the same as being 'too working class' and, predictably, the closer we move to the realm of class the clearer we find concerns of race and ethnicity.... The key is class. 'Scottishness' equates to class and class equals conflict. Even within Scotland we can be criticised for this. The work of writers deemed 'too Scottish' shares a class background. (119)

If class allegiance can be glossed over with the potent proxy of national belonging, it can be readily dismissed insofar as it challenges cosmopolitan bourgeois norms. The writer designated as such must be guilty of perpetuating "clannish confines" incommensurable with progressive politics in a globalized world, languishing as they do within outmoded, exclusionary group identities. Kelman rejects this posture without denying the existence of strategic elisions between nation and class; rather, he provides an explanation. The degree of explicit or implicit national belonging in literary expression is significant insofar as it can be explained by class conflict.

In his work on the Scottish industrial novel, Manfred Malzahn has described the importance of class in Scottish self-perception: due to "anglicised urban middle-class counterparts," any assertion of working class identity in Scotland is, he claims, "likely to appear also as the assertion of a Scottish identity"(230). But this account – of impressions given by writers and interpretations applied to their work – also leads to more complex anxieties about affectation and competing claims to authenticity. It has become a critical commonplace in Scottish literary studies since the 1980s that the dominance of unitary cultural "types" must be resisted: the mythopoeia of Red Clydeside radicalism as well as Kailyard sentimentalism should be scrutinized. Nevertheless, this insistence on criticism over myth does not go so far as to address the long-overwrought "predicament of the Scottish writer" (from the subtitle of Edwin Muir's 1936 study *Scott and Scotland*), that is, the question of what, if anything, is particular about the national designation, and the problem of how this singularity might be fully realized, or reaffirmed, in lieu of modernity. In other words, efforts to deploy the national framework yet resist essentialism cannot help but maintain what Christopher Whyte has identified as a persistent tautology: "What matters is not whether Scottish society is indeed democratic and egalitarian, but rather that a sufficient number of Scottish people should, even delusively, have believed this was the case, for a sufficient length of time"(11–14). Both the Kailyard and Red Clydeside are, as contested sites of "cultural heritage," characterized by a robust communitarian strain: one mythologizing spaces either beyond or on the outer reaches of industrialization, and the other among the urban working class on whose labor it was built. However, acknowledging the fecundity of these sites for mythmaking does not banish the emergent myths. Similarly, reaffirming our sense of the *national* literary tradition by insisting on its pluralism or hybridity does not help us transcend, or otherwise overcome, the problem posed by the "nation." It constitutes only a deferral.

Anxiety around the deficiencies of class and/or national identity in the late twentieth and early twenty-first centuries did not emerge uniformly from modern Scottish literary history. Certainly, writers have not always been averse to tackling the national "predicament" – though critics have carried the mantle in recent decades – and neither have they been shy, historically, of writing the working class into an undifferentiated mass. As his career advanced, Hugh MacDiarmid (1892–1978) positioned himself more visibly between the twin poles of Scottish nationalism and socialist internationalism. However, among his earliest editorials evangelizing on behalf of the ascendant literary renaissance, these principles were expressed purely in terms of creative and critical practice. Concentrated by a commitment to *Scottish* and *European* cultural contexts, and a calculated resistance to what he later terms the "English Ascendancy in British Literature,"[1] the inaugural issue of his *Scottish Chapbook* described in its editorial, "A New Movement in Scottish Literature." In its conclusion, MacDiarmid poses an imagined "mythical personage" of the typical Scotsman, only to have it immediately confounded by a painter-friend who, working to the same rubric, sketches

> a Glasgow 'keelie,'[2] a Polish pitman from Lanarkshire, a Dundee Irishman, an anarchist orator of a kind frequently seen at the Mound Edinburgh on Sunday nights, a Perthshire farmer, a Hebridean islander, and a Berwickshire bondager. (MacDiarmid, *Prose* 7)

MacDiarmid confirmed the need for a *new* literature that might not exclude these figures in favor of the dominie, the minister, and the "lad o' pairts" so familiar to the Kailyard. However, having insisted on this gesture toward another substantially gendered, but otherwise relatively diverse, cast of the "typical," MacDiarmid returns to a kind of solidarity that might easily be mistaken for coalescence. Difference or diversity is not the operative value, but underlying unity:

> The result was that each of these acutely differentiated faces acquired a peculiar unplaceable resemblance – an elusive likeness that had in each case a faintly ennobling air. A like task confronts Scottish writers today. I believe that forces are now discernable in Scottish life and literature which will have a similar unifying and uplifting effect. (MacDiarmid, *Prose* 8)

At this stage in his thought, containing the far-reaching political-philosophical precepts of romantic nationalism and internationalist socialism in such plain (if vague), faux-naïve terms, MacDiarmid seems to take on a greater risk of the parochialism his movement was intended to remedy. If, as MacDiarmid later claimed, "The cause of the Scots literary movement is the cause of the Scottish people," then we are asked to trust that these seemingly ineffable ideals are mutually affirming (*Prose* 162). In this rendering, therefore, national literary self-realization demands that the risk is taken and that the contradictory movement both beyond and within "clannish confines" be embraced.

Nationalism and socialism may be listed among the most recognizably impactful ideological precepts in twentieth-century geopolitics, but, in the context of the burgeoning renaissance, their cultural appeal was transmuted in less abstracted, more intuitively felt forms, not least in the inheritance and redeployment of the Scots vernacular and of Scottish folk culture. Another of MacDiarmid's most influential early proclamations was that the "Scots Vernacular" constituted a "vast unutilized mass of lapsed observation . . . an inchoate Marcel Proust – a Dostoeveskian [*sic*] debris of ideas – an inexhaustible quarry of subtle and significant sound"(*Prose* 22–3). MacDiarmid extolls the virtues of the vernacular, not only in terms of its capacity for modernistic experiment, but also in its apparent immunity to the excesses of condescension and didacticism on the one hand, and the lachrymose and specious, on the other. Its "democratic spirit" comes from its common heritage, and, therefore, its common touch, as with folk culture. And, in this sense, rather paradoxically, the traditions or folk inheritances of the nation come to inaugurate its modernistic credentials. This is borne out by some of the most celebrated poets of the renaissance, and especially in MacDiarmid's own lyrics.

In his early collection, *Penny Wheep* (1926), titles like "The Love-sick Lass," "Servant Girl's Bed," and "The Bonnie Lowe" make their allusion to the chapbook tradition of the eighteenth and nineteenth centuries clear (*Poems* I: 55, 65, 67). Meanwhile, a work like "Focherty" is set in the bucolic market town and describes the eponymous local "big man," a force of nature who tramples smaller men, like the speaker, with ease. The final lines imagine Focherty on Judgment Day, "like a bull in the sale-ring" (*Poems* I: 53). Both local lore and the settings and events of the everyday are suddenly transplanted to a supernatural plane and to the end of Time, but so, too, are petty village politics. Finally, in "Your Immortal Memory, Burns!" MacDiarmid redirects his subtle appropriation of the "bardic voice" to attack its most celebrated proponent, or, more specifically, the cult attached to his name: "Thy power alone / The spectacle attests / Of drunken bourgeois on the Muses' breasts!" (*Poems* I: 77–9). The part-vernacular, part-dictionary-dredged Scots that is common to these pieces derives its connotative heft and scope from the processes of folk culture, and from the accumulated histories and usages that are bound up in this lexicon, these meters and rhymes.

William Soutar (1898–1943) made frequent use of the ballad stanza and insisted on its importance in the literary movement to which he belonged: "the fact that the ballad is the most stimulating source of inspiration for the modern writer in Scots manifests the social implications of the vernacular revival: it is symptomatic of our need and our desire to recreate a true community" (*Diaries* 128). If this yearning is expressed in the writer's adoption of the vernacular or the ballad form, as critics, we have to recognize the absence-in-modernity that this reveals, as well as the retrograde grasping for old forms as antidotes to contemporary problems. This "true community" must, by implication, be situated at some productive intersection of class unity and national belonging, and it must extend both diachronically and synchronically to include the depth of the past and the breadth of the present.

While Soutar believed that the revival of the Scots vernacular was instrumental in both "the rediscovery of our national roots" and in a broader political "alignment with the worker," his use of these sources was less reflexive, and less cynical, than MacDiarmid's ("Vernacular" 50–51). Though he is often regarded as writing in the shadow of the latter, their poetics, in fact, diverged sharply. Soutar's has a formal clarity, through which it resembles more closely the products of the folk tradition, and, though it channels a transcendentalism familiar to readers of *Penny Wheep*, its imagery is not so concentrated or elliptical. "The Tryst," perhaps his most anthologized piece, is a pared-down lament that seems to hold within it the essence of all those antecedent ballads and folk songs built on the motif of the "night-visitor": "Sae luely, luely cam she in / Sae luely was she gaen" ("luely": quietly, softly) (Soutar, *Poems* 36). In "Ballad," another in the mode of the night-visitor, the speaker describes her response to the apparition of her dead lover in the half-light: "I thocht the hale o' the world was there / Sae sma' and in a sma' room" (Soutar, *Poems* 138). In their simultaneous examination of cosmic expansiveness and claustrophobic domesticity, these closing lines point to another of Soutar's characteristic themes: the limitations that seem implicit in the deployment of an individual poetic voice and the risk of over-extension that comes with assuming a communal or collective posture to anticipate this problem.

In his diaries, Soutar demonstrates a healthy skepticism toward both Marxian political philosophy and his cohort's flirtations with romantic nationalism: "the dogmatic Marxist can forget the individual in the class and thereby fail to differentiate between hating a system productive of classes and hating our fellow beings"; "[the vernacular revival] brings with it the dangerous seduction of taking refuge in the womb of the past and calling it a rebirth" (*Diaries*, 79–80, 50). However, these perfectly valid concerns are not, as with MacDiarmid, acknowledged in the structures and registers of his work. Where MacDiarmid might bulldoze these concerns or avoid them altogether in a way so conspicuous as to draw attention to the fact, Soutar does not embody this paradox of bullish nuance. Indeed, he was well aware of this limitation and knew that it led to a degree of avoidance or approximation in his poetry: "I am afraid I have as yet barely begun to accept that challenge [of reconciling himself, as a Scottish poet, with the tensions in his national identity and his class allegiance]. The acceptance will be...a vicarious answer" (*Diaries* 78). This vicariousness was to be adopted in different forms by subsequent Scottish writers.

Writing a Radical Tradition

In his efforts to triangulate the role of the poet between the poles of romantic nationalism, socialist internationalism, and "the people," who are the source and promise of the other two, MacDiarmid found that modernist avant-gardism and Leninist vanguardism provided him with the redeeming models of authorship and influence he sought. His resultant elitism was the most persistent cause of his public rifts with other Scottish writers and critics, and Henderson – champion of the Scottish folk revival and of MacDiarmid's poetic genius – was no exception. In their public "flytings" in the late 1950s and mid-1960s, they enacted a long-standing and definitive tension in the Scottish cultural tradition as generally conceived at the time: that between the accumulated cultural inheritance in its popular *living* form, and its future trajectory according to those who had both absorbed it very selectively and sought to shape its advance.[3] Such criticisms are, however, a little unfair, as neither poet was immune from his own projections and mediation, but the difference in emphasis is nevertheless vital: Henderson sought to foster a "genuine people's culture," while MacDiarmid promoted an art that would speak to an unrealized revolutionary future, that would refuse to patronize the people by disguising or excising its politics or its complexity (Gibson, *The Voice*). For both men, an independent socialist republic was the prize, but, as artists, they conceptualized their contributions to this end entirely differently.

In his later poetry, MacDiarmid often describes the importance and the *difficulty* of "winning up to the level of the proletariat," of truly being one with the working class (*Poems* 407). In a passage from his "Third Hymn to Lenin" admonishing the 1930s Group, he distinguishes himself from Auden and his peers in this endeavor: "Unlike the pseudos I am *of* – not *for* – the working class" (*Poems* 900). The difference in these prepositions is telling: "of" expresses the relationship of the part to the whole, whereas "for" – as "in support of" or "on behalf of" – speaks of a distance; it positions its subject outside of, but functioning as, representative of its object. MacDiarmid is not only indulging in a form of inverted snobbery – lauding his class background – he is reaffirming the importance of belonging to but being distinguished within a group belonging. This is the kind of negotiation intrinsic to a cultural politics constructed around the dialectic between national and class consciousness.

In John Maclean (1879–1923), Red Clydeside leader, Bolshevik consul to Scotland, and latter-day folk-hero of the Scottish left, MacDiarmid and many subsequent others found a modern martyr for this combined cause of revolutionary socialism and national self-determination. Maclean died at only 44 due to ill health, exacerbated, if not caused by, his cruel treatment while in prison for "sedition." Not only did the "great John Maclean" believe that the Scottish working class were disposed toward a more rapid revolutionary trajectory than their peers in England, Ireland, and Wales, he was convinced that the communist ideal was written into the people's history. He envisaged the clan system that had survived into the eighteenth century as a model of "Celtic" proto-communism that could still be recaptured in a modern struggle for "one clan" delineated along national lines. In Scotland, therefore, he thought it possible to accurately proclaim: "back to communism and forward to communism" (Maclean 133–9). Though this romantic mystification is quite baseless in terms of the economic, social, and cultural realities of Scottish history, its traction amid the violence and divisiveness of the twentieth century is perhaps not so difficult to explain. In the 1930s and 1940s, MacDiarmid developed what he variously described as "The Red Scotland Thesis" or "The Maclean Line," where Maclean embodied the nation: "The unification of Scotland – Highland and Lowland, rural and urban – was complete in himself" (MacDiarmid, "Maclean" 2–4). This image, of the martyred leader who had, in his life, combined philosophy and praxis, recurred in poems by MacDiarmid and by an emergent group of working class socialist Scots poets in the years following the Second World War. In collections like John Kincaid, George Todd, F. J. Anderson, and Thurso Berwick's *Fowrsom Reel* (1948), and T. S. Law's *Whit Tyme in the Day* (1948), these poets marked twenty-five years since Maclean's death by lining up behind his call for a Scottish Workers' Republic. In their epigrams they identified with the socialist MacDiarmid, foregoing the formal experimentation of the "Lallans Makars" (Scots-language poets) whom they dismissed as bourgeois nationalists (Hubbard). They heralded Maclean as representative of their political inheritance, and, extending their group to include a younger generation of poets in 1973, a further 25 years after his death, they published another collection of poems and songs, *Homage to John Maclean* (1973). Here, Maclean was canonized: placed in the radical national tradition alongside Wallace, Bruce, Burns, and Thomas Muir (martyr and political reformer of the late eighteenth century). He became the culmination of a tradition that was desperately seeking new forms for its continuation. In one of the more questioning and less hagiographical contributions, Edwin Morgan imagines "the rock of nations... saw-toothed, half-submerged," the ships "Workingclass Solidarity" and "International Brotherhood" wrecked nearby, while Maclean trims the lighthouse lamp, and thereby reveals a "Scottish Socialism" whereby nationhood might be transfigured and redeployed to guide the metaphorical ships on their journey, to act as a topographical reference point, rather than a final destination (Law and Berwick 18–20).

In James Barke's 1936 novel, *Major Operation*, the bourgeois coal-broker George Anderson is enlisted to the socialist cause by a John Maclean figure – an educator, and charismatic agitator – named Jock MacKelvie. In his later epic realist novel, *Land of the Leal* (1939), which describes the repeated relocations of the Ramsay family over two generations, from around the turn of the century to the time of the novel's publication, MacKelvie reappears among the dockworkers of the Clyde where the family finally find themselves, having originated in the Rhins of Galloway, and passed through the dairy farms of the Borders and the landed estates of Fife. Finding hardship and exploitation wherever they go, the Ramsays document the movement from the oft-idealized pre-proletarian communities of the late-nineteenth-century Kailyard to the urban industrial landscape that was more familiar to the realist novel of the 1930s. Though David and Jean Ramsay come to think fondly, in some respects, of the various pasts they gather behind them, the cruelty and poverty of these experiences is neither diminished, nor forgotten. We come to recognize both the falsity of poetic myth and the compulsion to compose such myths through the vagaries of memory and the fear of death. The phenomenological prompts for these projections are revealed to be indistinguishable from the narratives that grow out of our group belonging. Where David, the father, looks to the romantic poet: "he had felt with Burns that rank was indeed but the guinea stamp"; Andrew, the son, looks to Maclean the agitator, whose speech on a local street corner is a significant event in his developing class consciousness: "If they [his parents] didn't understand the nature and significance of the system that had driven them like beasts for the greater part of their lives, he did. He and his generation" (Barke, *Leal* 243, 518).

Both sons – Andrew, who dies fighting for the International Brigades in Spain, and Tom, the Church of Scotland minister – come under the tutelage of MacKelvie. The novel's denouement comes with Tom's rousing antifascist sermon, after which MacKelvie explains to him the virtues of a working class upbringing: "A worker knows what it is to suffer – and he's prepared to suffer for his political beliefs." Tom responds: "I feel that in working for Socialism ... I am working for something that justifies their whole existence – justifies all the suffering and hardship they have undergone" (*Leal* 609). In "Land o' the Leal," the popular ballad by Carolina Nairne (1766–1845), the title refers to heaven and the promise it affords as "the land of the faithful," but in Barke's novel, it incites an ironic reading and stands as a metonym for the persistent interrogation of the faith (or loyalties) that should be afforded to the powers that preside over, and the structures that maintain, such entrenched hardship. The only recompense available is an emerging class consciousness and another deferred promise: an historical end, still distant, but that must be met if innumerable lives like the Ramsays' are to consummate their historical purpose.

During the 1930s Barke was critical of the nationalist intelligentsia in Scotland, and particularly the writers. Though he was sympathetic to the national cause, he maintained that it should be subordinate to the struggle against capitalism, and he envisaged the only true reconciliation between national- and class-belonging would be one that united the artist and the people: "All that is truly national, all that is best and worthy of preservation in the various national cultures is the heritage of the workers and peasants concerned, of the class in whose hands the future lies" (Barke, "National Question" 369).[4] In *A Scots Quair*, Lewis Grassic Gibbon drew from a similar nexus in the communal culture, one drawing its significance from the accumulated past and the perpetually deferred promise of the future. Where the first of that trilogy closes with the titular "Sunset Song," lamenting the "Last of the Peasants, the last of the Old Scots folk" (256), Barke's *Major Operation* opens with an analogous sunset on Glasgow, "The Second City [of the British Empire]," looked upon by the upper and middle classes with "polite interest and polite unconcern," and, by the working class (if at all), with mere "indifference" (14). It signifies a transition that has been replayed *ad infinitum:* a brief distraction for the bourgeoisie and an irrelevance to the proletariat.

Gibbon's trilogy is marked throughout by two indelible forces sometimes articulated in alignment with one another, sometimes in stark opposition, and sometimes in subtle confusion: first is the much-vaunted hold of the "land" on these "Old Scots folk," that which, in Chris's eyes, "endures" through change; second is the hold of history, which her son, Ewan, comes to regard above all else in *Grey Granite*: "He was one with them all, a long wail of sobbing mouths and wrung flesh, tortured and tormented by the world's Masters while those Masters lied about Progress through Peace, Democracy, Justice, the Heritage of Culture" (*Scots Quair* 137).[5] Where Chris returns to the "land" in the closing pages, Ewan embarks on a hunger march to London. This division between the deep history that is indifferent to human agency and the history that is produced by it is prefigured throughout and has its attendant symbols, most prominently in *Sunset Song*, in the standing stones that look out over the village of Kinraddie. In one of the final passages of the trilogy, Chris and Ewan come to recognize the irreconcilable nature of this opposition: "It's the old fight that maybe will never have a finish, whatever the names we give to it – the fight in the end between FREEDOM and GOD" (202). It seems that for both Gibbon and Barke the arrival of modernity and the transition from the "peasant folk" to the urban proletariat is best expressed across generations and as an endlessly renewed, and rearticulated, struggle to find meaning and purpose for those who came before; and all in the face of a consistently unforgiving universe.[6] While these terms perhaps transcend the dialectic of romantic nationalism and socialist internationalism, the tension these poles encapsulate might be conceived as a possible response to the challenge set out in each of these novels. The appeals of a group belonging that has endured, that one inherits as a birthright, and that of a group belonging that casts one as an historical agent capable of affecting change are often contradictory *and* complementary.

Disaggregated Voices

If John Maclean stands as a symbol for this combination of political traditions, it is telling that Peter Stark of *No Mean City* (1935), the enormously popular and notoriously violent melodrama depicting life in the Gorbals of Glasgow in the 1920s, insists: "'Ah don't want to be a John MacLean or anything like that!' ... *He* thought MacLean was a saint and a martyr, but too unpractical for everyday life. And he himself had no instinct for martyrdom" (McArthur and Long 225). More intelligent than his brother, Johnnie Stark the "Razor King," Peter covets a different form of social aspiration: respectability over respect, an escape to the bourgeoisie rather than an ascent to folk-hero status. Despite his political sympathies, his aspirations, and his autodidacticism, Peter's efforts at self-improvement prove to be no less futile than his brother's. Indeed, as Sylvia Bryce-Wunder has argued, the novel's characters dehumanize themselves in their efforts to reject the humiliations of poverty and circumstance. While this larger reality is invisible to Peter, his narrowed focus on survival bears an attendant skepticism and demands that Maclean's communitarian ideals are admired but not pursued. The novel's popular claim to authenticity was based substantially on its authorship: on Alexander McArthur, described in the publicity as an unemployed worker who had lived in the Gorbals his entire life, and on the journalist, Kingsley Long. The large working class readership the book earned also served to validate the authors' appendix, which called upon newspaper excerpts as evidence: "the authors maintain that they have not drawn an exaggerated picture of conditions in the Glasgow tenements or of life as it is lived amongst the gangster element of the slum population" (McArthur and Long 314). Combined with the swift and often bewildering shifts in tone: from close observations of everyday spaces and routines, through sensationalist high drama, to the affected distance of the journalist (on sanitary conditions and public disorder) and the anachronistic sociologist (reflecting on the characteristics of the "slum mind") these claims to authenticity invite our scrutiny. How can the truth-value of a literary work reconcile these divergent sources: the lived impressionism, and the empirical reportage? Mediation and authenticity in the depiction of working class life in Glasgow, and the tensions that come with writing as one *of* as opposed to *for* this community, are issues that were revisited with meticulous self-awareness in the 1966 novel *The Dear Green Place*, by Archie Hind (1928–2008).

Following Mat Craig, an aspiring working class writer at turns liberated and trammeled by his art and his work (and the tension between the two), the novel provides an intimate and humane portrait of the artist struggling with that designation and its purpose. The nation as romantic construction falls victim to a symbolic and caustic attack in an early scene at a New Year's party. Playing the bagpipes, Mat notes with disgust how easily he can manipulate his audience: a slow air produces a "soulful and woebegone" look; a quick march incites them to become "staunch wee Scottish soldiers"; and "The Highland Cradle Song" makes them "weep for the sticky weans." Ending, cheekily, on "a few bars of a rumba, then a bit of an Orange song," he prompts a comic discussion over the politics of the pipes, the "Capitalistic and Imperialistic influence" instilled in the music historically, and speculation over the possibility of a "new Historical stage in pipe music" featuring such works as "Vladimir Ilyich's welcome to St Petersburg" and "Uncle Joes' Wee Cley Pipe." The historical contingency of this national symbol is laid bare, and politics and popular culture are riven. The scene ends with the drunk and injured on the streets, "viciousness and violence and a kind of bitter sentimentality" (Hind 37–40). Barke had his characters *reach for* Burns to point to an admired, if outmoded, radicalism. Whereas, Hind has Mat *subjected to* Burns in quotation. In this setting these nuggets of folk-wisdom stand only for the familiar frustrations of the working class, for limitations imposed from outside the community and for the resignation that those circumstances engender. "Ye labour soon, ye labour late, / To feed the titled knave, man," from "Tree of Liberty," is invoked while Mat discusses the paltry holiday allowance at the slaughterhouse where he works (Hind 135). "Facts are chiels that winna ding... [fellows that will not be overturned]," from "A Dream," is set against his failure to provide for his family as he pursues his art (Hind 240).

The struggles faced by the working class writer are documented throughout, from the "nights of labor" demanded by the craft, and the economic pressures; to the relevance of bourgeois cultural constructions of the author and prescription of literary value to an artist speaking out of this community (see Rancière). But, so too, are the apparent struggles of the *Scottish* writer, whose national context provides only a "null blot, a cessation of life, a dull absence": "The canny Scot with his deathly stultifying safety" as opposed to Mat's vision of the writer as one who ought to "Shove [his world] into the violent torrent of events. Make things happen" (Hind 84). Faced with a nation and a class-community that seem anathema to this model of authorship, Mat despairs that even books that had "formed the basis of a practical dream," by Marx or Shaw for example, were not deployed to change the world but were held among the working class as a "sentimentalised orthodoxy, a pathetic and futile hope for utopia" (Hind 208). In the closing pages, Mat's inner conflict reaches its apogee. His troubles, of inspiration, aspiration, and conceptualization, shift and transform: the noble endeavors of the artist become the tawdry extravagance of a delusional, and vice-versa. The novel ends, as it begins, with the City of Glasgow's coat of arms and the "piece of doggerel," which describes it:

> This is the tree that never grew,
> This is the bird that never flew,
> This is the fish that never swam,
> This is the bell that never rang.
> (Hind 10, 248)

This describes, rather enigmatically, the miracles of St. Mungo, patron saint of Glasgow, and it rings in Mat's (and the reader's) mind through the closing lines. While this might be read simply as a return to a kind of localism, and the belonging that comes with "home" and is rehearsed and reaffirmed in children's rhymes, it might also provide us with potent imagery for the contradictory forces that have distinguished Mat's life: the being without the doing, the dream that provides an identity but goes unrealized. Hind's Mat is a child of Red Clydeside. Separated from his father's struggle with history by his ambition as a writer, his conflict has a focus at once more personal and more fundamental than that of Doug Craig (his father), Andrew Ramsay (*Land of the Leal*), or Ewan Tavendale (*A Scots Quair*). His conflict asks if the novel can sustain this burden of representation, while showing that, to do so, it must depict a creative impasse, and an ambitious failure.

In *Lean Tales* (1985), a collection of short stories by James Kelman (b. 1946), Agnes Owens (1926–2014), and Alasdair Gray (b. 1934), the experience of the working class subject is delineated altogether more violently. Its isolated and interiorized narratives are unapologetic about their resistance to interpretation. They are "lean" in the sense that they are trim and economical, but also lithe and nimble – not beholden to profound negotiations with history and tradition. Again, national mystification is confounded immediately. Kelman's "Busted Scotch," the opening story, sees a cabaret act at a casino in England, "a scotchman doing this harrylauder thing complete with kilt and trimmings," in a bill also featuring "an Indian Squaw."[7] Hearing his accent, a female croupier identifies the narrator with the "scotch" performer ("one of your countrymen"), and, as if in response, he bets all of his wages on his first hand: "bust" (*Lean Tales* 13–14). The implied parity between these "native" performances, and the embarrassment that might only have been avoided, or embraced, with alcohol ("Fine if I had been drunk"), prompts him to take an inordinate risk, perhaps an attempt to prove his mastery over his fortune. His failure marks the first of many failures of the nation in this short story collection. As a model of identity politics capable of freeing or ennobling the Scottish working class, the nation falls woefully short. In "learning the Story," the nation's folk culture is further distanced from the landscapes and narratives it might once have conjured, as an "old lady under a bridge" plays the tune "Maxwelton Braes are Bonny" on her mouthorgan only to stop abruptly and commence to smoke her "Capstan full strength cigarettes" (*Lean Tales* 51–2).[8] Kelman's narrator recounts this event in detail, without explanation or judgment.

In Owens's "Arabella" we are given more extensive access to our narrator's worldview, though it diverges from the reality we come to recognize all the more dramatically. The titular character lives in squalor. She is illiterate, though she cultivates a reputation as a "healer" of considerable powers. We come to realize that the "magic," or "treatment," she proffers are in fact sex acts, given in return for contributions to the "money box" she keeps for her "children," that is, for the dogs with whom she shares her home. The Sanitary Inspector who threatens to evict her is murdered, drowned in a barrel of her "potion" made up of "cow-dung, mashed snails or frogs, or whatever dead creature was handy." The last word is given over entirely to Arabella's perspective: "As usual everything had worked out well for her" (*Lean Tales* 115, 119). In control of her own narrative and identity, she remains immune to the incursions of the state, to its representatives in public education and public health, and, by implication, to any broader group belonging. Hers is a story that ought to be unknowable, but that narrative fiction permits us to access. In "Fellow Travellers" Owens gives us a less self-assured character in Jean, who, sitting on the train, feels so besieged and scrutinized by the small talk of the others in the carriage that she disembarks and ends "going nowhere"; though we are left with the impression that such overwhelming feelings of directionlessness are widely shared, and only thinly veiled (*Lean Tales* 158). In "McIntyre," the eponymous union man and tenants' rights demonstrator comes to disappoint the narrator, who has long admired him: "he never understood that from many people's point of view smelly feet are worse than capitalism. Only to me it had been a comforting fault" (*Lean Tales* 165). Therefore, he who lives entirely in the struggle loses sight of the mundanities that make up so much of our conscious lives, and another avenue of group belonging, of political purpose, is found lacking.

Gray returns to Hind's concern with the Scottish working class artist in "A Report to the Trustees of the Bellahouston Travelling Scholarship," which purports to have been written by a young art student, and depicts a series of misadventures, illnesses, and debts, before arriving at the lesson: "My tour was spent in an effort to avoid the maturity gained from new experiences. Yet . . . that effort failed" (*Lean Tales* 212). Again, wisdom has come only with unattainable ambitions, inner conflict, self-sabotage, and a form of acknowledged failure. Gray maintains this metafictional bent in "Portrait of a Playwright," which describes the life and works of Joan Ure (1918–78), who wrote a story about

> a woman with a talent, who feels it is too small to matter, suppresses it, and faints. She is pleased, for that suggests the talent is genuine. To be absolutely certain she hides it again. 'Very soon she coughed up the first gobbets of blood. And there she saw brilliant at last, the brightness of the tiny talent she had.' The woman dies rejoicing. She knows her talent is genuine, for it *was* death to hide it. (*Lean Tales* 250)

In representing the magnitude of this need for validation in one so browbeaten, Gray/Ure constructs a model of individuated exploitation that runs so deeply as to connect the political and the creative endeavor in fundamental terms. Among Gray's final contributions to *Lean Tales* are the short pieces "The Grumbler" and the "Decision," both of which speak to the powerlessness of the subject. In the first, a man who has everything he wants cannot find happiness, and, in the second, a young woman thinks that to "decide" not to have children is enough: "I don't take precautions when I decide not to have a cigarette, why take precautions when I decide not to have a baby?" (*Lean Tales* 277).

Finally, Gray's "Ending," which is one sentence in length, reads: "Having beguiled with fiction until I had none left I resorted to facts, which also ran out" (*Lean Tales* 281). The speaker has neither fictions nor facts. If there is nothing left to be stated that he or she knows to be true or knows not to be true, only approximation and speculation remains. An understanding of this dilemma helps us to read *Lean Tales*, and the works of Kelman, Owens, and Gray, more generally. The "truths" of these shorn and stark narratives as measured against history, or understood in the context of nationality or class, is an irrelevance. Though "clannish confines" have been continually transcended in the works of these later writers, and any claim to group belonging is greeted, rightly, with suspicion and scrutiny, even the disaggregated voice of the individual does not go altogether unaffected by these inheritances. As we can glean from the common concern among these working class writers over the forces that press upon and seek to define, control, or otherwise exploit us, even as we reject "clannish" behavior, we only come up against other "confines" more difficult to discern and to combat.

This chapter began with a mid-twentieth-century product of the folk revival and the Scottish literary renaissance, one that very self-consciously coordinates the local, the national, and the universal. Though the national framework has, in the postmodern period, earned the distrust with which it is handled, "Glasclune and Drumlochy" serves as an example of the ways in which "clannish" divides are a perpetual, if tragic, presence in history. In light of this, we might come to see MacDiarmid's poetics as one that faces up to this fact, rather than evading it. The politics of a combined romantic nationalism and socialist internationalism must, by definition, inhabit this tension between the inward and the outward perspective. It must also, in turn, negotiate between the elitism that comes with interpreting and representing cultural history and setting out its future, and the populism that is risked in any appeal to "the people." In adopting and adapting the folk tradition and the Scots vernacular, poets like MacDiarmid and Soutar risked eliding class difference by reinforcing a common "folk" inheritance, but each in his way acknowledges this difficulty: the former by unapologetically situating himself "whaur extremes meet," (MacDiarmid, *Poems* I: 87) and the latter, by his vicariousness. Where the 1930s realist epics of Gibbon and Barke enter a dialogue with history, postwar writers were to embrace disaggregated voices, relinquishing their claim to speak for the community.

The lives they choose to depict make scant claims beyond themselves but respond in their idiosyncrasies to the same historical pressures. In so doing, they radically democratize the literary, validating diverse voices by scrutinizing the limits of their creative conceit. The "confines" that bear down upon these voices, though less "clannish," are exposed as no less parochial, and no less insular, and all the more inescapable for it.

NOTES

1. The title of one of MacDiarmid's essays published in T. S. Eliot's *Criterion* in 1931.
2. *OED*: "a low or vulgar boy; a street-loafer."
3. For a selection of the exchanges in these latter-day "flytings," see Henderson, *Armstrong* 117–41.
4. In a letter to Gibbon, Barke heaped praises on *Sunset Song* and compared it, in its stature and in the eagerness with which he read it, to *The Communist Manifesto*. In reply, Gibbon expressed his pleasure at the comparison and applauds Barke in turn: "there is at least one soul in Scotland unspotted by this dreary rash of nationalism" (McCulloch 90–93).
5. The most frequently cited passage describing this aspect is Ewan's comrade, Jim Trease's exclamation: "A hell of a thing to be History, Ewan!" (Gibbon, *Grey Granite* 147).
6. See Timothy C. Baker, who formulates this dialectic as that between "romance" and "realism" in response to modernity.
7. Harry Lauder (1870–1950) was a hugely successful music hall and vaudeville performer.
8. A once popular brand of unfiltered cigarettes in the UK renowned for their markedly high tar and nicotine content, and associated with only the most dedicated of smokers.

CHAPTER 24

A Critical Minefield
The Haunting of the Welsh Working Class Novel

Lisa Sheppard and Aidan Byrne

Davy Jones "ate William Trefor's buttocks over a three-day period . . . he found some of the younger colliers quite succulent" (Gower 112). He is a zombie cannibal, a miner trapped underground shortly after the 1926 strike and, having been forced up from the pits after 60 years by Margaret Thatcher's closure of his industry in the 1980s, reduced to "stalking unwitting prey through the aisles of late night supermarkets" in Jon Gower's 2012 short story "The Pit" (118). The undead have appeared in Welsh fiction at least since D. Griffith Jones's *Ofnadwy Ddydd* ("The Dreadful Day," 1966) as defenders of Christianity and Welsh-language culture, but "The Pit" is the *reductio ad absurdum* of a Welsh literary tradition that incorporated folk culture into nineteenth-century novels, introduced Gothic elements into apparently realist ideological texts, then documented the effects of late capitalism on individuals within multiply marginalized societies. Though progressive forces may wish to downplay the grotesque elements at play in Welsh society and culture, Gower's miner-zombie represents a lost generation of skilled craftsmen and the working class culture he outlived, succeeded by and haunting soft, consumerist prey with no apparent future.

We draw on Derridean and post-Freudian concepts of haunting to suggest that contemporary Welsh working class fiction in English is multiply haunted – and, therefore, culturally "stuck" – both by its history and by the tensions between it and the Welsh-language cultures that are both present and absent within its texts.[1] By drawing comparisons with some contemporary Welsh-language texts, however, we suggest that the characters presented to us know that they must create a new culture and new identities from these presences and absences but lack the agency to do so. While not every protagonist is a Davy Jones, there is a distinct sense that the contemporary literatures of working class Wales reflect a society that is indeed eating itself.

For Avery Gordon, "haunting . . . always registers the harm inflicted or the loss sustained by a social violence done in the past or in the present.

But haunting, unlike trauma, is distinctive for producing a something-to-be-done" (xvi). Recent Welsh urban novels in both languages are haunted by violent death and unorthodox sexualities: folk culture, rural ways of life, the fading *gwerin* and its language, and militant socialism are both present and absent in and to their protagonists. The postindustrial Welsh working class novel in English, however, is largely bereft of "something-to-be-done," unlike the preindustrial novels of Allen Raine, Amy Dillwyn, and others which incorporated folk cultures, legends, love, and resourceful women to plot a distinctively Welsh way forward. The 1936 Welsh-language classic, Kate Roberts's *Traed Mewn Cyffion* ("Feet in Chains"), set in the quarrying districts of north west Wales, depicts a similarly resolute woman, who, along with her children, is awoken to the possibility of doing something. Near the beginning of the novel, its heroine Jane Gruffudd is asked by her young son Owen, "'Mam, how would it be if there was nothing at all?'" She responds, bleakly, "'[i]t would be lovely my boy'" (Roberts 40).[2] By the end of the novel, however, having lost one son (Twm) in the trenches of the First World War, seen another (Wiliam) leave for the south Wales coalfield, and witnessed little improvement in her family's life over the decades, stoic Jane finally acts, hitting the military pensions officer over the head with a clothes brush after he boasts about reducing the pension of another mother who has lost a son in the War. While Wil is influenced by the politics of Kier Hardy, seeing his mother act opens Owen's eyes "to the possibility of doing something" (Roberts 203), and the novel ends with his own realization of his burgeoning national and social consciousness.

Despite the potential of a better future hinted at by *Traed Mewn Cyffion*, the industrial novel nurtured bitter defeat from Caradoc Evans's *My People* (1915) onward. He instituted a darkly ironic, naturalist or absurdist style to represent an articulate people left high and dry, rejecting the realism of the imperial center. Yet, postindustrial Welsh novels often lack that bitter resistance, haunted instead by the total defeat of collective traditions that sustained the industrial generations. The end of Welsh mass labor led to a sense of doom: M. Wynn Thomas finds "social and cultural disorientation" and predicts "the end of a distinctive Welsh identity," while Dai Smith refers to the "vacuum of contemporary South Wales... an historical process ended" (Thomas 170; Smith 156). The photographic cover of Smith's edited anthology *Story* (2014: vol. 2) reinforces this attitude: two drunk young women hold each other up, continuing a long and misogynistic tradition of female anthropomorphizations of Wales. Many of the volume's stories echo this position: without meaningful male employment and traditional social structures, passive desperation dominates, even for characters who find alternative sources of identity in sexuality, ethnicity, or religion. Lives are given shape by what *happens* to them (adolescence, class and racial prejudice, alienation) rather than what they *do*. Agency seems to be missing in virtually all contemporary representations of Welsh working class life even in speculative fiction: in Lloyd Jones's *Y Dŵr* (2009: *Water*, 2014), the protagonists wait for the rising waters to snuff out their lives and culture like hopeless descendants of R. S. Thomas's phlegmatic Iago Prytherch.

The imagined Welsh working class which haunts contemporary fiction is monolithic: white, male, anglophone, (ex-)industrial, and heterosexual. Stable roles – as worker, provider, patriarch – vanish, leaving behind populations of depressed and deprived men and women. Contemporary Welsh literature fitfully reveals competing and complementary versions of working class experiences – queer, rural, urban, anglophone, Welsh-speaking, male, female, and ethnic – in works by talented anglophone authors such as Charlotte Williams and Trezza Azzopardi and by Welsh-language writers such as Angharad Price. Price's 2010 novel *Caersaint*, for example, follows the tribulations of one Jamal Gwyn Jones, a half-Welsh, half-Pakistani, Welsh-speaking orphan, as he seeks election as mayor of the town (based on Caernarfon). Through its portrayal of his character, and of the Welsh-speaking, working class community that he seeks to represent, the novel deconstructs the idea that north and west Wales are rural and monocultural areas while also challenging the idea that the Welsh language is by now the preserve of the middle classes.

Despite such developments in contemporary working class fiction, the genre is largely inhabited by ghosts. One of these ghosts is the *gwerin*, or "folk." This Welsh class position embodied linguistic unity, respectability, Nonconformism, resistance to political radicalism, and was itself a reaction against "Brad y Gleision Llyfrau" ("the Treason of the Blue Books"), an 1847 British government report which depicted the Welsh as sexually incontinent and barely civilized (Aaron, "The Hoydens of Wild Wales" 24–6; Bohata 71). Valleys proletarianism rejected *gwerin* quietism and deference to authority: In Gwyn Thomas's *Sorrow For Thy Sons* (rejected for publication in 1935, published in 1986), three orphaned young men inherit their father's ceremonial chair, representing a patriarchal and cultural authority they reject. The uncomfortable and constricting seat leaves Alf "feeling he was starting a long stretch in jail" (G. Thomas, *Sorrow* 30). *My People*, Caradoc Evan's Gothic *succès de scandale* flayed the *gwerin*'s hypocrisy in English, while Rhys Davies's homoerotic work, Thomas's blend of socialism, absurdism, and naturalism, Ron Berry's sophisticated, witty consumers, and, more recently, works by Niall Griffiths and Rachel Trezise all represent those excluded from the *gweriniaeth* ideal: monoglot anglophones, urban dwellers, the workless, and the rootless.

A large swathe of contemporary Welsh writing in English represents the working class as culturally, spiritually, and politically (un)dead. Jane Aaron employed the term "Coalfield Gothic" to describe the alienation, sexual dysfunction, death fixation, and powerlessness so prominent in twentieth-century industrial fictions (*Welsh Gothic* 98). Even overtly political texts such as Lewis Jones's novels *Cwmardy* and *We Live* (1937, 1939) and the "export version" of Welsh industrial fictions, such as Richard Llewellyn's 1939 *How Green Was My Valley*, demonstrate the extent to which Welsh anglophone novels are "haunted" by cultural positions forgotten but not gone, subverting realist readings.[3] The central protagonist in the supposedly Communist *Cwmardy* and *We Live* is sexually fixated on his sister who dies in childbirth and, subsequently, on Mary, his tubercular lover. Len eventually volunteers to fight and die in Spain not as a socialist apotheosis but because he realizes that she will volunteer him: she is a vampiric figure whose coldly dogmatic Stalinism sustains her life and Party career at the cost of his life.

Women, though marginalized by industrial life and politics, are made to bear the weight of what was lost. Llewellyn's *How Green Was My Valley* expresses a fear of females and feminization (conflated with anglicization) in Gothic form. Huw Morgan is torn between two girls, Ceinwen and Shani. Ceinwen is a Valleys girl, an aspirant actor drawn to hedonistic anglophone culture. She is also a vampire who draws blood when she kisses Huw. Shani, though, like *Cwmardy*'s Mary, is ailing: "so small, and thin, and white" (Llewellyn 226), symbolizing a Welsh Wales too frail to compete with cosmopolitan Ceinwen. They haunt Huw's dreams and leave him in a state of limbo. Deprived of the racially and culturally pure Wales by industrialization, secularization, and socialism, Huw and his people in turn haunt the valley. Gwyn Thomas's novella "Simeon" (1946) repeats the theme of incest, while in his *Sorrow for thy Sons* Alf's sex with Annie, the mentally ill daughter of conservative neighbors, is an authorially approved act of class warfare. His fiancée Gwyneth is yet another dying, delicate woman, too pure to live in a hopeless society. Alf says, "'I planted a handful of dreams in Gwyneth.... But there's death mixed up in it and it's coming closer'" (*Sorrow for thy Sons* 240): the metaphor echoes Huw's sexual exploration of Ceinwen's "topsoil" (Llewellyn 309). These texts ostensibly promote totalizing ideological systems, but Gothic sexualities and vampiric women repeatedly subvert such readings.

While these earlier novels haunt realist, politically conscious texts via Gothic elements, many contemporary texts portray a state of depressed, individualist hedonism. Niall Griffiths's *Wreckage* (2005) tells the story of two minor Liverpool gangsters marauding around North Wales, intercut with accounts of how their Welsh and Irish ancestors were forced into the underclass, exactly the kind of social violence enunciated by Avery Gordon. Ianto, the central protagonist of Griffiths's *Sheepshagger*, embodies this condition: half Iago Prytherch, half Travis Bickle. He is "the world's best inbred backwoods feeb psycho mong" (*Sheepshagger* 73), eventually a killer of (English) walkers. Rural Wales is now the site of authentic horrors (as it is in Ed Thomas's 2014 TV drama *Y Gwyll / Hinterland*) rather than a nice place for a walk. Ianto's people feel marooned: "The Irish kill each other, the Scots kill emselves, an us, well, all we do is kill time" (*Sheepshagger* 74). They are neither ignorant nor inarticulate, discussing devolution, Meibion Glyndŵr, the Free Wales Army, Saunders Lewis, and Sion Aubrey Roberts, but they conclude that in "modern fuckin' times" the Welsh "write the odd fuckin' poem . . . fuckin' apathy, mun, the Welsh disease" (*Sheepshagger* 74–5). Ianto, Darren, and Alistair, the Welsh-Irish Scouse petty criminals of *Wreckage*, haunt abandoned farmhouses, near-derelict council estates, and the back roads of North and Mid-Wales. The past is all around, but for the former working class, it is an inaccessible reminder of their decline. They are neither ex-miners nor language campaigners, but they possess dim memories of better times and nobler origins. They drown personal and collective trauma in drink, drugs, and violence amid the wreckage of a potentially better Wales.

While men strike back against their marginalization through violence, Griffiths's women either accede to the brutal demands of men or – as in *A Great Big Shining Star* (2013) – internalize the demands of decultured consumer capitalism. In this novel, Griffiths refers occasionally to crossing an eastern border, but the main character Grace Allcock inhabits Cyberia rather than Wales, lacking roots or means of resistance. She is present yet absent, a hauntological figure referring back to the death of other (better?) cultural dispositions. Grace is transformed via plastic surgery and a sex tape into Gracie, a temporary "celebrity." The reader is relied upon to do the haunting because almost nobody in the text – parents, teachers, friends – has any cultural resources. To Grace, social media, surgery, and celebrity status cover a terrifying void: "Sometimes it bothers her . . . that the planet has no brakes. . . . She touches tenderly the wrappings on her face and thinks of the magic occurring . . . coming to her is as much of the world as she wants or needs" (*A Great Big Shining Star* 17). Welsh names, histories, and experiences do not exist in her electronic nonspace. Only the graveyard she uses for occasional trysts hints at alternative values: after her death, it is washed away in a storm, and all that remains of Gracie is a solitary breast implant. She, like Ianto or Gower's Davy Jones, is a grotesque, the figure who represents "the estranged or alienated world... from a perspective that suddenly renders it strange... either comic or terrifying" and who haunts Welsh working class fiction (Thomson, *The Grotesque* 18).

If "writing from a marginal position can – perhaps must – destabilize the norm of the literary and linguistic system by marking the unmarked, charging the neutral, colourising the colourless" (Kronfeld 72), Gracie's clichéd media-derived discourse ("end of the day" is a favorite way to avoid meaningful communication) signals Welsh, working class cultural defeat. In complete contrast, Mike Jenkins's uncompromising use of Merthyr dialect in *Graffiti Narratives* (1994) and other work indicates a more self-confident vision of autonomous Valleys culture. The reader is expected to learn a new language rather than have it explained by a narrator-translator whose standard English marginalizes the protagonists and their milieu. Jenkins's novels are, according to Pikoulis, "products of the devolved unitary state," and, like Griffiths's characters, have recruited an egalitarian, anglophone variation of the *gweriniaeth* of bottom dogs, or, in Pikoulis's words, "spoilt innocents" (124, 132).

Contemporary Welsh-language texts too, like those of authors Llwyd Owen and Owen Martell, destabilize literary and linguistic systems – Owen's 2006 novels *Ffawd, Cywilydd a Chelwyddau* ("Fate, Shame and Lies") and *Ffydd Gobaith Cariad* ("Faith Hope Love"), and Martell's *Dyn yr Eiliad* ("Man of the Moment," 2003) are narrated in a form of Welsh which is obviously influenced by English sentence idiom and vocabulary. This can be seen in Martell's character Daniel's description of his father: "A *jyst* fel petai i ddangos nad fi yn unig oedd yn *susceptible* i'r dylanwad, roedd fy nhad hefyd – 'solid, implacable Dad' – yn wahanol pan fyddai Davies yn *dod rownd* i'n tŷ ni" (*Dyn yr Eiliad* 27).[4] While the patois used by each author and how it reflects Welsh dialects in areas where English is more widely spoken would make an interesting study in itself, it is the reactions of reviewers and competition judges to both the language and content of Llwyd Owen's first offering which give us a greater sense of one ghost that haunts this genre of Welsh-language literature. *Ffawd, Cywilydd a Chelwyddau* was entered for the Daniel Owen Memorial Prize at the 2005 National Eisteddfod. Although all three judges agreed that Owen was the competition's "greatest genius," he was denied victory on the grounds that his use of "anglicised" Welsh demonstrated "the limit of the author's linguistic resources" and that some of the content was deemed extreme in the context of Welsh language publishing (Prichard, Mair, and Davies 92–100). While it could be argued that the specter of Y Llyfrau Gleision's attack on Welsh respectability was present, looming larger still was the threat to the linguistic standards of a language whose territory had been reduced and whose idiom had been diluted for a considerable amount of time. Gwenan Mared's review of Owen's 2007 third novel, *Yr Ergyd Olaf* ("The Last Hit"), also reflected this concern, noting that "the Welsh that is flourishing in the capital is not the same as the old language with which we are familiar. Perhaps this is not how we would wish things to be, but that is how it is" (Mared 154).

Mared's apparent resignation at the end of her review echoes the fatalism of Luc Swan, the protagonist of Owen's *Ffawd, Cywilydd a Chelwyddau*. As a result of his mother's alcoholism and his father's madness, Luc was put into care as a child and later finds solace from his dead-end job as a runner for a television company in drink, drugs, and prostitutes. The characters of this novel are not haunted by ghosts: they are visited by the devil. The real cause of Luc's lifelong misfortune is that his father, John, sold his son's soul to the devil, and many other characters strike bargains too. Luc's fate is sealed from birth – his name is an anagram of "anlwcus," the Welsh for "unlucky."[5] Unsurprisingly, the world of the media in which Luc works is not lacking in demons either. By the end of the novel, Luc discovers that members of a boyband featured on one of the company's popular children's programs are running a pedophile ring. Luc's past has returned to haunt him here as one of the band members is named "Stifyn," a Welsh rendering of "Steven," the name of Luc's childhood abuser. After witnessing their rape of a teenage girl, and being raped by them himself, he shoots and kills two of the band members and is sent to prison, while the wider world is left none the wiser as to the boyband's crimes. His attempt to do something goes horribly wrong.

Whereas the contemporary anglophone Welsh novel in the hands of Griffiths (and, as discussed later, Rachel Trezise and Lewis Davies) depicts a postindustrial generation with nothing to do, *Ffawd* introduces its reader to the new work that is to be found in the media. Luc is no "*cyfryngi*," the middle-class "luvvies" of the Welsh media: he is the son of a painter and decorator. As the mines before them attracted workers from across Wales and beyond to the Valleys, the promise of employment at one of Cardiff's numerous television production companies draws young people from far and wide to the Welsh capital. As a result, relations between television runners like Luc and their media bosses is reminiscent of that of industrial workers with their masters. "We know –," Luc says, "and more importantly, the bosses know – that there's a bottomless pit of people who are more than ready to take our places if we complain about the job" (*Ffawd* 15): the new proletariat may not be in danger of mine collapses, but it is exploited and insecure all the same.

Owen has inherited an older Welsh-language novelistic tradition stretching back to Saunders Lewis's *Monica* (1930), in which urban and suburban settings are used to challenge religious and social ideals. However, the inhabitants of his Cardiff underworld, and their violence, substance abuse, and scorn for the media, have much in common with the desperate figures depicted by Griffiths's fiction and that of other contemporary anglophone Welsh writers. The violence and abuse suffered and inflicted by Owen's characters is so graphic that it occasionally borders on the surreal, so much so that his first three novels refer loosely to each other in order to ground them in an apparent reality. At the end of *Ffawd, Cywilydd a Chelwyddau*, the imprisoned Luc sees a fellow prisoner named Alun Brady who is about to be released (*Ffawd* 281). Brady is, in fact, the main character of Owen's second novel *Ffydd Gobaith Cariad*, who comments in that novel's opening chapter that Luc Swan is "a celeb in the slammer" as the reader now witnesses the same scene from his perspective (*Ffydd* 17). Once Alun, formerly the apple of his middle class parents' eye, has descended into Cardiff's criminal underworld, he meets a gangster known as Tubs, who is, in fact, the protagonist of Owen's third novel, *Yr Ergyd Olaf* (2008). A similar tactic is employed by North Walian author Dewi Prysor in his series of three novels, *Brithyll* ("Trout," 2006), *Madarch* ("Mushrooms," 2007), and *Crawia* ("Slate Fence," 2008). Although set in rural Meirionydd rather than urban Cardiff, Prysor's characters too engage in recreational drug use and get drunk with often comic results – activities not often associated with a Welsh-speaking rural community. Revisiting the same characters over the course of three novels seems to solidify a portrayal which might otherwise seem unlikely to some.

Although Llwyd Owen's protagonists, such as Luc, often try to act against injustices, the societies to which they belong seem to be moral and ideological voids. Of the current generation of anglophone working class writers, Rachel Trezise's (sometimes autobiographical) work represents postindustrial working class Wales as a site of social, moral, and economic failure. Gwyn Thomas and Ron Berry's cosmopolitan, optimistic urban Welsh experience has disappeared. Trezise's *In and Out of the Goldfish Bowl* (2000) links poverty, sexual abuse, and economic decline, but promotes individual self-expression as a means of survival: reminiscent of

Alf in Gwyn Thomas's *Sorrow for thy Sons*, who loudly plays arias as a means of asserting his agency and masculinity despite unemployment confining him to domestic duties (63). Respite in Trezise's Valleys is temporary and individual: "the drugs and the records and the comics and the porn" are the solutions to "stress, strife, poverty, alcohol, drugs, chain-smoking; anything a Welsh person endured to stay alive" ("Valley Lines" 100, 103). Her Valleys too are haunted: Pontypridd is "a lonely Victorian wasteland" populated by "dusty phantom crowds" of miners congregating for "union meetings and rugby matches" ("The Brake Fluid at Gina's" 160). The Rhondda is "a valley of closing down coal mines and despairing, redundant men ... the world was somewhere else" ("Coney Island" 74). The loss is especially difficult for women: excluded from cultural activity in better days by the strong link between male labor and cultural activity, women's agency, as Aaron notes ("Valleys Women Writing" 86), remains limited. Trezise's second novel, *Sixteen Shades of Crazy* (2010), returns to the familiar themes of hopelessness and claustrophobia in the Valleys, "a classroom with no teacher" (293) in which drugs provide the only relief to the female protagonists whose lives and bonds are shaken up by the arrival of Johnny, the English drug dealer.

Much contemporary Welsh fiction replaces the exuberance of working class leisure activity with wearied, joyless attempts to fill time. The title of Lewis Davies's best-selling *Work, Sex and Rugby* (1993) does not celebrate masculinity: it lists duties unenthusiastically performed by a self-aware but directionless young protagonist-narrator. Laboring as a decorator's mate is far removed from miners' solidarity, while sex, rugby, and drinking merely pass the time in a valley characterized as grey, exhausted, and shrouded in drizzle: "Reality's shit all of the time ... sometimes you need to lose it" (*Work, Sex and Rugby* 82). The novel ends with a postmodern nod to self-fashioning, but the narrator ends his story having sex in a graveyard with a former girlfriend, an homage to the Welsh tradition of entwining sexuality and morbidity. Drizzle, greyness, exhaustion, talk, and recreational violence fill the pages of Davies's and Trezise's work. What is largely absent, however, is the Gothic presence found elsewhere. Instead, Davies and Trezise return to the realist project of representing "the Universal ... as a quality of the individual" (Lukács 76). While Trezise's characters resemble Gower's Davy Jones, "more than half the population are living dead, walking wounded" (*Goldfish Bowl* 119), they have lost the resistance and potential alterity provided by such Gothic elements.

In the case of contemporary Welsh-language fiction, Daniel Williams has suggested that, while it subverts realist conventions in a mode akin to postmodernist experimentation, Owen Martell's *Dyn yr Eiliad* ultimately offers a continuation of the realist project, not dissimilar to Davies's and Trezise's return to it (D. Williams, "Realaeth" 23–4). The novel charts Daniel and Anna's attempts to "create a new reality" following the death of their friend, Davies, the novel's third main character (D. Williams, "Realaeth" 23). The arguable return of the realist form at this point is significant in itself as 1990s Welsh-language fiction was characterized by bold postmodernist experimentation.[6] The telling of Martell's story is shared between Daniel, who speaks in the first person, and a narrator, who speaks in the third person, reminiscent of the realist mode. They share the same language, however, and the narration moves unnoticed at times between the two voices. Williams's reading links this reformulation of the realist mode to a process of national reimagining, and the process of attaching new meanings to "Welshness" in postdevolution Wales (D. Williams, "Realaeth" 25–6). Daniel and Davies have certainly inherited concepts of identity which Daniel, in light of Davies's death and other factors, must re-evaluate. Both men left Dowlais at 18 to go to university in Cardiff, seeking to distance themselves from the "Valleys" identity they inherited from their parents. Daniel's father

> would list the injustices – trying to make staunch socialists of us before we were eleven years old. Lord Crawshay, Dic Penderyn, who was hanged around this time, mid-August in 1831, underground working conditions, the miner's strike and the thousands in crisis. And Aberfan, of course. (Martell, 27)

The bringing together of events into a seemingly coherent narrative, as well as the concluding "of course," highlight the father's, and, to an extent, the reader's, unquestioning interpretation of Valleys' history and identity. It seems as certain and as unflinching as the mountains which surround the town, and upon which Daniel often reflects.

It is, however, an unstable and mobile "mountain" which haunts Daniel. The image of the colliery spoil tip at Aberfan collapsing in 1966, killing 144 people, is invoked by both Daniel and the third-person narrator in various different ways – numerous direct and indirect references are made to it. Near the beginning of the novel, as Daniel surveys the hills and valleys around him, noting how they have molded the inhabitants, the narrator describes Daniel's location: "Abercynon to the left. Nelson, Treharris, Aberfan to the right. 'Distant Drums' by Jim Reeves was number one when the mountain fell on the school" (Martell 15). Toward the novel's end, Daniel ponders the landfill sites that blight the Valleys' landscape:

> The lorries came every week carrying thrown-out prams, old food tins and doses of existentialism. . . . And that would be our gift to the world. An enormous mound of sludge – which would one of these days break free at the start of a school day and slide down the mountain to bury Merthyr. (Martell 250)

Although the image of the Aberfan disaster persists, it occurs in different ways, places, and contexts to each speaker.

For Daniel Williams, the image of the landfill is interesting in the context of Daniel's attempt to create a new identity out of what is left of the past ("Realaeth" 25). We argue that this is even more so the case in the context of much of the contemporary fiction discussed here, and its exploration of what is left of Welsh working class society. As his reference to Aberfan suggests, the mountains of rubbish Daniel looks at are not monolithic – they are made of bits and pieces, leftovers, remnants discarded by different people, communities, and industries. Even the mountains described early on in the novel, which seemed to symbolize the certainties offered by old identities, are, as Daniel tells us, made up of "[s]trata. Layers," a palimpsest of different influences (Martell 15). Like the characters of Rachel Trezise and Lewis Davies, Daniel seems to be aware that identity or history can be pieced together and that self-expression is an important medium – he writes notes throughout as he tries to draw the different strands of Davies's life and death, and, indeed, his own existence, together.

Martell's novel itself documents the adding of another layer to the Valleys' rocky identity, namely the return or revival of the Welsh language, achieved in part by the establishment of Welsh-medium schools in the area. Welsh-speakers Daniel and Davies are the children of English-speaking parents and so have presumably learned Welsh at school. Williams suggests that locating the novel in an area which has seen something of a Welsh-language revival is no coincidence, and it might be interesting to consider the anglophone novels discussed here in light of such a statement ("Realaeth" 25–6). That is not to say that learning Welsh is the answer to Trezise, Davies, and Griffiths's characters' problems. Instead, the language's return to the Valley offers a useful example of creating something new out of cultural remnants which had seemingly disappeared. As Daniel struggles to bring the fragments of Davies's story and his own history together, the novel's language, created from a mixture of Welsh and English, offers a model for forging identities out of the remnants of previously antagonistic cultures, languages, and communities.

Among these remnants, and given the hollowing out of the collective cultures and social structures that nurtured the anglophone working class novel, does an identifiably Welsh working class fiction still exist? We argue that it does, but in a new form. Gordon insists that "a disappearance is real only when it is apparitional," when "something lost or invisible or seemingly not there makes itself known or apparent to us" (63). What haunts Davy, Gracie, Lewis, and their counterparts are not the same things that haunt their English equivalents. What is present and absent in these texts is peculiarly Welsh: languages and dialects, the cultures and class formations lived through, and the traumatic loss of rural and industrial identities, however constructed or aspirational they may have been. Grace Allcock's experiences may look like those of any media-saturated British teenager under late capitalism, but she is haunted by different absences. The similarities between these anglophone texts and their Welsh-language contemporaries in terms of their focus on violence, sex, drink, and drugs, and in their characters' fragmented identities, might suggest that this new form is, in fact, a national form, too, or at least one which bridges the nation's linguistic divisions.

The outcast, the grotesque, the monster are central to twentieth-century and contemporary Welsh working class fiction. This is the revenge not only of the colonized but of the doubly excluded. The Gothic elements which have been recurrent features of these fictions are "an aesthetics of *making* monstrous, of demonstrative magnification and amplification" (Chow 16) which speak back to an audience implicated in constructing this marginalized monstrosity. The failure of socialism to transform social relations has merely added it to the list of ghosts. Phelps claims that "all English postwar literature has been overshadowed by a sense of social and cultural disintegration" (*Modern Britain* 198): although haunted by similar forces, the self-awareness of contemporary Welsh working class fiction suggests a need to construct new identities, even if the characters lack the agency to do so.

NOTES

1. See Jacques Derrida, *Spectres of Marx* (Abingdon: Routledge, 1994).
2. For the original Welsh, see Kate Roberts, *Traed Mewn Cyffion* ([1936]; 9th edition, Llandysul: Gwasg Gomer, 2001), 39.
3. See also Raymond Williams, "The Welsh Industrial Novel," in *Problems in Materialism and Culture* ([1978] London: Verso, 1980), 227.

4. The original Welsh demonstrates the type of language used in the novel, italicizing the words and patterns which demonstrate English influence ("jyst" is commonly used for "just," the use of "susceptible" is a case of code-switching, and "dod rownd i'n tŷ ni" draws on the English "come around to our house" – the standard Welsh word for 'around' would be "o gwmpas," and would not be used in this context). Further quotations from Welsh primary and secondary texts will be given in English translation by Lisa Sheppard unless stated otherwise.
5. Llwyd Owen revealed this detail during a discussion following a seminar paper on *Ffawd Cywilydd a Chelwyddau* at Cardiff University's School of Welsh (Sara Orwig, "Cyfnewid côd mewn llenyddiaeth: astudiaeth achos o *Ffawd Cywilydd a Chelwyddau*," 9 December 2014).
6. For academic studies discussing this trend, see Angharad Price, *Rhwng Gwyn a Du: Agweddau ar Ryddiaith Gymraeg yn 1990au* (Cardiff: University of Wales Press, 2002).

CHAPTER 25

Transforming Working Class Writers and Writing
Digital Editions, Projects, and Analyses

Cole Crawford

I work primarily with late-eighteenth- and early-nineteenth-century authors who produced printed texts, but my engagement with working class literary studies has always been mediated through a digital lens. As an undergraduate I double-majored in computer science and British literature, a combination that generally elicits quizzical looks. But as scholars working within the hybrid field of digital humanities (DH) have demonstrated, these seemingly unrelated disciplines often overlap to a surprising degree. Though traditional techniques such as close reading, rhetorical analysis, and literary criticism will remain necessary for scholarly research within the humanities, I believe that digital methodologies have increasingly become and will remain indispensable tools, both for supporting these established techniques and for asking and answering new questions, including questions that inform the study of laboring class authors. In what follows, I will provide a broad sketch of disciplinary trends in DH, discuss how other scholars of laboring class culture have employed digital methods, and finally discuss two of my own current projects which, in differing ways, demonstrate some possibilities and limitations for digital approaches to the study of the working class writing.

Digital humanities emerged from the older, more narrowly focused subdiscipline of humanities computing, which began as early as the 1940s.[1] John Unsworth coined the term "digital humanities" in 2001 during the prepublication process for *A Companion to Digital Humanities* (2004), preferring this new, broader description to the older label (Kirschenbaum). The Alliance of Digital Humanities Organizations – an international umbrella association for numerous groups and the sponsor of the annual Digital Humanities conference – was created in 2005, while the American National Endowment for the Humanities established the Digital Humanities Initiative (now the Office of Digital Humanities) in 2006. In the UK, the Arts and Humanities Research Council identified "Digital Transformations in the Arts and Humanities" as a priority area in 2011. The field has been served by the ADHO's flagship journal *Digital Humanities Quarterly* since 2007, and the *Journal of Digital Humanities* since 2012. These developments have affirmed DH as a legitimate and rapidly expanding academic field. Since around 2011, when William Pannapacker declared digital humanities not just the next big thing, but "The Thing – there's no Next about it," DH has gained significant traction and public exposure. Bolstered by funds from large NEH grants, the establishment of undergraduate and graduate programs, and the creation of digital humanities centers, the digital humanities are thriving in terms of institutional support, economic funding, and research output.

Despite this growth, or perhaps in part because of it, scholars have not yet reached a clear consensus on what "counts" as digital humanities research or agreed on a single definition of the field. As Matthew Kirschenbaum reminds us, essays that attempt to define the boundaries of digital humanities have been "genre pieces" for years (1). Dozens of such key definitional works have already been collected in *Defining Digital Humanities: A Reader* (Terras et al. 2013), *Debates in the Digital Humanities* (Gold 2012), and *Understanding Digital Humanities* (Berry 2012). While most authors concur about characteristics common to digital humanities, there is just as much disagreement, perhaps an inevitable consequence of a nascent field. Offering up another definitional essay is not my goal. The field is simply too expansive, with innumerable strains and variants of digital research all claiming the label of digital humanities and fitting (problematically and confusingly as well as inclusively) under the same "Big Tent" (see Terras, "Peering Inside"). For the purposes of this essay, Kathleen Fitzpatrick's description of the digital humanities is sufficiently broad: "a nexus of fields within which scholars use computing technologies to investigate the kinds of questions that are traditional to the humanities, or . . . who ask traditional kinds of humanities-oriented questions about computing technologies." This definition stresses that digital humanities researchers do more than just use technologies. They intentionally engage with them as central elements of their research, either as a component of a methodology or as an object of study.

The first part of this definition, which stresses the active use of technology, includes researchers performing tasks associated with the older humanities computing core of digital humanities: literary scholars using quantitative text analysis programs to perform distant readings of large collections of writing (see Moretti, *Graphs, Maps, Trees* and *Distant Reading*); historians creating interactive GIS (geographic information systems) maps; editors using TEI (Text Encoding Initiative) markup to create structured, machine-readable texts; librarians digitizing analog materials to birth new electronic archives; and archeologists reconstructing ancient ruins as 3D models and immersing users in vanished worlds through virtual reality displays. The second part of Fitzpatrick's definition – asking humanistic questions about technologies – sketches a broader understanding of the digital humanities as a field that also embraces researchers who focus on technology as an object of study. This includes scholars who work with new media texts, investigate how technology affects pedagogy or composition, or use technology to challenge the conventions of scholarly publishing. And though Fitzpatrick does not explicitly mention it, I would add to this definition the critical, theoretical discourse surrounding digital humanities itself, a meta-discussion which continues to define the field's boundaries and what should be considered digital humanities scholarship.

This meta-discussion has produced a framework that I find very productive for scholars of working class culture interested in creating significant digital projects. Unlike traditional written scholarship, which changes primarily in terms of content and ideas while maintaining a somewhat predictable and stable form, the presentation and organization of digital projects often changes rapidly because the underlying mode is transient and always advancing. This constant technological progression changes how projects are built from a technical standpoint, but more importantly, it also alters how users consume, interact with, and (re)interpret digital scholarship. DH projects have changed dramatically over the past several decades, much like the Internet, which has evolved from Web 1.0 (flat, read-only data designed for passive consumption) to Web 2.0 (interactive data that invites participation between users and websites) and looks forward to Web 3.0 (a semantic web that uses open, structured data to share information and connect different applications). In *The Digital Humanities Manifesto 2.0*, Schnapp and Presner refer to the iterative evolution of DH as a series of waves:

> The first wave of digital humanities work was quantitative, mobilizing the search and retrieval powers of the database, automating corpus linguistics, stacking hypercards into critical arrays. The second wave is **qualitative, interpretive, experiential, emotive, generative** in character. It harnesses digital toolkits in the service of the Humanities' core methodological strengths: attention to complexity, medium specificity, historical context, analytical depth, critique and interpretation. (original emphasis)

While I have encountered some digital working class projects that have tentatively engaged with this "second wave" which is characterized by experimental interpretation and interactivity, the vast majority of digital working class research relies on older first-wave technologies. There is nothing inherently wrong with or obsolete about Web 1.0 websites, or their first-wave DH counterparts; many admirably fulfill their stated purposes simply by presenting data digitally. Projects that archive and revive primary texts through digitization (including some of my own work, which I describe below) are certainly useful, but they are principally *reproductive* rather than *productive*, "replicat[ing] the world of scholarly communications that print gradually codified over five centuries" rather than fully exploiting the advantages of an entirely new mode (Schnapp and Presner). Newer second-wave projects move beyond this model, adopting standards and best practices posited by both humanistic scholars and HCI (human–computer interaction) researchers to provide opportunities for interpretation and emphasize the user's experience, rather than just recreating textual materials or crunching numbers. Engaging with both content and technology while seamlessly merging both aspects to craft a deeply theorized and interpretive argument is difficult, but potentially very productive. The most successful digital projects do not just captivate users, but rather invoke an entirely different model of knowledge generation and consumption for both the project creator and the user.

Most current laboring class DH projects can be considered digital editions or thematic research collections, though many blend together multiple elements and include critical components. Digital editions aim to present scholarly versions of literary texts or letters, usually produced by a single author. Single-author editions usually have more clearly defined critical approaches than large collections that include hundreds or thousands of texts. Examples of single-author digital editions of British working class writers include *The Letters of Robert Bloomfield and His Circle*; *John Clare Poems: The Lifetime Published Poetry*; *The Letters of James Currie (1756–1805)*; and the *William Golder Electronic Edition*. Though not strictly a digital edition, *Editing Robert Burns for the 21st Century* is a digital companion to the new Oxford University Press editions of Burns edited by Gerard Carruthers and his University of Glasgow team, and includes song and prose recordings, videos, and other interactive exhibits related to Burns's work. Thematic research collections aggregate heterogeneous items which share a common topic and emphasize connections between materials rather than a linear reading experience. Text-focused collections which incorporate works by laboring class authors include *Scottish Women Poets of the Romantic Period*; *Irish Women Poets of the Romantic Period*; *Women Writers Project*; *Eighteenth-Century Poetry Archive; The Poetess Archive*; and *British Women Romantic Poets (1789–1832)*.

Biographical collections principally present data about the writers rather than hosting primary sources, though they may include bibliographies. Chiefly biographical / bibliographic collections include *Orlando: Women's Writing in the British Isles from the Beginnings to the Present* and the *Archive of Working-Class Writing*. The *Archive of Working-Class Writing* is notable because it focuses exclusively on laboring class writers, especially those with memoirs in the Burnett Archive of Working-Class Autobiographies; digitizing this collection is the project's current objective. The sister sites *Locating London's Past, London Lives 1690–1800*, and *The Proceedings of the Old Bailey 1674–1913* recognize that how we read working class writers differs from how we read other authors and therefore approach biographies, using primary sources to "assess the role of plebeians in the evolution of social practices" ("About *London Lives*"). These three projects address how working class individuals (not necessarily writers) interacted with social institutions. *London Lives* and *The Old Bailey Online* are very large databases containing hundreds of thousands of documents. *The Old Bailey Online* specifically focuses on criminal trials, while *London Lives* incorporates proceedings from *The Old Bailey Online* alongside manuscripts from institutional sources, such as medical records, parish poor relief logs, guild and society notes, and tax records, merging all these sources and allowing users to search individual names and retrieve all the documents associated with that individual. *Locating London's Past* uses datasets from both projects to geographically map documents that contain spatial information, such as crime locations or home addresses of poor relief recipients, onto a georeferenced version of John Rocque's 1746 map of London. This fascinating interface allows users to construct stories about working class Londoners and generate new ways of seeing and interpreting the large-scale data that drives the project, thereby embodying many of the values characteristic of second-wave DH projects.

While not specifically focused on working class writing, there are several other large-scale digital resources that include working class texts or critical research on British working class writers. Gale Cengage's massive *Eighteenth* and *Nineteenth Century Collections Online* websites, which include many working class texts, artifacts, and curated collections, are likely to be familiar to readers. Two other projects from the University of Virginia – *NINES* (Networked Infrastructure for Nineteenth-Century Electronic Scholarship) and its sister site, *18thConnect* – function not as standalone archives, but as research aggregators, digital tool clearinghouses, and peer-review bodies for born-digital scholarship. Searching *NINES*, for example, will return results from hundreds of peer-reviewed projects associated with *NINES*. *Connected Histories* is a similar digital resource aggregator that covers a longer time period (1500–1900). The *Romantic Circles* website includes articles and digital editions of working class writers, such as the aforementioned Robert Bloomfield edition.

Many of these projects are heavily text-based and aim to present existing information rather than to generate new insights or invite user interaction and collaboration, and thus most can be considered first-wave DH projects in Schnapp and Presner's model. With some exceptions, such as *Locating London's Past*, which uses an innovative map interface, and the *Eighteenth-Century Poetry Archive*, which deploys quantitatively enhanced "layers" to assist users interested in reading poems closely, the majority of these undertakings barely experiment with new digital methods or push beyond text-centric modes of presentation. While nearly all the projects present primary texts accurately and achieve other project-specific goals, they are so deeply rooted in the textual tradition that they fail to capitalize on the advantages that the digital offers over print. Fully embracing the digital medium is a crucial shift necessary for projects on working class writers to actively engage their audiences and to help their users generate new knowledge. Providing open access to resources is another vital step. Several of the aforementioned projects are restricted to paid subscribers, and while I recognize the need for academic resource providers to receive compensation for their work, limiting access to digital projects through paywalls prevents the emergence of new scholarship and hinders collaboration.

The first of my current projects began as an edition that primarily reproduced extant texts, but my hope is to develop it further to become more interactive and experiential. *Transforming Robert Tannahill*, a digital edition of the Paisley weaver-poet Robert Tannahill (1774–1810), includes many of his poems, songs, and letters. Tannahill published his only lifetime collection of work via subscription in 1807 (Semple lxxiii). The entire print run of *The Soldier's Return: A Scottish Interlude in Two Acts, with Other Poems and Songs Chiefly in the Scottish Dialect* sold out in weeks, and though the featured dramatic interlude was criticized, Tannahill's poems were generally well-received and his songs hailed as some of the best since Burns's death (Semple lxxiv; Struthers 415–16; "A Memoir" 78). Despite his success, Tannahill was unsatisfied with this initial venture and wished to publish a revised edition that included an improved interlude and sheet music to accompany his songs (Semple lxxviii). Unhappy with the subscription method, he attempted to publish directly, and received several rejection notices because of the shrinking poetry market (Semple lxxix, lxxxii). Coupled with his depression, these rejections were too much for Tannahill to bear, and in 1810 he attempted to destroy all his manuscripts before committing suicide (Semple lxxviii, lxxxiv).

After his early death, Tannahill's work steadily rose in popularity, and a series of Tannahill Concerts in Paisley that ran from 1876 through 1936 attracted crowds of up to 30,000 who paid to hear a choir of hundreds sing his songs (Jolly; "Tannahill Anniversary" 11). Though Tannahill's poems went through several editions after his death, including German translations, the most recent edition of his work was compiled in 1876 by David Semple. While Semple's work is invaluable, especially his "Life of Tannahill" and appendices, he made numerous questionable editorial decisions, such as smoothing Tannahill's dialect voice and other substantives even when the meaning of the lines was perfectly clear. Semple's edition, while close to comprehensive in terms of the poems, also neglected a large collection of Tannahill's letters held by the University of Glasgow. With the recent recording of a CD collection of Tannahill's songs by Fred Freeman and the continued popularity of the traditional Scottish band "The Tannahill Weavers," it seemed an appropriate time to revive Tannahill's poems after over a century of editorial and critical neglect.

While I always conceived of the project as a digital product, it is first and foremost an edition of a literary work, and as such draws deeply on established print-based humanities methodologies, especially the traditions of textual criticism and archival research. I created a guiding editorial rationale for the project, incorporating ideas from W. W. Greg, Fredson Bowers, and Jerome McGann to provide a reading text with minimal editorial intervention that preserves Tannahill's dialect voice and style while also making this edition accessible to a wide audience through extensive but unobtrusive annotations. I originally transcribed a small selection of Tannahill's nature writing, focusing solely on poems and songs from his first collection, and edited the texts as necessary. I later expanded the scope of the project to include the entirety of *The Soldier's Return*, and have since added dozens of other recovered poems and most of Tannahill's correspondence. Tannahill's letters are quite fragile and I was unable to convince the University of Glasgow to professionally digitize the collection, so I traveled to Scotland to work with the holograph manuscripts in person for several weeks. I also visited the National Library of Scotland, where I found a copy of the periodical which published Tannahill's first poem, and the Paisley County Library, where I (re)discovered a lost sonnet of Tannahill's which has never before been included in a collection of his work. I intend to eventually add all Tannahill's known writings as well as additional background information and critical essays to create the most comprehensive version of his work available. From the beginning of the edition in early 2013, I conceived of it as an open-access digital project. Constructing the project digitally appealed to me because I wanted to reach a large and widely distributed audience; maintain the ability to easily extend, change, and update the project's content and form over time; integrate interactive content to connect with readers; and interpret texts using new methodologies.

Though I had previously developed several small websites, representing physical texts in a digital space was an entirely new experience for me. The form of the project changed several times as I progressed as a developer and editor. The first version was static and included only edited versions of Tannahill's texts – a project drawing strongly on first-wave DH methodologies. I then added annotations and English descriptions of difficult Scots-language terms, embedding these references directly in the texts themselves so readers could mouse over terms for more information. As part of my efforts to make the edition accessible and appealing to a wide audience, I also built several supplementary tools and visualizations. I used a named entity recognizer to find places mentioned in Tannahill's writing, then georeferenced each point and plotted the frequency of these markers with a GIS program, creating a map displaying all the locations Tannahill named in his work and how often each appears. The high frequency of Scottish locations, especially places quite near Paisley, helped me argue that Tannahill was a fundamentally local poet compared to more cosmopolitan writers such as Robert Burns. I also recreated a virtual version of historical Paisley through a combination of old survey maps, modern photographs, and the Google Maps Javascript API (application programming interface) to immerse my readers in Tannahill's world. Though certainly not cutting-edge, these visualizations helped make the project more interpretive and experiential, beginning to shift it toward a second-wave paradigm.

Not every endeavor was successful. Despite my desire to situate Tannahill in a rich historical context, I was unable to include musical recordings of Tannahill's songs from Fred Freeman's recent *Complete Songs of Robert Tannahill* series because of an ongoing copyright dispute. This was disappointing because Tannahill's songwriting was his greatest literary strength and placing settings of his songs in conversation with their texts was one of his most sustained ambitions. Another weakness is the digital platform for the website. I am currently using a proprietary CMS (content management system) with a simple drag-and-drop interface that also allows custom styling and web scripting because I wanted to focus primarily on adding well-edited, quality content rather than designing a bespoke website. As the project evolved, I encountered more and more limitations with this management system, and plan to eventually move to a more robust and standard open source CMS such as Drupal or Wordpress. I also did not initially consider the project's longevity. Only after completing much of the transcription process did I realize that I should have encoded texts with TEI-compliant XML (extensible markup language). TEI is both a set of guidelines for encoding text and an organization that maintains the guidelines; TEI-XML is the preferred format of the MLA's Committee on Scholarly Editions for digital editions. Unlike HTML, which describes how text should be formatted, TEI-XML explicitly encodes text with semantic meaning, which is useful both for presentation and computational analysis of textual structures. Using TEI-XML rather than HTML would have ensured the text's future usability, promoted reuse by other scholars or migration to another publishing platform, and enhanced my ability to perform computational textual analyses. Recoding all my transcriptions is thus my next goal for the project. Though these mishaps – copyright difficulties, platform problems, and textual markup issues – could perhaps have been minimized or prevented by consulting with developers or senior researchers who regularly create digital editions, I do not view them as failures, but rather as learning opportunities that have taught me far more about the process of building a digital humanities project than any direct advice could have achieved. *Transforming Robert Tannahill* demonstrates that digital humanities can be accessible to students at the undergraduate level and that individual scholars can create robust and complex digital projects without prior DH experience.

Along with my work on Tannahill, I have also contributed to another large-scale project, *Laboring-Class Poets Online* (LCPO). LCPO aims to present a comprehensive, online database of all working class British poets who published between 1700 and 1900, focusing primarily on biographical characteristics while also including basic bibliographic information about the texts each poet produced. In many ways LCPO is an extension of the groundbreaking six-volume anthology *Eighteenth and Nineteenth Century English Labouring-Class Poetry* (Goodridge et al.), but it both precedes and succeeds this collection of working class writing. This database has grown through multiple iterations as it has advanced both in terms of numbers of poets and technological complexity. What began as 300-poet checklist compiled by John Goodridge during his doctoral research on Stephen Duck and Mary Collier now contains biographical descriptions of over

2,030 laboring class poets contributed by a working group of over a dozen scholars, and this list is constantly growing. However, while the information contained within the list was rigorously collected and is of obvious interest to scholars of working class literature, its form more closely resembles a printed text than a structured database; though it exists digitally, the format does not currently leverage the potential benefits of the digital medium. Extending Schnapp and Presner's framework backward, it can be seen as a "DH wave beta" project. I consider a structured database that researchers can search with field-level specificity to be a first-wave project because it mostly adheres to the passive consumption, search-and-read-only model. Producing such a project is the current goal of LCPO, but moving from a first-wave to a second-wave paradigm is our ultimate objective, a task which will require providing new ways for users to interact with, interpret, and repurpose the collected data.

Converting this collection of biographical records into an online database is the primary purpose of LCPO because of the advantages of relational databases compared to text files. These benefits include an increase in sheer speed because of a computer-friendly structure; the ability to perform complicated, multipart queries rather than limiting users to only keyword-based text searches (returning, for example, all female poets who lived in Paisley between 1750 and 1800 with an occupation other than weaver); allowing multiple users to concurrently access and edit dynamic information; providing direct access within a web browser instead of requiring users to download and externally view text files; maintaining data integrity by enforcing rules about what information can be entered at the field level and preventing the duplication of data; general extensibility, reliability, and updateability; and authorizing other digital tools and projects to access and transform this structured data.

This last item, allowing other projects or tools to interface with exposed data, is particularly important for further research and for moving beyond the inherent limits of static, first-wave initiatives. Providing a way for other researchers to use our data, whether through a REST endpoint or static download, promotes collaboration by allowing new projects to continuously build on the original initiative. This also provides a way for researchers to extend the core project through data visualizations or other representations, which can assist scholars interested in approaching working class writers from this period in aggregate. Such approaches may reveal entirely new findings that we did not initially envision. After collecting the life narratives of thousands of working class poets over several decades and carefully distilling these biographies into discrete data points, the project investigators have already developed many productive ways to view and theorize working class culture, which will be incorporated into *Laboring-Class Poets Online*. Though the creation of any digital tool or archive is an implicit instantiation of a certain worldview, these arguments about how we understand working class writers will not exist in opaque isolation from the underlying information that generated them. Exposing the raw LCPO data can potentially strengthen the project by helping researchers understand why we made certain inferences and by providing material to further refine these assumptions. Relinquishing control over how datasets are used can be unsettling for scholars accustomed to deploying strong theories and crafting airtight arguments. However, releasing the data amassed by LCPO for reuse and reinterpretation could ultimately have a larger impact than only delivering our prepackaged conclusions.

Because the database is relatively comprehensive, we can use it not only to learn about individual authors, but also to approach British laboring class poets as a group. Creating ways besides search queries to interact with this information, such as data visualizations, can help researchers identify previously hidden patterns or trends by creating coherence out of confusion and raw numbers. For example, researchers could potentially use entries from the LCPO database to understand the spatial and temporal development of writing communities. A project with first-wave aims might present this data quantitatively, perhaps returning a dynamically generated table with relevant fields: poet names, the dates these poets were actively publishing, and the locations of their residences or publishers. A well-designed database could even assist the researcher by returning only poets who lived within a specific geographic area and wrote during a designated period. However, manually processing such data at scale – in this case, over 2,000 poets, but in larger data sets millions of records – is difficult or even impossible. A project with second-wave characteristics would provide a more qualitative and experiential way to interpret the lives of these poets while maintaining analytical depth and complexity. This could be accomplished by creating a geographic map with a timeline slider and georeferenced points representing the locations of actively publishing poets, which would allow users to manipulate the time factor to see how different writing communities formed and declined over time. Clicking on individual markers could redirect users to specific poet pages, while selecting multiple markers or filtering by field parameters could allow users to compare specific records. While scholars have already distinguished large groups of poets from Paisley, Manchester, Nottingham, Blackburn, and other locations, such a tool could help uncover unknown clusters. Other visualizations could address characteristics such as profession, gender, publications, publishers, genres, topics, dialect use, or networks of influence, thereby organizing and grouping poets by biographical characteristics other than geographic location.

Such data visualizations are intrinsically interesting, but their true utility lies in highlighting anomalies that require more thorough qualitative, humanistic inquiry. Computational analyses or visualizations may reveal such patterns or abnormalities, but algorithms can rarely provide satisfactory reasons for *why* they occurred. While this lack of complete objectivity even in a digitally mediated environment may be maddening for computer scientists, it should be encouraging for literary critics and historians. This is a potential point of entry for humanities scholars trained in synthesizing complex, ambiguous data from conflicting sources to produce comprehensive arguments. While datasets may contain sufficient observations to reach potential answers, they require human interpretation to turn these thousands or millions of disorganized, unprocessed, discrete measurements into significant information that can be used to craft a cohesive narrative. This shift from meaningless data to meaningful information is predicated on organization and interpretation. Implementing machine learning techniques or computational sorting algorithms to reach this point does not erase the human influence from the process; after all, humans coded the algorithms, and humans eventually interpret the results. Finding a way to effectively mesh quantitative and qualitative analyses with humanistic interpretation encourages deep, speculative exploration. Using data visualizations as a bridge to zoom in and out between large-scale quantitative analyses and close, interpretive readings and explications is conducive to a form of argument that is richer and more productive than using either close reading or distant reading in isolation. Researchers should not view close reading and distant reading as mutually exclusive approaches locked in an "either / or" binary, but rather look for ways to deploy them together in a "both / and" relationship. Ultimately, an approach that repeatedly applies both heuristics could help us learn not only what biographic or bibliographic features generally distinguished working class writers, but help us craft an argument about why these characteristics were endemic to the working class writers that appear in the LCPO database.

LCPO researchers and students have begun creating this database by selecting metadata fields to describe poets; re-keying information from the text-based poets list; compiling poet bibliographies and uncovering previously digitized and openly available manuscripts; and drafting extended entries about important poets. Theory is deeply embedded within these database design practices. As DH theorists such as Jean Bauer and Josh Honn have argued, just because a tool or project is digital rather than analog does not free it from the theoretical and ideological considerations by which we judge text-based work; digital tools and projects are never value-neutral because they are always crafted for a specific purpose and thus support a certain use or position. When trying to describe the professions of laboring class poets, for example, the project team decided to create not one but two fields, industry and occupations. The industry field uses a controlled vocabulary of 22 set terms so that poets who worked in similar trades can be grouped together, while the occupations field is unconstrained and thus infinitely more idiosyncratic, containing entries from "haberdasher" to "cordwainer" (Froid). This allows the database to maintain a balance between the human complexity needed to study these poets and the rigid field constraints conducive to database searches, ultimately adding more information rather than reducing the reality of eighteenth- and nineteenth-century employment to a tiny set of predefined terms. Even though the team had little experience with data curation or data management best practices, we understood the theoretical and historical significance of these choices; by creating this controlled vocabulary, we actively shaped the results users will receive and thus how thousands of poets will be presented. *Laboring-Class Poets Online* is an ongoing project because of its scale and complexity. The group plans to complete the digital development of the database and release a version with core database functionality for public access by summer 2017.

In closing, let me note that I am not suggesting that all literary researchers should begin using digital methods, or that digital projects will supplant traditional text-based scholarship as the primary product of the humanities. Close reading, ethnography, and other qualitative approaches will likely remain central to the humanities for the foreseeable future, and though some projects and papers could benefit by incorporating digital techniques, just as many can succeed entirely through written arguments. Nor am I suggesting that DH presents some sort of techno-utopian salvation where the pervasive issues afflicting the humanities and the modern university are magically solved by turning to the digital. DH has its own internal tensions. Movements such as #transformDH rightly argue that the field has been too exclusionary and needs to better consider "race, ethnicity, disability, and class" ("About #transformDH"); MLA panels like "The Dark Side of Digital Humanities" critique DH's supposed economic complicity with the neoliberal academy (Grusin et al.); and arguments between proponents of different "types" of DH (Ramsay), or ideology versus methodology (Scheinfeldt), or any of the other ways to frame the divide between a "materialist epistemology" of building (Ramsay and Rockwell) and other theories of knowledge generation threaten to divide the inclusive big tent that was only recently established.

Though these issues are certainly troubling, they are being actively grappled with and addressed by digital humanities scholars committed to improving the field. And though these problems affect DH as an area of study, they do not degrade the efficacy of digital methods and scholarship, which I am convinced will become increasingly vital for humanistic research in the twenty-first century. In an age where the underlying value of the humanities is increasingly questioned, public digital projects can make academic research more approachable for general readers and thereby attract a broader audience. Projects such as this collection of essays, which strives to recover and reappraise historical working class writing for nonspecialist readers, already further such egalitarian efforts. Public digital humanities projects can build on existing textual scholarship to help us construct a public literary studies movement to parallel the public history campaign – and like the public history movement, scholars can help ensure that this effort represents a people's history, a literary legacy that bubbles up from below. Digital projects – those without paywalls, at least – are more accessible than printed texts for most potential readers. As scholars of working class writing, we should attend to the modes of production chosen by the artists and writers we study and recognize that modern writers are composing digitally and multimodally rather than solely through printed texts. *Laboring-Class Poets Online* has uncovered a prodigious number of eighteenth- and nineteenth-century working class writers and texts because of the proliferation of print during this period and the opening of publishing both to new markets and new authors, including those from the working class. Reconstructing a culture of working class writing before 1700 or so is much harder because of the relative scarcity of texts. The opposite is true today: increased literacy rates and digital modes of distribution have greatly increased the number of writers and therefore the number of texts available for scholarly analysis.[2] But few modern texts are alphabetic and analog – they are predominantly multimodal and digital. Fifty years from now, even scholars using qualitative humanities heuristics will need to understand and interact with the digital because the content they will be studying will have been produced digitally. By creating born-digital scholarship that meets such works natively, we can connect modern readers with the rich heritage of historical working class writers while also expanding the existing archive to encompass contemporary texts. The field of working class literary studies is still young and growing; we are only just now realizing the full strength and extent of this tradition, and much work – both analog and digital – remains to be done. The entire past human record is rapidly being digitized, and the future human record will be primarily digital. It is up to humanities researchers to ensure that working class literature assumes its rightful place in this unfolding story.

NOTES

1. See Susan Hockey for a detailed humanities computing timeline.
2. Despite a technology-driven expansion of writing outlets, access-related problems continue to limit the agency of content producers, especially those from rural areas or limited economic means.

Afterword

Brian Maidment

This volume is already furnished with a foreword and an introduction which survey its substantial content. Accordingly, the aim in this afterword is to think more generally about the agenda that has informed the study of laboring class writing over the last 25 years in order to allow readers, having read through the sequence of essays in this volume, to come to their own conclusions about the extent to which that agenda has been acknowledged and explored. My qualification for undertaking this task lies largely in having produced, now over 25 years ago, a heavily annotated anthology of writing by "self-taught" nineteenth-century poets – *The Poorhouse Fugitives* – which was published by a relatively small literary press in 1987 and which has, much to Carcanet's credit, remained in print ever since. It is my hope that, in reengaging with the issues that were central to structuring this volume, it may be possible to suggest both some of the preoccupations that have informed the essays in this volume and to lay out some of the continuing tasks and complexities that will, I hope, drive future study in this field.

The primary motive for undertaking *The Poorhouse Fugitives* was to provide a teaching text that would give students access not just to unfamiliar and obscure texts written by authors existing on the margins of recoverable literary history but also to provide some sort of context for a discussion of the cultural significance of such writing. Such a project was very much of its particular time and place in the history of higher education in the UK, in this case the English and History departments of Manchester Polytechnic. "Polytechnic English," as it was sometimes called, was part of a wider movement which aimed to re-write British humanities degrees in order to provide a cultural history that would challenge the syllabus "from below" through a broad-based attack on the structures of "canonicity" and the privileging of complexity and aesthetic achievement over socio-historical significance in the study of literature. The formal processes through which polytechnic degree programs were "validated" by a national body drawn from established universities had proved a jousting ground for such discussion along with many fraught conferences based on discussion of how to "fire the canon." This project was driven both by the kinds of students who went to Polytechnics (a high percentage of mature and "self-educated" students along with a range of students from culturally and economically deprived backgrounds) and by a sense of polemical zeal, widely exhibited by polytechnic teachers, in producing socially questioning and dissenting graduates who would challenge traditional values. The study of writing by "working class," politically oppositional, or radical authors was clearly the kind of project "Polytechnic English" would relish.

Manchester, with many defining characteristics of Engels's "shock city" still clearly visible in the 1980s, but also full of reminders of the cotton industry as a form of "people's history," served as a further impetus to bring together a collection of writing by obscure local authors. Regional identity certainly needed acknowledgment and restatement. Such scholarly work as had been undertaken up to that time, somewhat embarrassingly, had come from anthologies written with a clear ideological purpose in Russia (Kovalev's 1956 *An Anthology of Chartist Writing*) and East Germany (Mary Ashraf's two-volume *Introduction to Working Class Literature* from 1977 and 1978). The key book that alerted us to the range and importance of "industrial writing," Martha Vicinus's *The Industrial Muse* (1974), emanated from the American mid-west. Why was there so little British acknowledgment, in both scholarly publications and undergraduate syllabi, of the wealth of resources that might be recovered from the major libraries and scattered local history collections that had served as the cultural reservoirs for provincial industrial culture?

If the context that made *The Poorhouse Fugitives* a necessary project lay in the politics of British higher education, the questions it sought to answer also belonged to wider discussions about cultural memory. The primary intention was to enact a process of *recovery*, to bring back what had been lost and re-instate it within the possibility of further discussion. But clearly the process of "recovery" is not a neutral process. At its least value laden, "recovering" laboring class literary expression is merely making available what has previously been unavailable, a process hugely assisted over the last decade by the mass digitization of literary texts, especially periodicals and newspapers. But such a definition of "recovery" avoids the more difficult issues at stake. Why was this literature "lost"? Given the political agenda of the 1980s, explanations for the invisibility of laboring class writing ran through a spectrum of possibilities that ran from historical accident (it had been "overlooked" because of its mode of publication and, crucially, its aesthetic failings) through cultural snobbery (it was "avoided" because of its stridency and lowly origins) and on to overtly political responses – writing by laboring men and women had been effectively "repressed" because of its implicit social challenge. In the ideological struggles that preoccupied higher education in the 1980s, it was tempting to look no further than "repression" as an explanation for the historical occlusion of a large body of literary work by socially marginal authors. "Repression" was an extremely valuable term not just for the implicit critique of an authoritarian society that it suggested, but also because it made writing by laboring class authors an exemplary site for an investigation of the processes and structures through which societies manage – the Williamsite term would be "assimilate" – politically oppositional literature. Accordingly, *The Poorhouse Fugitives* included a large amount of material that sought to identify the print dialogues and responses through which liberal metropolitan opinion engaged with the literary aspirations of the emergent artisan classes for just this reason.

The quest for an "oppositional" literature raised, and still raises, a series of questions about "difference" – in what sense, apart from its invisibility, was laboring class literature different from that produced elsewhere in society? In the 1980s, any such difference was perceived largely in terms of class. In its clumsiest and least precise definition, this was distinctively "working class" literature. The difficulties of such a definition are immediately obvious – was this literature narrowly defined by being *produced by* working class writers, and in what terms was it possible to say if a writer *was* working class? While the incentive to detailed biographical study of individual authors that such an approach required was often extremely helpful in providing a necessary socio-historical context for further study, it was an approach that failed to address a number of key issues. In what senses was working class writing *formally* distinctive from other published literature? What sense of a distinctive readership did it display? Was such writing addressed upwards in an attempt to influence sophisticated and powerful readers or sideways to enhance shared consciousness among fellow working class readers? How far was working class writing identifiable by its particular modes of publication, distribution, and reception? Was such writing in any meaningful sense "proletarian" as historians and polemicists on the far left would have most liked? Even the most committed and naïve Marxist historians had by this time abandoned the idea of a single working class as an historical category, but the differentiations available (the artisans, the labor elite, and so on) if anything made definitions even more unhelpful. In an attempt to avoid the crudities of a predominantly socioeconomic definition, I used a cultural definition – "self-taught" – to differentiate the writers I gathered together in *The Poorhouse Fugitives*, thus making education and cultural experience rather than economic status a central mode of "difference." Subsequently, it has become general scholarly practice to echo John Goodridge's preferred designation – "labouring class" – as the most useful term largely because it simultaneously acknowledges ideas of class, economic status, and cultural experience. It is a recognition of the extent to which "working class" writing has become an integral part of the everyday repertoire of research and scholarship, and how widely recognition of the terminological complexities has been assimilated into general awareness, that "labouring class" has become both a useful and largely uncontentious marker of a shared field of study.

Underlying this emphasis on class as the central defining characteristic of the field was the hope that "working class" literature would offer an "authentic" account of industrial experience not to be found in any other sources. This aspiration to identify and celebrate the "real" voice of working people had informed Martha Vicinus's *The Industrial Muse*, a book which had made a huge impact on my colleagues at Manchester Polytechnic and led us to introduce a cross-disciplinary program on "Manchester in the 1840s." Also in the late 1970s a range of school and educational textbooks, including Roy Palmer's *A Touch on the Times* (1974) and Jon Raven's *Victoria's Inferno* (1978), had been published, joining A. L. Lloyd's *Folksong in England* (1967) in seeking to identify a range of literature about the British industrial experience that was "authentically" of the people. Yet as we worked with the poems, broadsides, lyrics, and fiction that we had gathered for the program we became increasingly conscious of the highly mediated nature of the texts that we were seeking to understand and their refusal to be simply "alternative" or "oppositional."

We were also perpetually anxious about issues to do with literary quality – how important was the aesthetic achievement of a poem in making it effective? Did poems need to be highly accomplished in order to celebrate the cultural achievement represented by their making, or did issues to do with address, occasion, and performance outweigh literary qualities through a shared sense of social purposefulness? Was laboring class writing always forced to ventriloquize the literary characteristics of the dominant culture, or were there ways in which it could speak authentically through the use of alternative literary modes and languages? The use of dialect served as a rallying place for these discussions, much indebted to Brian Hollingworth's invaluable anthology *Songs of the People* (1977). And how far did regional factors – a shared idiolect, local distribution networks, the publishers, printers, and bookshops to be found springing up in industrial cities – structure the production, consumption and understanding of laboring class writing? Did regionality, through the establishment of bardic communities, cut across differences of social class? And how far, in particular, were newspapers and magazines crucial in the construction of a regional identity that was available to the laboring classes?

Looking back now, the insistence on social class as the primary "difference" expressed by laboring class writing seems naïve or even misleading, a view confirmed by reading through the subtle and complex notions of personal and literary identity contained in this volume. *The Poorhouse Fugitives* was extremely limited in expressing the importance of forms of "difference" other than class, most obviously gender, but also region, locality, language, and performance. There were a few women writers in *The Poorhouse Fugitives*, and Florence Boos was only the first of subsequent commentators to suggest how inadequately female writers had been represented. Other critics pointed out the considerable attention paid to the industrial northwest at the expense of other significant localities, both urban and rural, where laboring class writers were extremely active and important in defining the particular regional characteristics that informed their work. Some acknowledgment was made of the performative elements to be found in Chartist poetry, but there was nothing of the sophisticated awareness of performance elements to be found in, for example, Mike Sanders's recent work on Chartist poetry.

While this volume does not form a definitive history of working class or laboring class writing – as the editors note it is *a* history rather than *the* history – it does suggest how deeply absorbed, and shared, an awareness of the central issues that define the field has become. The recovery over the last 25 years of the "lost" literature produced by and for the laboring classes has been remarkable, and has been well supported by major digitization projects. "Availability" is certainly not the central difficulty for future study, and the chapters of this volume are largely based on texts that are now accessible to a wide range of readers. In terms of "canonicity," writing by laboring class men and women has been widely assimilated into literary history. Yet much more work remains to be done, especially in developing study of laboring class writing within undergraduate and postgraduate programs. This volume represents a key moment of celebration of, and reflection upon, traditions of writing which embody a challenging sociocultural complexity. It is this complexity that forces us to ask persistent and still pertinent questions about how societies forget, about how cultural identity is formed, and about the power structures expressed and constructed through literary texts.

Works Cited

PRIMARY SOURCES

Addison, Joseph. *The Spectator* 160 (3 September 1711). www.networkedcorpus.com/spectator/index.html.

Addressed to the Serious Considerations of the Peers. No Slaves – No Sugar. Containing new and irresistible Arguments in Favour of the African Trade. By a Liverpool Merchant. London: W. J. and J. Richardson, 1804.

Allan, Dot. *Hunger March.* London: Hutchinson, 1934.

Allan, Thomas, ed. *Allan's Illustrated Edition of Tyneside Songs and Readings. With Lives, Portraits, and Autographs of the Writers, and Notes on the Songs.* 1891. Newcastle: Frank Graham, 1972.

Anderson, Robert. *Robert Anderson: The Cumberland Bard: Centenary Celebration Souvenir.* Ed. W. T. McIntyre. Carlisle: Thurnam and Sons, 1933.

——— "Dedication." *Poetical Works of Robert Anderson, author of "Cumberland Ballads" to which is prefixed the life of the author, written by himself with an essay on the character, manners, and customs of the peasantry of Cumberland; and observations on the style and genius of the author by Thomas Sanderson.* Carlisle: B. Scott, 1820.

Arnold, Matthew. *Culture and Anarchy.* London: Smith, Elder, 1869.

Ashford, Mary Ann. *Life of a Licensed Victualler's Daughter.* London: Saunders and Ottley, 1844.

"The Authoress of Our New Serial Story." *The Co-operative News* 21 July 1915: 998–9.

Bancks, John. *The Weaver's Miscellany or Poems on Several Subjects.* London: For the Author, 1730.

Barke, James. *Land of the Leal.* 1939. Edinburgh: Canongate, 1987.

——— *Major Operation.* 1936. London: Collins, 1955.

——— "The Scottish National Question." 1936. *Modernism and Nationalism.* Ed. Margery Palmer McCulloch. Glasgow: ASLS, 2004. 367–70.

Baron, Alexander. *King Dido.* 1969. Nottingham: Five Leaves, 2009.

——— *The Lowlife.* 1963. London: The Harvill Press, 2001.

——— *The Human Kind.* 1953. Bath: New Portway Editions, Cedric Chivers Ltd., 1973.

——— *Rosie Hogarth.* 1951. Nottingham: Five Leaves, 2010.

There's No Home. London: Jonathan Cape, 1950. London: Sort of Books, 2011.
From the City, From the Plough. 1948. London: Triad Paperbacks, 1979.
Barstow, Stan. *A Kind of Loving*. London: Penguin, 1962.
Basker, James, ed. *Amazing Grace: An Anthology of Poems about Slavery, 1660–1810*. New Haven: Yale University Press, 2002.
Bathgate, Janet. *Aunt Janet's Legacy to Her Nieces: Recollections of Humble Life in Yarrow in the Beginning of the Century*. Selkirk: George Lewis and Sons, 1894.
The Bays Miscellany. London: For A. Moore, 1730.
Bede. *Ecclesiastical History of the English People*. Trans. Leo Sherley-Price. Ed. R. E. Latham. Harmondsworth: Penguin, 1990.
Beggs, Thomas. *The Minstrel's Offering: Original Poems and Songs*. Belfast: Hugh Clark, 1836.
Bell, John, ed. *Rhymes of Northern Bards: Being a Curious Collection of Old and New Songs and Poems, Peculiar to the Counties of Newcastle Upon Tyne, Northumberland, and Durham*. 1812. Rpt. with an introduction by David Harker. Newcastle upon Tyne: Frank Graham, 1971.
Bell, Lady Florence. *At the Works: A Study of a Manufacturing Town*. London: Virago, 1985.
Bernstein, Marion. *A Song of Glasgow Town: The Collected Poems of Marion Bernstein*. Eds. Edward H. Cohen, Anne R. Fertig and Linda Fleming. Glasgow: Association for Scottish Literary Studies, 2013.
Besant, Walter. *The Pen and the Book*. London: Thomas Burleigh, 1899.
"Biography." *Literary Gazette* 1162 (27 April 1839): 267–68.
Black, Clementina. *The Agitator*. London: Bliss, Sands and Foster, 1894.
Black, P. Cameron, and Alex Wallace. *Sketch of the Late Mrs Janet Hamilton, with Addresses at her Funeral and Grave. With a Prefatory Note by the Rev. George Gilfillan*. Glasgow: Aird and Coghill, 1873.
Blackwood's Edinburgh Magazine. January–June 1857.
Blair, Eric [George Orwell]. "The Spike." 1931. *The Collected Essays, Journalism and Letters of George Orwell*. Vol. 1: 1920–1940. Ed. Sonia Orwell and Ian Angus. Harmondsworth: Penguin, 1970. 58–66.
Bloomfield, Robert. *The Letters of Robert Bloomfield and His Circle. Romantic Circles Electronic Editions*. Eds. Tim Fulford and Lynda Pratt. University of Maryland, 2009.
Boos, Florence S., ed. *Working-Class Women Poets in Victorian Britain: An Anthology*. Peterborough: Broadview, 2008.
Booth, William. *"In Darkest England" and "The Way Out."* New York and London: Funk and Wagnalls, 1890.
Bramsbury, H. J. "A Working Class Tragedy." 1888–89. *British Socialist Fiction 1884–1914*. Ed. Deborah Mutch. Vol. 1: 1884–1891. London: Pickering and Chatto, 2013. 51–211.
British Library Board. *Royal Literary Fund Archives*. London: British Library, 2016.
"The Broken Contract; or, the Betrayed Virgin's Complaint." [London?]: [1736? 1763?].

Brontë, Charlotte. *Jane Eyre*. 1847. Ed. Margaret Smith. Oxford: Oxford University Press, 2000.
Bruce, John Collingwood, and John Stokoe, eds. *Northumbrian Minstrelsy: A Collection of Ballads, Melodies, and Small-Pipe Tunes of Northumbria*. 1882. Hatboro, PA: Folklore Associates, 1965.
Buffon, Georges Louis Leclerc, Comte de. *The Natural History of Animals, Vegetables, and Minerals; with the Theory of the Earth in General*. Trans. W. Kenrick and J. Murdoch. 6 vols. London: Printed for, and Sold by T. Bell, 1775–6.
Burns, Robert. *Poems and Songs*. Ed. James Kinsley. 3 vols. Oxford: Clarendon, 1969.
— *The Letters of Robert Burns*. Vol. 1: 1780–1789. Ed. John DeLancey Ferguson. 2nd edition, ed. G. Ross Roy. 2 vols. Oxford: Clarendon, 1985.
— *The Life and Works of Robert Burns*. Ed. Robert Chambers. 4 vols. Edinburgh: William and Robert Chambers, 1852.
Campbell, Elizabeth Duncan. *Songs of My Pilgrimage*. Edinburgh: Andrew Elliot, 1875.
The Candidates for the Bays: A Poem. London: For A. Moore, 1730.
Carlyle, Jane. *"I Too Am Here": Selections from the Letters of Jane Welsh Carlyle*. Ed. Alan McQueen Simpson and Mary McQueen Simpson. Cambridge: Cambridge University Press, 1977.
Carlyle, Thomas. *Past and Present*. London: Oxford University Press, 1938.
Carnie Holdsworth, Ethel [An-Ex-Mill-Girl]. *Helen of Four Gates*. Ed. Nicola Wilson. Kilkerran: Kennedy and Boyd, 2016.
— [Ethel Carnie]. *Miss Nobody*. Ed. Nicola Wilson. Kilkerran: Kennedy and Boyd, 2013.
— *This Slavery*. Ed. Nicola Wilson. Nottingham: Trent Editions, 2011.
— [Ethel Holdsworth]. "The Beggar Prince." *The Age* [Melbourne] 28 November–30 December 1932. National Library of Australia.
— *This Slavery*. London: Labour, 1925.
— "Letter." *The Sunday Worker* 26 July 1925: 6.
— [Ethel Holdsworth]. *General Belinda*. London: Herbert Jenkins, 1924.
— "This Slavery." *The Daily Herald* Oct. 1923–Feb. 1924.
— [Ethel Holdsworth]. "The Great Experiment." *The Queenslander* [Brisbane] 30 Dec. 1922–17 March 1923.
— [Ethel Carnie]. "The Iron Horses." *The Co-operative News* 31 July–11 Dec. 1915.
— [Ethel Carnie] "Book-makers and Bookbinders." *Daily Herald* 16 June 1914.
— [Ethel Carnie]. "Miss Nobody: A Working Girl's Love Story." *The Christian Commonwealth* 11 June–24 Sept. 1913.
— [Ethel Carnie]. "Living Pictures." *The Woman Worker* [London] 3 Nov. 1909: 416.
— [Ethel Carnie]. "How Colour Is Introduced." *The Woman Worker* [London] 7 April 1909: 323.
— [Ethel Carnie]. "The Factory and Content." *The Woman Worker* [London] 31 March 1909: 312.

[Ethel Carnie]. "Factory Intelligence." *The Woman Worker* [London] 10 March 1909: 219.

Chesterton, Cecil. *In Darkest London*. London: Stanley Paul, 1926.

Clare, John. *By Himself*. Ed. Eric Robinson and David Powell. New York: Routledge, 2002.

"John Clare's Journal." *John Clare: By Himself*. Ed. Eric Robinson and David Powell. 1996. New York: Routledge, 2002. 171–243.

John Clare: Poems of the Middle Period, 1822–1837. Ed. Eric Robinson, David Powell, and P. M. S. Dawson. 5 vols. Oxford: Clarendon, 1996–2003.

The Early Poems of John Clare, 1804–1822. Ed. Eric Robinson, David Powell, and Margaret Grainger. 2 vols. Oxford: Clarendon, 1989.

The Letters of John Clare. Ed. Mark Storey. Oxford: Clarendon, 1985.

"The Mores." c. 1812–1831. *The Oxford Authors: John Clare*. Ed. Eric Robinson and David Powell. Oxford: Oxford University Press, 1984.

The Shepherd's Calendar; with Village Stories, and Other Poems. London: John Taylor, 1827.

"Helpstone." *Poems Descriptive of Rural Life and Scenery*. London and Stamford: Taylor and Hessey and E. Drury, 1820.

Clarke, Allen. *The Knobstick: A Story of Love and Labour*. Manchester: John Heywood, 1893.

The Red Flag. 1907. *British Socialist Fiction*. Ed. Deborah Mutch. Vol. 4: 1907–1910. Routledge, 2013. 147–211.

Clarkson, Thomas. *Essay on the Slavery and Commerce of the Human Species*. London: Printed by J. Phillips, 1786.

Cobbett, William. *Rural Rides*. Vol. 1. 1830. New York: Cosimo Classics, 2003.

The Autobiography of William Cobbett. Ed. William Reitzel. London: Faber and Faber, 1967.

Rural Rides. Ed. Asa Briggs. 2 vols. London: Dent, 1966.

Cockburn, Catharine. *The Works of Mrs. Catharine Cockburn*. 2 vols. London: J. and P. Knapton, 1751.

Collier, Mary. *The Woman's Labour: An Epistle to Mr. Stephen Duck*. *Eighteenth-Century English Labouring-Class Poets*. Ed. William J. Christmas. Gen. Ed. John Goodridge. Vol. 1: 1700–1740. London: Pickering and Chatto, 2003. 314–20.

The Woman's Labour. 1739. *The Thresher's Labour by Stephen Duck; The Woman's Labour by Mary Collier: Two Eighteenth-century Poems*. Ed. E. P. Thompson and Marian Sugden. London: The Merlin Press, 1989.

Poems on Several Occasions. Winchester: For the Author, by Mary Ayres, 1762.

The Woman's Labour: An Epistle to Mr. Stephen Duck. London: For the Author, 1739.

Cooper, Thomas. *The Purgatory of Suicides*. London: Jeremiah How, 1845.

Corvan, Edward. *Corvan's Song Books*. 4 vols. Newcastle upon Tyne: W. Stewart, 1857–66.

Random Rhymes, Being a Collection of Local Songs and Ballads, Illustrative of the Habits and Character of the "Sons of Coaly Tyne." Newcastle, 1850.

"The Cruel Mother." *The English and Scottish Ballads*. Ed. Francis J. Child. 5 vols. Boston: Houghton Mifflin; London: Henry Stevens, Son and Stiles. 1882. 218–26.

Davies, John H., ed. *The Letters of Lewis, Richard, William and John Morris of Anglesey (Morrisiaid Môn) 1728–1765*. 2 vols. Aberystwyth: John H. Davies, 1907, 1909.

Davies, Lewis. *Work, Sex and Rugby*. 1993. Cardigan: Parthian, 1999.

Davies, Margaret Llewelyn, ed. *Life as We Have Known It: The Voices of Working-Class Women*. 1931. London: Virago, 1977.

Davies, W. H. *The Autobiography of a Super-Tramp*. 1908. London: Jonathan Cape, 1926.

Dayus, Kathleen. *The Ghosts of Yesteryear*. London: Virago, 2007.

—. *The Girl from Hockley: Growing up in Working-Class Birmingham*. Ed. Joanna Goldsworthy. London: Virago, 2006.

—. *The Best of Times*. London: Virago, 1991.

—. *All My Days*. London: Virago, 1988.

—. *Where There's Life*. London: Virago, 1985.

—. *Her People*. London: Virago, 1982.

Dickens, Charles. *Hard Times*. 1854. London: Vintage Classics, 2009.

Dodsley, Robert. *The Correspondence of Robert Dodsley, 1733–1764*. Ed. James E. Tierney. Cambridge: Cambridge University Press, 1988.

—. *A Muse in Livery: A Collection of Poems*. 2nd ed. London: For T. Osborn and J. Nourse, 1732.

—. *A Muse in Livery, or The Footman's Miscellany*. London: For the Author, 1732.

—. *An Epistle from a Footman to the Celebrated Stephen Duck*. London: For J. Brindley, 1731.

—. *The Footman's Friendly Advice to His Brethren of the Livery*. London: For T. Worrall, 1730.

—. *Servitude, a Poem*. London: For T. Worrall, 1729.

"Drake, James." *The Complaint: A Lyric Rhapsody*. Dublin: James Hoey, 1730.

Drummond, William Hamilton. *Trafalgar: An Heroic Poem*. 2 vols. Belfast, 1806.

—. *The Giant's Causeway: A Poem*. 2 vols. Belfast: For the Author, 1811.

"Duck, Arthur." *The Thresher's Miscellany or, Poems on Several Subjects*. London: For A. Moore, 1730.

Duck, Stephen. "The Thresher's Labour." *Eighteenth-Century English Labouring-Class Poets*. Ed. William J. Christmas. Gen. Ed. John Goodridge. Vol. 1: 1700–1740. London: Pickering and Chatto, 2003. 139–46.

—. *The Thresher's Labour*. 1730. *The Thresher's Labour by Stephen Duck; The Woman's Labour by Mary Collier: Two Eighteenth-century Poems*. Ed. E. P. Thompson and Marian Sugden. London: The Merlin Press, 1989.

—. *Poems on Several Subjects*. 7th ed. London: For J. Roberts, 1730.

Duff, William. *Critical Observations on the Writings of the Most Celebrated Geniuses in Poetry*. London, 1770.

—. *Essay on Original Genius*. London, 1767.

Engels, Frederick. *Condition of the Working Class in England*. 1845.

Evans, Caradoc. *My People*. London: Andrew Melrose, 1915.
"Ex-Mill Girl Who Became a Literary Celebrity." *The Yorkshire Observer* 5 April 1932: 11.
Ferguson, Moira, ed. *The Thresher's Labour, Stephen Duck (1736) and The Woman's Labour, Mary Collier (1739)*. Los Angeles: William Andrews Clark Memorial Library, 1985.
Fletcher, Alfred H. *Lost in the Mine: A Tale of the Great Coal Strike*. London: Simpkin and Marshall, 1895.
Fordyce, W., and T. Fordyce, eds. *The Newcastle Song Book; Or, Tyne-side Songster. Being a Collection of Comic and Satirical Songs, Descriptive of Eccentric Characters, and the Manners and Customs of a Portion of the Labouring Population of Newcastle and the Neighbourhood. Chiefly in the Newcastle Dialect*. Newcastle upon Tyne: W. and T. Fordyce, 1842.
Fox, R. M. *Drifting Men*. London: Hogarth, 1930.
Frizzle, John. "An Irish Miller, to Mr. Stephen Duck." *Eighteenth-Century English Labouring-Class Poets*. Ed. William J. Christmas. Gen. Ed. John Goodridge. Vol. 1: 1700–1740. London: Pickering and Chatto, 2003. 232.
Fullerton, John. ["Wild Rose"]. *Poems*. Peterhead: P. Scrogie, Observer Works, 1905.
Gerard, Alexander. *Essay on Genius*. London, 1774.
—. *Essay on Taste*. London, 1759.
Gibbon, Lewis Grassic. *Grey Granite*. London: Jarrolds, 1934.
—. *A Scots Quair*. 1932–34. Edinburgh: Canongate, 1995.
Gissing, George. *The Nether World*. 1889. Oxford: Oxford University Press, 2008.
Goodridge, John, Simon Kövesi, David Fairer, William Christmas, Bridget Keegan, Tim Burke, Scott McEathron, and Kaye Kossick, eds. *Eighteenth and Nineteenth-Century English Labouring-Class Poets*. 6 vols. Florence, KY: Routledge, 2003 and 2005.
"Goose, Philip." *The Duck Drowned in Parnassus or, The Goose Triumphant*. London: For T. Roberts, 1730.
Gower, Jon. "The Pit." *Too Cold for Snow*. Cardigan: Parthian, 2012. 111–19.
Gray, Thomas. *Elegy Written in a Country Churchyard*. 1751. *The Thomas Gray Archive*. 2000.
Greenwood, Walter. *Love on the Dole*. London: Jonathan Cape, 1933.
Griffiths, Niall. *A Great Big Shining Star*. London: Jonathan Cape, 2013.
—. *Sheepshagger*. London: Random House, 2011.
—. *Wreckage*. London: Jonathan Cape, 2005.
—. *Grits*. London: Jonathan Cape, 2000.
Hamilton, Janet. *Poems, Essays, and Sketches: Comprising the Principal Pieces from Her Complete Works*. Glasgow: James Maclehose, 1880.
—. *Poems and Ballads*. Glasgow: James Maclehose, 1873.
—. *Poems of Purpose*. Glasgow: Thomas Murray, 1865.
Hanway, Jonas. *A Candid Historical Account of the Hospital for the Reception of Exposed and Deserted Young Children*. London, 1759.
Hardy, Thomas. *Memoir of Thomas Hardy*. London: James Ridgway, 1832.

Harkness, Margaret [John Law]. *Out of Work*. London: Swan Sonnenschein, 1888.
Harrison, Tony. *Selected Poems*. London: Penguin, 1984.
Heaney, Seamus. "Birl for Burns." *Addressing the Bard: Twelve Contemporary Poets Respond to Robert Burns*. Ed. Douglas Gifford. Edinburgh: Scottish Poetry Library, 2009.
Henderson, Hamish. *Collected Poems and Songs*. Edinburgh: Curly Snake, 2000.
The Armstrong Nose. Edinburgh: Polygon, 1996.
Henrietta, F. *Poems and Lyrics*. Airdrie: Baird and Hamilton, Advertiser Office, 1879.
Hewitt, John. *Rhyming Weavers and Other Country Poets of Antrim and Down*. Belfast: Blackstaff, 1974.
Higgs, Mary. *Glimpses into the Abyss*. London: P. S. King, 1906.
Hill, Geoffrey. "Ovid in the Third Reich." *New and Selected Poems, 1952–1992*. Boston: Houghton Mifflin Harcourt, 1992.
Hilton, Jack. *Caliban Shrieks*. London: Cobden-Sanderson, 1935.
Hind, Archie. *The Dear Green Place*. 1966. Edinburgh: Polygon, 2008.
H. O. B. "A Propaganda Novel." *The Plebs* 17 (Oct. 1925): 408–9.
Holcroft, Thomas, and William Hazlitt. *Memoirs of the Late Thomas Holcroft*. 3 vols. London: Longman, Hurst, Rees, Orme and Brown, 1816.
Holt & Gregson Papers. Vol. 10. Liverpool Record Office. 1787–1790. [942 HOL 10].
Huddleston, Robert. *A Collection of Poems and Songs, on Rural Subjects*. Belfast: J. Smyth, 1844.
Hunt, Henry. *Memoirs of Henry Hunt*. 3 vols. London: T. Dalby, 1820.
Hunter, Edward. *The Road the Men Came Home*. London: National Labour Company, 1920.
Jenkins, Mike. *The Fugitive Three*. Blaenau Ffestiniog: Cinnamon Press, 2008.
Wanting to Belong. Bridgend: Seren, 1998.
Graffiti Narratives. Aberystwyth: Planet, 1994.
Johnson, Samuel. *Life of Savage*. Ed. Clarence Tracy. Oxford: Clarendon Press, 1971.
A Dictionary of the English Language. 2 vols. London, 1755–56.
"The History of Misella." *The Rambler*. Vol. 2. London: J. Payne, 1752: 86–303. 6 vols.
Johnston, Ellen. *Autobiography, Poems and Songs*. Glasgow: W. Love, 1867; 2nd ed., 1869.
Jones, D. Griffith. *Ofnadwy Ddydd*. Abercynon: Cwmni Cyhoeddiadau Modern Cymreig, 1966.
Jones, Lloyd. *Water [Y Dwr]*. Trans. Lloyd Jones. Talybont: Y Lolfa, 2014.
Y Dwr. Talybont: Y Lolfa, 2009.
Jones, Lewis. *We Live*. London: Lawrence and Wishart, 1939.
Cwmardy. London: Lawrence and Wishart, 1937.
Joseph, Michael, and Marten Cumberland. *How to Write Serial Fiction*. London: Hutchinson, 1927.

"Joyful News to Batchelors and Maids: Being a Song in Praise of the Foundling Hospital." London: T. Price, n.d.

Keating, Peter, ed. *Into Unknown England, 1866–1913: Selections from the Social Explorers*. Glasgow: Collins, 1976.

Kelman, James, Agnes Owens, and Alasdair Gray. *Lean Tales*. London: Jonathan Cape, 1985.

Kennedy, Bart. *A Sailor Tramp*. London: Grant Richards, 1902.

Kincaid, John, George Todd, F. J. Anderson, and Thurso Berwick. *Fowrsom Reel: A Collection of New Poetry*. Glasgow: Caledonia Press, 1949.

Kitson, Peter, ed. *Theories of Race*. Vol. 8 of *Slavery, Abolition and Emancipation: Writings in the British Romantic Period*. London: Pickering and Chatto, 1999.

Knox, James. *Airdrie Bards, Past and Present*. Airdrie: Baird and Hamilton, 1930.

Kovalev, Yuri, ed. *An Anthology of Chartist Literature*. Moscow: Foreign Languages Publishing House, 1956.

Lamming, George. *The Pleasures of Exile*. London: Michael Joseph, 1960.

Landon, Letitia E. *Poetical Works of Letitia Elizabeth Landon in Four Volumes*. Vol. 4. London: Longman, Brown, Green, and Longman, 1844.

Law, T. S. *Whit Tyme in the Day and Other Poems*. Glasgow: Caledonian Press, 1948.

Law, T. S., and Thurso Berwick, eds. *Homage to John Maclean*. Larkhall: John Maclean Society, 1973.

Leonard, Tom, ed. *Radical Renfrew: Poetry from the French Revolution to the First World War*. Edinburgh: Polygon, 1990.

Levene, Alysa, ed. *Narratives of the Poor in Eighteenth-Century Britain*. Vol. 3. London: Pickering and Chatto, 2006.

Lewis, George. *The Life Story of Aunt Janet*. Selkirk, 1902.

Lewis, Saunders. *Monica*. Aberystwyth: Gwasg Aberystwyth, 1930.

A School of Welsh Augustans. Wrexham: Hughes, 1924.

Linton, Eliza Lynn. *The True History of Joshua Davidson*. 1872. London: Strahan, 1873.

List of Communications Laid Before the Literary and Philosophical Society of Liverpool, since Its Institution in 1812, to the End of Session Tenth, 1821. Liverpool: Printed by Harris and Co., 1821.

Llewellyn, Richard. *How Green Was My Valley*. 1939. London: Penguin, 1989.

Llwyd, Richard. *Richard Llwyd: Beaumaris Bay and Other Poems*. Ed. Elizabeth Edwards. Nottingham: Trent Editions, 2016.

London, Jack. *The People of the Abyss*. 1903. London: Journeyman, 1977.

"The Road" and "Rods and Gunnels." 1902. *Jack London on the Road: The Tramp Diary and Other Hobo Writings*. Ed. Richard W. Etulain. Logan: Utah State University Press, 1979. 69–79 and 89–95.

Longfellow, Henry Wadsworth. *The Poems of Henry Wadsworth Longfellow, Complete in One Volume*. New York: Harper, 1846.

Lorde, Audre. *Sister Outsider: Essays and Speeches*. New York: Ten Speed Press, 2007.

MacDiarmid, Hugh. *Complete Poems*. 2 vols. Manchester: Carcanet, 1993–4.

Selected Prose. Manchester: Carcanet, 1992.

"John Maclean, Scotland, and the Communist Party." *John Maclean: Scottish Martyr and Revolutionary Socialist*. Spec. issue of *Scots Socialist* 5 (Nov.–Dec. 1940): 2–4.

MacGill, Patrick. *Children of the Dead End: The Autobiography of a Navvy*. London: Herbert Jenkins, 1914.

MacInnes, Colin. *England, Half English*. London: MacGibbon and Kee, 1961.

Mackay, Charles. *Voices from the Crowd; and Other Poems*. London: W. S. Orr, 1846.

Maclean, John. *In the Rapids of Revolution*. London: Allison and Busby, 1978.

Macpherson, James. *The Poems of Ossian and Related Works*. Edinburgh: Edinburgh University Press, 1996.

Maidment, Brian, ed. *The Poorhouse Fugitives: Self-Taught Poets and Poetry in Victorian Britain*. Manchester: Carcanet, 1987.

Markham, E. A. *The Penguin Book of Caribbean Short Stories*. London: Penguin, 1996.

Marshall, John, ed. *A Collection of Songs, Comic, Satirical, and Descriptive, Chiefly in the Newcastle Dialect, and Illustrative of the Language and Manners of the Common People on the Banks of the Tyne and Neighbourhood*. By T. Thompson, J. Shield, W. Midford, H. Robson, et al. Newcastle: John Marshall, 1827.

Martell, Owen. *Dyn yr Eiliad*. 2003. Llandysul: Gwasg Gomer, 2004.

Martin, Sarah. *A Brief Sketch of the Life of the Late Sarah Martin, of Great Yarmouth: with Extracts from Her Writings and Prison Journal*. London: The Religious Tract Society, 1847.

Mayer Papers. Liverpool Record Office. [920 MAY].

McArthur, Alexander, and H. Kingsley Long. *No Mean City*. 1935. London: Corgi Books, 1984.

McHutchison, W. *Poems and Songs*. Airdrie: Baird and Hamilton, Advertiser Office, 1877.

"A Memoir of the Unfortunate Renfrewshire Bard, Robert Tannahill." *The Kaleidoscope: Or, Literary and Scientific Mirror* [Liverpool] 11 September 1827: 78.

Midford, William. *A Collection of Songs, Comic and Satirical, Chiefly in the Newcastle Dialect. By William Midford. To which are added, a few Choice Local Songs, by Various Authors*. Newcastle upon Tyne: J. Marshall, 1818.

Millar, A. H. *The Dundee Advertiser, 1801–1901: A Centenary Memoir*. Dundee: John Leng, 1901.

Miller, Hugh. *My Schools and Schoolmasters, or The Story of My Education*. Edinburgh: Johnstone and Hunter, 1854.

Miller, Thomas. *Godfrey Malvern: The Life of an Author*. London, 1842.

Millhouse, Robert. *Sonnets and Songs of Robert Millhouse*. Ed. John Potter Briscoe. Nottingham and London, 1881.

—. *The Song of the Patriot, Sonnets, and Songs*. London, 1826.

—. *Blossoms*. London, 1823.

Millward, E. G., ed. *Blodeugerdd Barddas o Gerddi Rhydd y Ddeunawfed Ganrif*. Llandybïe: Cyhoeddiadau Barddas, 1991.

Milton, John. "Lycidas." 1638. *English Poetry 1579–1830: Spenser and the Tradition.*
"'Miss Nobody'–and its Author." *The Wheatsheaf.* November 1913: 85–86.
M'Kenzie, Andrew. "M'Kenzie, Andrew–J.R. Semple, Moilena Turnpike, near Antrim, 9 Jul. 1832." MA Thesis. John Hewitt. University of Ulster Lib., Coleraine.
More, Hannah. "A Prefatory Letter to Mrs Montagu. By a Friend." Preface. *Poems on Several Occasions.* By Ann Yearsley. London: Thomas Cadell, 1785. iii–xii.
Morrison, Arthur. *A Child of the Jago.* 1896. Oxford: Oxford World's Classics, 2012.
Morrison, D. H. *Poems and Songs.* Airdrie: Baird and Hamilton, Advertiser Office, 1870.
The Museum: or, the Literary and Historical Register: Volume the First. London, 1756.
Mutch, Deborah, ed. *British Socialist Fiction, 1884–1914.* 5 vols. London: Pickering and Chatto, 2013.
Newbery, John. *The Art of Poetry on a New Plan.* 2 vols. London: J. Newbery, 1702.
Noble, Mark. *Memoirs of the Protectoral-House of Cromwell.* 2nd ed. Vol. 2. Lynn, 1787.
Oakley, Elizabeth. "The Autobiography of Elizabeth Oakley (1831–1900)." *A Miscellany.* Ed. R. Wilson. Norwich: Norfolk Historical Society, 1991.
O'Flaherty, Liam. "The Tramp." 1924. *Tramps, Workmates and Revolutionaries: Working-Class Stories of the 1920s.* Ed. H. Gustav Klaus. London: Journeyman, 1993. 15–24.
Orwell, George. *The Collected Essays, Journalism and Letters of George Orwell.* Vol. 2: My Country Right or Left, 1940–1943. London: Secker and Warburg, 1968.
Down and Out in Paris and London. 1933. Harmondsworth: Penguin, 1966.
Owen, Hugh, ed. *Additional Letters of the Morrises of Anglesey (1735–1786).* 2 vols. London: The Honourable Society of Cymmrodorion, 1947, 1949.
Owen, Llywd. *Yr Ergyd Olaf.* Talybont: Y Lolfa, 2007.
Ffawd, Cywilydd a Chelwyddau. Talybont: Y Lolfa, 2006.
Ffydd Gobaith Cariad. Talybont: Y Lolfa, 2006.
Paine, Thomas. *Rights of Man.* Ed. Eric Foner. Harmondsworth: Penguin, 1984.
"Petition of Liverpool to the House of Commons." 14 February 1788. *History of the Liverpool Privateers and Letters of Marque, with an Account of the Liverpool Slave Trade, 1744–1812.* By Gomer Williams. 1897. Liverpool and Montreal: Liverpool University Press/McGill-Queen's University Press, 2004.
Price, Angharad. *Caersaint.* Talybont: Y Lolfa, 2010.
Rhwng Gwyn a Du: Agweddau ar Ryddiaith Gymraeg yn 1990au. Cardiff: University of Wales Press, 2002.
Prince, Mary. *The History of Mary Prince, a West Indian Slave, Related by Herself.* Ed. Moira Ferguson. Rev. ed. Ann Arbor: University of Michigan Press, 1997.
Prysor, Dewi. *Crawia.* Talybont: Y Lolfa, 2008.
Madarch. Talybont: Y Lolfa, 2007.
Brithyll. Talybont: Y Lolfa, 2006.

Purbeck, Jane. *Honoria Somerville: A Novel*. 4 vols. London: G. G. J. and J. Robinson, 1789.
Ramsay, Allan. "Elegy of Maggy Johnston." *Poems*. Edinburgh, 1721. 44–49.
Ramsay, James. *Essay on the Treatment and Conversion of the African Slaves in the British Sugar Colonies*. London: Printed and Sold by James Phillips, 1784.
Regulations for Managing the Hospital for the Maintenance and Education of Exposed and Deserted Young Children. By Order of the Governors of this Said Hospital. London, 1796.
"Rhyming Epistle to Mr R– B–, Ayrshire." *Edinburgh Evening Courant*. Edinburgh, 23 June 1787.
Ritson, Joseph, ed. "The Northumberland Garland; or, Newcastle Nightingale: A Matchless Collection of Famous Songs." *Northern Garlands*. Ed. Joseph Ritson. 1793. London: R. Triphook, 1810.
Roberts, Kate. *Feet in Chains*. Trans. Katie Gramich. Cardigan: Parthian, 2012.
   Traed Mewn Cyffion. 1936. Llandysul: Gwasg Gomer, 2001.
Robson, Joseph Philip, ed. *Songs of the Bards of the Tyne; or, a Choice Selection of Original Songs, Chiefly in the Newcastle Dialect. With a Glossary of 800 Words*. Newcastle: France and Co., [c. 1849].
Rousseau, Jean-Jacques. "The Social Contract." *The Portable Enlightenment Reader*. Ed. Isaac Kramnick. London: Penguin, 1995.
Rushton, Edward. *The Collected Writings of Edward Rushton (1756–1814)*. Ed. Paul Baines. Liverpool: Liverpool University Press, 2014.
   Poems and Other Writings by the Late Edward Rushton, to Which Is Added, a Sketch of the Life of the Author, by the Rev. William Shepherd. London: Effingham Wilson, Royal Exchange, 1824.
   Poems. London: T. Ostell, 1806.
Rushton, Edward. "Biographical Sketch of Edward Rushton, Written by His Son." *Belfast Monthly Magazine* 31 December 1814: 474–85.
Sayers, Dorothy L., trans. *The Divine Comedy 1: Hell*. London: Penguin, 1949.
Selvon, Sam. *The Lonely Londoners*. London: Penguin, 2006.
   Foreday Morning: Selected Prose, 1946–1986. Harlow: Longman, 1989.
   Ways of Sunlight. Harlow: Longman, 1987.
Semple, David. "Life of Tannahill." Introduction. *The Poems and Songs and Correspondence of Robert Tannahill*. By Robert Tannahill. Ed. David Semple. Paisley: Alexander Gardner, 1876. xxv–lxxxviii.
Sharpe, William. *Dissertation on Genius*. London, 1755.
Shepherd, William. "A Sketch of the Life of the Author." *Poems and Other Writings by the Late Edward Rushton*. Ed. William Shepherd. London: Effingham Wilson, Royal Exchange, 1824. ix–xxviii.
Sillitoe, Alan. *Saturday Night and Sunday Morning*. London: Flamingo, 1994.
   The Death of William Posters. London: W. H. Allen, 1965.
Sinclair, Iain. Introduction. *The Lowlife*. By Alexander Baron. London: The Harvill Press, 2001. v–xii.
Smiles, Samuel. *Self Help: With Illustrations of Character and Conduct*. London: John Murray, 1859.

Smith, Mary. *The Autobiography of Mary Smith, Schoolmistress and Nonconformist. A Fragment of a Life. With Letters from Jane Welsh Carlyle and Thomas Carlyle.* Carlisle: Wordsworth Press, 1892.

Sommerfield, John. *May Day.* 1936. London: London Books, 2010.

Soutar, William. *Into a Room: Selected Poems of William Soutar.* Argyll: Argyll Publishing, 2000.

Diaries of a Dying Man. 1954. Edinburgh: Canongate, 2000.

"Faith in the Vernacular." 1938. *Modernism and Nationalism.* Ed. Margery Palmer McCulloch. Glasgow: ASLS, 2004. 50–51.

Southey, Robert. *The Lives and Works of the Uneducated Poets, to Which Are Added Attempts in Verse, by John Jones, an Old Servant.* London: John Murray, 1831.

"Disraeli's Calamities of Authors." *Quarterly Review,* September and December *1812.* London, 1813. 93–114.

"Letter 1019." *The Collected Letters of Robert Southey, Part Three, 1804–1809.* Ed. Carol Bolton and Tim Fulford. *Romantic Circles Electronic Editions.* University of Maryland, August 2013.

[Southey, Robert]. "Art. IV." *The Annual Review, and History of Literature, for 1804.* Vol. 3. Ed. Arthur Aikin. London: Longman, Hurst, Rees, and Orme, 1805. 644–48.

Stewart, James. *The Twa Elders, and Other Poems.* Airdrie: Baird and Hamilton, Advertiser Office, 1886.

Storie, Elizabeth. *The Autobiography of Elizabeth Storie, a Native of Glasgow, Who Was Subjected to Much Injustice at the Hands of Some Members of the Medical, Legal, and Clerical Professions.* Glasgow, 1859.

Struthers, John. *The Harp of Caledonia: A Collection of Songs, Ancient and Modern (Chiefly Scottish).* Vol. 2. Glasgow: Khull, Blackie, 1821.

"Tannahill Anniversary: Concert at Gleniffer Braes." *The Glasgow Herald* 4 June 1906: 11.

Tannahill, Robert. *The Poems and Songs.* Paisley: Alexander Gardner, 1874.

The Soldier's Return: A Scottish Interlude in Two Acts, with Other Poems and Songs Chiefly in the Scottish Dialect. Paisley, 1807.

Tatersal, Robert. "The Introduction, to Mr. Stephen Duck." *Eighteenth-Century English Labouring-Class Poets.* Ed. William J. Christmas. Gen. Ed. John Goodridge. Vol. 1: 1700–1740. London: Pickering and Chatto, 2003. 291–92.

"To Stephen Duck, the Famous Threshing Poet." *Eighteenth-Century English Labouring-Class Poets.* Ed. William J. Christmas. Gen. Ed. John Goodridge. Vol. 1: 1700–1740. London: Pickering and Chatto, 2003. 283–84.

The Bricklayer's Miscellany, the Second Part. London: For the Author, 1735.

The Bricklayer's Miscellany. 2nd ed. London: For the Author, 1734.

Tennant, R. *Poems and Songs.* Glasgow: H. Nisbet, 1865.

Thelwall, John. "Memoir of the Life of the Author." *Poems Chiefly Written in Retirement.* London: R. Phillips, 1801.

Thomas, Ed, dir. *Y Gwyll / Hinterland.* S4C/BBC. 2014. Television.

Thomas, Gwyn. "Simeon." 1946. *The Dark Philosophers.* Cardigan: Parthian, 2005. 243–95.

Sorrow for Thy Sons. London: Lawrence and Wishart, 1986.

Thomson, Katherine Byerly. *Memoirs of Viscountess Sundon, Mistress of the Robes to Queen Caroline*. 2 vols. London: Henry Colburn, 1847.
Thompson, Samuel. *The Correspondence of Samuel Thomson (1766–1816): Fostering an Irish Writers' Circle*. Ed. Jennifer Orr. Dublin: Four Courts, 2012.
　Simple Poems on a Few Subjects, Partly in the Scottish Dialect. Belfast: Smyth and Lyons, 1806.
　New Poems on a Variety of Different Subjects, Partly in the Scottish Dialect. Belfast: Doherty and Simms, 1799.
　Poems on Different Subjects, Partly in the Scottish Dialect. Belfast: Printed for the Author, 1793.
Tirebuck, W. E. *Miss Grace of All Souls.'* London: Heinemann, 1895.
Torbuck, J. *Collection of Welch Travels and Memoirs of Wales*. London, 1742.
"Tour in North Wales." 1776. National Library of Wales. MS 16351C.
Tressell, Robert. *The Ragged Trousered Philanthropists*. Oxford: Oxford University Press, 2005.
Trezise, Rachel. *Sixteen Shades of Crazy*. London: Blue Door, 2010.
　"The Brake Fluid at Gina's." *Fresh Apples*. Cardigan: Parthian, 2006. 159–70.
　"Valley Lines." *Fresh Apples*. Cardigan: Parthian, 2006. 95–110.
　"Coney Island." *Fresh Apples*. Cardigan: Parthian, 2006. 71–94.
　In and Out of the Goldfish Bowl. Cardigan: Parthian, 2000.
Vincent, David, ed. *Testaments of Radicalism: Memoirs of Working Class Politicians 1790–1885*. London: Europa, 1977.
Wakeman, Annie. *The Autobiography of a Charwoman*. London: Macqueen, 1900.
Wallace, James. *A General and Descriptive History of the Antient and Present State of the Town of Liverpool [. . .] Together with a Circumstantial Account of the True Causes of Its Extensive African Trade*. 1795. 2nd ed. Liverpool: Crane and Jones, 1797.
Walpole, Horace. *Correspondence*. Ed. W. S. Lewis, et al. Vol. 31. New Haven: Yale University Press, 1961.
Warton, Joseph. *Essay on the Genius and Writings of Pope*. London, 1756.
Watson, Roderick, ed. *The Poetry of Scotland*. Edinburgh: Edinburgh University Press, 1995.
Watt, Christian. *The Christian Watt Papers*. Ed. David Fraser. Edinburgh: Paul Harris, 1983.
Wells, H. G. *The Time Machine*. London: Heinemann, 1895.
Welsh, James C. *The Morlocks*. London: Herbert Jenkins, 1924.
West, Alan. "On the Inside Looking In." Rev. of *Saturday Night and Sunday Morning*, by Alan Sillitoe. *The New Yorker* 5 Sept. 1959: 99–100.
Wheeler, Thomas Martin. "Sunshine and Shadow: A Tale of the Nineteenth Century." 1849–50. *Chartist Fiction*. Ed. Ian Haywood. Aldershot: Ashgate, 1999. 65–200.
White, Henry Kirke. *The Life and Remains of Henry Kirke White: of Nottingham*. London: J. F. Dove, 1827.
Whitehead, Andrew. Introduction. *Rosie Hogarth*. By Alexander Baron. Nottingham: Five Leaves, 2010. 5–11.

Williams, David. *Incidents in My Own Life Which Have Been Thought of Some Importance*. Ed. Peter France. Brighton: University of Sussex Library, 1980.

Williams, Edward. *Poems, Lyric and Pastoral*. 2 vols. London: S. Rousseau, 1794.

Williams, Edward ("Iolo Morganwg"). *The Correspondence of Iolo Morganwg*. Eds. Geraint H. Jenkins, Ffion Mair Jones, and David Ceri Jones. 3 vols. Cardiff: University of Wales Press, 2007.

Williams, Merryn, and Raymond Williams. Introduction. *John Clare, Selected Poetry and Prose*. London: Methuen, 1986.

Wilson, Alexander. *Poems and Miscellaneous Prose*. 2 vols. Ed. Alexander Grosart. Paisley: Alexander Gardner, 1876.

Wilson, Joe. *Tyneside Songs and Drolleries, Readings and Temperance Songs*. 1890. Ed. Thomas Allan. Wakefield: S. R. Publishing, 1970.

Joe Wilson's Tyneside Songs, Ballads, and Drolleries. Original Fireside Pictors, Drawn i' Wor Awn Awd Canny Toon Style, by Joe Wilson, and Sung by Him with Immense Success at the "Tyne" and "Oxford" Music Halls, Newcastle. Newcastle: J. Wilson, [c. 1865].

Woodhouse, James. *The Life and Poetical Works of James Woodhouse*. Ed. R. I. Woodhouse. London: The Leadenhall Press, 1896.

Poems on Several Occasions. London: Mills, 1766.

Poems on Sundry Occasions. London: Richardson and Clark, 1764.

Woodward, Kathleen. *Jipping Street*. 1928. London: Virago, 1983.

Wright, Joseph. *Janet Hamilton, and Other Papers*. Edinburgh: R. and R. Clark, 1889.

Yearsley, Ann. *The Collected Works of Ann Yearsley*. Ed. Kerri Andrews. 3 vols. London: Pickering and Chatto, 2014.

Selected Poems. Ed. Tim Burke. Cheltenham: The Cyder Press, 2003. 23–25.

Poems on Various Subjects. London: G. G. and J. Robinson, 1787.

Poems on Several Occasions. London: Thomas Cadell, 1785.

[Milkwoman of Clifton, near Bristol]. "Addressed to Ignorance, Occasioned by a Gentleman's Desiring the Author Never to Assume a Knowledge of the Ancients." *Poems, on Various Subjects*. London: Printed for the Author and Sold by G. G. J. and J. Robinson, 1767. 93–99.

Young, Edward. *Conjectures on Original Composition*. London, 1759.

Zola, Émile. *Germinal*. 1885. Trans. Peter Collier. Oxford: Oxford University Press, 1998.

SECONDARY SOURCES

Aaron, Jane. "'The Hoydens of Wild Wales': Representations of Welsh Women in Edwardian and Victorian Fiction." *Welsh Writing in English: A Yearbook of Critical Essays* 1 (1995): 23–39.

"Valleys' Women Writing." *Beyond the Difference: Welsh Literature in Comparative Contexts*. Ed. Alyce von Rothkirch and Daniel Williams. Cardiff: University of Wales Press, 2004. 84–96.

Welsh Gothic. Cardiff: University of Wales Press, 2013.

"About #TransformDH." *TransformDH*, n.d.
"About London Lives." *London Lives, 1690 to 1800: Crime, Poverty, and Social Policy in the Metropolis.*
Adams, J. R. R. *The Printed Word and the Common Man.* Belfast: Blackstaff, 1987.
Adams, Theresa. "Representing Rural Leisure: John Clare and the Politics of Popular Culture." *Studies in Romanticism* 47.3 (Fall 2008): 371–92.
Agha, Asif. "The Social Life of Cultural Value." *Language and Communication* 23 (2003): 231–73.
Alpers, Paul. *What Is Pastoral?* Chicago: University of Chicago Press, 1996.
Andrews, Corey E. *The Genius of Scotland: The Cultural Production of Robert Burns, 1785–1834.* Leiden and Boston: Brill Rodopi, 2015.
——— "'Far Fam'd RAB': Scottish Labouring-Class Poets Writing in the Shadow of Robert Burns, 1785–1792." *Studies in Hogg and His World* 23 (2013): 41–67.
——— "Work Poems: Assessing the Georgic Mode of Eighteenth-Century Working-Class Poetry." *Experiments in Genre in Eighteenth-Century Literature.* Ed. Sandro Jung. Ghent: Academia Scientific, 2011. 105–33.
Andrews, Kerri. *Ann Yearsley and Hannah More, Patronage and Poetry.* London: Pickering and Chatto, 2013.
Aravamudan, Srinivas. *Tropicopolitans: Colonialism and Agency, 1688–1804.* Durham: Duke University Press, 1999.
Armstrong, Isobel. *Victorian Poetry: Poetry, Poetics, and Politics.* London: Routledge, 1996.
Astley, Neil, ed. *Tony Harrison: A Critical Anthology.* Newcastle: Bloodaxe, 1991.
Baer, Marc. *Theatre and Disorder in Late Georgian London.* Oxford: Clarendon Press, 1992.
Bailey, Peter. *Popular Culture and Performance in the Victorian City.* Cambridge: Cambridge University Press, 1998.
——— "Conspiracies of Meaning: Music-Hall and the Knowingness of Popular Culture." *Past and Present* 144.1 (1994): 138–70.
Baker, Timothy C. "The Romantic and the Real: James Leslie Mitchell and the Search for a Middle Way." *Journal of Modern Literature* 36.4 (Summer 2013): 44–61.
Bakhtin, M. M. *The Dialogic Imagination.* Trans. Caryl Emerson and Michael Holquist. Ed. Michael Holquist. Austin: University of Texas Press, 1981.
Baraniuk, Carol. "'Things Tragic and Bitter': Samuel Ferguson, *Congal* and the Northern Romantic Tradition." *Forging the Anchor: Samuel Ferguson and His Legacy.* Ed. Frank Ferguson and Jan Jedrzejewski. Dublin: Four Courts, forthcoming.
——— *James Orr: Poet and Patriot.* London: Pickering and Chatto, 2014.
Barrell, John. *Imagining the King's Death: Figurative Treason, Fantasies of Regicide, 1793–1796.* Oxford: Oxford University Press, 2000.
——— *Poetry, Language and Politics.* Manchester: Manchester University Press, 1988.
——— *The Dark Side of the Landscape: The Rural Poor in English Painting, 1730–1840.* Cambridge: Cambridge University Press, 1983.

The Idea of Landscape and the Sense of Place, 1730–1840. Cambridge: Cambridge University Press, 1972.
Barthes, Roland. *Camera Lucida*. London: Jonathan Cape, 1982.
Batchelor, Jennie. "'The Claims of Literature': Women Applicants to the Royal Literary Fund, 1790–1810." *Women's Writing* 12.3 (2005): 505–21.
——. "'Industry in Distress': Reconfiguring Femininity and Labor in the Magdalen House." *Eighteenth-Century Life* 28.1 (2004): 1–20.
Bate, Jonathan. *John Clare: A Biography*. New York: Farrar, Straus and Giroux, 2003.
Bauer, Carol, and Lawrence Ritt, eds. *Free and Ennobled: Source Readings in the Development of Victorian Feminism*. Oxford: Pergamon, 1979.
Bauer, Jean. "Who You Calling Untheoretical?" *Journal of Digital Humanities* 1.1 (2011).
Beal, Joan. "Enregisterment, Commodification and Historical Context: 'Geordie' versus 'Sheffieldish.'" *American Speech* 84.2 (2009): 138–56.
——. "From Geordie Ridley to *Viz*: Popular Literature in Tyneside English." *Language and Literature* 9.4 (2000): 343–59.
——. "'Geordie Nation': Language and Regional Identity in the Northeast of England." *Lore and Language* 17.1–2 (1999): 33–48.
Belchem, John. *"Orator" Hunt: Henry Hunt and Working-Class Radicalism*. Oxford: Clarendon, 1985.
Bell, Eleanor. *Questioning Scotland*. Basingstoke: Palgrave Macmillan, 2004.
Bennett, Louise. "Colonization in Reverse." *Writing Black Britain: 1948–1998*. Ed. James Proctor. Manchester: Manchester University Press, 2000.
Berry, David M., ed. *Understanding Digital Humanities*. Basingstoke: Palgrave Macmillan, 2012.
Binfield, Kevin. "Ned Ludd and Labouring-Class Autobiography." *Romantic Autobiography in England*. Ed. Eugene Stelzig. Aldershot: Ashgate, 2010.
Binhammer, Katherine. *The Seduction Narrative in Britain, 1747–1800*. Cambridge: Cambridge University Press, 2009.
Blair, Kirstie. "'Let the Nightingales Alone': Correspondence Columns, the Scottish Press, and the Making of the Working-Class Poet." *Victorian Periodicals Review* 47.2 (2014): 188–207.
——. "'A Very Poetical Town': Newspaper Poetry and the Working-Class Poet in Victorian Dundee." *Victorian Periodical Poetry*. Ed. A. Chapman and C. Ehnes. Spec. issue of *Victorian Poetry*. 52.1 (2014): 89–109.
——. "Introduction." *Class and the Canon: Constructing Labouring-Class Poetry and Poetics, 1750–1900*. Ed. Kirstie Blair and Mina Gorji. Palgrave: Basingstoke, 2013. 1–15.
Blair, Kirstie, and Mina Gorji, eds. *Class and the Canon: Constructing Labouring-Class Poetry and Poetics*. Basingstoke: Palgrave Macmillan, 2013.
Bohata, Kirsti. *Postcolonialism Revisited*. Cardiff: University of Wales Press, 2004.
Bonehill, John, and Stephen Daniels, eds. *Paul Sandby: Picturing Britain*. London: Royal Academy, 2009.

Boos, Florence S. "Queen of the Far-Famed Penny Post: Ellen Johnston, 'The Factory Girl' and Her Audiences." *Women's Writing* 10.3 (2003): 503–26.
— "'The Homely Muse' in Her Diurnal Setting: The Periodical Poems of 'Marie,' Janet Hamilton, and Fanny Forester." *Victorian Poetry* 39.2 (2001): 255–86.
Bourdieu, Pierre. *The Field of Cultural Production: Essays on Art and Literature.* New York: Columbia University Press, 1993.
— "The Forms of Capital." *Handbook of Theory and Research for the Sociology of Education.* John Richardson, ed. New York: Greenwood, 1986. 241–58.
Bresnihan, Patrick. "John Clare and the Manifold Commons." *Environmental Humanities* 3 (2013): 71–91.
Broadhead, Alex. *The Language of Robert Burns: Style, Ideology and Identity.* Lewisburg, PA: Bucknell University Press, 2014.
Brockett, John Trotter. *A Glossary of North Country Words, in Use, from an Original Manuscript, in the Library of John George Lambton, Esq., M.P. with Considerable Additions.* Newcastle: E. Charnley, 1825.
Bruce, Robert. *William Thom: The Inverurie Poet — A New Look.* Aberdeen: Reid & Son, 1970.
Bryce-Wunder, Sylvia. "Of Hard Men and Haries: *No Mean City* and Modern Urban Scottish Fiction." *Scottish Studies Review* 4.1 (Spring 2003): 112–25.
Bucholtz, Mary, and Kira Hall. "Identity and Interaction: A Sociocultural Linguistic Approach." *Discourse Studies* 7.4–5 (2005): 585–614.
Burchardt, Jeremy. *Paradise Lost: Rural Idyll and Social Change since 1800.* London: I. B. Tauris, 2002.
Burke, Tim. "'Humanity Is Now the Pop'lar Cry': Laboring-Class Writers and the Liverpool Slave Trade, 1787–1789." *Eighteenth Century* 42.3 (2001): 245–63.
Burnett, John, ed. *Destiny Obscure: Autobiographies of Childhood, Education and the Family from the 1820s to the 1920s.* London: Allen Lane, 1982.
— ed. *Useful Toil: Autobiographies of Working People from the 1820s to the 1920s.* London: Allen Lane, 1974.
Burnett, John, David Vincent, and David Mayall, eds. *The Autobiography of the Working Class: An Annotated Critical Bibliography.* 3 vols. New York: New York University Press, 1984–89.
Burtt, Edward H., Jr., and William E. Davis, Jr. *Alexander Wilson: The Scot Who Founded American Ornithology.* Cambridge, MA: The Belknap Press of Harvard University Press, 2013.
Butler, Marilyn. *Burke, Paine, Godwin and the Revolution Controversy.* Cambridge: Cambridge University Press, 1984.
Cafarelli, Annette Wheeler. "The Romantic 'Peasant' Poets and Their Patrons." *The Wordsworth Circle* 26.2 (1995): 77–87.
Cairnie, Julie. "The Ambivalence of Ann Yearsley: Laboring and Writing, Submission and Resistance." *Nineteenth-Century Contexts* 27.4 (2005): 353–64.
Calhoun, Craig. *The Roots of Radicalism: Tradition, the Public Sphere, and Early Nineteenth-Century Social Movements.* Chicago: Chicago University Press, 2012.

Cantwell, Robert. *Alexander Wilson, Naturalist and Pioneer.* Philadelphia: J. B. Lippincott, 1961.
Carruthers, Gerard. "Robert Burns's Scots Poetry Contemporaries." *Burns and Other Poets.* Ed. David Sergeant and Fiona Stafford. Edinburgh: Edinburgh University Press, 2012. 37–52.
Robert Burns. Northcote: Tavistock, 2006.
Carter, Jefferson Matthew. "The Unletter'd Muse: The Uneducated Poets and the Concept of Natural Genius in Eighteenth-Century England." Diss. University of Arizona, 1972.
Castellano, Katey. *The Ecology of Romantic Conservatism: 1790–1837.* Basingstoke and New York: Palgrave Macmillan, 2013.
Charnell-White, C. *Beirdd Ceridwen: Blodeugerdd Barddas o Ganu Menywod hyd tua 1800.* Llandybïe: Cyhoeddiadau Barddas, 2005.
Chirico, Paul. *John Clare and the Imagination of the Reader.* Basingstoke: Palgrave Macmillan, 2007.
Chow, Rey. *Ethics after Idealism: Theory, Culture, Ethnicity, Reading.* Basingstoke: Palgrave Macmillan, 1998.
Christmas, William J. "Lyric Modes: The Soliloquy Poems of Mary Leapor and Ann Yearsley." *Tulsa Studies in Women's Literature* 34.1 (2015): 33–50.
"The Farmer's Boy and Contemporary Politics." *Robert Bloomfield: Lyric, Class, and the Romantic Canon.* Ed. Simon White, John Goodridge, and Bridget Keegan. Lewisburg, PA: Bucknell University Press, 2006.
The Lab'ring Muses: Work, Writing, and the Social Order in English Plebiean Poetry, 1730–1830. Newark: University of Delaware Press, 2001.
Chun, Wendy H., Richard A. Gruson, Patrick Jagoda, and Rita Raley. "307: The Dark Side of Digital Humanities." *Proceedings of the Modern Language Association, January 3–6, 2013: A Special Session.* Boston: Modern Language Association, 2016.
Claeys, Gregory. "Paine and Cobbett: How to Radicalise a Conservative." *Cobbett's New Register* 11.6 (2015): 2–14.
Clare, Johanne. *John Clare and the Bounds of Circumstance.* Kingston, ON: McGill-Queen's University Press, 1987.
Cohen, Edward H., and Anne R. Fertig. "Marion Bernstein and the Glasgow Weekly Mail in the 1870s." *Victorian Periodicals Review*, forthcoming.
Coleman, Linda S., ed. *Women's Life-Writing: Finding Voice, Building Community.* Bowling Green: Bowling Green State University Popular Press, 1997.
Colls, Robert. *The Pitmen of the Northern Coalfield: Work, Culture, and Protest, 1790–1850.* Manchester and Wolfeboro, NH: Manchester University Press, 1987.
The Collier's Rant: Song and Culture in the Industrial Village. London: Croom Helm; Totowa, NJ: Rowman and Littlefield, 1977.
Constantine, Mary-Ann. "'A Subject of Conversation': Iolo Morganwg, Hannah More and Ann Yearsley." *Wales and the Romantic Imagination.* Ed. Damian Walford Davies and Lynda Pratt. Cardiff: University of Wales Press, 2007. 65–85.

The Truth against the World: Iolo Morganwg and Romantic Forgery. Cardiff: University of Wales Press, 2007.

"'This Wildernessed Business of Publication': The Making of Poems, Lyric and Pastoral (1794)." *Rattleskull Genius: The Many Faces of Iolo Morganwg.* Ed. G. Jenkins. Cardiff: University of Wales Press, 2005. 123–45.

Cook, Daniel. *Thomas Chatterton and Neglected Genius, 1760–1830.* Basingstoke: Palgrave, 2013.

Cox, Jeffrey. *Romanticism in the Shadow of War: Literary Culture in the Napoleonic War Years.* Cambridge: Cambridge University Press, 2014.

Crawford, Rachel. *Poetry, Enclosure, and the Vernacular Landscape, 1700–1830.* Cambridge University Press, 2002.

Crawford, Robert. *Scotland's Books.* London: Penguin, 2007.

Cross, Nigel. *The Common Writer: Life in Nineteenth-Century Grub Street.* Cambridge: Cambridge University Press, 1985.

A Select Catalogue of Applicants to the Royal Literary Fund 1790–1918. Diss. University College London, 1980.

Curran, Stuart. "Romantic Elegiac Hybridity." *The Oxford Handbook of the Elegy.* Ed. Karen Weisman. Oxford and New York: Oxford University Press, 2010. 238–50.

Davies, Damian Walford. *Presences that Disturb: Models of Romantic Identity in the Literature and Culture of the 1790s.* Cardiff: University of Wales Press, 2002.

Davies, Hywel M. "Wales in English Travel Writing, 1791–98: The Welsh Critique of Theophilus Jones." *Welsh History Review* 23.3 (2007): 65–93.

Dawson, Ashley. *Mongrel Nation: Diasporic Culture and the Making of Modern Britain.* Ann Arbor: University of Michigan Press, 2007.

Dawson, P. M. S. "Common Sense or Radicalism? Some Reflections on Clare's Politics." *Romanticism* 2.1 (April 1996): 81–97.

Dellarosa, Franca. *Talking Revolution: Edward Rushton's Rebellious Poetics, 1782–1814.* Liverpool: Liverpool University Press, 2014.

Denney, Peter. "Popular Radicalism, Religious Parody and the Mock Sermon in the 1790s." *History Workshop* 74.1 (2012): 51–78.

"The Talk of the Tap-Room: Bloomfield, Politics, and Popular Culture." *Robert Bloomfield: The Inestimable Blessing of Letters.* Ed. John Goodridge and Bridget Keegan. *Romantic Circles Praxis.* December 2011.

"'Unpleasant, tho' Arcadian Spots': Plebeian Poetry, Polite Culture, and the Sentimental Economy of the Landscape Park." *Criticism* 47.4 (2005): 493–514.

Deppman, Jed, Daniel Ferrer, and Michael Groden. *Genetic Criticism: Texts and Avant-Textes.* Philadelphia: University of Pennsylvania Press, 2004.

Derrida, Jacques. *Spectres of Marx: The State of the Debt, the Work of Mourning, and the New International.* London: Routledge, 1994.

Devine, T. M. "Making the Caledonian Connection: The Development of Irish and Scottish Studies." *Radharc* 3 (2002): 3–15.

Dictionary of Welsh Biography. The National Library of Wales, 2015.

Digital Miscellanies Index, 2010.

Diniejko, Andrzej. "Slums and Slumming in Late Victorian London." *The Victorian Web: Literature, History and Culture in the Age of Victoria*. October 2013.
Donaldson, William. *Popular Literature in Victorian Scotland: Language, Fiction and the Press*. Aberdeen: Aberdeen University Press, 1986.
Drexler, Peter. "Labour and Gender: Ford Madox Brown's Work and Victorian Navvy Stories." *Victorian Highways and Byways: New Approaches to Nineteenth-Century British Literature and Culture*. Ed. Dietmar Böhnke et al. Berlin: trafo Wissenschaftsverlag, 2010. 67–101.
Duffy, Seán. "The Bruce Brothers and the Irish Sea World, 1306–1329." *Cambridge Medieval Celtic Studies* 21 (1991): 55–86.
Eckert, Penelope. "Variation and the Indexical Field." *Journal of Sociolinguistics* 12.4 (2008): 453–76.
Egerton, Frank N. "Alexander Wilson." *Oxford Dictionary of National Biography*. Oxford University Press, 2015.
"Elegy, n." *OED Online*. Oxford University Press.
The English Dialect Dictionary. 6 vols. London and New York: Henry Frowde, for the English Dialect Society, 1898–1905.
Evans, Tanya. "'Blooming Virgins All Beware': Love, Courtship, and Illegitimacy in Eighteenth-Century British Popular Literature." *Illegitimacy in Britain, 1700–1920*. Eds. Alysa Levene, Thomas Nutt, and Samantha Williams. Basingstoke: Palgrave Macmillan, 2005. 18–33.
"Unfortunate Objects": Lone Mothers in Eighteenth-Century London. Basingstoke: Palgrave Macmillan, 2005.
Fairer, David. "Persistence, Adaptations and Transformations in Pastoral and Georgic Poetry." *Cambridge History of English Literature, 1660–1780*. Ed. John Richetti. Cambridge: Cambridge University Press, 2005. 259–86.
"'Where Fuming Trees Refresh the Thirsty Air': The World of Eco-Georgic." *Studies in Eighteenth-Century Culture* 40 (2011): 201–18.
English Poetry of the Eighteenth Century, 1700–1789. Harlow and London: Pearson Education, 2003.
Felsenstein, Frank. "Ann Yearsley and the Politics of Patronage: The Thorp Arch Archive." Part 2. *Tulsa Studies in Women's Literature* 22.1 (2003): 13–56.
"Ann Yearsley and the Politics of Patronage: The Thorp Arch Archive." Part 1. *Tulsa Studies in Women's Literature* 21.2 (2000): 346–92.
Ferguson, Frank, and Andrew Holmes, eds. *Revising Robert Burns and Ulster: Literature, Religion and Politics c. 1770–1920*. Dublin: Four Courts, 2009.
Ferguson, Frank, and James McConnel, eds. *Ireland and Scotland in the Nineteenth Century*. Dublin: Four Courts, 2009.
Ferguson, Moira. *Eighteenth-Century Women Poets: Nation, Class and Gender*. Albany: SUNY Press, 1995.
Findlay, William. "Reclaiming Local Literature: William Thom and Janet Hamilton." *The History of Scottish Literature*. Ed. Douglas Gifford. Vol. 3. Aberdeen: Aberdeen University Press, 1989.
Fisher, Kate. *Birth Control, Marriage and Sex in Britain 1918–1960*. Oxford: Oxford University Press, 2006.

Fitzpatrick, Kathleen. "Reporting from the Digital Humanities 2010 Conference." *The Chronicle of Higher Education* 13 July 2010.
Fox, Pamela. Introduction. *Helen of Four Gates*. Ed. Nicola Wilson. Kilkerran: Kennedy and Boyd, 2016. ix–xxxiii.
Freedman, Jean R. "With Child: Illegitimate Pregnancy in Scottish Traditional Ballads." *Folklore Forum* (1991): 3–18.
Froid, Dan. "What Does a Haberdasher Really Do? Creating a Controlled Vocabulary for LCPO." *Laboring Class Poets Online*.
Frow, John. *Genre*. London: Routledge, 2006.
Frow, Ruth, and Edmund Frow. "Ethel Carnie: Writer, Feminist and Socialist." *The Rise of Socialist Fiction, 1880–1914*. Ed. H. Gustav Klaus. Sussex: Harvester Press, 1987. 251–6.
Gagnier, Regenia. *Subjectivities: A History of Self-Representation in Britain, 1832–1920*. New York and Oxford: Oxford University Press, 1991.
Garner, Stephen. *Whiteness: An Introduction*. London: Routledge, 2007.
Genette, Gérard. *Paratexts: Thresholds of Interpretation*. Trans. Jane E. Lewin. Cambridge: Cambridge University Press, 1997.
George, M. Dorothy. *English Political Caricature, 1793–1832*. Oxford: Clarendon Press, 1959.
Gibson, Corey. *The Voice of the People*. Edinburgh: Edinburgh University Press, 2015.
Gifford, Douglas. "Scottish Literature in the Victorian and Edwardian Era." *Scottish Literature in English and Scots*. Ed. Douglas Gifford, S. Dunnigan, and Alan MacGillivray. Edinburgh: Edinburgh University Press, 2002. 321–32.
Gilbert, Pamela K. "History and Its Ends in Chartist Epic." *Victorian Literature and Culture* 37.1 (2009): 27–42.
Gilmartin, Kevin. *Print Politics: The Press and Radical Opposition in Early Nineteenth-Century England*. Cambridge: Cambridge University Press, 1996.
Gilroy, Paul. *Postcolonial Melancholia*. New York: Columbia University Press, 2004.
Gold, Matthew K., and Lauren F. Klein, eds. *Debates in the Digital Humanities*. Minneapolis: University of Minnesota Press, 2012.
Goodridge, John. "Introduction to the Database of British and Irish Labouring-Class Poets and Poetry, 1700–1900." *Laboring-Class Poets Online*. 2013.
John Clare and Community. Cambridge: Cambridge University Press, 2012.
"Stephen Duck, The Thresher's Labour, and Mary Collier, The Woman's Labour." *A Companion to Eighteenth-Century Poetry*. Ed. Christine Gerrard. Malden, MA and Oxford: Blackwell, 2006. 209–22.
Introduction. *Nineteenth-Century English Labouring-Class Poets: 1800–1900*. Ed. John Goodridge, Scott McEathron, and Kaye Kossick. Vol. 3. London: Pickering and Chatto. xv–xxiii.
General Editor's Introduction. *Eighteenth-Century English Labouring-Class Poets*. Ed. William J. Christmas. Vol. 1: 1700–1740. London: Pickering and Chatto, 2003. xiii–xvii.

Rural Life in Eighteenth Century Poetry. Cambridge: Cambridge University Press, 1995.
"Some Predecessors of Clare: The Response to Duck." *John Clare Society Journal* 9 (1990): 17–26.
Goodridge, John, and Bridget Keegan. "John Clare and the Traditions of Labouring-Class Verse." *The Cambridge Companion to English Literature, 1740–1830.* Ed. Thomas Keymer and Jon Mee. Cambridge: Cambridge University Press, 2004. 280–95.
Gordon, Avery. *Ghostly Matters: Haunting and the Sociological Imagination.* Minneapolis: University of Minneapolis Press, 2008.
Gorji, Mina. *John Clare and the Place of Poetry.* Liverpool: Liverpool University Press, 2008.
Grande, James. *William Cobbett, the Press and Rural England: Radicalism and the Fourth Estate, 1792–1835.* Basingstoke: Palgrave, 2014.
Grande, James, and John Stevenson. *William Cobbett, Romanticism and the Enlightenment.* London: Pickering and Chatto, 2015.
Green, Georgina. *The Majesty of the People: Popular Sovereignty and the Role of the Writer in the 1790s.* Oxford: Oxford University Press, 2014.
Gregson, Keith, and Mike Huggins. "Sport, Music-Hall Culture and Popular Song in Nineteenth-Century England." *Culture, Sport, Society* 2.2 (1999): 82–102.
Griffin, Dustin. *Literary Patronage, 1650–1800.* Cambridge: Cambridge University Press, 1996.
Griffin, Emma. *Liberty's Dawn: A People's History of the Industrial Revolution.* New Haven: Yale University Press, 2013.
Griffiths, Bill. *A Dictionary of North East Dialect.* 2nd ed. Newcastle: Northumbria University Press, 2005.
Gros, Frédéric. *A Philosophy of Walking.* London: Verso, 2014.
Hall, Edith. "Classics, Class, and Cloaca: Harrison's Humane Coprology." *Arion: A Journal of Humanities and the Classics* 15.2 (2007): 83–108.
Hames, Scott. Introduction. *Unstated: Writers on Scottish Independence.* Ed. Scott Hames. Edinburgh: Word Power, 2012. 1–18.
Hames, Scott, ed. *Unstated: Writers on Scottish Independence.* Edinburgh: Word Power, 2012.
Hammond, Mary. *Reading, Publishing and the Formation of Literary Taste in England, 1880–1914.* Farnham: Ashgate, 2006.
Harker, David. "The Original Bob Cranky?" *Folk Music Journal* 5.1 (1985): 48–82.
"The Making of the Tyneside Concert Hall." *Popular Music* 1 (1981): 27–56.
"Thomas Allan and 'Tyneside Song.'" *Allan's Illustrated Edition of Tyneside Songs and Readings.* 1891. Rpt. with introduction by David Harker. Newcastle upon Tyne: Frank Graham, 1972. vii–xxviii.
"John Bell, the Great Collector." *Rhymes of Northern Bards: Being a Curious Collection of Old and New Songs and Poems, Peculiar to the Counties of Newcastle Upon Tyne, Northumberland, and Durham.* Rpt. with introduction by David Harker. Newcastle upon Tyne: Frank Graham, 1971. v–liii.

Harrison, Gary. *Wordsworth's Vagrant Muse: Poetry, Poverty and Power*. Detroit: Wayne State University Press, 1994.
Haughton, Hugh, and Adam Phillips. "Introduction: Relocating John Clare." *John Clare in Context*. Ed. Hugh Haughton, Adam Phillips, and Geoffrey Summerfield. Cambridge: Cambridge University Press, 1994.
Haywood, Ian. *Romanticism and Caricature*. Cambridge: Cambridge University Press, 2013.
Heidegger, Martin. *Basic Writings*. Ed. David Farrell Krell. London: Routledge, 1993.
Hermeston, Rod. "Indexing Bob Cranky: Social Meaning and the Voices of Pitmen and Keelmen in Early Nineteenth-Century Tyneside Song." *Victoriographies* 4.2 (2014): 156–80.
——. "Linguistic Identity in Nineteenth-Century Tyneside Dialect Songs." Diss. University of Leeds, 2009.
Heslop, Richard Oliver. *Northumberland Words: A Glossary of Words used in the County of Northumberland and on the Tyneside*. 2 vols. London: English Dialect Society, 1892.
Higgins, David. *Romantic Englishness: Local, National and Global Selves, 1780–1850*. Basingstoke: Palgrave, 2014.
Hill, Draper. *Mr Gillray the Caricaturist*. London: Phaidon, 1965.
Hitchcock, Tim, Peter King, and Pamela Sharpe, eds. *Chronicling Poverty: The Voices and Strategies of the Poor, 1640–1840*. Basingstoke: Palgrave Macmillan, 1997.
Hobbs, Andrew. "Five Million Poems, or the Local Press as Poetry Publisher, 1800–1900." *Victorian Periodicals Review* 45.5 (2012): 488–92.
Hobbs, Andrew, and Claire Januszewski. "How Local Newspapers Came to Dominate Victorian Poetry Publishing." *Victorian Periodical Poetry*. Ed. A. Chapman and C. Ehnes. Spec. issue of *Victorian Poetry* 52.1 (2014): 65–87.
Hockey, Susan. "The History of Humanities Computing." *A Companion to Digital Humanities*. Ed. Susan Schreibman, Ray Siemens, and John Unsworth. Oxford: Blackwell, 2004.
Honeybone, Patrick, and Kevin Watson. "Salience and the Sociolinguistics of Scouse Spelling: Exploring the Phonology of the Contemporary Humorous Localised Dialect Literature of Liverpool." *English World-Wide* 34.3 (2013): 305–40.
Honn, Josh. "Never Neutral: Critical Approaches to Digital Tools and Culture in the Humanities." *Proceedings of the Digital Humanities Speaker Series, October 16, 2013, University of Western Ontario*. University of Western Ontario.
Houston, Natalie. "Newspaper Poems: Material Texts in the Public Sphere." *Victorian Studies* 50.2 (2008): 233–42.
Howarth, Janet. "Gender, Domesticity, and Sexual Politics." *Short Oxford History of the British Isles: The Nineteenth Century*. Ed. Colin Matthew. Oxford: Oxford University Press, 2000. 161–93.

Howell, David. *Patriarchs and Parasites: The Gentry of South-West Wales in the Eighteenth Century.* Cardiff: University of Wales Press, 1986.

Howkins, Alun, and Ian Dyck. "'The Time's Alteration': Popular Ballads, Rural Radicalism and William Cobbett." *History Workshop Journal* 23 (Spring 1987): 20–38.

Hubbard, Tom. "Reintegrated Scots: The Post-MacDiarmid Makars." *The History of Scottish Literature.* Ed. Cairns Craig. Vol. 4. Aberdeen: Aberdeen University Press, 1987. 179–93.

Hudson, Nicholas. "From 'Nation' to 'Race': The Origin of Racial Classification in Eighteenth-Century Thought." *Eighteenth-Century Studies* 29.3 (1996): 247–64.

Hughes, Glyn Tegai. "Life and Thought." *A Guide to Welsh Literature c. 1700–1800.* Ed. Branwen Jarvis. Cardiff: University of Wales Press, 2000. 1–22.

Hulme, Peter. "Introduction: The Cannibal Scene." *Cannibalism and the Colonial World.* Eds. Francis Barker, Peter Hulme, and Margaret Iverson. Cambridge: Cambridge University Press, 1998. 1–38.

Huws, Daniel. "Iolo Morganwg and Traditional Music." *Rattleskull Genius: The Many Faces of Iolo Morganwg.* Ed. Geraint H. Jenkins. Cardiff: University of Wales Press, 2005. 333–56.

Ingrams, Richard. *The Life and Adventures of William Cobbett.* London: Harper Perennial, 2012.

James, E. Wyn. "Cushions, Copy-books and Computers: Ann Griffiths (1776–1805), Her Hymns and Letters and Their Transmission." *Bulletin of the John Rylands Library* 90.2 (2014): 163–183.

"The Evolution of the Welsh Hymn." *Dissenting Praise: Religious Dissent and the Hymn in England and Wales.* Ed. Isabel Rivers and David L. Wykes. Oxford: Oxford University Press, 2011. 229–68.

James, Louis. "Miller, Thomas (1807–1874)." *Oxford Dictionary of National Biography.* Oxford University Press, 2004.

Janowitz, Anne. *Lyric and Labour in the Romantic Tradition.* Cambridge: Cambridge University Press, 1998.

Jarvis, Branwen H. *Goronwy Owen.* Cardiff: University of Wales Press, 1986.

Jarvis, Branwen H., ed. *A Guide to Welsh Literature c. 1700–1800.* Cardiff: University of Wales Press, 2000.

Jaworski, Adam, Nikolas Coupland, and Dariusz Galasiński. "Metalanguage: Why Now?" *Metalanguage: Social and Ideological Perspectives.* Ed. Adam Jaworski, Nikolas Coupland, and Dariusz Galasiński. Berlin: Mouton de Gruyter, 2004. 3–8.

Jenkins, Lee M. "On Not Being Tony Harrison: Tradition and the Individual Talent of David Dabydeen." *ARIEL: A Review of International English Literature* 32.2 (2001): 69–88.

Jenkins, Robert Thomas, and Helen M. Ramage. *The History of the Honourable Society of Cymmrodorion and of the Gwyneddigion and Cymreigyddion Societies, 1751–1951.* London: The Honourable Society of Cymmrodorion, 1951.

Johnston, D. R. *The Literature of Wales*. Cardiff: University of Wales Press, revised ed. 2017.
Johnstone, Barbara, Jennifer Andrus, and Andrew E. Danielson. "Mobility, Indexicality, and the Enregisterment of 'Pittsburghese.'" *Journal of English Linguistics* 34.2 (2006): 77–104.
Jolly, Lynn. "Delight as Pamphlets from the Glen Concerts Held in Honour of Paisley's Bard Tannahill Are Found." *Daily Record* 18 May 2010.
Jones, Dafydd Glyn. "The Interludes." *A Guide to Welsh literature: 1700–1800*. Ed. B. Jarvis. Cardiff: University of Wales Press, 2000. 210–55.
Jones, Fion Mair. "Welsh Balladry and Literacy." *Street Ballads in Nineteenth Century Britain, Ireland and North America: The Interface between Print and Oral Traditions*. Ed. David Atkinson and Steve Roud. London: Ashgate, 2014.
Welsh Ballads of the French Revolution. Cardiff: University of Wales Press, 2012.
Jones, Owen. *Chavs: The Demonisation of the Working Class*. London: Verso, 2011.
Joyce, Patrick. *Visions of the People: Industrial England and the Question of Class, 1848–1914*. Cambridge: Cambridge University Press, 1991.
Jung, Sandro. "Shenstone, Woodhouse, and Mid-Eighteenth-Century Poetics: Genre and the Elegiac-Pastoral Landscape." *Philological Quarterly* 88.1/2 (2009): 127–49.
Kanner, Barbara. *Women in Context: Two Hundred Years of British Women Autobiographers: A Reference Guide*. Boston: G. K. Hall, 1997.
Kay, Billy. *Scots: The Mither Tongue*. Edinburgh: Mainstream, 2006.
Keane, John. *Tom Paine: A Political Life*. London: Bloomsbury, 2009.
Kear, Jon, and Ben Thomas. *In Elysium: Prints by James Barry*. Canterbury: University of Kent, 2010.
Keegan, Bridget. *British Labouring-Class Nature Poetry, 1730–1837*. Basingstoke: Palgrave Macmillan, 2008.
"Mysticisms and Mystifications: The Demands of Laboring-Class Religious Poetry." *Criticism* 47.4 (2005): 471–91.
"Cobbling Verse: Shoemaker Poets of the Long Eighteenth Century." *The Eighteenth Century: Theory and Interpretation* 42.3 (2001): 195–217.
"Georgic Transformations and Stephen Duck's 'The Thresher's Labour.'" *SEL* 41.3 (Summer 2001): 545–62.
Kelly, James. "Review of Jennifer Orr (ed.) *The Correspondence of Samuel Thomson: fostering an Irish writers' circle*. Dublin: Four Courts, 2012." *Irish University Review* 42.2 (2012): 444–47.
Kelman, James. *Unstated: Writers on Scottish Independence*. Ed. Scott Hames. Edinburgh: Word Power, 2012. 118–25.
Kidd, Colin. *Subverting Scotland's Past*. Cambridge: Cambridge University Press, 2003.
Kidd, Helen. "'Writing Near the Fault Line.'" *Kicking Daffodils: Twentieth-Century Women Poets*. Ed. Vicki Bertram. Edinburgh: Edinburgh University Press, 1997. 95–109.
Kift, Dagmar. *The Victorian Music Hall: Culture, Class, and Conflict*. Cambridge: Cambridge University Press, 1996.

Kirschenbaum, Matthew. "What Is Digital Humanities and What's It Doing in English Departments?" *Debates in the Digital Humanities*. Ed. Matthew K. Gold. Minneapolis: University of Minnesota Press, 2013.
Klancher, Jon. *The Making of English Reading Audiences, 1790–1832*. Madison: University of Wisconsin Press, 1987.
Klaus, H. Gustav. *Factory Girl: Ellen Johnston and Working-Class Poetry in Victorian Scotland*. Frankfurt: Peter Lang, 1998.
― *The Literature of Labour: Two Hundred Years of Working-Class Writing*. Brighton: The Harvester Press, 1985.
Klaus, H. Gustav, ed. *Tramps, Workmates and Revolutionaries: Working-Class Stories of the 1920s*. London: Journeyman, 1993.
― ed. *The Socialist Novel in Britain: Towards the Recovery of a Tradition*. Brighton: Harvester, 1982.
Knox, W. W. *A History of the Scottish People: Urban Housing in Scotland, 1840–1940*.
― *A History of the Scottish People: Health in Scotland, 1840–1940*.
Kövesi, Simon. "John Clare & . . . & . . . & . . . : Deleuze and Guattari's Rhizome." *Ecology and the Literature of the British Left: The Red and the Green*. Ed. John Rignall, H. Gustav Klaus, and Valentine Cunningham. Farnham, Surrey: Ashgate, 2012. 75–88.
Krishnamurthy, Aruna, ed. *The Working-Class Intellectual in Eighteenth and Nineteenth-Century Britain*. Aldershot: Ashgate, 2009.
Kronfeld, Chana. *On the Margins of Modernism*. Berkeley: University of California Press, 1996.
Kuduk, Stephanie. "Sedition, Criticism and Epic Poetry in Thomas Cooper's *The Purgatory of Suicides*." *Victorian Poetry* 39.2 (2001): 165–86.
Lake, A. Cynfael. *Blodeugerdd Barddas o Ganu Caeth y Ddeunawfed Ganrif*. Llandybïe: Cyhoeddiadau Barddas, 1993.
Landry, Donna. "Georgic Ecology." *Robert Bloomfield: Lyric, Class, and the Romantic Canon*. Ed. Simon White, John Goodridge, and Bridget Keegan. Lewisburg, PA: Bucknell University Press, 2006. 253–68.
― *The Muses of Resistance: Laboring-Class Women's Poetry in Britain, 1739–1796*. Cambridge: Cambridge University Press, 1990, 2005.
Landry, Donna, and William J. Christmas. Introduction. *Criticism* 47.4 (2005): 413–20.
Langhamer, Claire. *Women's Leisure in England, 1920–60*. Manchester: Manchester University Press, 2000.
Larsen, Timothy. *Crisis of Doubt: Honest Faith in Nineteenth-Century England*. Oxford: Oxford University Press, 2006.
Latham, Sean. "New Age Scholarship: The Work of Criticism in the Age of the Digital." *New Literary History* 35.3 (2004): 411–26.
Law, Graham. *Serializing Fiction in the Victorian Press*. London: Palgrave, 2000.
Leader, Zachary. *Revision and Romantic Authorship*. Oxford: Clarendon Press, 1996.
Leask, Nigel. "Was Burns a Labouring-Class Poet?" *Class and the Canon: Constructing Labouring-Class Poetry and Poetics*. Ed. Kirstie Blair and Mina Gorji. Basingstoke: Palgrave Macmillan, 2013. 16–33.

Leerssen, J. *Remembrance and Imagination: Patterns in the Historical and Literary Representation of Ireland in the Nineteenth Century*. Cork: Cork University Press, 1996.

Lessa, Richard. "Time and John Clare's Calendar." *Critical Quarterly* 24.1 (Spring 1982): 59–71.

Levene, Alysa. *The Childhood of the Poor: Welfare in Eighteenth-Century London*. Basingstoke: Palgrave Macmillan, 2012.

Levene, Alysa, Thomas Nutt, and Samantha Williams, eds. *Illegitimacy in Britain, 1700–1920*. Basingstoke: Palgrave Macmillan, 2005.

Lindsay, Maurice. *The Scottish Renaissance*. Edinburgh: Serif, 1948.

Linebaugh, Peter, and Marcus Rediker. *The Many-Headed Hydra: The Hidden History of the Revolutionary Atlantic*. London: Verso, 2000.

"Literary Fund." *North British Review* 29 (1858): 244–56.

Livingstone, David N. "Race, Space and Moral Climatology: Notes toward a Genealogy." *Journal of Historical Geography* 28.2 (2002): 159–80.

Lodge, David. "Richard Hoggart: A Personal Appreciation." *Re-Reading Richard Hoggart: Life, Literature, Language, Education*. Ed. Sue Owen. Newcastle: Cambridge Scholars, 2008.

Lucas, John. "Bloomfield and Clare." *The Independent Spirit: John Clare and the Self-Taught Tradition*. Ed. John Goodridge. Helpston: The John Clare Society and Margaret Grainger Memorial Trust, 1994. 55–68.

——. "Clare's Politics." *John Clare in Context*. Ed. Hugh Haughton, Adam Phillips, and Geoffrey Summerfield. Cambridge: Cambridge University Press, 1994. 148–77.

——. *John Clare*. Plymouth: Northcote House, 1994.

Lukács, Georg. "Writer and Critic, 1970." *Pictures of Reality*. By Terry Lovell. London: Athlone, 1980.

Lynch, Deidre Shauna. *The Economy of Character: Novels, Market Culture, and the Business of Inner Meaning*. Chicago and London: University of Chicago Press, 1998.

Mack, Douglas. *Scottish Fiction and the British Empire*. Edinburgh: Edinburgh University Press, 2006.

Macksey, Richard. Foreword. *Paratexts: Thresholds of Interpretation*. By Gérard Genette. Trans. Jane E. Lewin. Cambridge: Cambridge University Press. xi–xxii.

Maidment, B. E. "Imagining the Cockney University: Humorous Poetry, the March of Intellect, and the Periodical Press, 1820–1860." *Victorian Periodical Poetry*. Ed. A. Chapman and C. Ehnes. Spec. issue of *Victorian Poetry* 52.1 (2014): 21–40.

——. "Class and Cultural Production in the Industrial City: Poetry in Victorian Manchester." *City, Class and Culture: Studies of Cultural Production and Social Policy in Victorian Manchester*. Ed. A. J. Kidd and K. W. Roberts. Manchester: Manchester University Press, 1985. 148–66.

Malcolm, David. "Bedazzled." *TLS* 7 March 2014: 28.

Malzahn, Manfred. "The Industrial Novel." *The History of Scottish Literature*. Ed. Cairns Craig. Vol. 4. Aberdeen: Aberdeen University Press, 1987. 229–42.

Mandell, Laura. "Nineteenth-Century Scottish Poetry." *The Edinburgh History of Scottish Literature*. Ed. Susan Manning, Ian Brown, Thomas Owen Clancy, and Murray Pittock. Vol. 2 of *Enlightenment, Britain and Empire (1707–1918)*. Edinburgh: Edinburgh University Press, 2007. 301–7.

Mannheim, Bruce, and Dennis Tedlock. Introduction. *The Dialogic Emergence of Culture*. Ed. Dennis Tedlock and Bruce Mannheim. Urbana and Chicago: University of Illinois Press, 1995.

Mared, Gwenan. "Ein tynnu o fywyd beunyddiol." *Taliesin* 133 (2008): 152–54.

Martin, Nicole. "BBC Series 'Labels White Working Class Racist.'" *Telegraph* 28 March 2008.

Marx, Leo. *The Machine in the Garden: Technology and the Pastoral Ideal in America*. London and New York: Oxford University Press, 1964.

Mason, Rowena. "Liz Kendall 'Will Back White Working-Class Young.'" *Guardian* 29 May 2015.

Matthew, Colin, ed. *Short Oxford History of the British Isles: The Nineteenth Century*. Oxford: Oxford University Press, 2000.

McCalman, Iain. *The Radical Underworld: Prophets, Revolutionaries and Pornographers in London, 1795–1840*. Cambridge: Cambridge University Press, 1988.

McClure, Ruth. *Coram's Children: The London Foundling Hospital in the Eighteenth Century*. New Haven: Yale University Press, 1981.

McCrone, David. *Understanding Scotland*. London: Routledge, 1992.

McCulloch, Margery Palmer, ed. *Modernism and Nationalism*. Glasgow: ASLS, 2004.

McDonagh, Josephine. *Child Murder and British Culture, 1720–1900*. Cambridge: Cambridge University Press, 2003.

McFarland, Elaine. *Ireland and Scotland in the Age of Revolution: Planting the Green Bough*. Edinburgh: Edinburgh University Press, 1994.

McKusick, James. "William Cobbett, John Clare and the Agrarian Politics of the English Revolution." *Radicalism in British Literary Culture, 1650–1830*. Ed. Timothy Morton and Nigel Smith. Cambridge: Cambridge University Press, 2002. 167–82.

"John Clare's Version of Pastoral." *The Wordsworth Circle* 30.2 (Spring 1999): 80–84.

Medhurst, Andy. *A National Joke: Popular Comedy and English Cultural Identities*. London and New York: Routledge, 2007.

Mellor, Anne K. "'Anguish no Cessation Knows': Elegy and the British Woman Poet, 1660–1834." *The Oxford Handbook of the Elegy*. Ed. Karen Weisman. Oxford and New York: Oxford University Press, 2010. 442–62.

Merchant, J. "'An Insurrection of Maids': Domestic Servants and the Agitation of 1872." *Victorian Dundee: Images and Realities*. Ed. L. Miskell, C. A. Whatley, and B. Harris. East Linton: Tuckwell Press, 2000. 104–21.

Mitchell, Jack. "Early Harvest: Three Anti-Capitalist Novels Published in 1914." *The Socialist Novel in Britain: Towards the Recovery of a Tradition*. Ed. H. Gustav Klaus. Brighton: Harvester, 1982. 67–88.

Moretti, Franco. *Distant Reading*. London: Verso, 2013.
— *Graphs, Maps, Trees: Abstract Models for Literary History*. London: Verso, 2007.
Morgan, Prys. "From a Death to a View: The Hunt for the Welsh Past in the Romantic Period." *The Invention of Tradition*. Ed. Eric Hobsbawn and Terence Ranger. Cambridge: Cambridge University Press, 1992. 43–100.
— *The Eighteenth Century Renaissance*. Llandybïe: Christopher Davies, 1981.
— *Iolo Morganwg (Writers of Wales)*. Cardiff: University of Wales Press, 1975.
Muir, Edwin. *Scott and Scotland: The Predicament of the Scottish Writer*. London: Routledge, 1936.
Mumm, S. D. "Writing for Their Lives: Women Applicants to the Royal Literary Fund, 1840–1880." *Publishing History* 27 (1990): 27–49.
Murdoch, John. "The Landscape of Labor: Transformations of the Georgic." *Romantic Revolutions: Criticism and Theory*. Ed. Kenneth R. Johnson, Gilbert Chaitin, Karen Hanson, and Herbert Marks. Bloomington: Indiana University Press, 1990. 176–93.
Nash, Andrew. "Victorian Scottish Literature." *The Cambridge Companion to Scottish Literature*. Ed. G. Carruthers and M. McIlvanney. Cambridge: Cambridge University Press, 2012. 145–58.
— "The Production of the Novel, 1880–1940." *The Oxford History of the Novel in English*. Volume 4. Ed. Patrick Parrinder and Andrzej Gasiorek. Oxford: Oxford University Press, 2011. 3–19.
Nasta, Susheila, ed. *Critical Perspective on Sam Selvon*. Washington: Three Continents Press, 1988.
Nasta, Susheila, and Anna Rutherford, eds. *Tiger's Triumph: Celebrating Sam Selvon*. Hebden Bridge: Dangaroo, 1995.
Nattrass, Leonora. *William Cobbett: The Politics of Style*. Cambridge: Cambridge University Press, 1995.
Nicholson, Colin. "'Reciprocal Recognitions': Race, Class and Subjectivity in Tony Harrison's *The Loiners*." *Race and Class* 51.4 (2010): 59–78.
Norman, Marc, and Tom Stoppard. *Shakespeare in Love*. London: Faber, 1999.
Ochs, Elinor. "Indexing Gender." *Rethinking Context: Language as an Interactive Phenomenon*. Ed. Alessandro Duranti and Charles Goodwin. Cambridge: Cambridge University Press, 1992. 335–58.
O'Donoghue, D. J. "*Ulster Poets and Poetry*": *Ulster Journal of Archaeology (Second Series)* 1 (1895): 1, 20–22.
Orr, Jennifer. *Literary Networks and Dissenting Print Culture in Romantic-Period Ireland*. Basingstoke: Palgrave Macmillan, 2015.
Orwig, Sara. "Cyfnewid côd mewn llenyddiaeth: astudiaeth achos o *Ffawd Cywilydd a Chelwyddau*." Unpublished seminar paper. University of Cardiff. 9 Dec. 2014.
Osborn, James M. "Spence, Natural Genius and Pope." *Philological Quarterly* 45.1 (1966): 123–44.
— "Thomas Birch and the 'General Dictionary' (1734–41)." *Modern Philology* 36.1 (1938): 25–46.

Outhwaite, R. B. "'Objects of Charity': Petitions to the London Foundling Hospital, 1768–72." *Eighteenth-Century Studies* 32.4 (1999): 497–510.
Overton, Bill. "Mary Leapor's Verse and Genre." *Tulsa Studies in Women's Literature* 34.1 (2015): 19–32.
— *The Eighteenth-Century British Verse Epistle*. Houndmills, Basingstoke and New York: Palgrave Macmillan, 2007.
Pannapacker, William. "Digital Humanities Triumphant?" *Debates in the Digital Humanities*. 2012. Ed. Matthew K. Gold. Minneapolis: University of Minnesota Press, 2013.
Parisot, Eric. *Graveyard Poetry: Religion, Aesthetics and the Mid-Eighteenth-Century Poetic Tradition*. Farnham: Ashgate, 2013.
Patterson, Annabel. *Pastoral and Ideology: Virgil to Valéry*. Berkeley: University of California Press, 1987.
Pearce, Michael. "'That Word So Fraught with Meaning': The History, Cultural Significance and Current Use of *Canny* in North East England." *English Studies* 94.5 (2013): 562–81.
Pegge, Samuel. *Anecdotes of the English Language; Chiefly Regarding the Local Dialect of London*. Ed. Henry Christmas. 3rd ed. London: J. B. Nichols, 1844.
Perry, Jeffrey. "Theodore W. Allen and His Insights on How White Skin Privileges Divide the 99 Percent." *ChickenBones: A Journal for Literary and Artistic African-American Themes* (2010).
Perry, Ruth. *Novel Relations: The Transformation of Kinship in English Literature and Culture, 1748–1818*. Cambridge: Cambridge University Press, 2004.
Peterson, Linda H. *Traditions of Victorian Women's Autobiography: The Poetics and Politics of Life Writing*. Charlottesville: University Press of Virginia, 1999, 2001.
Phelps, Gilbert. *Modern Britain: The Cambridge Cultural History*. Cambridge: Cambridge University Press, 1972.
Pierrot, Grégory. "Sable Warriors and Neglected Tars: Edward Rushton's Atlantic Politics." *Race, Romanticism, and the Atlantic*. Ed. Paul Youngquist. Farnham and Burlington, VT: Ashgate, 2013. 125–44.
Pikoulis, John. "'Some Kind o' Beginnin': Mike Jenkins and the Voices of Cwmtaff." *Welsh Writing in English* 10 (2005): 121–43.
Pittock, Murray. *Burns and Other Poets*. Edinburgh: Edinburgh University Press, 2012.
— *Scottish and Irish Romanticism*. Oxford: Oxford University Press, 2008.
Pittock, Murray, ed. *The Edinburgh Companion to Scottish Romanticism*. Edinburgh: Edinburgh University Press, 2011.
Pordzik, Ralph. *Victorian Wastelands: Apocalyptic Discourse in Nineteenth-Century Poetry*. Heidelberg: Universitätsverlag Winter, 2012.
Prescott, Sarah. *Eighteenth-Century Writing from Wales: Bards and Britons*. Cardiff: University of Wales Press, 2008.
Prichard, Elfyn, Bethan Mair, and Catrin Puw Davies. "Beirniadaeth Gwobr Goffa Daniel Owen." *Cyfansoddiadau a Beirniadaethau Eisteddfod Genedlaethol

Cymru, Eryri a'r Cyffiniau 2005. Ed. J. Elwyn Hughes. Llys yr Eisteddfod, 2005. 92–100.
Ramsay, Stephen. "DH Types One and Two." *StephenRamsay.us.* May 2013.
Ramsay, Stephen, and Geoffrey Rockwell. "Developing Things: Notes toward an Epistemology of Building in the Digital Humanities." *Debates in the Digital Humanities.* 2012. Ed. Matthew K. Gold. Minneapolis: University of Minnesota Press, 2013.
Rancière, Jacques. *Nights of Labor: The Workers' Dream in Nineteenth-Century France.* 1981. Trans. John Drury. Philadelphia: Temple University Press, 1989.
Rendall, Jane. "'A Short Account of My Unprofitable Life': Autobiographies of Working Class Women in Britain c. 1775–1845." *Women's Lives/Women's Times.* Ed. Trev Broughton and Linda Anderson. Albany: SUNY Press, 1997.
Richardson, Catherine. "Household Writing." *The History of British Women's Writing, 1500–1610.* Ed. Caroline Bicks and Jennifer Summit. Vol. 2. Basingstoke: Palgrave Macmillan, 2011.
Ridley, George. *George Ridley: Gateshead Poet and Vocalist.* Ed. David Harker. Newcastle: Frank Graham, 1973.
Rignall, John, and H. Gustav Klaus, eds. *Ecology and the Literature of the British Left: The Red and the Green.* Farnham, Surrey: Ashgate, 2012.
Rizzo, Betty. "The Patron as Poet-Maker: The Politics of Benefaction." *Studies in Eighteenth-Century Culture* 20 (1991): 241–66.
Robinson, Eric. Introduction. *John Clare: A Champion for the Poor–Political Verse and Prose.* Ed. P. M. S. Dawson, Eric Robinson, and David Powell. Manchester: Carcanet, 2000. ix–lxiii.
"John Clare and the Newspapers: Reader and Contributor." *John Clare Society Journal* 6 (1987): 37–47.
Rosen, J. "Class and Poetic Communities: The Works of Ellen Johnston, 'The Factory Girl.'" *Victorian Poetry* 39.2 (2001): 207–27.
Rosenthal, Laura J. *Infamous Commerce: Prostitution in Eighteenth-Century British Literature and Culture.* Ithaca and London: Cornell University Press, 2006.
Rosser, Siwan. *Y Ferch ym Myd y Faled.* Caerdydd: Gwasg Prifysgol Cymru, 2005.
Rowbotham, Sheila. *Hidden from History.* London: Pluto, 1973.
Rubery, M. *The Novelty of Newspapers: Victorian Fiction after the Invention of the News.* Oxford: Oxford University Press, 2009.
Russell, Dave. *Looking North: Northern England and the National Imagination.* Manchester and New York: Manchester University Press, 2004.
Popular Music in England, 1840–1914: A Social History. 2nd ed. Manchester and New York: Manchester University Press, 1997.
Russell, Gillian, and Clara Tuite, eds. *Romantic Sociability: Social Networks and Literary Culture in Britain, 1770–1800.* Cambridge: Cambridge University Press, 2002.
Russo, John, and Sherry Lee Linkon, eds. *New Working-Class Studies.* Ithaca and London: Cornell University Press, 2005.
Sacks, Peter. *The English Elegy: Studies in the Genre from Spenser to Yeats.* Baltimore and London: The Johns Hopkins University Press, 1985.

Said, Edward. *Orientalism*. 1978. 3rd ed. London: Penguin Modern Classics, 2003.
Sales, Roger. *English Literature in History, 1780–1830: Pastoral and Politics*. London: Hutchinson, 1983.
Sanders, Mike. *The Poetry of Chartism: Aesthetics, Politics, History*. Cambridge: Cambridge University Press, 2009.
Sangster, Matthew. *Living as an Author in the Romantic Period: Remuneration, Recognition and Self-Fashioning*. Diss. Royal Holloway, University of London, 2012.
Scheinfeldt, Tom. "Sunset for Ideology, Sunrise for Methodology?" *Found History*. 13 March 2008.
Schenck, Celeste M. "Feminism and Deconstruction: Re-Constructing the Elegy." *Tulsa Studies in Women's Literature* 5.1 (1986): 13–27.
Schnapp, Jeffrey, and Todd Presner. *The Digital Humanities Manifesto 2.0. UCLA Digital Humanities*. University of California, Los Angeles, 29 May 2009.
Scodel, Joshua. *The English Poetic Epitaph: Commemoration and Conflict from Jonson to Wordsworth*. Ithaca and London: Cornell University Press, 1991.
Scrivener, Michael. "Laboring-Class Poetry in the Romantic Era." *A Companion to Romantic Poetry*. Ed. Charles Mahoney. Chichester: Wiley-Blackwell, 2011. 234–50.
Sebba, Mark. "Orthography as Social Action: Scripts, Spelling, Identity and Power." *Orthography as Social Action: Scripts, Spelling, Identity and Power*. Ed. Alexandra Jaffe, Jannis Androutsopoulos, Mark Sebba, and Sally Johnson. Boston and Berlin: Mouton de Gruyter, 2012. 1–19.
"Sociolinguistic Approaches to Writing Systems Research." *Writing Systems Research* 1.1 (2009): 35–49.
Spelling and Society: The Culture and Politics of Orthography around the World. Cambridge: Cambridge University Press, 2007.
Sergeant, David, and Fiona Stafford, eds. *Burns and Other Poets*. Edinburgh: Edinburgh University Press, 2011.
Sharratt, Bernard. *Reading Relations*. Brighton: Harvester, 1982.
Shiells, Robert. *The Lives of the Poets of Great Britain and Ireland*. 5 vols. London: For R. Griffiths, 1753.
Shuttleton, David. "'Nae Hottentots': Thomas Blacklock, Robert Burns, and the Scottish Vernacular Revival." *Eighteenth-Century Life* 37.1 (Winter 2013): 21–50.
Siskin, Clifford. *The Work of Writing: Literature and Social Change in Britain, 1700–1830*. Baltimore and London: The Johns Hopkins University Press, 1998.
Skeggs, Beverley. *Class, Self, Culture*. London: Routledge, 2004.
Smalley, Roger. *Breaking the Bonds of Capitalism: The Political Vision of a Lancashire Mill Girl*. Lancaster: Lancaster University, 2014.
Smith, Dai. "A Novel History." *Wales: The Imagined Nation: Studies in Cultural and National Identity*. Ed. Tony Curtis. Bridgend: Poetry Wales Press, 1986. 131–58.
Smith, Dai, ed. *Story*. Vol. 2. Cardigan: Parthian, 2014.

Smith, G. Gregory. *Scottish Literature: Character and Influence*. London: Macmillan, 1919.
Smith, Jeremy. "Copia Verborum: The Linguistic Choices of Robert Burns." *Review of English Studies* 58.233 (2007): 73–88.
Solomon, Harry M. *The Rise of Robert Dodsley: Creating the New Age of Print*. Carbondale and Edwardsville: Southern Illinois University Press, 1996.
Spater, George. *William Cobbett: The Poor Man's Friend*. 2 vols. Cambridge: Cambridge University Press, 1982.
Spence, Peter. *The Rise of Romantic Radicalism*. Aldershot: Scolar, 1996.
Spencer, Luke. *The Poetry of Tony Harrison*. London: Harvester Wheatsheaf, 1994.
Stafford, Fiona. "Pastoral Elegy in the 1820s: *The Shepherd's Calendar*." *Victoriographies* 2.2 (November 2012): 103–27.
      "Scottish Poetry and Regional Literary Expression." *The Cambridge Companion to English Literature, 1660–1780*. Ed. J. J. Richetti. Cambridge: Cambridge University Press, 2005.
Staves, Susan. *A Literary History of Women's Writing in Britain, 1660–1789*. Cambridge: Cambridge University Press, 2006.
Steedman, Carolyn. *An Everyday Life of the English Working Class: Work, Self and Sociability in the Early Nineteenth Century*. Cambridge: Cambridge University Press, 2013.
Storey, Edward. *A Right to Song: The Life of John Clare*. London: Methuen, 1982.
Storey, Mark, ed. *Clare: The Critical Heritage*. London: Routledge and Kegan Paul, 1973.
Super, R. H. "Trollope at the Royal Literary Fund." *Nineteenth-Century Fiction* 37.3 (1982): 316–28.
Swann, Joan, Ana Deumert, Theresa Lillis, and Rajend Mesthrie. *A Dictionary of Sociolinguistics*. Tuscaloosa: University of Alabama Press, 2004.
Taylor, Barbara. *Eve and the New Jerusalem: Socialism and Feminism in the Nineteenth Century*. London: Virago, 1983.
Terras, Melissa, Julianne Nyhan, and Edward Vanhoutte, eds. *Defining Digital Humanities: A Reader*. New York: Routledge, 2014.
Terras, Melissa. "Peering Inside the Big Tent." *Defining Digital Humanities: A Reader*. Ed. Melissa Terras, Julianne Nyhan, and Edward Vanhoutte. Burlington, VT: Ashgate, 2013. 263–70. Rpt. of "Peering Inside the Big Tent: Digital Humanities and the Crisis of Inclusion." 26 July 2011.
Thomas, M. Wynn. *Internal Difference: Literature in 20th-Century Wales*. Cardiff: University of Wales Press, 1992.
Thompson, E. P. *The Making of the English Working Class*. 1963. Harmondsworth: Penguin, 1980.
Thompson, Noel. *The Real Rights of Man: Political Economies for the Working Class, 1775–1850*. London: Pluto Press, 1998.
Thomson, Alex. "'You Can't Get There from Here': Devolution and Scottish Literary History." *International Journal of Scottish Literature* 3 (Autumn/Winter 2007): 1–20.
Thomson, Philip. *The Grotesque*. London: Methuen, 1972.

Todd, Selina. *The People: The Rise and Fall of the Working Class*. London: John Murray, 2015.
Treadwell, James. *Autobiographical Writing and British Literature, 1783–1834*. Oxford: Oxford University Press, 2005.
Treadwell, Michael. "James Roberts." *Dictionary of Literary Biography*. Vol. 154: The British Literary Book Trade, 1720–1820. Ed. James K. Bracken and Joel Silver. Detroit and London: Gale Research, 1995.
Trehane, Emma. "'Emma and Johnny': The Friendship between Eliza Emmerson and John Clare." *John Clare Society Journal* 24 (2005): 69–77.
Trolander, Paul. *Literary Sociability in Early Modern England: The Epistolary Record*. Newark: University of Delaware Press, 2014.
Tucker, Herbert. *Epic: Britain's Heroic Muse 1790–1910*. Oxford: Oxford University Press, 2008.
Uglow, Jenny. *Nature's Engraver: A Life of Thomas Bewick*. London: Faber and Faber, 2006.
Unwin, Rayner. *The Rural Muse: Studies in the Peasant Poetry of England*. London: George Allen and Unwin, 1954.
Van-Hagen, Steve. "Patrons, Influences, and Poetic Communities in James Woodhouse's *The Life and Lucubrations of Crispinus Scriblerus*." *Social Networks in the Long Eighteenth Century: Clubs, Literary Salons, Textual Coteries*. Ed. Ileana Baird. Newcastle upon Tyne: Cambridge Scholars, 2014. 309–33.
"The Life, Works and Reception of an Evangelical Radical: James Woodhouse (1735–1820), the 'Poetical Shoemaker.'" *Literature Compass* 6.2 (2009): 384–406.
"The Poetry of Physical Labour 1730–1800: The Duckian Tradition." Diss. University of Kent, 2006.
Vardy, Alan D. *John Clare, Politics and Poetry*. Basingstoke: Palgrave Macmillan, 2003.
Vicinus, Martha. *The Industrial Muse: A Study of Nineteenth-Century British Working-Class Literature*. London: Croom Helm, 1974.
Vincent, David. *Literacy and Popular Culture: England 1750–1914*. Cambridge: Cambridge University Press, 1989.
Bread, Knowledge and Freedom: A Study of Nineteenth-Century Working Class Autobiography. London: Methuen, 1982.
Wahrman, Dror. *The Making of the Modern Self: Identity and Culture in Eighteenth-Century England*. New Haven and London: Yale University Press, 2004.
Waldron, Mary. *Lactilla, Milkwoman of Clifton: The Life and Writings of Ann Yearsley, 1753–1806*. Athens: University of Georgia Press, 1996.
Wales, Katie. "Northern English in Writing." *Varieties of English in Writing: The Written Word as Linguistic Evidence*. Ed. Raymond Hickey. Amsterdam and Philadelphia: John Benjamins, 2010. 61–80.
Northern English: A Cultural and Social History. Cambridge and New York: Cambridge University Press, 2006.

"'North of Watford Gap': A Cultural History of Northern English (from 1700)." *Alternative Histories of English*. Ed. Richard. J. Watts and Peter Trudgill. London: Routledge, 2002. 45–66.

Wallace, Anne. *Walking, Literature, and English Culture: The Origins and Uses of Peripatetic in the Nineteenth Century*. Oxford: Clarendon, 1993.

"Farming on Foot: Tracking Georgic in Clare and Wordsworth." *Texas Studies in Literature and Language* 34.4 (Winter 1992): 509–40.

Wallerstein, Immanuel. *The Capitalist World Economy*. Cambridge: Cambridge University Press, 1979.

Ward, Sam. "'This Is Radical Slang': John Clare, Lord Radstock and the Queen Caroline Affair." *New Essays on John Clare*. Ed. Simon Kövesi and Scott McEathron. Cambridge: Cambridge University Press, 2015. 189–208.

Watson, Roderick. *The Literature of Scotland*. London: Palgrave Macmillan, 1984.

Weber, Max. *The Protestant Ethic and the Spirit of Capitalism*. New York: Scribner, 1953.

Werkmeister, Lucyle. "Robert Burns and the London Daily Press." *Modern Philology* 63.4 (1966): 322–35.

Wheeler, Roxann. *The Complexion of Race: Categories of Difference in Eighteenth-Century British Culture*. Philadelphia: University of Pennsylvania Press, 2000.

White, Simon J. *Robert Bloomfield, Romanticism, and the Poetry of Community*. Aldershot and Burlington: Ashgate, 2007.

Whiters, Charles W. J. *Placing the Enlightenment: Thinking Geographically about the Age of Reason*. Chicago and London: University of Chicago Press, 2007.

Whyte, Christopher. *Modern Scottish Poetry*. Edinburgh: Edinburgh University Press, 2004.

Williams, Daniel. "Realaeth a Hunaniaeth: O T. Rowland Hughes i Owen Martell." *Taliesin* 125 (Summer 2005): 12–27.

Williams, David. *Claims of Literature: The Origin, Motives, Objects, and Transactions of the Society for the Establishment of a Literary Fund*. London, 1802.

Williams, G. J. *Iolo Morganwg: y Gyfrol Gyntaf*. Cardiff: University of Wales Press, 1956. 464–5.

Traddodiad Llenyddol Morganwg. Cardiff: University of Wales Press, 1948.

Williams, Gwyn. *Artisans and Sans-culottes: Popular Movements in Britain and France during the French Revolution*. 2nd ed. London: Libris, 1989.

Williams, Raymond. *Keywords: A Vocabulary of Culture and Society*. London: Fontana Press, 1983.

Culture and Materialism. 1980. London: Verso, 2005.

"The Press and Popular Culture: A Historical Perspective." *Newspaper History, from the Seventeenth Century to the Present Day*. Ed. G. Boyce, J. Curran, and P. Wingate. London: Constable, 1978. 40–50

"The Welsh Industrial Novel." 1978. *Problems in Materialism and Culture*. London: Verso, 1980. 213–32.

The Country and the City. Oxford: Oxford University Press, 1975.

Williamson, Karina. "Voice, Gender, and the Augustan Verse Epistle." *Presenting Gender: Changing Sex in Early-Modern Culture*. Ed. Chris Mounsey. Lewisburg, PA: Bucknell University Press, 2001. 76–93.

Wilson, Amrit. *Finding a Voice: Asian Women in Britain*. London: Virago, 1978.

Wilson, Arline. *William Roscoe: Commerce and Culture*. Liverpool: Liverpool University Press, 2008.

Wilson, David A. *Paine and Cobbett: The Transatlantic Connection*. Kingston and Montreal: McGill-Queen's University Press, 1988.

Windle, Jack. "'What Life Means to Those at the Bottom': *Love on the Dole* and Its Reception since the 1930s." *Literature and History* 20.2 (2011): 35–50.

Winks, W. E. *Lives of Illustrious Shoemakers*. London: Sampson Low, 1883.

Wittig, Kurt. *The Scottish Tradition in Literature*. Westport, CT: Greenwood, 1958.

Wolfreys, Julian. *Victorian Hauntings: Spectrality, Gothic, the Uncanny and Literature*. Basingstoke: Palgrave, 2002.

Worpole, Ken. *Dockers and Detectives*. 1983. London. Five Leaves, 2008.

Introduction. *King Dido*. By Alexander Baron. Nottingham: Five Leaves, 2009. 5–19.

Wright, Austin. *Joseph Spence: A Critical Biography*. Chicago: University of Chicago Press, 1950.

Wylie, William Howie. *Old and New Nottingham*. London and Nottingham, 1853.

Index

Aaron, Jane, 393
Aberdeen Herald, 276
abolitionism, 118, 122, 124–7
Adams, Theresa, 206
aesthetics, xix, 13–14, 26, 85, 196–9, 203–7.
    See also form
The Age (newspaper), 320
agency, 16–17, 19, 124–7, 386
agrarian idyll, 6, 181, 199–207
agricultural labor, xvii, 34–5, 48–9. *See also* Clare, John; Duck, Stephen
Airdrie and Coatbridge Advertiser, 272–5
Akenside, Mark, 50
A. L. B.
    "A Scottish Servant Maid", 278
alcoholism. *See* drunkenness
Alighieri, Dante
    The Inferno, 215
Aliquis
    "Lines from a Sentimentalist", 274–5
Allan, Thomas
    Allan's Illustrated Edition of Tyneside Songs and Readings, 292–3
Allen, Theodore W., 365
Alpers, Paul
    What is Pastoral, 196
A. M. B.
    "Song of the Servant Maid", 277
ambition
    Chartist movement, 227–8
    funding, 27–30, 154–61, 164–5
    masculine literary inheritance, 89–90
    newspaper poets, 265–6
    shift towards admiration of, 5
    women, 218, 248–62
Anderson, F. J.
    Fowrsom Reel, 375
Anderson, James, 53, 82
Anderson, Robert, 141–6
    Centenary, 143

"Dedication", 142, 143, 146
"Epistle to Burns", 141
Angry Young Men, 358
Aravamudan, Srinivas, xxii
Armstrong, Isobel
    Victorian Poetry: Poetry, Poetics and Politics, 228
Armstrong, William
    "The Skipper in the Mist", 288
Arnold, Matthew, 215
Ashford, Mary Ann
    The Life of a Licensed Victualler's Daughter, 250–5
audience
    consciousness of in charity petitions, 11, 12
    potential patrons, 43–5
    social meaning, 282, 285–9, 291, 294
    use of vernacular, 133–4, 357–8, 390
Austen, Jane, xvii
    Northanger Abbey, 316
authenticity
    claims of biographical texts, 32, 108–9, 143, 378
    fantasies of, 3–5
    Foundling Hospital petitions, 12
    recovery of writings, 8–9
Authors' Syndicate Ltd., 319
autobiography. *See also* biographical texts; lifewriting
    communal function, 343–4
    ego, 188, 190
    fake or satirical, 168, 176, 177–88, 192
    mainstays of radical, 191–2
    poetry as implied, 33–6, 47
    political efficacy of radical, 188–93
    prefaces, 63, 131, 135, 136–8, 142
    recovery of women's, 340–2
    typologies, 340
    Victorian women's, 248–62

Bakhtin, Mikhail, 282
    The Dialogic Imagination, 200

Index

ballads
  ballad stanza, 372
  Cumberland, 141–6
  marine, 125
  working class familiarity with, 13, 18–20
  "The Broken Contract; or, the Betrayed Virgin's Complaint", 18
  "The Cruel Mother", 19
  "Joyful News to Batchelors and Maids", 20
  "The Yarmouth Tragedy; or, the Perjur'd Sailor", 19
Bancks, John, 25, 26, 31
  Weaver's Miscellany, 30, 31
  "The Introduction", 35
Banffshire Journal, 276
Barbauld, Anna Letitia
  Eighteen Hundred and Eleven, A Poem, 140
Barber, Mary, 26, 28
  Poems on Several Occasions, 30
Barbour, John
  The Brus, 136
bards
  English primitivist attitudes, 101–2
  patronage, 103, 113
  poetic personae, 108–9, 131
  romanticization by reading classes, 130
  social classes, 103–6
  Welsh concepts, 103, 110, 114
Barke, James, 377
  Land of the Leal, 376–7
  Major Operation, 376
Barnardo homes, 349–50
Barnsley, Dorothy, 19–20
Baron, Alexander
  community vs. individual, 336–8
  influence of Dickens, 329–30
  insidership, 333–4
  life of, 328
  masculine community, 337
  movement in, 327–8, 332–3
  sense of place, 334–6
  voice, 333
  work of, 327–8
  From the City, From the Plough, 332, 334, 336–7
  The Human Kind, 330, 332, 333
  King Dido, 331–2, 333–5, 336–7, 338
  The Lowlife, 333–6
  Rosie Hogarth, 333–6, 338
  There's No Home, 330, 334, 337
Barrell, John, xix–xx, 206, 211
  The Idea of Landscape and the Sense of Place, xxii, 197
  The Dark Side of the Landscape, xvii, xix–xx, xxii
  Imagining, xxi–xxii
Barry, James, xviii
Barstow, Stan
  A Kind of Loving, 353
Barthes, Roland, 181
Bate, Jonathan, 55, 199
Bathgate, Janet Greenfield
  Aunt Janet's Legacy to Her Nieces: Recollections of Humble Life in Yarrow in the Beginning of the Century, 250, 255–7
Beattie, James, 52
Becker, Lydia, 262
Bede, 3
  History, 1
The Bee (periodical), 53, 82
Beggs, Thomas
  The Minstrel's Offering, 136
Bell, John
  Rhymes of Northern Bards: Being a Curious Collection of Old and New Songs and Poems . . ., 292, 293
Bell, Lady Florence
  At the Works, 312
Bennet, Louise
  "Colonization in Reverse", 352
Bernstein, Alec. *See* Baron, Alexander
Berwick, Thurso
  Fowrsom Reel, 375
  Homage to John Maclean, 375
Besant, Walter, 317
  The Pen and The Book, 317
Bethnal Green, 331–2, 334, 335
"Betty Martin", 278, 280, 309
Bewick, Thomas, 294
Binhammer, Katherine
  The Seduction Narrative in Britain, 16
biographical texts. *See also* autobiography
  caricatures, 180
  claims of affinity with Duck, 30–1
  depictions of natural genius, 63
  distortion through caricature, 177–8
  education, 31–2
  fantasy of personae, 73–4
  identification with working class, 32–3
  instructional use of, 25
  poetry as implied, 33–6
  role in readers' understanding of Duck, 25
  self-conscious modesty, 31, 47, 63, 142
  to establish claims of authenticity, 32, 108–9, 143, 378
Birmingham, 339–51
Black, Clementina
  The Agitator, 307
Blacklock, Thomas, 41, 51–3
Blair, Eric (George Orwell), 302, 305

Blair, Robert
    "The Grave", 78
Blake, William, xviii
    "London", 140
Blamire, Susanna, 141
Blatchford, Robert, 312, 317
Bloomfield, Robert, 152–4, 198
    The Farmer's Boy, 152, 153, 205
    May Day with the Muses, 152
Bob Cranky (song character), 282, 288, 289
Booker, Luke, 155, 157–8
Booth, William, 331
Borrow, George, 329
Bramsbury, H. J. (pseud.)
    "A Working Class Tragedy", 297
Bresnihan, Patrick, 206
Briggs, Asa, 188
Britannia (newspaper), 227
British Nationality Act (1948), 356
Brockett, John Trotter, 287
    A Glossary of North Country Words, 285
Brontë, Charlotte
    Jane Eyre, 296
Brooks, Elizabeth, 12, 20
Bruce, John Collingwood
    Northumbrian Minstrelsy, 292
Bucholtz, Mary, 281
Buffon, Georges-Louis Leclerc, Comte de, 121, 122
    Natural History of Animals, Vegetables and Minerals, 120, 126
Burchardt, Jeremy, 195
Burges, James Bland, 150
Burke, Edmund, 82, 83
Burke, Tim, 55, 56
Burnett, John
    The Autobiography of the Working Class, 1790–1940, 248
Burns, Robert
    championship of Scots, 72–3, 75–6
    cultural and political pressures, 208
    English exploitation of Scotland, 221
    influence on others, 109, 141
    insecurities regarding use of Scots, 210
    poetic persona, 131
    public reception of, 72–3
    use of "Standard Habbie" stanzas, 132
    verse correspondence with Blacklock, 52–3
    "Holy Willie's Prayer", 73
    "The Ordination", 73
    Poems, Chiefly in the Scottish Dialect (Edinburgh ed.), 72
    Poems, Chiefly in the Scottish Dialect (Kilmarnock ed.), 52, 72
    "Tam o' Shanter", 75

Cadell, Thomas, 58
Caedmon
    "Hymn", 1, 3
Callender, James Thomson, 81
Campbell, Thomas
    "The Battle of Maciejowice", 212
canny, 285–9
canu caeth (strict-meter poetry), 103–4
canu rhydd (free-meter poetry), 103, 104–5, 106
Caribbean, 357–8
caricature, 177–8, 180–8
Carlisle Woman's Suffrage Society, 262
Carlyle, Thomas, 216
Carnie Holdsworth, Ethel
    championship of print culture, 313–15
    critical assessments of, 320–1
    early life, 313
    experiments with genre, 321–4
    film rights, 319
    genre stratification, 315–16, 320–1
    journalism career, 317–18
    literary output, 313, 318
    on imagination and pleasure, 315
    radicalism, 324–5
    serial fiction, 318–20
    "All On Her Own", 324
    "The Beggar Prince", 320
    "Book-makers and Bookbinders", 314
    "A Bookworm", 313
    "Factory Intelligence", 312, 315
    General Belinda, 314, 315
    "The Great Experiment", 320, 321
    Helen of Four Gates, 318, 319
    Miss Nobody, 311–12, 314, 316, 317, 321
    "Miss Nobody: A Working Girl's Love Story", 318, 319
    The Taming of Nan, 319
    "The Iron Horses", 318, 319
    "This Slavery", 318, 322
    This Slavery, 298, 314, 320, 323
Caroline, Queen, 4, 24–5, 27–30, 44, 47
Carter, Jefferson Matthew
    The Unletter'd Muse, 58, 61–2
Cassell, John, 211
Castellano, Katey, 203
charity. *See also* Foundling Hospital petitions; patronage; Royal Literary Fund
    Barnardo homes, 349–50
    importance of good character, 17–18
    religious institutions, 348–9
    social ideals of private, 149–51
    use of lifewriting to obtain, 4
Chartist movement, 5, 227–8, 305
Chatterton, Thomas, 94–6, 109, 111
Chester Chronicle (newspaper), 113

children. *See also* Foundling Hospital petitions
  as source of redemption, 15–16
  Barnardo Homes, 349–50
  infanticide, 19, 219–20
  neglect, 216
Chrichton, Thomas, 73, 77
Christianity. *See* religion
Christmas, William J., 13, 26, 56
  The Lab'ring Muses, 22, 65
  "Learning to Read in the Long Revolution", 85, 86
"Christ's Kirk" stanza, 78
City and Country, 110, 112, 144, 195, 370
clannishness, 367–71, 383. *See also* identity
Clare, Johanne
  John Clare and the Bounds of Circumstance, 197
Clare, John, xvii, xix
  agrarian idyll, 195, 199–207
  identity, 2
  limited travels of, 8
  on pastoral, 198–9
  patronage of, 4
  representation of rural idyll, 6
  rural idyll, 195–6
  "Helpstone", 195, 201–3
  "Last of March, Written at Lolham Brigs", 197–8
  "Recollections After a Ramble", 195
  "The Mores", xx
  The Shepherd's Calendar, 195, 201, 203–7
Clarke, Allen
  The Knobstick, 298
  The Red Flag, 302
Clarkson, Thomas, 121, 122
  Essay on the Slavery and Commerce of the Human Species, 120
class
  challenges to mainstream culture, 120–2
  changes in Welsh social structures, 103–6
  concepts and definitions of, 1–2
  cultural capital, 212
  depictions of rural life, 106–7
  discourses of respectability, 282–4, 285–6, 387, 391
  education inequalities, 212–13
  exclusivity, 344–5
  genre stratification, 315–16, 320–1
  gwerin, 387
  intersections with national identity, 358, 370, 374–5, 383–4
  intersections with race, 8, 358, 359–65
  in tramp narratives, 302, 305
  religious issues, 276
  Royal Literary Fund applications, 163
  servants, 250–2, 259, 277–9
  solidarity, 190
  subaltern status, 208
  use of dehumanizing language as means of stratification, 330–1
classical learning
  displays of, xxi, 228–9
  disregard for, 130–1, 214
  influence on verse epistles, 39, 47
  role in genius debates, 58–61
Clayton, Charlotte, 28–30
The Clear Light (periodical), 318
Coalfield Gothic, 388
Coatbridge, 214
Cobbett, William
  admiration of Paine, 192
  court martial, 178
  criticism of, 201
  fragmentation of autobiographical texts, 188, 193
  radicalism, 176–80
  The Life of Peter Porcupine, 178
  The Progress of a Ploughboy to a Seat in Parliament, 193
  Rural Rides, 333
  The Soldier's Friend, 184
  "To the Independent People of Hampshire", 178, 184
Cockburn, Catherine
  Vindication of Mr. Locke's Christian Principles, 29
Coleman, Linda S.
  Women's Life Writing, 343
Colles, William Morris, 319
Collier, Mary, xix
  biographical texts, 31
  declaration of affinity with Duck, 30
  Duck as inspiration, 25
  education, 31
  Poems on Several Occasions, 31
  The Woman's Labour, 7, 25, 30, 31, 46–9
Colls, Robert, 282, 283
colonialism
  decolonization, 361–5
  English primitivist attitudes in Wales, 101–2
  of Scotland by England, 220–1
  patois, 357–8, 390–1
  postcolonialism, 352–3
  use of English, 210–12, 386, 396
The Comic Miscellany, 50
Commercial Road, London, 332, 335
community. *See also* intersectionalism
  among northern regions, 141
  around verse epistles addressed to Duck, 40–9
  communal function of autobiography, 343–4
  expression through non-standard spellings, 289–91

Four Nations, 113
identification as writers, 5–7
in competition with individual, 336–8
literary sociability, 39
masculine, 337
of humans and nature, 197, 202–7
of oppressed, 48–9
Paisley literary, 77
racism as threat to, 353
role of verse epistles in building, 39–40
surrounding Dodsley's publishing business, 49–51
teaching of poetic craft, 107–8, 109, 112
tensions among various meanings of words, 285–9
tramp narratives, 301
transatlanticism, 139–40
women's oral tradition, 209
working class internationalism, 360–1, 365
Cook, James, 124
Journals, 124
Cooper, Mary, 50, 54
Cooper, Thomas
bookseller, 50, 54
career, 227, 245–6
Chartism, 226
classical references, 228–9
evolution of humanity, 237–9
handling of nihilism, 232–3
identification with figure of Judas, 243
loss of belief in Christianity, 235–7, 240–2
rejection of Hell, 245
rejection of priestcraft, 229–32
reverence for figure of Christ, 239–40, 243–5
truth in politics, 233–5
The Purgatory of Suicides, 5, 227–45
Corvan, Ned, 293
"Ha'e ye seen wor Jimmy", 286
"The Happy Keelman", 290
"Lads o' Tyneside", 288
"O, maw bonnie Nannie O", 286
"The Shades Saloon", 284, 290
"Wor Tyneside Champions", 285
Country and City, 110, 112, 144, 195, 370
Coward, George, 262
Crabbe, George, xxii
Cranky, Bob (song character), 282, 288, 289
Crawford, Rachel
Poetry, Enclosure and the Vernacular Landscape, 197
Cross, Nigel, 160, 162, 164
cultural capital, 212
Cumberland, 143, 250, 258–62
Cumberland, Marten
How to Write Serial Fiction, 319, 322
Cumbrian dialect, 141

Cunningham, Allan, 198
Currie, James, 210
"The Influence of Climate on Human Nature", 116

Dafydd ap Gwilym, 109
Dafydd, John, 106
Dafydd, Morgan, 106
Dalraida (Gaelic kingdom), 137
Dante
The Inferno, 215
Davenport, Allen, 199
Davies, Lewis
Work, Sex and Rugby, 393
Davies, W. H.
background, 300
Autobiography of a Super-Tramp, 299, 301, 302, 304
Dawson, Ashley
Mongrel Nation, 358–9
Dayus, Kathleen
atypical narratives, 341–2
background, 339
community, 343–4
domestic abuse, 345–6
enameling industry, 350
limited escape, 351
motherhood, 347–50
publishing of, 340–1
relationship with mother, 345–6, 347
sexual ignorance, 346–8
social class, 344–5
All My Days, 342
The Best of Times, 342
The Ghosts of Yesteryear, 342
Her People, 341, 342, 346
Where There's Life, 341, 342
decolonization, 361–5
Delaney, Shelagh
A Taste of Honey, 353
Delany, Patrick, 28, 30
De Wilde, Samuel
The Porcupine's Den, 185, 187
De Wint, Peter, 198
dialect. *See also* Scots language
Anderson's use of, 141
Cumbrian, 141
in Welsh novels, 390
narrative voice, 357–8
Northumbrian, 285–91
of Merthyr Tydfil, 390
Scots folk revival, 369–74
Ulster, 133, 146
use of in narrative voice, 357–8
Dickens, Charles, 163–4
Bleak House, 332

Dickens, Charles (*cont.*)
  David Copperfield, 330
  Hard Times, 329–30
digital humanities
  benefits of, 411–12
  critiques of, 410–11
  data visualization, 407–9
  definition, 398–400
  iterative evolution, 400
  Laboring-Class Poets Online, 406–10
  Tannahill project, 403–6
  working-class literature studies, 400–3
discursive poetry, 46
Dissenters, 134, 139, 140, 146
Dodd, Anne, 41
Dodsley, James, 50
Dodsley, Robert
  biographical texts, 32
  correspondence, 41, 51–2
  Duck as inspiration, 25, 26
  education, 32
  patronage, 36
  publishing business, 40, 49–51
  A Collection of Poems by Several Hands, 50
  An Epistle from a Footman in London to the Celebrated Stephen Duck, 30, 32, 41–2
  The Footman's Friendly Advice to his Brethren of the Livery, 41
  Footman's Miscellany, 36
  A Muse in Livery, 36
  Servitude, 41
  The Toy Shop, 49
domestic abuse, 216, 286, 345–6
Donaldson, William, 279
Doric, 210–12, 215–16, 222–3. *See also* Scots language
Drake, James, 27, 32
Drummond, William Hamilton
  Giant's Causeway, 138
drunkenness
  alcoholism, 216, 347
  as class marker, 219, 282–4
  temperance movement, 216, 286–7, 290
Duck, Arthur, 26, 31
  The Thresher's Miscellany, 27, 32
Duck school
  constraints of labor on art, 33–7
  conventions of, 26
  creation of biographies, 31–3
  criticism, 26
  emergence, 24–6
  establishment of conventions, 26, 30–1, 37
  fictitious poets, 26
  opportunism, 26
Duck, Stephen, xix. *See also* Collier, Mary
  as model for other writers, 4, 25
  patronage of Queen Caroline, 24–5, 27–30
  publication and distribution, 50
  verse epistles addressed to, 40–9
  Caesar's Camp: or, St. George's Hill, 54
  "Contentment", 54
  Every Man in his Own Way, 54
  Hints to a School-Master, 54
  "Honour'd Sir", 34
  An Ode on the Battle of Dettingen, 50
  "On Poverty", 34
  Poems on Several Subjects by Stephen Duck, 24, 33, 34, 41
  "The Shunammite", 34, 36
  "Some Account of the Author", 31
  "The Thresher's Labour", 4, 25, 33, 34, 46, 196
  "The Two Beavers", 50
Duff, William
  Critical Observations, 62
Dyck, Ian, 205

Eames, Anna Maria, 98
Eames, Levi, 98
East End of London, 328
Edinburgh Parthenon, 75
education
  claims in biographical texts, 31–2
  class issues, xxi, 212–13, 355–6
  maternal role, 216–17
  role in genius debates, 58–61, 62–5
  schoolmistresses, 250, 257, 259
  women's oral tradition, 209
Education Act (1944), 356
Edwards, Elizabeth, 112
Edwards, Thomas, 102
elegy
  as expression of identity, 6
  assumptions of literary inheritance, 89–90
  definitions, 87–8
  enclosure elegies, 201–3, 204
  origins, 88–9
  patriarchal nature, 86
  Scottish mock-elegy, 132
  subversion by women, 90–1, 92–3, 96–9
Elliott, Ebenezer, 212
Emery, Robert
  "Paganini", 286
emigration, 139–40
Emmerson, Eliza, 201
enclosure, xx, 201–3, 204
environmental consciousness, 83, 197, 202–7, 304
epic poetry, 228–9. *See also* Cooper, Thomas
Eusden, Laurence
  "The Battle of the Poets", 27
Evans, Caradoc
  My People, 386
Evans, Evan, 104

Index

Evans, Tanya
  "*Unfortunate Objects*", 13, 16
Exeter, 4

Fairer, David, 196
  English Poetry of the Eighteenth Century, 39
Ferguson, Samuel, 134
Fergusson, Robert, 75
film, 6, 319
Finchley, 328, 333, 335
Fitzgerald, William T., 152
Fletcher, John, 113
Fordyce and Fordyce
  The Newcastle Song Book, 292, 293
form. *See also* verse epistles; ballads; elegy; genre; novels; georgic-pastoral doublings
  as expression of identity, 6–7
  hymns, 106
  serial fiction, 318–20
Foundling Hospital petitions. *See also* seduction narratives
  admission process, 10
  as literature, xix, 13–14, 20–2
  authenticity, 12
  Barnsley petition, 19–20
  King petition, 17–18
  Logdon petition, 12, 14–17
  male behavior, 11, 19
  Smith petition, 11
  threat of death, 10, 19
  Wapshott petition, 10, 19
Four Nations, 113
Fox, Pamela, 315
"fratriotism", 213
French Revolution, xx, 77, 81, 112, 182–8
Freneau, Philip, 121
Frizzle, John, 25, 31, 34
  "An Irish Miller, to Mr. Stephen Duck", 35, 42–4
Frow, John, 86, 324

Gagnier, Regenia
  Subjectivities: Self-Representation in Britain 1832–1920, 248, 343
Garibaldi, Guiseppe, 273
Garner, Stephen, 354
Gay, John, xvi
Geddes, Alexander, 81
Genette, Gérard, 291
genius. *See also* natural genius; original genius
  natural vs. original debates, 58–62
  reclamation of, 56, 57, 59–60, 62–5
genre. *See also* autobiography; form; novels; poetry
  construction through paratexts, 291–4
  evolution of systems, 86
  experiments with, 85, 321–4
  stratification, 315–16, 320–1
Gentleman's Magazine, xxii, 108
George III, xxi
georgic-pastoral doublings, xvii, xix, 196–9, 203–7
Gibbon, Lewis Grassic, 377–8
  Grey Granite, 377
  A Scots Quair trilogy, 377–8
  Sunset Song, 378
Gilfillan, George, 210, 211
Gillray, James, 178
  Life of William Cobbett, 168, 176, 178, 180–8
  A Peep into the Cave of Jacobinism, 185, 186
  Search Night – or – State Watchmen mistaking Honest Men for Conspirators, 183, 184
  Smelling Out a Rat, Or, The Atheistical Revolutionist disturbed in his Midnight Calculations, 183, 185
Gilroy, Paul, 354
Gissing, George
  The Nether World, 329, 330
Glamorgan, 110
Glasgow, 221–2
Goldsmith, Oliver, xxii
Goodridge, John, 26, 37, 56, 199, 204
  Eighteenth Century English Labouring-Class Poetry, 406
  Nineteenth Century English Labouring-Class Poetry, 406
Goose, Philip, 26, 27
Gordon, Avery, 385
Gorji, Mina
  John Clare and the Place of Poetry, 204
Gothic, 385–8, 396
Gower, Jon, xix
  "The Pit", 385
Gray, Alasdair
  Lean Tales, 381
  "A Report to the Trustees of the Bellahouston Travelling Scholarship", 382–3
Gray, Thomas
  The Bard, a Pindaric Ode, 130
  Elegy Written in a Country Churchyard, 89, 97, 130, 363
Griffin, Dustin, 55
Griffiths, Ann, 106
Griffiths, Niall, xix
  A Great Big Shining Star, 389
  Sheepshagger, 389
  Wreckage, 389
Grosart, Alexander, 75, 77
Grub-street Journal, 27

Hackney, 328, 332, 335, 336
Hall, Kira, 281

Hames, Scott
  Unstated: Writers on Scottish Independence, 369
Hamilton, Janet
  early life, 208–9
  feminism, 218–19
  linguistic facility, 210
  literary epiphany, 213–14
  newspaper poetry, 272
  poetic career, 208, 209–10
  Scotland's relationship to England, 220–1
  use of Doric, 215–16, 222–3
  use of English, 210–12
  women's roles, 216–20, 221–2
  "Address to Working Women", 218
  "Auld Mither Scotland", 220–1
  "Crinoline", 218
  "The Drunkard's Wife", 216
  "The Feast of the 'Mutches'", 221–2
  "A Lay of the Tambour Frame", 217–18
  "March of the mind", 218
  "Oor Location", 219
  "Our Local Scenery", 215–16
  "A Plea for the Doric", 211
  Poems, Essays, and Sketches, 218
  "Rhymes for the Times II", 218, 220
  "Rhymes for the Times III", 214, 219
  "Scottish Peasant Life and Character", 209
  "The Uses of Poetry to the Working Classes", 211–13
  "Woman", 217
Harker, Dave, 282, 292
Harkness, Margaret
  Out of Work, 297, 305
Harrison, Gary
  Wordsworth's Vagrant Muse, 200
Harrison, Tony
  early career, 355–6
  intertextuality, 363–5
  portrayal of women, 358
  postcolonial perspective, 352
  "Clearing II", 365
  "Heredity", 3
  "Next Door" sequence, 361–3
  "Old Soldiers", 361, 363
  "On Not Being Milton", 3, 354–5, 363
  The School of Eloquence, 354, 361, 363
  v., 361, 363–5
Haughton, Hugh
  John Clare in Context, 204
haunting, 185–8, 385–8, 395
Heaney, Seamus
  "A Birl for Burns", 132, 133
Henderson, Hamish, 374–5
  "Glascune and Drumlochy", 367–8

Henry, William, 78–9
Heslop, Richard Oliver, 287
  "Newcastle Toon Nee Mair", 290
  Northumberland Words, 286
Hewitt, John, 134
  Rhyming Weavers, 140
Higgs, Mary, 302
Hill, Peter, 75
Hind, Archie
  The Dear Green Place, 379–81
hinny, 287–9
Hobbes, Thomas
  Leviathan, 122
Hogarth, William
  Industry and Idleness, 180
Hogg, James
  The Shepherd's Calendar, 203
Holdsworth, Ethel Carnie. *See* Carnie Holdsworth, Ethel
homosexuality, 353, 387
Hood, Thomas
  "Song of the Shirt", 217
Horace
  The Art of Poetry, 46
Howitt, Godfrey, 162
How, Jeremiah, 226
Howkins, Alun, 205
Huddleston, Robert, 137–8
  Collection of Poems and Songs on Rural Subjects, 137
Hume, David, 51
Hunter, Edward
  The Road the Men Went Home, 307–8
Hunt, Henry, 189
hymns, 106
Hyndman, Henry Myers, 297

identity. *See also* poetic personae
  as writers, 5–7, 24
  dehumanizing language as means of class stratification, 330–1
  empowerment through self-definition, 1
  expression through non-standard spellings, 289–91
  internationalism, 360–1, 365
  intersection of nationality and class, 367–70, 374–5, 383–4
  intersection of race and class, 358, 359–65
  Irish, 133
  local loyalty, 281, 284–8, 294
  narrative objectivity, 300
  public roles, 2, 5, 111–12
  reclamation of genius, 56, 57, 62–5
  regional, 7–8, 131
  Scottish, 367–70, 375

Index   463

self-determination, 395
transnationalism, 134–6
use of artistic forms to express, 6–7
Welsh working class, 387, 395, 396
immigration, 352–3, 361–5
indexicality
  audience response, 282–4
  definition, 281–2
  non-standard spellings, 289–91
  tensions among various meanings of words, 285–9
Industrial Revolution. *See also* textile industry
  exploitation, 217–20
  rural destruction, 214–16
  working conditions, 209, 312–14
infanticide, 19, 219–20
Inskip, Thomas, 198
internationalism. *See also* transnationalism
  importance of celebrating, 354, 365
  responses to racism, 353–4
  working class origins, 360
intersectionalism
  race and class, 358, 359–65
  Scottish national identity and class, 367–70, 374–5, 383–4
Ireland. *See also* Ulster
  Irish roots of tramp storytellers, 299
  poetry, 132
  republicanism, 133, 134
Irwin, Lady Anne
  "An Epistle to Mr. Pope . . . Occasion'd by his Characters of Women", 46
Irwin, Margaret, 323
Islington, 334
Ivy Stories (periodical), 324

Jacobinism, 182–8
Jamaica, 352
James, C. L. R.
  "Triumph", 357
Janowitz, Anne, 199, 208
J. C. (Elie)
  response to "A Servant Maid", 278
Jenkins, Herbert, 319
Jenkins, Mike
  Graffiti Narratives, 390
Jewish writers, 328
Jimpwaist, Jessie
  "A Factory Lassie's Sang", 279
Johnson, James
  Scots Musical Museum, 52, 141
Johnson, Samuel, 88
  "The History of Misella", 15

Johnston, Ellen, 273, 279
Jones, D. Griffith
  Ofnadwy Ddydd, 385
Jones, Henry
  The Earl of Essex, 50
  Merit: A Poem, 50
  Poems on Several Occasions, 50
  Verses to His Grace the Duke of Newcastle, 50
Jones, Huw
  "Dyrifau Digrifol", 106
Jones, Lewis
  Cwmardy, 388
  We Live, 388
Jones, Lloyd
  Y Dŵr, 387
Jones, Owen
  Chavs, 9
Joseph, Michael
  How to Write Serial Fiction, 319, 322
Joyce, Patrick, 286, 287
Justice (newspaper), 297

Kames, Henry Home, Lord
  Sketches of the History of Man, 119
Kanner, Barbara, 248
Kay, Billy, 210
Keating, Peter, 323
Keegan, Bridget, 199
Kelman, James, 369
  "Busted Scotch", 381
  Lean Tales, 381
Kenna Fa
  "The Udny Case", 276–7
Kennedy, Bart
  background, 300
  A Sailor Tramp, 299, 300–3, 304–5
Kennedy, James, 73
Kidd, Colin
  Subverting Scotland's Past, 135
Kincaid, John
  Fowrsom Reel, 375
King, Millicent, 17–18
Kipling, Rudyard, 361
Klaus, H. Gustav, 273
Kovalev, Yuri
  Anthology of Chartist Literature, 228
Kövesi, Simon, 200

Laboring-Class Poets Online (LCPO), xix, 406–10
laboring class. *See* working class
Lamming, George, 357
Lanarkshire, Scotland, 214
Landon, Letitia, 217

Landry, Donna, 13
  "Learning to Read in the Long Revolution", 85, 86
landscape, 206–7. *See also* rural idyll
Langloan, 213, 214
Latto, William, 272
Lawrie, George, 52
Law, T. S.
  Homage to John Maclean, 375
  Whit Tyme in the Day, 375
Leapor, Mary, xix, 85
Leerssen, Joep, 112
leftists. *See* radicalism
Leicestershire Mercury (newspaper), 226
Leng, John, 272
Leonard, Tom
  Radical Renfrew: Poetry from the French Revolution to the First World War, 77
Leslie, John, 276
letters. *See* verse epistles
Lewis, George, 255
life-narratives. *See* lifewriting
lifewriting. *See also* autobiography; biographical texts; Foundling Hospital petitions
  aesthetic study of, 13–14
  as authentication, 4
  ego in, 188
  fragmented nature, 188–90, 193
  literary view of Foundling Hospital petitions, 20–2
  women's challenges, 7
Linkon, Sherry Lee
  New Working-class Studies, 8
literary sociability. *See also* community
  definition, 39
  identification as writers, 5–7
  of oppressed, 48–9
  personal letters, 50–2
  surrounding Dodsley's publishing business, 49–51
  verse epistles, 39–49, 52–3
Liverpool, 116, 117
Liverpool Philosophical and Literary Society, 116
Llewellyn, Richard
  How Green Was My Valley, 388
Llwyd, Richard, 112–14
  Beaumaris Bay, 113
  "Hymn to Temperance", 112
locality
  formula in biographical introductions, 32
  Tyneside dialect songs, 281, 284–5, 288, 294
Lochhead, Liz, 210
Lockman, John, 25, 28
Logdon, Mary, 12, 14–17

London
  autobiography, 250–5
  hostility to, 285
  postwar novels of Baron, 327–9, 331–8
  slum novels, 330–2
London, Jack, 300, 302
  The People of the Abyss, 299, 301, 303, 331
  "Rods and Gunnels", 302
Lorde, Audre, 212
Love-Merit, Richard, 27, 32
Lucas, John, 205
Lynton, Eliza Lynn
  The True History of Joshua Davidson, 303, 306

MacDiarmid, Hugh
  championship of vernacular, 371–2
  radicalism, 374–6
  Scottish literary renaissance, 369–74
  "The Bonnie Love", 372
  "Focherty", 372
  "The Love-sick Lass", 372
  Penny Wheep, 372
  "Servant Girl's Bed", 372
  "Third Hymn to Lenin", 374
  "Your Immortal Memory, Burns!", 372
MacGill, Patrick, 300
  Children of the Dead End, 299, 301–2, 303–4
Mackay, Charles
  "Wait a Little Longer", 304
MacLean, John, 375–6
Macpherson, James
  Fragments of Ancient Poetry Collected in the Highlands of Scotland, 131
Maidment, Brian, 211
  The Poorhouse Fugitives, 413
Malcolm, David, 321
Malzahn, Manfred, 370
Mared, Gwenan, 391
marine ballads, 125
Markham, E. A., 357
Marshall, John
  A Collection of Songs, Comic, Satirical, and Descriptive, 292–3
Martell, Owen, xix
  Dyn yr Eiliad, 390, 393–6
Martin, Betty, 278
  "The Grubses", 277
Marx, Leo
  The Machine in the Garden, 196
masculinity
  community, 337
  critical reverence for, 209
  literary inheritance, 89–90
  tramp narratives, 301–2
  violence, 389

Index

Mayall, David
  The Autobiography of the Working Class, 1790–1940, 248
McArthur, Alexander
  No Mean City, 378–9
McCalman, Iain, 188
McDougall, A.
  "Farewell to Bute", 273–4
McKusick, James, 203
Mellor, Anne K., 94, 97, 99
Merthyr Tydfil, dialect of, 390
Methodism, 229
Midford, William
  A Collection of Songs, Comic and Satirical, 292
  "The Royal Arch Dukes", 286
Miller, Thomas, 162–3, 164
  Godfrey Malvern, 163
Millhouse, Robert, 154–61, 164–5
  "The Bard", 155
  Blossoms, 157, 158
  The Destinies of Man, 154
  "Gold", 156
  "The Insolent in Office", 155
  "The Lot of Genius", 156
  "The Proud Man's Contumely", 155
  The Song of the Patriot, Sonnets, and Songs, 158
  "To Beneficence", 157, 158
  "To Charity", 165
  "To Genius", 156
  "To Poverty", 156
  Vicissitude, 154
Milton, John, 33, 34
  "Lycidas", 92
mining
  Coalfield Gothic, 388
  destructiveness, 214–16
  itinerant agitators, 306–8
  Welsh post-industrialism, 385, 392, 393
M'Kenzie, Andrew, 138
  "The Mount of Dromore", 145
Monboddo, James Burnett, Lord, 119
Montagu, Elizabeth, 58, 61
Moore, John, 52
moral climatology, 116, 122–4
More, Hannah, 5, 56, 58, 60
Morgan, Edwin, 376
Morgan, Prys, 112
Morganwg, Iolo. *See* Williams, Edward (Iolo Morganwg)
Morris, Lewis, 105
Morrison, Arthur
  A Child of the Jago, 331
Morris, William
  News from Nowhere, or an Epoch of Rest, 314
motherhood, 216–17, 219–20, 347–50

Muir, Thomas, 81
Mumms, S. D., 163
Murdoch, John, 197
The Museum (periodical), 50
music halls, 283–4, 292
Mutch, Deborah, 323

Napoleonic Wars, 186
Nash, Andrew, 275
national identity
  concepts of, 7
  importance of class to identity, 370, 374–5
  intersections with class, 358, 370, 374–5, 383–4
natural genius. *See also* original genius
  acceptable education, 62
  biographical depictions of, 63
  definition, 55
  limiting expectations, 3–5
  reclamation of, 56, 57, 59–60
natural sublime, 83
Neilson, John, 73
Nettle, Lowrie (pseud.), 80, 139
Newbery, John
  The Art of Poetry on a New Plan, 87
Newcassel (Newcastle), 285
New Cyclopaedia, 83
new formalism, 13–14, 22
newspapers
  Burns's reliance on, 266
  community building, 279–80
  correspondents' columns, 264–5
  educational aim, 272
  greed, 353
  in Scotland, 270
  local cultures, 270
  love poems, 274–5
  mass-market penny, 317–18
  patronage role, 267–8, 279
  poetry columns, 265–6
  political interests, 272–9
  radical poetry, 267
  rate of pay for writers, 317
  recovery of poetry, 268, 270
  relationship with working class poets, 266–7
  Scots-language, 272
  self-identification of poets, 269–70
  serial fiction, 318–20
  types, 270–2
  women reporters, 261
  working class leisure, 273–4
Nicholson, Margaret, xxi–xxii
"The Northamptonshire Peasant". *See* Clare, John
Northern Star (newspaper), 139, 227
Northumbrian dialect, 285–91

No Slaves – No Sugar (pamphlet), 118–19
novels
  dehumanizing language, 329–31
  experiments with genre, 321–4
  growth in popularity, 6
  poetry succeeded by, 6
  postwar London, 327–9, 331–8
  serial publication, 318–20
  slum novels, 330–2
  use of dialect in narrative voice, 357–8
novels, Welsh
  Coalfield Gothic, 388
  cultural decay, 389–93
  devolution, 393
  English-language, 386, 396
  Gothic elements, 385–8, 396
  haunting, 385
  identity, 387
  individualism, 393
  in English, 386, 396
  in Welsh, 386–7, 395–6
  post-industrialism, 392, 393
  postmodern representation, 393
  realism, 393–5
  violence, 389
  Welsh-English patois, 390–1
  women in, 389–90, 393

Ochs, Elinor, 282
O'Flaherty, Liam
  "The Tramp", 302
Oldys, Francis (George Chalmers), 192
oral narratives, 249
original genius. *See also* natural genius
  application to Yearsley, 58
  definition, 55
  reclamation of, 62–5
Orr, James, 132, 145
  "To the Potatoe", 133
Orwell, George (Eric Blair), 302, 305, 361, 362
Overton, Bill, 40, 46, 85
Owen, Goronwy, 104
Owen, Llwyd
  Ffawd, Cywilydd a Chelwyddau, 390, 391–2
  Ffydd Gobaith Cariad, 390, 392
  Yr Ergyd Olaf, 392
Owens, Agnes
  "Arabella", 381–2
  Lean Tales, 381
Owens, Samuel, 24
Oxford English Dictionary (OED), 1

Paine, Thomas, 80
  autobiography, 191–2
  fragmentation of autobiographical texts, 189
  Rights of Man, 184, 191–2
Paisley, Scotland, 71, 73, 77, 78–80, 405
parenthood, 216–17, 219–20, 347–50
Parisot, Eric, 89
parodies, 26, 27–8
pastoral-georgic doublings, xvii–xviii, 196–9, 203–7
patronage. *See also* Royal Literary Fund
  access to proceeds, 58
  autobiographies, 249
  biographical texts as bids for, 109
  charity, 4, 253, 254
  claims inspired by Duck's success, 27–30
  criticism of royalty, 24–5, 27
  education of writers by patrons, 62
  from established poets, 113
  in Church of Scotland, 81
  local, 73
  maintenance of class order, 56
  mediation, 2–5, 11
  newspapers, 113, 267–8, 279
  of bards, 103, 113
  perceptions of writing and writers, 2–5
  social implications of charitable support of literature, 149–51, 163–4
  subscription model, 73–4, 110–11, 137, 144–6
  support of employers, 36
  Yearsley's revolt against More, 58, 60
Patterson, Annabel, 196
Peacock, John Macleay, 8
Pearson, Susannah, 353
"peasant poet" phenomenon. *See* natural genius
Peasants' Revolt, xxi
peddlers, 73, 81–2
pennillion verse form, 104
People's Journal (newspaper), 272
Peterson, Linda
  Traditions of Victorian Women's Autobiography, 248
Philips, John
  Cyder, 204
Phillips, Adam
  John Clare in Context, 204
Pikoulis, John, 390
Pinkerton, John, 210
Pittock, Murray, 213
The Plebs (periodical), 320
plein air, 83
poetic personae. *See also* identity
  bardic, 108–9, 131
  construction of, 25, 111–12, 131
  fantasy, 73–4
  Welsh working-class, 102

poetry. *See also* ballads; elegy; form; verse epistles
  epic, 228–9
  establishment of conventions, 26
  superseded by novel, 6
poetry, Scots
  Burns's championship of, 72–3, 75–6
  "Christ's Kirk" stanzas, 78
  criticism of Calvinist culture, 78, 80–1
  criticism of Whig culture, 72–3, 77, 78
  French Revolution, 77, 81
  radicalism, 77–82
  rural sentimentality, 77, 78
  Scottish literary renaissance, 367–70, 374–5
  "Standard Habbie" stanzas, 78, 81, 132, 276
poetry, Welsh
  bards, 103, 110, 114
  depictions of rural life, 106–7
  hierarchies, 103
  in English, 108–9, 113
  influence of English culture, 108–9, 111–14
  nonconformist vein, 106
  poetic personae, 102
  religious vein, 106
  revival, 104, 107–8
  role of working class, 111–12
politics
  idealization of working class, xvii, 5
  right-wing provocation of racism, 353
Pope, Alexander, xvii, 49, 198
  "Of the Characters of Women: An Epistle to a Lady", 46
popular reading
  expectations of, 3–5
  experiments with genre, 321–4
  fantasies of authenticity, 3–5
  genre stratification, 320–1
  radicalism, 324–5
  romanticization of working class poets, 130
  serial fiction, 318–20
  stereotypes of working class, 311–12
  working-class as, 211–13, 279
  writers' attempts to win, 30–1
  yellowbacks, 316
postcolonialism, 352–65
prefaces
  self-conscious modesty, 63, 142
  self-identification in, 131, 135, 136–8
pregnancy
  redemption through motherhood, 15–16
  women's sexual ignorance, 346–8
Price, Angharad, xix
  Caersaint, 387
primitivism, 101–2
print culture
  championship of working class access, 313–15
  construction of genre through paratexts, 291–4
  genre stratification, 315–16, 320–1
  serial fiction, 318–20
  working conditions, 314
Proceedings of a General Court Martial, 179
prostitution, 15
proto-Thatcherism, 336
Prysor, Dewi
  Brithyll, 392
  Crawia, 392
  Madarch, 392
Pye, Anne, 152
Pye, Henry James, 152
Pye, Walter, 152

The Queenslander (newspaper), 320

race
  abolitionist poetry, 124–7
  as category, 117
  climatological hypothesis, 116, 122–4
  debates on nature of, 118–20, 123
  decolonization, 361–5
  erasure of internationalist working class history, 354
  internationalist responses to, 353–4, 365
  intersections with class, 8, 358, 359–65
  Liverpool slave trade, 116, 118
  myth of Welsh whiteness, 387
  post-war responses to racism, 353–4
  racism in tramp narratives, 304–5
  right-wing provocation of racism, 353
radicalism
  contestation of rural countryside, xvii–xviii, 195
  efficacy of autobiography, 188–93
  "fratriotism", 213
  hauntology, 185–8
  loyalist attacks on, 176–80
  of agrarian idyll, xix–xx, 199–207
  poetic agency, 124–7
  popular fiction, 324–5
  power of individuals' challenges to mainstream culture, 120–2
  rejection of *gwerin*, 387
  Scottish literary renaissance, 374–8
  tramp narratives, 302–4, 305–8
  use of caricature, 185
radical spectrality, 176
Ramsay, Allan, 75, 78, 121
  The Gentle Shepherd, 76
Ramsay, James, 123
  Essay on the Treatment and Conversion of African Slaves, 120

Raymond, Harold, 323
Rayner Parkes, Bessie, 218
reading and the reading classes
    expectations of, 3–5
    experiments with genre, 321–4
    fantasies of authenticity, 3–5
    genre stratification, 315–16, 320–1
    radicalism, 324–5
    romanticization of working class poets, 130
    serial fiction, 318–20
    stereotypes of working class, 311–12
    while at work, 33, 213–14, 312–13, 318
    working class as, 211–13, 279
    working-class championship, 313
    writers' attempts to win, 30–1
    yellowbacks, 316
realism, 330–2, 338, 393–5
recovery research
    authenticity in, 8–9
    challenges, 117
    feminist literature, 325
    issues of, 414–15, 416–17
    of autobiography, 188–91
    purpose of, 117
    theoretical approaches, 8, 400–3
Reitzel, William
    Autobiography of William Cobbett, 188
religion
    class issues, 276
    complicity with state, 230
    criticism of kirk in Scots poetry, 80–1
    in autobiography, 250, 255–7, 259
    Judaism, 328
    nonconformist vein in Welsh poetry, 106
    politics of Presbyterianism, 72–3
    Puritan work ethic, 209
    reclamation of natural genius, 59–60
    rejection of priestcraft, 229–32
    skepticism, 240–5
    triumph of enlightenment over, 237–9
    view of original genius, 62–5
Rendall, Jane, 248, 249
Renfrewshire, Scotland, 77
Rhys, Evan Thomas
    "Cân y Tri Slave", 107
Richardson, Catherine, 21
Ridley, George, 293
    "Johnny Luik-Up", 290
Rippingille, Edward, 198
Ritson, Joseph
    The Northumberland Garland; Or, Newcastle Nightingale, 292
Rizzo, Betty, 56
Roberts, Ellis, 101–2
    "Cwynfan Brydain", 106
Roberts, James, 41, 50

Roberts, Kate
    Traed Mewn Cyffion, 386
Robert the Bruce, 136
Robson, Joseph Philip, 290
    Songs of the Bards of the Tyne, 292, 293
Rogers, Samuel, 152, 162
Rousseauvian language, 139
Royal Literary Fund
    applicants, 151
    as charity vs. payment for literary production, 151
    biases, 163
    Bloomfield petitions, 152–4
    charges of extravagance, 153
    Miller petitions, 162–3, 164
    Millhouse petitions, 154–61, 164–5
    number of grants, 160
    political leanings, 153–4
    reform attempt by Dickens, 163–4
    refusal of public endorsements, 151, 157, 158
    stated purpose, 149–51, 160, 164
Ruddiman, Walter, 75
Rudd, John, 341
rural idyll
    caricature of, 181
    doubling of agrarian idyll, 203–7
    pastoral-georgic doublings, 196–9
    socio-political appropriation, 195–6
rural life
    community with nature, 197, 202–7
    depictions in Welsh poetry, 106–7
    in opposition to urban, 110, 112, 144, 195, 370
Rushton, Edward
    cosmopolitanism of, 8
    debates on nature of race, 119–20, 123
    political radicalism, 117, 124–7
    scholarly recovery, 117
    An Attempt to Prove that Climate, Food and Manners, Are Not the Causes of the Dissimilarity of Colour in the Human Species, 119–24
    "The Coromantees", 126–7
    "The Leviathan", 121–2
    Lucy's Ghost, 125
    Poems and Other Writings, 119
    "Toussaint to His Troops", 125
    West Indian Eclogues, 124–5
Russell, Dave, 283
Russo, John
    New Working-class Studies, 8

Sacks, Peter, 89, 90, 96
Said, Edward, 331
sailors, 120–2, 125, 298–9. *See also* Tyneside dialect songs

Index

469

Sandby, Paul
  North West View of Wakefield Lodge in Whittlebury Forest, 1767, xvii–xviii
Sanderson, Thomas
  "Address to the Reader", 142
satire, loss of meaning, 291
Saunders, John, 160
Savage, Richard, 26, 29, 30
Schenck, Celeste M., 86, 90, 96
Scotland
  autobiography, 250, 255–7
  importance of class to identity, 370, 374–5
  Industrial Revolution, 214–16, 218–20
  national identity, 367–70, 375, 383–4
  newspaper culture, 270, 275
  subaltern relationship to England, 208, 210–12, 220–1
  sympathies with Italian nationalism, 272
Scots language
  Blacklock's relationship to, 52
  Burns's insecurities regarding use of, 210
  Doric dialect, 210–12, 215–16, 222–3
  influence in Ulster, 133, 136–8
  means of construction of personae, 131
  newspaper poetry, 272
  subaltern status, 208, 210–12
  Ulster political associations, 146
Scots poetry
  Burns' championship of, 72–3, 75–6
  "Christ's Kirk" stanzas, 78
  criticism of Calvinist culture, 78, 80–1
  criticism of Whig culture, 72–3, 77, 78
  French Revolution, 77, 81
  radicalism, 77–82
  rural sentimentality, 77, 78
  Scottish literary renaissance, 367–70, 374–5
  "Standard Habbie" stanzas, 78, 81, 132, 276
Scott, Sir Walter, 131
sea poetry, 120–2, 125
seduction narratives
  agency in, 16–17, 19
  Foundling Hospital petitions as responses to, 20–1
  "The History of Misella", 15
  interpretations of character, 17–18
  social constructs, 14–15
  social expectations of charities, 11, 12–13
self-publishing, 250–5, 260
Selkirk, John
  "Bob Cranky's 'Size Sunday", 282, 288
Selvon, Sam
  as important figure, 352
  early life, 356
  internationalism, 365
  intersectionalism, 358, 359–65

portrayal of women, 358
  use of dialect, 357–8
  The Lonely Londoners, 353, 358–61
  Ways of Sunlight, 357
Semple, David
  "Life of Tannahill", 404
serial fiction, 318–20
sexism
  double standards, 17–18
  in popular reading, 74–5
  misogynistic portrayals, 358, 386, 388
sexuality
  double standards, 17–18
  homosexuality, 353
  incest, 388
  in tramp narratives, 301
  seduction narratives, 11, 12–21
  women's ignorance, 346–8
Sharp, William, 80
Shelley, Percy Bysshe
  "The Mask of Anarchy", 140, 199
Shenstone, William, 61, 198
Shield, John
  "Bob Cranky's Adieu", 289
Sillitoe, Alan, 357
Skeggs, Beverly, 354
Skelton, John, 227
slavery
  abolitionist poetry, 124–7
  centrality of Liverpool, 116, 118
  debates on nature of race, 118–20, 122
Smalley, Roger, 323
Smith, Adam, 150
Smith, Ann, 11
Smith, Dai, 386
Smith, Mary
  Autobiography of Mary Smith, 250, 258–62
  Poems, 260
  Progress, and Other Poems, 260
Snow, Joseph, 160–1
sociability. *See* literary sociability, community
social meaning
  differing, 282
  loss of, 291, 294
  of *canny*, 285–9
  of *hinny*, 287–9
Society of Authors, 319
Solomon, Harry M., 41
Sommerfield, John
  May Day, 333
"Song of the Servant Maid", 277
Soulby, Anthony
  The Harmonist; or, Musical Olio, A choice Selection of new and much-approved songs; Also, several Cumberland Ballads, By Mr Anderson, 141

Soutar, William
  use of ballad stanza, 372
  "Ballad", 373
  "The Tryst", 373
Southey, Robert, 5, 118, 126, 153
Spence, Joseph, 36
  Account of Blacklock, 51
Spence, Peter, 176
Spence, Thomas, 200
  The Real Rights of Man, 82
Spencer, Luke, 362–5
The Sports of the Muses, 50
Stafford, Fiona, 141
  "Pastoral Elegy in the 1820s", 203
Staves, Susan, 13
Stewart, W.
  Burns' Songs and Anderson's Cumberland Ballads, 141
Stoke Newington, 334
Stokoe, John
  Northumbrian Minstrelsy, 292
Storey, Edward, 204
Super, R. H., 159

Tannahill, Robert, 76–7, 403–6
  The Soldier's Return, 403, 404
Tatersal, Robert
  biographical texts, 32
  Duck as inspiration, 25, 26
  poetic persona, 25
  unlikelihood of royal patronage, 30
  "The Bricklayer's Labours", 25, 36
  Bricklayer's Miscellany, 31, 32, 34, 35, 36
  Second Part, 30, 37
  "To Stephen Duck, The famous Threshing Poet", 44–6
Taylor, John (publisher), 201
Taylor, John (the "Water Poet"), 5
temperance movement, 216, 286–7, 290
Tennant, George
  "To the Patriots of Italy – an Ode", 272
  "The Wee Beggar Wean", 272
Tennant, Robert, 272
textile industry. *See also* Millhouse, Robert; Tannahill, Robert
  criticisms of mill owners, 78–80
  exploitation of women, 217–20
  weaver poets, 30, 35, 139, 140–2, 272, 363
Thicknesse, Anna, 96
Thomas, Gwyn
  "Simeon", 388
  Sorrow for thy Sons, 388, 393
Thomas, M. Wynn, 386
Thompson, E. P.
  The Making of The English Working Class, 229

Thompson, Tommy
  "Canny Newcassel", 285, 287
Thomson, James, xvii
  The Seasons, 204
Thomson, Samuel
  artistic circle, 134
  transnationalist identity, 134–6
  "The Bard's Farewell!", 139–40
  New Poems, 135
  Simple Poems on a Few Subjects, Partly in the Scottish Dialect, 136
  "To a Hedgehog", 133
  "To Captain McDougal, Castle-Upton, with a copy of the author's poems", 134–6
Thom, William, 211
Tierney, James E., 51
The Time-Piece and Literary Companion (newspaper), 121
Todd, George
  Fowrsom Reel, 375
Tollett, Elizabeth
  Pastoral. In Memory of Mrs. Elizabeth Blackler, 94
tramp narratives
  activism in, 305–8
  Alexander Wilson inspired by tramping, 83
  anarchists, 302–4
  class in, 302
  commentary on widespread unemployment, 296–8, 305
  environmentalism, 304
  intentional trampdom, 298, 308
  kinship with sailors, 298–9
  masculinity, 301–2
  racism, 304–5
  women, 296, 298, 301–2
transatlantic radical culture
  abolitionism, 124–7
  promulgation of Paine's ideas, 81
    Alexander Wilson's contributions to, 83
  Revolutionary America, 139–40
  working class Ulster networks, 130
transnationalism. *See also* internationalism
  Anderson, Robert, 142, 144, 146
  conflict with localized print market, 144–6
  Irish identity, 132
  Ulster, 134–6, 139–40, 147
Tressell, Robert
  The Ragged Trousered Philanthropists, 353
Trezise, Rachel
  In and Out of the Goldfish Bowl, 392, 393
  Sixteen Shades of Crazy, 393
Trinidad, 357–8
Trolander, Paul

Index

Literary Sociability in Early Modern England, 39
Trotter, Catherine. *See* Cockburn, Catherine
Tully's Head, 50
Tyneside dialect songs
  construction of genre through paratexts, 291–4
  discourses of respectability, 282–4, 285–6
  interpreting, 282
  locality, 281, 284–5, 288, 294
  meanings of *canny*, 285–9
  meanings of *hinny*, 287–9
  narrowing of meaning, 291, 294
  non-standard spellings, 289–91
Tytler, James "Balloon", 81
Tyler, Wat, xxi

Uglow, Jenny, 283
Ulster
  connections to Revolutionary America, 139–40
  identity, 132
  legitimacy of language, 146
  linguistic culture, 133
  poetry, 133
  Scottish-Irish tensions, 136
  transnationalism, 130, 147
  weaver community, 139, 140–2
United States, emigration to, 76, 82, 139–40
urban life. *See also* London
  Birmingham, 339–51
  in opposition to rural, 110, 112, 144, 195, 370
  slum novels, 330–2
vernacular. *See* dialect
verse epistles
  by women addressed to men, 46
  definition, 39
  private letters, 52–4
  published addresses to Duck, 40–9
  sociability value, 6, 39–40
  Yearsley's use of, 58–61

Vicinus, Martha
  The Industrial Muse, 228
Victorian era
  feminism, 258–62
  schoolteachers, 250, 257, 259
  servant class, 250–2, 259, 277–9
  widespread unemployment, 296–8
  women's autobiography, 248–62
Vincent, David
  The Autobiography of the Working Class, 1790–1940, 248
  Bread, Knowledge, and Freedom, 248
Virago Press, 340–1

Virgil
  Eclogues, 196

Wahrman, Dror, 119
Wakefield, Thomas, 161, 162
Wales
  bardic traditions, 103, 110, 114
  changing social structure, 103–6
  contemporary working class identity, 387
  development of working class personae, 102
  English primitivist attitudes, 101–2
  gwerin, 387
  industrial novels, 386
  post-industrial novels, 386
  working class identity, 387, 395, 396
Wales, Katie, 286
Walker, Hugh, 227
Wallace, Alexander, 210
Wallace, William, 221
Walpole, Horace, 24
Walton, Isaac
  The Compleat Angler, 199
Wapshott, Anne, 10, 19
Ward, Sam, 201
Watkins, John, 160
weaver poets, 30, 35, 139, 140–2, 272, 363. *See also* Hamilton, Janet; Millhouse, Robert; Tannahill, Robert; Wilson, Alexander
Webb, Belinda, 322
Weekly Magazine, 75
Wells, H. G.
  The Time Machine, 304
Welsh, James C.
  The Morlocks, 306–7
Welsh language
  identity, 387
  loss of, 103
  novels, 386–7, 395–6
  Welsh-English patois, 390–1
Welsh novels
  Coalfield Gothic, 388
  cultural decay, 389–90, 391–2, 393
  devolution, 393
  Gothic elements, 385–8, 396
  haunting, 385
  identity, 387
  individualism, 393
  in English, 386, 396
  in Welsh, 386–7, 395–6
  post-industrialism, 392, 393
  postmodern representation, 393
  realism, 393–5
  violence, 389
  Welsh-English patois, 390–1
  women in, 389–90, 393

Welsh poetry
   bards, 103, 110, 114
   depictions of rural life, 106–7
   hierarchies, 103
   in English, 108–9, 113
   influence of English culture, 108–9, 111–14
   nonconformist vein, 106
   poetic personae, 102
   religious vein, 106
   revival, 104, 107–8
   role of working class, 111–12
The Wheatsheaf (periodical), 311
Wheeler, Thomas Martin
   "Sunshine and Shadow", 296–7, 305
Whigs, 72–3, 77, 78
Whitby Abbey, 1
Whitehead, Andrew, 333
Williams, Daniel, 393, 395
Williams, David, 164
   Claims of Literature, 149–51
Williams, Edward (Iolo Morganwg)
   biographical introduction, 108–9
   dual identities, 110
   fabrication of poems by Dafydd ap Gwilym, 109
   life of, 109–10, 111
   patronage bids, 109, 110–11
   poetic persona, 111–12
   Poems, Lyric and Pastoral, 112
Williams, Gwyn Alf, 111
Williamson, Karina, 46
Williams, Raymond, 195
   Keywords, 1
   "The Welsh Industrial Novel", 329, 330, 338
Wilson, Alexander
   career, 70
   cosmopolitanism of, 8
   emigration to United States, 76, 82
   legal troubles, 79, 80, 81
   natural sublime, 83
   ornithological work, 83
   patronage, 73
   posthumous interest in, 70–1
   subscriptions, 73–4
   Tannahill's lament for, 76–7
   travels, 73
   travels/walking trips, 83
   "The Address to the Synod of Glasgow and Ayr", 80–1
   American Ornithology, 83
   "The Foresters", 83
   "The Hollander, or Light Weight", 78–9
   "The Insulted Peddlar", 78, 81–2
   "Journal as a Peddlar, 1789–90", 73–4
   "The Laurel Disputed; or the merits of Allan Ramsay and Robert Fergusson contrasted", 75
   Poems (1790), 73
   Poems, Chiefly in the Scottish Dialect, 73
   Poems: Humorous, Satirical and Serious (1791), 75
   "The Shark, or Lang Mills Detected", 78, 80, 139
   "Watty and Meg, or the Wife Reformed", 74–5
Wilson, Joe, 286–7, 293
   "Aw'll Sing Ye a Tyneside Sang", 281, 285
   "Aw Wish Yor Fethur wes Here", 287
   "Canny Man", 287
   "Keep Yor Feet Still!", 289
   "Pride", 288
   "Tyneside Lads for Me", 287
   "Ungrateful Bill", 288
   "Varry Canny", 287
Wisbech, 8
The Woman Worker (newspaper), 312, 315, 317
women. *See also* Foundling Hospital petitions
   aesthetic study of writings of, 13–14
   as moral guardians, 216–17
   autobiography, 248–62, 339–51
   communal function, 343–4
   denigration of, 151
   female constancy, 18, 288
   feminism, 218–19, 258–62, 325
   in tramp narratives, 296, 298, 301–2
   in Welsh novels, 389–90, 393
   leisure, 312–13
   literacy, 21–2
   meanings of *hinny*, 287–9
   misogynistic portrayals, 358, 386, 388
   mother-daughter relationships, 345–6, 347
   motherhood, 347–50
   old, 221–2
   oral tradition, 209
   recovery of autobiographical writings, 340–2
   reputations of, 5, 17–18
   Royal Literary Fund biases, 163
   sexual double standards, 17–18
   sexual ignorance, 346–8
   subversion of form, 86
   tensions between artistic and class or social identities, 7
   "triple shift", 7
   value as workers, 20
   working conditions, 217–20, 250–2, 277–9, 314
women's elegy
   conventions, 90

disruptive nature, 90–1
nature of grief, 92–4, 96–8, 99
Woodhouse, James
  life of, 61
  natural genius of, 61–2
  patronage, 61
  reclamation of natural genius, 62–5
  "The Author's Apology", 63
  The Life and Lucubrations of Crispinus Scriblerus, 57, 61, 62, 63–5
  Poems on Several Occasions, 63
  Poems on Sundry Occasions, 50, 63
Woodward, Kathleen
  Jipping Street, 345
Wordsworth, William, 199
work
  as obstacle to art, 33–7
  as subject, 4
  in service, 250–2, 259, 277–9
  working conditions, 209, 312–14
working class
  concepts and definitions of, xvii, 1–2
  contemporary attitudes towards, 9
  literary innovations, xviii
working class writing
  awareness of roles and class in study of, 2–3
  conflicting roles, 2–6
  definition, 1, 415–16
  forms, 6–7
  loss of, 413–14
  regional identities, 7–8, 131
  study of, 8–9, 417–18
Wright, Joseph, 210
"writing back", 1–2

Yearsley, Ann, xix, xxi–xxii
  classical learning, xxi, 60–1
  elegy as expression of identity, 6
  failure to occupy conventional elegaic role, 93–4
  inconsistent use of elegy, 91
  life of, 57–8
  nature of grief, 92–3, 96–8, 99
  poetic output, 78, 86
  response to muting of female poets, 56
  revolt against patronage of More, 56, 58
  Southey's description of, 5
  use of poetic inheritance, 94–6
  "Addressed by Mrs. Yearsley to a recent Widower, with whom she had had a disagreement", 96, 98
  "Addressed to Ignorance, Occasioned by a Gentleman's desiring the Author never to assume a Knowledge of the Ancients", xxi–xxii, 57, 58, 60–1
  "Bristol Elegy", 98
  "Elegy, on Mr. Chatterton", 94–6, 99
  "Elegy, On Visiting the Hermitage, near Bath", 96
  "On the Death of Her Grace, the Duchess Dowager of Portland", 93–4
  "On the Death of Mr. Richard Smith, Surgeon", 96
  "On the Sudden Death of a Friend", 91–3, 99
  Poems on Several Occasions, 58, 91
  Poems on Various Subjects, xxi, xxii, 57, 93
  The Rural Lyre, 58, 96
  "To Mr ****, an Unlettered Poet, on Genius Unimproved", 57, 58–60
  "Verses on the Death of Miss Scrafton, who Died Sept, 1, 1788 Aged Twenty Two Years", 96–7
Yeats, W. B., 134
yellowbacks, 316
Young, Edward
  Conjectures on Original Composition, 64

Zola, Émile
  Germinal, 306–7

Lightning Source UK Ltd.
Milton Keynes UK
UKHW011428250721
387729UK00003B/6